GREASE Monkey

Written and drawn by

Tim Eldred

A TOM DOHERTY ASSOCIATES BOOK   TOR®   NEW YORK

This is a work of fiction. All the characters and events portrayed in this novel are either fictitious or are used fictitiously.

GREASE MONKEY

This book is printed on acid-free paper.

Edited by Teresa Nielsen Hayden

A Tor Book
Published by Tom Doherty Associates, LLC
175 Fifth Avenue
New York, NY 10010

www.tor.com

Library of Congress Cataloging-in-Publication Data

Eldred, Tim.
Grease monkey / written and drawn by Tim Eldred.—1st ed.
p. cm.
ISBN-13: 978-0-765-31325-6 (acid-free paper)
ISBN-10: 0-765-31325-1 (acid-free paper)
1. Graphic novels. I. Title

PN6727.E44G74 2006
741.5—dc22

2006040396

First Edition: June 2006

Printed in the United States of America

0 9 8 7 6 5 4 3 2 1

CONTENTS

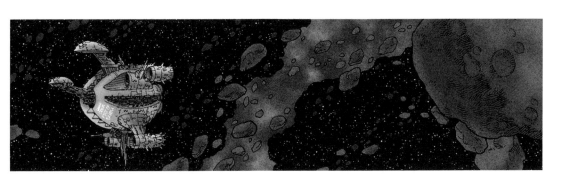

FOREWORD

UNFORGETTABLE

There are some things you don't remember. And some you'll never forget.

I don't remember when I first met Tim Eldred, for instance. The earliest I remember talking to him is at lunch at a comic-professionals' convention about ten years back, when the whole table full of creators we were eating with spent the time cocreating a hilarious, unpublishable team of scatological superheroes. I think Tim was lettering for Malibu Comics at the time, but I could be mistaken.

Whatever. It was a fun lunch, and I enjoyed talking with Tim.

Sometime later, I started getting *Grease Monkey* in the mail. I don't remember much about how that came about, either. Something I should mention here: I work alone at a keyboard all day, in an office above my garage. I'm used to silence and solitude. So when I go to a convention—and I don't think I've seen Tim outside of cons—I'm hit by instant sensory overload. Too many people, too much noise, things happening in all directions—I'm overwhelmed by it all and am lucky to remember where I'm supposed to be at any given time. But I'm not so good with names and faces and short-term memory and things like that, not with so much Convention happening all around me.

I think Tim asked if he could send me some of his stuff. I usually say no to that kind of thing—back when I was a literary agent, I saw the result of a plagiarism accusation where a fan accused an author of swiping material from fan fiction he'd sent her, and I've been wary of reading unpublished fiction ever since—but Tim was a good guy and a fellow pro and I'd enjoyed chatting with him and it seemed rude to say no.

Or it might have happened some other way. Like I said, I'm hazy on how it happened.

In any case, I'm glad it did. Because I found *Grease Monkey* funny and charming and clever and crisply drawn. I liked the setting; I liked the fact that the leads were support staff, not the "heroes," which is unusual for comics but gave an interesting perspective to it all. I liked the contrast between young, insecure Robin Plotnik and the tough-as-nails, all-female Barbarian squadron. And that Tim Eldred draws good gorillas. It was a fun comic, more like the YA SF I liked to read when I was a kid than anything I could think of in comics.

I would have liked to see more.

And I did. Over the next decade, *Grease Monkey* stories kept showing up in my mailbox. Sometimes there were long stretches between them, and sometimes they turned up two or three at a time, like buses, but they kept coming. I was amazed at Tim's tenacity. He didn't have a publisher, at least not most of the time. He was producing this stuff for a very small group—himself and whomever he showed it to—apparently with the faith that someday, somehow, he'd reach a wider group. (I did, at one point, suggest he pitch it to Image Comics, which I think wound up costing him money, so I apologize for that. I was just enjoying what I was reading and wanted more people to be able to discover how much fun it all was. It just wasn't a good time in the comics industry for fun, that's all.)

But Tim's tenacity wasn't the only thing that amazed me. Oh, I still admired the craft—every *Grease Monkey* story was well-constructed, briskly paced, and engaging, and Tim's skills grew over the years. As a series of light SF adventure, it was a consistent winner. But that wasn't it, either.

What snuck up on me over the years was just how much is actually going on in this series. What I thought of as a loose string of stories—almost a sitcom set on a space station—was turning out more and more to be a single work, more ambitious, more structured, and deeper than I'd realized. This wasn't a series, it was a novel—an episodic novel, to be sure, but a novel nonetheless. For all the surface fun, Tim had a lot going on underneath, from personal issues to group dynamics to cultural resentments, and he'd thought it out far more thoroughly than those early episodes hinted at.

And as each chapter—by now I was thinking of them as chapters, not as stories—arrived, I was more and more caught up in the building momentum, as minor threads grew into major issues, and long-simmering character issues surfaced and clashed. And I got more and more eager for the next chapter, which was frustrating in that I never knew when a new one would show up.

And now here it is, all done, all presented nice and tidy in one volume, instead of as innumerable piles of photocopies scattered around my house. In some ways, I'm envious of you new readers, who are first encountering it like this. You get to see it as a single work, you get to experience it as a novel from the get-go, and don't have to wait years for it all. But on the other hand, you won't have that anticipation, that growing sense of discovery sneaking up on you over time as what seemed to be a light adventure-comedy turns out to have some bite underneath the polished surface.

What I envy you most, though, is that whatever the package, whatever the presentation, you haven't read it yet. You get to experience it all for the first time, fresh and new and unknown.

Me? I've got to wait ten years for Tim to finish his next project.

Unless I start getting chapters in the mail again, in which case I'm in for a decade of torture, knowing from the start this time that it'll all be going somewhere, and I just have to wait till it gets there.

But that's not important. What's important is this: Turn the pages.

You're about to meet Robin and Mac and the Barbarians and Admiral Stettler and Kara and Jeff and more.

And in the end, it won't matter where you came across this book or why you picked it up. It's *Grease Monkey*, the book itself, that matters.

And whatever else you might remember or not, I'm sure of one thing, in my convention-addled brain:

The book is unforgettable.

—Kurt Busiek
September 2004

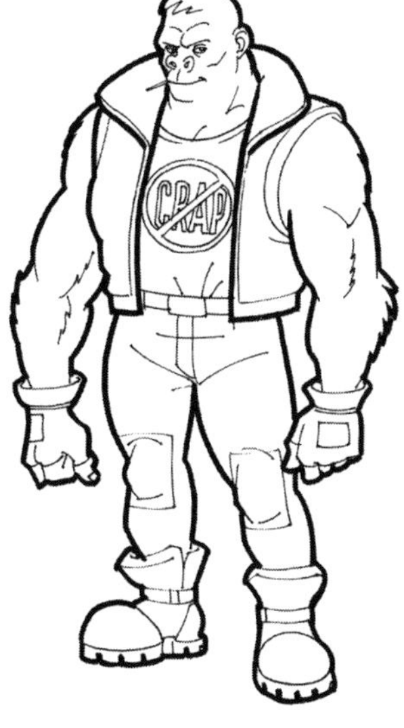
CRAP

Early in the 21st Century (2:55 a.m., in fact),
the history of Planet Earth took a left turn into
oncoming traffic. ALIEN traffic.
A million, zillion, hostile spaceships descended
on humanity and blasted civilization
into chili powder. Then they left.

Shocked by the impoliteness of this alien horde,
an alliance of galactic powers sent emissaries
to Earth in order to repair the damage
as best they could.
This alliance, known as the Galactic Alliance
Against the Alien Horde (or G.A.A.A.H.),
needed allies in their ongoing space war,
and helped humankind back to its feet.

When humankind stood up, however, it found
a leg missing. Over sixty percent of all the
people on Earth had been killed in the attack.
Since G.A.A.A.H. scientists had the ability
to bestow high intelligence on other species,
it was decided to invite some of Earth's other
inhabitants and restore the number of humans lost.

The dolphins wanted nothing to do with this,
but were glad to learn that there would now be
sixty percent less pollution in their water.

The gorillas, on the other hand, were more
than happy to bask in a higher I.Q. pool
in exchange for their services. . . .

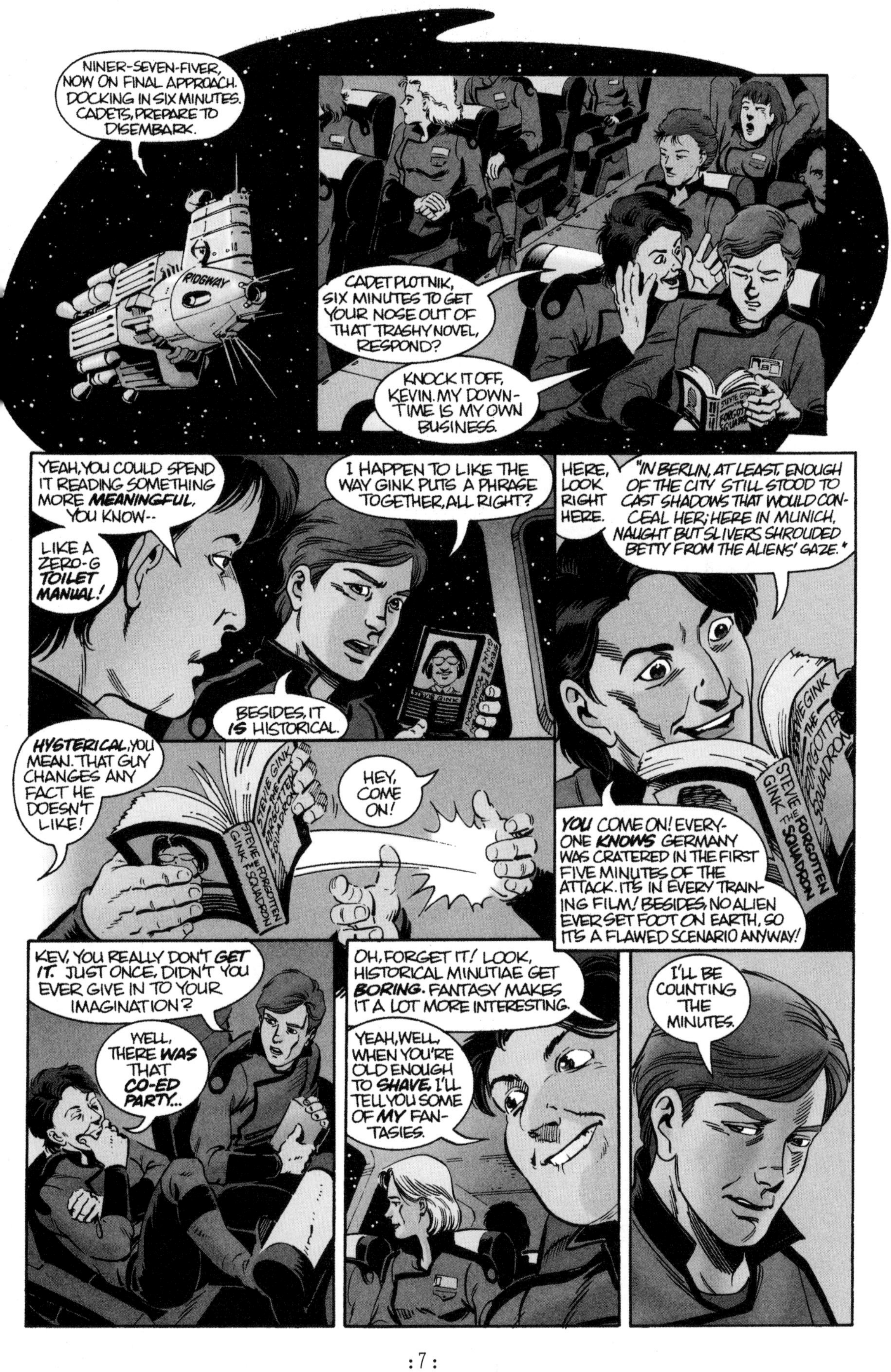
NINER-SEVEN-FIVER, NOW ON FINAL APPROACH. DOCKING IN SIX MINUTES. CADETS, PREPARE TO DISEMBARK.
RIDGWAY
CADET PLOTNIK, SIX MINUTES TO GET YOUR NOSE OUT OF THAT TRASHY NOVEL, RESPOND?
KNOCK IT OFF, KEVIN. MY DOWN-TIME IS MY OWN BUSINESS.
YEAH, YOU COULD SPEND IT READING SOMETHING MORE MEANINGFUL, YOU KNOW--
LIKE A ZERO-G TOILET MANUAL!
I HAPPEN TO LIKE THE WAY GINK PUTS A PHRASE TOGETHER, ALL RIGHT?
BESIDES, IT IS HISTORICAL.
HERE, LOOK RIGHT HERE.
"IN BERLIN, AT LEAST, ENOUGH OF THE CITY STILL STOOD TO CAST SHADOWS THAT WOULD CONCEAL HER; HERE IN MUNICH, NAUGHT BUT SLIVERS SHROUDED BETTY FROM THE ALIENS' GAZE."
HYSTERICAL, YOU MEAN. THAT GUY CHANGES ANY FACT HE DOESN'T LIKE!
HEY, COME ON!
YOU COME ON! EVERYONE KNOWS GERMANY WAS CRATERED IN THE FIRST FIVE MINUTES OF THE ATTACK. IT'S IN EVERY TRAINING FILM! BESIDES, NO ALIEN EVER SET FOOT ON EARTH, SO IT'S A FLAWED SCENARIO ANYWAY!
STEVIE GINK THE FORGOTTEN SQUADRON
KEV, YOU REALLY DON'T GET IT. JUST ONCE, DIDN'T YOU EVER GIVE IN TO YOUR IMAGINATION?
WELL, THERE WAS THAT CO-ED PARTY...
OH, FORGET IT! LOOK, HISTORICAL MINUTIAE GET BORING. FANTASY MAKES IT A LOT MORE INTERESTING.
YEAH, WELL, WHEN YOU'RE OLD ENOUGH TO SHAVE, I'LL TELL YOU SOME OF MY FANTASIES.
I'LL BE COUNTING THE MINUTES.

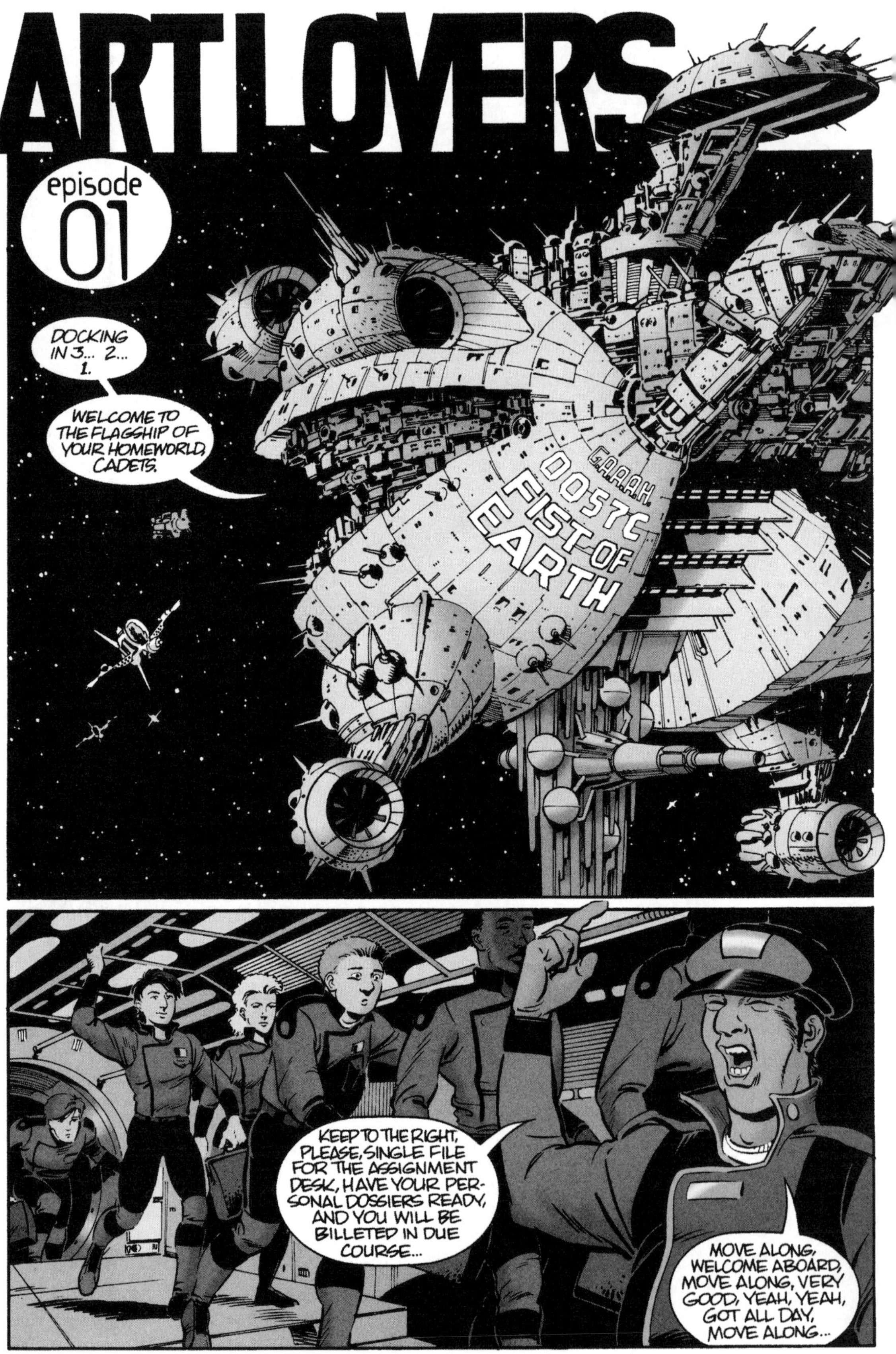
ARTLOVERS
episode 01
DOCKING IN 3... 2... 1.
WELCOME TO THE FLAGSHIP OF YOUR HOMEWORLD, CADETS.
G.A.A.A.H. 0057C FIST OF EARTH
KEEP TO THE RIGHT, PLEASE, SINGLE FILE FOR THE ASSIGNMENT DESK, HAVE YOUR PERSONAL DOSSIERS READY, AND YOU WILL BE BILLETED IN DUE COURSE...
MOVE ALONG, WELCOME ABOARD, MOVE ALONG, VERY GOOD, YEAH, YEAH, GOT ALL DAY, MOVE ALONG...

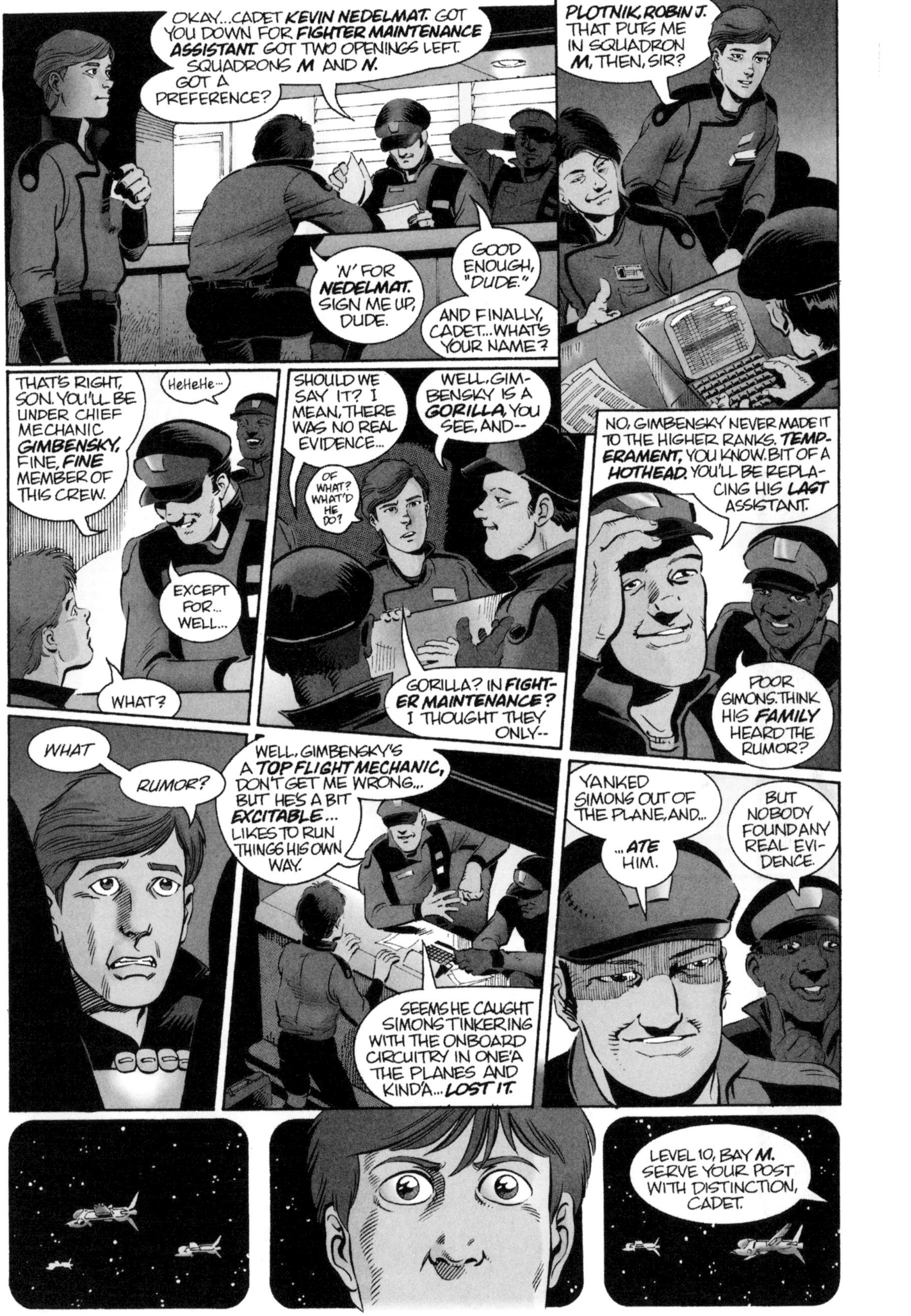

OKAY...CADET KEVIN NEDELMAT. GOT YOU DOWN FOR FIGHTER MAINTENANCE ASSISTANT. GOT TWO OPENINGS LEFT. SQUADRONS M AND N. GOT A PREFERENCE?
'N' FOR NEDELMAT. SIGN ME UP, DUDE.
GOOD ENOUGH, "DUDE."
AND FINALLY, CADET...WHAT'S YOUR NAME?
PLOTNIK, ROBIN J. THAT PUTS ME IN SQUADRON M, THEN, SIR?
THAT'S RIGHT, SON. YOU'LL BE UNDER CHIEF MECHANIC GIMBENSKY, FINE, FINE MEMBER OF THIS CREW.
HeHeHe...
EXCEPT FOR... WELL...
WHAT?
SHOULD WE SAY IT? I MEAN, THERE WAS NO REAL EVIDENCE...
WELL, GIMBENSKY IS A GORILLA, YOU SEE, AND--
OF WHAT? WHAT'D HE DO?
GORILLA? IN FIGHTER MAINTENANCE? I THOUGHT THEY ONLY--
NO, GIMBENSKY NEVER MADE IT TO THE HIGHER RANKS. TEMPERAMENT, YOU KNOW. BIT OF A HOTHEAD. YOU'LL BE REPLACING HIS LAST ASSISTANT.
POOR SIMONS. THINK HIS FAMILY HEARD THE RUMOR?
WHAT RUMOR?
WELL, GIMBENSKY'S A TOP FLIGHT MECHANIC, DON'T GET ME WRONG... BUT HE'S A BIT EXCITABLE... LIKES TO RUN THINGS HIS OWN WAY.
SEEMS HE CAUGHT SIMONS TINKERING WITH THE ONBOARD CIRCUITRY IN ONE'A THE PLANES AND KIND'A... LOST IT.
YANKED SIMONS OUT OF THE PLANE, AND...
...ATE HIM.
BUT NOBODY FOUND ANY REAL EVIDENCE.
LEVEL 10, BAY M. SERVE YOUR POST WITH DISTINCTION, CADET.

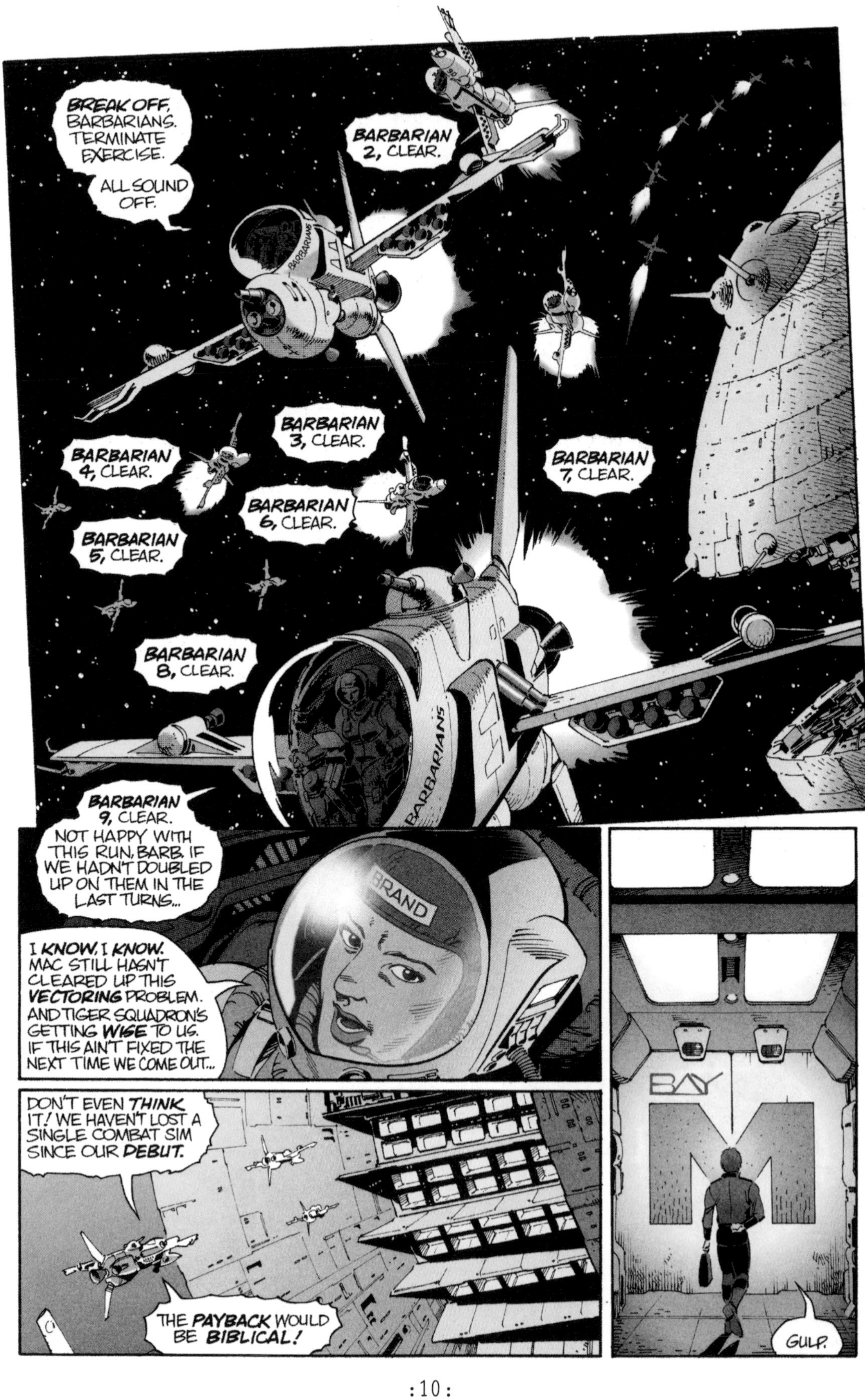
BREAK OFF, BARBARIANS. TERMINATE EXERCISE.
ALL SOUND OFF.
BARBARIAN 2, CLEAR.
BARBARIAN 3, CLEAR.
BARBARIAN 4, CLEAR.
BARBARIAN 7, CLEAR.
BARBARIAN 6, CLEAR.
BARBARIAN 5, CLEAR.
BARBARIAN 8, CLEAR.
BARBARIANS
BARBARIAN 9, CLEAR.
NOT HAPPY WITH THIS RUN, BARB. IF WE HADN'T DOUBLED UP ON THEM IN THE LAST TURNS...
BRAND
I KNOW, I KNOW. MAC STILL HASN'T CLEARED UP THIS VECTORING PROBLEM. AND TIGER SQUADRON'S GETTING WISE TO US. IF THIS AIN'T FIXED THE NEXT TIME WE COME OUT...
DON'T EVEN THINK IT! WE HAVEN'T LOST A SINGLE COMBAT SIM SINCE OUR DEBUT.
THE PAYBACK WOULD BE BIBLICAL!
BAY
M
GULP.

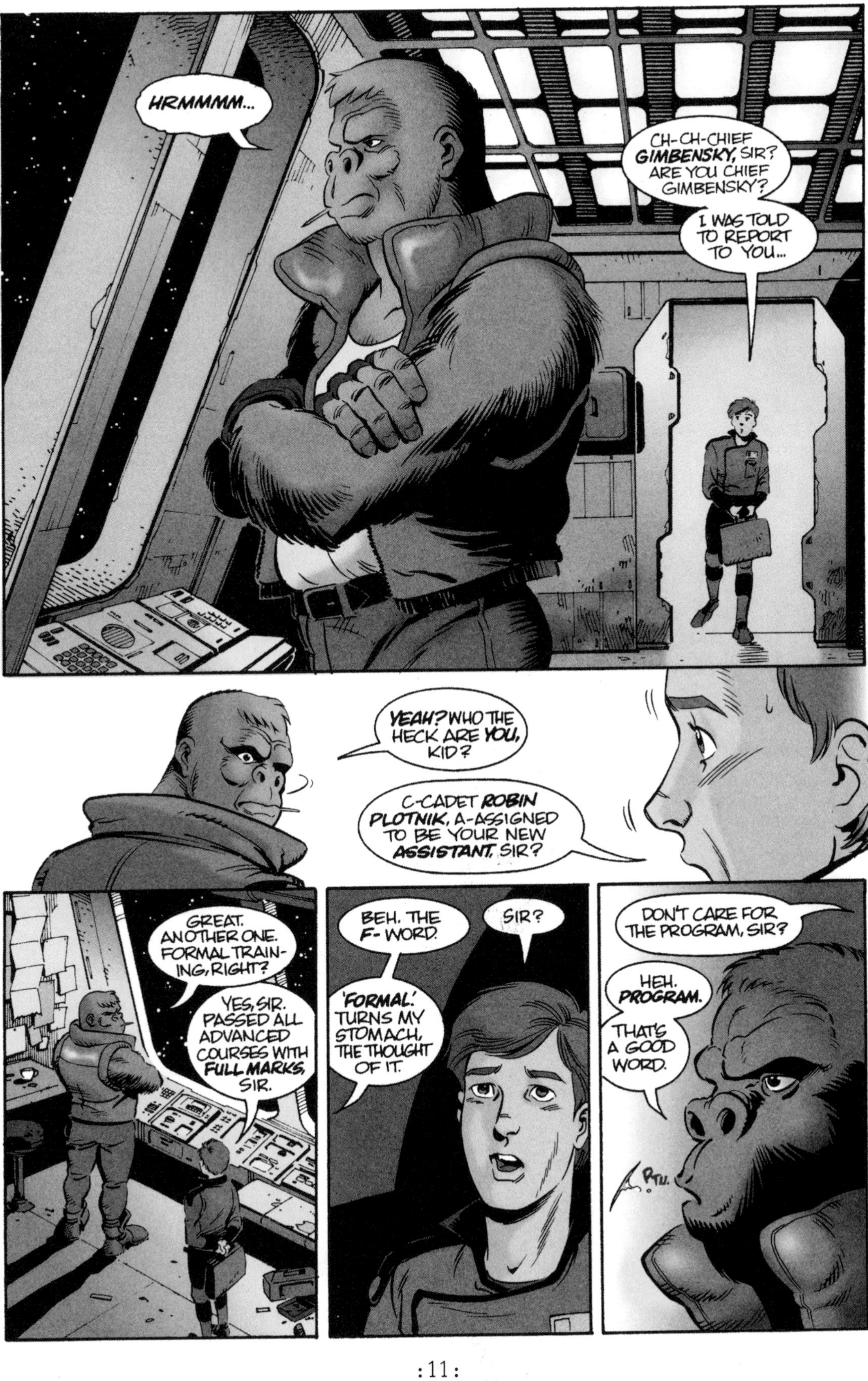
HRMMMM...
CH-CH-CHIEF GIMBENSKY, SIR? ARE YOU CHIEF GIMBENSKY?
I WAS TOLD TO REPORT TO YOU...
YEAH? WHO THE HECK ARE YOU, KID?
C-CADET ROBIN PLOTNIK, A-ASSIGNED TO BE YOUR NEW ASSISTANT, SIR?
GREAT. ANOTHER ONE. FORMAL TRAINING, RIGHT?
YES, SIR. PASSED ALL ADVANCED COURSES WITH FULL MARKS, SIR.
BEH. THE F-WORD.
SIR?
'FORMAL.' TURNS MY STOMACH, THE THOUGHT OF IT.
DON'T CARE FOR THE PROGRAM, SIR?
HEH. PROGRAM.
THAT'S A GOOD WORD.

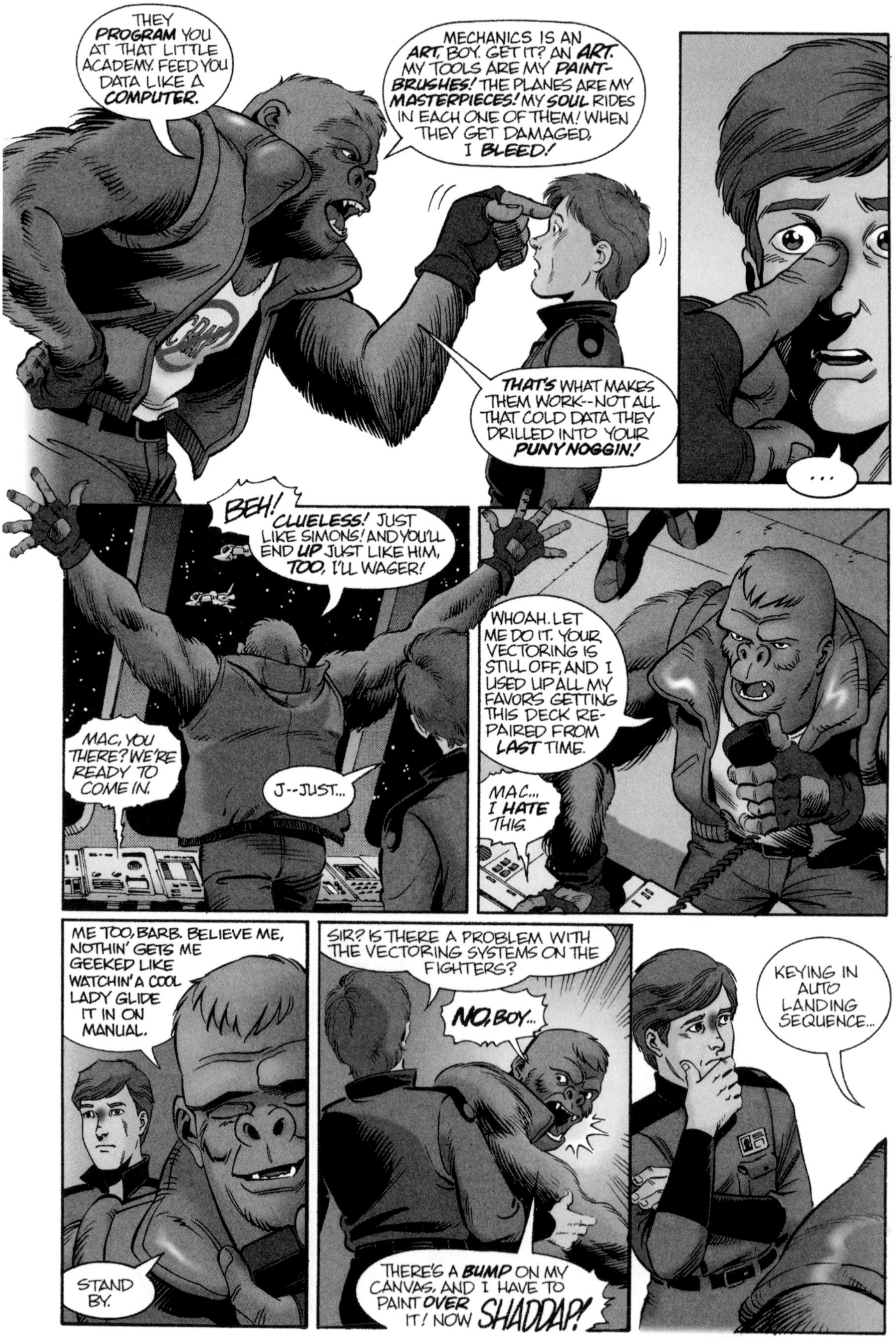
THEY PROGRAM YOU AT THAT LITTLE ACADEMY. FEED YOU DATA LIKE A COMPUTER.
MECHANICS IS AN ART, BOY. GET IT? AN ART. MY TOOLS ARE MY PAINT-BRUSHES! THE PLANES ARE MY MASTERPIECES! MY SOUL RIDES IN EACH ONE OF THEM! WHEN THEY GET DAMAGED, I BLEED!
THAT'S WHAT MAKES THEM WORK--NOT ALL THAT COLD DATA THEY DRILLED INTO YOUR PUNY NOGGIN!
...
BEH! CLUELESS! JUST LIKE SIMONS! AND YOU'LL END UP JUST LIKE HIM, TOO, I'LL WAGER!
MAC, YOU THERE? WE'RE READY TO COME IN.
J--JUST...
WHOAH. LET ME DO IT. YOUR VECTORING IS STILL OFF, AND I USED UP ALL MY FAVORS GETTING THIS DECK RE-PAIRED FROM LAST TIME.
MAC... I HATE THIS.
ME TOO, BARB. BELIEVE ME, NOTHIN' GETS ME GEEKED LIKE WATCHIN' A COOL LADY GLIDE IT IN ON MANUAL.
STAND BY.
SIR? IS THERE A PROBLEM WITH THE VECTORING SYSTEMS ON THE FIGHTERS?
NO, BOY...
THERE'S A BUMP ON MY CANVAS, AND I HAVE TO PAINT OVER IT! NOW SHADDAP!
KEYING IN AUTO LANDING SEQUENCE...

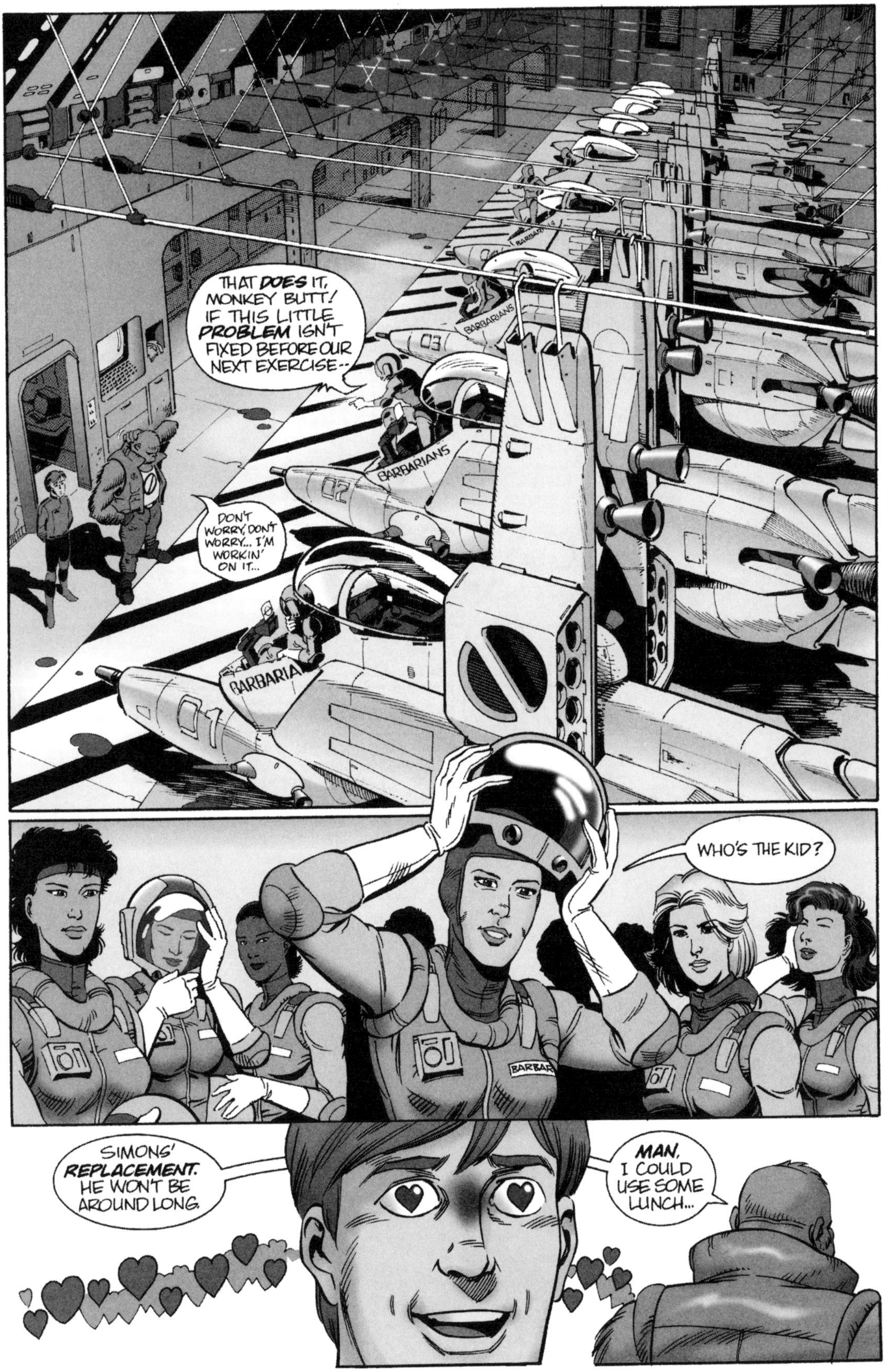
THAT DOES IT, MONKEY BUTT! IF THIS LITTLE PROBLEM ISN'T FIXED BEFORE OUR NEXT EXERCISE--
DON'T WORRY, DON'T WORRY... I'M WORKIN' ON IT...
BARBARIANS
BARBARIANS
BARBARIA
WHO'S THE KID?
SIMONS' REPLACEMENT. HE WON'T BE AROUND LONG.
MAN, I COULD USE SOME LUNCH...

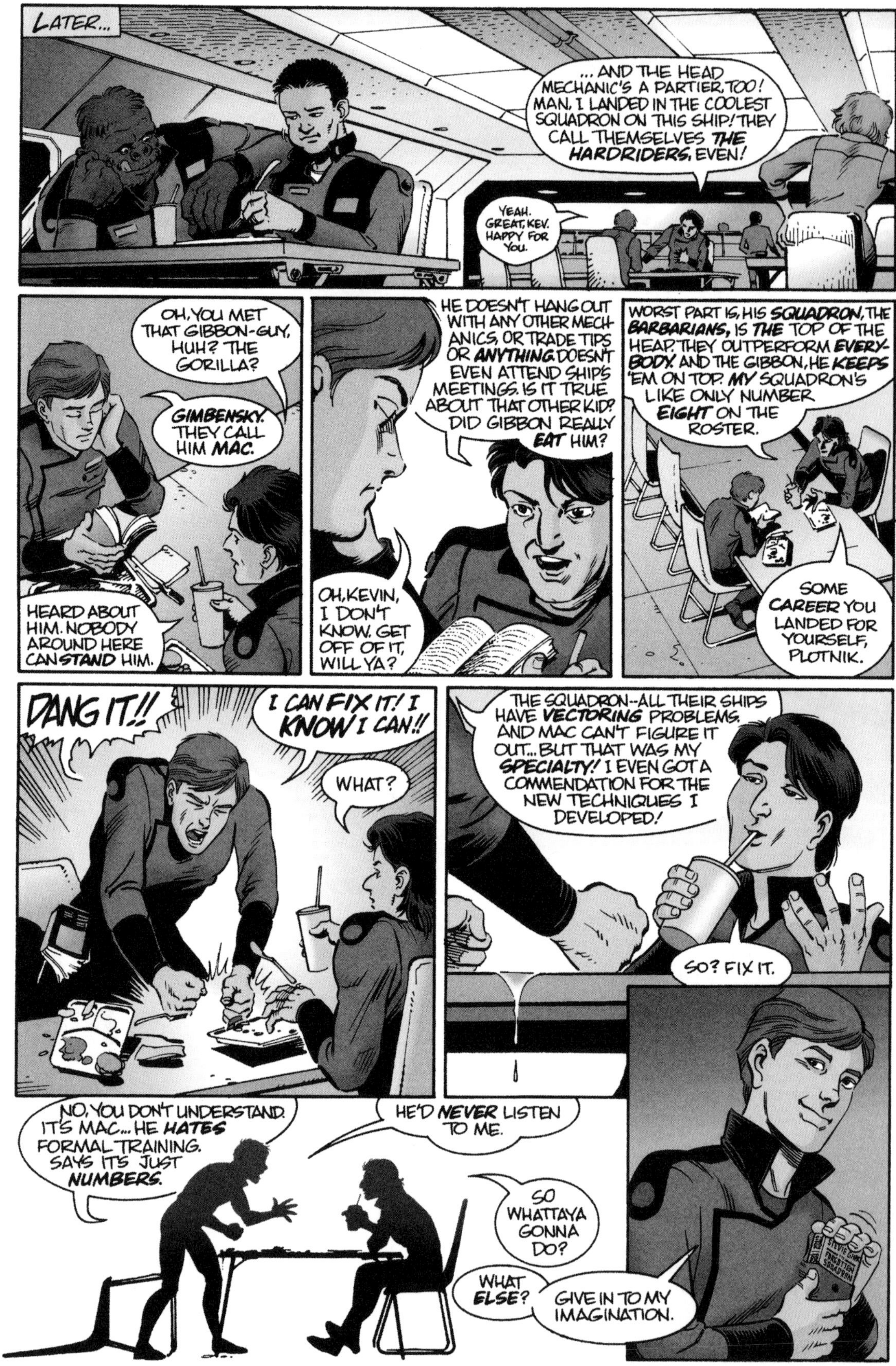
LATER...
...AND THE HEAD MECHANIC'S A PARTIER, TOO! MAN, I LANDED IN THE COOLEST SQUADRON ON THIS SHIP! THEY CALL THEMSELVES THE HARDRIDERS, EVEN!
YEAH. GREAT, KEV. HAPPY FOR YOU.
OH, YOU MET THAT GIBBON-GUY, HUH? THE GORILLA?
GIMBENSKY. THEY CALL HIM MAC.
HEARD ABOUT HIM. NOBODY AROUND HERE CAN STAND HIM.
HE DOESN'T HANG OUT WITH ANY OTHER MECHANICS, OR TRADE TIPS OR ANYTHING. DOESN'T EVEN ATTEND SHIP'S MEETINGS. IS IT TRUE ABOUT THAT OTHER KID? DID GIBBON REALLY EAT HIM?
OH, KEVIN, I DON'T KNOW. GET OFF OF IT, WILL YA?
WORST PART IS, HIS SQUADRON, THE BARBARIANS, IS THE TOP OF THE HEAP. THEY OUTPERFORM EVERYBODY. AND THE GIBBON, HE KEEPS 'EM ON TOP. MY SQUADRON'S LIKE ONLY NUMBER EIGHT ON THE ROSTER.
SOME CAREER YOU LANDED FOR YOURSELF, PLOTNIK.
DANG IT!!
I CAN FIX IT! I KNOW I CAN!!
WHAT?
THE SQUADRON--ALL THEIR SHIPS HAVE VECTORING PROBLEMS. AND MAC CAN'T FIGURE IT OUT... BUT THAT WAS MY SPECIALTY! I EVEN GOT A COMMENDATION FOR THE NEW TECHNIQUES I DEVELOPED!
SO? FIX IT.
NO, YOU DON'T UNDERSTAND. IT'S MAC... HE HATES FORMAL TRAINING. SAYS IT'S JUST NUMBERS.
HE'D NEVER LISTEN TO ME.
SO WHATTAYA GONNA DO?
WHAT ELSE?
GIVE IN TO MY IMAGINATION.

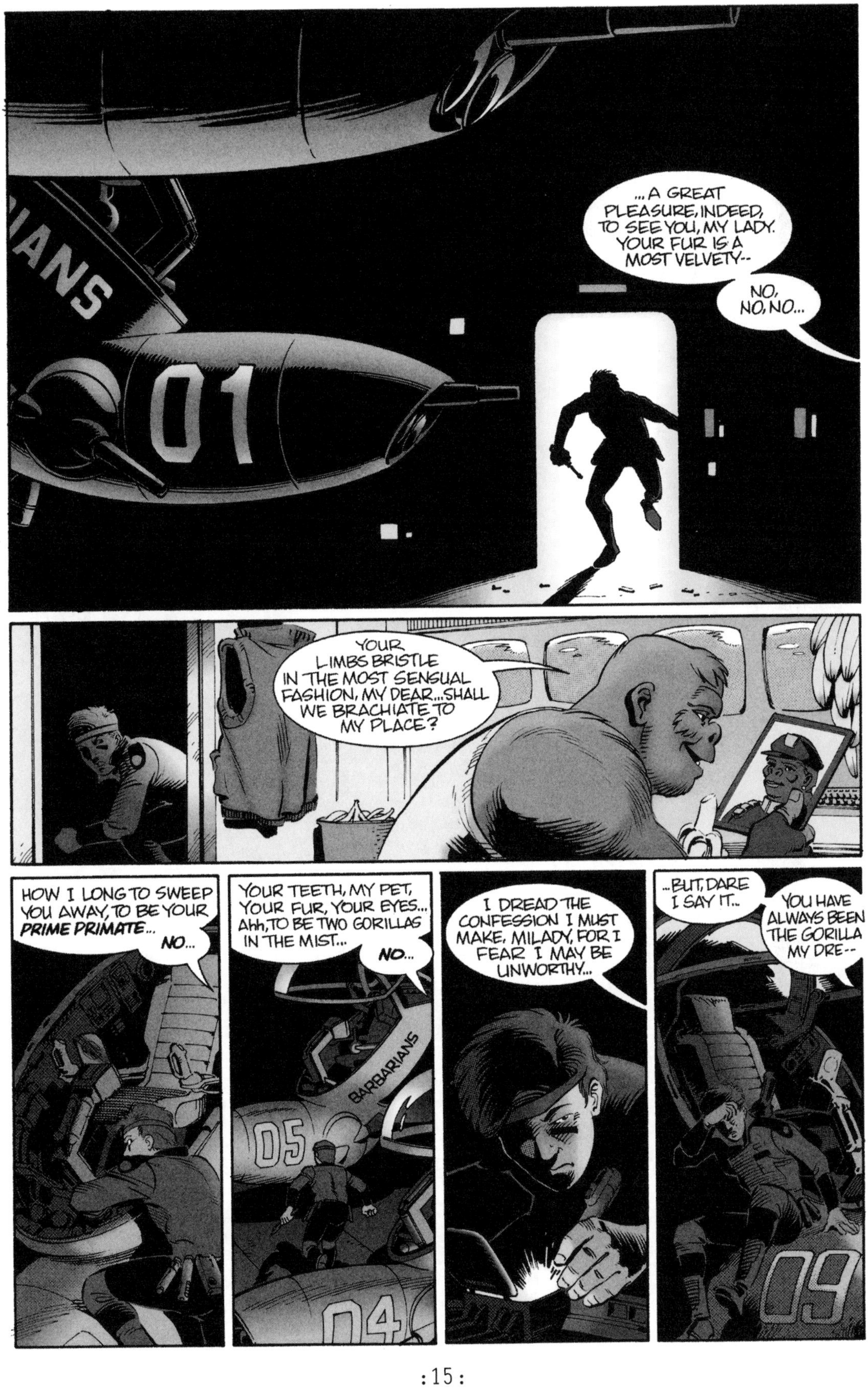
...A GREAT PLEASURE, INDEED, TO SEE YOU, MY LADY. YOUR FUR IS A MOST VELVETY--
NO, NO, NO...
IANS
01
YOUR LIMBS BRISTLE IN THE MOST SENSUAL FASHION, MY DEAR...SHALL WE BRACHIATE TO MY PLACE?
HOW I LONG TO SWEEP YOU AWAY, TO BE YOUR *PRIME PRIMATE*...
NO...
YOUR TEETH, MY PET, YOUR FUR, YOUR EYES... Ahh, TO BE TWO GORILLAS IN THE MIST...
NO...
BARBARIANS
05
04
I DREAD THE CONFESSION I MUST MAKE, MILADY, FOR I FEAR I MAY BE UNWORTHY...
...BUT, DARE I SAY IT...
YOU HAVE ALWAYS BEEN THE GORILLA MY DRE--
09

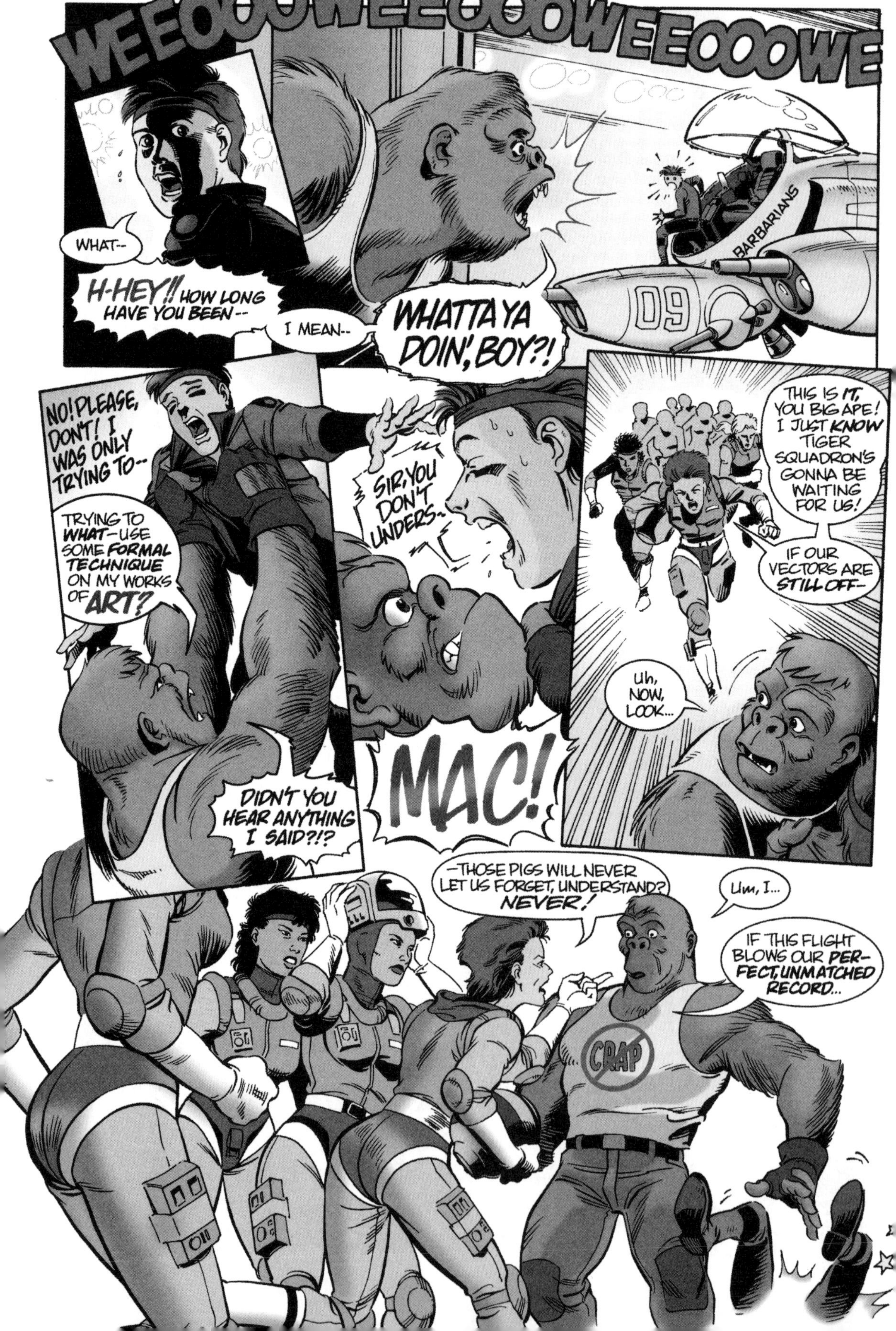
WEEOOOWEEOOOWEEOOOWE
BARBARIANS
09
WHAT--
H-HEY!! HOW LONG HAVE YOU BEEN--
I MEAN--
WHATTA YA DOIN', BOY?!
NO! PLEASE, DON'T! I WAS ONLY TRYING TO--
TRYING TO WHAT--USE SOME FORMAL TECHNIQUE ON MY WORKS OF ART?
DIDN'T YOU HEAR ANYTHING I SAID?!?
SIR, YOU DON'T UNDERS--
MAC!
THIS IS IT, YOU BIG APE! I JUST KNOW TIGER SQUADRON'S GONNA BE WAITING FOR US!
IF OUR VECTORS ARE STILL OFF--
Uh, NOW, LOOK...
--THOSE PIGS WILL NEVER LET US FORGET, UNDERSTAND? NEVER!
Um, I...
IF THIS FLIGHT BLOWS OUR PERFECT, UNMATCHED RECORD...
CRAP

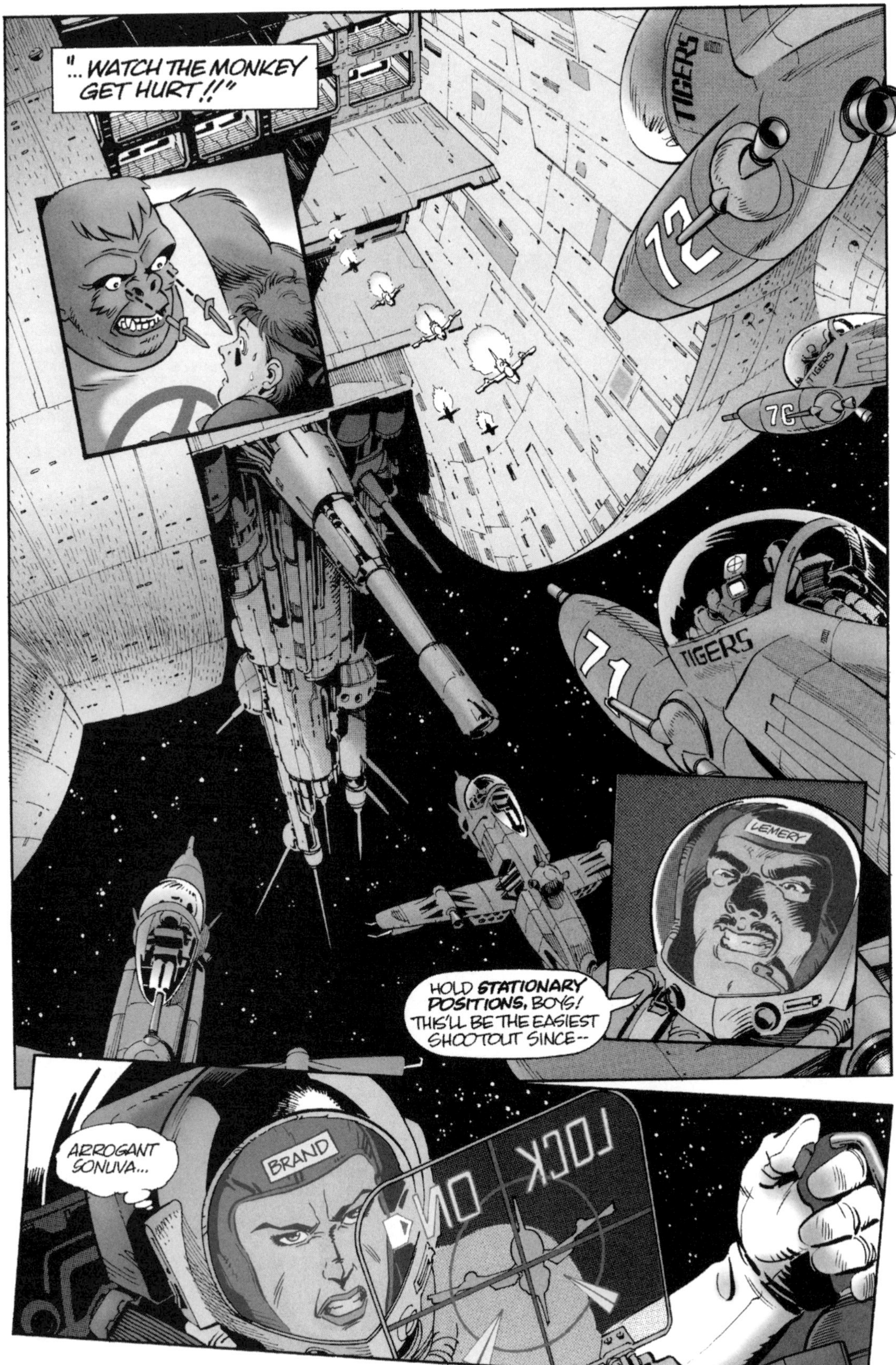
"...WATCH THE MONKEY GET HURT!!"
TIGERS
72
TIGERS
70
TIGERS
71
LEMERY
HOLD STATIONARY POSITIONS, BOYS! THIS'LL BE THE EASIEST SHOOTOUT SINCE--
ARROGANT SONUVA...
BRAND

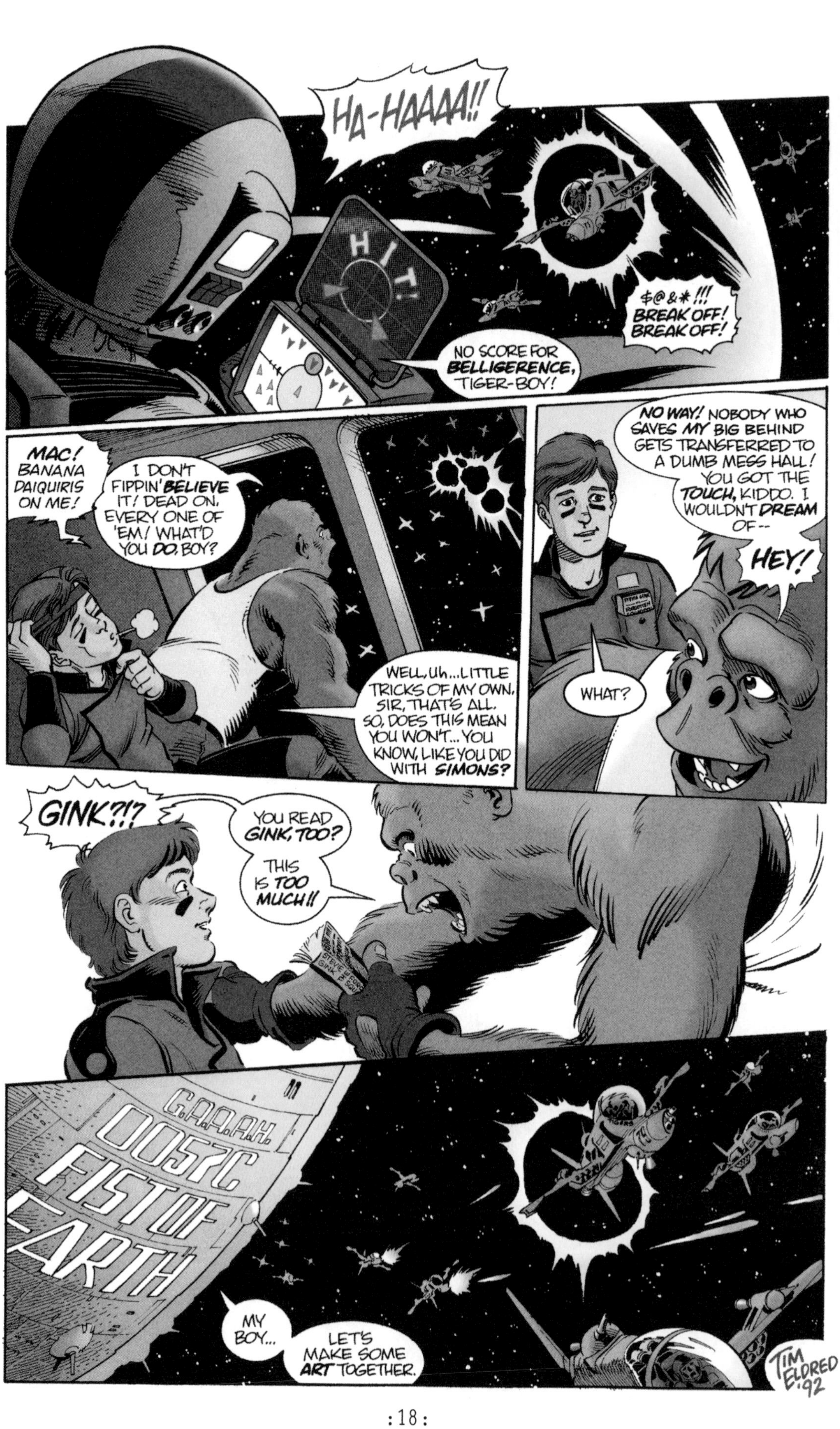
HA-HAAAA!!
HIT!
$@&*!!! BREAK OFF! BREAK OFF!
NO SCORE FOR BELLIGERENCE, TIGER-BOY!
MAC! BANANA DAIQUIRIS ON ME!
I DON'T FIPPIN' BELIEVE IT! DEAD ON, EVERY ONE OF 'EM! WHAT'D YOU DO, BOY?
WELL, Uh... LITTLE TRICKS OF MY OWN, SIR, THAT'S ALL. SO, DOES THIS MEAN YOU WON'T... YOU KNOW, LIKE YOU DID WITH SIMONS?
NO WAY! NOBODY WHO SAVES MY BIG BEHIND GETS TRANSFERRED TO A DUMB MESS HALL! YOU GOT THE TOUCH, KIDDO. I WOULDN'T DREAM OF--
HEY!
WHAT?
GINK?!?
YOU READ GINK, TOO?
THIS IS TOO MUCH!!
G.A.A.A.H. 005.C FIST OF EARTH
MY BOY...
LET'S MAKE SOME ART TOGETHER.
TIM ELDRED '92

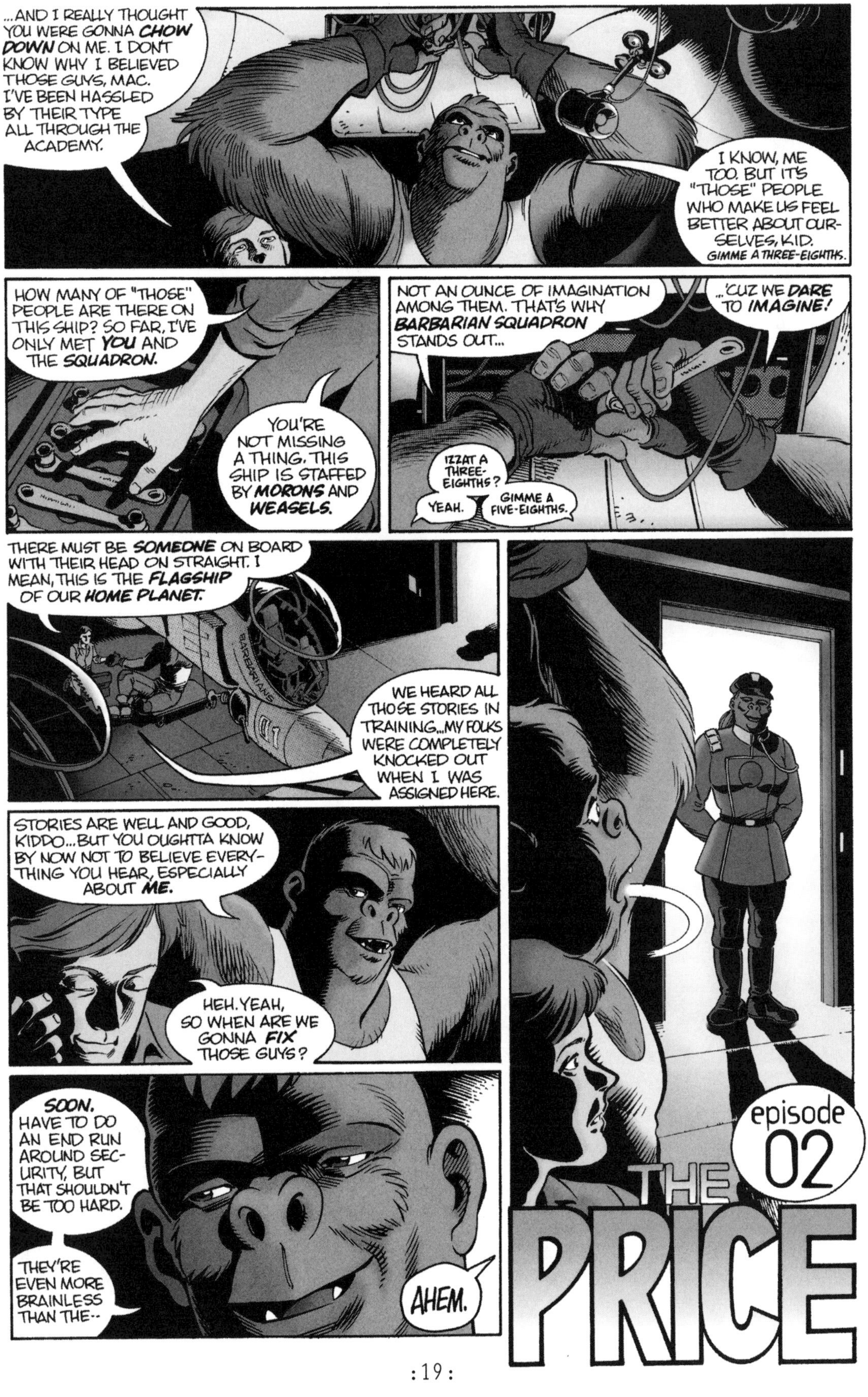
...AND I REALLY THOUGHT YOU WERE GONNA CHOW DOWN ON ME. I DON'T KNOW WHY I BELIEVED THOSE GUYS, MAC. I'VE BEEN HASSLED BY THEIR TYPE ALL THROUGH THE ACADEMY.
I KNOW, ME TOO. BUT IT'S "THOSE" PEOPLE WHO MAKE US FEEL BETTER ABOUT OURSELVES, KID. GIMME A THREE-EIGHTHS.
HOW MANY OF "THOSE" PEOPLE ARE THERE ON THIS SHIP? SO FAR, I'VE ONLY MET YOU AND THE SQUADRON.
YOU'RE NOT MISSING A THING. THIS SHIP IS STAFFED BY MORONS AND WEASELS.
NOT AN OUNCE OF IMAGINATION AMONG THEM. THAT'S WHY BARBARIAN SQUADRON STANDS OUT...
...'CUZ WE DARE TO IMAGINE!
IZZAT A THREE-EIGHTHS?
YEAH.
GIMME A FIVE-EIGHTHS.
THERE MUST BE SOMEONE ON BOARD WITH THEIR HEAD ON STRAIGHT. I MEAN, THIS IS THE FLAGSHIP OF OUR HOME PLANET.
BARBARIANS
WE HEARD ALL THOSE STORIES IN TRAINING...MY FOLKS WERE COMPLETELY KNOCKED OUT WHEN I WAS ASSIGNED HERE.
STORIES ARE WELL AND GOOD, KIDDO...BUT YOU OUGHTTA KNOW BY NOW NOT TO BELIEVE EVERYTHING YOU HEAR, ESPECIALLY ABOUT ME.
HEH. YEAH, SO WHEN ARE WE GONNA FIX THOSE GUYS?
SOON. HAVE TO DO AN END RUN AROUND SECURITY, BUT THAT SHOULDN'T BE TOO HARD.
THEY'RE EVEN MORE BRAINLESS THAN THE--
AHEM.
episode 02
THE PRICE

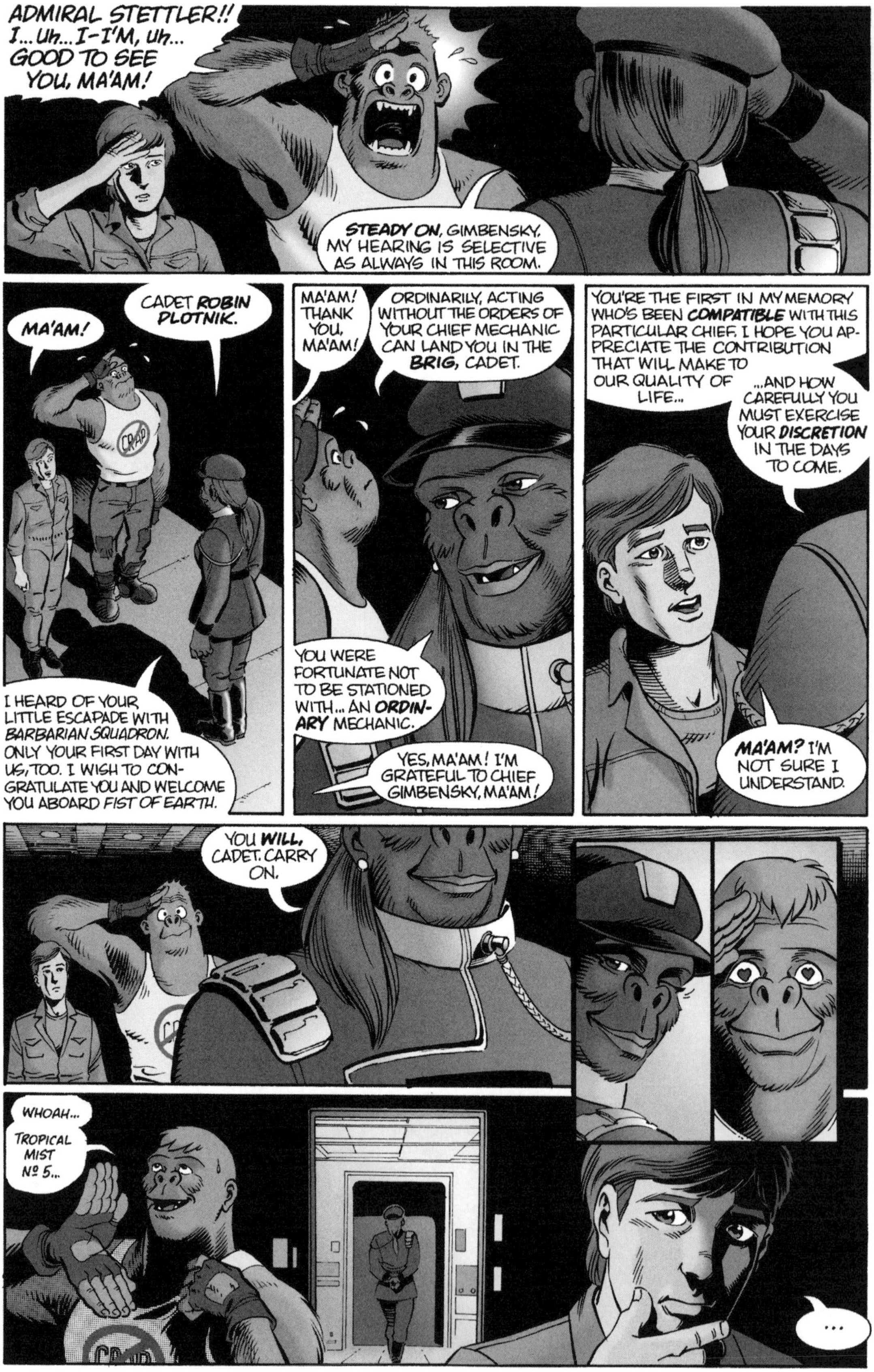
ADMIRAL STETTLER!! I... Uh... I-I'M, uh... GOOD TO SEE YOU, MA'AM!
STEADY ON, GIMBENSKY. MY HEARING IS SELECTIVE AS ALWAYS IN THIS ROOM.
MA'AM!
CADET ROBIN PLOTNIK.
CRAP
I HEARD OF YOUR LITTLE ESCAPADE WITH BARBARIAN SQUADRON. ONLY YOUR FIRST DAY WITH US, TOO. I WISH TO CONGRATULATE YOU AND WELCOME YOU ABOARD FIST OF EARTH.
MA'AM! THANK YOU, MA'AM!
ORDINARILY, ACTING WITHOUT THE ORDERS OF YOUR CHIEF MECHANIC CAN LAND YOU IN THE BRIG, CADET.
YOU WERE FORTUNATE NOT TO BE STATIONED WITH... AN ORDINARY MECHANIC.
YES, MA'AM! I'M GRATEFUL TO CHIEF GIMBENSKY, MA'AM!
YOU'RE THE FIRST IN MY MEMORY WHO'S BEEN COMPATIBLE WITH THIS PARTICULAR CHIEF. I HOPE YOU APPRECIATE THE CONTRIBUTION THAT WILL MAKE TO OUR QUALITY OF LIFE...
...AND HOW CAREFULLY YOU MUST EXERCISE YOUR DISCRETION IN THE DAYS TO COME.
MA'AM? I'M NOT SURE I UNDERSTAND.
YOU WILL, CADET. CARRY ON.
WHOAH...
TROPICAL MIST Nº 5...
...

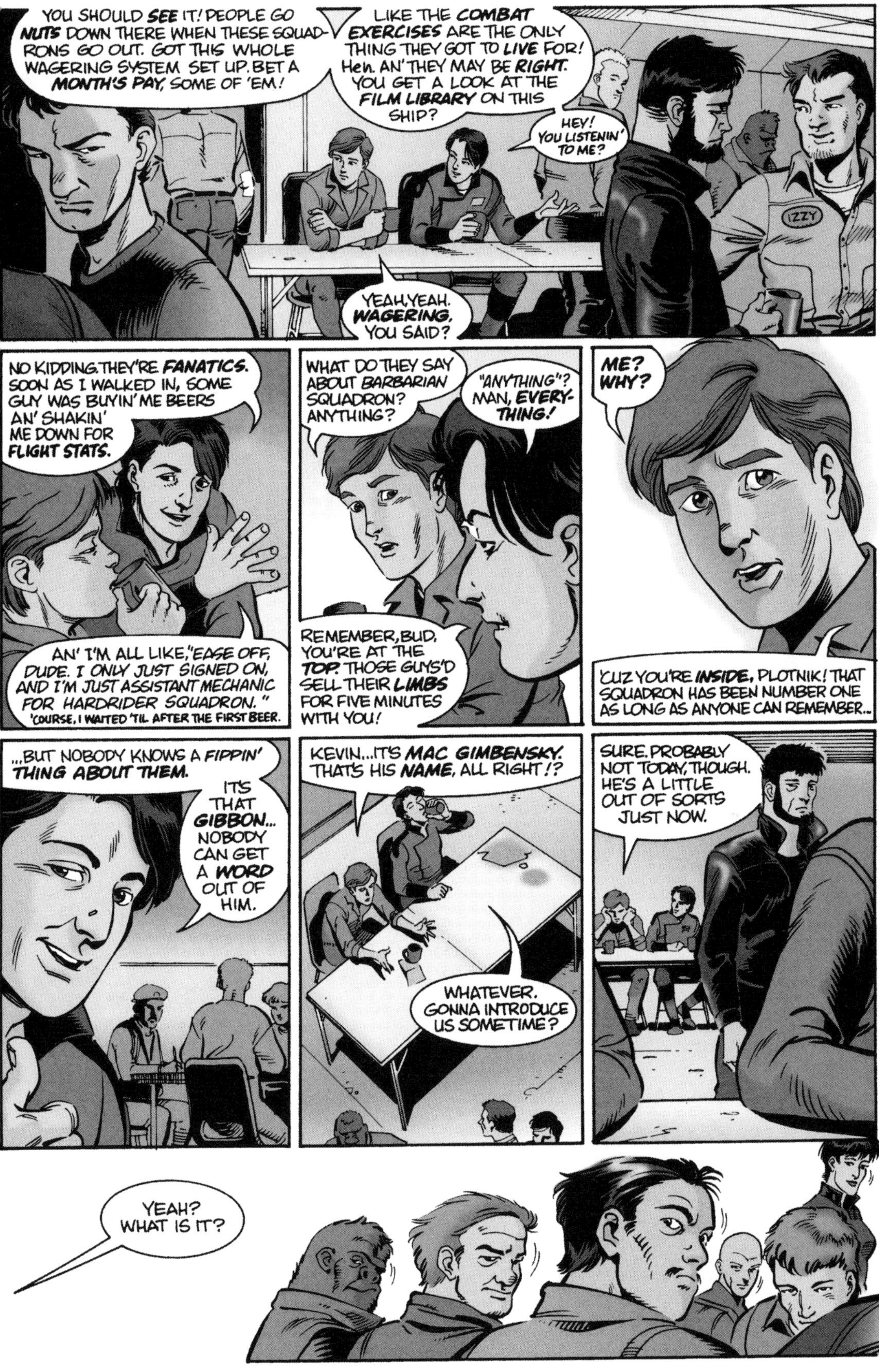
YOU SHOULD SEE IT! PEOPLE GO NUTS DOWN THERE WHEN THESE SQUADRONS GO OUT. GOT THIS WHOLE WAGERING SYSTEM SET UP. BET A MONTH'S PAY, SOME OF 'EM!
LIKE THE COMBAT EXERCISES ARE THE ONLY THING THEY GOT TO LIVE FOR! Heh. AN' THEY MAY BE RIGHT. YOU GET A LOOK AT THE FILM LIBRARY ON THIS SHIP?
HEY! YOU LISTENIN' TO ME?
IZZY
YEAH, YEAH. WAGERING, YOU SAID?
NO KIDDING. THEY'RE FANATICS. SOON AS I WALKED IN, SOME GUY WAS BUYIN' ME BEERS AN' SHAKIN' ME DOWN FOR FLIGHT STATS.
AN' I'M ALL LIKE, "EASE OFF, DUDE. I ONLY JUST SIGNED ON, AND I'M JUST ASSISTANT MECHANIC FOR HARDRIDER SQUADRON."
'COURSE, I WAITED 'TIL AFTER THE FIRST BEER.
WHAT DO THEY SAY ABOUT BARBARIAN SQUADRON? ANYTHING?
"ANYTHING"? MAN, EVERYTHING!
REMEMBER, BUD, YOU'RE AT THE TOP. THOSE GUYS'D SELL THEIR LIMBS FOR FIVE MINUTES WITH YOU!
ME? WHY?
'CUZ YOU'RE INSIDE, PLOTNIK! THAT SQUADRON HAS BEEN NUMBER ONE AS LONG AS ANYONE CAN REMEMBER...
...BUT NOBODY KNOWS A FIPPIN' THING ABOUT THEM.
IT'S THAT GIBBON... NOBODY CAN GET A WORD OUT OF HIM.
KEVIN...IT'S MAC GIMBENSKY. THAT'S HIS NAME, ALL RIGHT!?
WHATEVER. GONNA INTRODUCE US SOMETIME?
SURE. PROBABLY NOT TODAY, THOUGH. HE'S A LITTLE OUT OF SORTS JUST NOW.
YEAH? WHAT IS IT?

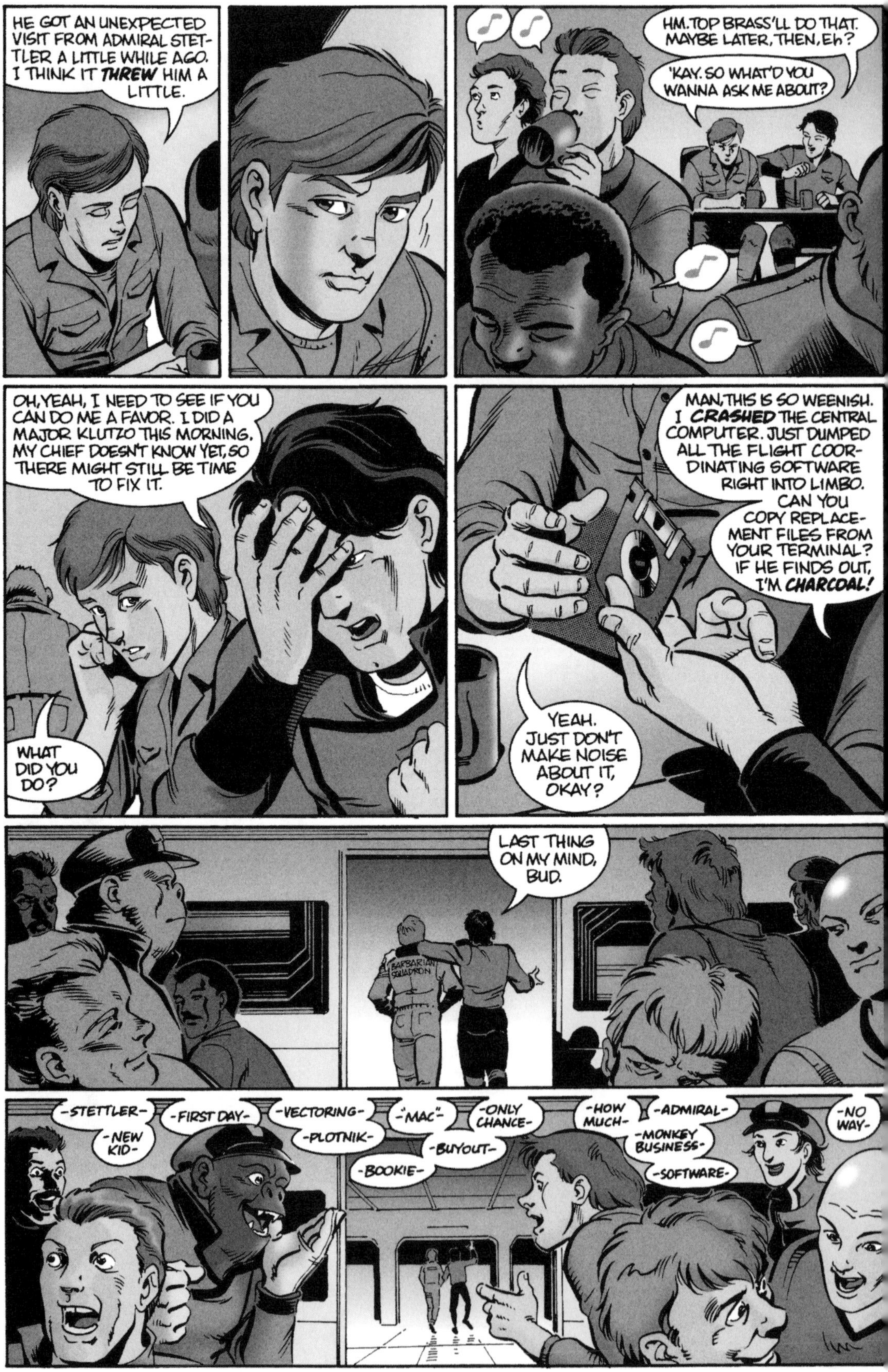
HE GOT AN UNEXPECTED VISIT FROM ADMIRAL STETTLER A LITTLE WHILE AGO. I THINK IT THREW HIM A LITTLE.
HM. TOP BRASS'LL DO THAT. MAYBE LATER, THEN, Eh?
'KAY. SO WHAT'D YOU WANNA ASK ME ABOUT?
OH, YEAH, I NEED TO SEE IF YOU CAN DO ME A FAVOR. I DID A MAJOR KLUTZO THIS MORNING. MY CHIEF DOESN'T KNOW YET, SO THERE MIGHT STILL BE TIME TO FIX IT.
WHAT DID YOU DO?
MAN, THIS IS SO WEENISH. I CRASHED THE CENTRAL COMPUTER. JUST DUMPED ALL THE FLIGHT COORDINATING SOFTWARE RIGHT INTO LIMBO. CAN YOU COPY REPLACEMENT FILES FROM YOUR TERMINAL? IF HE FINDS OUT, I'M CHARCOAL!
YEAH. JUST DON'T MAKE NOISE ABOUT IT, OKAY?
LAST THING ON MY MIND, BUD.
BARBARIAN SQUADRON
-STETTLER-
-NEW KID-
-FIRST DAY-
-VECTORING-
-PLOTNIK-
-"MAC"-
-BUYOUT-
-BOOKIE-
-ONLY CHANCE-
-HOW MUCH-
-ADMIRAL-
-MONKEY BUSINESS-
-SOFTWARE-
-NO WAY-

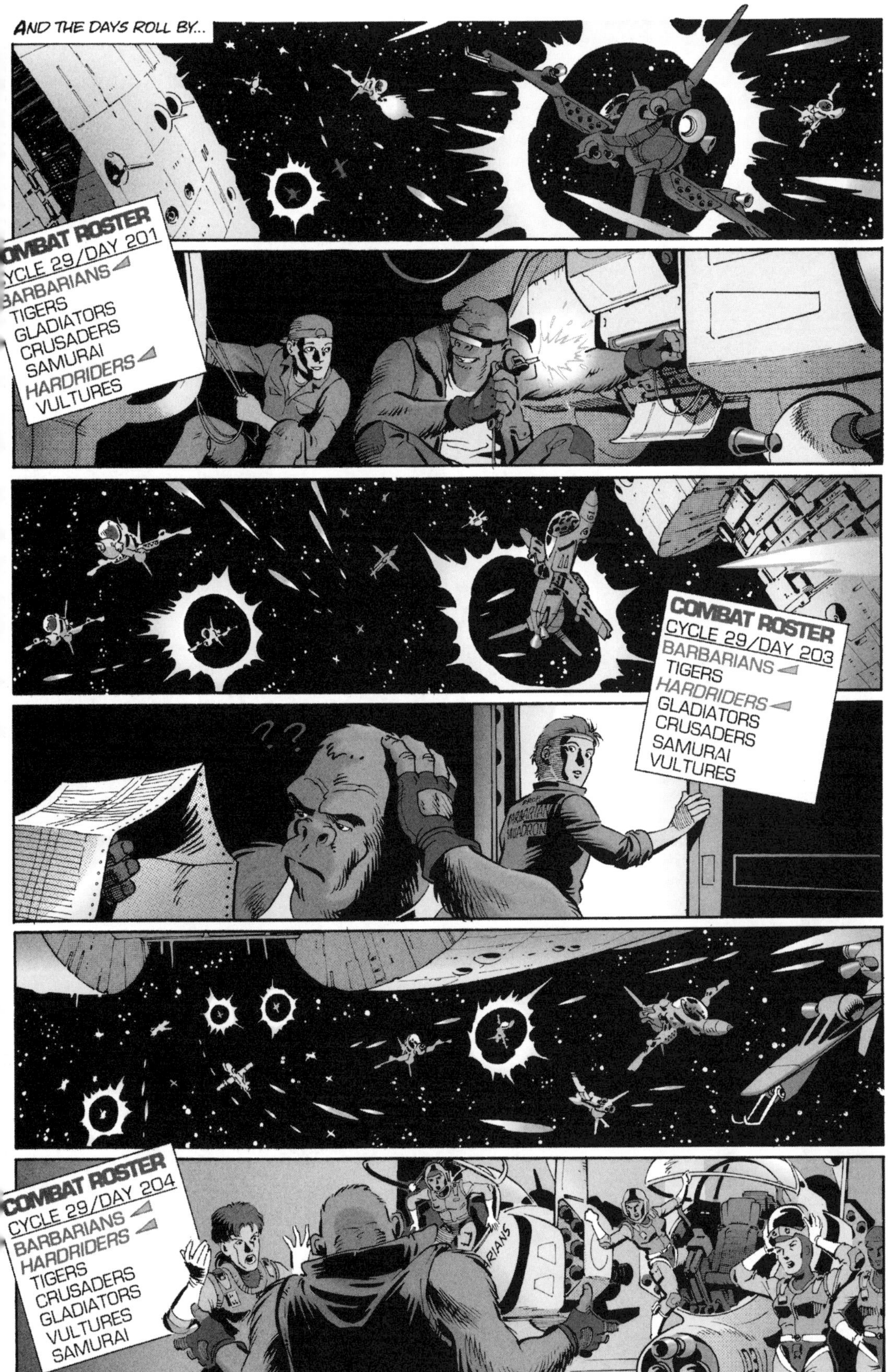
AND THE DAYS ROLL BY...
COMBAT ROSTER
CYCLE 29/DAY 201
BARBARIANS
TIGERS
GLADIATORS
CRUSADERS
SAMURAI
HARDRIDERS
VULTURES
COMBAT ROSTER
CYCLE 29/DAY 203
BARBARIANS
TIGERS
HARDRIDERS
GLADIATORS
CRUSADERS
SAMURAI
VULTURES
??
COMBAT ROSTER
CYCLE 29/DAY 204
BARBARIANS
HARDRIDERS
TIGERS
CRUSADERS
GLADIATORS
VULTURES
SAMURAI

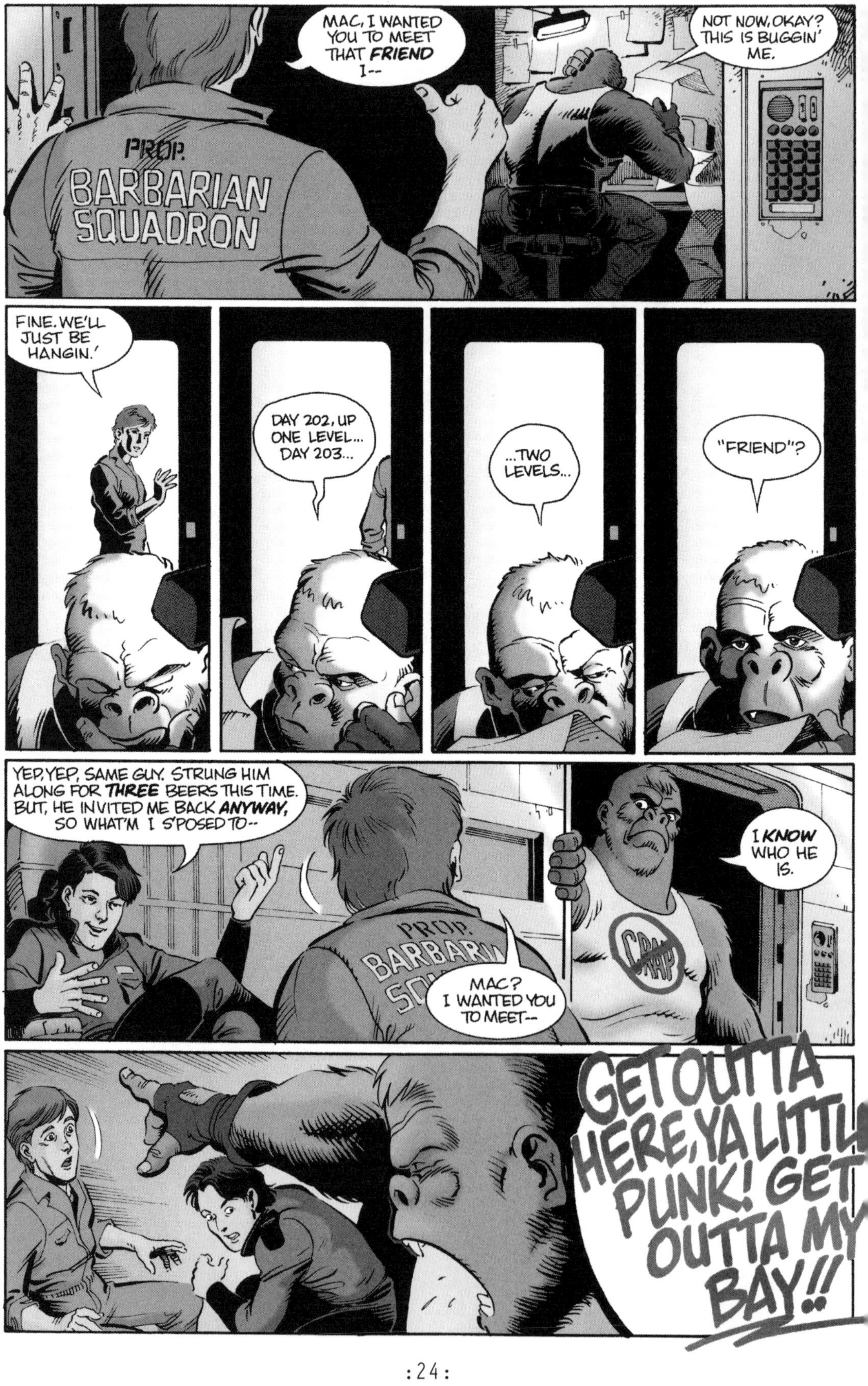
MAC, I WANTED YOU TO MEET THAT FRIEND I--
NOT NOW, OKAY? THIS IS BUGGIN' ME.
PROP.
BARBARIAN SQUADRON
FINE. WE'LL JUST BE HANGIN.'
DAY 202, UP ONE LEVEL... DAY 203...
...TWO LEVELS...
"FRIEND"?
YEP, YEP, SAME GUY. STRUNG HIM ALONG FOR THREE BEERS THIS TIME. BUT, HE INVITED ME BACK ANYWAY, SO WHAT'M I S'POSED TO--
I KNOW WHO HE IS.
MAC? I WANTED YOU TO MEET--
GET OUTTA HERE, YA LITTL PUNK! GET OUTTA MY BAY!!

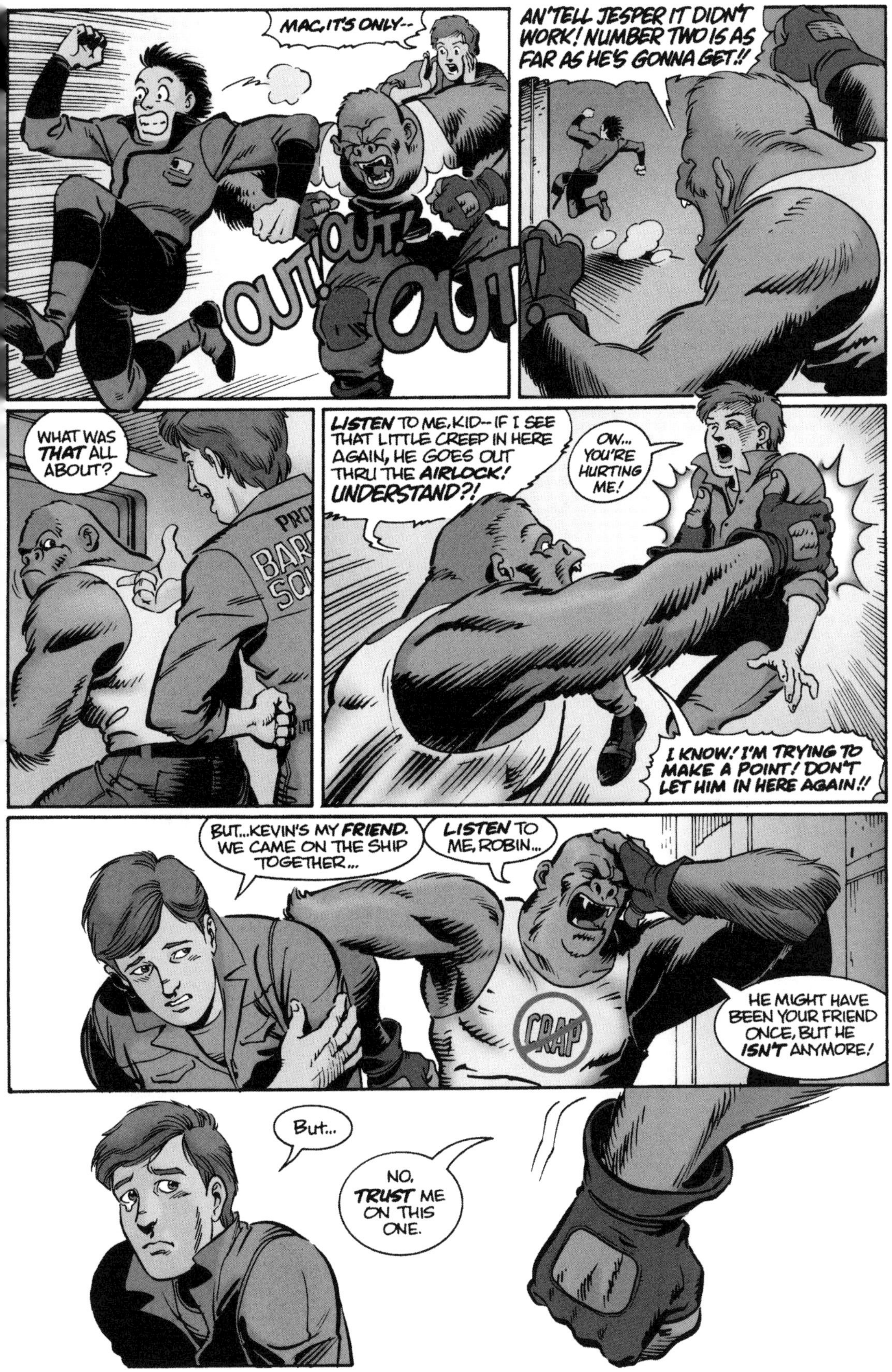

MAC, IT'S ONLY--
OUT! OUT! OUT!
AN' TELL JESPER IT DIDN'T WORK! NUMBER TWO IS AS FAR AS HE'S GONNA GET!!
WHAT WAS THAT ALL ABOUT?
LISTEN TO ME, KID-- IF I SEE THAT LITTLE CREEP IN HERE AGAIN, HE GOES OUT THRU THE AIRLOCK! UNDERSTAND?!
OW... YOU'RE HURTING ME!
I KNOW! I'M TRYING TO MAKE A POINT! DON'T LET HIM IN HERE AGAIN!!
BUT...KEVIN'S MY FRIEND. WE CAME ON THE SHIP TOGETHER...
LISTEN TO ME, ROBIN...
CRAP
HE MIGHT HAVE BEEN YOUR FRIEND ONCE, BUT HE ISN'T ANYMORE!
But...
NO. TRUST ME ON THIS ONE.

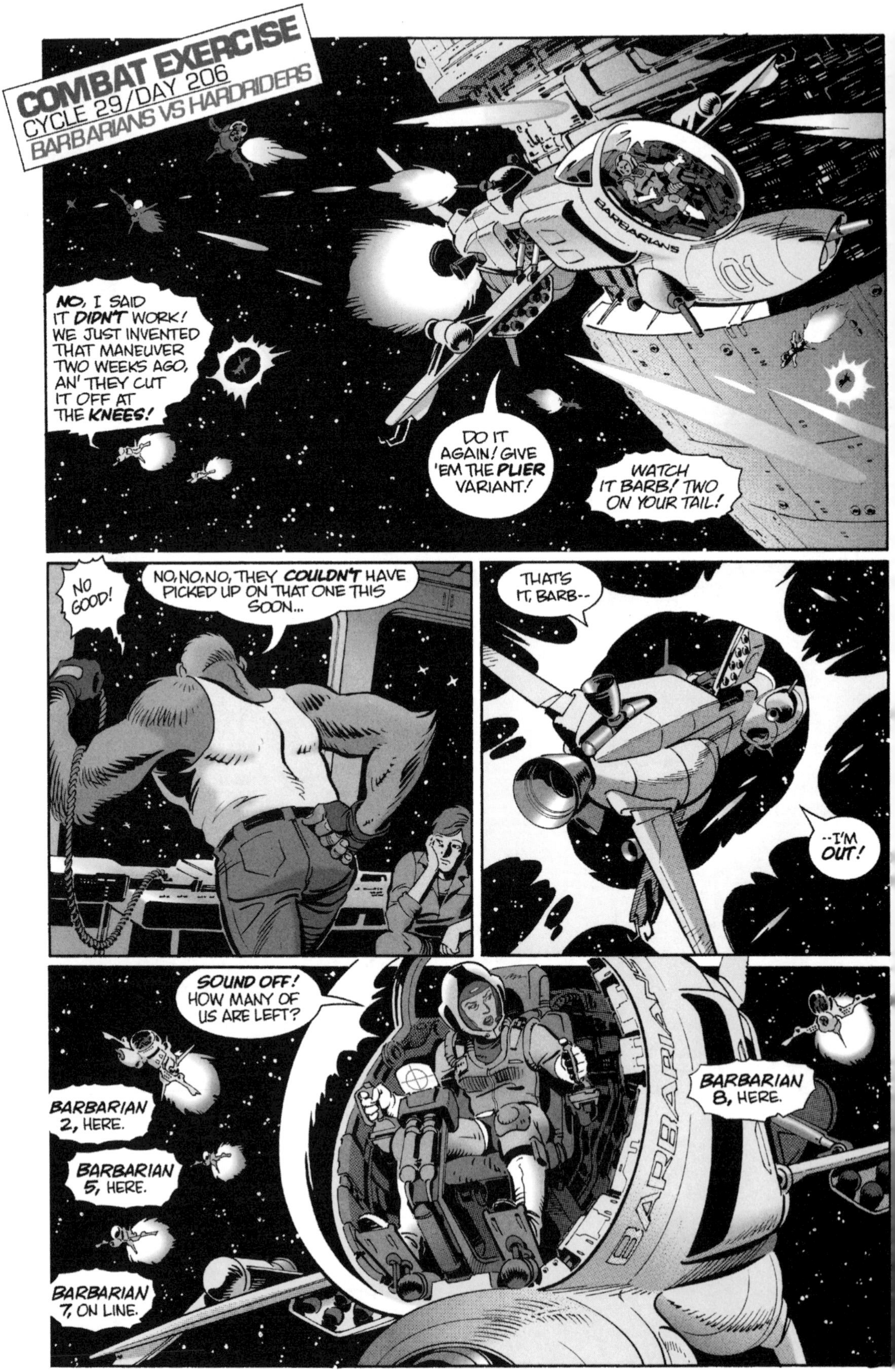
COMBAT EXERCISE
CYCLE 29/DAY 206
BARBARIANS VS HARDRIDERS
NO, I SAID IT DIDN'T WORK! WE JUST INVENTED THAT MANEUVER TWO WEEKS AGO, AN' THEY CUT IT OFF AT THE KNEES!
DO IT AGAIN! GIVE 'EM THE PLIER VARIANT!
WATCH IT BARB! TWO ON YOUR TAIL!
NO GOOD!
NO, NO, NO, THEY COULDN'T HAVE PICKED UP ON THAT ONE THIS SOON...
THAT'S IT, BARB--
--I'M OUT!
SOUND OFF! HOW MANY OF US ARE LEFT?
BARBARIAN 2, HERE.
BARBARIAN 5, HERE.
BARBARIAN 7, ON LINE.
BARBARIAN 8, HERE.

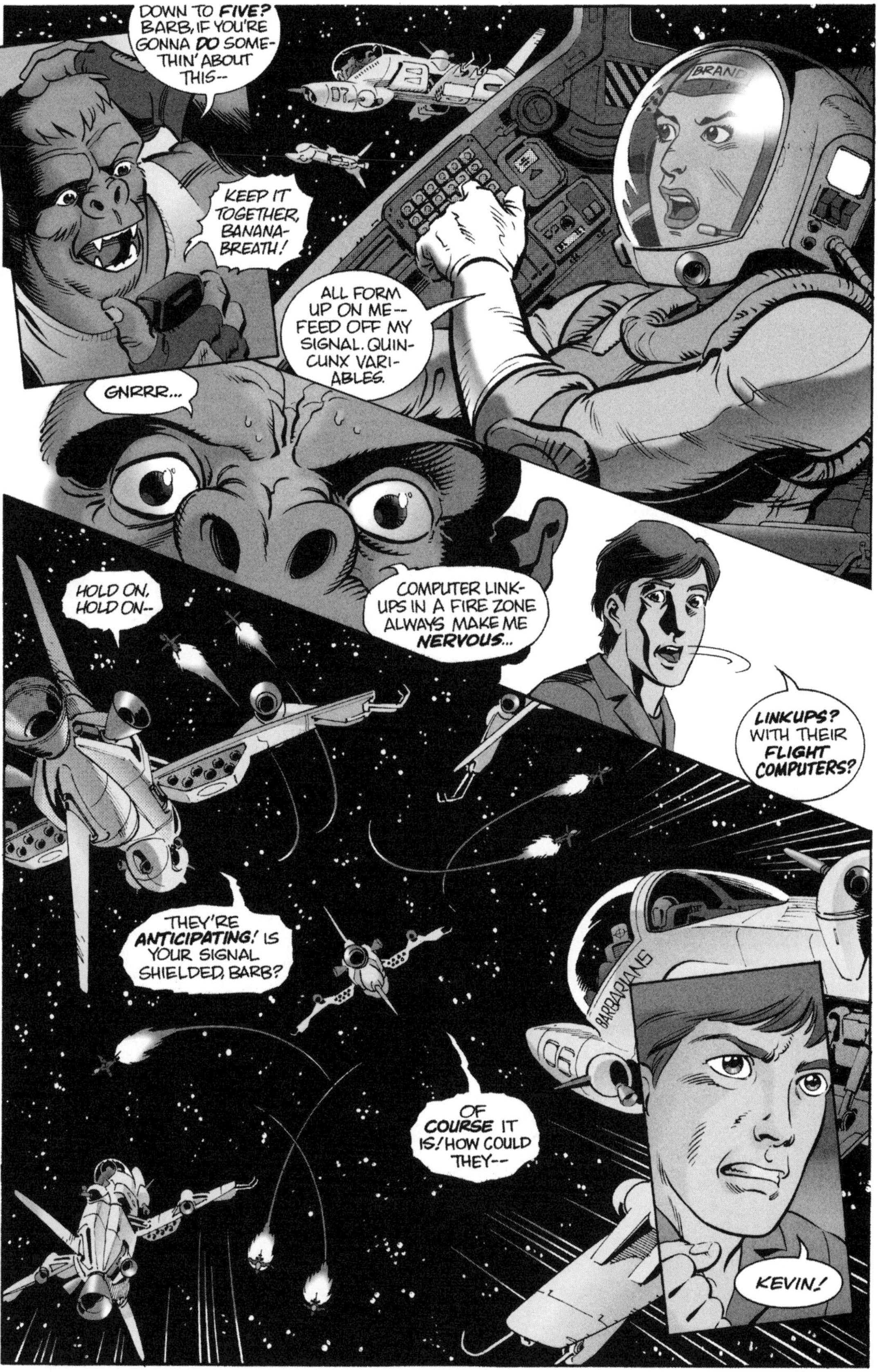
DOWN TO FIVE? BARB, IF YOU'RE GONNA DO SOMETHIN' ABOUT THIS--
KEEP IT TOGETHER, BANANA-BREATH!
ALL FORM UP ON ME-- FEED OFF MY SIGNAL. QUINCUNX VARIABLES.
GNRRR...
BRAND
HOLD ON, HOLD ON--
COMPUTER LINK-UPS IN A FIRE ZONE ALWAYS MAKE ME NERVOUS...
LINKUPS? WITH THEIR FLIGHT COMPUTERS?
THEY'RE ANTICIPATING! IS YOUR SIGNAL SHIELDED, BARB?
BARBARIANS
OF COURSE IT IS! HOW COULD THEY--
KEVIN!

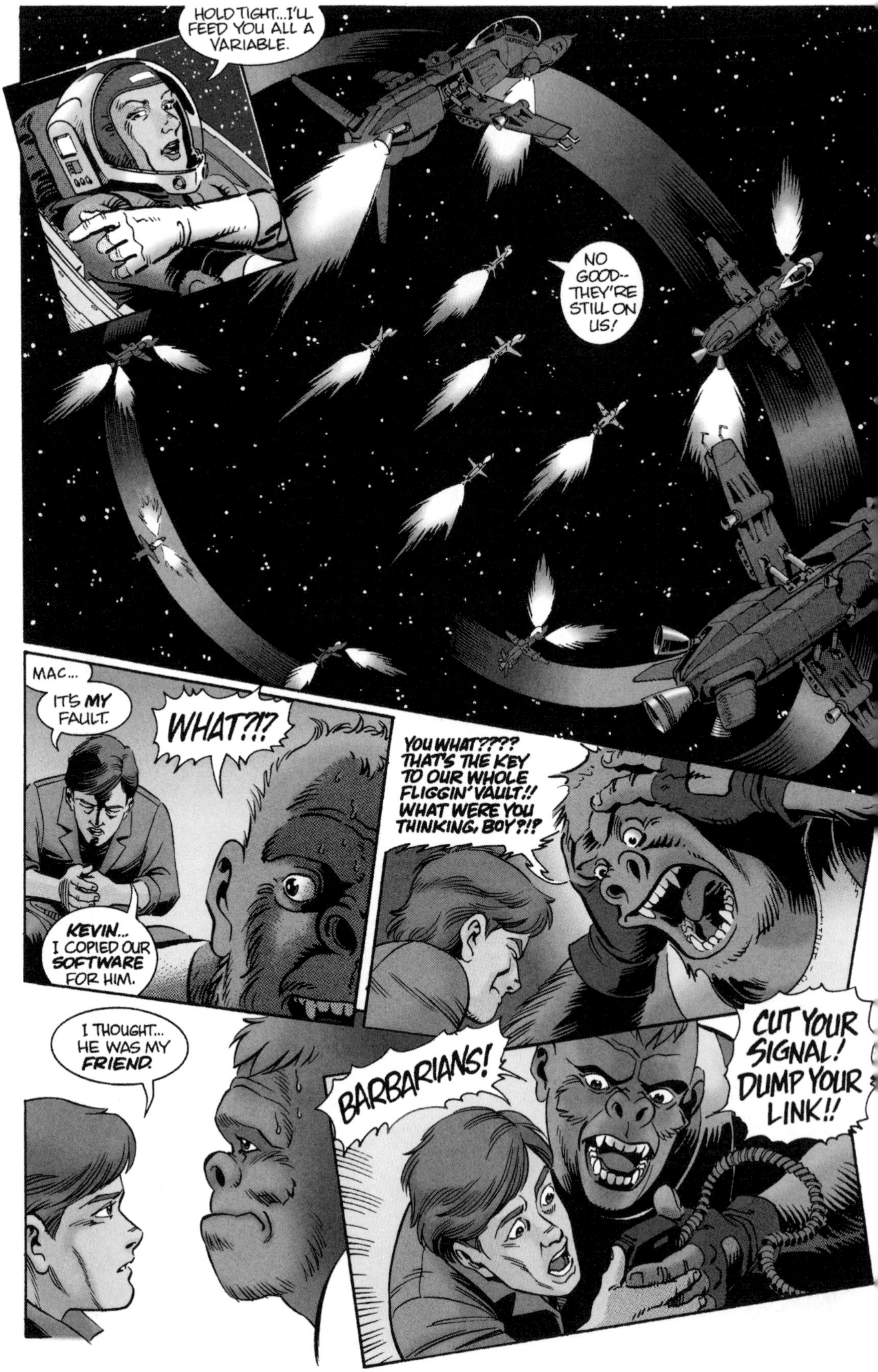
HOLD TIGHT...I'LL FEED YOU ALL A VARIABLE.
NO GOOD-- THEY'RE STILL ON US!
MAC...
IT'S MY FAULT.
WHAT?!?
KEVIN... I COPIED OUR SOFTWARE FOR HIM.
YOU WHAT???? THAT'S THE KEY TO OUR WHOLE FLIGGIN' VAULT!! WHAT WERE YOU THINKING, BOY?!?
I THOUGHT... HE WAS MY FRIEND.
BARBARIANS!
CUT YOUR SIGNAL! DUMP YOUR LINK!!

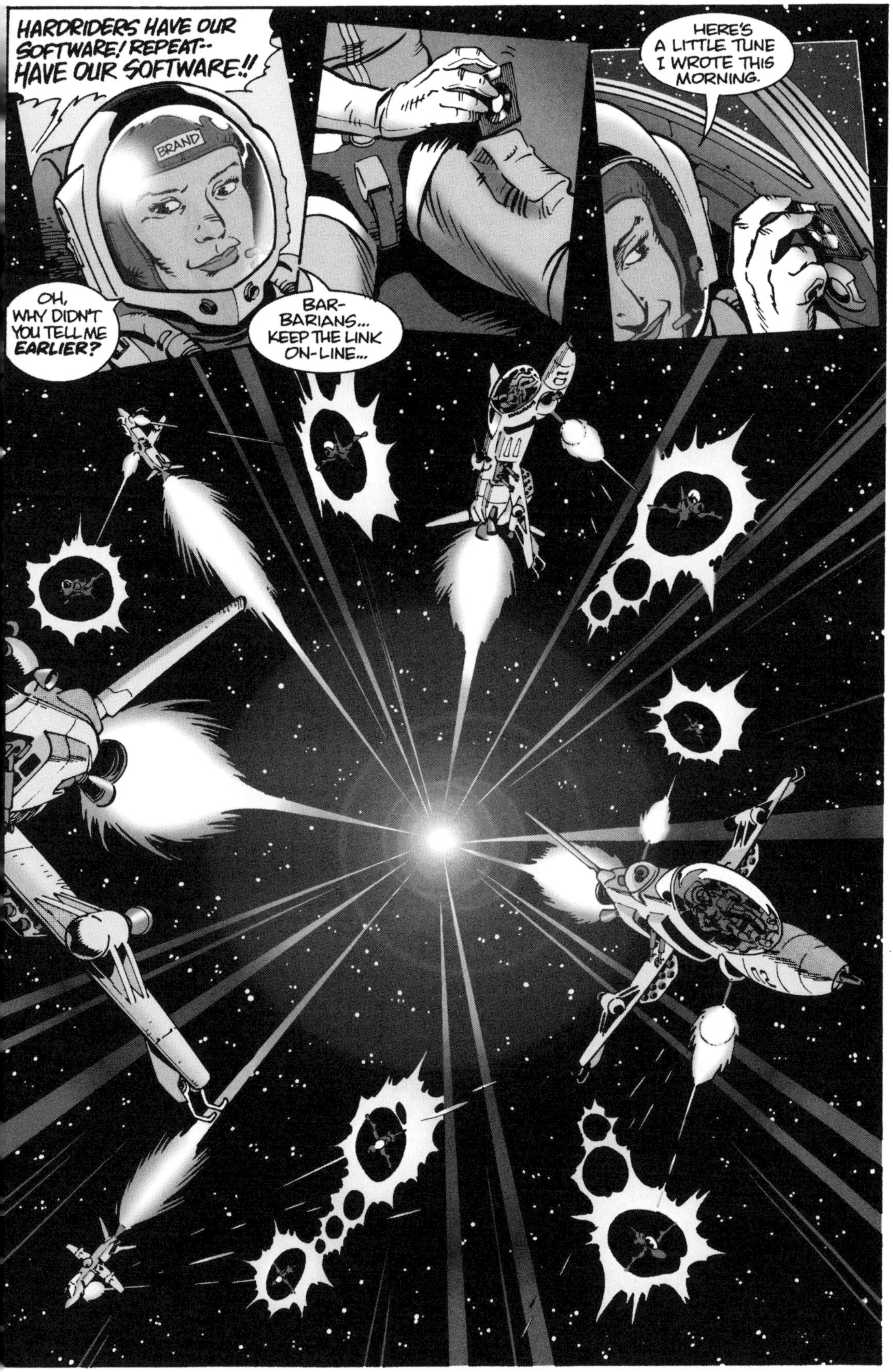
HARDRIDERS HAVE OUR SOFTWARE! REPEAT-- HAVE OUR SOFTWARE!!
BRAND
HERE'S A LITTLE TUNE I WROTE THIS MORNING.
OH, WHY DIDN'T YOU TELL ME EARLIER?
BAR- BARIANS... KEEP THE LINK ON-LINE...
02

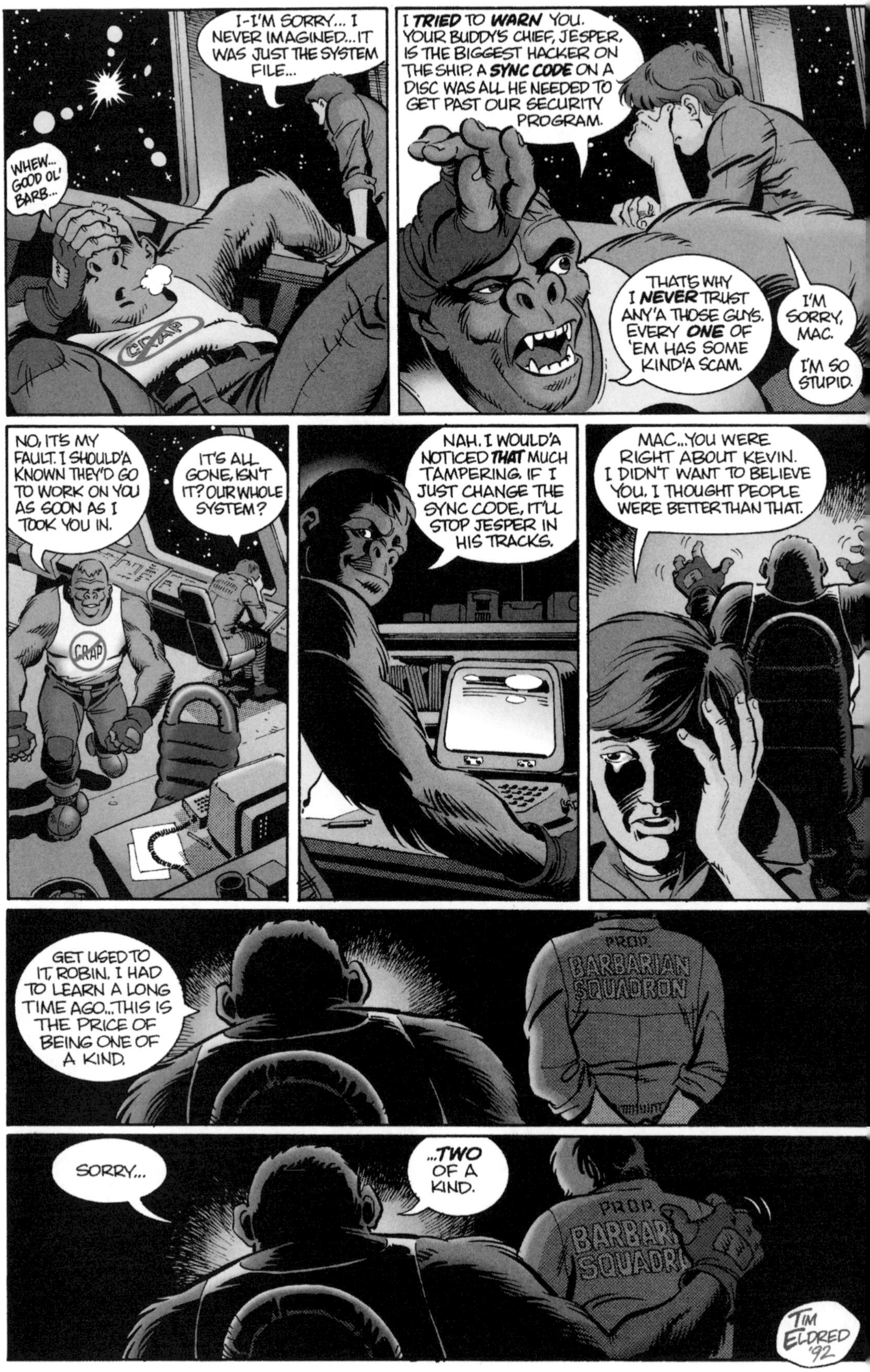

I-I'M SORRY... I NEVER IMAGINED... IT WAS JUST THE SYSTEM FILE...
WHEW... GOOD OL' BARB...
CRAP
I TRIED TO WARN YOU. YOUR BUDDY'S CHIEF, JESPER, IS THE BIGGEST HACKER ON THE SHIP. A SYNC CODE ON A DISC WAS ALL HE NEEDED TO GET PAST OUR SECURITY PROGRAM.
THAT'S WHY I NEVER TRUST ANY'A THOSE GUYS. EVERY ONE OF 'EM HAS SOME KIND'A SCAM.
I'M SORRY, MAC.
I'M SO STUPID.
NO, IT'S MY FAULT. I SHOULD'A KNOWN THEY'D GO TO WORK ON YOU AS SOON AS I TOOK YOU IN.
IT'S ALL GONE, ISN'T IT? OUR WHOLE SYSTEM?
CRAP
NAH. I WOULD'A NOTICED THAT MUCH TAMPERING. IF I JUST CHANGE THE SYNC CODE, IT'LL STOP JESPER IN HIS TRACKS.
MAC... YOU WERE RIGHT ABOUT KEVIN. I DIDN'T WANT TO BELIEVE YOU. I THOUGHT PEOPLE WERE BETTER THAN THAT.
GET USED TO IT, ROBIN. I HAD TO LEARN A LONG TIME AGO... THIS IS THE PRICE OF BEING ONE OF A KIND.
PROP. BARBARIAN SQUADRON
SORRY...
...TWO OF A KIND.
TIM ELDRED '92

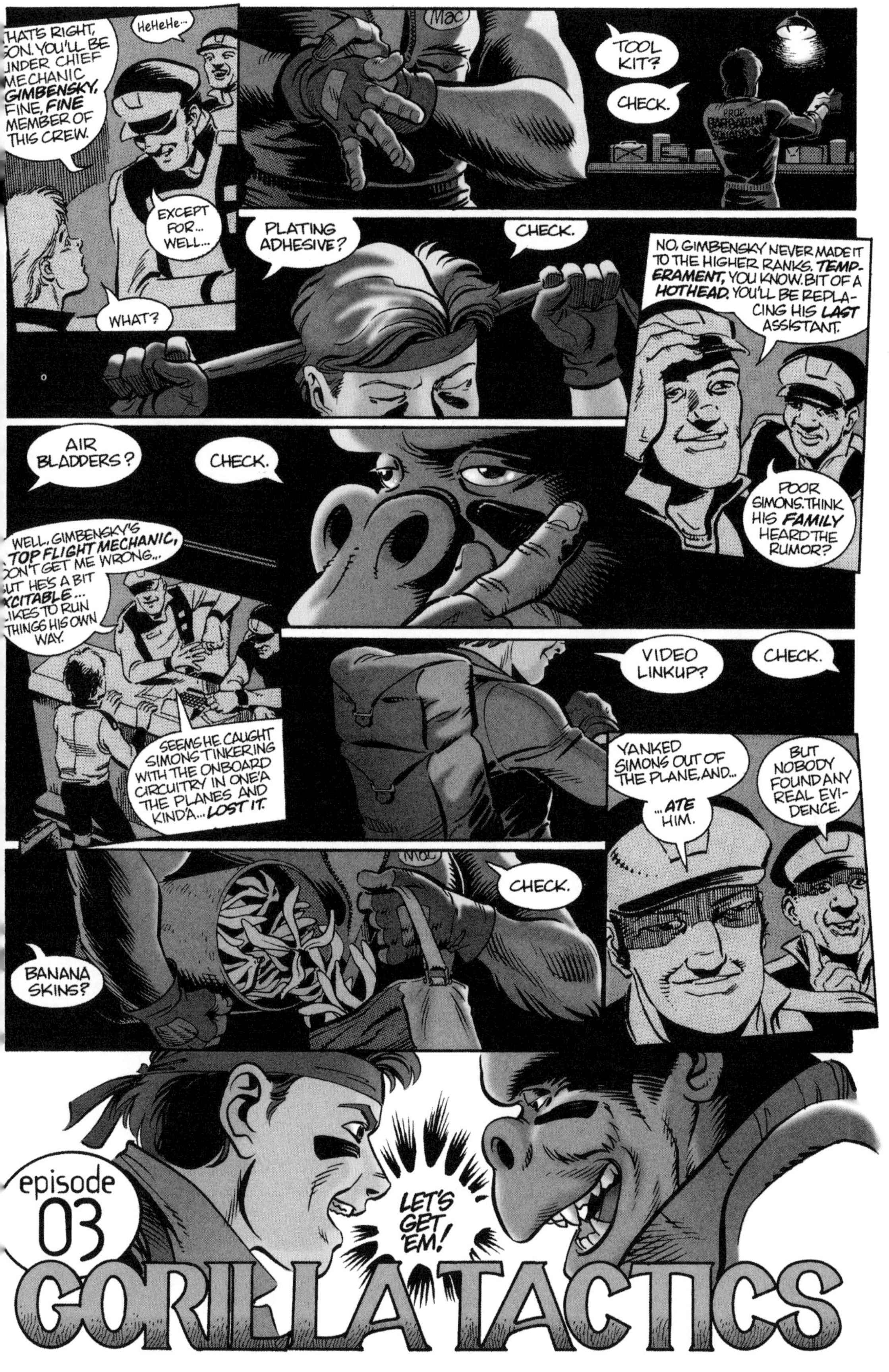
THAT'S RIGHT, SON. YOU'LL BE UNDER CHIEF MECHANIC GIMBENSKY. FINE, FINE MEMBER OF THIS CREW.
HeHeHe...
TOOL KIT?
CHECK.
EXCEPT FOR... WELL...
WHAT?
PLATING ADHESIVE?
CHECK.
NO, GIMBENSKY NEVER MADE IT TO THE HIGHER RANKS. TEMPERAMENT, YOU KNOW. BIT OF A HOTHEAD. YOU'LL BE REPLACING HIS LAST ASSISTANT.
AIR BLADDERS?
CHECK.
POOR SIMONS. THINK HIS FAMILY HEARD THE RUMOR?
WELL, GIMBENSKY'S TOP FLIGHT MECHANIC, DON'T GET ME WRONG... BUT HE'S A BIT EXCITABLE... LIKES TO RUN THINGS HIS OWN WAY.
SEEMS HE CAUGHT SIMONS TINKERING WITH THE ONBOARD CIRCUITRY IN ONE'A THE PLANES AND KIND'A... LOST IT.
VIDEO LINKUP?
CHECK.
YANKED SIMONS OUT OF THE PLANE, AND...
...ATE HIM.
BUT NOBODY FOUND ANY REAL EVIDENCE.
BANANA SKINS?
CHECK.
episode 03
LET'S GET 'EM!
GORILLA TACTICS

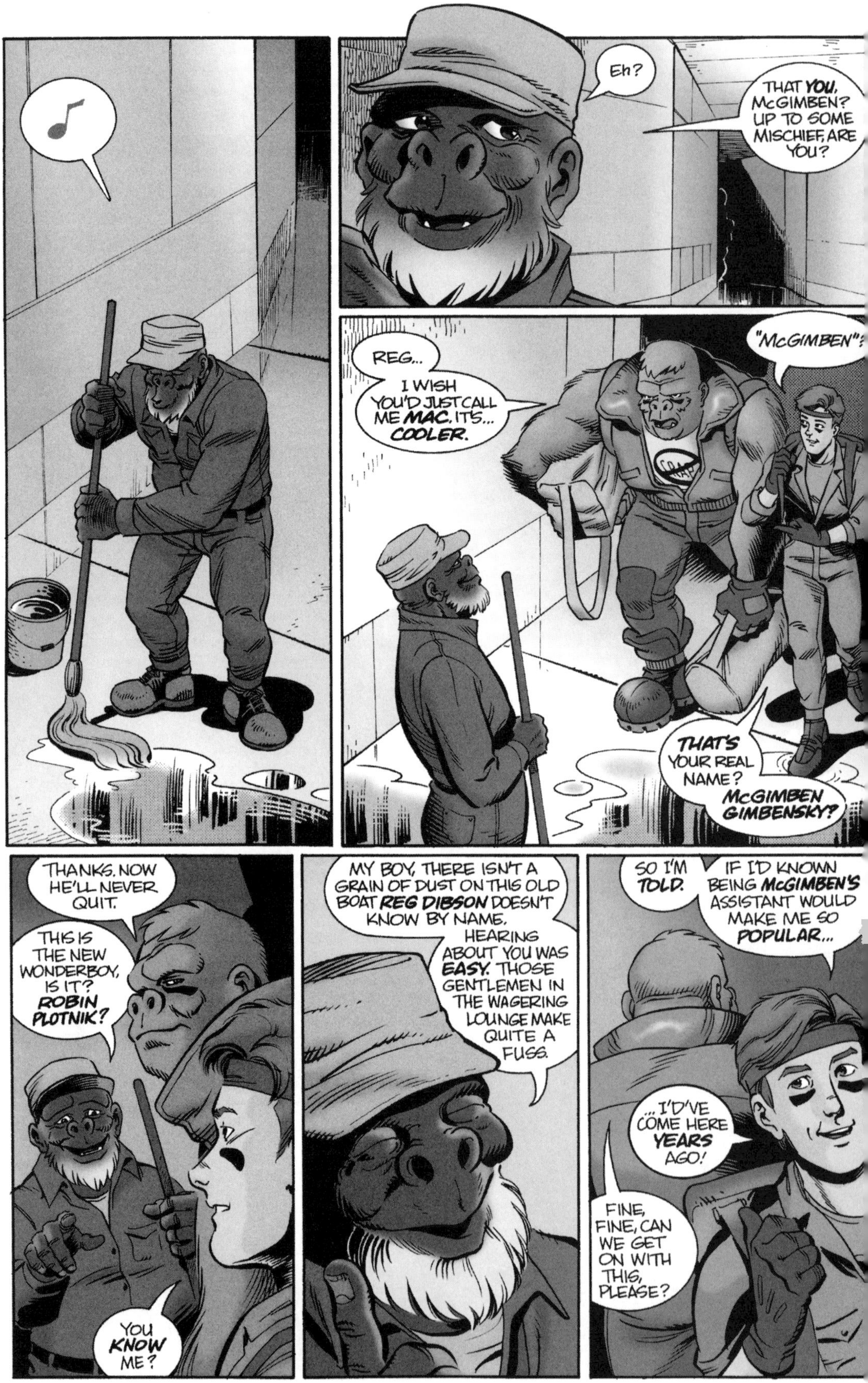
♪
Eh?
THAT YOU, McGIMBEN? UP TO SOME MISCHIEF, ARE YOU?
REG... I WISH YOU'D JUST CALL ME MAC. IT'S... COOLER.
"McGIMBEN"?
THAT'S YOUR REAL NAME? McGIMBEN GIMBENSKY?
THANKS. NOW HE'LL NEVER QUIT.
THIS IS THE NEW WONDERBOY, IS IT? ROBIN PLOTNIK?
YOU KNOW ME?
MY BOY, THERE ISN'T A GRAIN OF DUST ON THIS OLD BOAT REG DIBSON DOESN'T KNOW BY NAME.
HEARING ABOUT YOU WAS EASY. THOSE GENTLEMEN IN THE WAGERING LOUNGE MAKE QUITE A FUSS.
SO I'M TOLD.
IF I'D KNOWN BEING McGIMBEN'S ASSISTANT WOULD MAKE ME SO POPULAR...
...I'D'VE COME HERE YEARS AGO!
FINE, FINE, CAN WE GET ON WITH THIS, PLEASE?

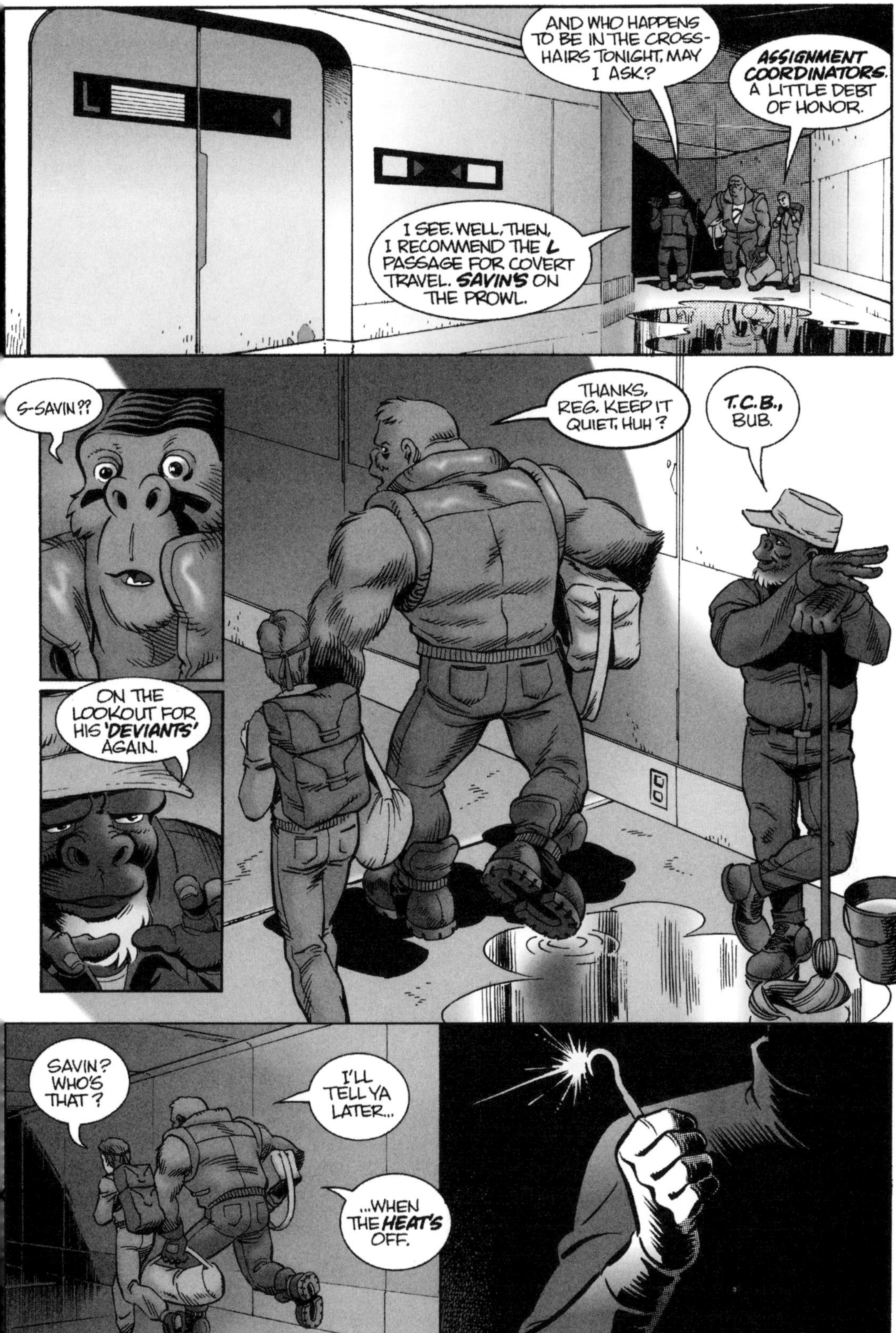
AND WHO HAPPENS TO BE IN THE CROSS-HAIRS TONIGHT, MAY I ASK?
ASSIGNMENT COORDINATORS. A LITTLE DEBT OF HONOR.
I SEE. WELL, THEN, I RECOMMEND THE L PASSAGE FOR COVERT TRAVEL. SAVIN'S ON THE PROWL.
S-SAVIN??
ON THE LOOKOUT FOR HIS 'DEVIANTS' AGAIN.
THANKS, REG. KEEP IT QUIET, HUH?
T.C.B., BUB.
SAVIN? WHO'S THAT?
I'LL TELL YA LATER...
...WHEN THE HEAT'S OFF.

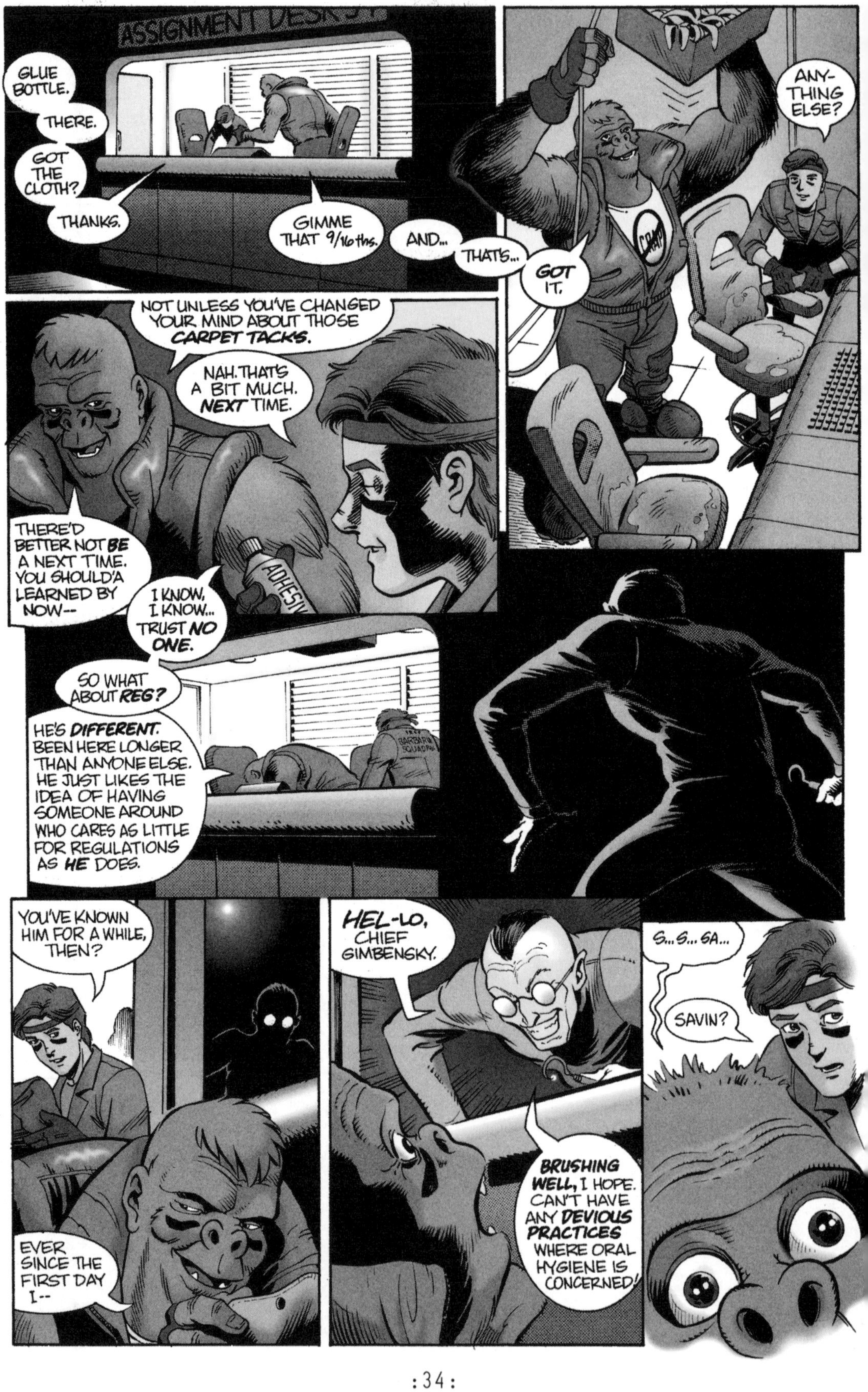
ASSIGNMENT DESK
GLUE BOTTLE.
THERE.
GOT THE CLOTH?
THANKS.
GIMME THAT 9/16ths.
AND...
THAT'S...
GOT IT.
ANY-THING ELSE?
NOT UNLESS YOU'VE CHANGED YOUR MIND ABOUT THOSE CARPET TACKS.
NAH. THAT'S A BIT MUCH. NEXT TIME.
THERE'D BETTER NOT BE A NEXT TIME. YOU SHOULD'A LEARNED BY NOW--
I KNOW, I KNOW... TRUST NO ONE.
ADHESIV
SO WHAT ABOUT REG?
HE'S DIFFERENT. BEEN HERE LONGER THAN ANYONE ELSE. HE JUST LIKES THE IDEA OF HAVING SOMEONE AROUND WHO CARES AS LITTLE FOR REGULATIONS AS HE DOES.
YOU'VE KNOWN HIM FOR A WHILE, THEN?
EVER SINCE THE FIRST DAY I--
HEL-LO, CHIEF GIMBENSKY.
BRUSHING WELL, I HOPE. CAN'T HAVE ANY DEVIOUS PRACTICES WHERE ORAL HYGIENE IS CONCERNED!
S...S...SA...
SAVIN?

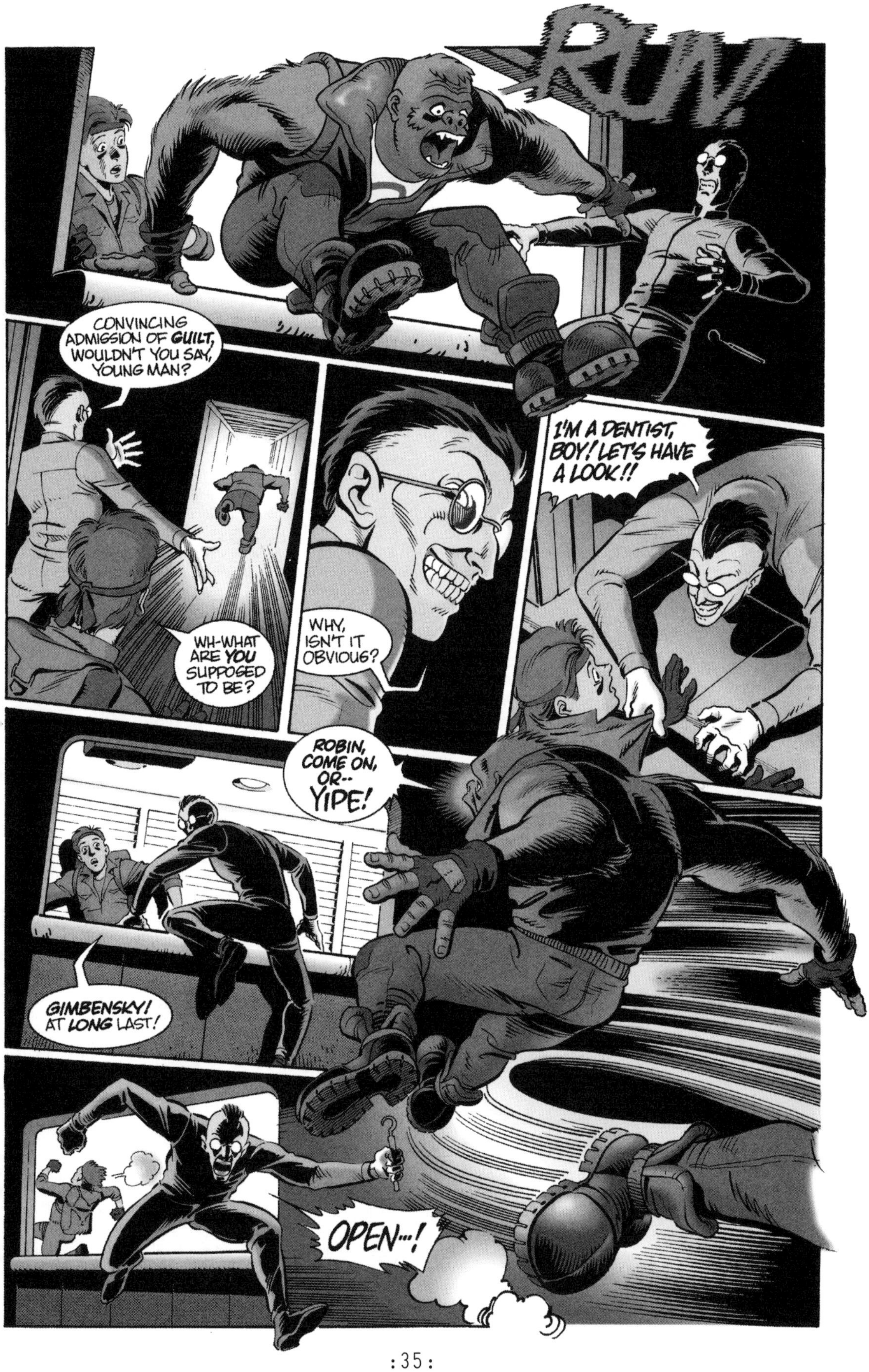
RUN!
CONVINCING ADMISSION OF GUILT, WOULDN'T YOU SAY, YOUNG MAN?
WH-WHAT ARE YOU SUPPOSED TO BE?
WHY, ISN'T IT OBVIOUS?
I'M A DENTIST, BOY! LET'S HAVE A LOOK!!
ROBIN, COME ON, OR-- YIPE!
GIMBENSKY! AT LONG LAST!
OPEN--!

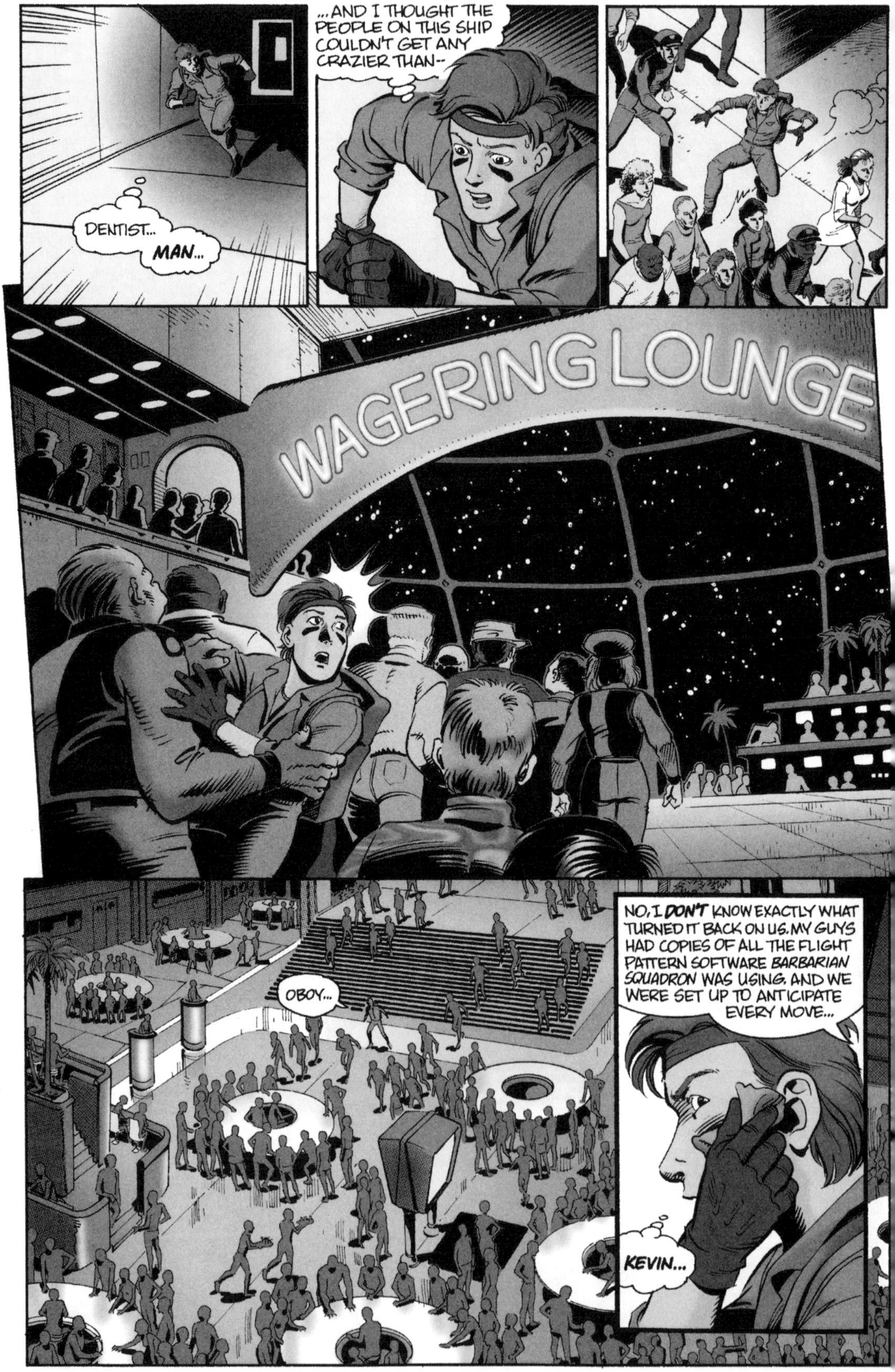
DENTIST...
MAN...
...AND I THOUGHT THE PEOPLE ON THIS SHIP COULDN'T GET ANY CRAZIER THAN--
WAGERING LOUNGE
OBOY...
NO, I DON'T KNOW EXACTLY WHAT TURNED IT BACK ON US. MY GUYS HAD COPIES OF ALL THE FLIGHT PATTERN SOFTWARE BARBARIAN SQUADRON WAS USING, AND WE WERE SET UP TO ANTICIPATE EVERY MOVE...
KEVIN...

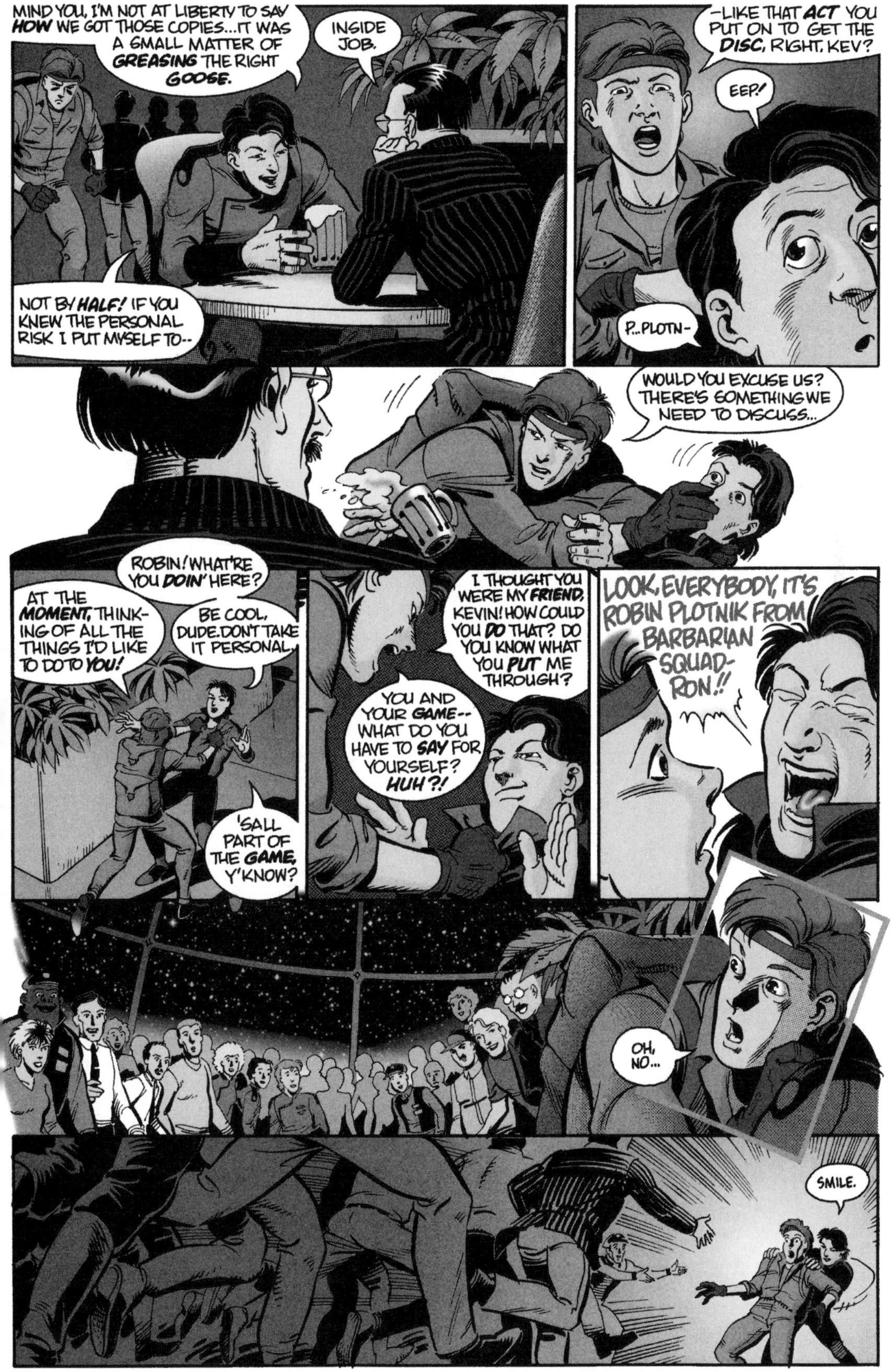
MIND YOU, I'M NOT AT LIBERTY TO SAY HOW WE GOT THOSE COPIES...IT WAS A SMALL MATTER OF GREASING THE RIGHT GOOSE.
INSIDE JOB.
NOT BY HALF! IF YOU KNEW THE PERSONAL RISK I PUT MYSELF TO--
-LIKE THAT ACT YOU PUT ON TO GET THE DISC, RIGHT, KEV?
EEP!
P...PLOTN-
WOULD YOU EXCUSE US? THERE'S SOMETHING WE NEED TO DISCUSS...
ROBIN! WHAT'RE YOU DOIN' HERE?
AT THE MOMENT, THINKING OF ALL THE THINGS I'D LIKE TO DO TO YOU!
BE COOL, DUDE. DON'T TAKE IT PERSONAL.
'SALL PART OF THE GAME, Y'KNOW?
I THOUGHT YOU WERE MY FRIEND, KEVIN! HOW COULD YOU DO THAT? DO YOU KNOW WHAT YOU PUT ME THROUGH?
YOU AND YOUR GAME-- WHAT DO YOU HAVE TO SAY FOR YOURSELF? HUH?!
LOOK, EVERYBODY, IT'S ROBIN PLOTNIK FROM BARBARIAN SQUADRON!!
OH, NO...
SMILE.

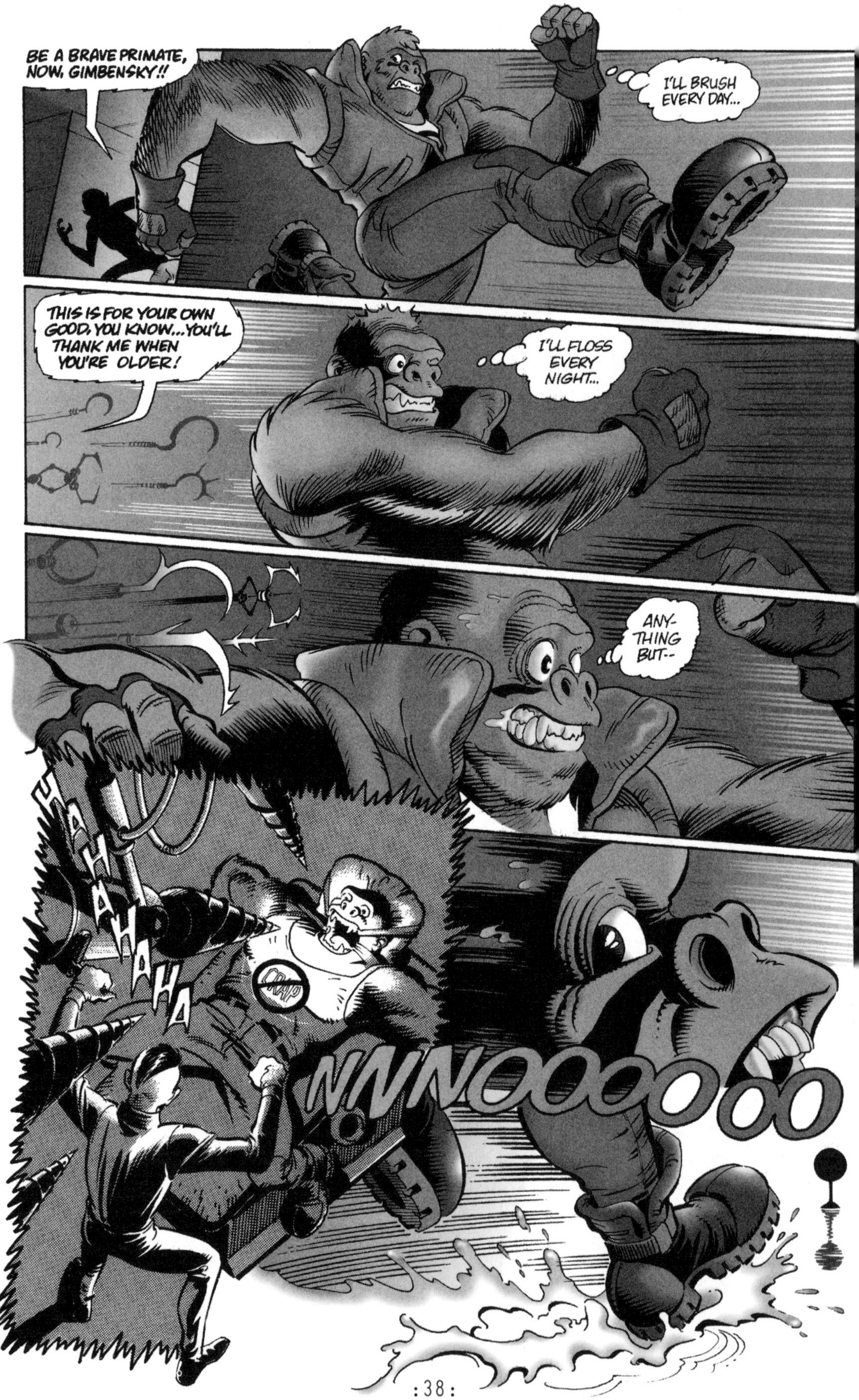
BE A BRAVE PRIMATE, NOW, GIMBENSKY!!
I'LL BRUSH EVERY DAY...
THIS IS FOR YOUR OWN GOOD, YOU KNOW... YOU'LL THANK ME WHEN YOU'RE OLDER!
I'LL FLOSS EVERY NIGHT...
ANY-THING BUT--
HAHAHAHAHAHA
CRAP
NNNOOOOOOO

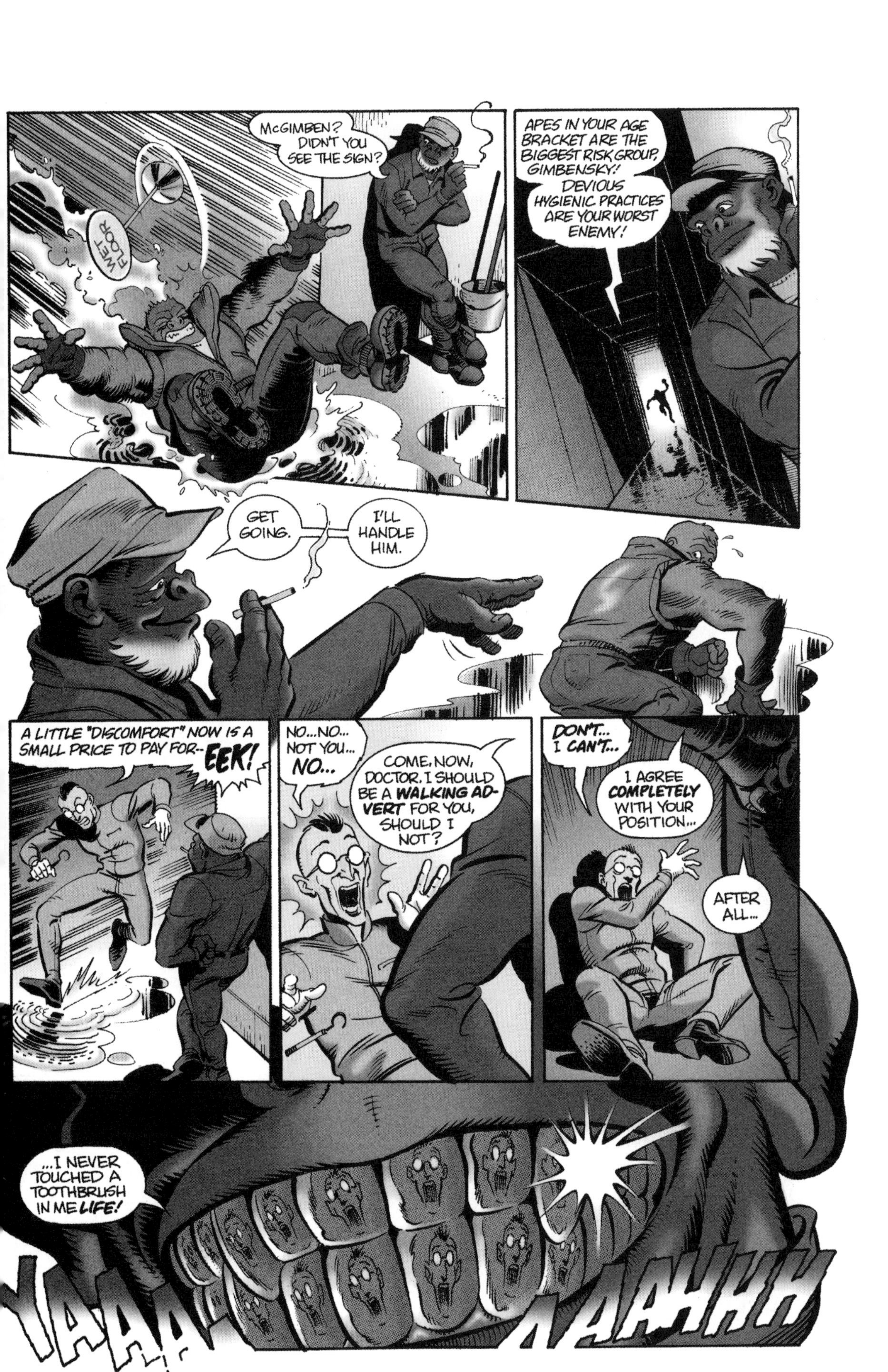
McGIMBEN? DIDN'T YOU SEE THE SIGN?
WET FLOOR
APES IN YOUR AGE BRACKET ARE THE BIGGEST RISK GROUP, GIMBENSKY! DEVIOUS HYGIENIC PRACTICES ARE YOUR WORST ENEMY!
GET GOING.
I'LL HANDLE HIM.
A LITTLE "DISCOMFORT" NOW IS A SMALL PRICE TO PAY FOR--EEK!
NO...NO... NOT YOU... NO...
COME, NOW, DOCTOR. I SHOULD BE A WALKING AD-VERT FOR YOU, SHOULD I NOT?
DON'T... I CAN'T...
I AGREE COMPLETELY WITH YOUR POSITION...
AFTER ALL...
...I NEVER TOUCHED A TOOTHBRUSH IN ME LIFE!
YAAA—AAHHH

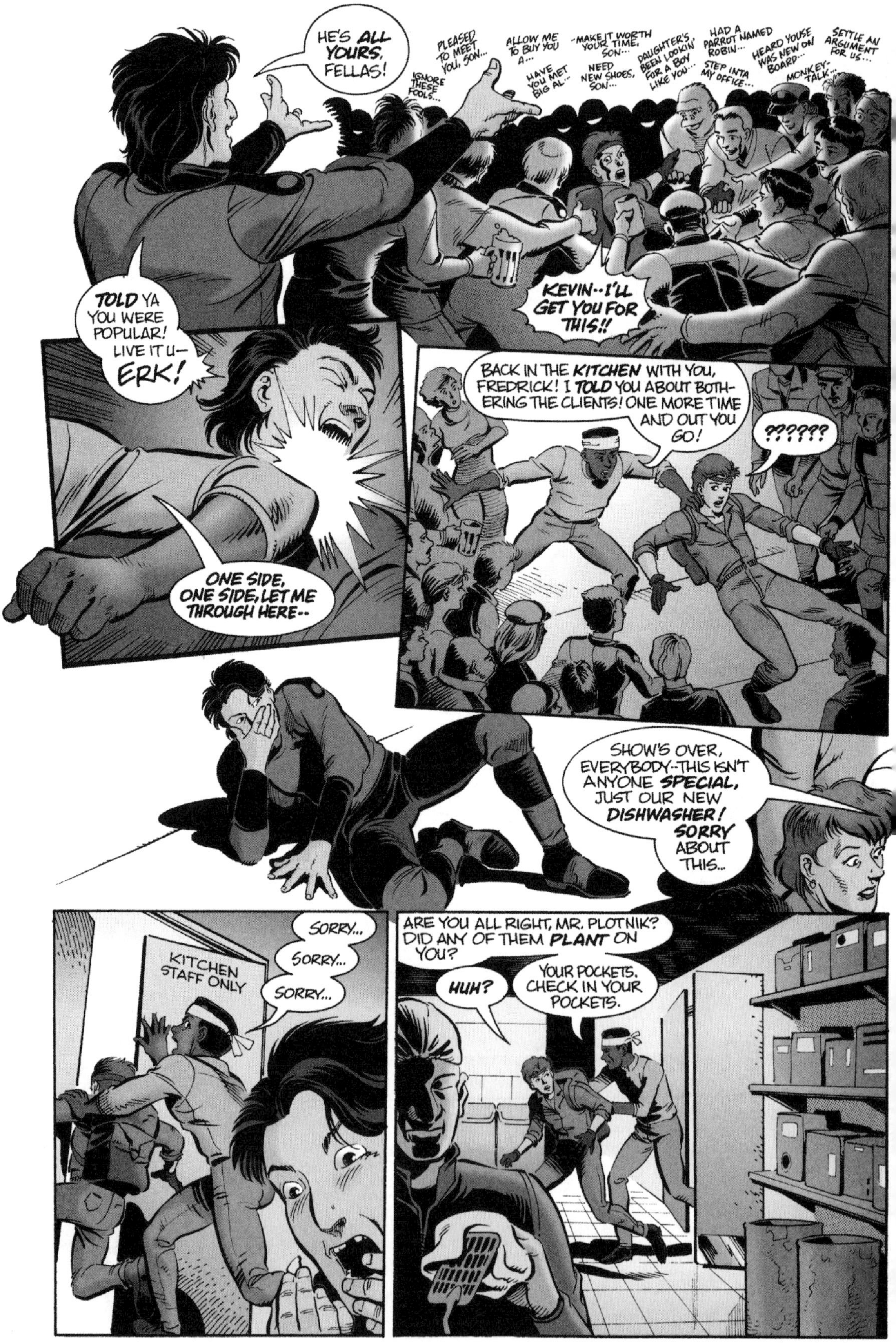
HE'S **ALL YOURS,** FELLAS!
IGNORE THESE FOOLS...
PLEASED TO MEET YOU, SON...
ALLOW ME TO BUY YOU A...
HAVE YOU MET BIG AL...
-MAKE IT WORTH YOUR TIME, SON...
NEED NEW SHOES, SON...
DAUGHTER'S BEEN LOOKIN' FOR A BOY LIKE YOU...
HAD A PARROT NAMED ROBIN...
STEP INTA MY OFFICE...
HEARD YOUSE WAS NEW ON BOARD...
MONKEY-TALK...
SETTLE AN ARGUMENT FOR US...
TOLD YA YOU WERE POPULAR! LIVE IT U-
ERK!
KEVIN--I'LL GET YOU FOR THIS!!
ONE SIDE, ONE SIDE, LET ME THROUGH HERE--
BACK IN THE **KITCHEN** WITH YOU, FREDRICK! I **TOLD** YOU ABOUT BOTHERING THE CLIENTS! ONE MORE TIME AND OUT YOU GO!
??????
SHOW'S OVER, EVERYBODY--THIS ISN'T ANYONE **SPECIAL,** JUST OUR NEW **DISHWASHER!** **SORRY** ABOUT THIS...
SORRY...
SORRY...
SORRY...
KITCHEN STAFF ONLY
ARE YOU ALL RIGHT, MR. PLOTNIK? DID ANY OF THEM **PLANT** ON YOU?
HUH?
YOUR POCKETS. CHECK IN YOUR POCKETS.

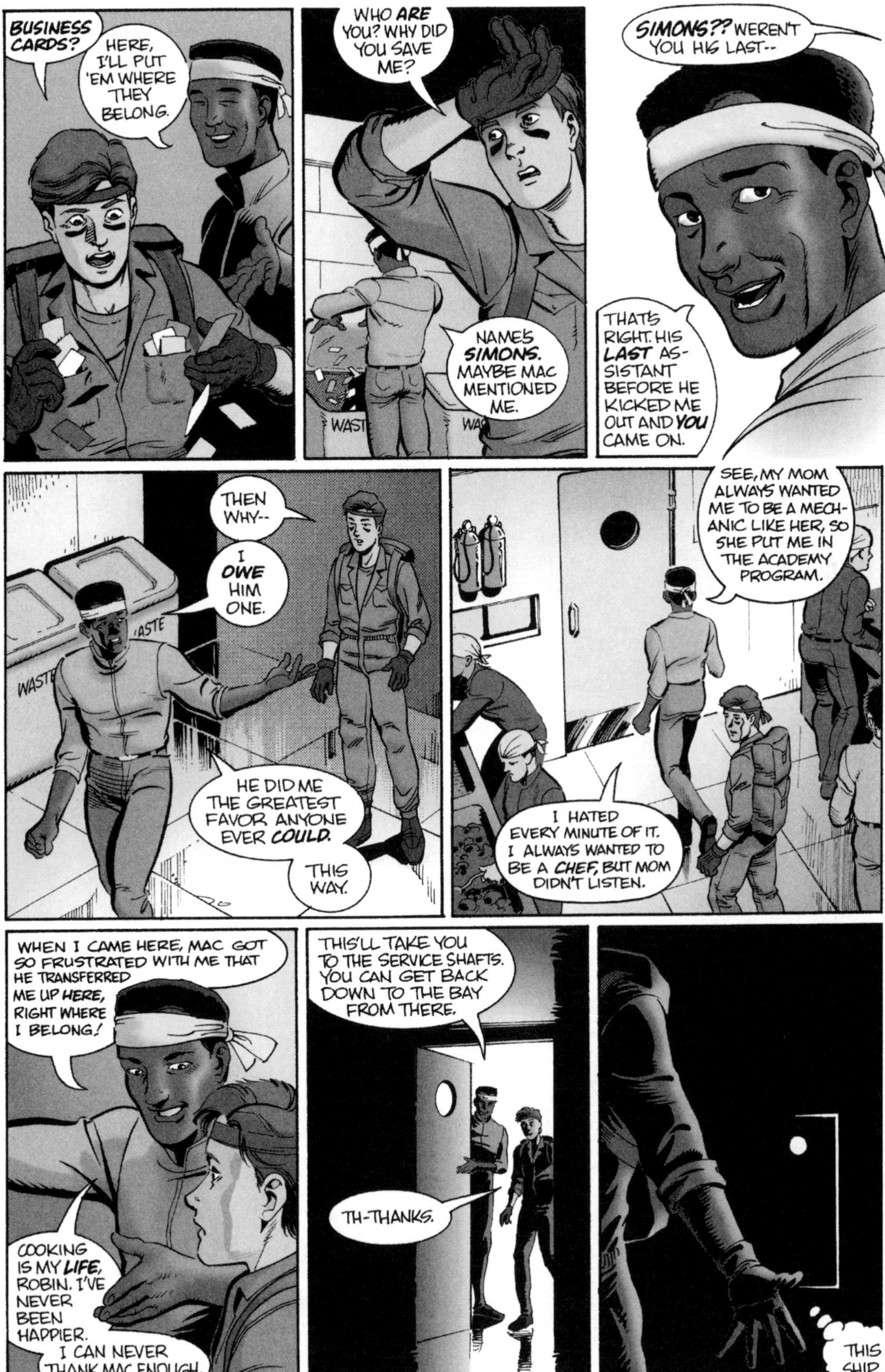
BUSINESS CARDS?
HERE, I'LL PUT 'EM WHERE THEY BELONG.
WHO ARE YOU? WHY DID YOU SAVE ME?
NAME'S SIMONS. MAYBE MAC MENTIONED ME.
WASTE
SIMONS?? WEREN'T YOU HIS LAST--
THAT'S RIGHT. HIS LAST ASSISTANT BEFORE HE KICKED ME OUT AND YOU CAME ON.
THEN WHY--
I OWE HIM ONE.
WASTE
HE DID ME THE GREATEST FAVOR ANYONE EVER COULD.
THIS WAY.
SEE, MY MOM ALWAYS WANTED ME TO BE A MECHANIC LIKE HER, SO SHE PUT ME IN THE ACADEMY PROGRAM.
I HATED EVERY MINUTE OF IT. I ALWAYS WANTED TO BE A CHEF, BUT MOM DIDN'T LISTEN.
WHEN I CAME HERE, MAC GOT SO FRUSTRATED WITH ME THAT HE TRANSFERRED ME UP HERE, RIGHT WHERE I BELONG!
COOKING IS MY LIFE, ROBIN. I'VE NEVER BEEN HAPPIER.
I CAN NEVER THANK MAC ENOUGH.
THIS'LL TAKE YOU TO THE SERVICE SHAFTS. YOU CAN GET BACK DOWN TO THE BAY FROM THERE.
TH-THANKS.
THIS SHIP...

NEXT MORNING...

KEVIN NEDELMAT?

UH.

DR. SAVIN WILL SEE YOU NOW.

SEDATION IS FOR BABIES

WHILE...

ASSIGNMENT DESK J7

ASSIGNMENT DESK J7

MORNIN'.

ASSIGNMENT DESK J7

HEY.

ASSIGNMENT DESK J7

WHAT'S WITH THIS CHAIR?

SPROING YAAH! THUD! SQUIK! BLATT! LOOK OUT! WHOAH! SMOOT! OW!

Tim Eldred '92

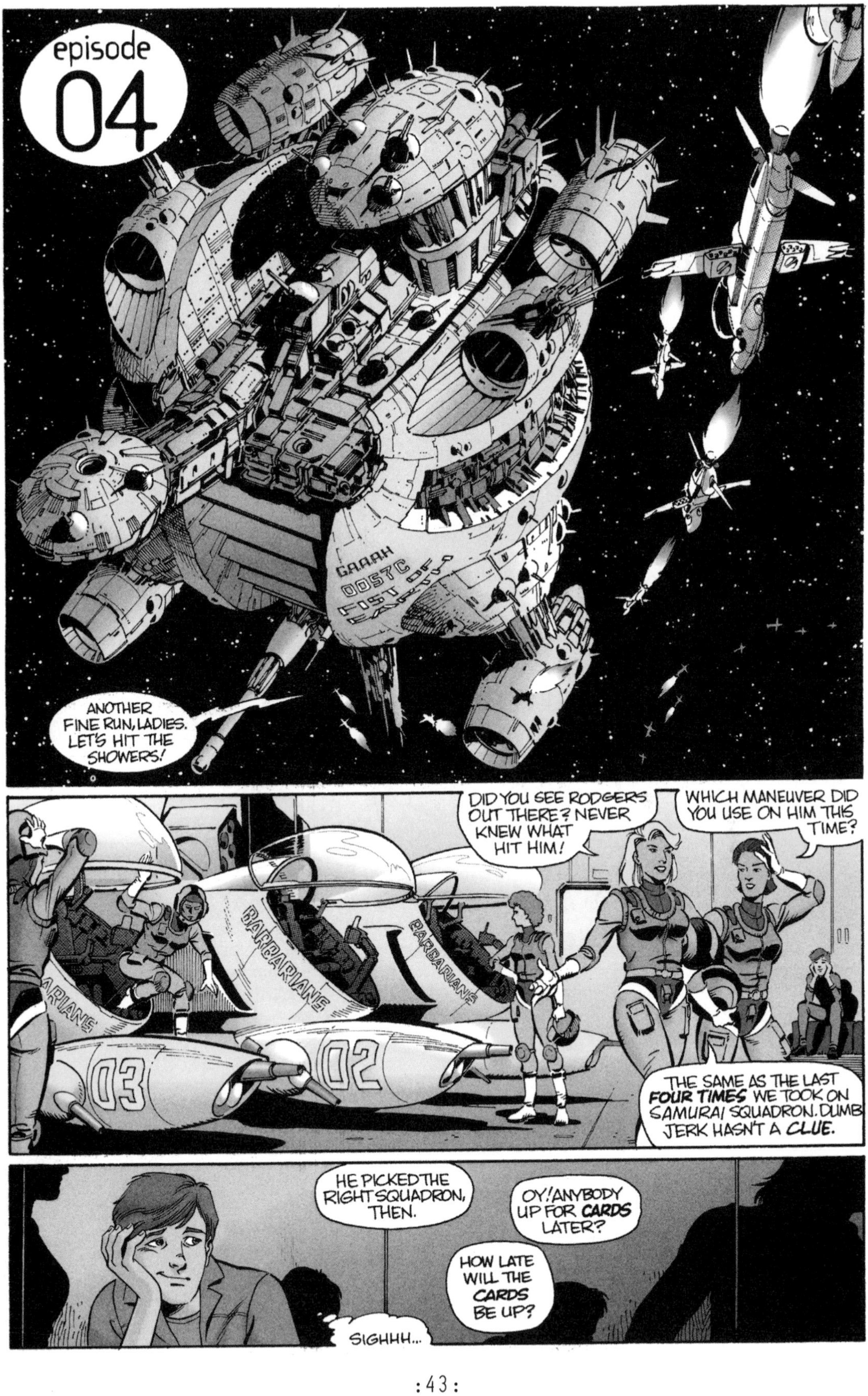
episode
04
ANOTHER FINE RUN, LADIES. LET'S HIT THE SHOWERS!
DID YOU SEE RODGERS OUT THERE? NEVER KNEW WHAT HIT HIM!
WHICH MANEUVER DID YOU USE ON HIM THIS TIME?
THE SAME AS THE LAST **FOUR TIMES** WE TOOK ON SAMURAI SQUADRON. DUMB JERK HASN'T A **CLUE**.
BARBARIANS
BARBARIANS
ARIANS
03
02
HE PICKED THE RIGHT SQUADRON, THEN.
OY! ANYBODY UP FOR **CARDS** LATER?
HOW LATE WILL THE **CARDS** BE UP?
SIGHHH...

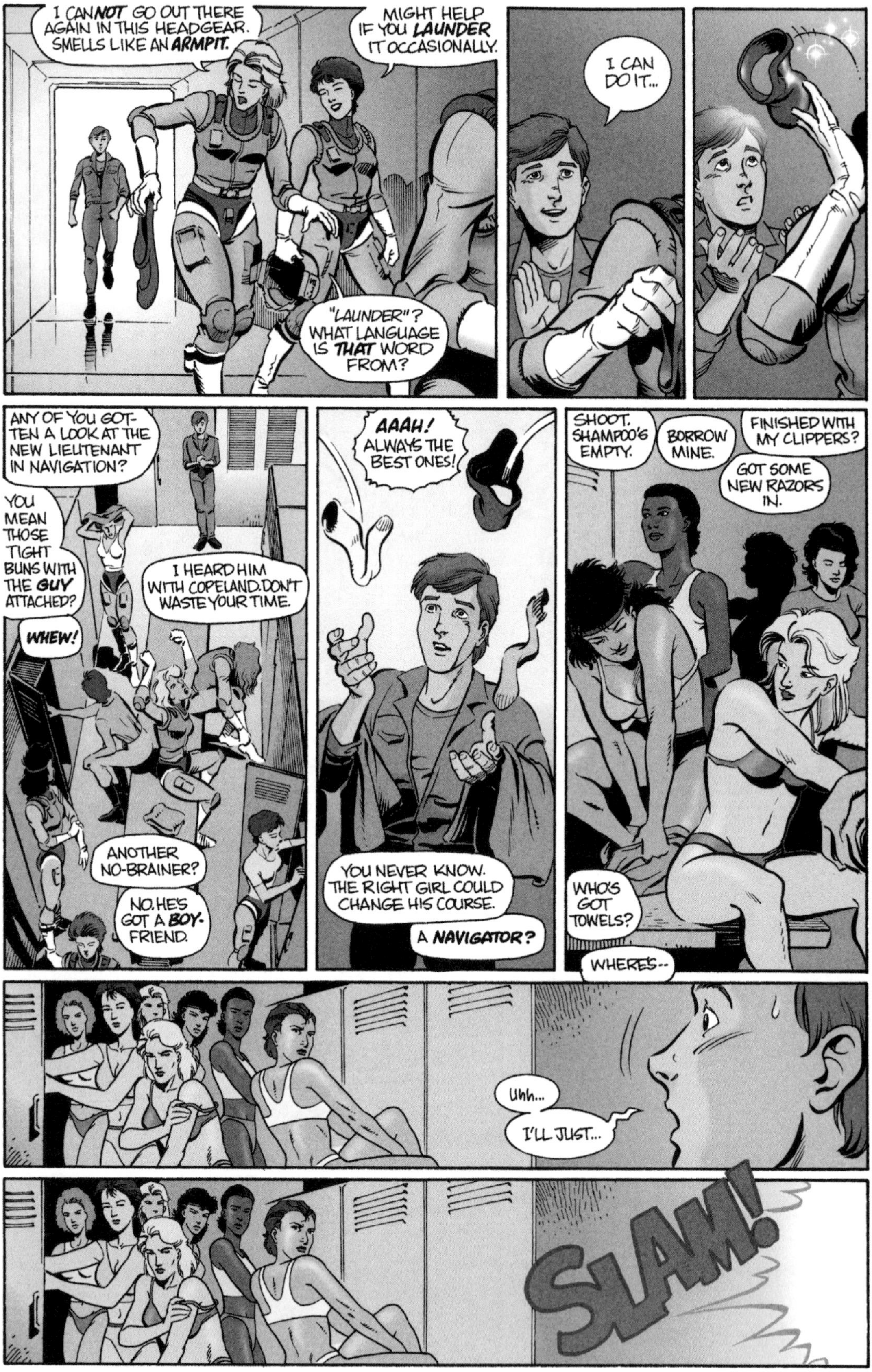
I CAN NOT GO OUT THERE AGAIN IN THIS HEADGEAR. SMELLS LIKE AN ARMPIT.
MIGHT HELP IF YOU LAUNDER IT OCCASIONALLY.
"LAUNDER"? WHAT LANGUAGE IS THAT WORD FROM?
I CAN DO IT...
ANY OF YOU GOTTEN A LOOK AT THE NEW LIEUTENANT IN NAVIGATION?
YOU MEAN THOSE TIGHT BUNS WITH THE GUY ATTACHED?
WHEW!
I HEARD HIM WITH COPELAND. DON'T WASTE YOUR TIME.
ANOTHER NO-BRAINER?
NO. HE'S GOT A BOY-FRIEND.
AAAH! ALWAYS THE BEST ONES!
YOU NEVER KNOW. THE RIGHT GIRL COULD CHANGE HIS COURSE.
A NAVIGATOR?
SHOOT. SHAMPOO'S EMPTY.
BORROW MINE.
FINISHED WITH MY CLIPPERS?
GOT SOME NEW RAZORS IN.
WHO'S GOT TOWELS?
WHERE'S--
Uhh...
I'LL JUST...
SLAM!

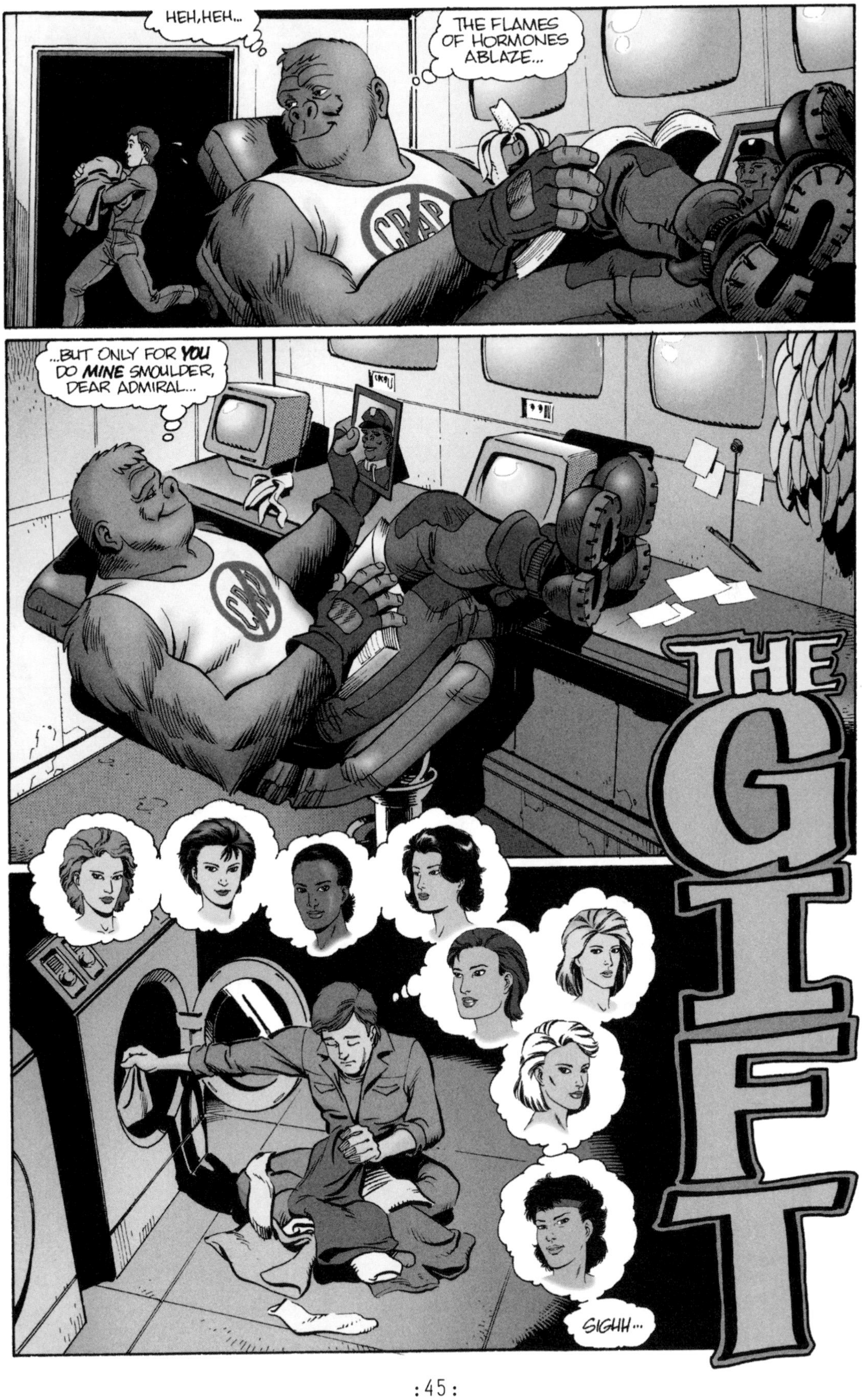
HEH, HEH...
THE FLAMES OF HORMONES ABLAZE...
...BUT ONLY FOR YOU DO MINE SMOULDER, DEAR ADMIRAL...
THE GIFT
SIGHH...

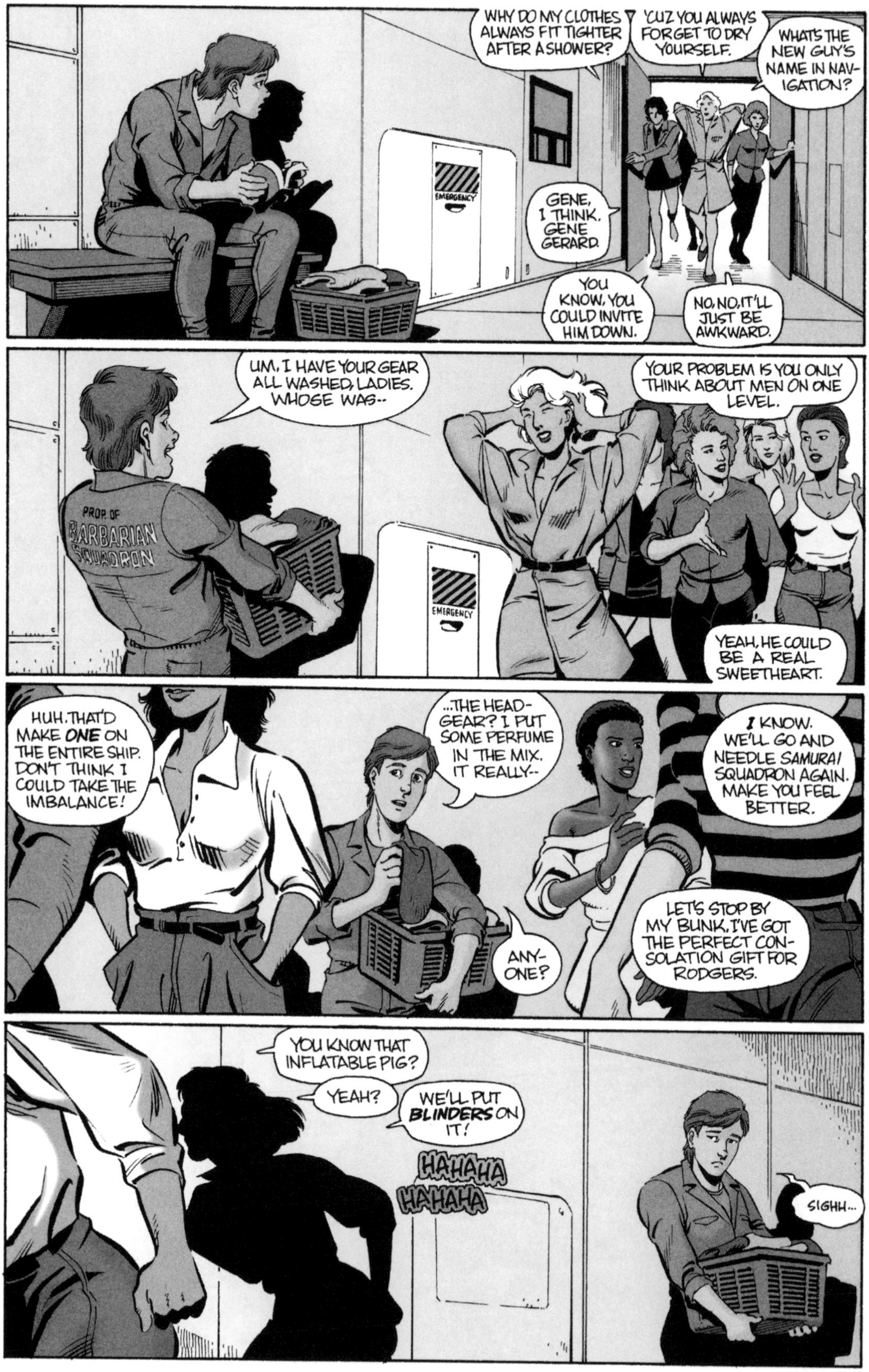
WHY DO MY CLOTHES ALWAYS FIT TIGHTER AFTER A SHOWER?
'CUZ YOU ALWAYS FORGET TO DRY YOURSELF.
WHAT'S THE NEW GUY'S NAME IN NAVIGATION?
GENE, I THINK. GENE GERARD.
YOU KNOW, YOU COULD INVITE HIM DOWN.
NO, NO, IT'LL JUST BE AWKWARD.
UM, I HAVE YOUR GEAR ALL WASHED, LADIES. WHOSE WAS--
YOUR PROBLEM IS YOU ONLY THINK ABOUT MEN ON ONE LEVEL.
PROP. OF BARBARIAN SQUADRON
EMERGENCY
YEAH, HE COULD BE A REAL SWEETHEART.
HUH. THAT'D MAKE ONE ON THE ENTIRE SHIP. DON'T THINK I COULD TAKE THE IMBALANCE!
...THE HEAD-GEAR? I PUT SOME PERFUME IN THE MIX. IT REALLY--
I KNOW. WE'LL GO AND NEEDLE SAMURAI SQUADRON AGAIN. MAKE YOU FEEL BETTER.
ANY-ONE?
LET'S STOP BY MY BUNK, I'VE GOT THE PERFECT CON-SOLATION GIFT FOR RODGERS.
YOU KNOW THAT INFLATABLE PIG?
YEAH?
WE'LL PUT BLINDERS ON IT!
HAHAHA HAHAHA
SIGHH...

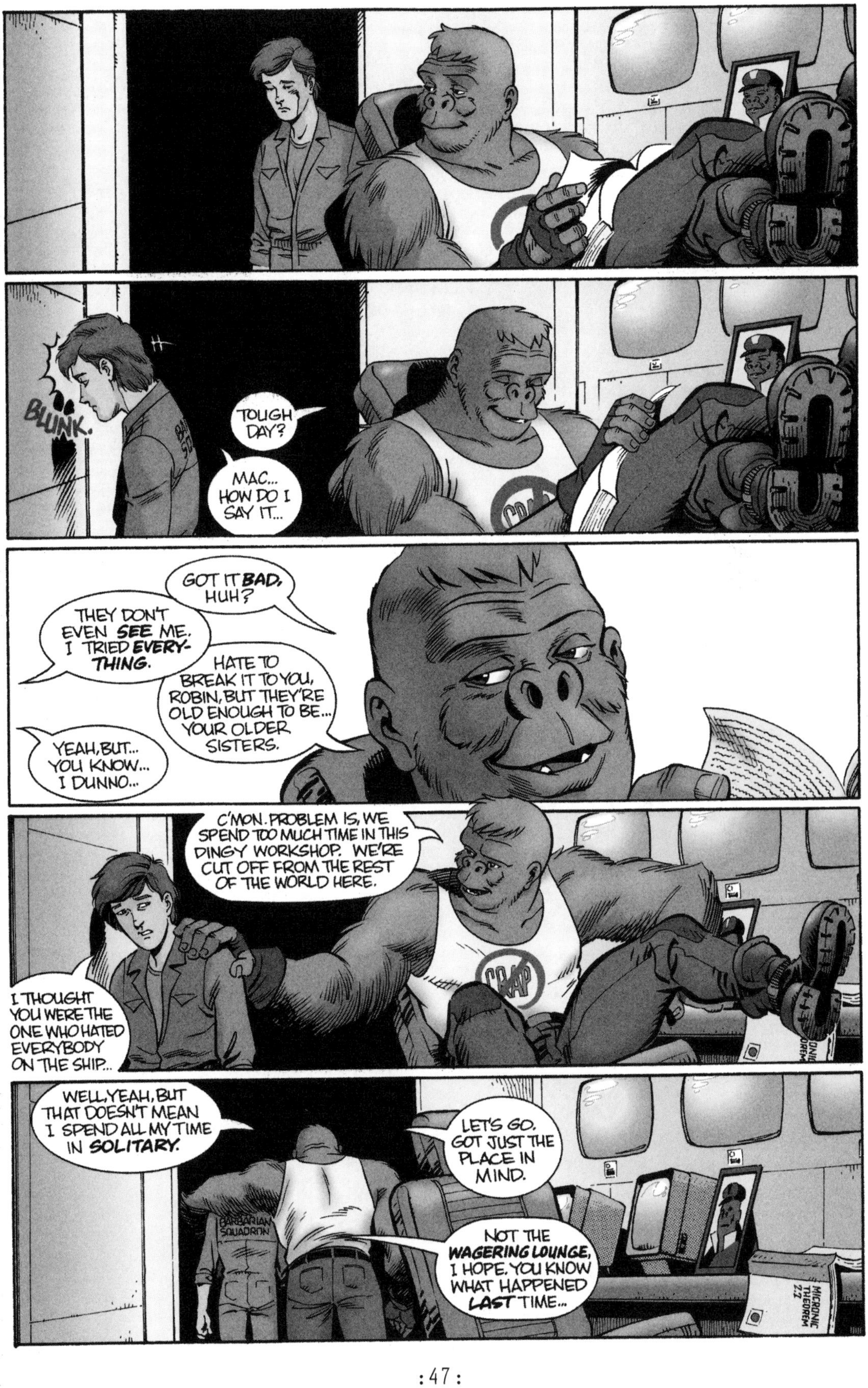

BLUNK.
TOUGH DAY?
MAC... HOW DO I SAY IT...
GOT IT BAD, HUH?
THEY DON'T EVEN SEE ME. I TRIED EVERY-THING.
HATE TO BREAK IT TO YOU, ROBIN, BUT THEY'RE OLD ENOUGH TO BE... YOUR OLDER SISTERS.
YEAH, BUT... YOU KNOW... I DUNNO...
C'MON. PROBLEM IS, WE SPEND TOO MUCH TIME IN THIS DINGY WORKSHOP. WE'RE CUT OFF FROM THE REST OF THE WORLD HERE.
CRAP
I THOUGHT YOU WERE THE ONE WHO HATED EVERYBODY ON THE SHIP...
WELL, YEAH, BUT THAT DOESN'T MEAN I SPEND ALL MY TIME IN SOLITARY.
LET'S GO. GOT JUST THE PLACE IN MIND.
BARBARIAN SQUADRON
NOT THE WAGERING LOUNGE, I HOPE. YOU KNOW WHAT HAPPENED LAST TIME...
MICRONIC THEOREM 2.2

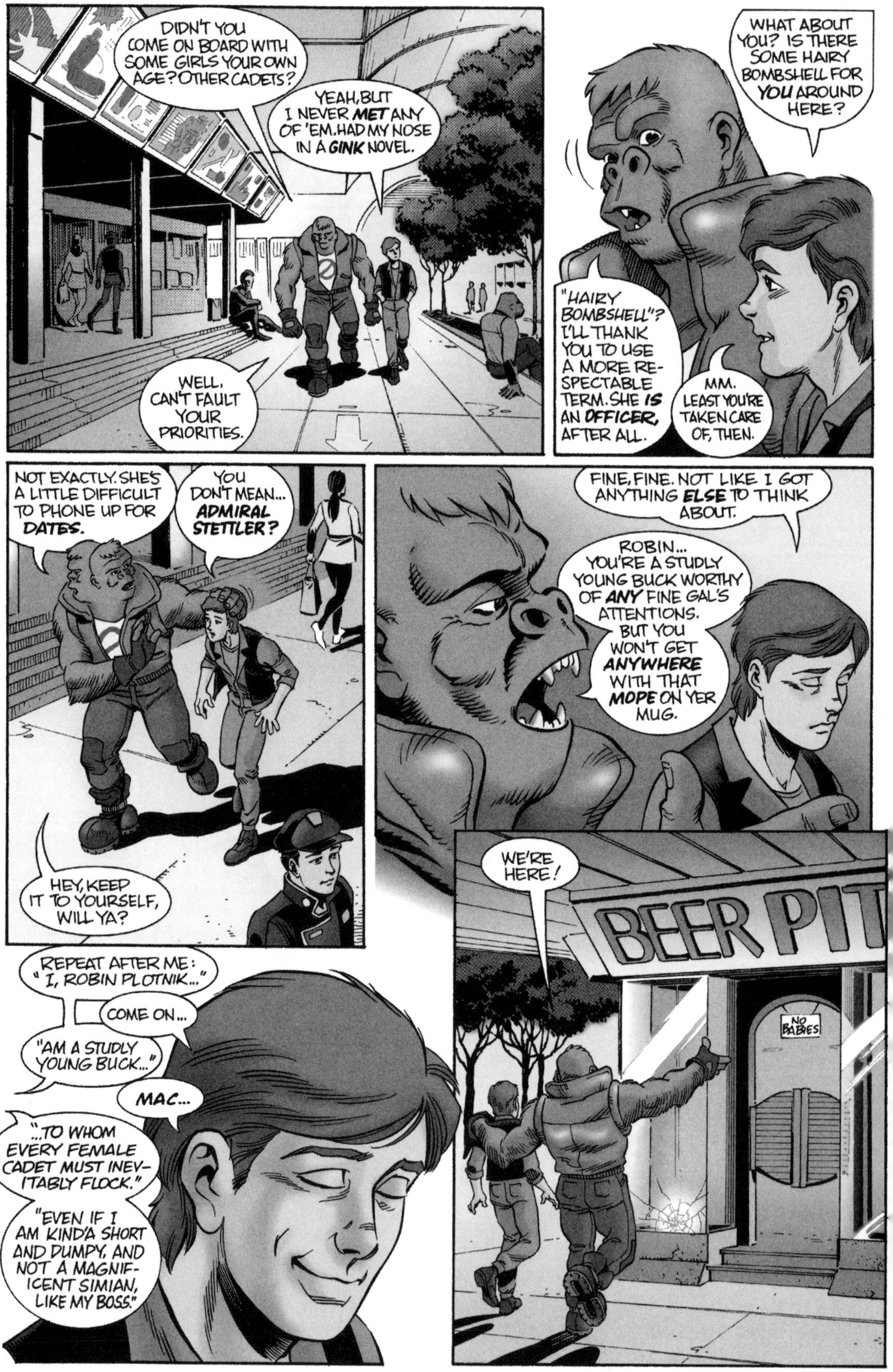

DIDN'T YOU COME ON BOARD WITH SOME GIRLS YOUR OWN AGE? OTHER CADETS?
YEAH, BUT I NEVER **MET** ANY OF 'EM. HAD MY NOSE IN A **GINK** NOVEL.
WELL, CAN'T FAULT YOUR PRIORITIES.
WHAT ABOUT YOU? IS THERE SOME HAIRY BOMBSHELL FOR **YOU** AROUND HERE?
"HAIRY BOMBSHELL"? I'LL THANK YOU TO USE A MORE RE-SPECTABLE TERM. SHE **IS** AN **OFFICER,** AFTER ALL.
MM. LEAST YOU'RE TAKEN CARE OF, THEN.
NOT EXACTLY. SHE'S A LITTLE DIFFICULT TO PHONE UP FOR **DATES.**
YOU DON'T MEAN... **ADMIRAL STETTLER?**
HEY, KEEP IT TO YOURSELF, WILL YA?
FINE, FINE. NOT LIKE I GOT ANYTHING **ELSE** TO THINK ABOUT.
ROBIN... YOU'RE A STUDLY YOUNG BUCK WORTHY OF **ANY** FINE GAL'S ATTENTIONS. BUT YOU WON'T GET **ANYWHERE** WITH THAT **MOPE** ON YER MUG.
REPEAT AFTER ME: "I, ROBIN PLOTNIK..."
COME ON...
"AM A STUDLY YOUNG BUCK..."
MAC...
"...TO WHOM EVERY FEMALE CADET MUST INEV-ITABLY FLOCK."
"EVEN IF I AM KIND'A SHORT AND DUMPY, AND NOT A MAGNIF-ICENT SIMIAN, LIKE MY BOSS."
WE'RE HERE!
BEER PIT
NO BABIES

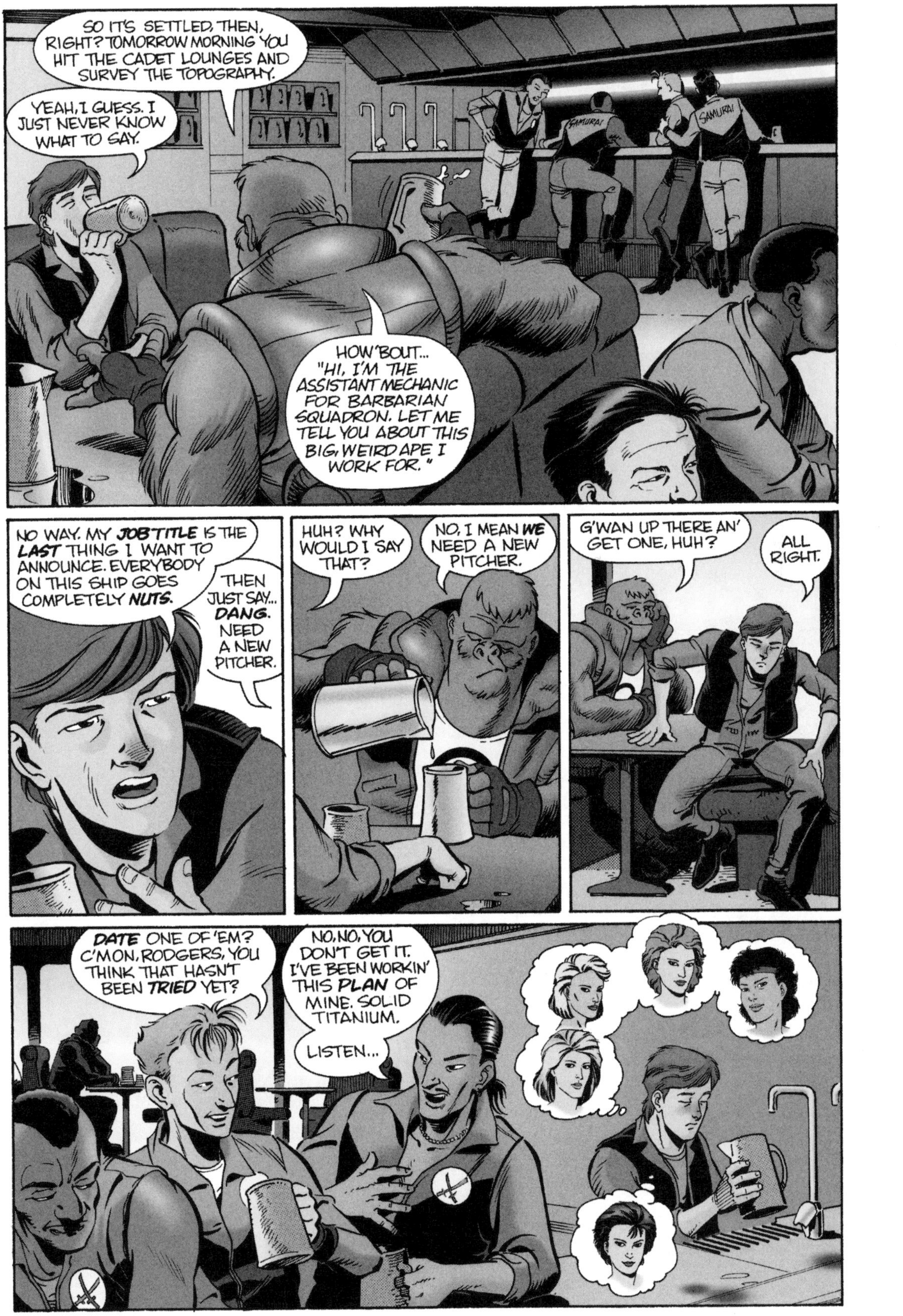
SO IT'S SETTLED, THEN, RIGHT? TOMORROW MORNING YOU HIT THE CADET LOUNGES AND SURVEY THE TOPOGRAPHY.
YEAH, I GUESS. I JUST NEVER KNOW WHAT TO SAY.
SAMURAI
SAMURAI
HOW 'BOUT... "HI, I'M THE ASSISTANT MECHANIC FOR BARBARIAN SQUADRON. LET ME TELL YOU ABOUT THIS BIG, WEIRD APE I WORK FOR."
NO WAY. MY JOB TITLE IS THE LAST THING I WANT TO ANNOUNCE. EVERYBODY ON THIS SHIP GOES COMPLETELY NUTS.
THEN JUST SAY... DANG. NEED A NEW PITCHER.
HUH? WHY WOULD I SAY THAT?
NO, I MEAN WE NEED A NEW PITCHER.
G'WAN UP THERE AN' GET ONE, HUH?
ALL RIGHT.
DATE ONE OF 'EM? C'MON, RODGERS, YOU THINK THAT HASN'T BEEN TRIED YET?
NO, NO, YOU DON'T GET IT. I'VE BEEN WORKIN' THIS PLAN OF MINE. SOLID TITANIUM.
LISTEN...

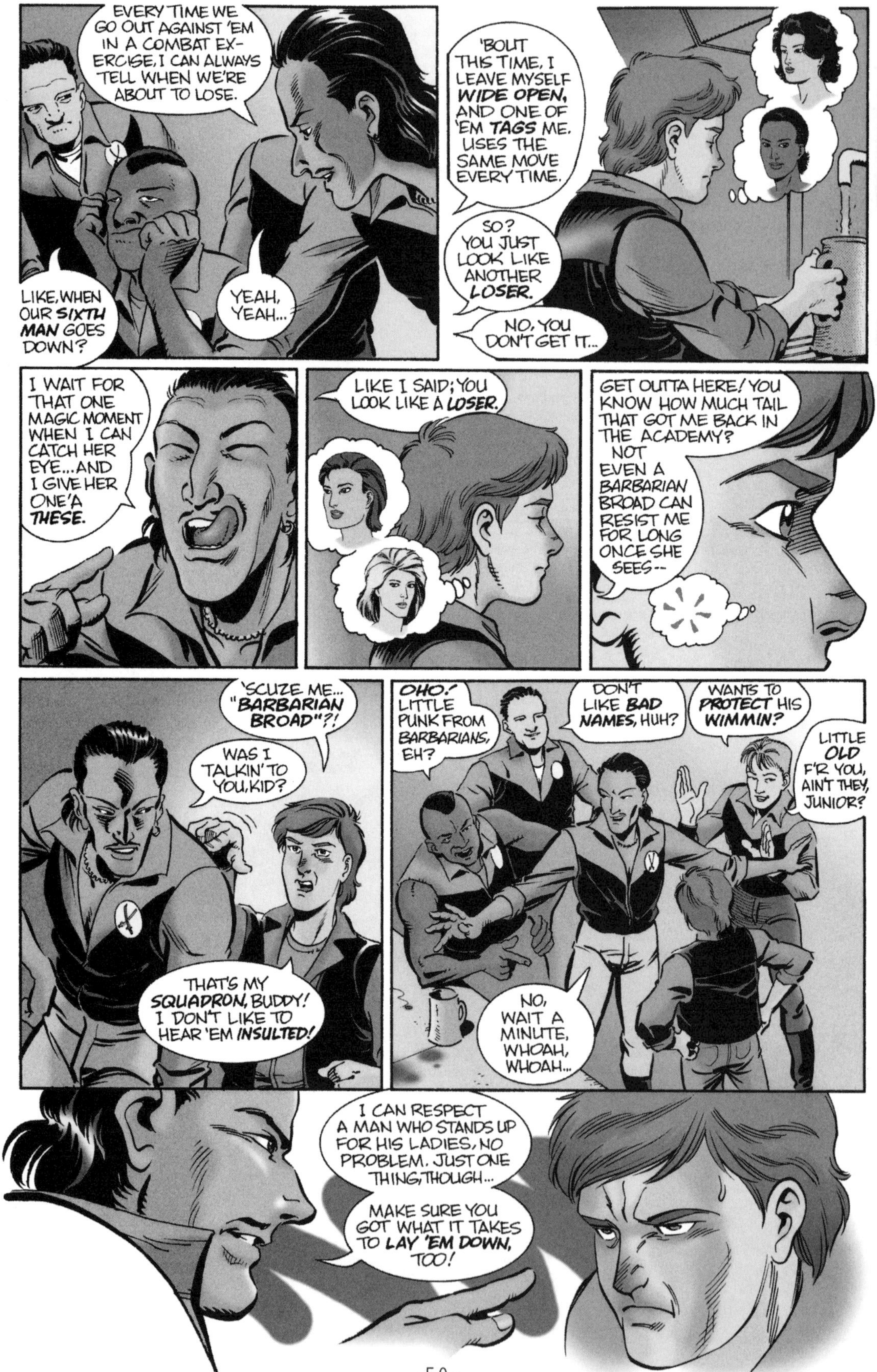
EVERY TIME WE GO OUT AGAINST 'EM IN A COMBAT EX-ERCISE, I CAN ALWAYS TELL WHEN WE'RE ABOUT TO LOSE.
LIKE, WHEN OUR SIXTH MAN GOES DOWN?
YEAH, YEAH...
'BOUT THIS TIME, I LEAVE MYSELF WIDE OPEN, AND ONE OF 'EM TAGS ME. USES THE SAME MOVE EVERY TIME.
SO? YOU JUST LOOK LIKE ANOTHER LOSER.
NO, YOU DON'T GET IT...
I WAIT FOR THAT ONE MAGIC MOMENT WHEN I CAN CATCH HER EYE... AND I GIVE HER ONE'A THESE.
LIKE I SAID; YOU LOOK LIKE A LOSER.
GET OUTTA HERE! YOU KNOW HOW MUCH TAIL THAT GOT ME BACK IN THE ACADEMY? NOT EVEN A BARBARIAN BROAD CAN RESIST ME FOR LONG ONCE SHE SEES--
'SCUZE ME... "BARBARIAN BROAD"?!
WAS I TALKIN' TO YOU, KID?
THAT'S MY SQUADRON, BUDDY! I DON'T LIKE TO HEAR 'EM INSULTED!
OHO! LITTLE PUNK FROM BARBARIANS, EH?
DON'T LIKE BAD NAMES, HUH?
WANTS TO PROTECT HIS WIMMIN?
LITTLE OLD F'R YOU, AIN'T THEY, JUNIOR?
NO, WAIT A MINUTE, WHOAH, WHOAH...
I CAN RESPECT A MAN WHO STANDS UP FOR HIS LADIES, NO PROBLEM. JUST ONE THING, THOUGH...
MAKE SURE YOU GOT WHAT IT TAKES TO LAY 'EM DOWN, TOO!

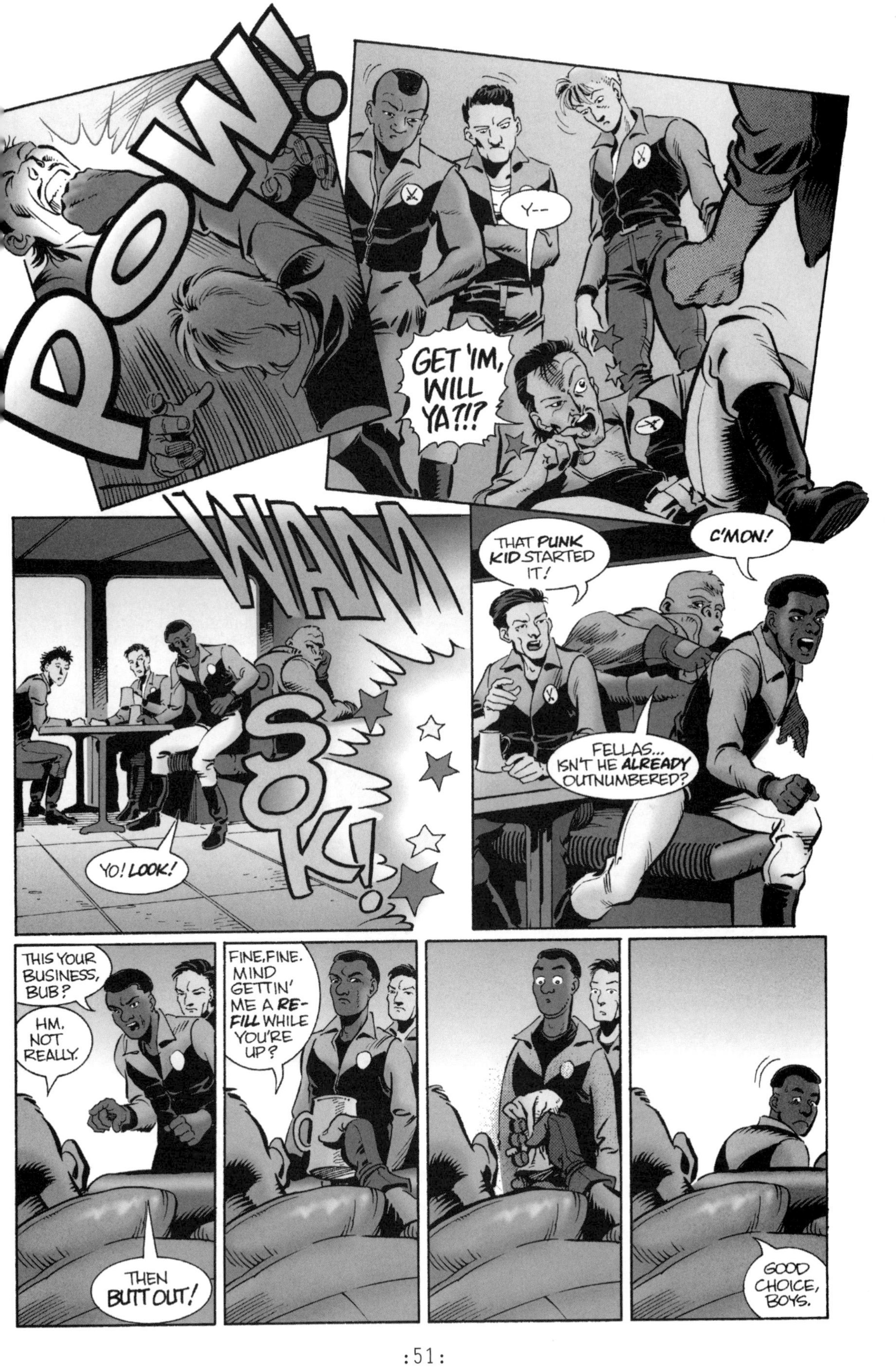
POW!
Y--
GET 'IM, WILL YA?!?
WAM
SOK!
YO! LOOK!
THAT PUNK KID STARTED IT!
C'MON!
FELLAS... ISN'T HE ALREADY OUTNUMBERED?
THIS YOUR BUSINESS, BUB?
HM. NOT REALLY.
THEN BUTT OUT!
FINE, FINE. MIND GETTIN' ME A RE-FILL WHILE YOU'RE UP?
GOOD CHOICE, BOYS.

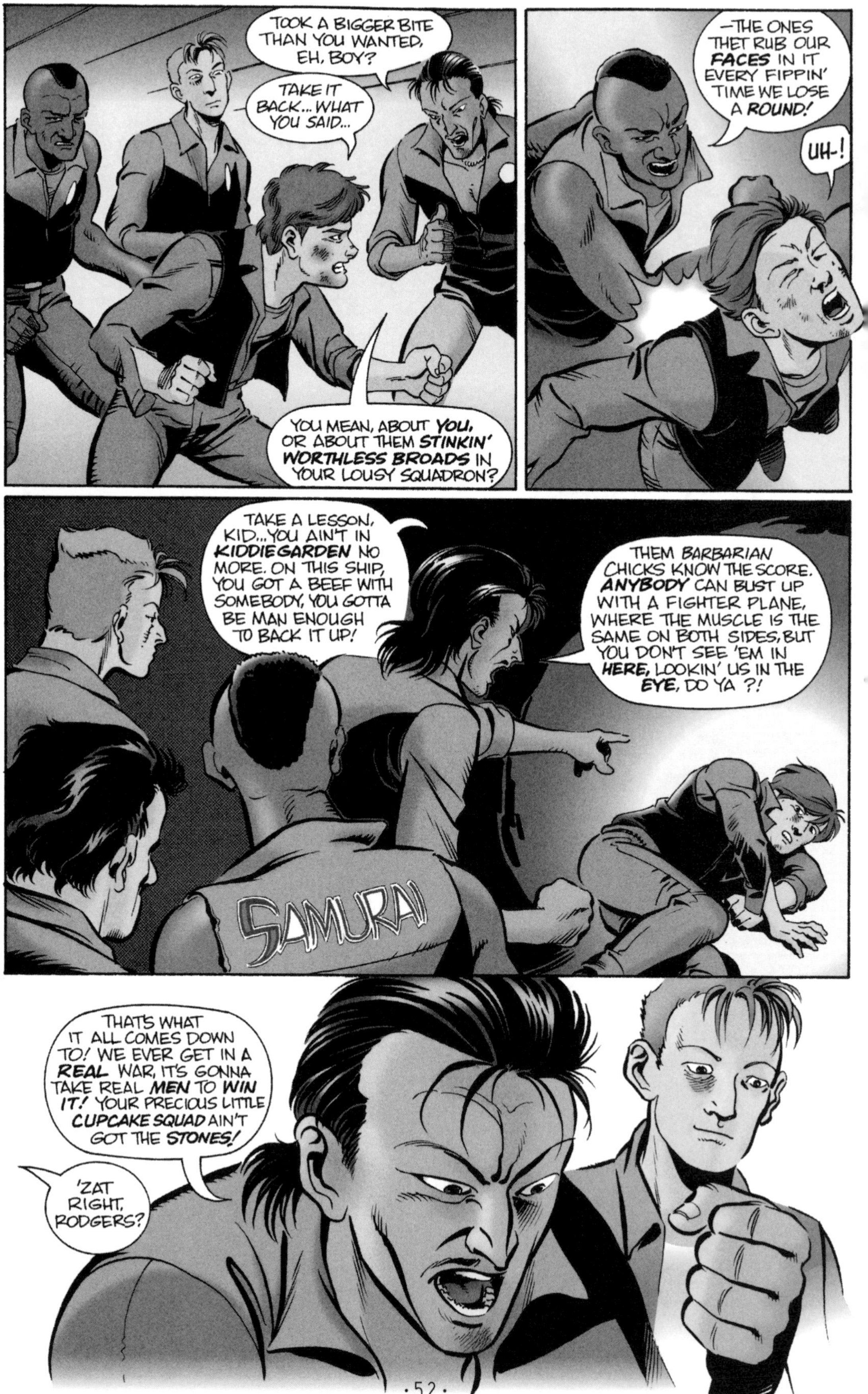
TOOK A BIGGER BITE THAN YOU WANTED, EH, BOY?
TAKE IT BACK... WHAT YOU SAID...
YOU MEAN, ABOUT YOU, OR ABOUT THEM STINKIN' WORTHLESS BROADS IN YOUR LOUSY SQUADRON?
—THE ONES THET RUB OUR FACES IN IT EVERY FIPPIN' TIME WE LOSE A ROUND!
UH-!
TAKE A LESSON, KID... YOU AIN'T IN KIDDIEGARDEN NO MORE. ON THIS SHIP, YOU GOT A BEEF WITH SOMEBODY, YOU GOTTA BE MAN ENOUGH TO BACK IT UP!
THEM BARBARIAN CHICKS KNOW THE SCORE. ANYBODY CAN BUST UP WITH A FIGHTER PLANE, WHERE THE MUSCLE IS THE SAME ON BOTH SIDES, BUT YOU DON'T SEE 'EM IN HERE, LOOKIN' US IN THE EYE, DO YA ?!
SAMURAI
THAT'S WHAT IT ALL COMES DOWN TO! WE EVER GET IN A REAL WAR, IT'S GONNA TAKE REAL MEN TO WIN IT! YOUR PRECIOUS LITTLE CUPCAKE SQUAD AIN'T GOT THE STONES!
'ZAT RIGHT, RODGERS?

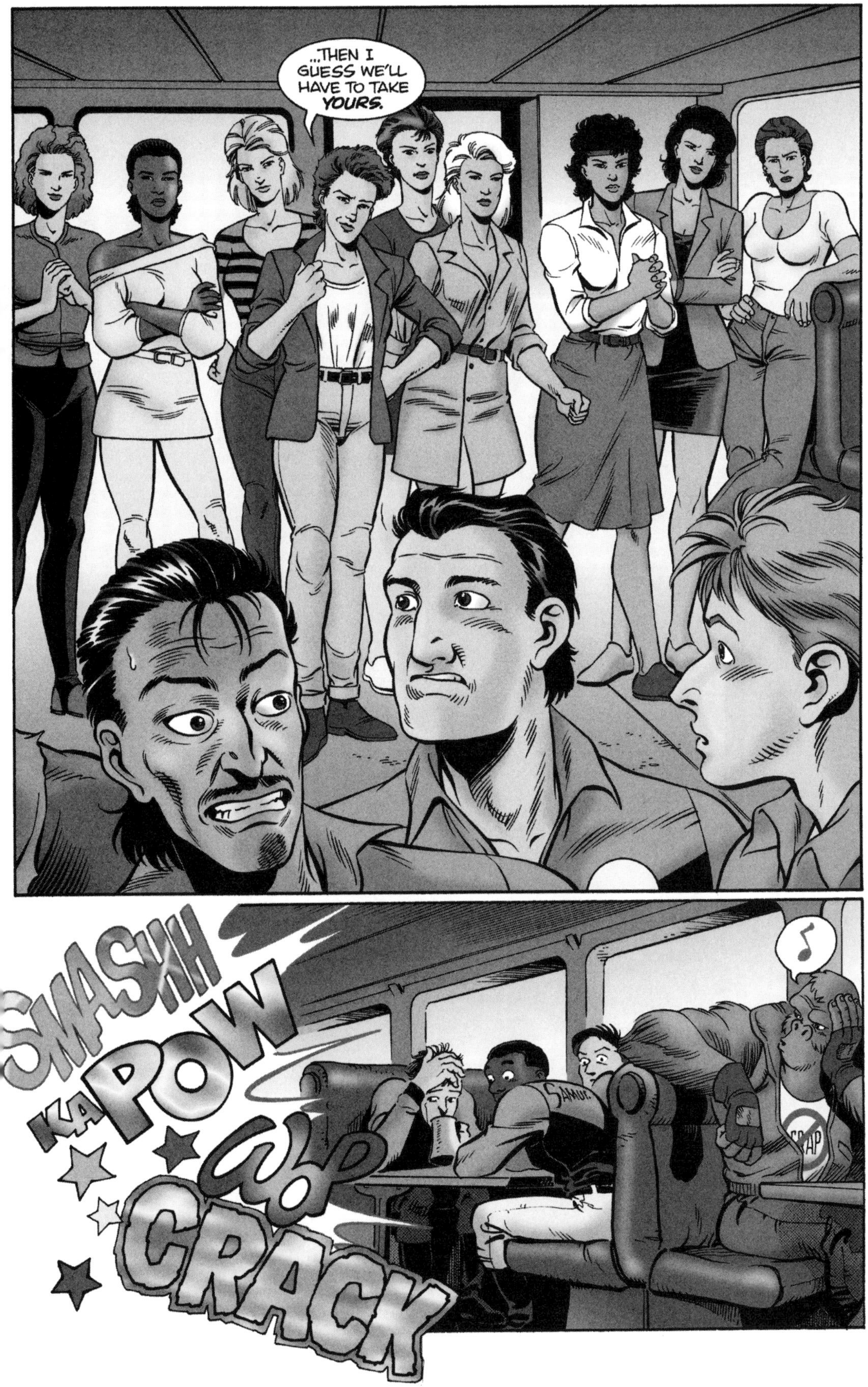
...THEN I GUESS WE'LL HAVE TO TAKE YOURS.
SMASHH
KA POW
CRACK

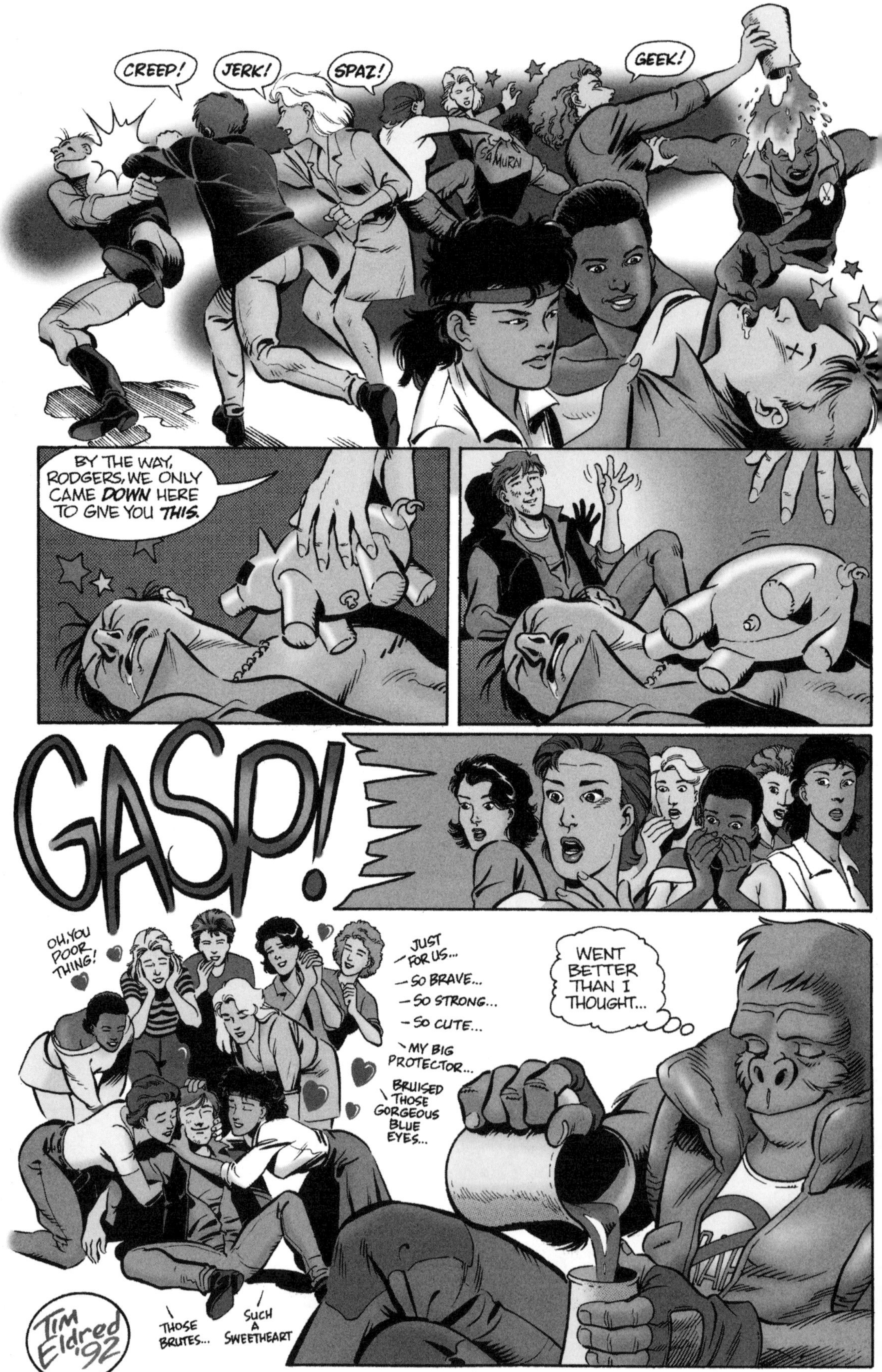
CREEP!
JERK!
SPAZ!
GEEK!
SAMURAI
BY THE WAY, RODGERS, WE ONLY CAME DOWN HERE TO GIVE YOU THIS.
GASP!
OH, YOU POOR THING!
JUST FOR US...
SO BRAVE...
SO STRONG...
SO CUTE...
MY BIG PROTECTOR...
BRUISED THOSE GORGEOUS BLUE EYES...
THOSE BRUTES...
SUCH A SWEETHEART
WENT BETTER THAN I THOUGHT...
TIM Eldred '92

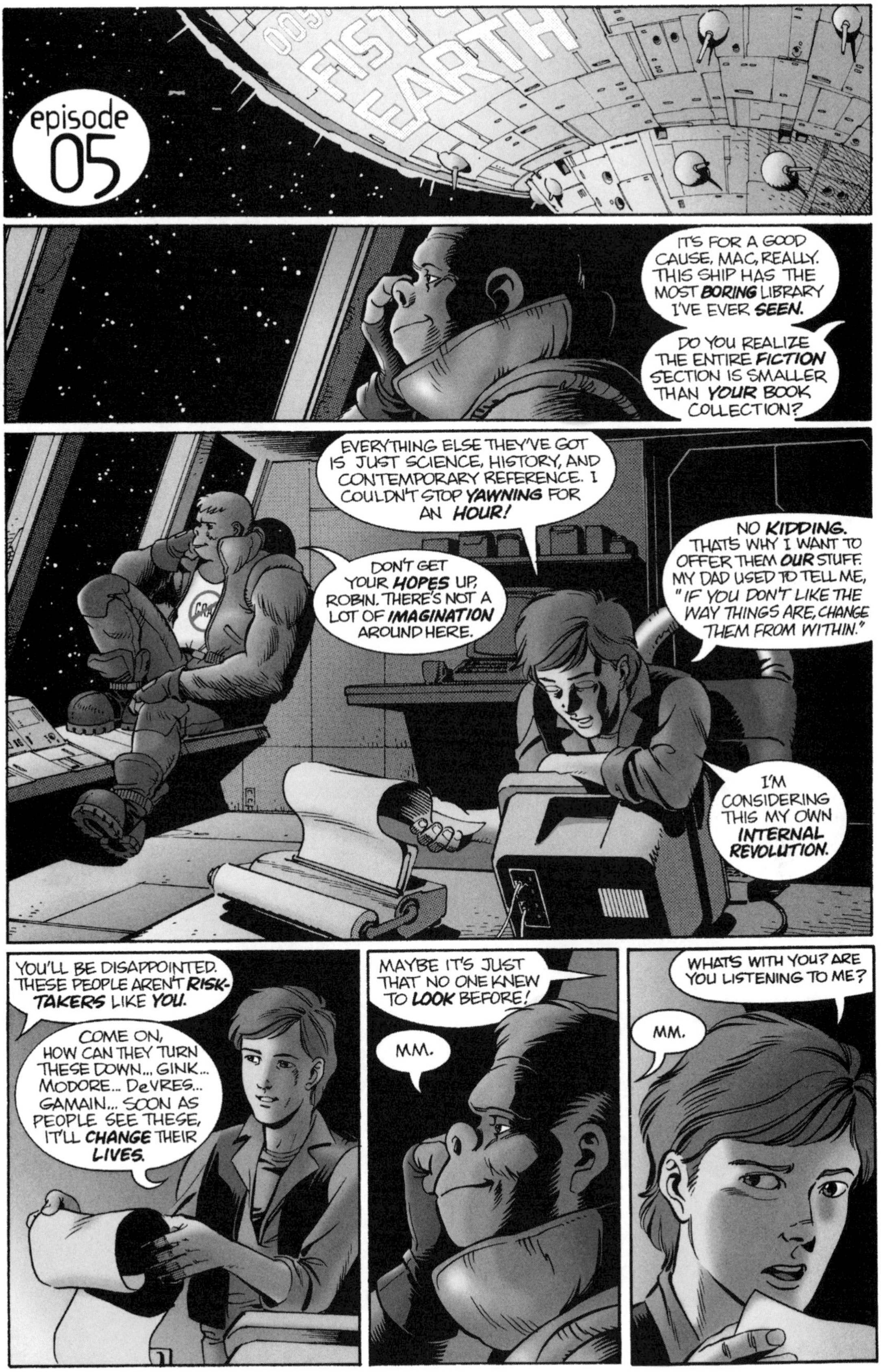
episode 05
005 FIST OF EARTH
IT'S FOR A GOOD CAUSE, MAC, REALLY. THIS SHIP HAS THE MOST BORING LIBRARY I'VE EVER SEEN.
DO YOU REALIZE THE ENTIRE FICTION SECTION IS SMALLER THAN YOUR BOOK COLLECTION?
EVERYTHING ELSE THEY'VE GOT IS JUST SCIENCE, HISTORY, AND CONTEMPORARY REFERENCE. I COULDN'T STOP YAWNING FOR AN HOUR!
DON'T GET YOUR HOPES UP, ROBIN. THERE'S NOT A LOT OF IMAGINATION AROUND HERE.
NO KIDDING. THAT'S WHY I WANT TO OFFER THEM OUR STUFF. MY DAD USED TO TELL ME, "IF YOU DON'T LIKE THE WAY THINGS ARE, CHANGE THEM FROM WITHIN."
I'M CONSIDERING THIS MY OWN INTERNAL REVOLUTION.
YOU'LL BE DISAPPOINTED. THESE PEOPLE AREN'T RISK-TAKERS LIKE YOU.
COME ON, HOW CAN THEY TURN THESE DOWN... GINK... MODORE... DeVRES... GAMAIN... SOON AS PEOPLE SEE THESE, IT'LL CHANGE THEIR LIVES.
MAYBE IT'S JUST THAT NO ONE KNEW TO LOOK BEFORE!
MM.
WHAT'S WITH YOU? ARE YOU LISTENING TO ME?
MM.

I'VE FINISHED THE LIST. I'D LIKE TO TAKE IT UP PERSONALLY.

FINE.

ARE YOU SURE? I MEAN, WE *ARE* SUPPOSED TO BE ON *ALERT* STATUS. THE ALARM COULD SOUND FOR BARBARA AND THE SQUADRON TO FLY A COMBAT EXERCISE *ANY* MOMENT.

BEH.

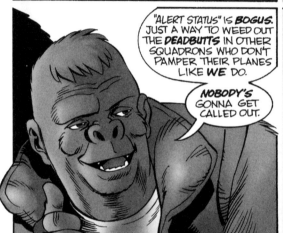

"ALERT STATUS" IS *BOGUS.* JUST A WAY TO WEED OUT THE *DEADBUTTS* IN OTHER SQUADRONS WHO DON'T PAMPER THEIR PLANES LIKE *WE* DO.

NOBODY'S GONNA GET CALLED OUT.

OKAY.

YOU WATCH. THIS IS GONNA BE SOMETHING *BIG!*

UH-HUH.

BIG...

THE CALLING

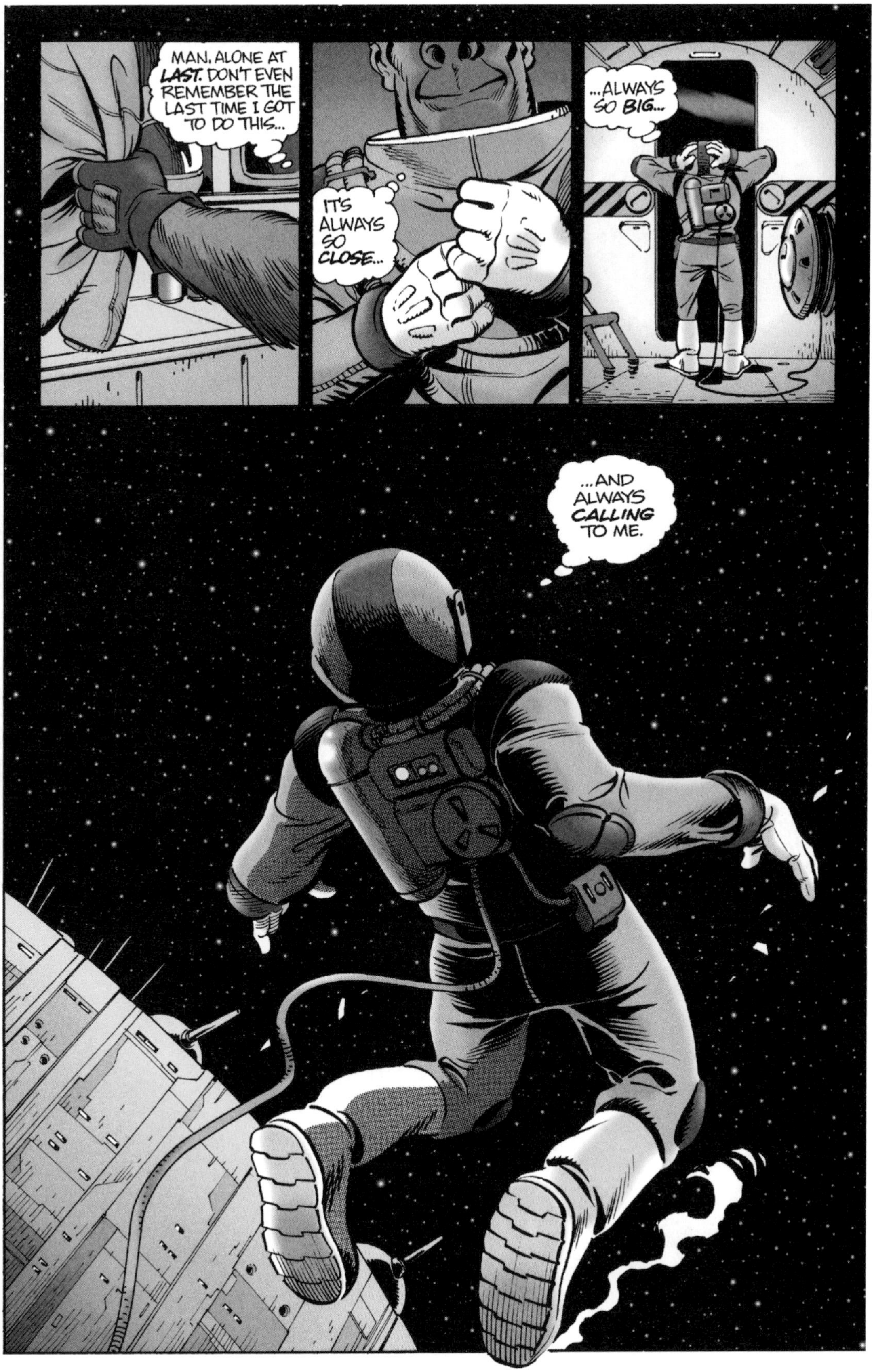
MAN. ALONE AT LAST. DON'T EVEN REMEMBER THE LAST TIME I GOT TO DO THIS...
IT'S ALWAYS SO CLOSE...
...ALWAYS SO BIG...
...AND ALWAYS CALLING TO ME.

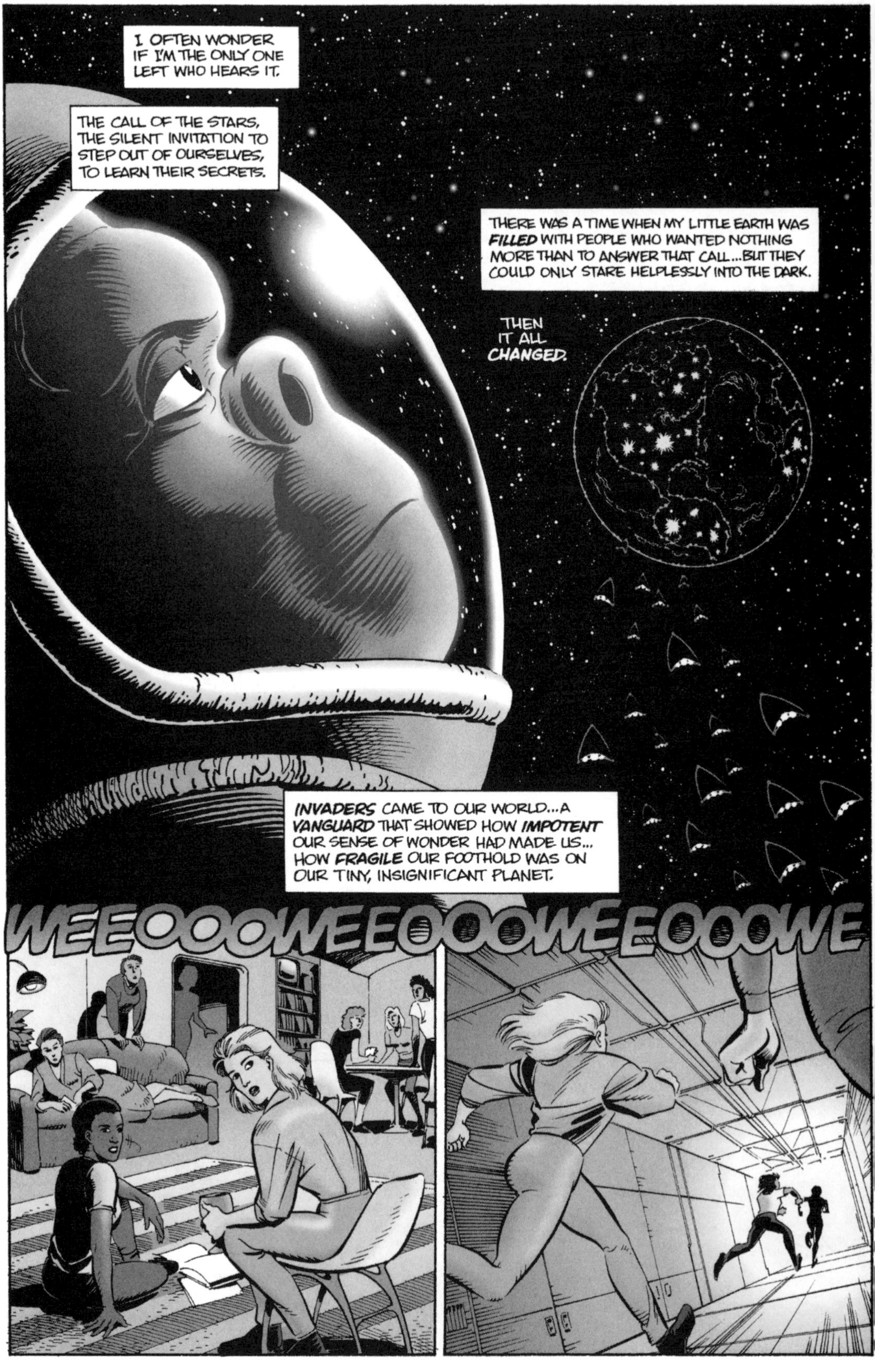
I OFTEN WONDER IF I'M THE ONLY ONE LEFT WHO HEARS IT.
THE CALL OF THE STARS, THE SILENT INVITATION TO STEP OUT OF OURSELVES, TO LEARN THEIR SECRETS.
THERE WAS A TIME WHEN MY LITTLE EARTH WAS FILLED WITH PEOPLE WHO WANTED NOTHING MORE THAN TO ANSWER THAT CALL...BUT THEY COULD ONLY STARE HELPLESSLY INTO THE DARK.
THEN IT ALL CHANGED.
INVADERS CAME TO OUR WORLD...A VANGUARD THAT SHOWED HOW IMPOTENT OUR SENSE OF WONDER HAD MADE US... HOW FRAGILE OUR FOOTHOLD WAS ON OUR TINY, INSIGNIFICANT PLANET.
WEEOOOWEEOOOWEEOOOWE

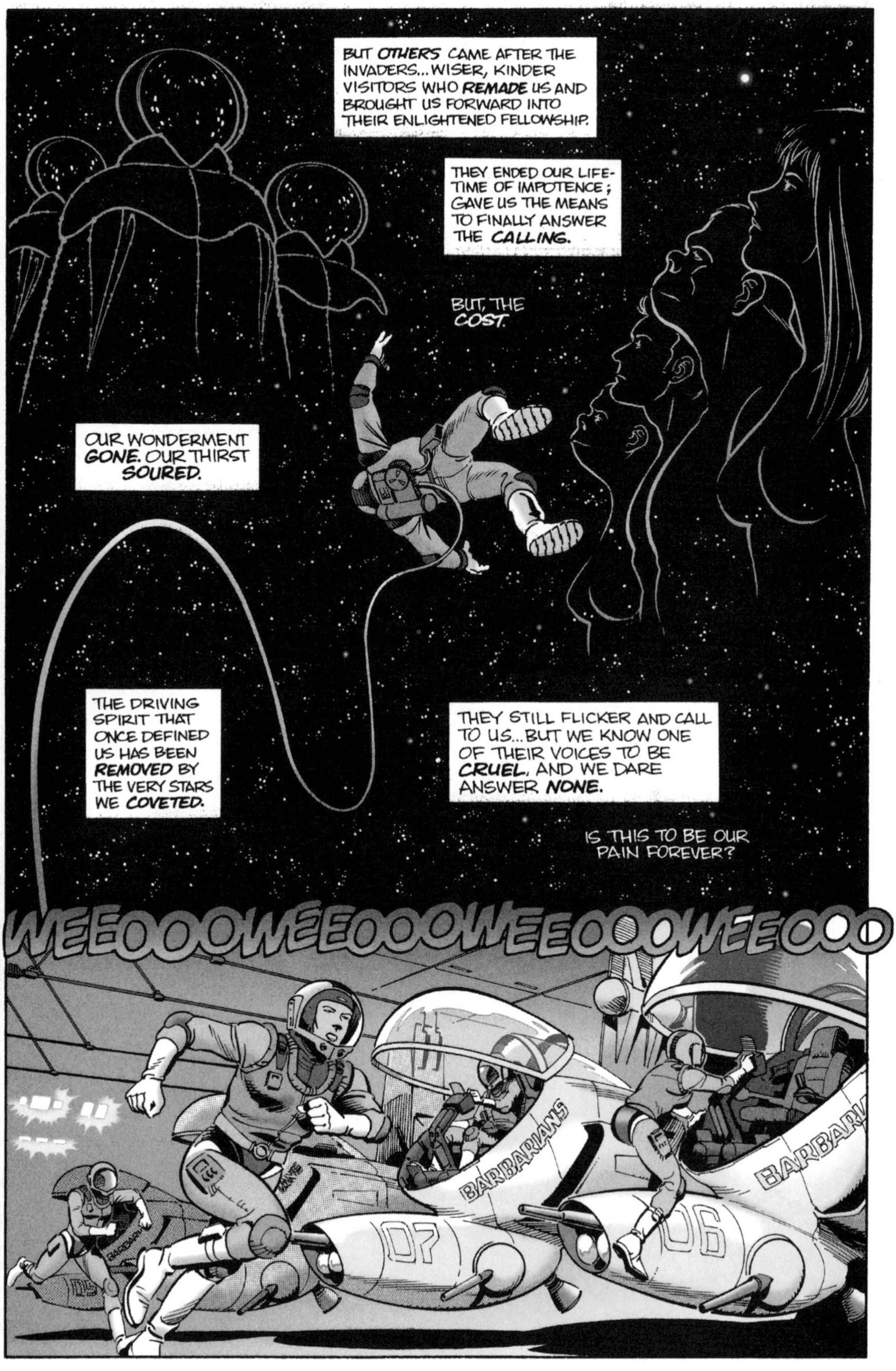
BUT OTHERS CAME AFTER THE INVADERS...WISER, KINDER VISITORS WHO REMADE US AND BROUGHT US FORWARD INTO THEIR ENLIGHTENED FELLOWSHIP.
THEY ENDED OUR LIFE-TIME OF IMPOTENCE; GAVE US THE MEANS TO FINALLY ANSWER THE CALLING.
BUT, THE COST.
OUR WONDERMENT GONE. OUR THIRST SOURED.
THE DRIVING SPIRIT THAT ONCE DEFINED US HAS BEEN REMOVED BY THE VERY STARS WE COVETED.
THEY STILL FLICKER AND CALL TO US...BUT WE KNOW ONE OF THEIR VOICES TO BE CRUEL, AND WE DARE ANSWER NONE.
IS THIS TO BE OUR PAIN FOREVER?
WEEOOOWEEOOOWEEOOOWEEOOO
BARBARIANS
07
06

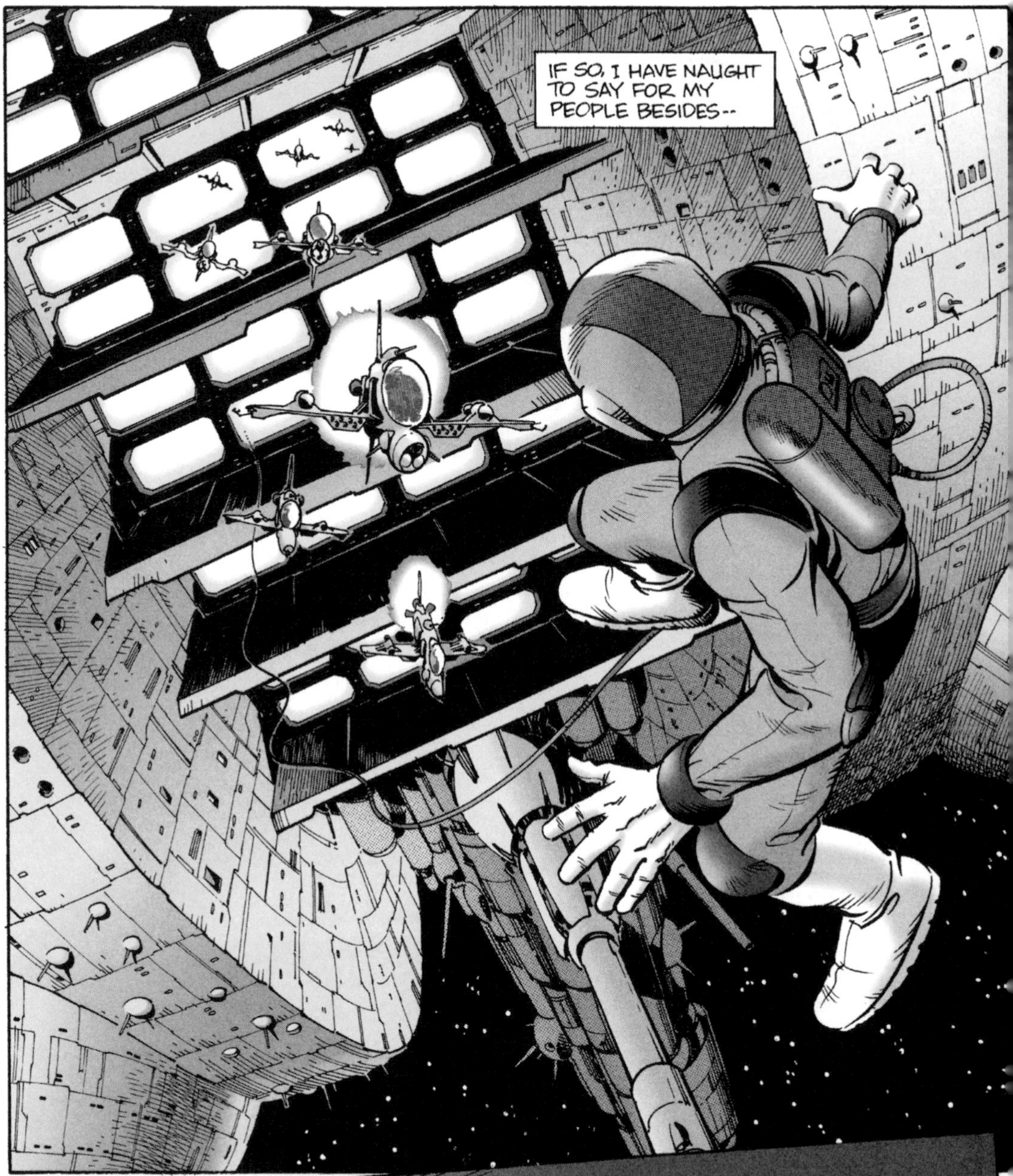
IF SO, I HAVE NAUGHT TO SAY FOR MY PEOPLE BESIDES--

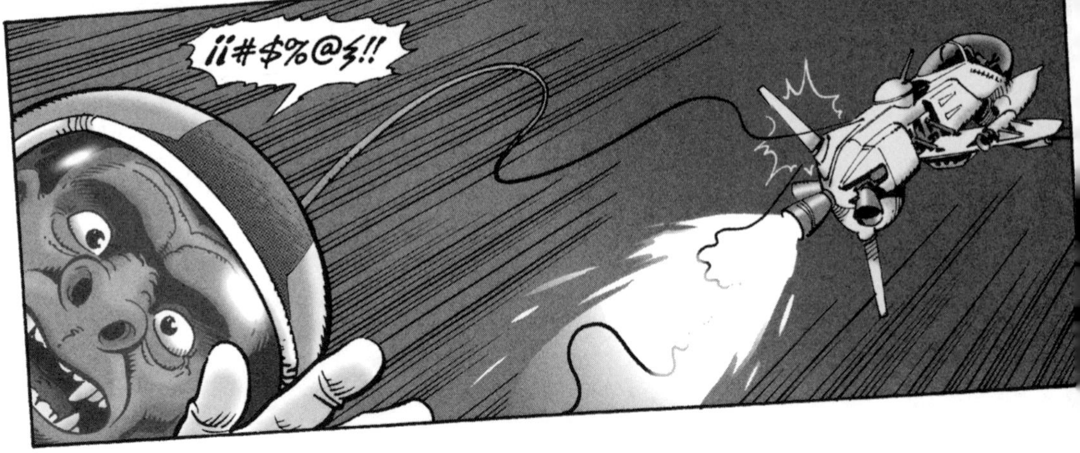
¡¡#$%@ξ!!

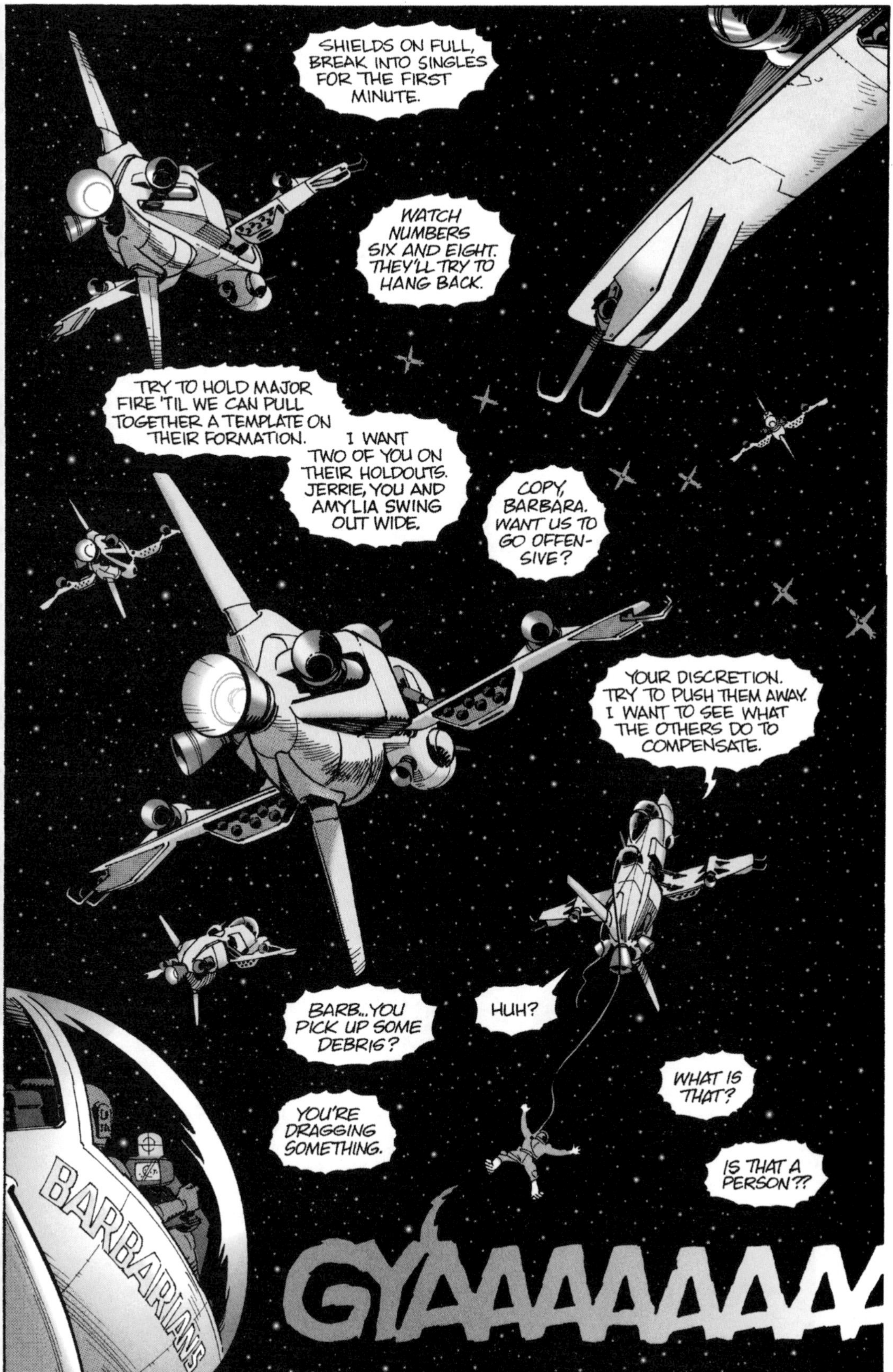
SHIELDS ON FULL, BREAK INTO SINGLES FOR THE FIRST MINUTE.
WATCH NUMBERS SIX AND EIGHT. THEY'LL TRY TO HANG BACK.
TRY TO HOLD MAJOR FIRE 'TIL WE CAN PULL TOGETHER A TEMPLATE ON THEIR FORMATION.
I WANT TWO OF YOU ON THEIR HOLDOUTS. JERRIE, YOU AND AMYLIA SWING OUT WIDE.
COPY, BARBARA. WANT US TO GO OFFEN-SIVE?
YOUR DISCRETION. TRY TO PUSH THEM AWAY. I WANT TO SEE WHAT THE OTHERS DO TO COMPENSATE.
BARB...YOU PICK UP SOME DEBRIS?
HUH?
YOU'RE DRAGGING SOMETHING.
WHAT IS THAT?
IS THAT A PERSON??
BARBARIANS
GYAAAAAAA

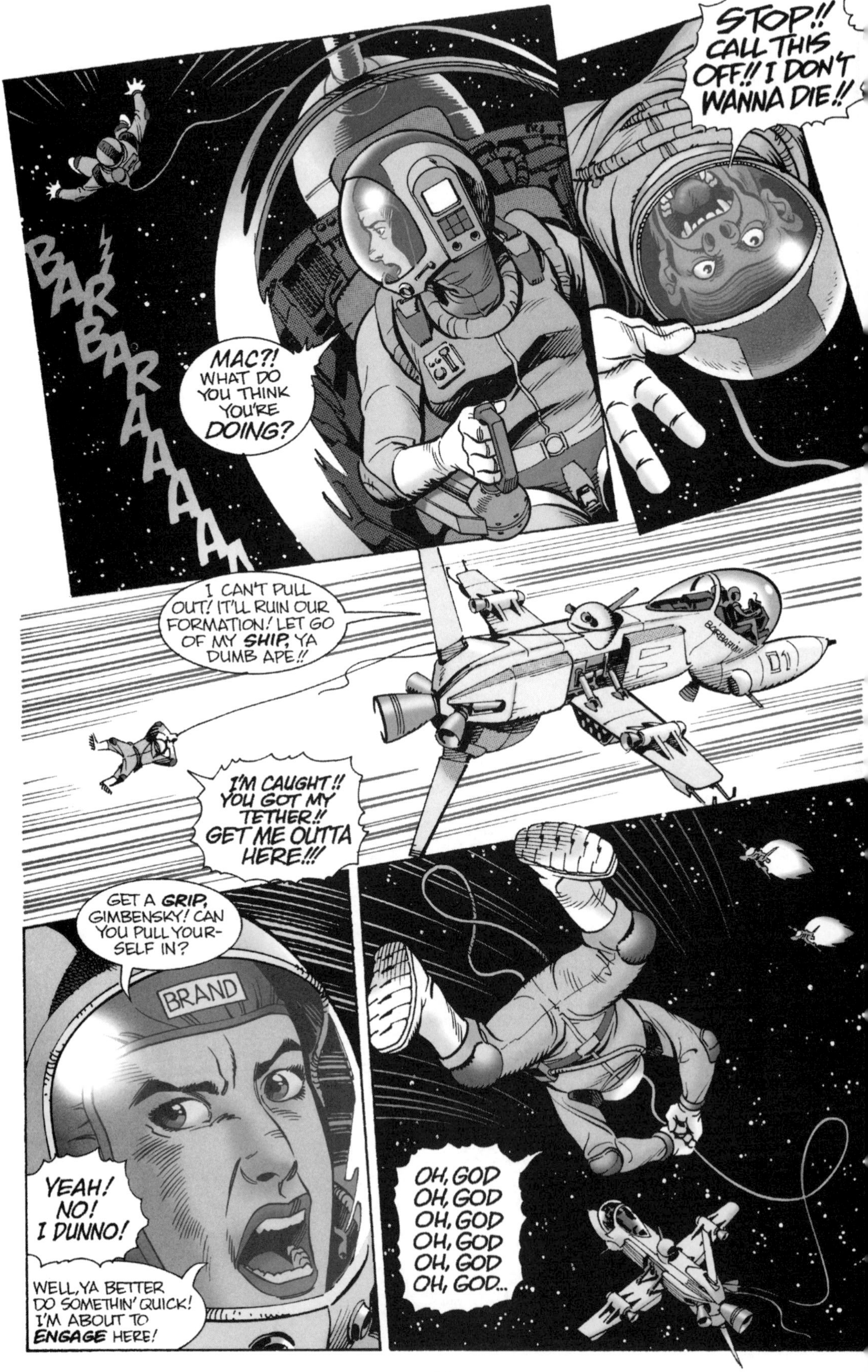
BARBARAAAAA
MAC?! WHAT DO YOU THINK YOU'RE DOING?
STOP!! CALL THIS OFF!! I DON'T WANNA DIE!!
I CAN'T PULL OUT! IT'LL RUIN OUR FORMATION! LET GO OF MY SHIP, YA DUMB APE!!
BARBARI
01
I'M CAUGHT!! YOU GOT MY TETHER!! GET ME OUTTA HERE!!!
GET A GRIP, GIMBENSKY! CAN YOU PULL YOURSELF IN?
BRAND
YEAH! NO! I DUNNO!
WELL, YA BETTER DO SOMETHIN' QUICK! I'M ABOUT TO ENGAGE HERE!
OH, GOD OH, GOD OH, GOD OH, GOD OH, GOD OH, GOD...

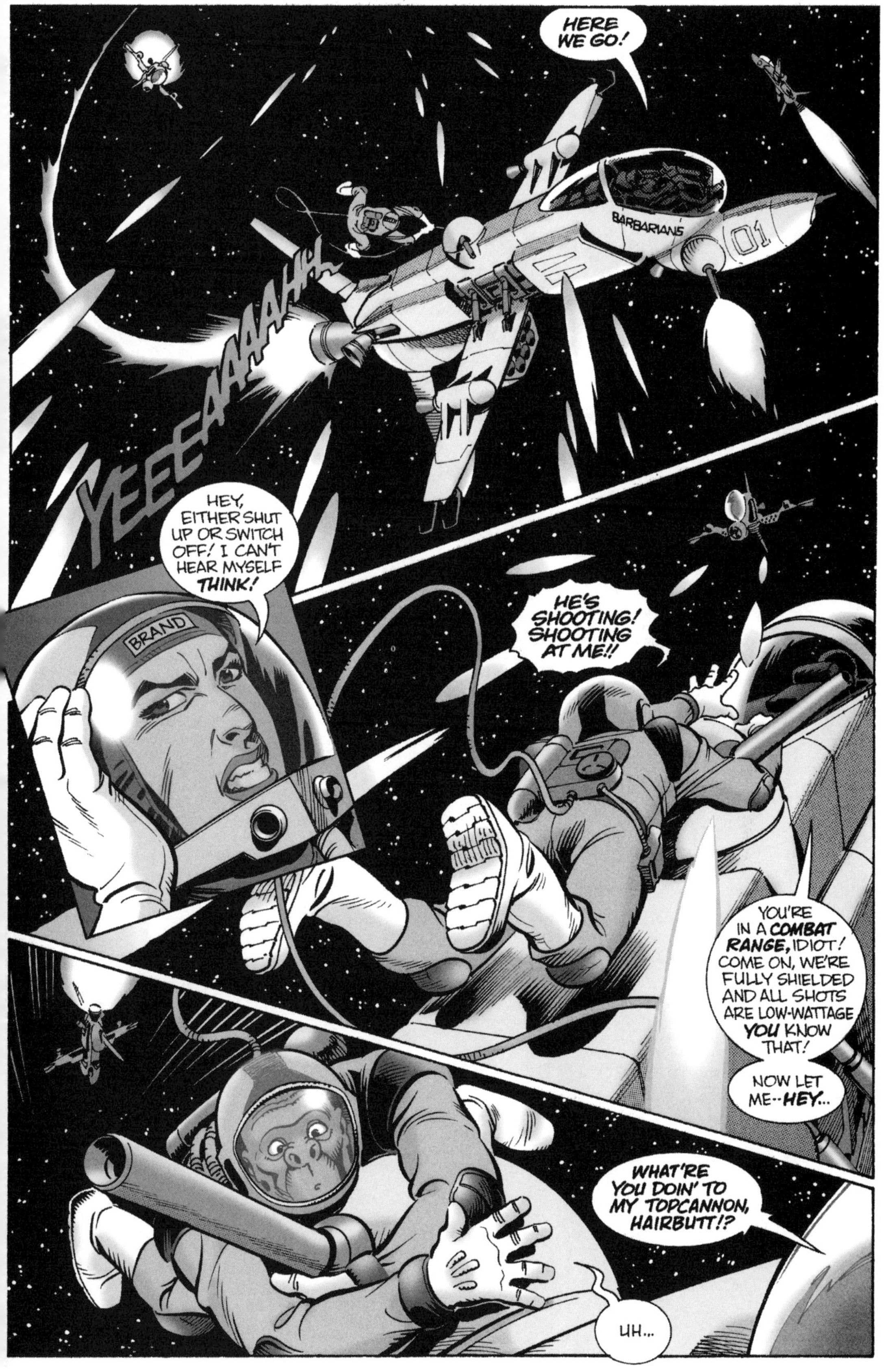
HERE WE GO!
YEEEAAAAHH
HEY, EITHER SHUT UP OR SWITCH OFF! I CAN'T HEAR MYSELF THINK!
BRAND
HE'S SHOOTING! SHOOTING AT ME!!
YOU'RE IN A COMBAT RANGE, IDIOT! COME ON, WE'RE FULLY SHIELDED AND ALL SHOTS ARE LOW-WATTAGE YOU KNOW THAT!
NOW LET ME--HEY...
WHAT'RE YOU DOIN' TO MY TOPCANNON, HAIRBUTT!?
UH...

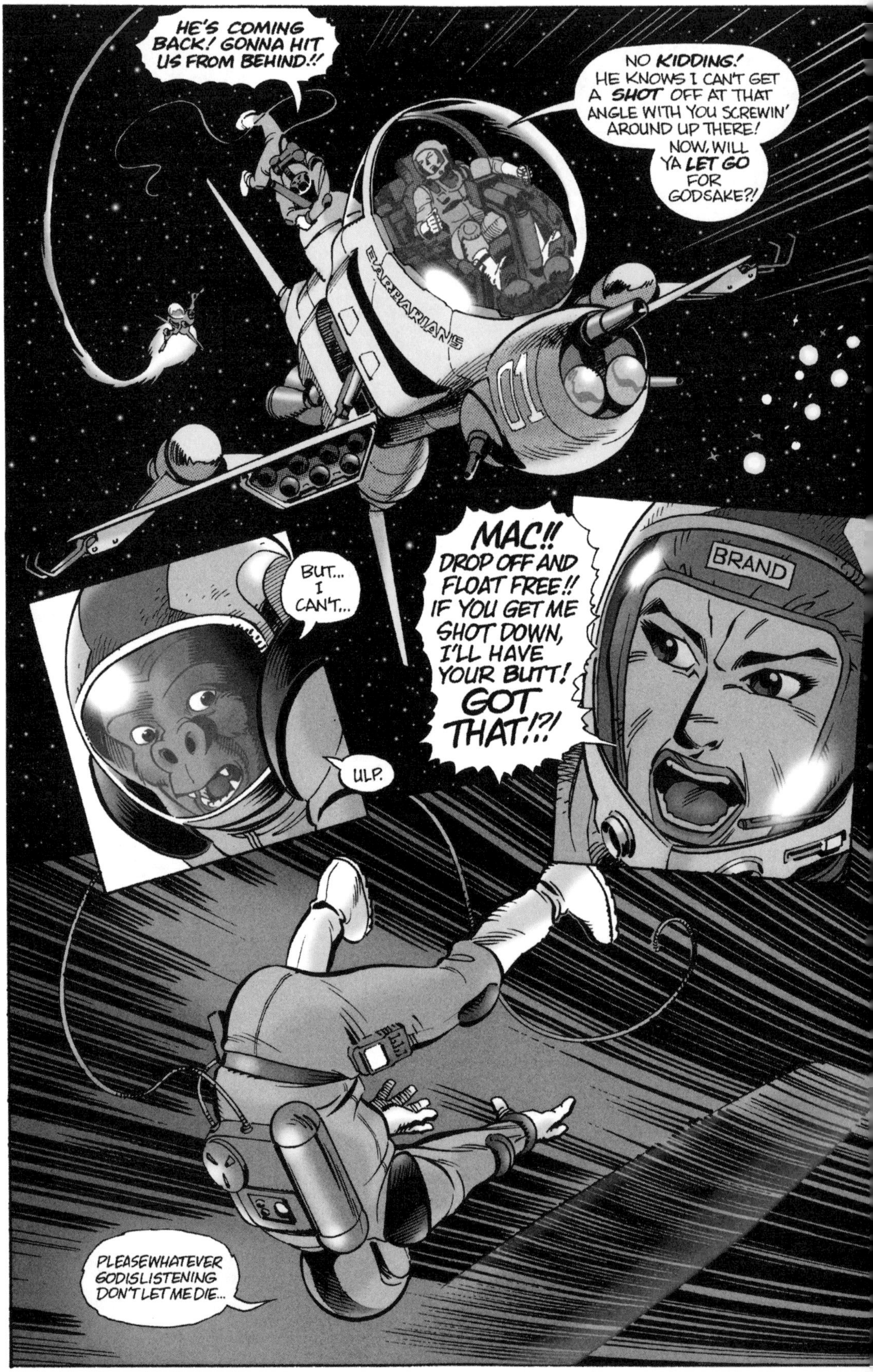
HE'S COMING BACK! GONNA HIT US FROM BEHIND!!
NO KIDDING! HE KNOWS I CAN'T GET A SHOT OFF AT THAT ANGLE WITH YOU SCREWIN' AROUND UP THERE! NOW, WILL YA LET GO FOR GODSAKE?!
BARBARIANS
01
BRAND
MAC!! DROP OFF AND FLOAT FREE!! IF YOU GET ME SHOT DOWN, I'LL HAVE YOUR BUTT! GOT THAT!?!
BUT... I CAN'T...
ULP.
PLEASEWHATEVER GODISLISTENING DON'TLETMEDIE...

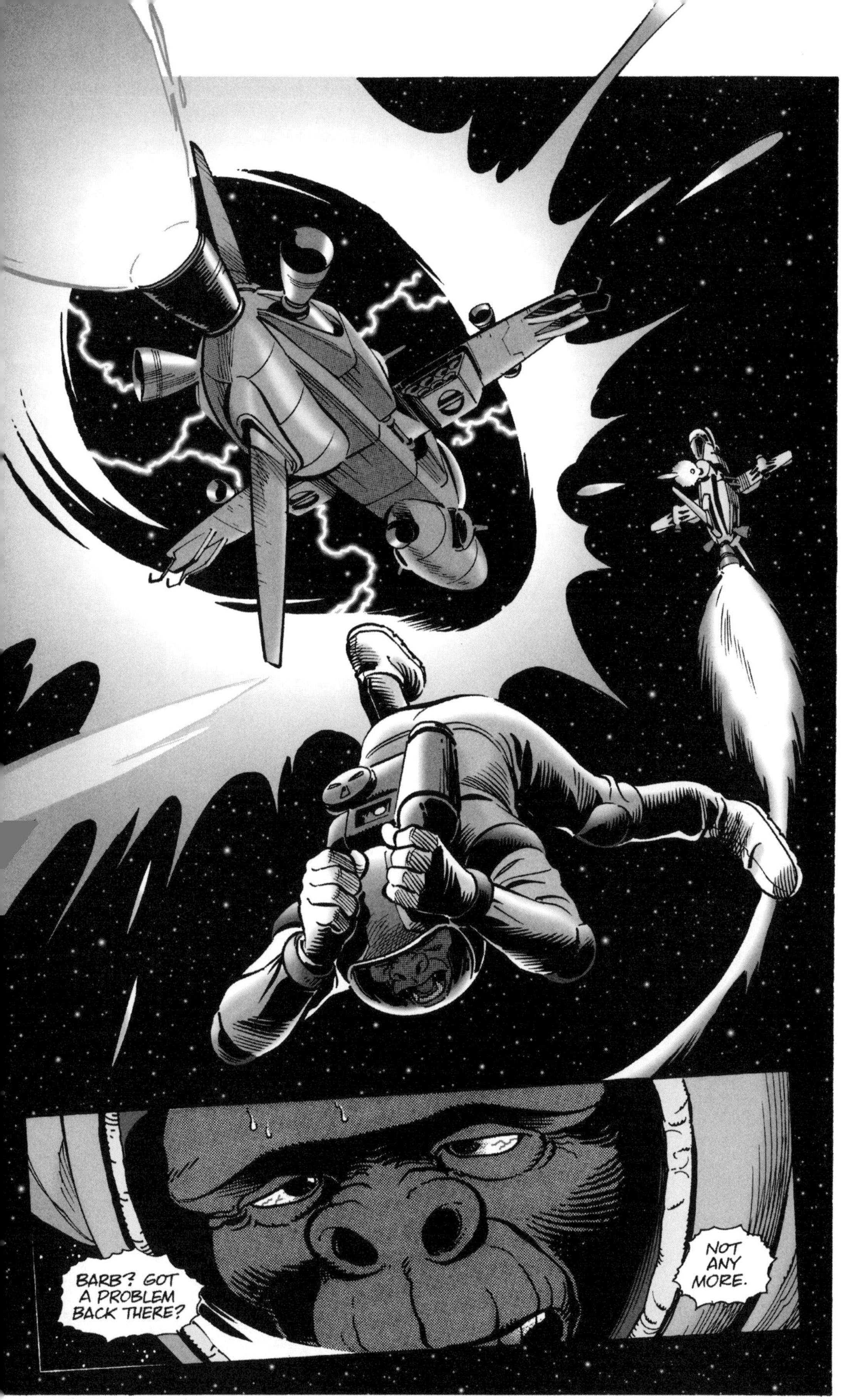
BARB? GOT A PROBLEM BACK THERE?
NOT ANY MORE.

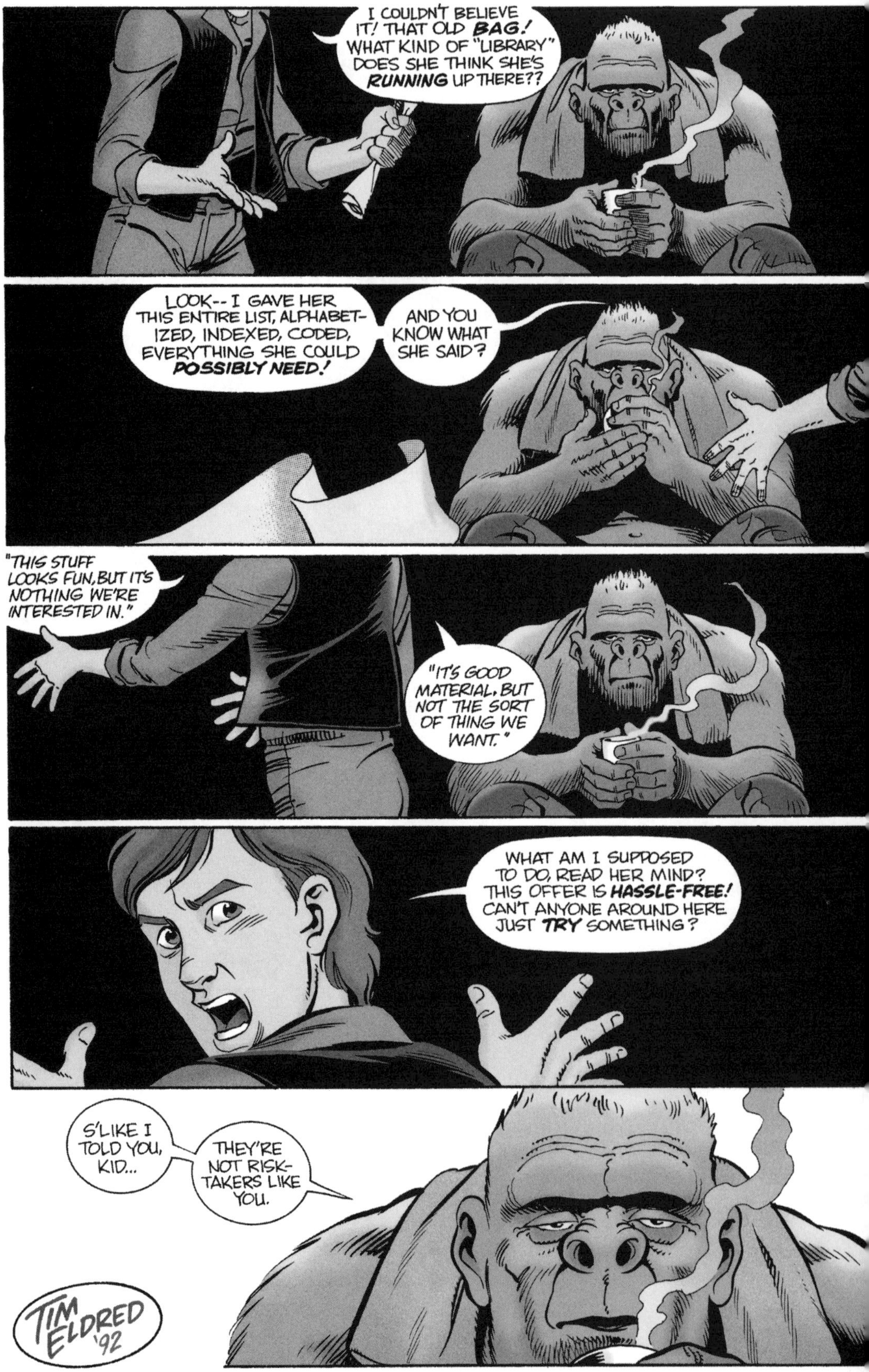
I COULDN'T BELIEVE IT! THAT OLD BAG! WHAT KIND OF "LIBRARY" DOES SHE THINK SHE'S RUNNING UP THERE??
LOOK-- I GAVE HER THIS ENTIRE LIST, ALPHABETIZED, INDEXED, CODED, EVERYTHING SHE COULD POSSIBLY NEED!
AND YOU KNOW WHAT SHE SAID?
"THIS STUFF LOOKS FUN, BUT IT'S NOTHING WE'RE INTERESTED IN."
"IT'S GOOD MATERIAL, BUT NOT THE SORT OF THING WE WANT."
WHAT AM I SUPPOSED TO DO, READ HER MIND? THIS OFFER IS HASSLE-FREE! CAN'T ANYONE AROUND HERE JUST TRY SOMETHING?
S'LIKE I TOLD YOU, KID...
THEY'RE NOT RISK-TAKERS LIKE YOU.
TIM ELDRED '92

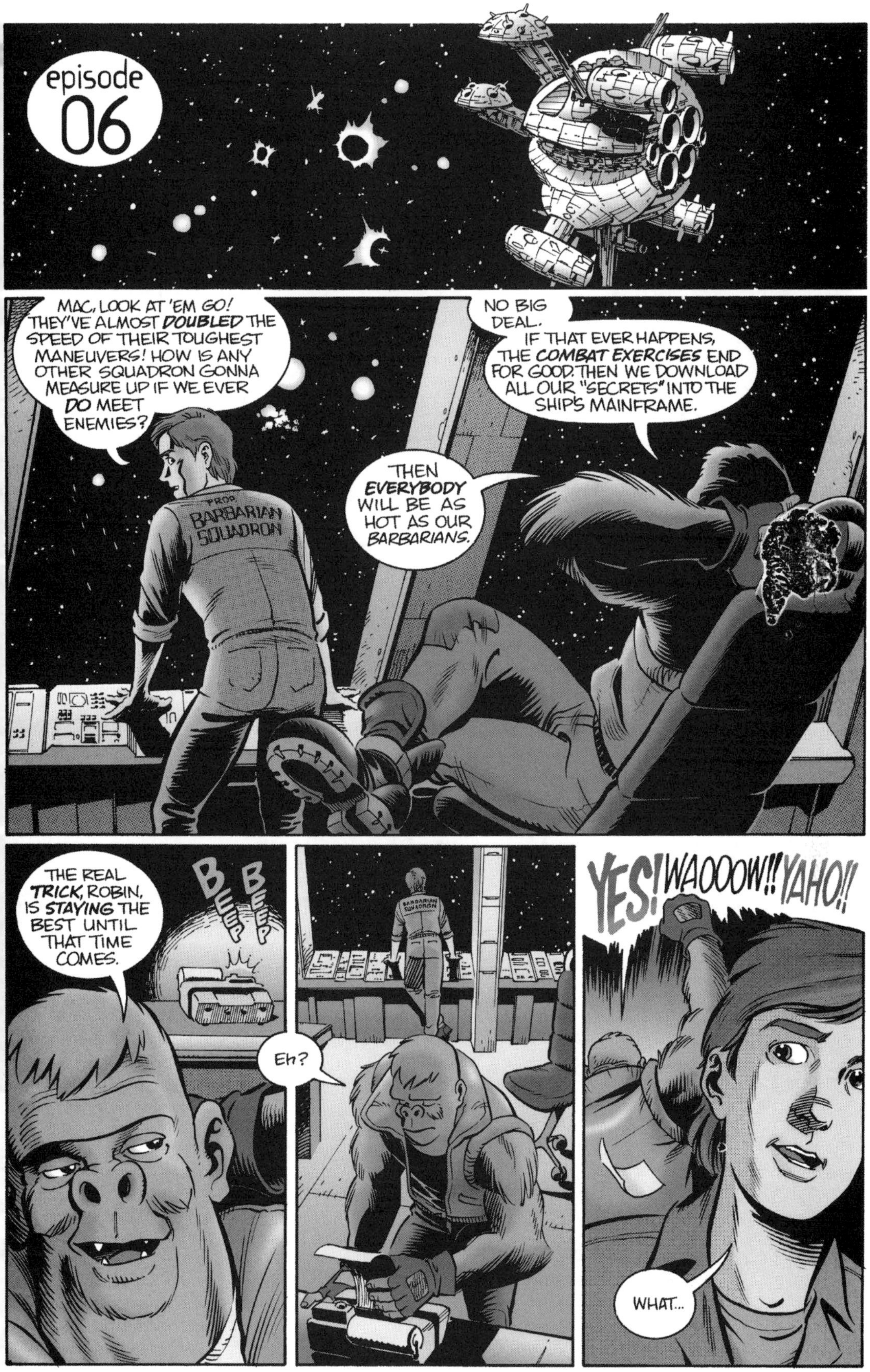
episode 06
MAC, LOOK AT 'EM GO! THEY'VE ALMOST DOUBLED THE SPEED OF THEIR TOUGHEST MANEUVERS! HOW IS ANY OTHER SQUADRON GONNA MEASURE UP IF WE EVER DO MEET ENEMIES?
NO BIG DEAL.
IF THAT EVER HAPPENS, THE COMBAT EXERCISES END FOR GOOD. THEN WE DOWNLOAD ALL OUR "SECRETS" INTO THE SHIP'S MAINFRAME.
THEN EVERYBODY WILL BE AS HOT AS OUR BARBARIANS.
PROP.
BARBARIAN SQUADRON
THE REAL TRICK, ROBIN, IS STAYING THE BEST UNTIL THAT TIME COMES.
BEEP BEEP
Eh?
YES! WAOOOW!! YAHO!!
WHAT...

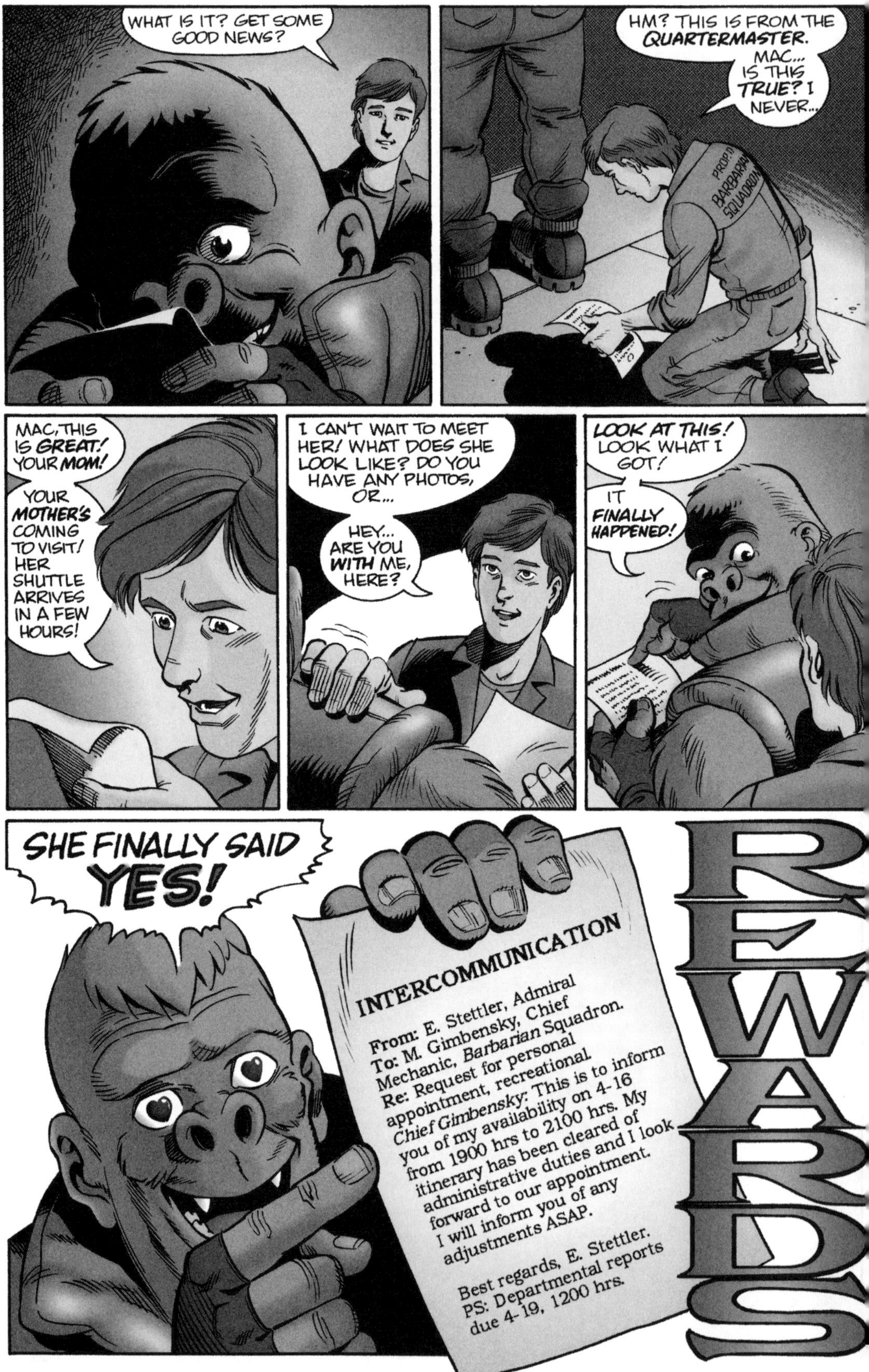
WHAT IS IT? GET SOME GOOD NEWS?
HM? THIS IS FROM THE QUARTERMASTER.
MAC... IS THIS TRUE? I NEVER...
BARBARIAN SQUADRON
MAC, THIS IS GREAT! YOUR MOM!
YOUR MOTHER'S COMING TO VISIT! HER SHUTTLE ARRIVES IN A FEW HOURS!
I CAN'T WAIT TO MEET HER! WHAT DOES SHE LOOK LIKE? DO YOU HAVE ANY PHOTOS, OR...
HEY... ARE YOU WITH ME, HERE?
LOOK AT THIS! LOOK WHAT I GOT!
IT FINALLY HAPPENED!
SHE FINALLY SAID YES!
INTERCOMMUNICATION
From: E. Stettler, Admiral
To: M. Gimbensky, Chief Mechanic, Barbarian Squadron.
Re: Request for personal appointment, recreational.
Chief Gimbensky: This is to inform you of my availability on 4-16 from 1900 hrs to 2100 hrs. My itinerary has been cleared of administrative duties and I look forward to our appointment. I will inform you of any adjustments ASAP.
Best regards, E. Stettler.
PS: Departmental reports due 4-19, 1200 hrs.
REWARDS

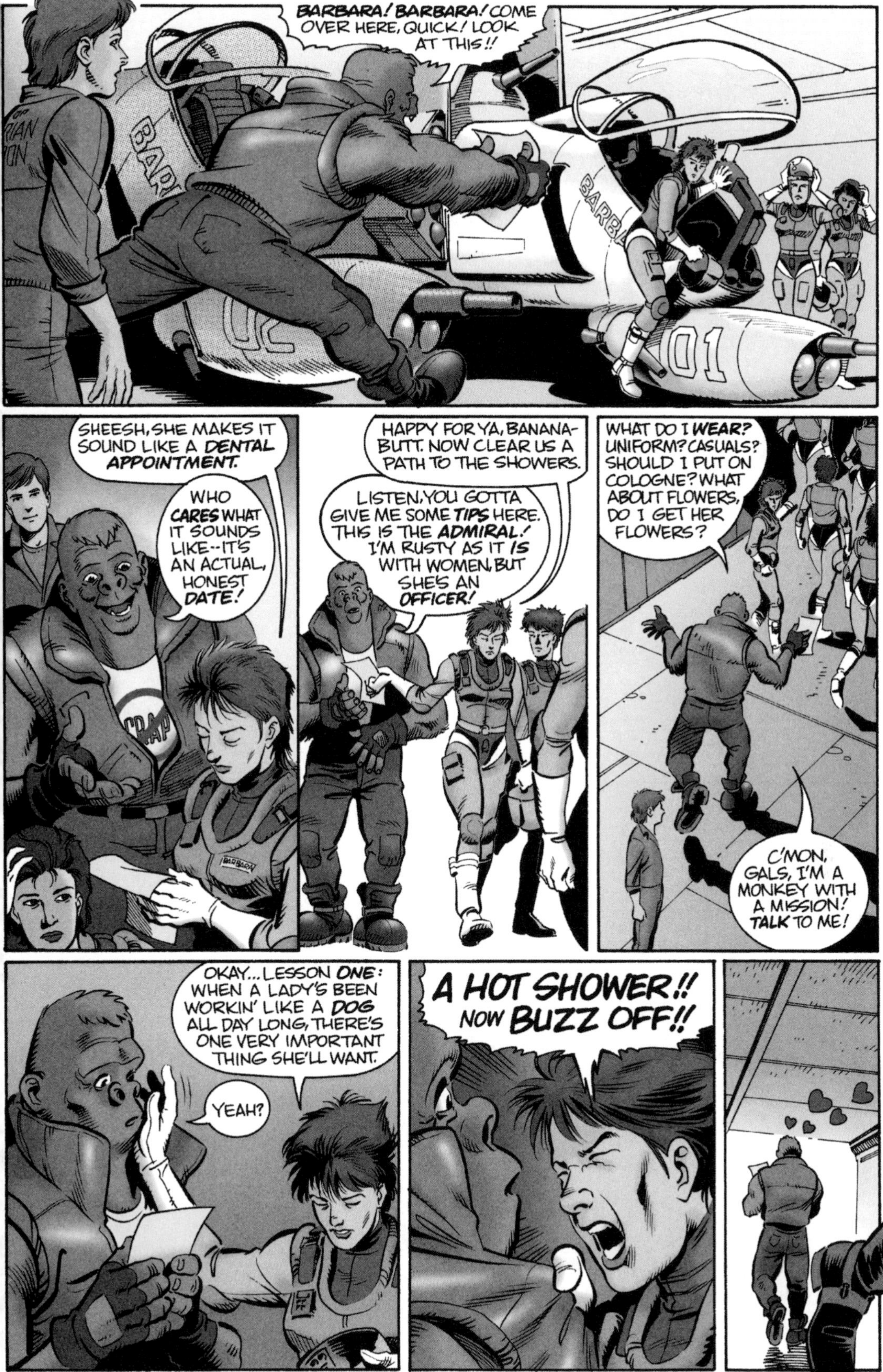
BARBARA! BARBARA! COME OVER HERE, QUICK! LOOK AT THIS!!
SHEESH, SHE MAKES IT SOUND LIKE A DENTAL APPOINTMENT.
WHO CARES WHAT IT SOUNDS LIKE--IT'S AN ACTUAL, HONEST DATE!
HAPPY FOR YA, BANANA-BUTT. NOW CLEAR US A PATH TO THE SHOWERS.
LISTEN, YOU GOTTA GIVE ME SOME TIPS HERE. THIS IS THE ADMIRAL! I'M RUSTY AS IT IS WITH WOMEN, BUT SHE'S AN OFFICER!
WHAT DO I WEAR? UNIFORM? CASUALS? SHOULD I PUT ON COLOGNE? WHAT ABOUT FLOWERS, DO I GET HER FLOWERS?
C'MON, GALS, I'M A MONKEY WITH A MISSION! TALK TO ME!
OKAY... LESSON ONE: WHEN A LADY'S BEEN WORKIN' LIKE A DOG ALL DAY LONG, THERE'S ONE VERY IMPORTANT THING SHE'LL WANT.
YEAH?
A HOT SHOWER!! NOW BUZZ OFF!!

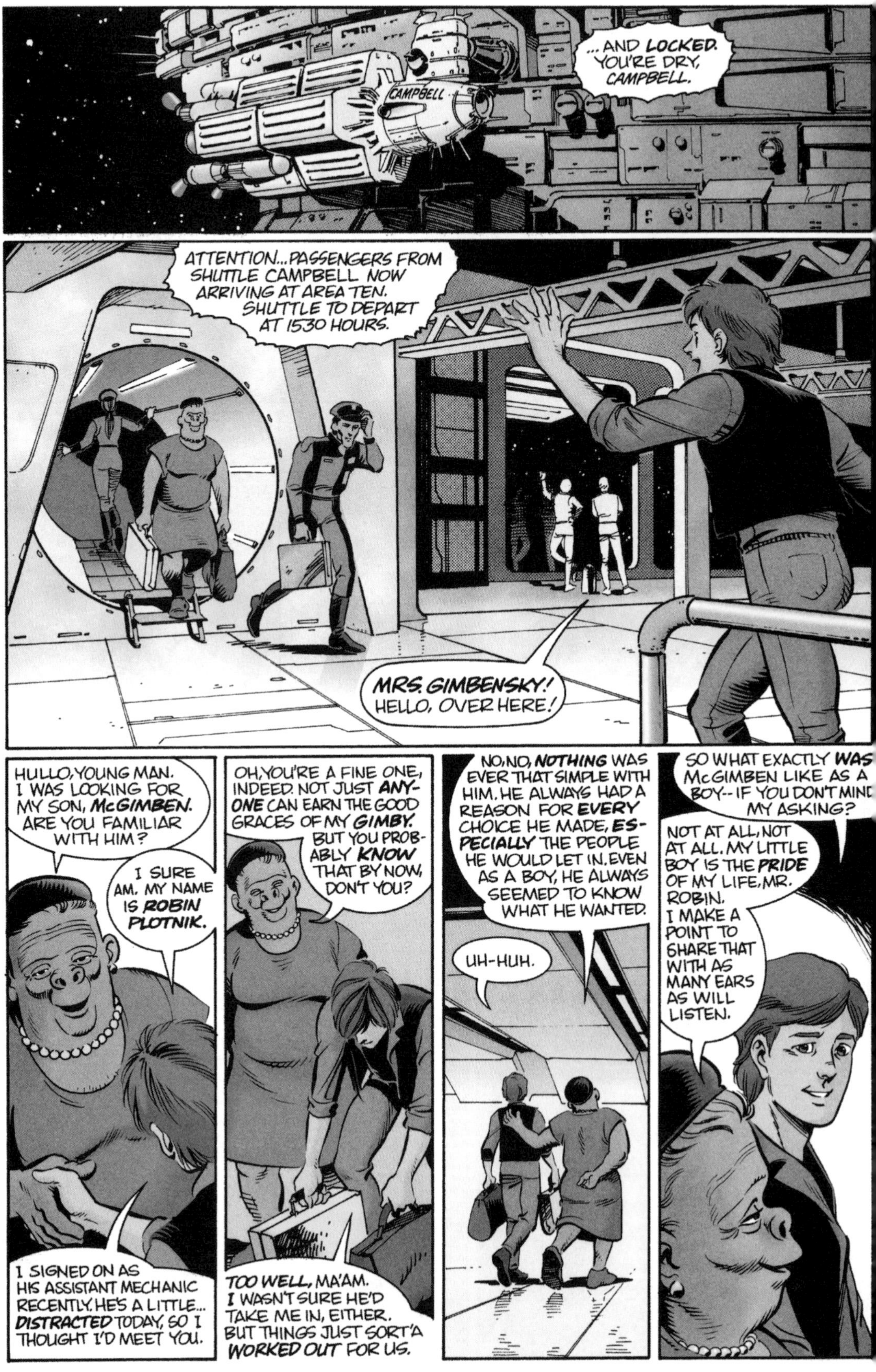
...AND LOCKED. YOU'RE DRY, CAMPBELL.
CAMPBELL
ATTENTION...PASSENGERS FROM SHUTTLE CAMPBELL NOW ARRIVING AT AREA TEN. SHUTTLE TO DEPART AT 1530 HOURS.
MRS. GIMBENSKY! HELLO, OVER HERE!
HULLO, YOUNG MAN. I WAS LOOKING FOR MY SON, McGIMBEN. ARE YOU FAMILIAR WITH HIM?
I SURE AM. MY NAME IS ROBIN PLOTNIK.
I SIGNED ON AS HIS ASSISTANT MECHANIC RECENTLY. HE'S A LITTLE... DISTRACTED TODAY, SO I THOUGHT I'D MEET YOU.
OH, YOU'RE A FINE ONE, INDEED. NOT JUST ANYONE CAN EARN THE GOOD GRACES OF MY GIMBY.
BUT YOU PROBABLY KNOW THAT BY NOW, DON'T YOU?
TOO WELL, MA'AM. I WASN'T SURE HE'D TAKE ME IN, EITHER. BUT THINGS JUST SORT'A WORKED OUT FOR US.
NO, NO, NOTHING WAS EVER THAT SIMPLE WITH HIM. HE ALWAYS HAD A REASON FOR EVERY CHOICE HE MADE, ESPECIALLY THE PEOPLE HE WOULD LET IN. EVEN AS A BOY, HE ALWAYS SEEMED TO KNOW WHAT HE WANTED.
UH-HUH.
SO WHAT EXACTLY WAS McGIMBEN LIKE AS A BOY-- IF YOU DON'T MIND MY ASKING?
NOT AT ALL, NOT AT ALL. MY LITTLE BOY IS THE PRIDE OF MY LIFE, MR. ROBIN. I MAKE A POINT TO SHARE THAT WITH AS MANY EARS AS WILL LISTEN.

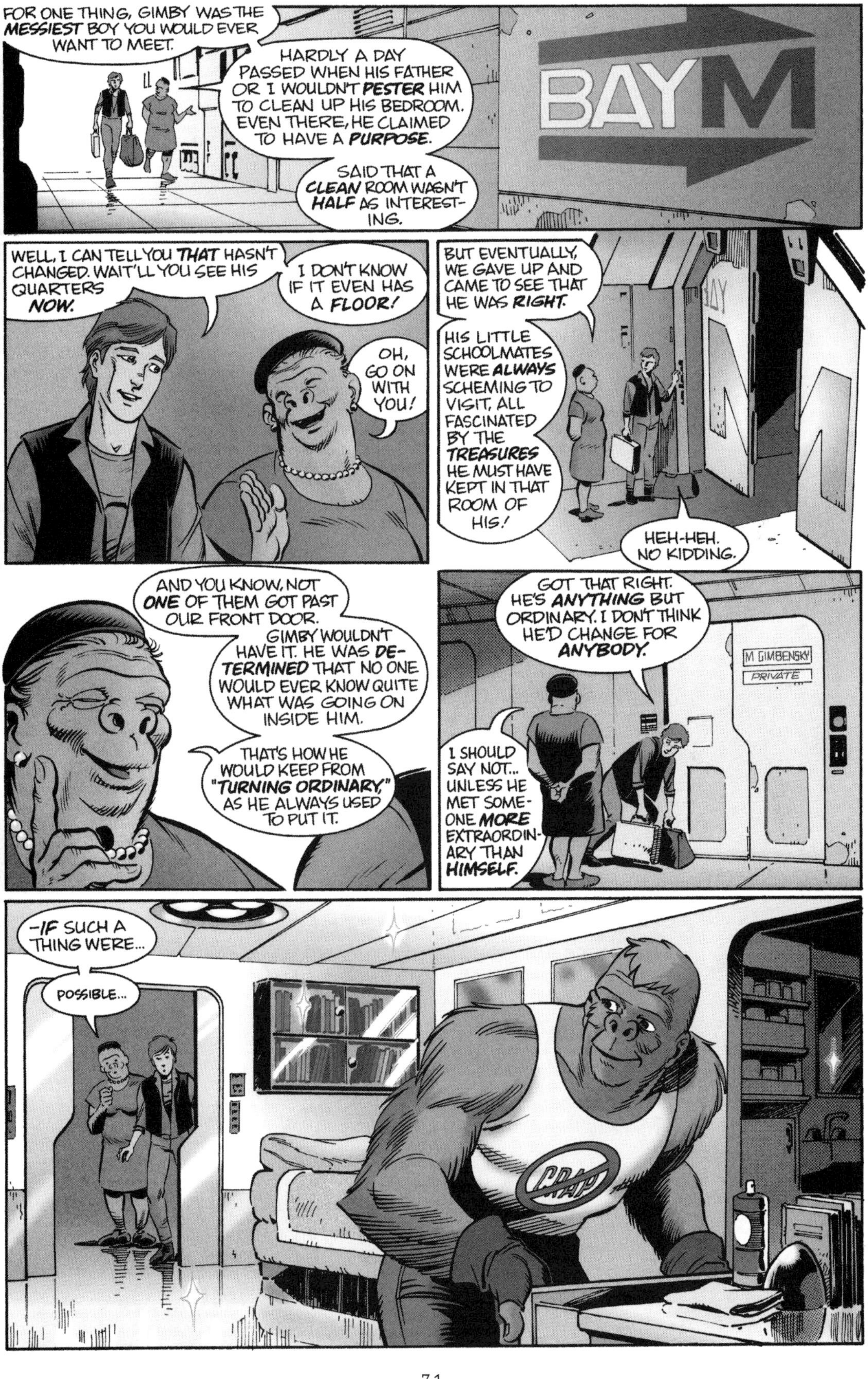

FOR ONE THING, GIMBY WAS THE MESSIEST BOY YOU WOULD EVER WANT TO MEET.
HARDLY A DAY PASSED WHEN HIS FATHER OR I WOULDN'T PESTER HIM TO CLEAN UP HIS BEDROOM. EVEN THERE, HE CLAIMED TO HAVE A PURPOSE.
SAID THAT A CLEAN ROOM WASN'T HALF AS INTEREST-ING.
BAY M
WELL, I CAN TELL YOU THAT HASN'T CHANGED. WAIT'LL YOU SEE HIS QUARTERS NOW.
I DON'T KNOW IF IT EVEN HAS A FLOOR!
OH, GO ON WITH YOU!
BUT EVENTUALLY, WE GAVE UP AND CAME TO SEE THAT HE WAS RIGHT.
HIS LITTLE SCHOOLMATES WERE ALWAYS SCHEMING TO VISIT, ALL FASCINATED BY THE TREASURES HE MUST HAVE KEPT IN THAT ROOM OF HIS!
HEH-HEH. NO KIDDING.
AND YOU KNOW, NOT ONE OF THEM GOT PAST OUR FRONT DOOR.
GIMBY WOULDN'T HAVE IT. HE WAS DE-TERMINED THAT NO ONE WOULD EVER KNOW QUITE WHAT WAS GOING ON INSIDE HIM.
THAT'S HOW HE WOULD KEEP FROM "TURNING ORDINARY," AS HE ALWAYS USED TO PUT IT.
GOT THAT RIGHT. HE'S ANYTHING BUT ORDINARY. I DON'T THINK HE'D CHANGE FOR ANYBODY.
M GIMBENSKY
PRIVATE
I SHOULD SAY NOT... UNLESS HE MET SOME-ONE MORE EXTRAORDIN-ARY THAN HIMSELF.
-IF SUCH A THING WERE...
POSSIBLE...

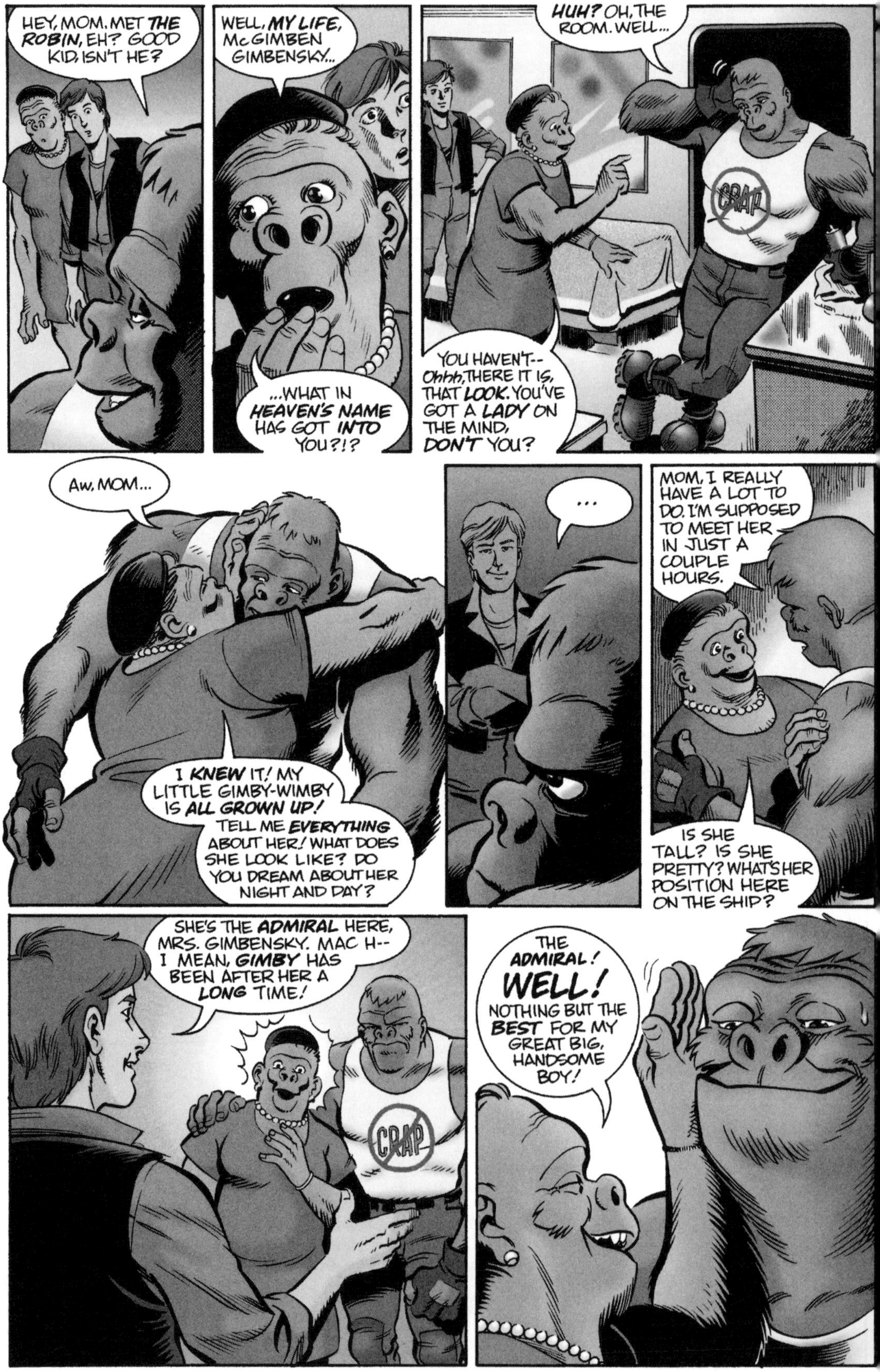
HEY, MOM. MET THE ROBIN, EH? GOOD KID, ISN'T HE?
WELL, MY LIFE, McGIMBEN GIMBENSKY...
...WHAT IN HEAVEN'S NAME HAS GOT INTO YOU?!?
HUH? OH, THE ROOM. WELL...
YOU HAVEN'T-- Ohhh, THERE IT IS, THAT LOOK. YOU'VE GOT A LADY ON THE MIND, DON'T YOU?
CRAP
AW, MOM...
I KNEW IT! MY LITTLE GIMBY-WIMBY IS ALL GROWN UP!
TELL ME EVERYTHING ABOUT HER! WHAT DOES SHE LOOK LIKE? DO YOU DREAM ABOUT HER NIGHT AND DAY?
...
MOM, I REALLY HAVE A LOT TO DO. I'M SUPPOSED TO MEET HER IN JUST A COUPLE HOURS.
IS SHE TALL? IS SHE PRETTY? WHAT'S HER POSITION HERE ON THE SHIP?
SHE'S THE ADMIRAL HERE, MRS. GIMBENSKY. MAC H-- I MEAN, GIMBY HAS BEEN AFTER HER A LONG TIME!
CRAP
THE ADMIRAL! WELL! NOTHING BUT THE BEST FOR MY GREAT BIG, HANDSOME BOY!

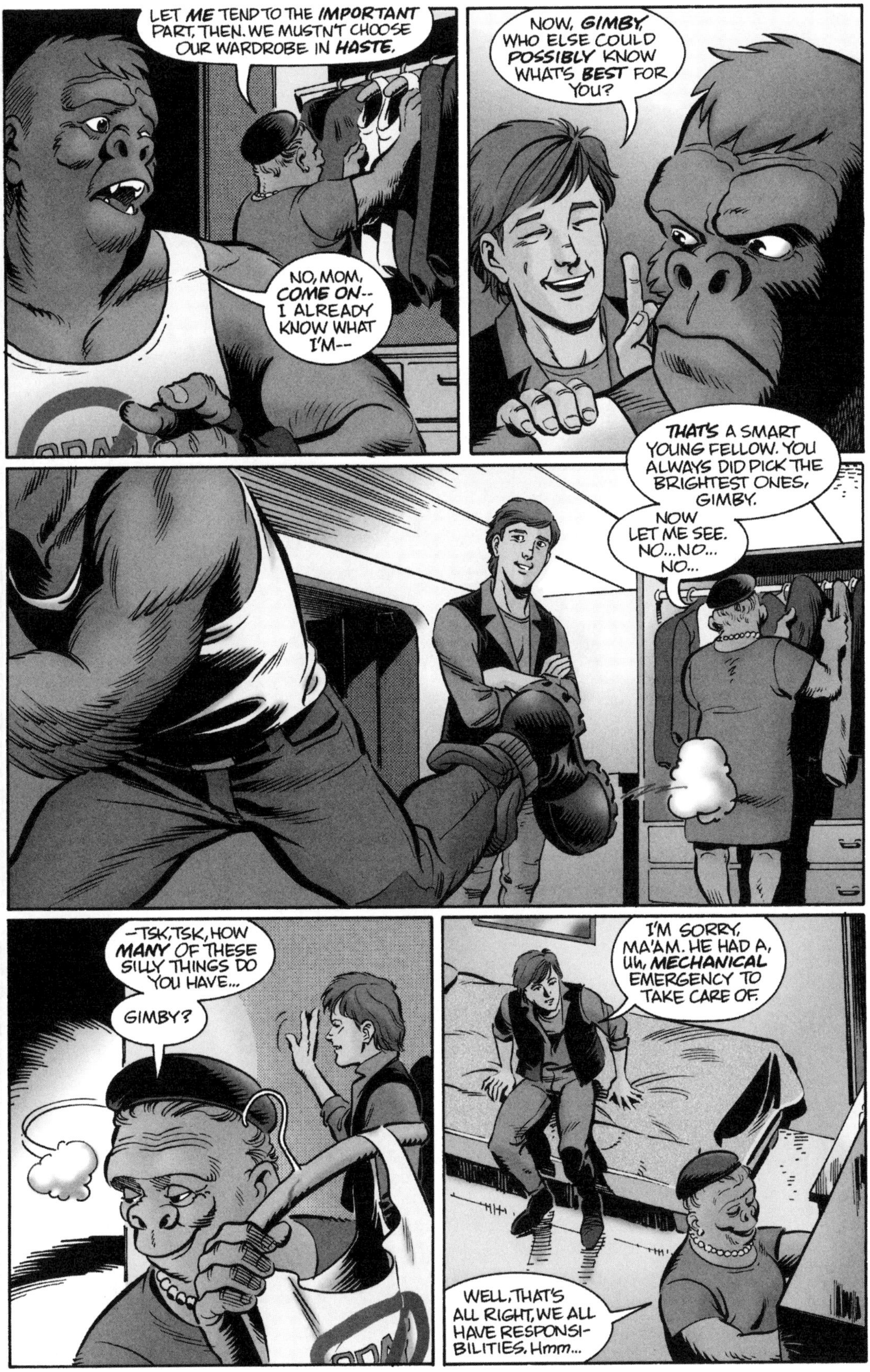
LET ME TEND TO THE IMPORTANT PART, THEN. WE MUSTN'T CHOOSE OUR WARDROBE IN HASTE.
NO, MOM, COME ON-- I ALREADY KNOW WHAT I'M--
NOW, GIMBY, WHO ELSE COULD POSSIBLY KNOW WHAT'S BEST FOR YOU?
THAT'S A SMART YOUNG FELLOW. YOU ALWAYS DID PICK THE BRIGHTEST ONES, GIMBY.
NOW LET ME SEE. NO...NO... NO...
-TSK, TSK, HOW MANY OF THESE SILLY THINGS DO YOU HAVE...
GIMBY?
I'M SORRY, MA'AM. HE HAD A, Uh, MECHANICAL EMERGENCY TO TAKE CARE OF.
WELL, THAT'S ALL RIGHT, WE ALL HAVE RESPONSI-BILITIES. Hmm...

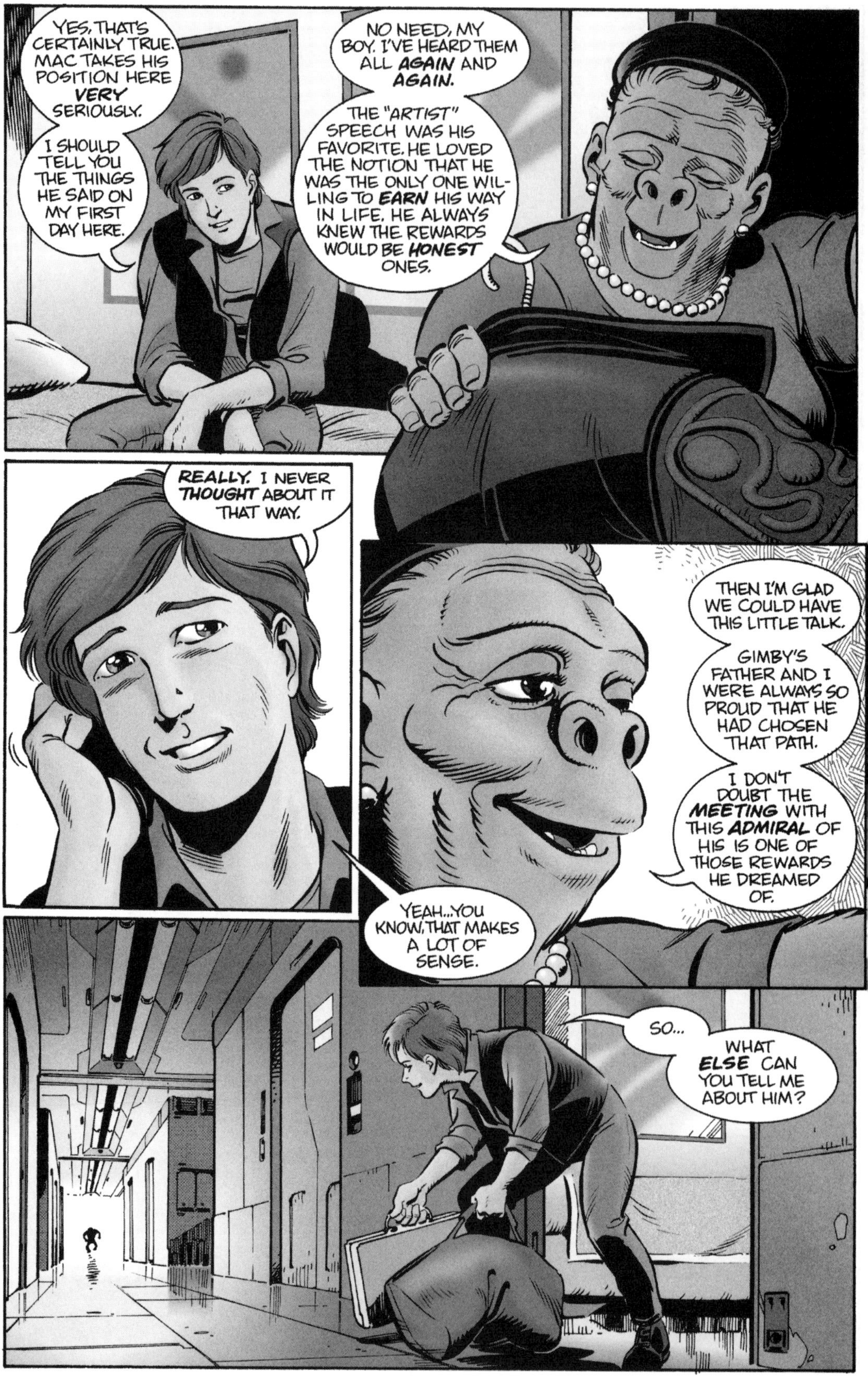

YES, THAT'S CERTAINLY TRUE. MAC TAKES HIS POSITION HERE **VERY** SERIOUSLY.
I SHOULD TELL YOU THE THINGS HE SAID ON MY FIRST DAY HERE.
NO NEED, MY BOY. I'VE HEARD THEM ALL **AGAIN** AND **AGAIN**.
THE "ARTIST" SPEECH WAS HIS FAVORITE. HE LOVED THE NOTION THAT HE WAS THE ONLY ONE WIL-LING TO **EARN** HIS WAY IN LIFE. HE ALWAYS KNEW THE REWARDS WOULD BE **HONEST** ONES.
REALLY. I NEVER **THOUGHT** ABOUT IT THAT WAY.
THEN I'M GLAD WE COULD HAVE THIS LITTLE TALK.
GIMBY'S FATHER AND I WERE ALWAYS SO PROUD THAT HE HAD CHOSEN THAT PATH.
I DON'T DOUBT THE **MEETING** WITH THIS **ADMIRAL** OF HIS IS ONE OF THOSE REWARDS HE DREAMED OF.
YEAH...YOU KNOW, THAT MAKES A LOT OF SENSE.
SO...
WHAT **ELSE** CAN YOU TELL ME ABOUT HIM?

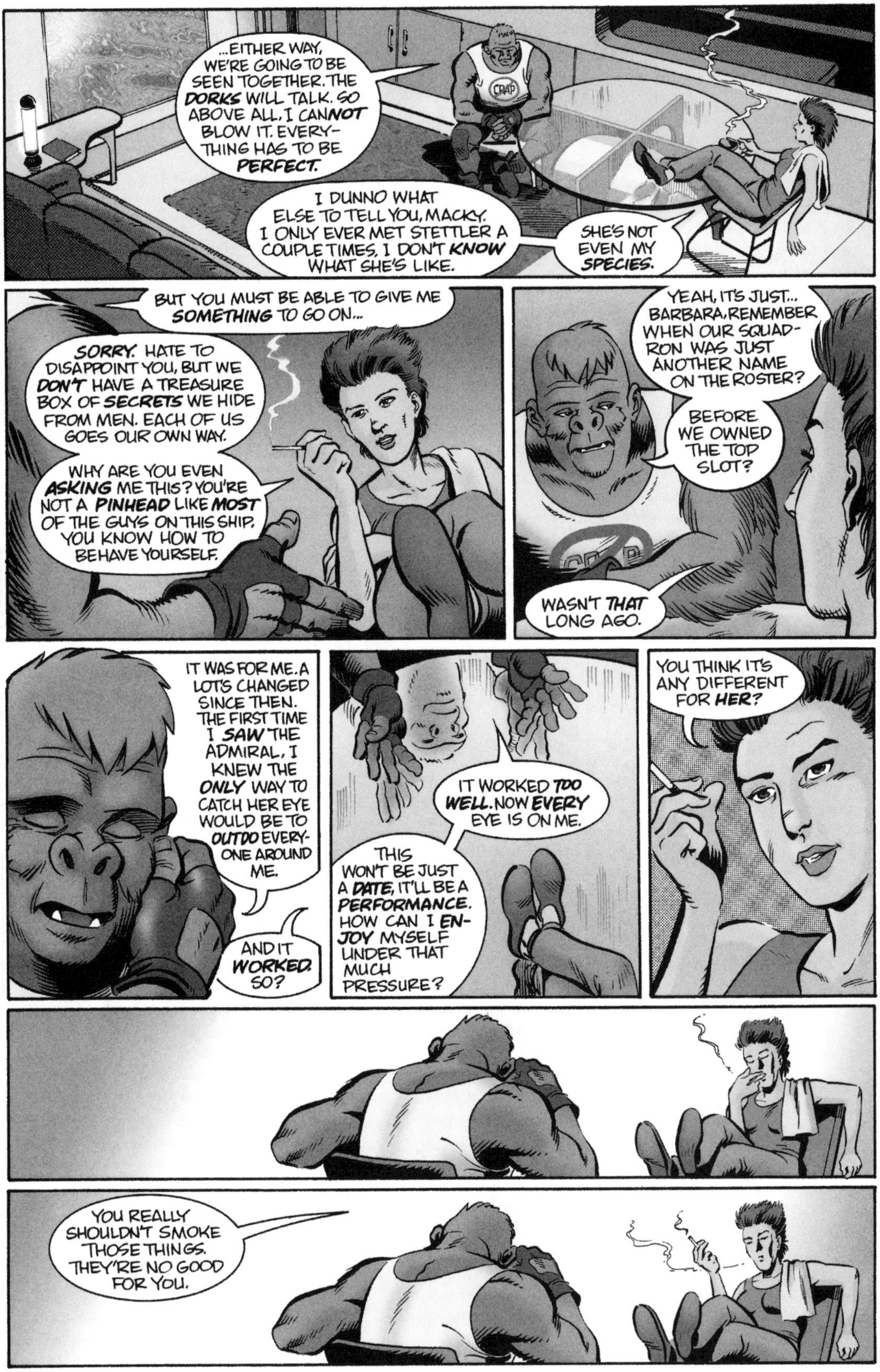
...EITHER WAY, WE'RE GOING TO BE SEEN TOGETHER. THE DORKS WILL TALK. SO ABOVE ALL, I CANNOT BLOW IT. EVERY-THING HAS TO BE PERFECT.
CRAP
I DUNNO WHAT ELSE TO TELL YOU, MACKY. I ONLY EVER MET STETTLER A COUPLE TIMES. I DON'T KNOW WHAT SHE'S LIKE.
SHE'S NOT EVEN MY SPECIES.
BUT YOU MUST BE ABLE TO GIVE ME SOMETHING TO GO ON...
SORRY. HATE TO DISAPPOINT YOU, BUT WE DON'T HAVE A TREASURE BOX OF SECRETS WE HIDE FROM MEN. EACH OF US GOES OUR OWN WAY.
WHY ARE YOU EVEN ASKING ME THIS? YOU'RE NOT A PINHEAD LIKE MOST OF THE GUYS ON THIS SHIP. YOU KNOW HOW TO BEHAVE YOURSELF.
YEAH, IT'S JUST... BARBARA, REMEMBER WHEN OUR SQUADRON WAS JUST ANOTHER NAME ON THE ROSTER?
BEFORE WE OWNED THE TOP SLOT?
WASN'T THAT LONG AGO.
IT WAS FOR ME. A LOT'S CHANGED SINCE THEN. THE FIRST TIME I SAW THE ADMIRAL, I KNEW THE ONLY WAY TO CATCH HER EYE WOULD BE TO OUTDO EVERY-ONE AROUND ME.
AND IT WORKED. SO?
IT WORKED TOO WELL. NOW EVERY EYE IS ON ME.
THIS WON'T BE JUST A DATE, IT'LL BE A PERFORMANCE. HOW CAN I EN-JOY MYSELF UNDER THAT MUCH PRESSURE?
YOU THINK IT'S ANY DIFFERENT FOR HER?
YOU REALLY SHOULDN'T SMOKE THOSE THINGS. THEY'RE NO GOOD FOR YOU.

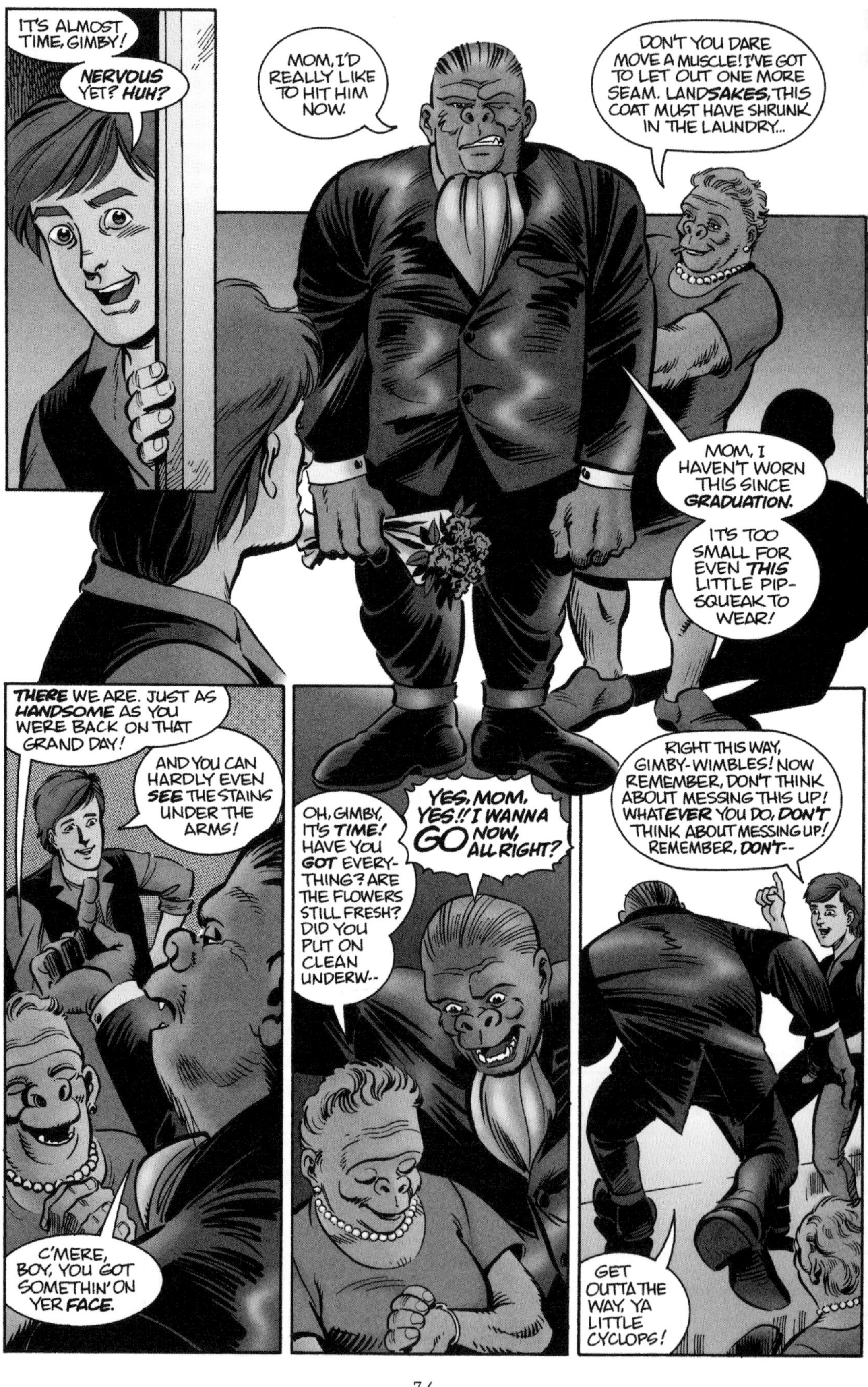
IT'S ALMOST TIME, GIMBY!
NERVOUS YET? HUH?
MOM, I'D REALLY LIKE TO HIT HIM NOW.
DON'T YOU DARE MOVE A MUSCLE! I'VE GOT TO LET OUT ONE MORE SEAM. LANDSAKES, THIS COAT MUST HAVE SHRUNK IN THE LAUNDRY...
MOM, I HAVEN'T WORN THIS SINCE GRADUATION.
IT'S TOO SMALL FOR EVEN THIS LITTLE PIP-SQUEAK TO WEAR!
THERE WE ARE. JUST AS HANDSOME AS YOU WERE BACK ON THAT GRAND DAY!
AND YOU CAN HARDLY EVEN SEE THE STAINS UNDER THE ARMS!
C'MERE, BOY, YOU GOT SOMETHIN' ON YER FACE.
OH, GIMBY, IT'S TIME! HAVE YOU GOT EVERY-THING? ARE THE FLOWERS STILL FRESH? DID YOU PUT ON CLEAN UNDERW--
YES, MOM, YES!! I WANNA GO NOW, ALL RIGHT?
RIGHT THIS WAY, GIMBY-WIMBLES! NOW REMEMBER, DON'T THINK ABOUT MESSING THIS UP! WHATEVER YOU DO, DON'T THINK ABOUT MESSING UP! REMEMBER, DON'T--
GET OUTTA THE WAY, YA LITTLE CYCLOPS!

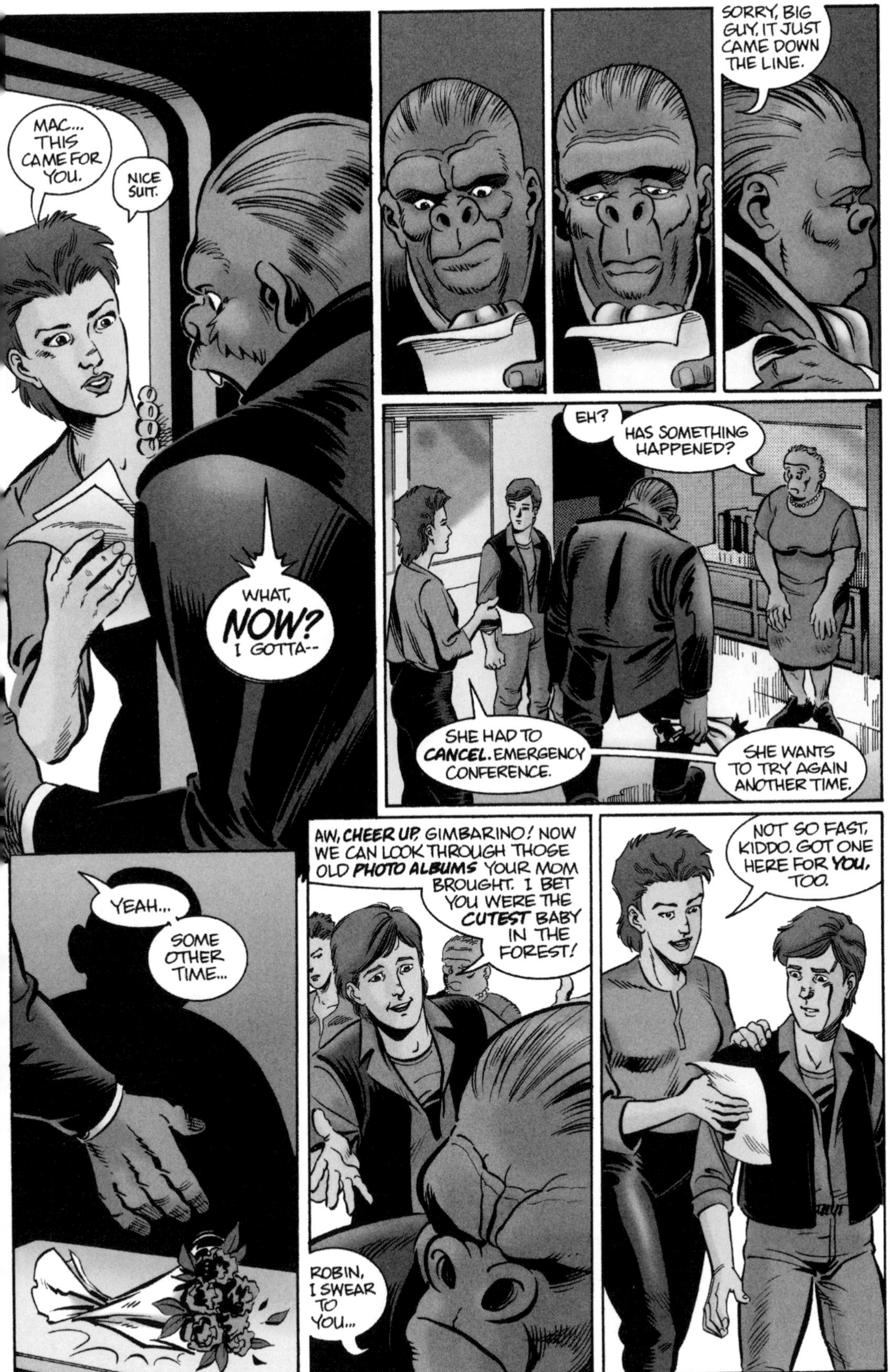
MAC... THIS CAME FOR YOU.
NICE SUIT.
WHAT, NOW? I GOTTA--
SORRY, BIG GUY, IT JUST CAME DOWN THE LINE.
EH?
HAS SOMETHING HAPPENED?
SHE HAD TO CANCEL. EMERGENCY CONFERENCE.
SHE WANTS TO TRY AGAIN ANOTHER TIME.
YEAH...
SOME OTHER TIME...
AW, CHEER UP, GIMBARINO! NOW WE CAN LOOK THROUGH THOSE OLD PHOTO ALBUMS YOUR MOM BROUGHT. I BET YOU WERE THE CUTEST BABY IN THE FOREST!
ROBIN, I SWEAR TO YOU...
NOT SO FAST, KIDDO. GOT ONE HERE FOR YOU, TOO.

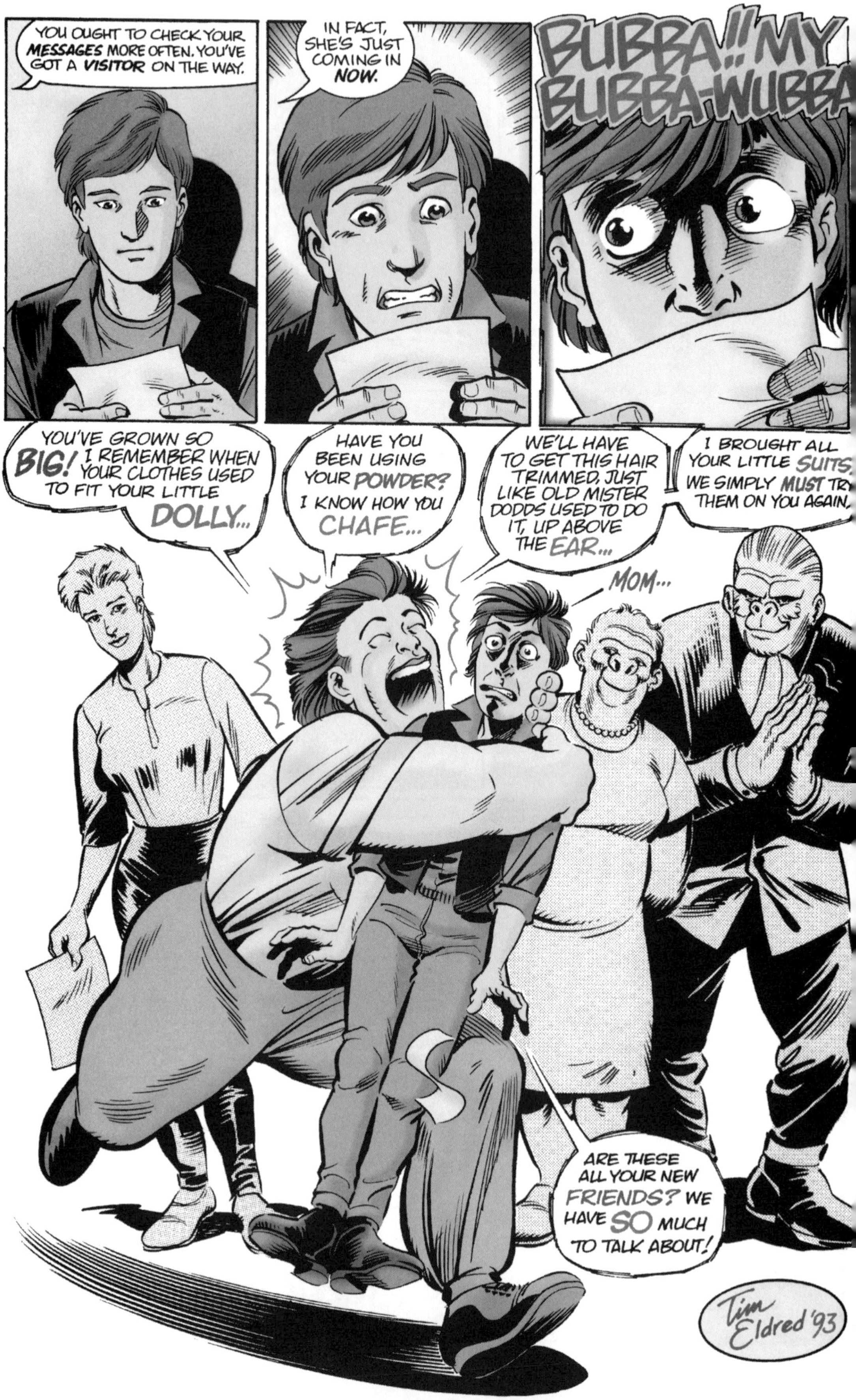
YOU OUGHT TO CHECK YOUR MESSAGES MORE OFTEN. YOU'VE GOT A VISITOR ON THE WAY.
IN FACT, SHE'S JUST COMING IN NOW.
BUBBA!! MY BUBBA-WUBBA
YOU'VE GROWN SO BIG! I REMEMBER WHEN YOUR CLOTHES USED TO FIT YOUR LITTLE DOLLY...
HAVE YOU BEEN USING YOUR POWDER? I KNOW HOW YOU CHAFE...
WE'LL HAVE TO GET THIS HAIR TRIMMED, JUST LIKE OLD MISTER DODDS USED TO DO IT, UP ABOVE THE EAR...
I BROUGHT ALL YOUR LITTLE SUITS. WE SIMPLY MUST TR THEM ON YOU AGAIN.
MOM...
ARE THESE ALL YOUR NEW FRIENDS? WE HAVE SO MUCH TO TALK ABOUT!
Tim Eldred '93

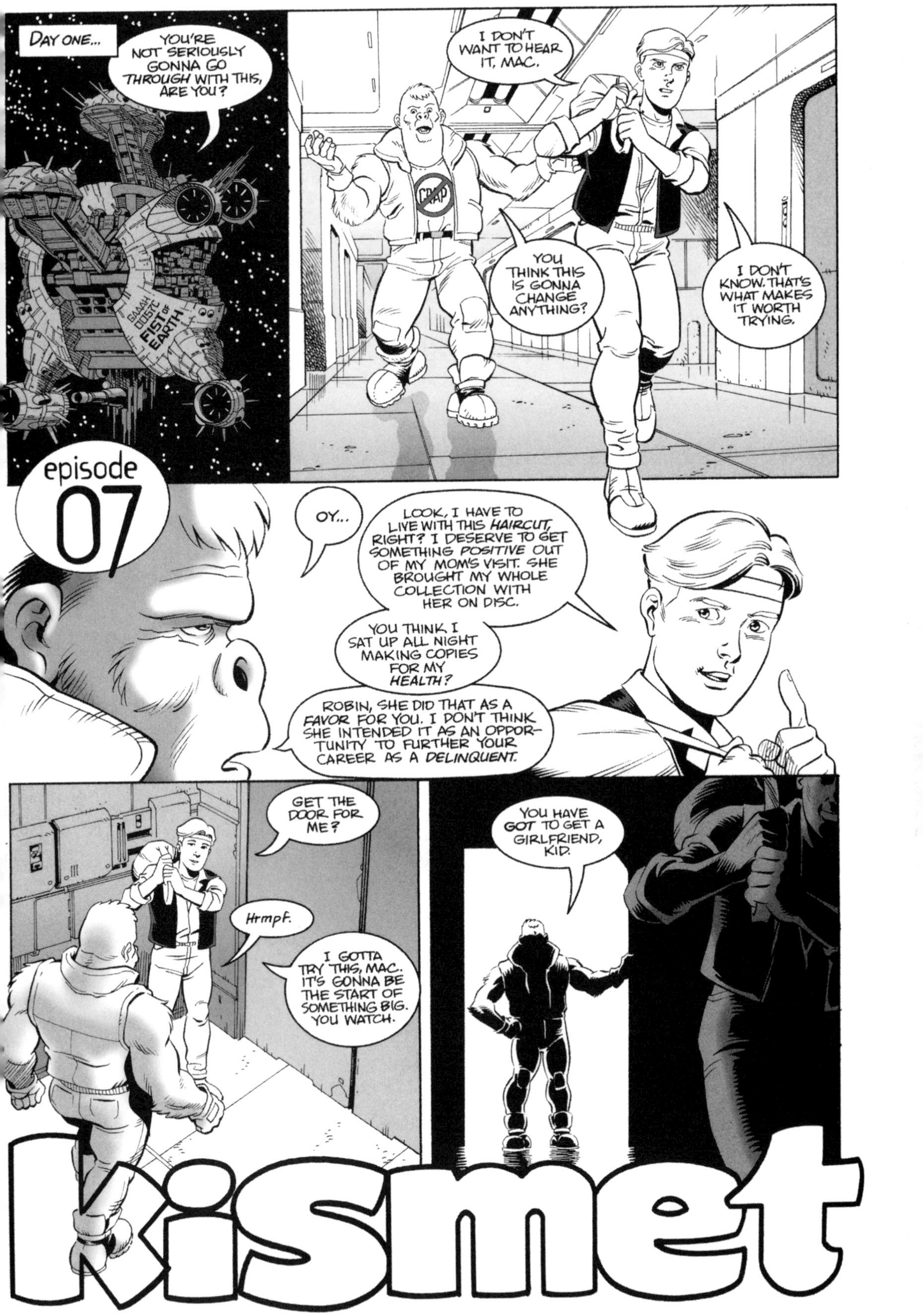
DAY ONE...
YOU'RE NOT SERIOUSLY GONNA GO THROUGH WITH THIS, ARE YOU?
FIST OF EARTH
I DON'T WANT TO HEAR IT, MAC.
CRAP
YOU THINK THIS IS GONNA CHANGE ANYTHING?
I DON'T KNOW. THAT'S WHAT MAKES IT WORTH TRYING.
episode 07
OY...
LOOK, I HAVE TO LIVE WITH THIS HAIRCUT, RIGHT? I DESERVE TO GET SOMETHING POSITIVE OUT OF MY MOM'S VISIT. SHE BROUGHT MY WHOLE COLLECTION WITH HER ON DISC.
YOU THINK I SAT UP ALL NIGHT MAKING COPIES FOR MY HEALTH?
ROBIN, SHE DID THAT AS A FAVOR FOR YOU. I DON'T THINK SHE INTENDED IT AS AN OPPORTUNITY TO FURTHER YOUR CAREER AS A DELINQUENT.
GET THE DOOR FOR ME?
Hrmpf.
I GOTTA TRY THIS, MAC. IT'S GONNA BE THE START OF SOMETHING BIG. YOU WATCH.
YOU HAVE GOT TO GET A GIRLFRIEND, KID.
Kismet

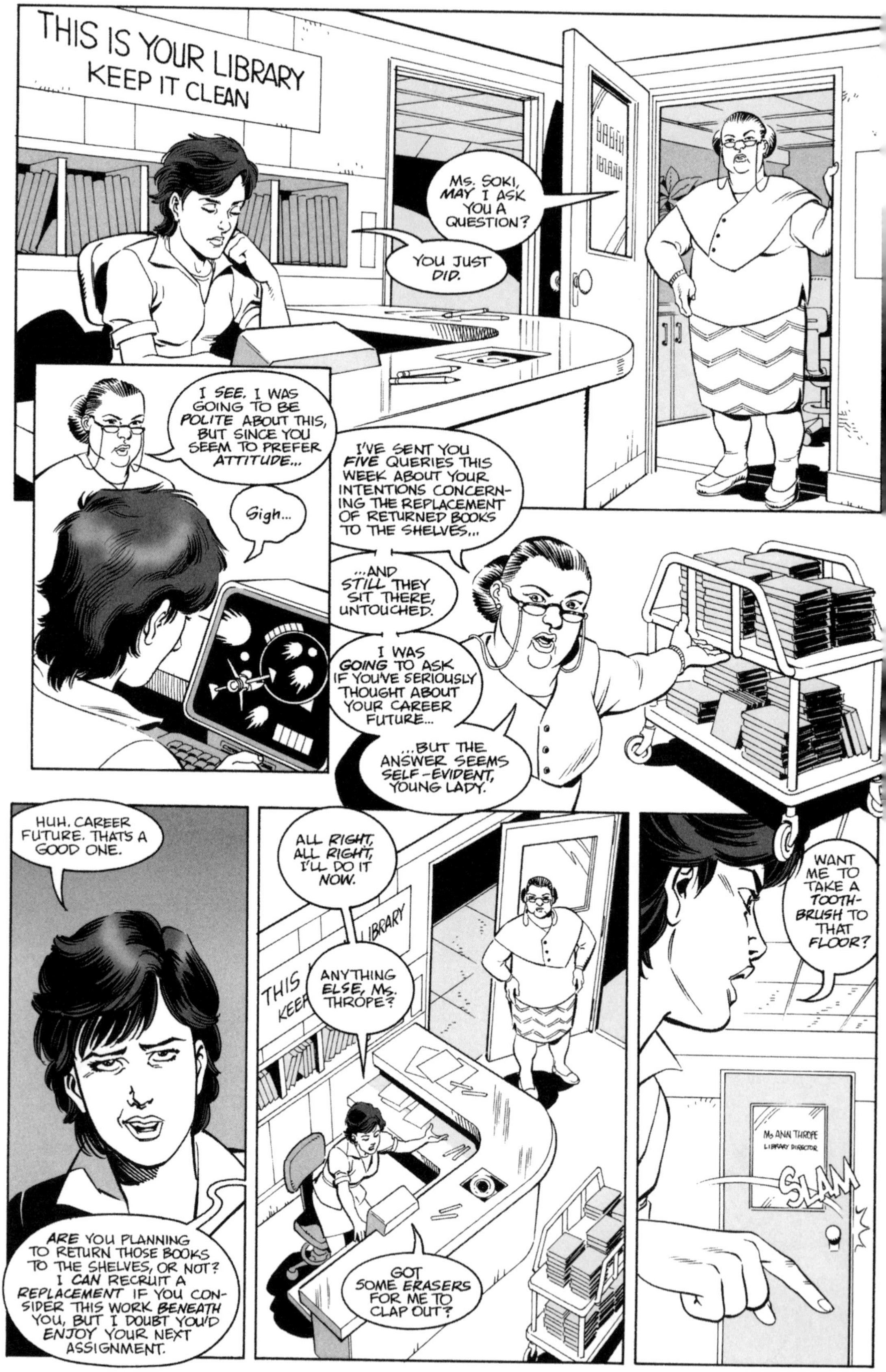

THIS IS YOUR LIBRARY
KEEP IT CLEAN
Ms. SOKI, MAY I ASK YOU A QUESTION?
YOU JUST DID.
I SEE. I WAS GOING TO BE POLITE ABOUT THIS, BUT SINCE YOU SEEM TO PREFER ATTITUDE...
Sigh...
I'VE SENT YOU FIVE QUERIES THIS WEEK ABOUT YOUR INTENTIONS CONCERNING THE REPLACEMENT OF RETURNED BOOKS TO THE SHELVES...
...AND STILL THEY SIT THERE, UNTOUCHED.
I WAS GOING TO ASK IF YOU'VE SERIOUSLY THOUGHT ABOUT YOUR CAREER FUTURE...
...BUT THE ANSWER SEEMS SELF-EVIDENT, YOUNG LADY.
HUH. CAREER FUTURE. THAT'S A GOOD ONE.
ARE YOU PLANNING TO RETURN THOSE BOOKS TO THE SHELVES, OR NOT? I CAN RECRUIT A REPLACEMENT IF YOU CONSIDER THIS WORK BENEATH YOU, BUT I DOUBT YOU'D ENJOY YOUR NEXT ASSIGNMENT.
ALL RIGHT, ALL RIGHT, I'LL DO IT NOW.
ANYTHING ELSE, Ms. THROPE?
GOT SOME ERASERS FOR ME TO CLAP OUT?
WANT ME TO TAKE A TOOTHBRUSH TO THAT FLOOR?
Ms ANN THROPE
LIBRARY DIRECTOR
SLAM

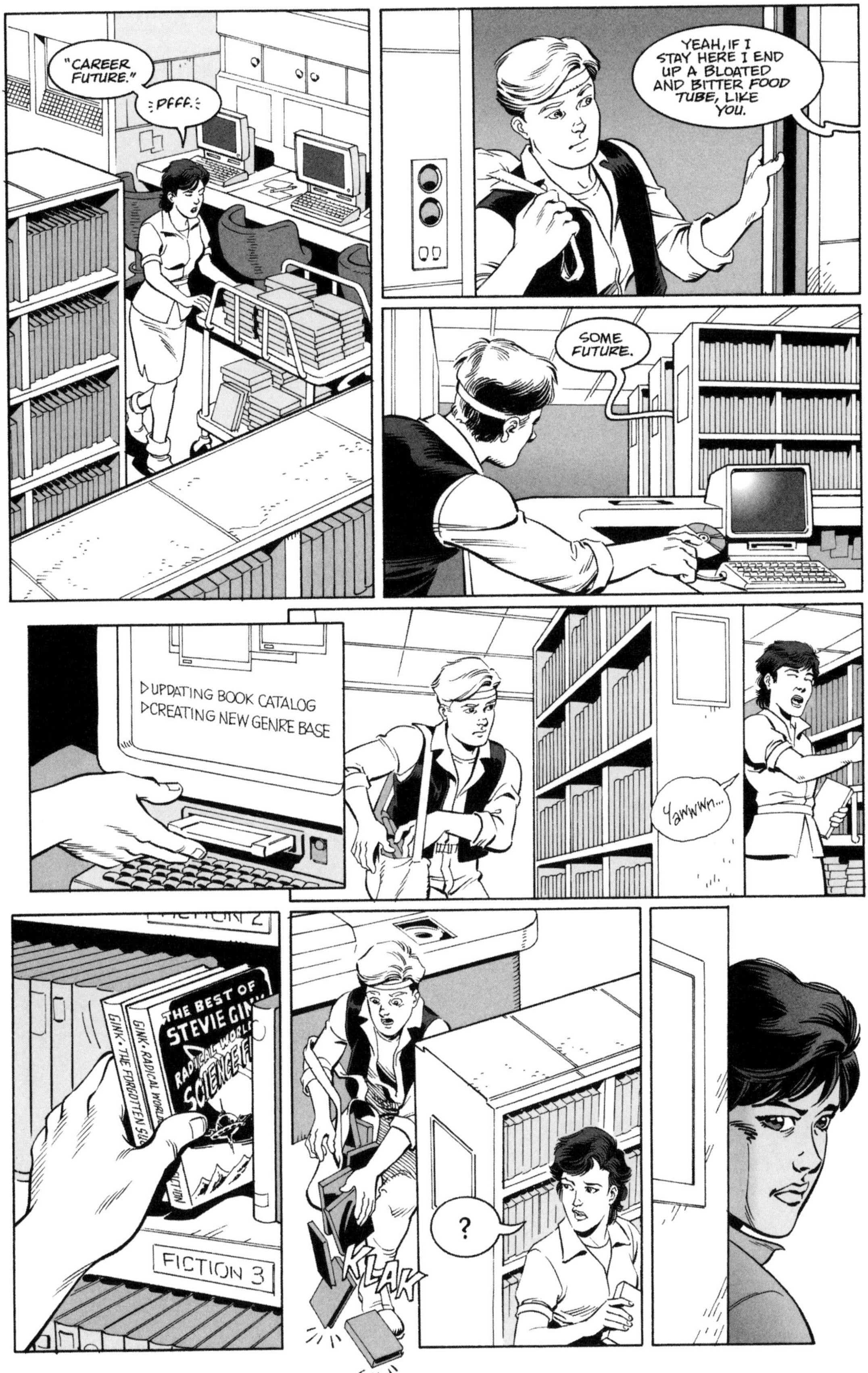
"CAREER FUTURE."
PFFF.
YEAH, IF I STAY HERE I END UP A BLOATED AND BITTER FOOD TUBE, LIKE YOU.
SOME FUTURE.
▷UPDATING BOOK CATALOG
▷CREATING NEW GENRE BASE
Yawwwn...
FICTION 2
THE BEST OF STEVIE GINK
RADICAL WORLDS OF SCIENCE FI
GINK · RADICAL WORLD
GINK · THE FORGOTTEN S
FICTION
FICTION 3
?
KLAK

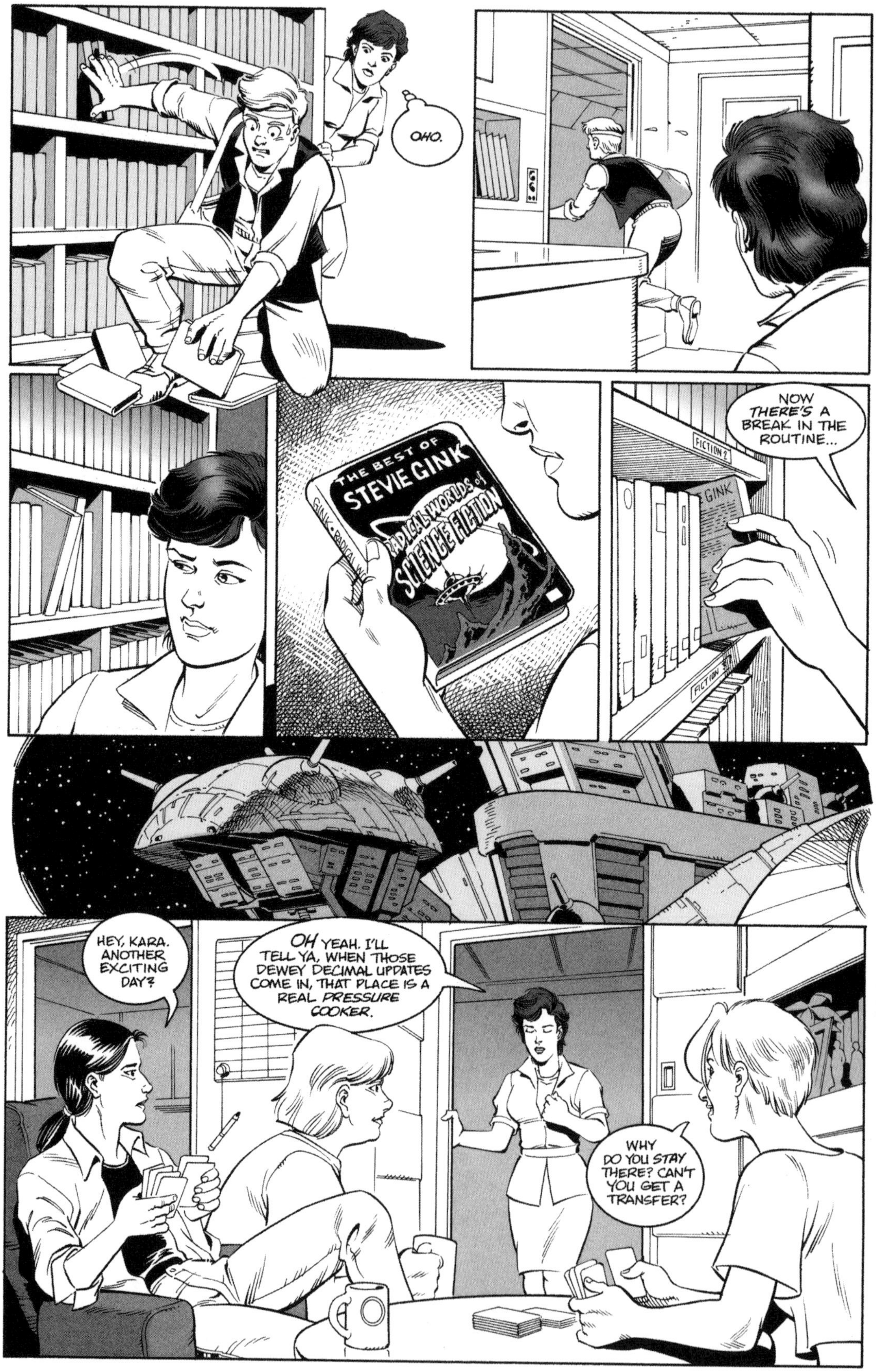
OHO.
NOW THERE'S A BREAK IN THE ROUTINE...
THE BEST OF STEVIE GINK
RADICAL WORLDS of SCIENCE FICTION
FICTION 2
HEY, KARA. ANOTHER EXCITING DAY?
OH YEAH. I'LL TELL YA, WHEN THOSE DEWEY DECIMAL UPDATES COME IN, THAT PLACE IS A REAL PRESSURE COOKER.
WHY DO YOU STAY THERE? CAN'T YOU GET A TRANSFER?

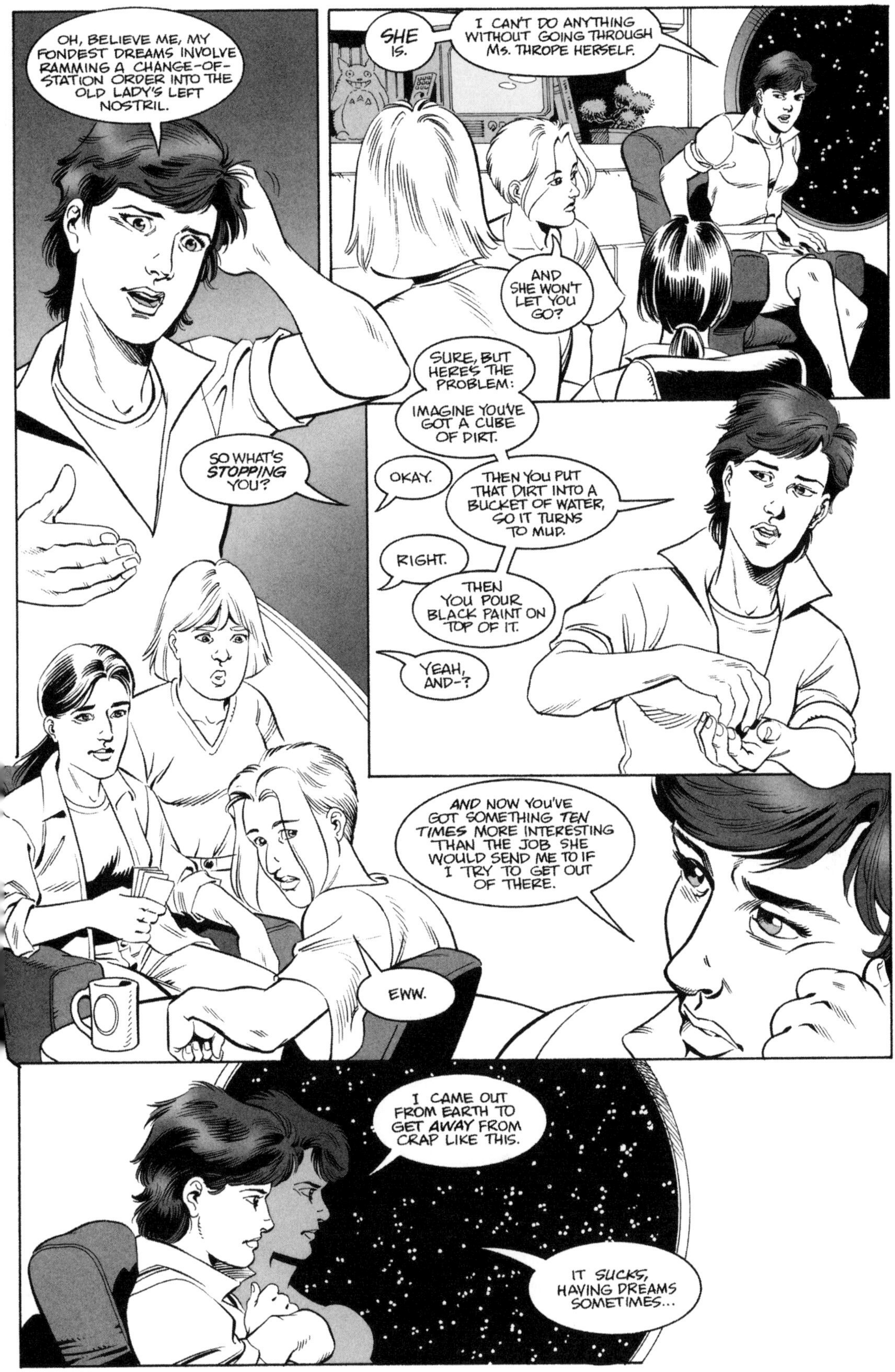
OH, BELIEVE ME, MY FONDEST DREAMS INVOLVE RAMMING A CHANGE-OF-STATION ORDER INTO THE OLD LADY'S LEFT NOSTRIL.
SO WHAT'S STOPPING YOU?
SHE IS.
I CAN'T DO ANYTHING WITHOUT GOING THROUGH Ms. THROPE HERSELF.
AND SHE WON'T LET YOU GO?
SURE, BUT HERE'S THE PROBLEM:
IMAGINE YOU'VE GOT A CUBE OF DIRT.
OKAY.
THEN YOU PUT THAT DIRT INTO A BUCKET OF WATER, SO IT TURNS TO MUD.
RIGHT.
THEN YOU POUR BLACK PAINT ON TOP OF IT.
YEAH, AND-?
AND NOW YOU'VE GOT SOMETHING TEN TIMES MORE INTERESTING THAN THE JOB SHE WOULD SEND ME TO IF I TRY TO GET OUT OF THERE.
EWW.
I CAME OUT FROM EARTH TO GET AWAY FROM CRAP LIKE THIS.
IT SUCKS, HAVING DREAMS SOMETIMES...

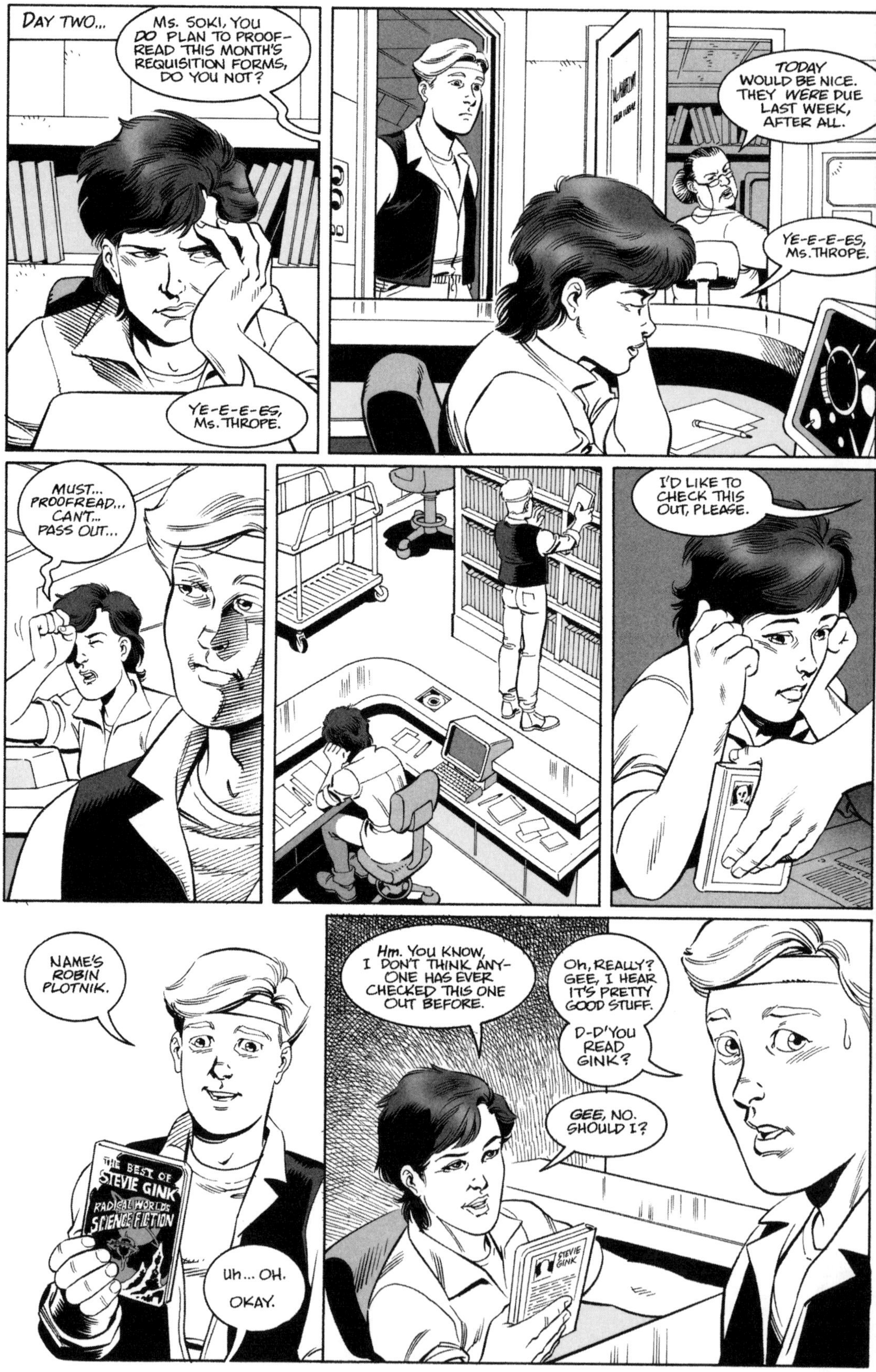

DAY TWO...
Ms. SOKI, YOU DO PLAN TO PROOF-READ THIS MONTH'S REQUISITION FORMS, DO YOU NOT?
YE-E-E-ES, Ms. THROPE.
TODAY WOULD BE NICE. THEY WERE DUE LAST WEEK, AFTER ALL.
YE-E-E-ES, Ms. THROPE.
MUST... PROOFREAD... CAN'T... PASS OUT...
I'D LIKE TO CHECK THIS OUT, PLEASE.
NAME'S ROBIN PLOTNIK.
THE BEST OF STEVIE GINK
RADICAL WORLDS SCIENCE FICTION
Uh... OH. OKAY.
Hm. YOU KNOW, I DON'T THINK ANY-ONE HAS EVER CHECKED THIS ONE OUT BEFORE.
Oh, REALLY? GEE, I HEAR IT'S PRETTY GOOD STUFF.
D-D'YOU READ GINK?
GEE, NO. SHOULD I?
STEVIE GINK

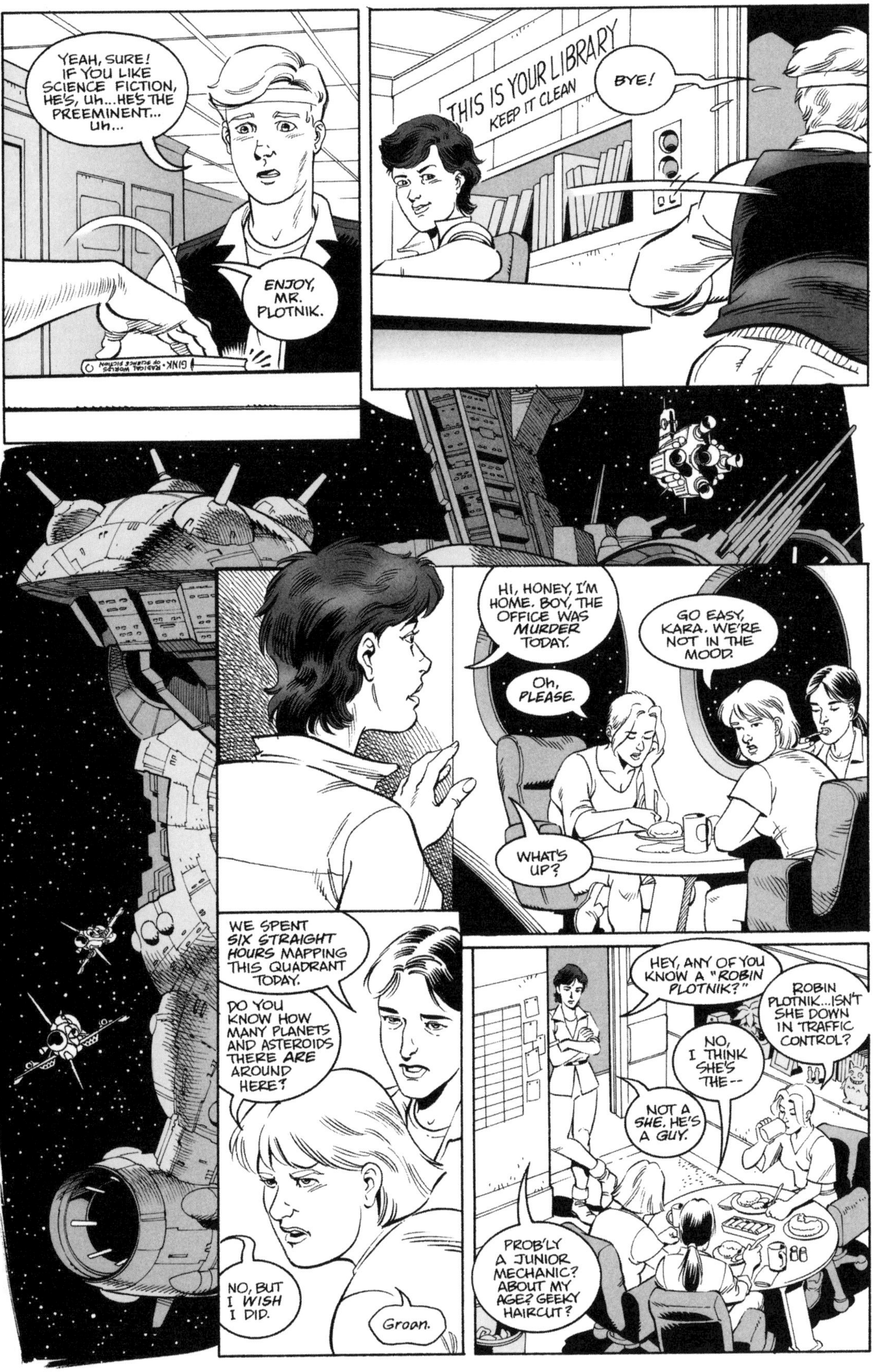

YEAH, SURE! IF YOU LIKE SCIENCE FICTION, HE'S, UH...HE'S THE PREEMINENT... UH...
ENJOY, MR. PLOTNIK.
GINK · RADICAL WORLDS OF SCIENCE FICTION
THIS IS YOUR LIBRARY
KEEP IT CLEAN
BYE!
HI, HONEY, I'M HOME. BOY, THE OFFICE WAS MURDER TODAY.
GO EASY, KARA. WE'RE NOT IN THE MOOD.
Oh, PLEASE.
WHAT'S UP?
WE SPENT SIX STRAIGHT HOURS MAPPING THIS QUADRANT TODAY.
DO YOU KNOW HOW MANY PLANETS AND ASTEROIDS THERE ARE AROUND HERE?
NO, BUT I WISH I DID.
Groan.
HEY, ANY OF YOU KNOW A "ROBIN PLOTNIK?"
ROBIN PLOTNIK...ISN'T SHE DOWN IN TRAFFIC CONTROL?
NO, I THINK SHE'S THE--
NOT A SHE. HE'S A GUY.
PROB'LY A JUNIOR MECHANIC? ABOUT MY AGE? GEEKY HAIRCUT?

Oh, A GUY, HUH?

TELL ME MORE!

KARA'S GOT A FEL-LAH!

YEAH, YOU'RE A BIG HELP.

A GUY. WELL, THAT MIGHT LIVEN THINGS UP A LITTLE.

DAY THREE...

MS. SOKI, THE HISTORY SHELF ISN'T GOING TO REORGANIZE ITSELF.

OH, FINE!

SLAM

Ms. ANN THROPE
LIBRARY DIRECTOR

HI.

HELLO.

FINISH THAT GINK BOOK ALREADY, DID YOU?

STILL WORKING ON IT. IT'S GREAT.

HELP YOU FIND SOMETHING ELSE?

THIS IS YO
KEEP CLEAN

AH, NO, I WAS JUST WONDERING HOW MANY OTHER GINK BOOKS YOU HAVE HERE.

LOOKS LIKE A FEW. I SUPPOSE SOME OF THEM ARE OUT AT THE MOMENT, EH?

NO, THEY'RE ALL HERE.

NO ONE BUT YOU HAS TOUCHED THEM, MR. PLOTNIK.

Ms A
LIBRAR

FICTION
◁1-5
6-10▷

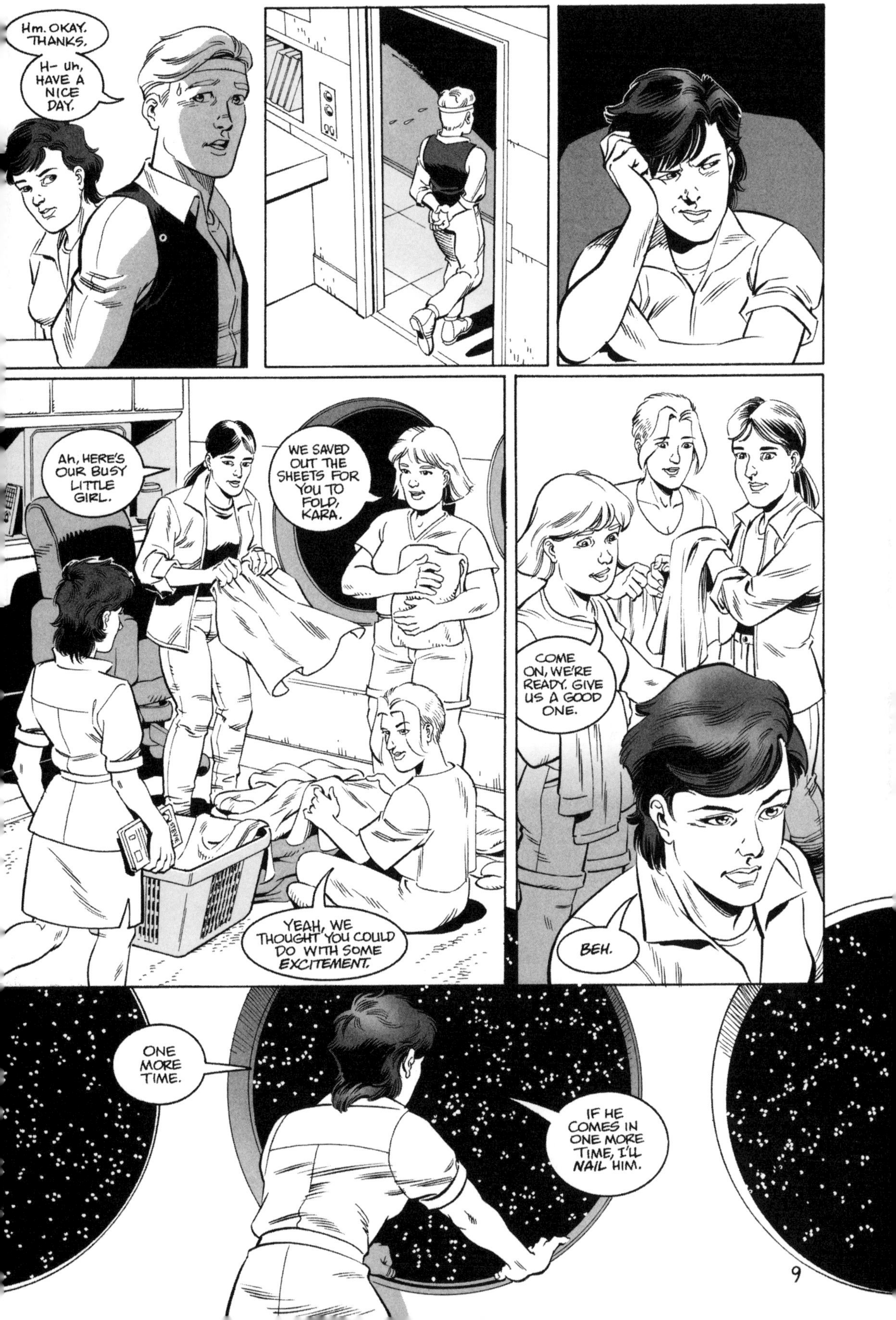
Hm. OKAY. THANKS.
H- uh, HAVE A NICE DAY.
Ah, HERE'S OUR BUSY LITTLE GIRL.
WE SAVED OUT THE SHEETS FOR YOU TO FOLD, KARA.
YEAH, WE THOUGHT YOU COULD DO WITH SOME *EXCITEMENT.*
STEVE
COME ON, WE'RE READY. GIVE US A GOOD ONE.
BEH.
ONE MORE TIME.
IF HE COMES IN ONE MORE TIME, I'LL *NAIL* HIM.

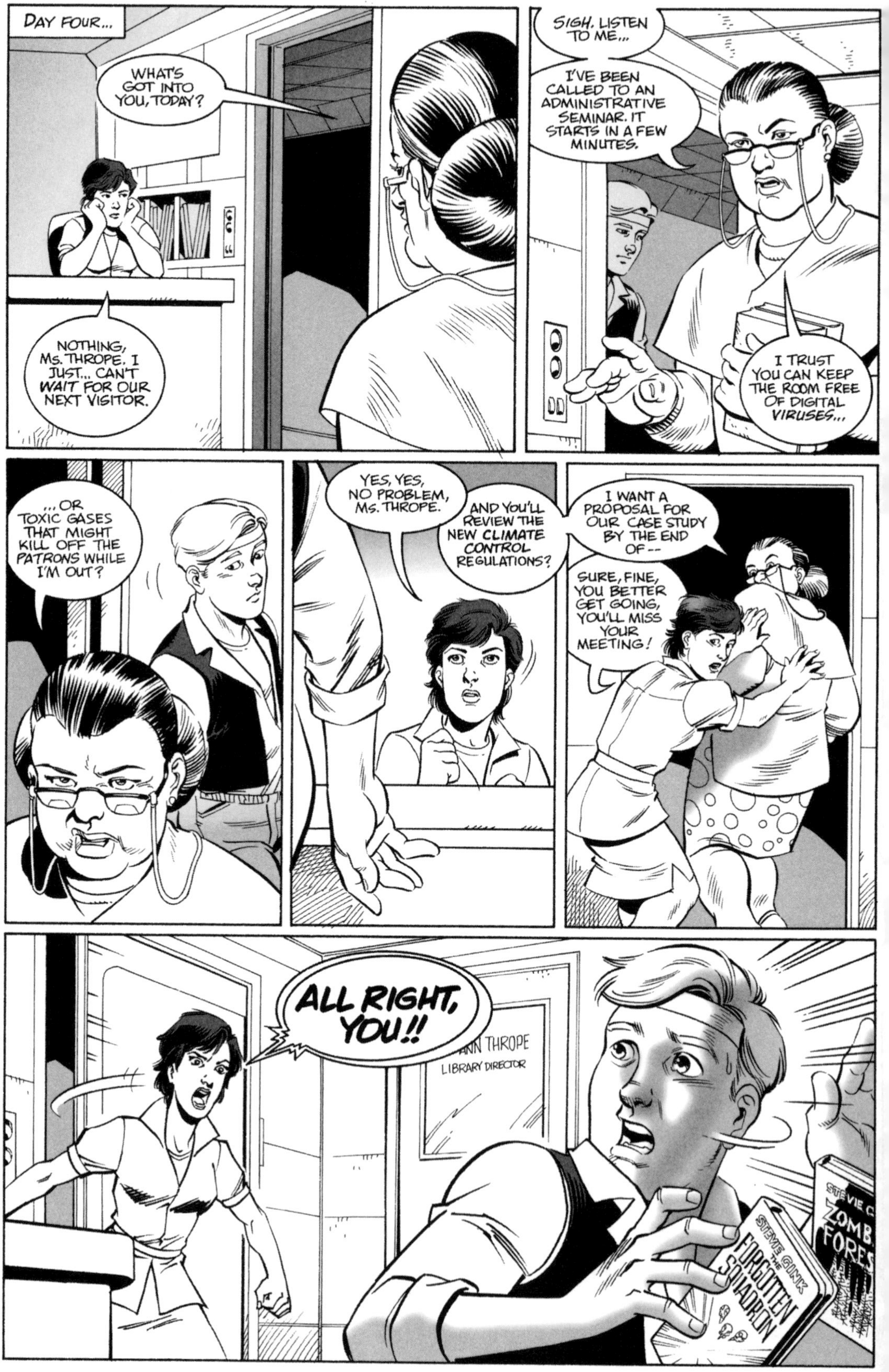
DAY FOUR...
WHAT'S GOT INTO YOU, TODAY?
NOTHING, Ms. THROPE. I JUST... CAN'T WAIT FOR OUR NEXT VISITOR.
SIGH. LISTEN TO ME...
I'VE BEEN CALLED TO AN ADMINISTRATIVE SEMINAR. IT STARTS IN A FEW MINUTES.
I TRUST YOU CAN KEEP THE ROOM FREE OF DIGITAL VIRUSES...
...OR TOXIC GASES THAT MIGHT KILL OFF THE PATRONS WHILE I'M OUT?
YES, YES, NO PROBLEM, Ms. THROPE.
AND YOU'LL REVIEW THE NEW CLIMATE CONTROL REGULATIONS?
I WANT A PROPOSAL FOR OUR CASE STUDY BY THE END OF--
SURE, FINE, YOU BETTER GET GOING, YOU'LL MISS YOUR MEETING!
ALL RIGHT, YOU!!
ANN THROPE
LIBRARY DIRECTOR
STEVE GINK
THE FORGOTTEN SQUADRON
STEVIE G
ZOMB
FORES

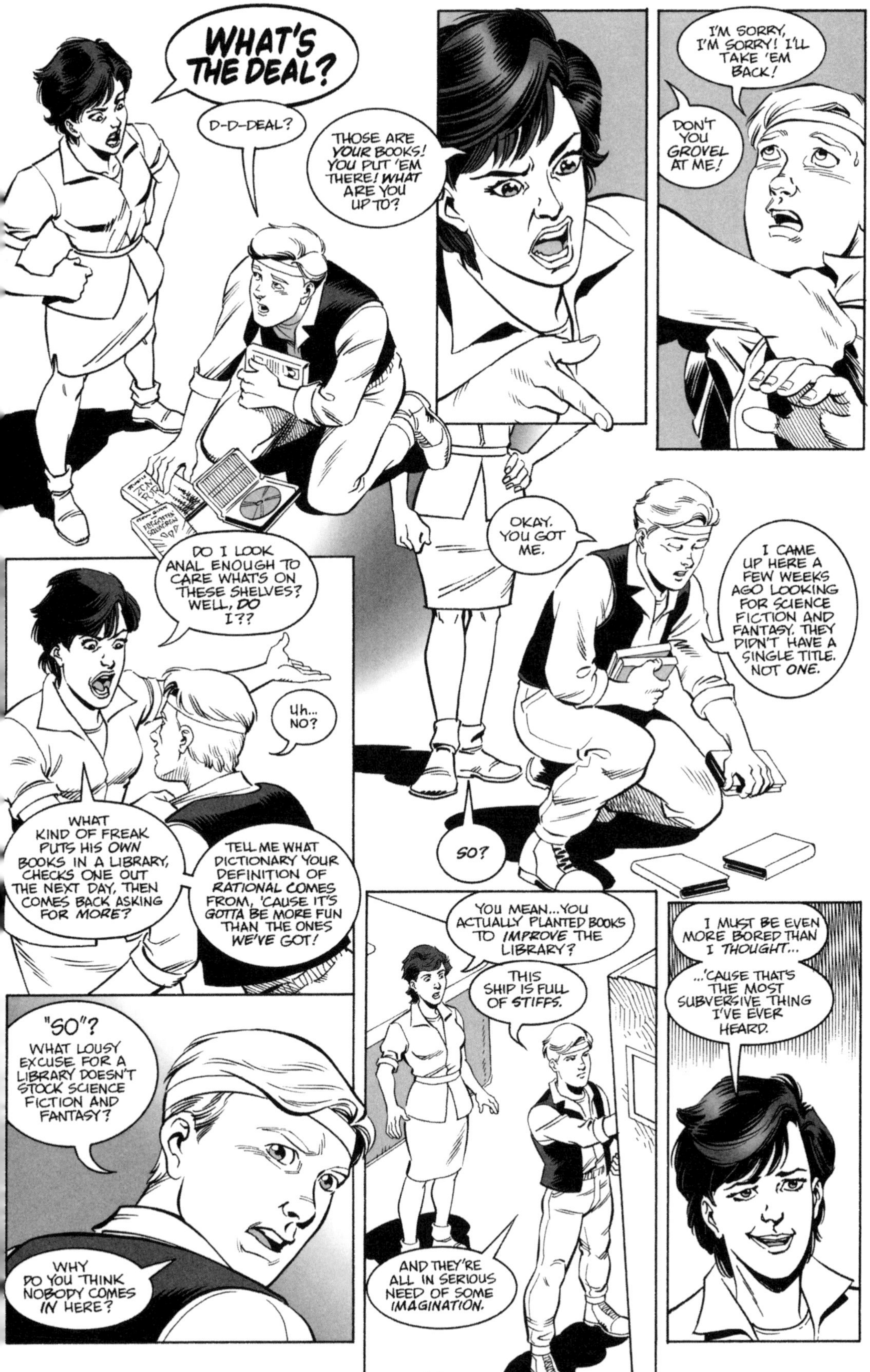
WHAT'S THE DEAL?
D-D-DEAL?
THOSE ARE YOUR BOOKS! YOU PUT 'EM THERE! WHAT ARE YOU UP TO?
I'M SORRY, I'M SORRY! I'LL TAKE 'EM BACK!
DON'T YOU GROVEL AT ME!
DO I LOOK ANAL ENOUGH TO CARE WHAT'S ON THESE SHELVES? WELL, DO I??
UH... NO?
WHAT KIND OF FREAK PUTS HIS OWN BOOKS IN A LIBRARY, CHECKS ONE OUT THE NEXT DAY, THEN COMES BACK ASKING FOR MORE?
TELL ME WHAT DICTIONARY YOUR DEFINITION OF RATIONAL COMES FROM, 'CAUSE IT'S GOTTA BE MORE FUN THAN THE ONES WE'VE GOT!
OKAY. YOU GOT ME.
I CAME UP HERE A FEW WEEKS AGO LOOKING FOR SCIENCE FICTION AND FANTASY. THEY DIDN'T HAVE A SINGLE TITLE. NOT ONE.
SO?
"SO"? WHAT LOUSY EXCUSE FOR A LIBRARY DOESN'T STOCK SCIENCE FICTION AND FANTASY?
WHY DO YOU THINK NOBODY COMES IN HERE?
YOU MEAN...YOU ACTUALLY PLANTED BOOKS TO IMPROVE THE LIBRARY?
THIS SHIP IS FULL OF STIFFS.
AND THEY'RE ALL IN SERIOUS NEED OF SOME IMAGINATION.
I MUST BE EVEN MORE BORED THAN I THOUGHT...
...'CAUSE THAT'S THE MOST SUBVERSIVE THING I'VE EVER HEARD.

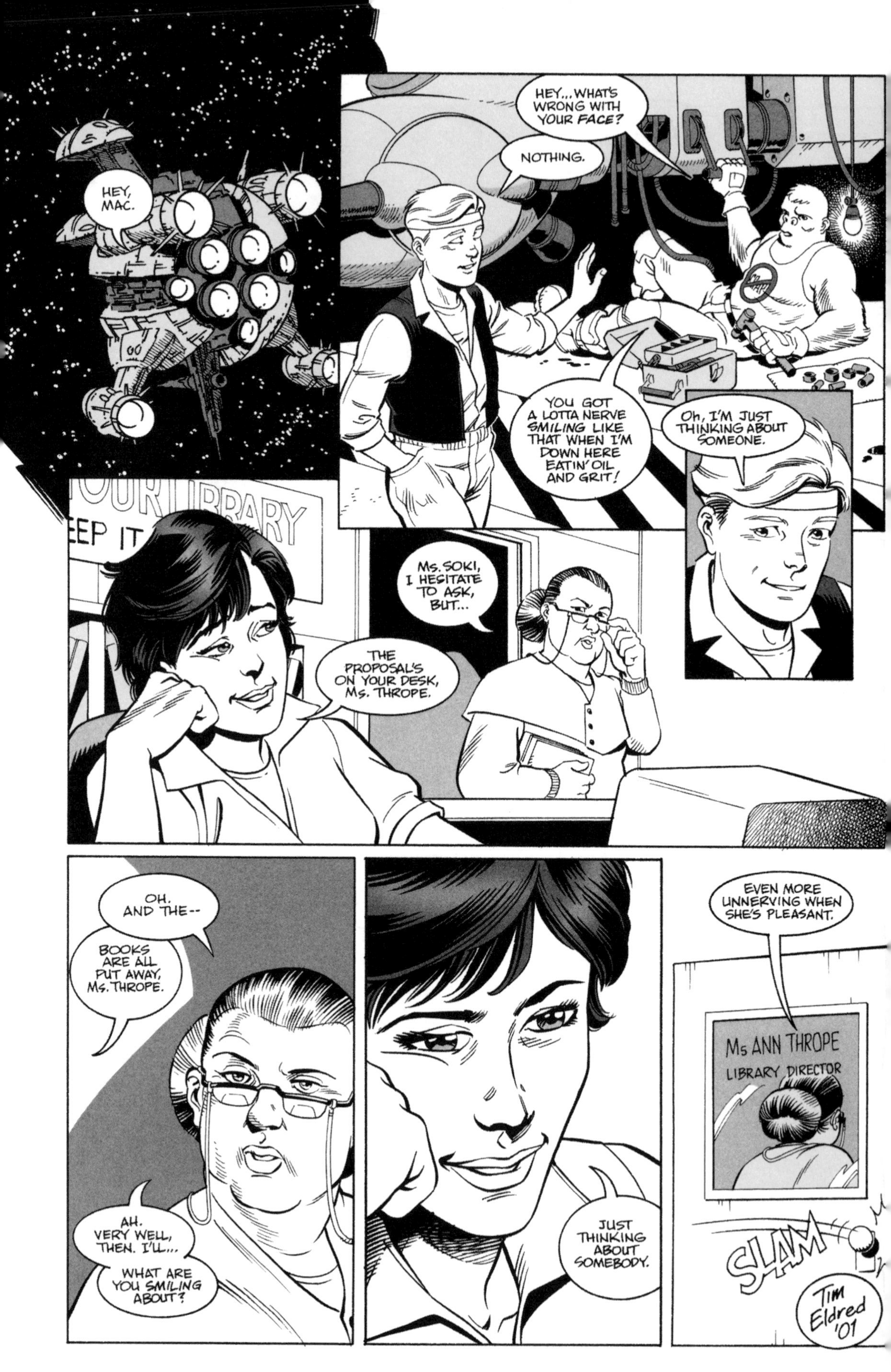
HEY, MAC.
HEY... WHAT'S WRONG WITH YOUR FACE?
NOTHING.
YOU GOT A LOTTA NERVE SMILING LIKE THAT WHEN I'M DOWN HERE EATIN' OIL AND GRIT!
Oh, I'M JUST THINKING ABOUT SOMEONE.
OUR LIBRARY
EEP IT
Ms. SOKI, I HESITATE TO ASK, BUT...
THE PROPOSAL'S ON YOUR DESK, Ms. THROPE.
OH. AND THE--
BOOKS ARE ALL PUT AWAY, Ms. THROPE.
AH. VERY WELL, THEN. I'LL...
WHAT ARE YOU SMILING ABOUT?
JUST THINKING ABOUT SOMEBODY.
EVEN MORE UNNERVING WHEN SHE'S PLEASANT.
Ms ANN THROPE
LIBRARY DIRECTOR
SLAM
Tim Eldred '01

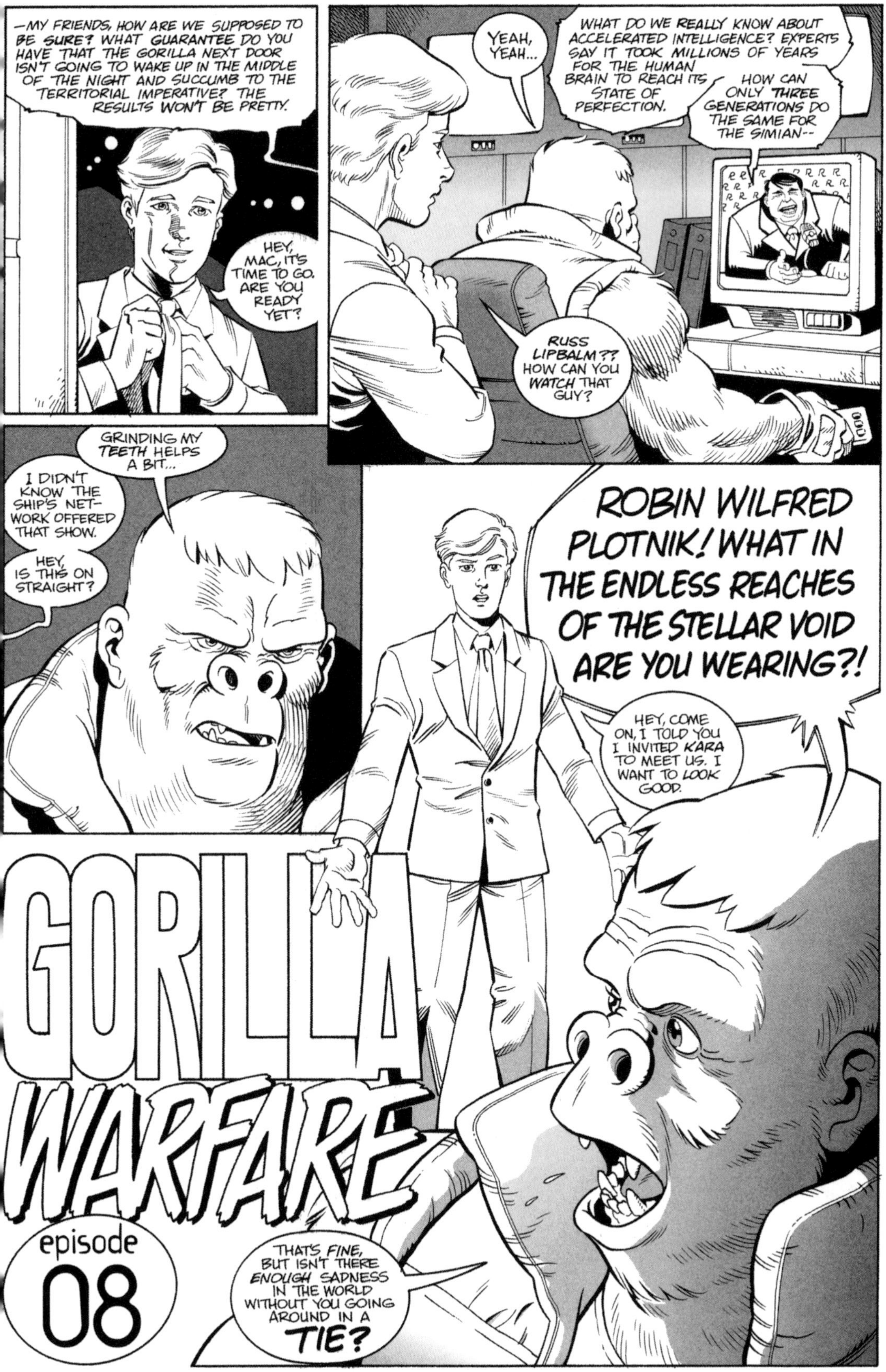
—MY FRIENDS, HOW ARE WE SUPPOSED TO BE SURE? WHAT GUARANTEE DO YOU HAVE THAT THE GORILLA NEXT DOOR ISN'T GOING TO WAKE UP IN THE MIDDLE OF THE NIGHT AND SUCCUMB TO THE TERRITORIAL IMPERATIVE? THE RESULTS WON'T BE PRETTY.
HEY, MAC, IT'S TIME TO GO. ARE YOU READY YET?
YEAH, YEAH...
WHAT DO WE REALLY KNOW ABOUT ACCELERATED INTELLIGENCE? EXPERTS SAY IT TOOK MILLIONS OF YEARS FOR THE HUMAN BRAIN TO REACH ITS STATE OF PERFECTION.
HOW CAN ONLY THREE GENERATIONS DO THE SAME FOR THE SIMIAN--
RUSS LIPBALM?? HOW CAN YOU WATCH THAT GUY?
GRINDING MY TEETH HELPS A BIT...
I DIDN'T KNOW THE SHIP'S NETWORK OFFERED THAT SHOW.
HEY, IS THIS ON STRAIGHT?
ROBIN WILFRED PLOTNIK! WHAT IN THE ENDLESS REACHES OF THE STELLAR VOID ARE YOU WEARING?!
HEY, COME ON, I TOLD YOU I INVITED KARA TO MEET US. I WANT TO LOOK GOOD.
GORILLA WARFARE
episode 08
THAT'S FINE, BUT ISN'T THERE ENOUGH SADNESS IN THE WORLD WITHOUT YOU GOING AROUND IN A TIE?

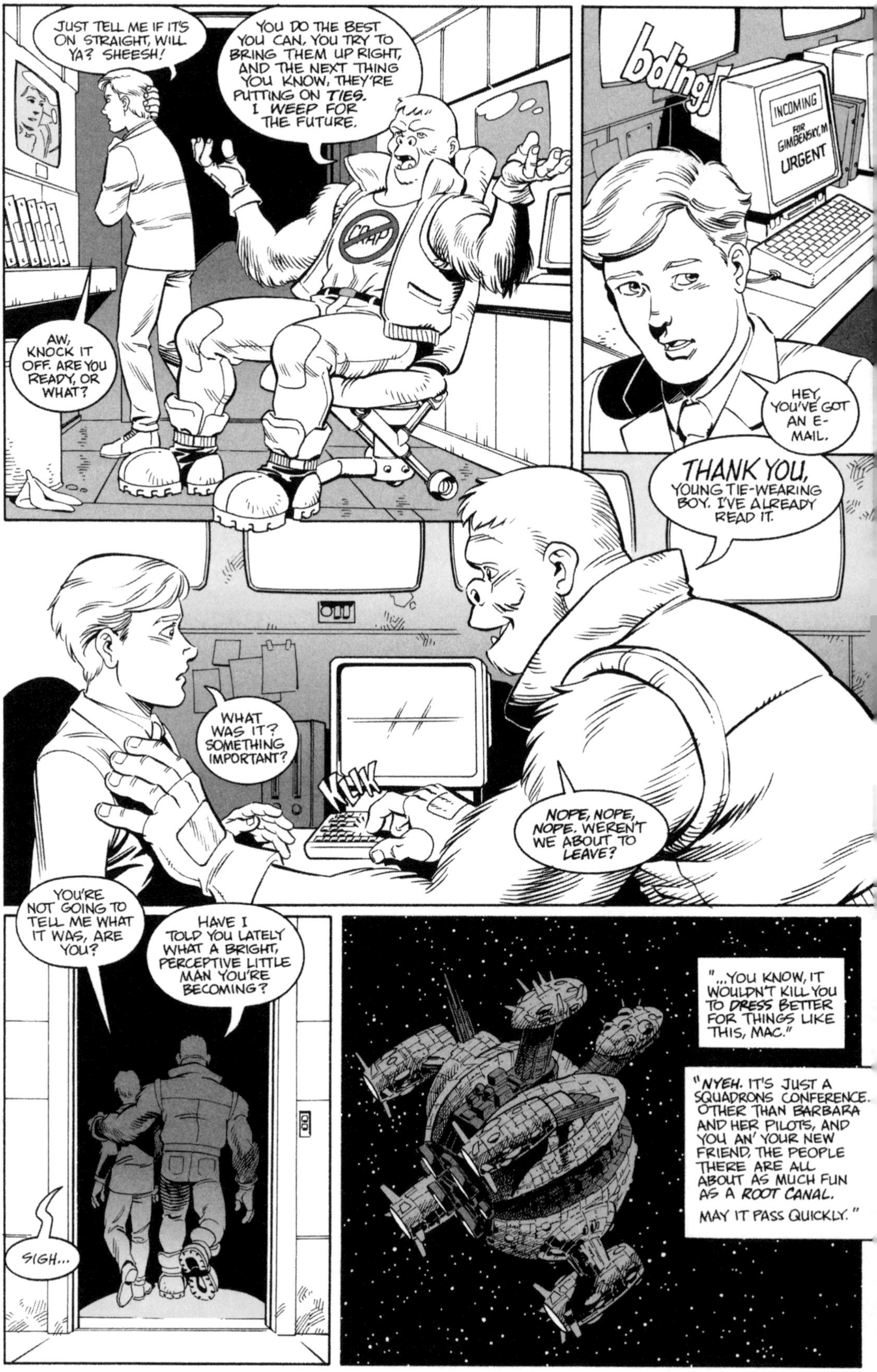
JUST TELL ME IF IT'S ON STRAIGHT, WILL YA? SHEESH!
YOU DO THE BEST YOU CAN, YOU TRY TO BRING THEM UP RIGHT, AND THE NEXT THING YOU KNOW, THEY'RE PUTTING ON *TIES*. I *WEEP* FOR THE FUTURE.
AW, KNOCK IT OFF. ARE YOU READY, OR WHAT?
bding!
INCOMING
FOR GIMBENSKY, M
URGENT
HEY, YOU'VE GOT AN E-MAIL.
THANK YOU, YOUNG TIE-WEARING BOY. I'VE ALREADY READ IT.
WHAT WAS IT? SOMETHING IMPORTANT?
KLIK
NOPE, NOPE, NOPE. WEREN'T WE ABOUT TO *LEAVE*?
YOU'RE NOT GOING TO TELL ME WHAT IT WAS, ARE YOU?
HAVE I TOLD YOU LATELY WHAT A BRIGHT, PERCEPTIVE LITTLE MAN YOU'RE BECOMING?
SIGH...
"...YOU KNOW, IT WOULDN'T KILL YOU TO *DRESS* BETTER FOR THINGS LIKE THIS, MAC."
"*NYEH*. IT'S JUST A SQUADRONS CONFERENCE. OTHER THAN BARBARA AND HER PILOTS, AND YOU AN' YOUR NEW FRIEND, THE PEOPLE THERE ARE ALL ABOUT AS MUCH FUN AS A *ROOT CANAL*.
MAY IT PASS QUICKLY."

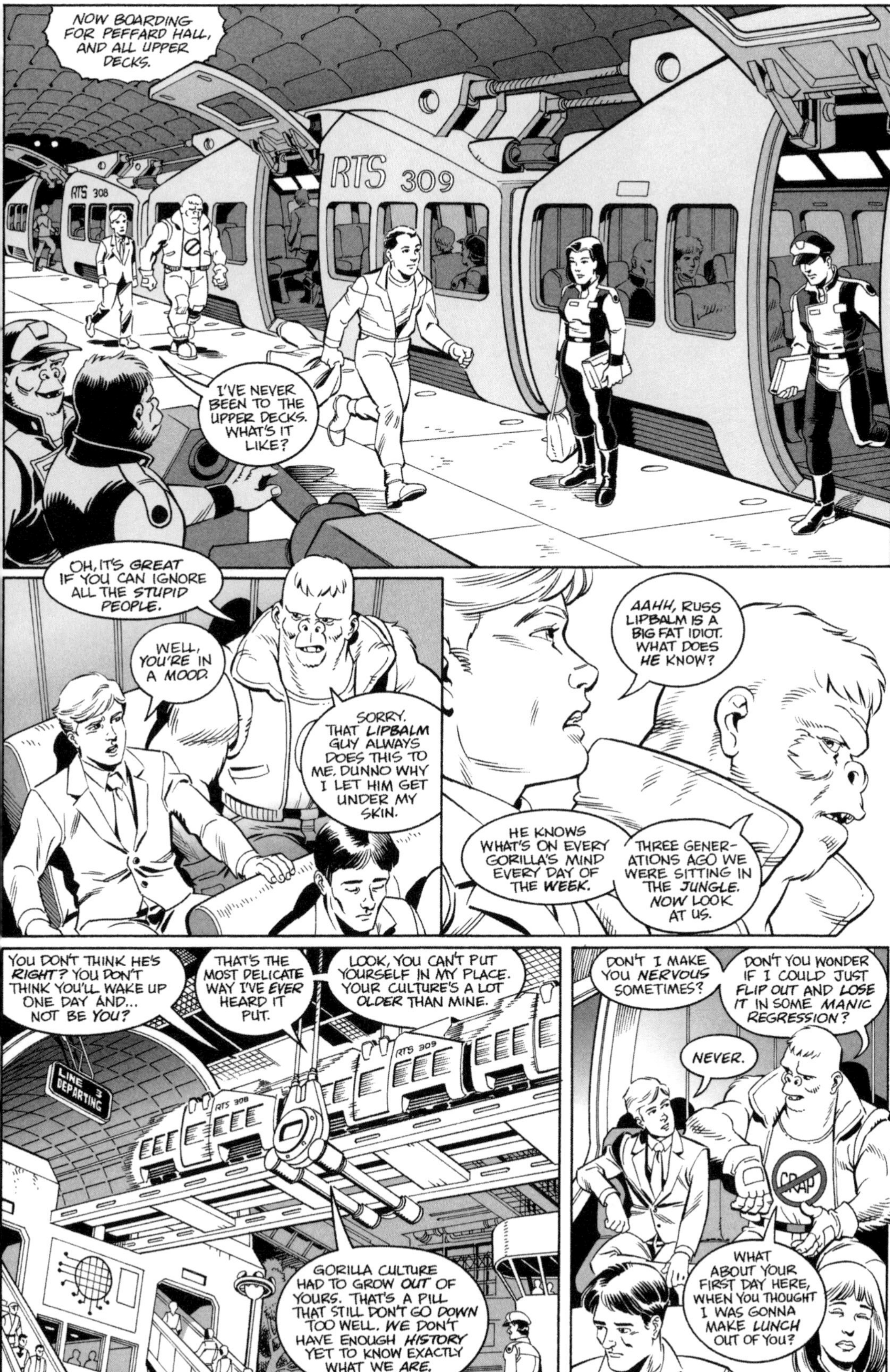
NOW BOARDING FOR PEFFARD HALL, AND ALL UPPER DECKS.
RTS 308
RTS 309
I'VE NEVER BEEN TO THE UPPER DECKS. WHAT'S IT LIKE?
OH, IT'S GREAT IF YOU CAN IGNORE ALL THE STUPID PEOPLE.
WELL, YOU'RE IN A MOOD.
SORRY. THAT LIPBALM GUY ALWAYS DOES THIS TO ME. DUNNO WHY I LET HIM GET UNDER MY SKIN.
AAHH, RUSS LIPBALM IS A BIG FAT IDIOT. WHAT DOES HE KNOW?
HE KNOWS WHAT'S ON EVERY GORILLA'S MIND EVERY DAY OF THE WEEK.
THREE GENERATIONS AGO WE WERE SITTING IN THE JUNGLE. NOW LOOK AT US.
YOU DON'T THINK HE'S RIGHT? YOU DON'T THINK YOU'LL WAKE UP ONE DAY AND... NOT BE YOU?
THAT'S THE MOST DELICATE WAY I'VE EVER HEARD IT PUT.
LOOK, YOU CAN'T PUT YOURSELF IN MY PLACE. YOUR CULTURE'S A LOT OLDER THAN MINE.
LINE 3 DEPARTING
RTS 308
RTS 309
GORILLA CULTURE HAD TO GROW OUT OF YOURS. THAT'S A PILL THAT STILL DON'T GO DOWN TOO WELL. WE DON'T HAVE ENOUGH HISTORY YET TO KNOW EXACTLY WHAT WE ARE.
DON'T I MAKE YOU NERVOUS SOMETIMES?
DON'T YOU WONDER IF I COULD JUST FLIP OUT AND LOSE IT IN SOME MANIC REGRESSION?
NEVER.
CRAP
WHAT ABOUT YOUR FIRST DAY HERE, WHEN YOU THOUGHT I WAS GONNA MAKE LUNCH OUT OF YOU?

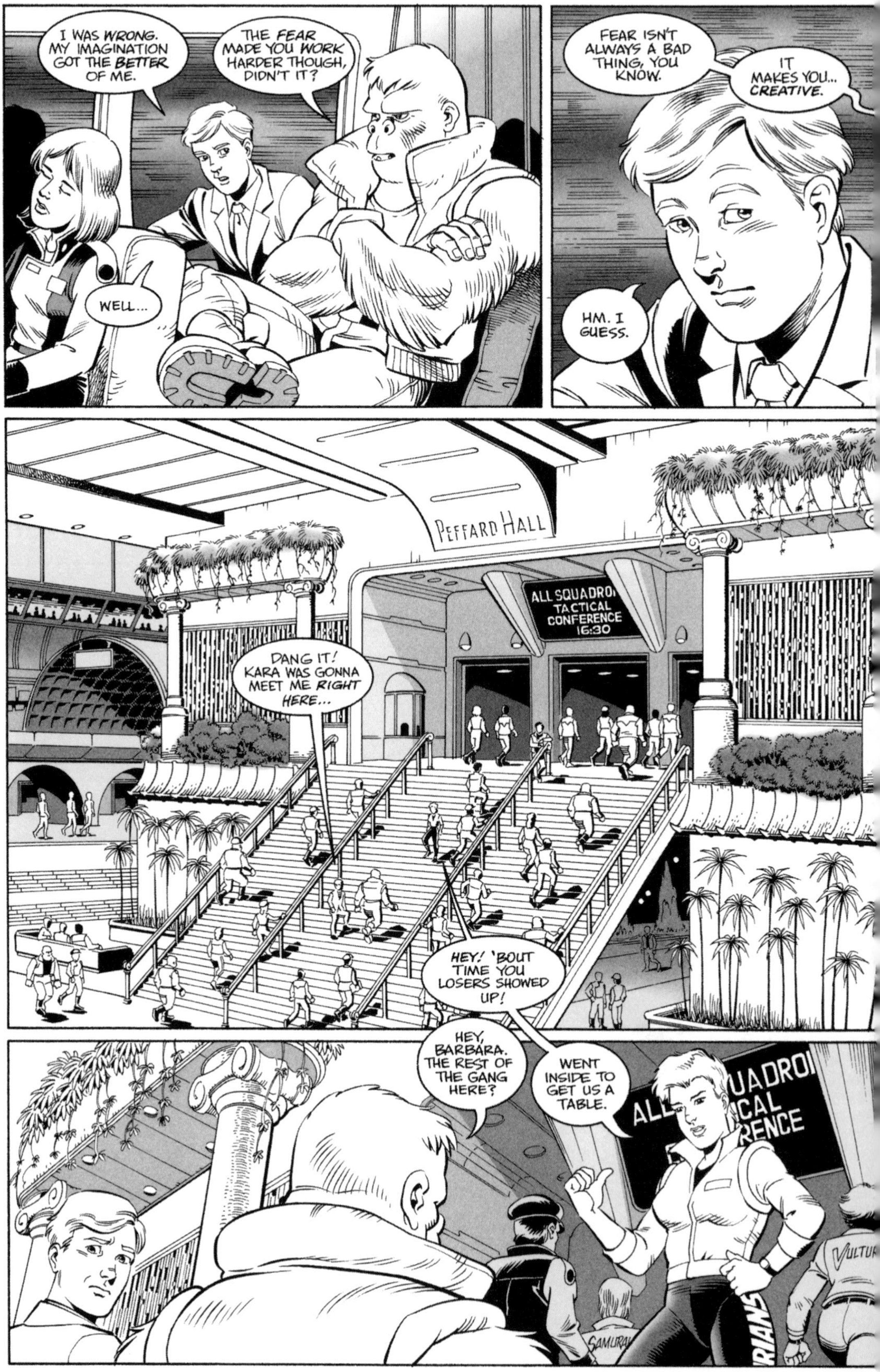
I WAS WRONG. MY IMAGINATION GOT THE BETTER OF ME.
THE FEAR MADE YOU WORK HARDER THOUGH, DIDN'T IT?
WELL...
FEAR ISN'T ALWAYS A BAD THING, YOU KNOW.
IT MAKES YOU... CREATIVE.
HM. I GUESS.
PEFFARD HALL
ALL SQUADRO
TACTICAL CONFERENCE 16:30
DANG IT! KARA WAS GONNA MEET ME RIGHT HERE...
HEY! 'BOUT TIME YOU LOSERS SHOWED UP!
HEY, BARBARA. THE REST OF THE GANG HERE?
WENT INSIDE TO GET US A TABLE.

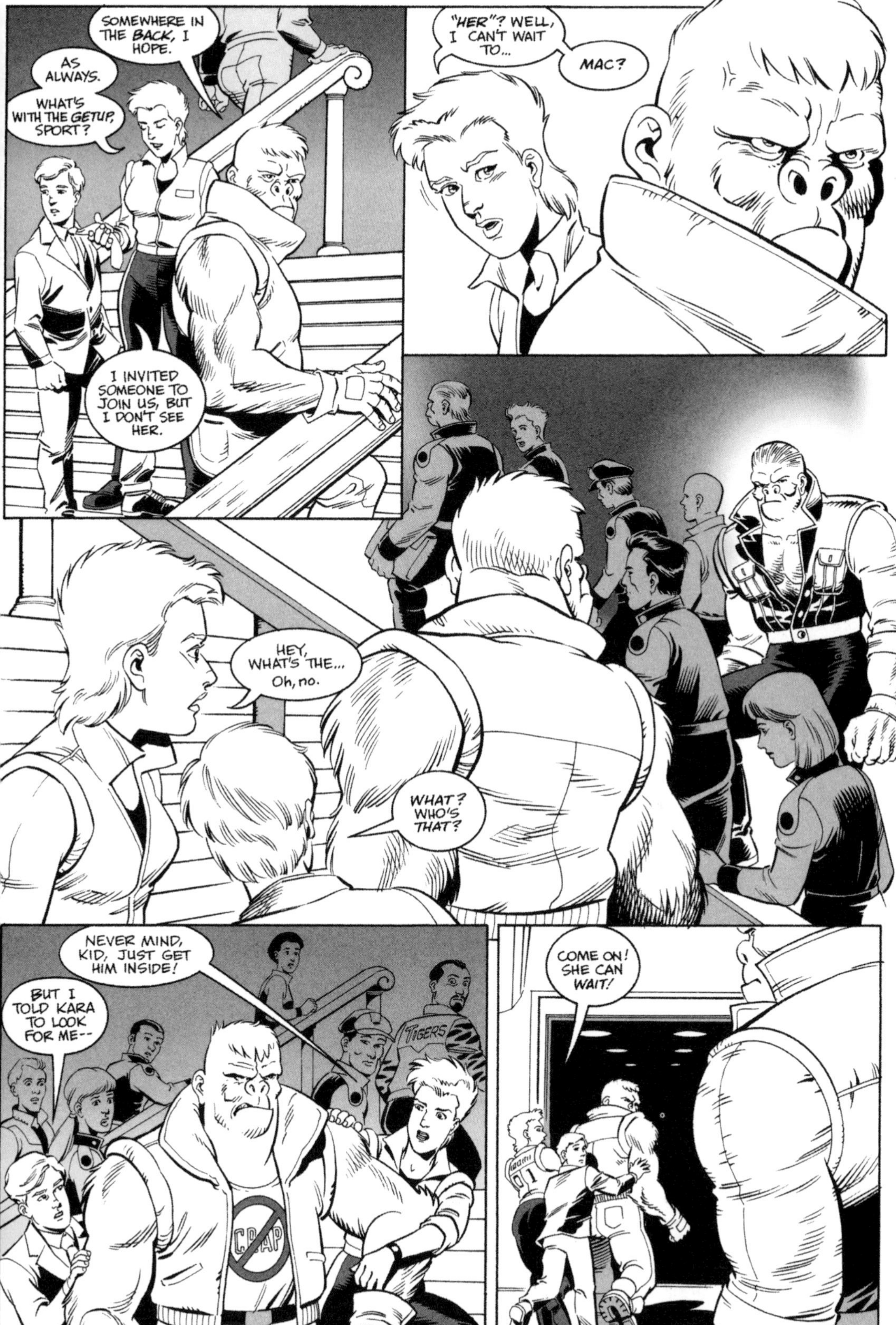
SOMEWHERE IN THE BACK, I HOPE.
AS ALWAYS.
WHAT'S WITH THE GETUP, SPORT?
I INVITED SOMEONE TO JOIN US, BUT I DON'T SEE HER.
"HER"? WELL, I CAN'T WAIT TO...
MAC?
HEY, WHAT'S THE... Oh, no.
WHAT? WHO'S THAT?
NEVER MIND, KID, JUST GET HIM INSIDE!
BUT I TOLD KARA TO LOOK FOR ME--
TIGERS
COME ON! SHE CAN WAIT!

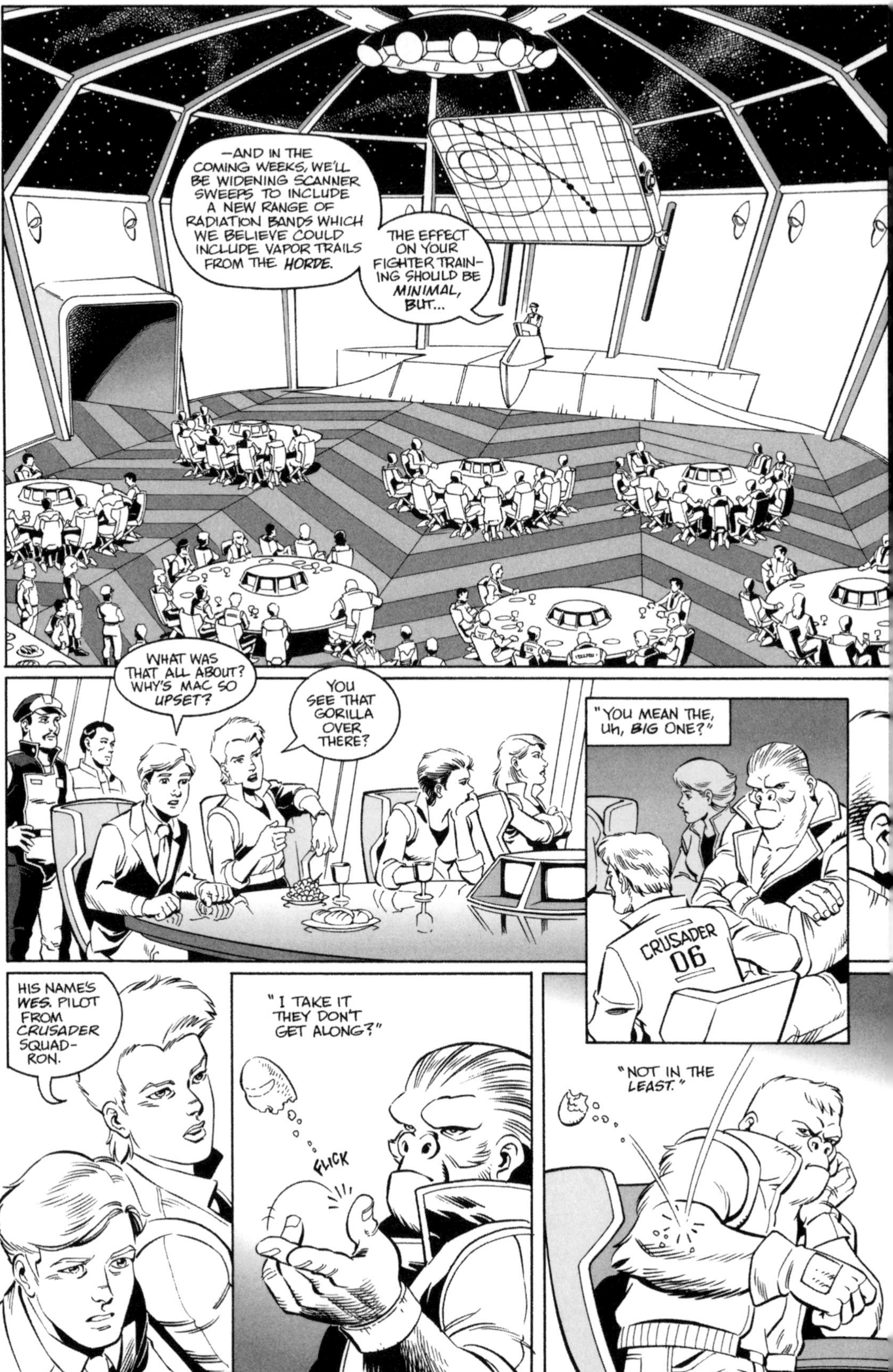
—AND IN THE COMING WEEKS, WE'LL BE WIDENING SCANNER SWEEPS TO INCLUDE A NEW RANGE OF RADIATION BANDS WHICH WE BELIEVE COULD INCLUDE VAPOR TRAILS FROM THE HORDE.
THE EFFECT ON YOUR FIGHTER TRAINING SHOULD BE MINIMAL, BUT...
WHAT WAS THAT ALL ABOUT? WHY'S MAC SO UPSET?
YOU SEE THAT GORILLA OVER THERE?
"YOU MEAN THE, Uh, BIG ONE?"
CRUSADER 06
HIS NAME'S WES. PILOT FROM CRUSADER SQUADRON.
"I TAKE IT THEY DON'T GET ALONG?"
FLICK
"NOT IN THE LEAST."

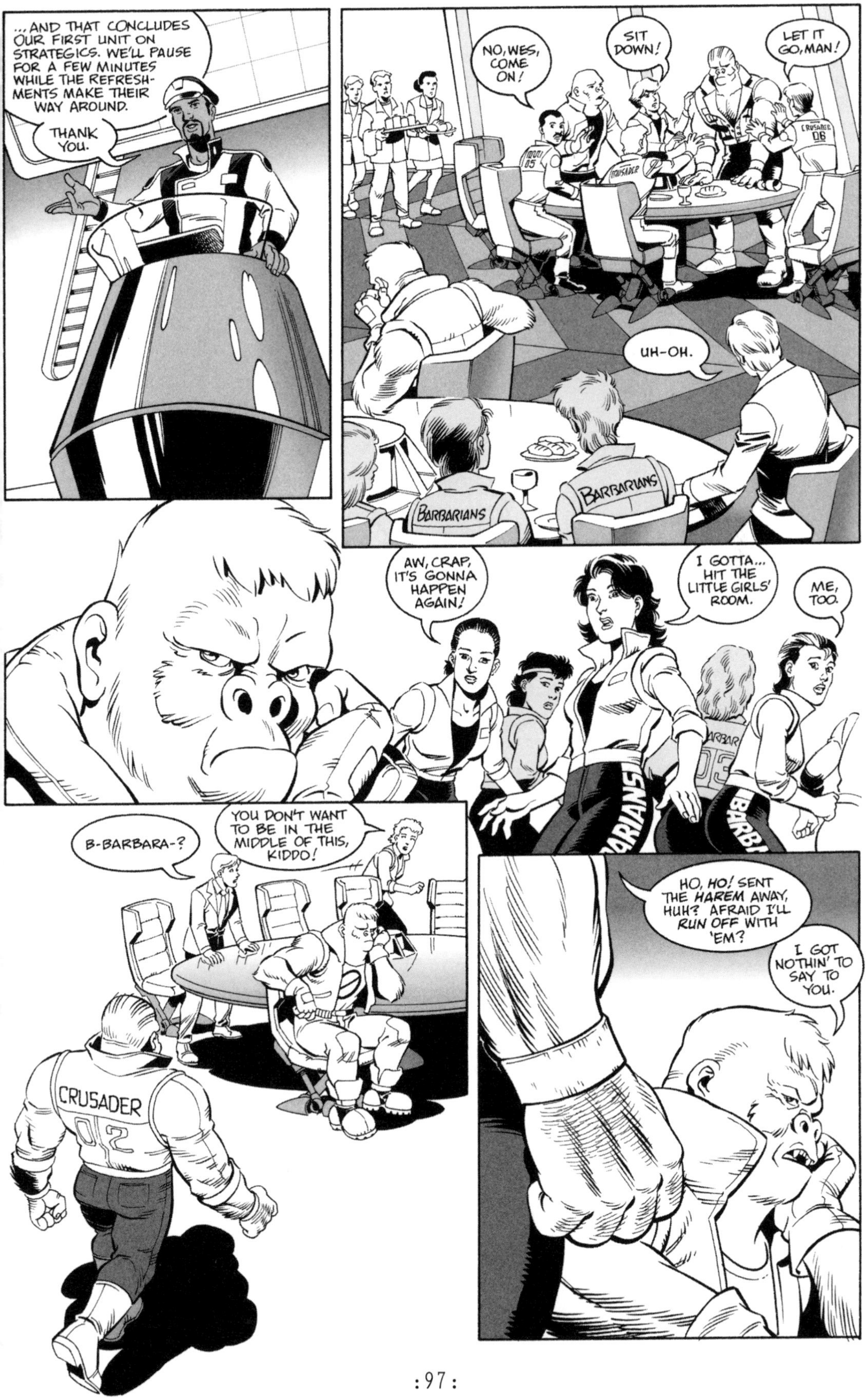

...AND THAT CONCLUDES OUR FIRST UNIT ON STRATEGICS. WE'LL PAUSE FOR A FEW MINUTES WHILE THE REFRESHMENTS MAKE THEIR WAY AROUND.
THANK YOU.
NO, WES, COME ON!
SIT DOWN!
LET IT GO, MAN!
CRUSADER 06
05
CRUSADER
UH-OH.
BARBARIANS
BARBARIANS
AW, CRAP, IT'S GONNA HAPPEN AGAIN!
I GOTTA... HIT THE LITTLE GIRLS' ROOM.
ME, TOO.
BARBARIANS
B-BARBARA-?
YOU DON'T WANT TO BE IN THE MIDDLE OF THIS, KIDDO!
CRUSADER 02
HO, HO! SENT THE HAREM AWAY, HUH? AFRAID I'LL RUN OFF WITH 'EM?
I GOT NOTHIN' TO SAY TO YOU.

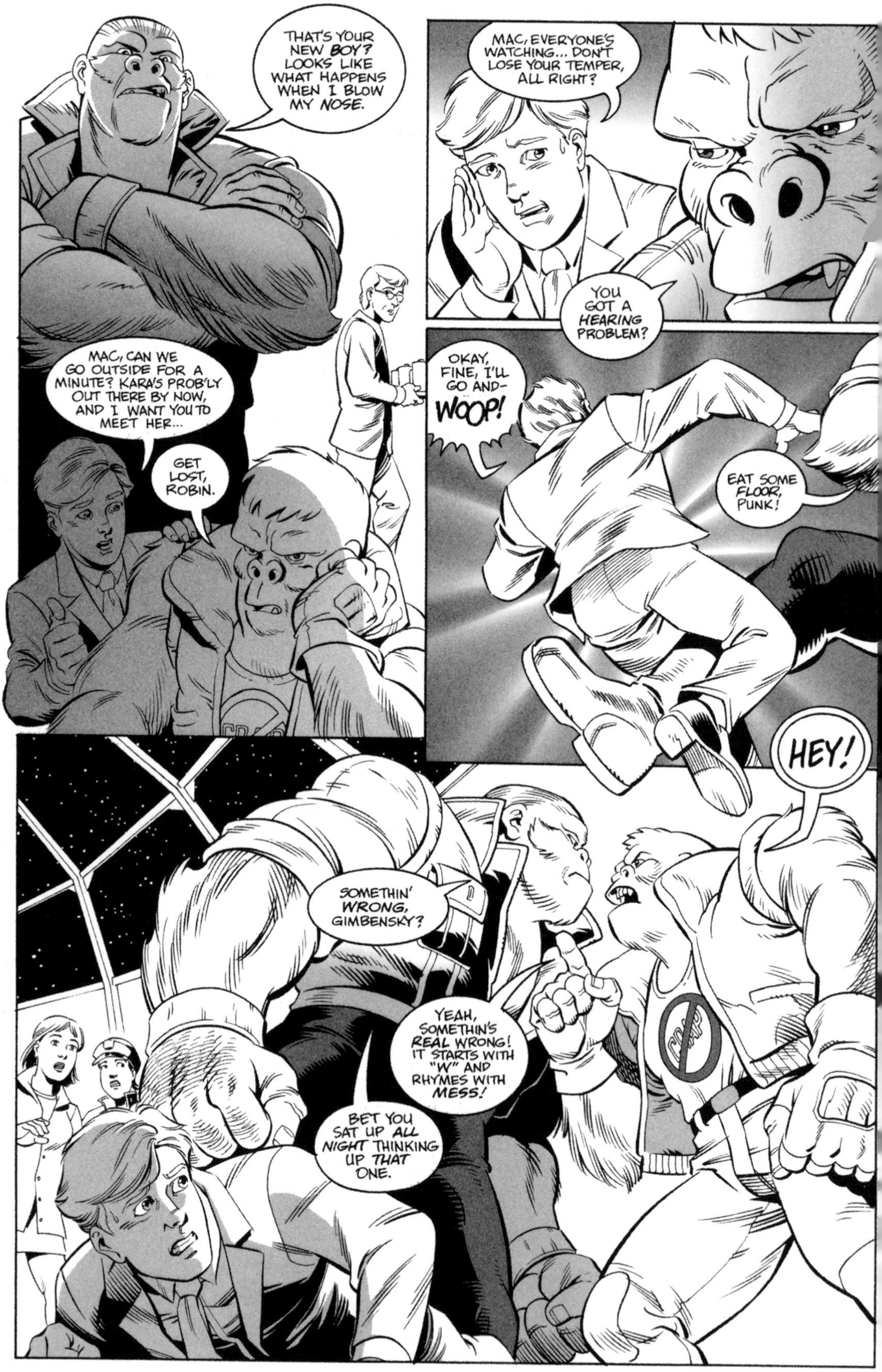
THAT'S YOUR NEW BOY? LOOKS LIKE WHAT HAPPENS WHEN I BLOW MY NOSE.
MAC, EVERYONE'S WATCHING... DON'T LOSE YOUR TEMPER, ALL RIGHT?
YOU GOT A HEARING PROBLEM?
MAC, CAN WE GO OUTSIDE FOR A MINUTE? KARA'S PROB'LY OUT THERE BY NOW, AND I WANT YOU TO MEET HER...
GET LOST, ROBIN.
OKAY, FINE, I'LL GO AND-
WOOP!
EAT SOME FLOOR, PUNK!
HEY!
SOMETHIN' WRONG, GIMBENSKY?
YEAH, SOMETHIN'S REAL WRONG! IT STARTS WITH "W" AND RHYMES WITH MESS!
BET YOU SAT UP ALL NIGHT THINKING UP THAT ONE.

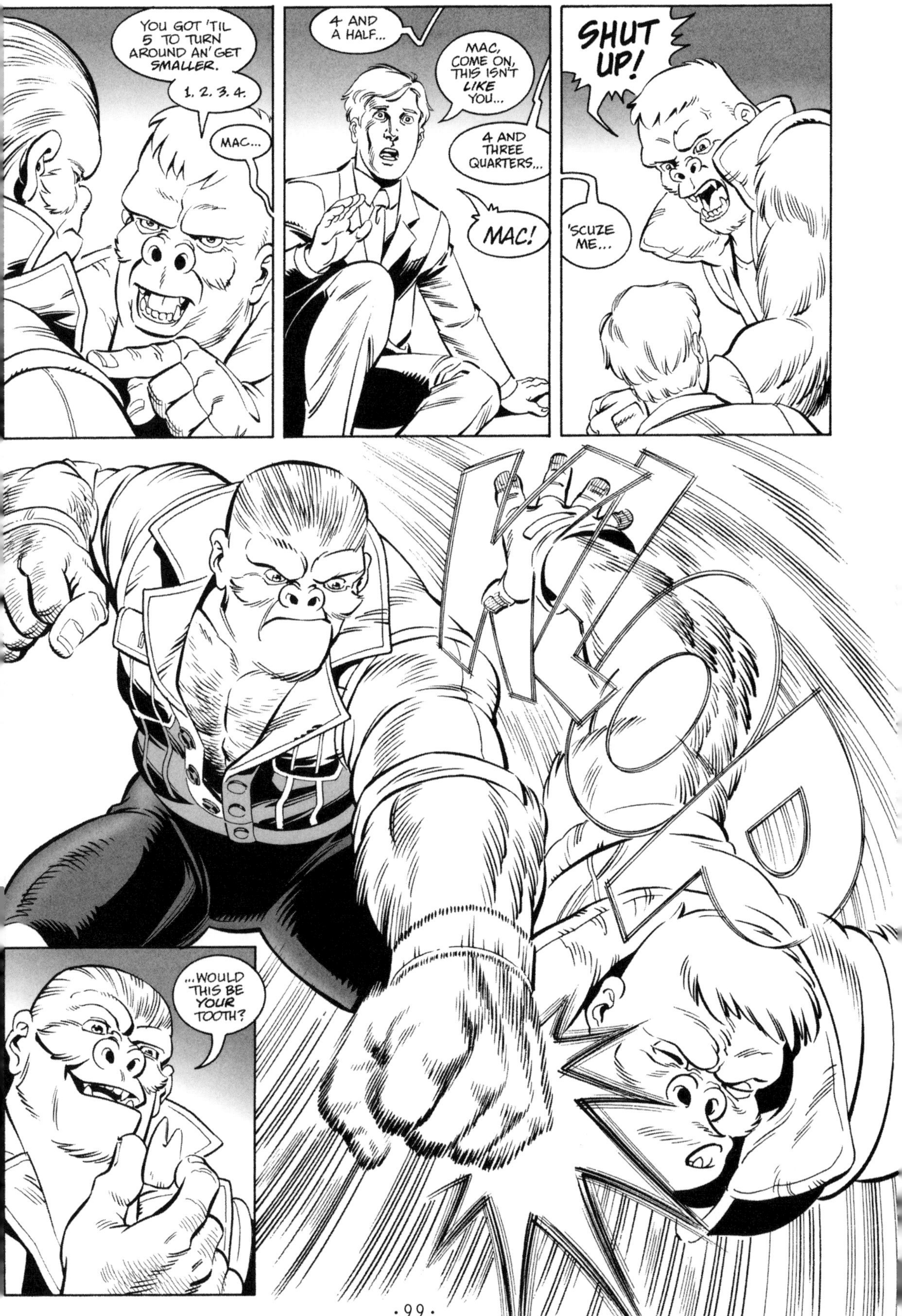
YOU GOT 'TIL 5 TO TURN AROUND AN' GET SMALLER.
1. 2. 3. 4.
MAC...
4 AND A HALF...
MAC, COME ON, THIS ISN'T LIKE YOU...
4 AND THREE QUARTERS...
MAC!
SHUT UP!
'SCUZE ME...
...WOULD THIS BE YOUR TOOTH?

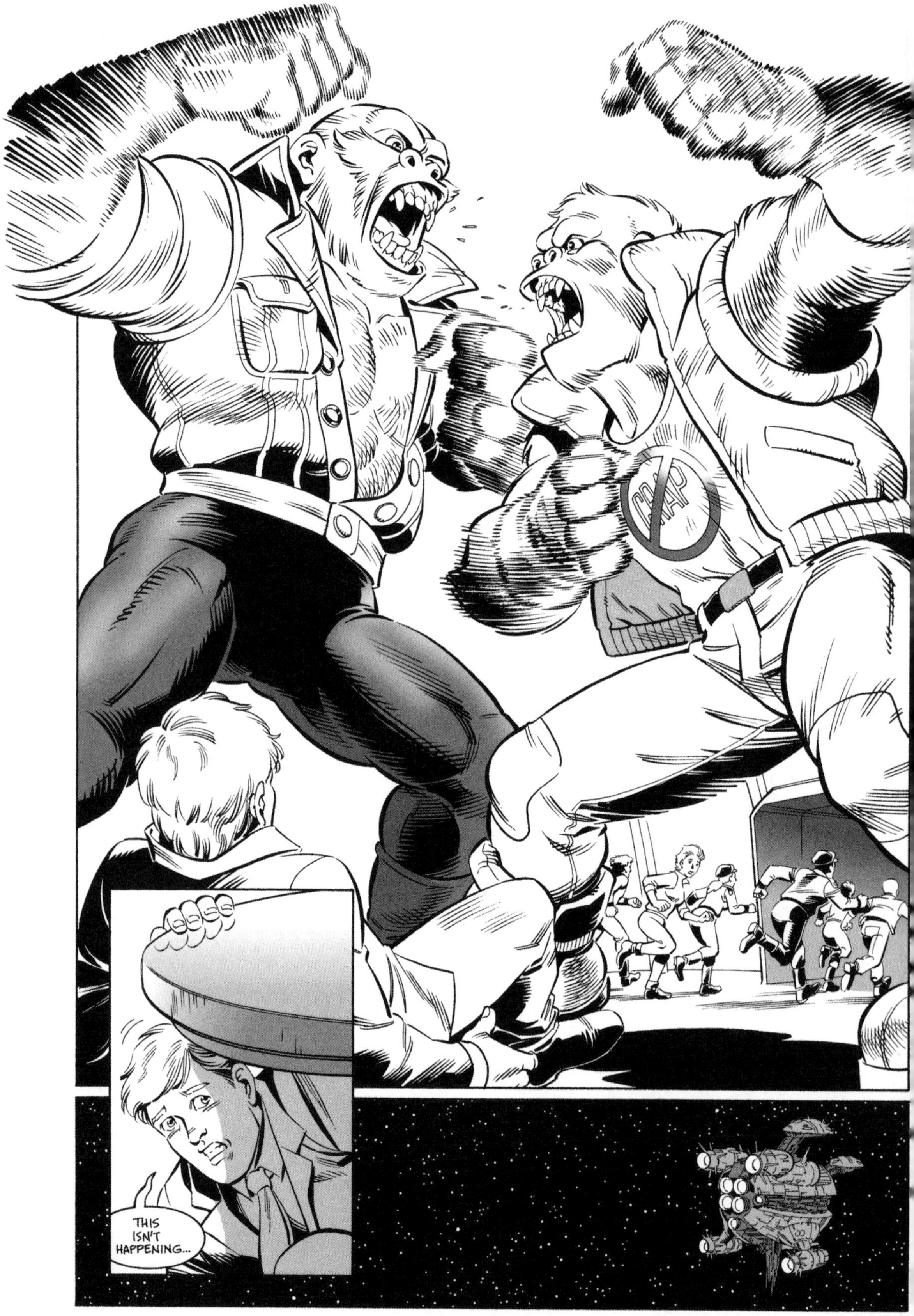
THIS ISN'T HAPPENING...

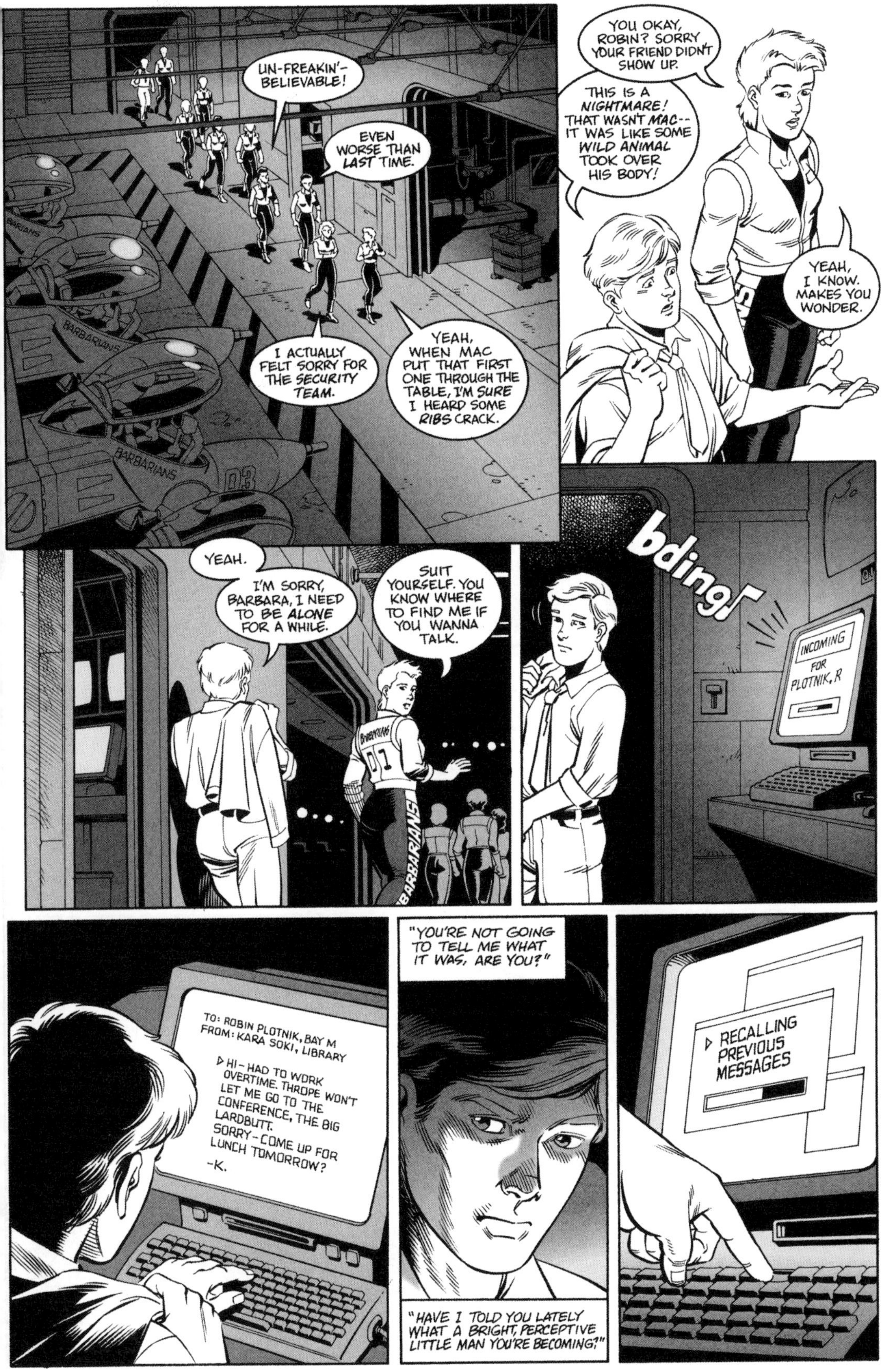
UN-FREAKIN'-BELIEVABLE!
EVEN WORSE THAN LAST TIME.
I ACTUALLY FELT SORRY FOR THE SECURITY TEAM.
YEAH, WHEN MAC PUT THAT FIRST ONE THROUGH THE TABLE, I'M SURE I HEARD SOME RIBS CRACK.
BARBARIANS
D3
YOU OKAY, ROBIN? SORRY YOUR FRIEND DIDN'T SHOW UP.
THIS IS A NIGHTMARE! THAT WASN'T MAC-- IT WAS LIKE SOME WILD ANIMAL TOOK OVER HIS BODY!
YEAH, I KNOW. MAKES YOU WONDER.
YEAH.
I'M SORRY, BARBARA, I NEED TO BE ALONE FOR A WHILE.
SUIT YOURSELF. YOU KNOW WHERE TO FIND ME IF YOU WANNA TALK.
BARBARIANS
bding!
INCOMING FOR PLOTNIK, R
TO: ROBIN PLOTNIK, BAY M
FROM: KARA SOKI, LIBRARY
HI- HAD TO WORK OVERTIME. THROPE WON'T LET ME GO TO THE CONFERENCE, THE BIG LARDBUTT. SORRY- COME UP FOR LUNCH TOMORROW?
-K.
"YOU'RE NOT GOING TO TELL ME WHAT IT WAS, ARE YOU?"
"HAVE I TOLD YOU LATELY WHAT A BRIGHT, PERCEPTIVE LITTLE MAN YOU'RE BECOMING?"
RECALLING PREVIOUS MESSAGES

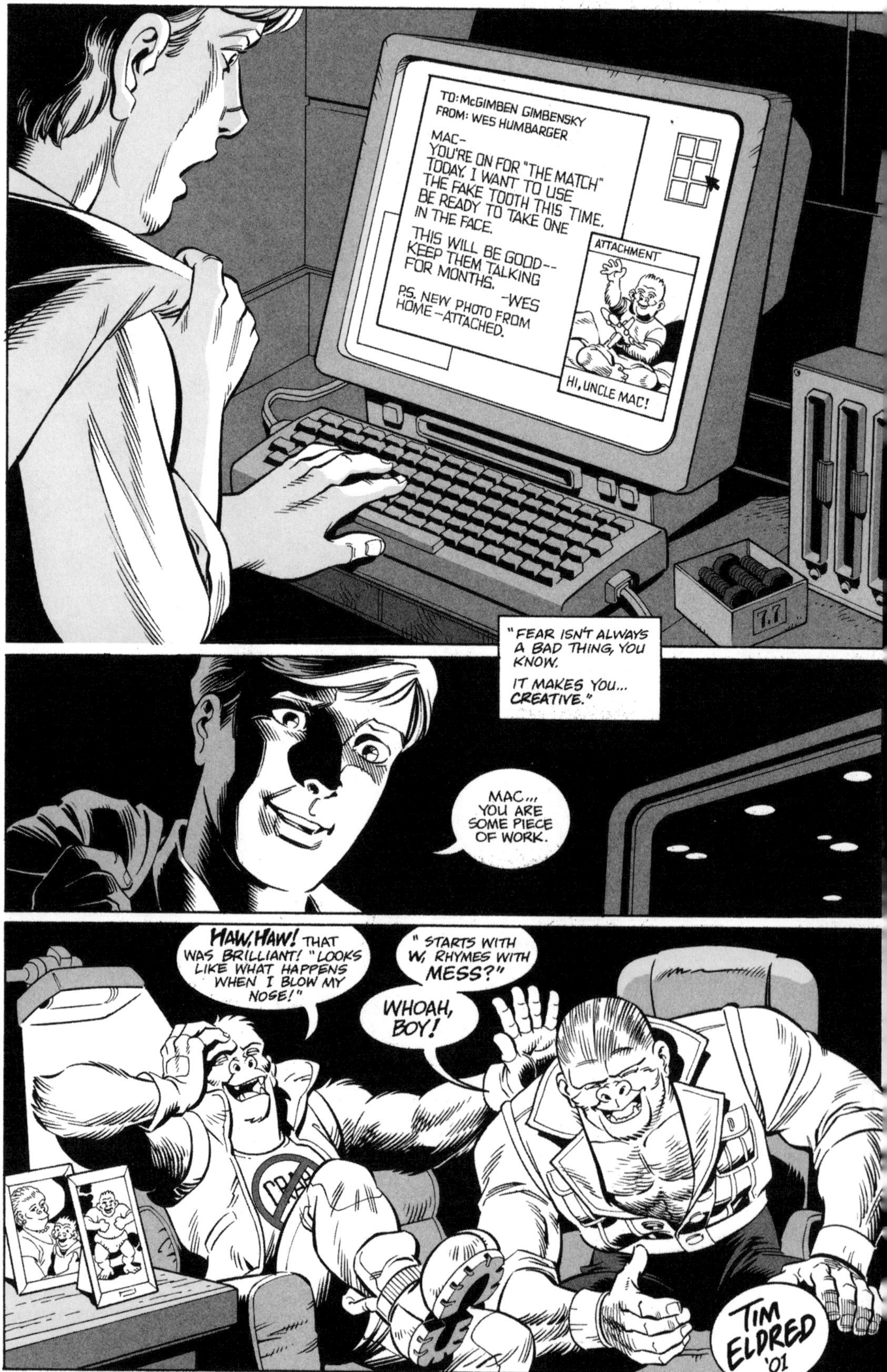
TO: McGIMBEN GIMBENSKY
FROM: WES HUMBARGER
MAC-
YOU'RE ON FOR "THE MATCH" TODAY. I WANT TO USE THE FAKE TOOTH THIS TIME. BE READY TO TAKE ONE IN THE FACE.
THIS WILL BE GOOD-- KEEP THEM TALKING FOR MONTHS.
-WES
P.S. NEW PHOTO FROM HOME--ATTACHED.
ATTACHMENT
HI, UNCLE MAC!
"FEAR ISN'T ALWAYS A BAD THING, YOU KNOW.
IT MAKES YOU... CREATIVE."
MAC... YOU ARE SOME PIECE OF WORK.
HAW, HAW! THAT WAS BRILLIANT! "LOOKS LIKE WHAT HAPPENS WHEN I BLOW MY NOSE!"
"STARTS WITH W, RHYMES WITH MESS?"
WHOAH, BOY!
TIM ELDRED '01

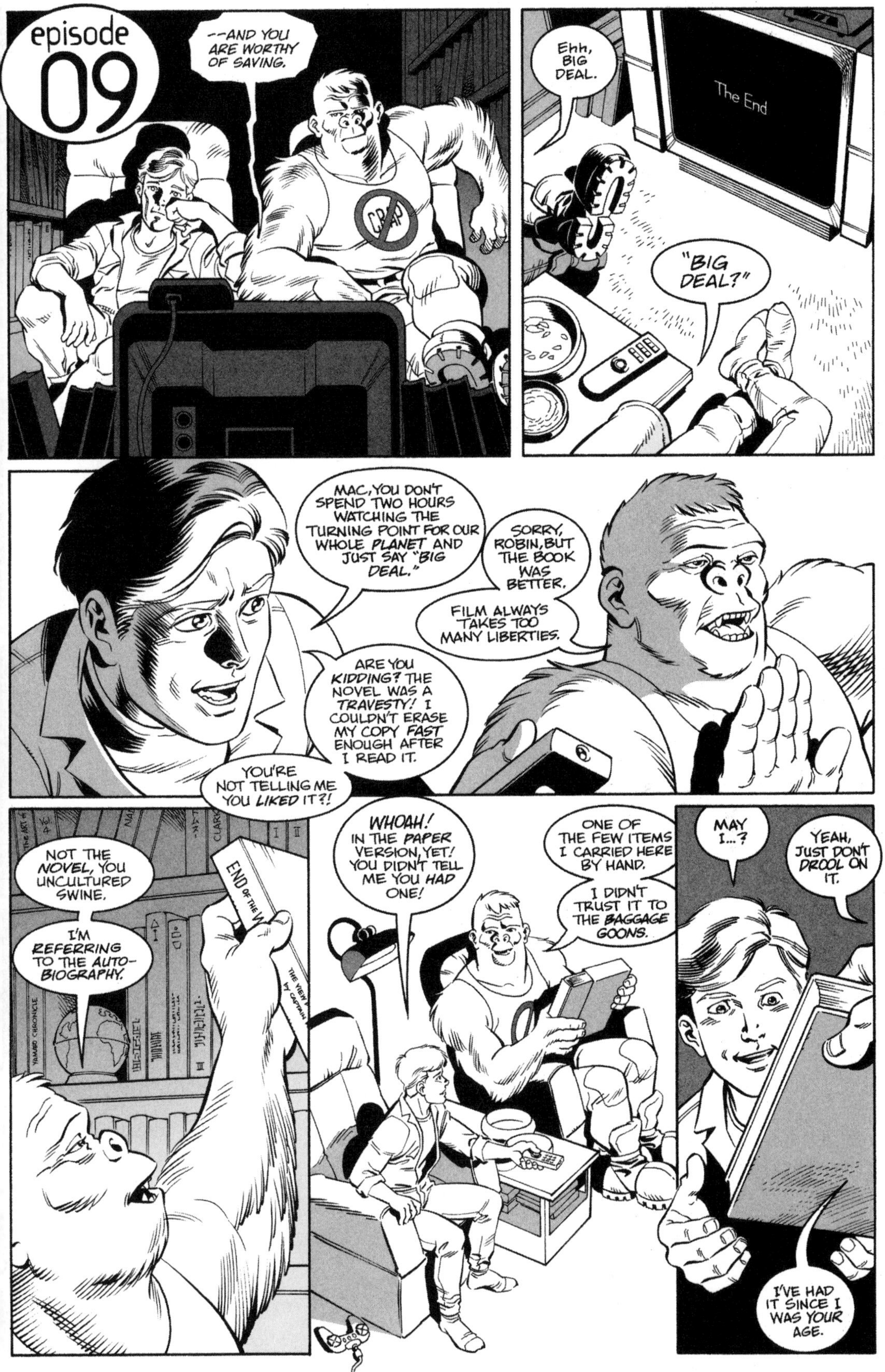
episode 09
--AND YOU ARE WORTHY OF SAVING.
Ehh, BIG DEAL.
The End
"BIG DEAL?"
MAC, YOU DON'T SPEND TWO HOURS WATCHING THE TURNING POINT FOR OUR WHOLE PLANET AND JUST SAY "BIG DEAL."
SORRY, ROBIN, BUT THE BOOK WAS BETTER.
FILM ALWAYS TAKES TOO MANY LIBERTIES.
ARE YOU KIDDING? THE NOVEL WAS A TRAVESTY! I COULDN'T ERASE MY COPY FAST ENOUGH AFTER I READ IT.
YOU'RE NOT TELLING ME YOU LIKED IT?!
NOT THE NOVEL, YOU UNCULTURED SWINE.
I'M REFERRING TO THE AUTO-BIOGRAPHY.
WHOAH! IN THE PAPER VERSION, YET! YOU DIDN'T TELL ME YOU HAD ONE!
ONE OF THE FEW ITEMS I CARRIED HERE BY HAND.
I DIDN'T TRUST IT TO THE BAGGAGE GOONS.
MAY I...?
YEAH, JUST DON'T DROOL ON IT.
I'VE HAD IT SINCE I WAS YOUR AGE.

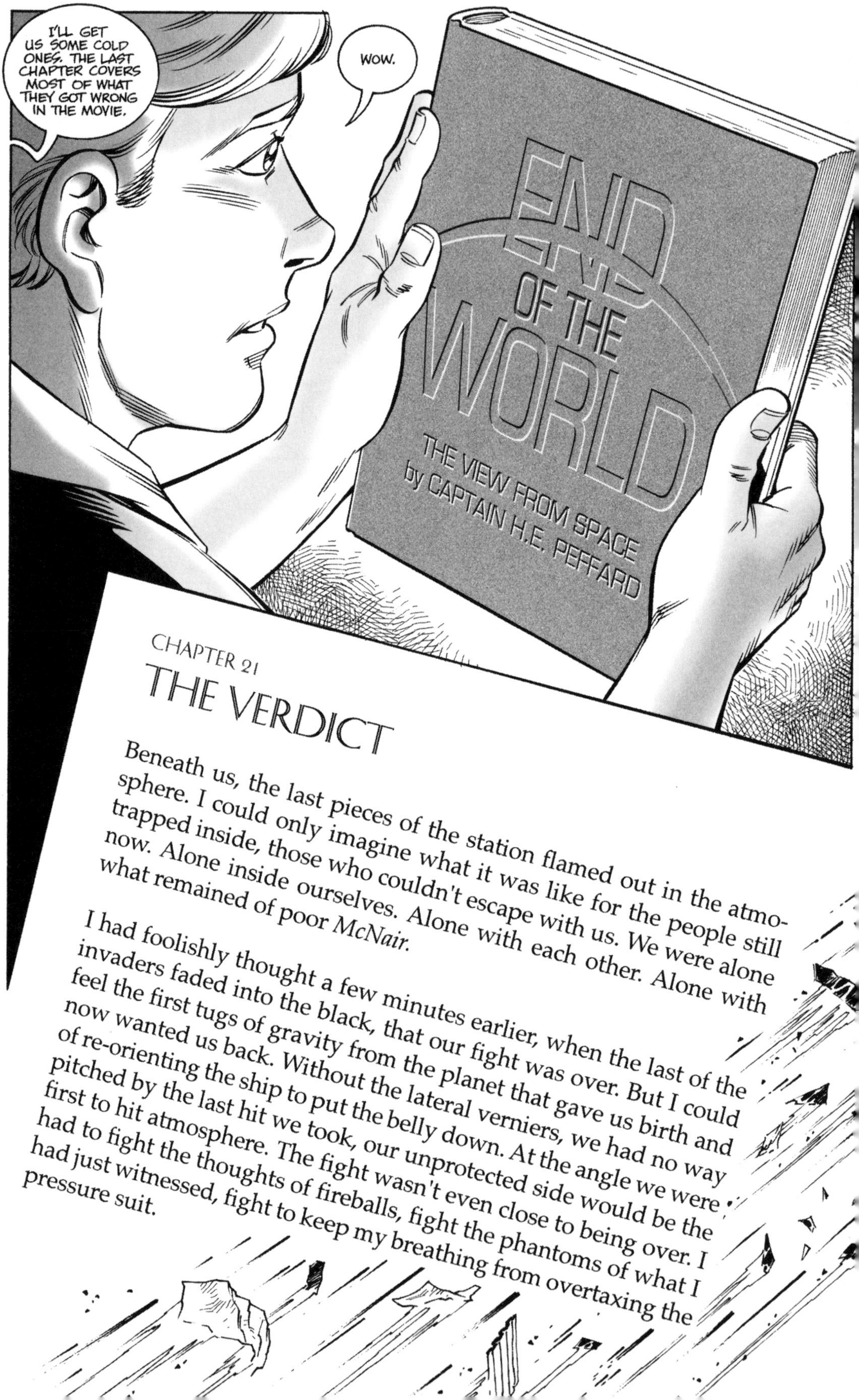
I'LL GET US SOME COLD ONES. THE LAST CHAPTER COVERS MOST OF WHAT THEY GOT WRONG IN THE MOVIE.
WOW.
END OF THE WORLD
THE VIEW FROM SPACE
by CAPTAIN H.E. PEFFARD
CHAPTER 21
THE VERDICT
Beneath us, the last pieces of the station flamed out in the atmosphere. I could only imagine what it was like for the people still trapped inside, those who couldn't escape with us. We were alone now. Alone inside ourselves. Alone with each other. Alone with what remained of poor *McNair.*
I had foolishly thought a few minutes earlier, when the last of the invaders faded into the black, that our fight was over. But I could feel the first tugs of gravity from the planet that gave us birth and now wanted us back. Without the lateral verniers, we had no way of re-orienting the ship to put the belly down. At the angle we were pitched by the last hit we took, our unprotected side would be the first to hit atmosphere. The fight wasn't even close to being over. I had to fight the thoughts of fireballs, fight the phantoms of what I had just witnessed, fight to keep my breathing from overtaxing the pressure suit.

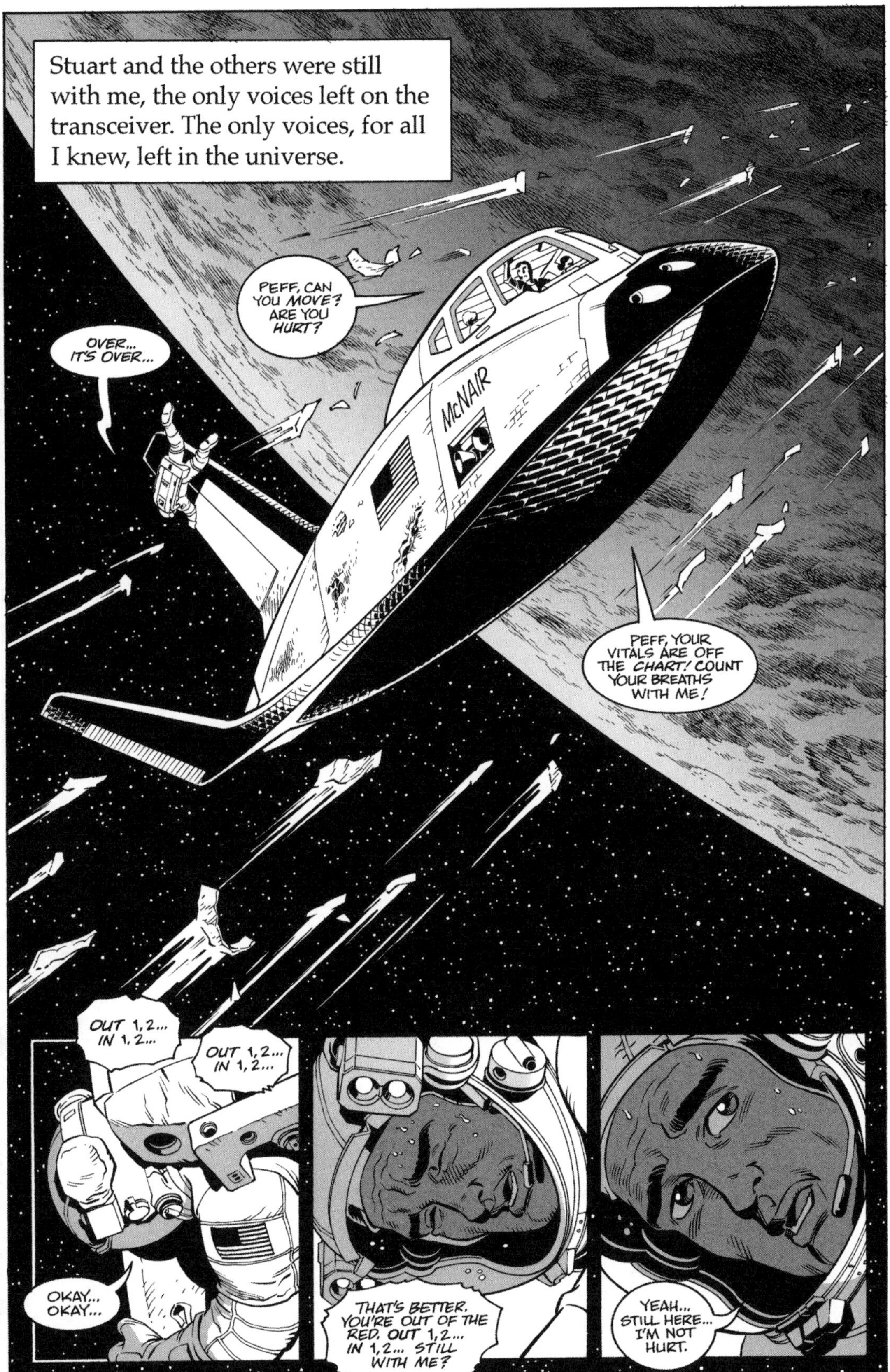
Stuart and the others were still with me, the only voices left on the transceiver. The only voices, for all I knew, left in the universe.
PEFF, CAN YOU MOVE? ARE YOU HURT?
OVER... IT'S OVER...
McNAIR
PEFF, YOUR VITALS ARE OFF THE CHART! COUNT YOUR BREATHS WITH ME!
OUT 1,2... IN 1,2...
OUT 1,2... IN 1,2...
OKAY... OKAY...
THAT'S BETTER. YOU'RE OUT OF THE RED. OUT 1,2... IN 1,2... STILL WITH ME?
YEAH... STILL HERE... I'M NOT HURT.

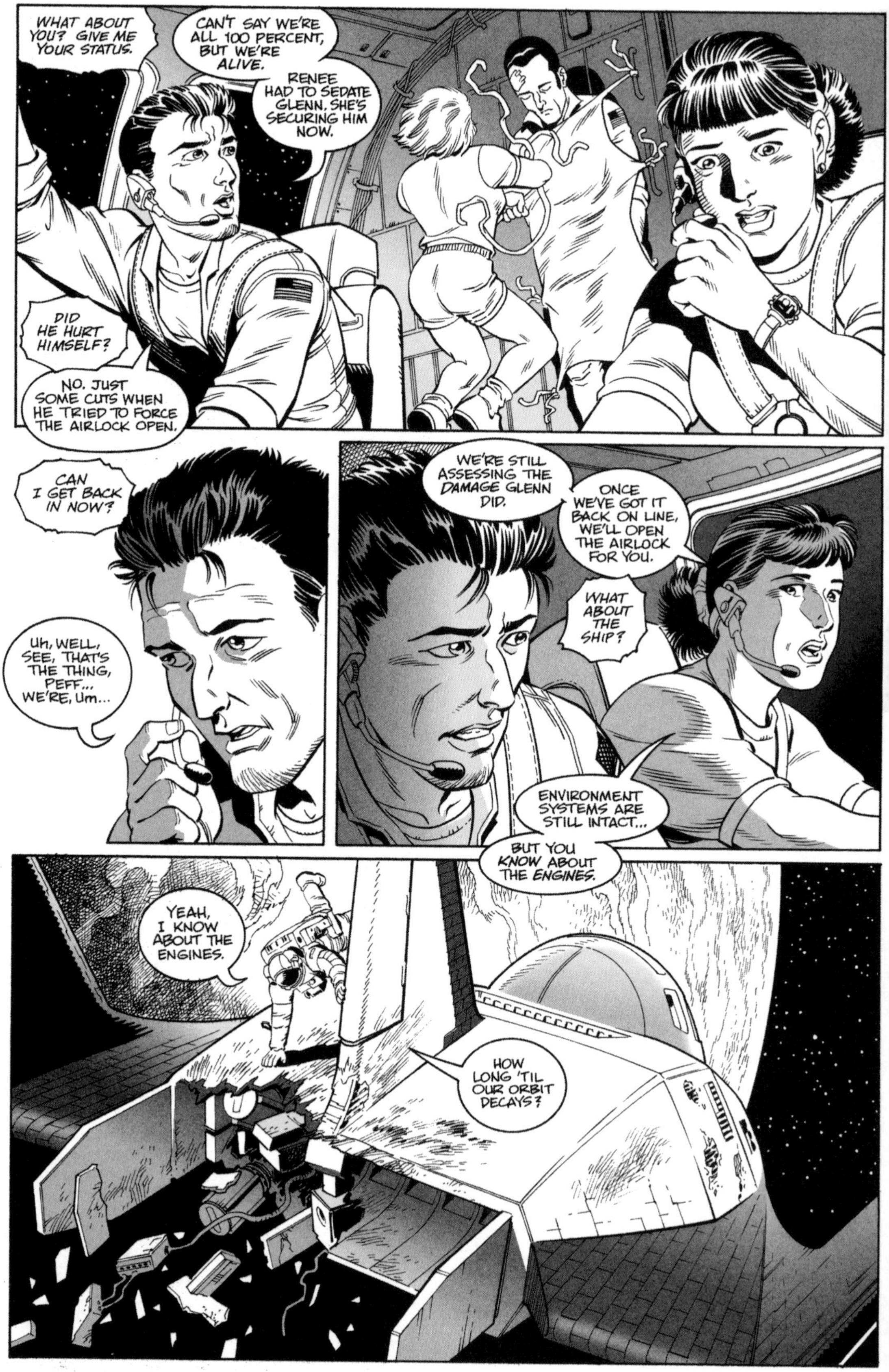
WHAT ABOUT YOU? GIVE ME YOUR STATUS.
CAN'T SAY WE'RE ALL 100 PERCENT, BUT WE'RE ALIVE.
RENEE HAD TO SEDATE GLENN. SHE'S SECURING HIM NOW.
DID HE HURT HIMSELF?
NO. JUST SOME CUTS WHEN HE TRIED TO FORCE THE AIRLOCK OPEN.
CAN I GET BACK IN NOW?
Uh, WELL, SEE, THAT'S THE THING, PEFF... WE'RE, Um...
WE'RE STILL ASSESSING THE DAMAGE GLENN DID.
ONCE WE'VE GOT IT BACK ON LINE, WE'LL OPEN THE AIRLOCK FOR YOU.
WHAT ABOUT THE SHIP?
ENVIRONMENT SYSTEMS ARE STILL INTACT...
BUT YOU KNOW ABOUT THE ENGINES.
YEAH, I KNOW ABOUT THE ENGINES.
HOW LONG 'TIL OUR ORBIT DECAYS?

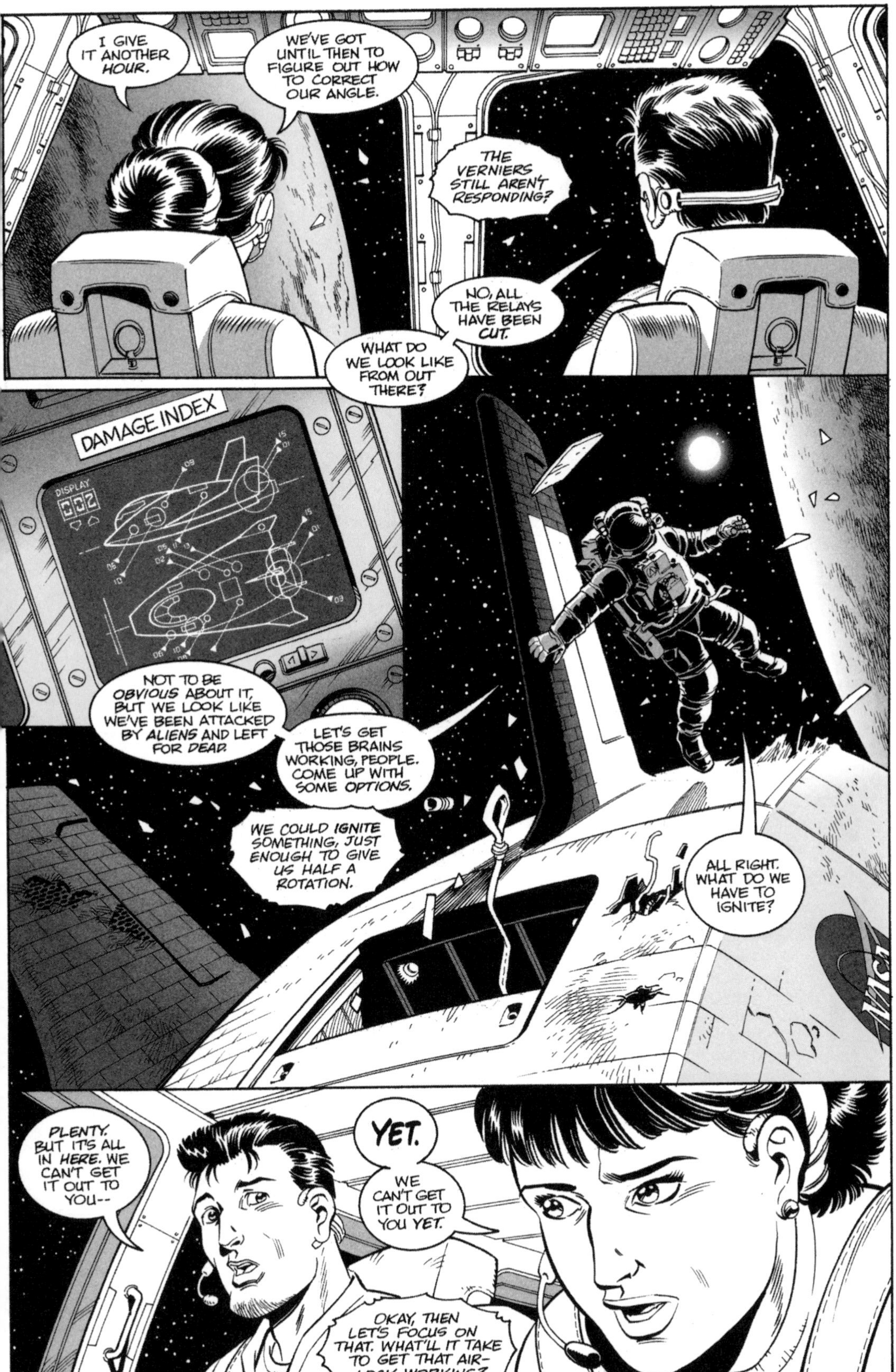

I GIVE IT ANOTHER HOUR.
WE'VE GOT UNTIL THEN TO FIGURE OUT HOW TO CORRECT OUR ANGLE.
THE VERNIERS STILL AREN'T RESPONDING?
NO, ALL THE RELAYS HAVE BEEN CUT.
WHAT DO WE LOOK LIKE FROM OUT THERE?
DAMAGE INDEX
DISPLAY
NOT TO BE OBVIOUS ABOUT IT, BUT WE LOOK LIKE WE'VE BEEN ATTACKED BY ALIENS AND LEFT FOR DEAD.
LET'S GET THOSE BRAINS WORKING, PEOPLE. COME UP WITH SOME OPTIONS.
WE COULD IGNITE SOMETHING, JUST ENOUGH TO GIVE US HALF A ROTATION.
ALL RIGHT. WHAT DO WE HAVE TO IGNITE?
PLENTY. BUT IT'S ALL IN HERE. WE CAN'T GET IT OUT TO YOU--
YET.
WE CAN'T GET IT OUT TO YOU YET.
OKAY, THEN LET'S FOCUS ON THAT. WHAT'LL IT TAKE TO GET THAT AIR-LOCK WORKING?

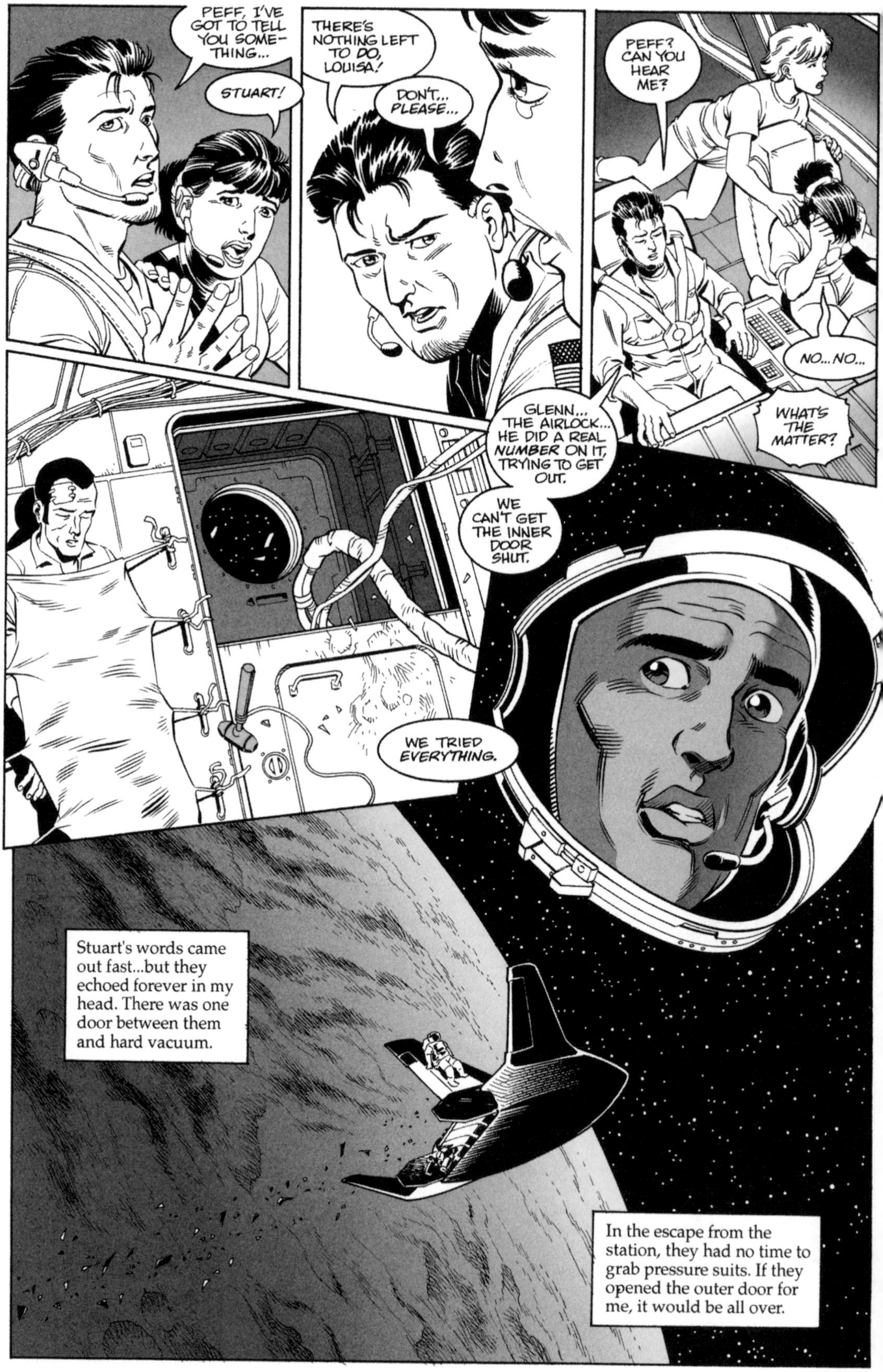
PEFF, I'VE GOT TO TELL YOU SOME-THING...
STUART!
THERE'S NOTHING LEFT TO DO, LOUISA!
DON'T... PLEASE...
PEFF? CAN YOU HEAR ME?
NO... NO...
WHAT'S THE MATTER?
GLENN... THE AIRLOCK... HE DID A REAL NUMBER ON IT, TRYING TO GET OUT.
WE CAN'T GET THE INNER DOOR SHUT.
WE TRIED EVERYTHING.
Stuart's words came out fast...but they echoed forever in my head. There was one door between them and hard vacuum.
In the escape from the station, they had no time to grab pressure suits. If they opened the outer door for me, it would be all over.

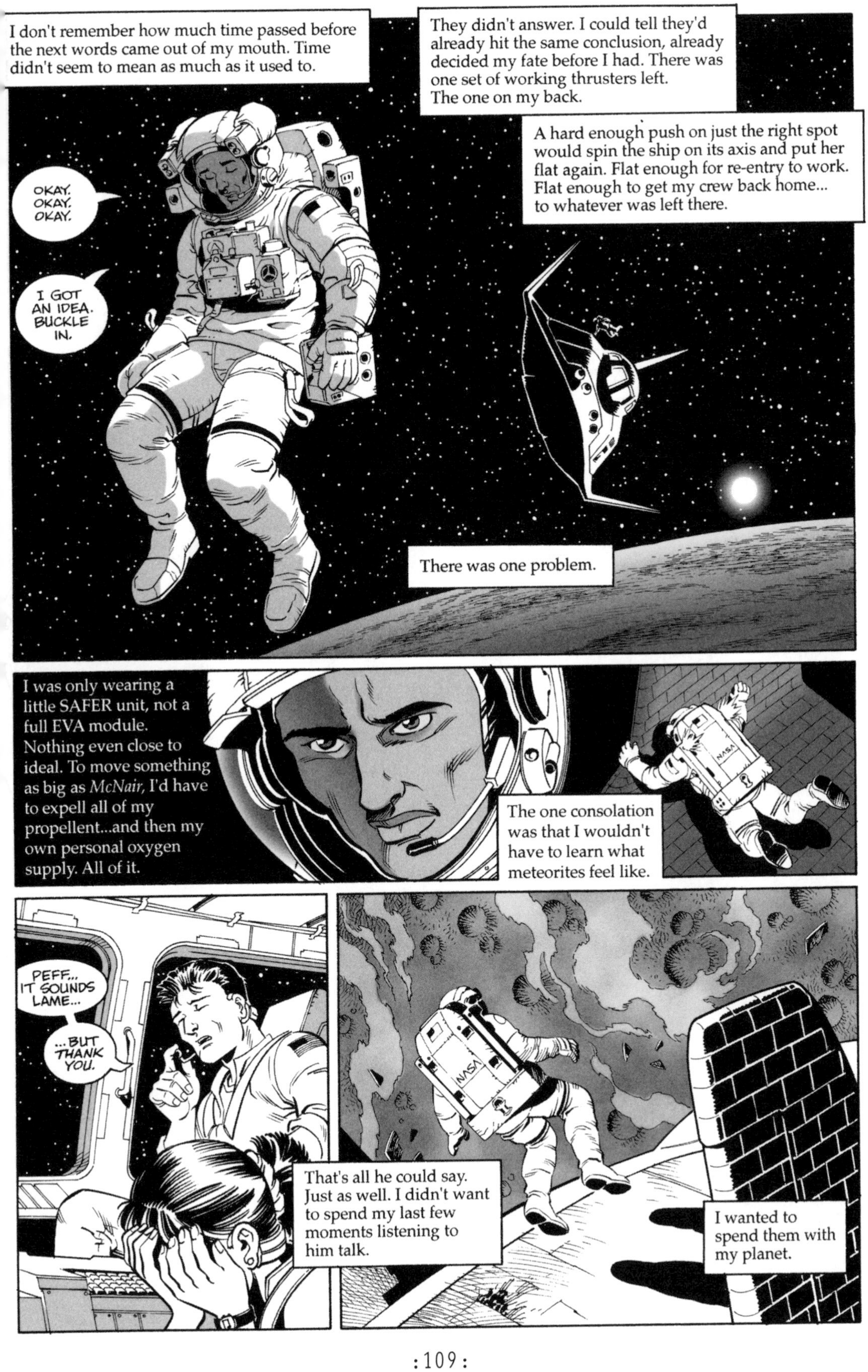

I don't remember how much time passed before the next words came out of my mouth. Time didn't seem to mean as much as it used to.
OKAY. OKAY. OKAY.
I GOT AN IDEA. BUCKLE IN.
They didn't answer. I could tell they'd already hit the same conclusion, already decided my fate before I had. There was one set of working thrusters left. The one on my back.
A hard enough push on just the right spot would spin the ship on its axis and put her flat again. Flat enough for re-entry to work. Flat enough to get my crew back home... to whatever was left there.
There was one problem.
I was only wearing a little SAFER unit, not a full EVA module. Nothing even close to ideal. To move something as big as *McNair,* I'd have to expell all of my propellent...and then my own personal oxygen supply. All of it.
The one consolation was that I wouldn't have to learn what meteorites feel like.
NASA
PEFF... IT SOUNDS LAME...
...BUT THANK YOU.
That's all he could say. Just as well. I didn't want to spend my last few moments listening to him talk.
NASA
I wanted to spend them with my planet.

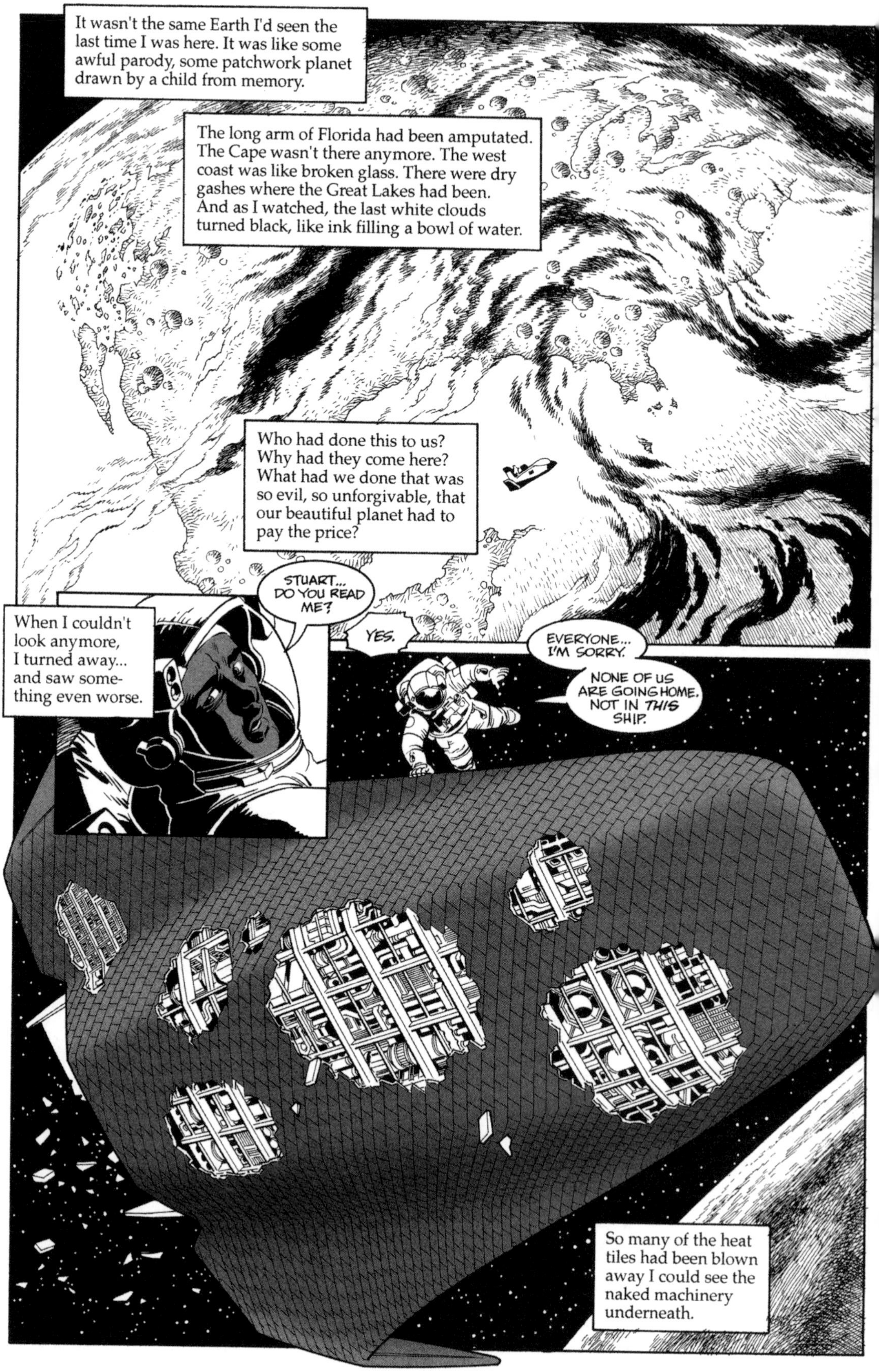
It wasn't the same Earth I'd seen the last time I was here. It was like some awful parody, some patchwork planet drawn by a child from memory.
The long arm of Florida had been amputated. The Cape wasn't there anymore. The west coast was like broken glass. There were dry gashes where the Great Lakes had been. And as I watched, the last white clouds turned black, like ink filling a bowl of water.
Who had done this to us? Why had they come here? What had we done that was so evil, so unforgivable, that our beautiful planet had to pay the price?
When I couldn't look anymore, I turned away... and saw something even worse.
STUART... DO YOU READ ME?
YES.
EVERYONE... I'M SORRY.
NONE OF US ARE GOING HOME. NOT IN THIS SHIP.
So many of the heat tiles had been blown away I could see the naked machinery underneath.

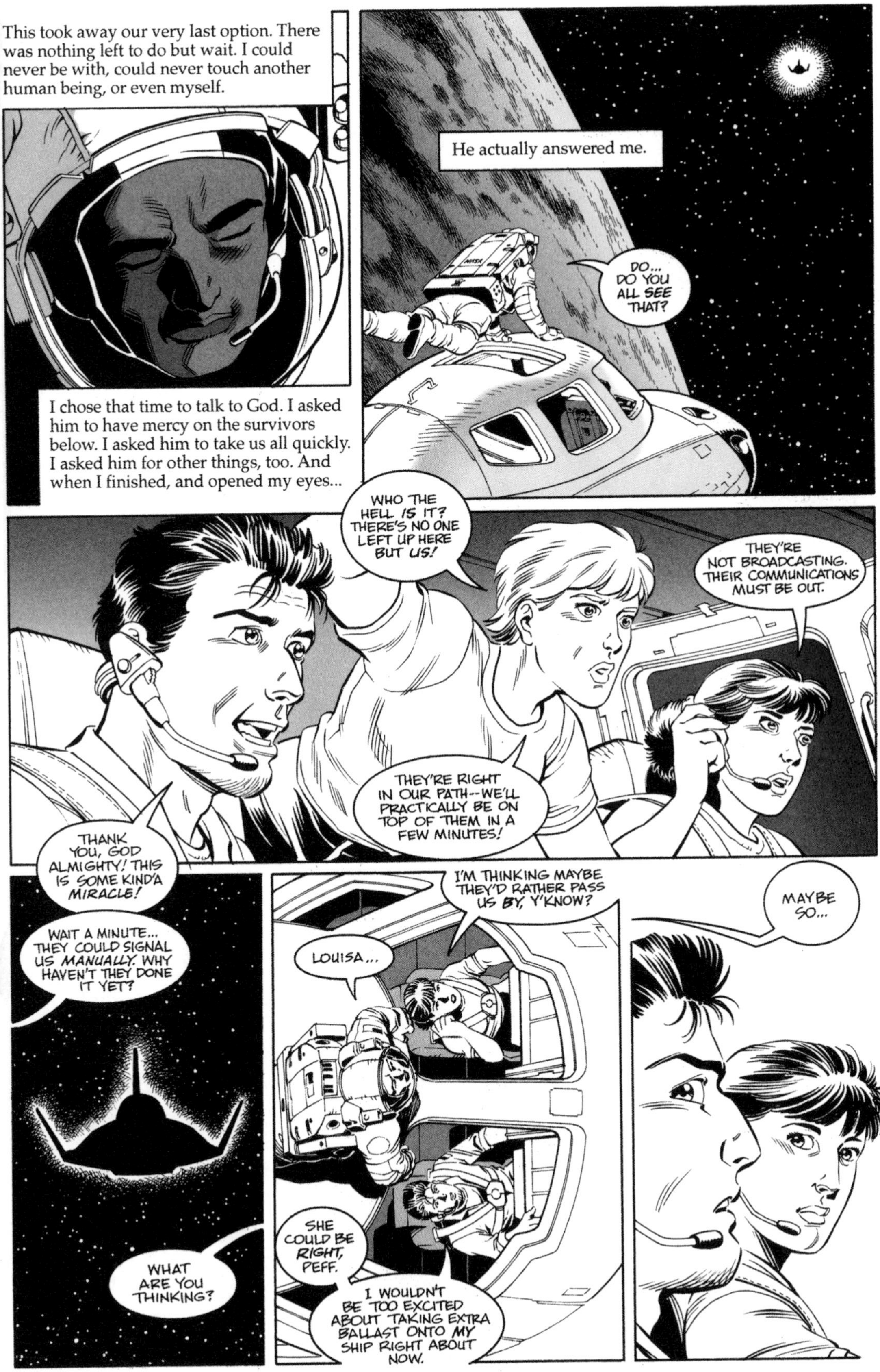

This took away our very last option. There was nothing left to do but wait. I could never be with, could never touch another human being, or even myself.
I chose that time to talk to God. I asked him to have mercy on the survivors below. I asked him to take us all quickly. I asked him for other things, too. And when I finished, and opened my eyes...
He actually answered me.
DO... DO YOU ALL SEE THAT?
THANK YOU, GOD ALMIGHTY! THIS IS SOME KIND'A MIRACLE!
WHO THE HELL IS IT? THERE'S NO ONE LEFT UP HERE BUT US!
THEY'RE NOT BROADCASTING. THEIR COMMUNICATIONS MUST BE OUT.
THEY'RE RIGHT IN OUR PATH--WE'LL PRACTICALLY BE ON TOP OF THEM IN A FEW MINUTES!
WAIT A MINUTE... THEY COULD SIGNAL US MANUALLY. WHY HAVEN'T THEY DONE IT YET?
WHAT ARE YOU THINKING?
LOUISA...
I'M THINKING MAYBE THEY'D RATHER PASS US BY, Y'KNOW?
SHE COULD BE RIGHT, PEFF.
I WOULDN'T BE TOO EXCITED ABOUT TAKING EXTRA BALLAST ONTO MY SHIP RIGHT ABOUT NOW.
MAYBE SO...

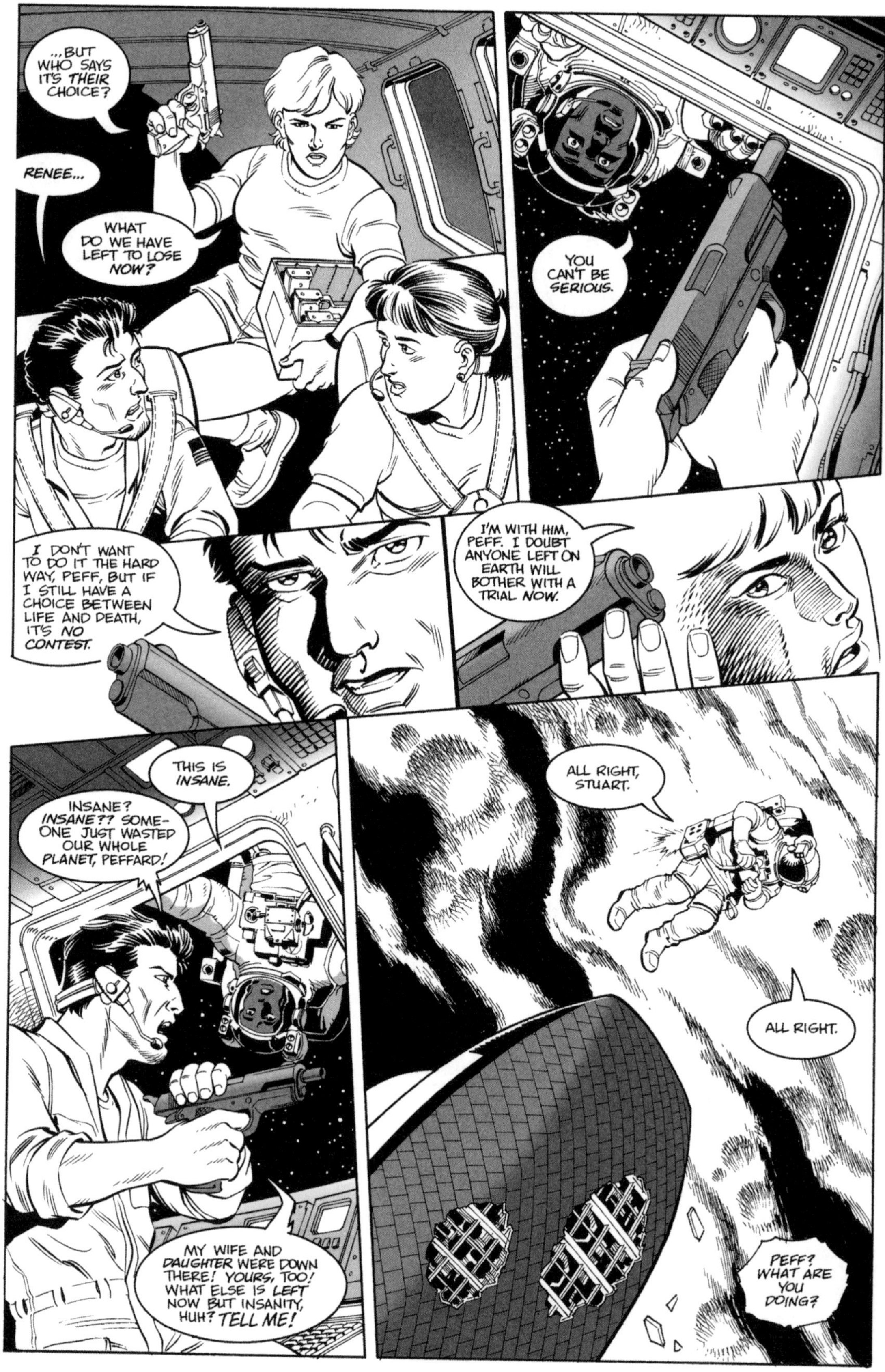

...BUT WHO SAYS IT'S THEIR CHOICE?
RENEE...
WHAT DO WE HAVE LEFT TO LOSE NOW?
YOU CAN'T BE SERIOUS.
I DON'T WANT TO DO IT THE HARD WAY, PEFF, BUT IF I STILL HAVE A CHOICE BETWEEN LIFE AND DEATH, IT'S NO CONTEST.
I'M WITH HIM, PEFF. I DOUBT ANYONE LEFT ON EARTH WILL BOTHER WITH A TRIAL NOW.
THIS IS INSANE.
INSANE? INSANE?? SOMEONE JUST WASTED OUR WHOLE PLANET, PEFFARD!
MY WIFE AND DAUGHTER WERE DOWN THERE! YOURS, TOO! WHAT ELSE IS LEFT NOW BUT INSANITY, HUH? TELL ME!
ALL RIGHT, STUART.
ALL RIGHT.
PEFF? WHAT ARE YOU DOING?

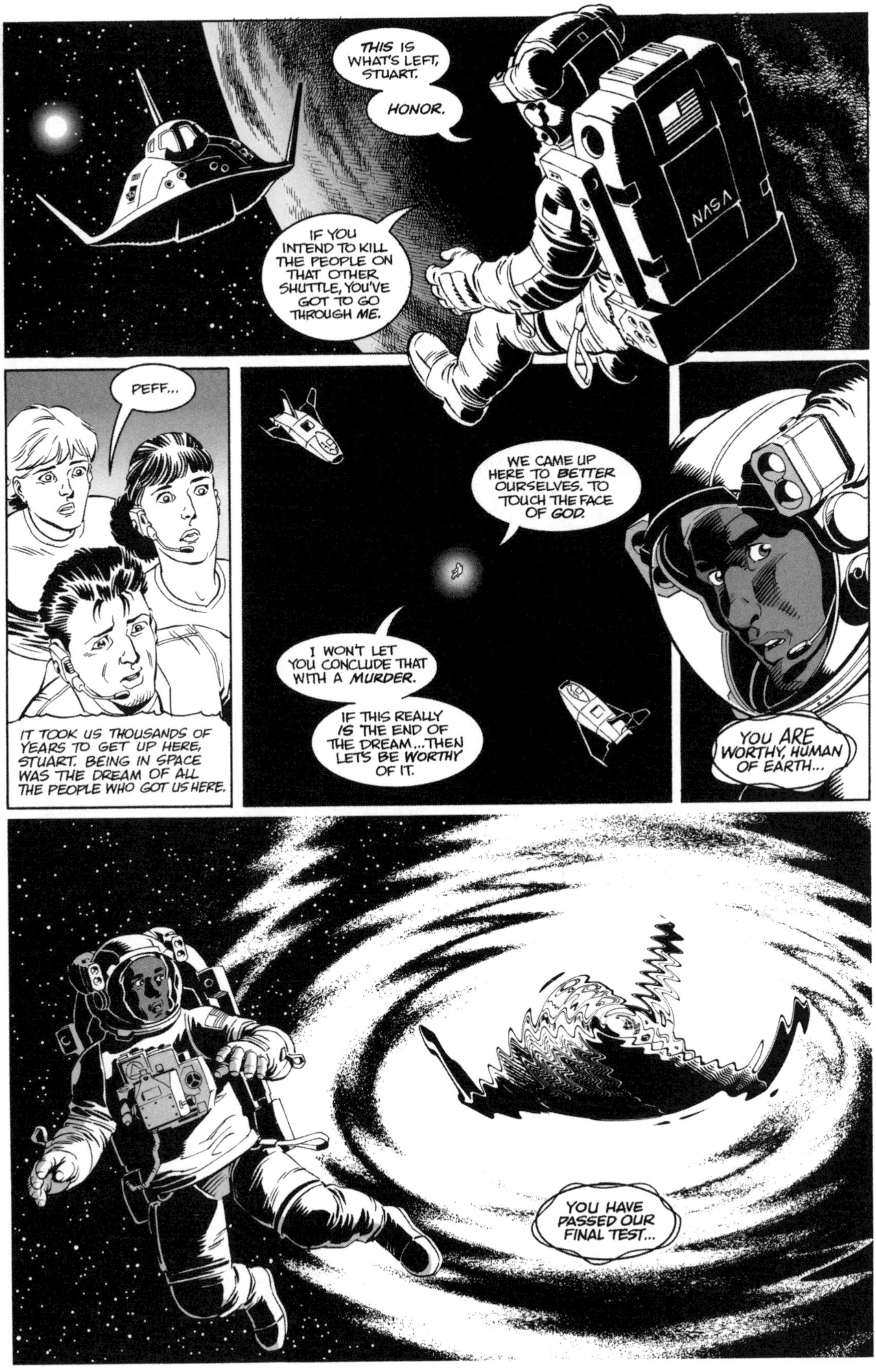
THIS IS WHAT'S LEFT, STUART.
HONOR.
IF YOU INTEND TO KILL THE PEOPLE ON THAT OTHER SHUTTLE, YOU'VE GOT TO GO THROUGH ME.
NASA
PEFF...
IT TOOK US THOUSANDS OF YEARS TO GET UP HERE, STUART. BEING IN SPACE WAS THE DREAM OF ALL THE PEOPLE WHO GOT US HERE.
WE CAME UP HERE TO BETTER OURSELVES. TO TOUCH THE FACE OF GOD.
I WON'T LET YOU CONCLUDE THAT WITH A MURDER.
IF THIS REALLY IS THE END OF THE DREAM...THEN LET'S BE WORTHY OF IT.
YOU ARE WORTHY, HUMAN OF EARTH...
YOU HAVE PASSED OUR FINAL TEST...

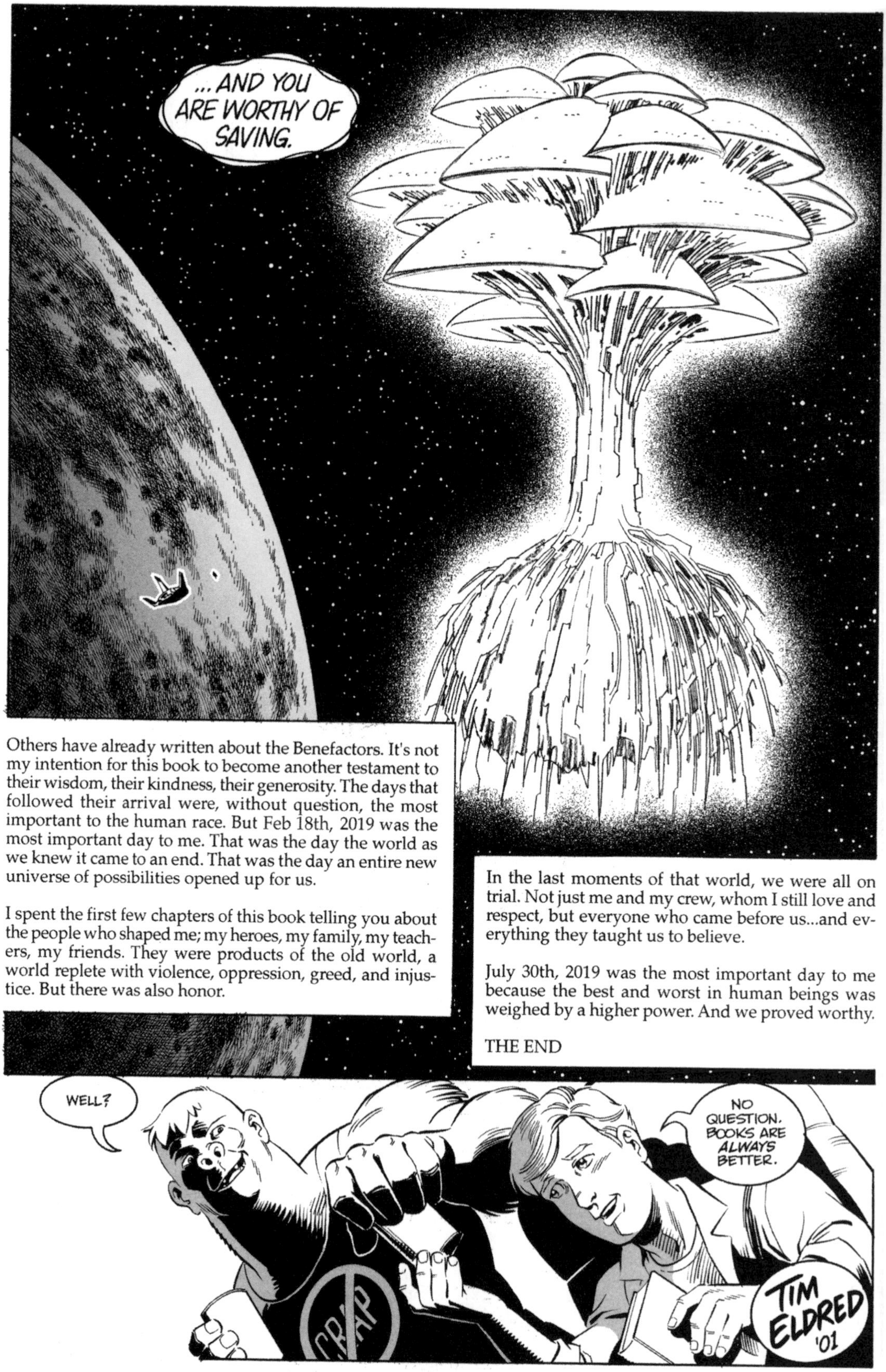
...AND YOU ARE WORTHY OF SAVING.
Others have already written about the Benefactors. It's not my intention for this book to become another testament to their wisdom, their kindness, their generosity. The days that followed their arrival were, without question, the most important to the human race. But Feb 18th, 2019 was the most important day to me. That was the day the world as we knew it came to an end. That was the day an entire new universe of possibilities opened up for us.
I spent the first few chapters of this book telling you about the people who shaped me; my heroes, my family, my teachers, my friends. They were products of the old world, a world replete with violence, oppression, greed, and injustice. But there was also honor.
In the last moments of that world, we were all on trial. Not just me and my crew, whom I still love and respect, but everyone who came before us...and everything they taught us to believe.
July 30th, 2019 was the most important day to me because the best and worst in human beings was weighed by a higher power. And we proved worthy.
THE END
WELL?
NO QUESTION. BOOKS ARE ALWAYS BETTER.
C.R.A.P.
TIM ELDRED '01

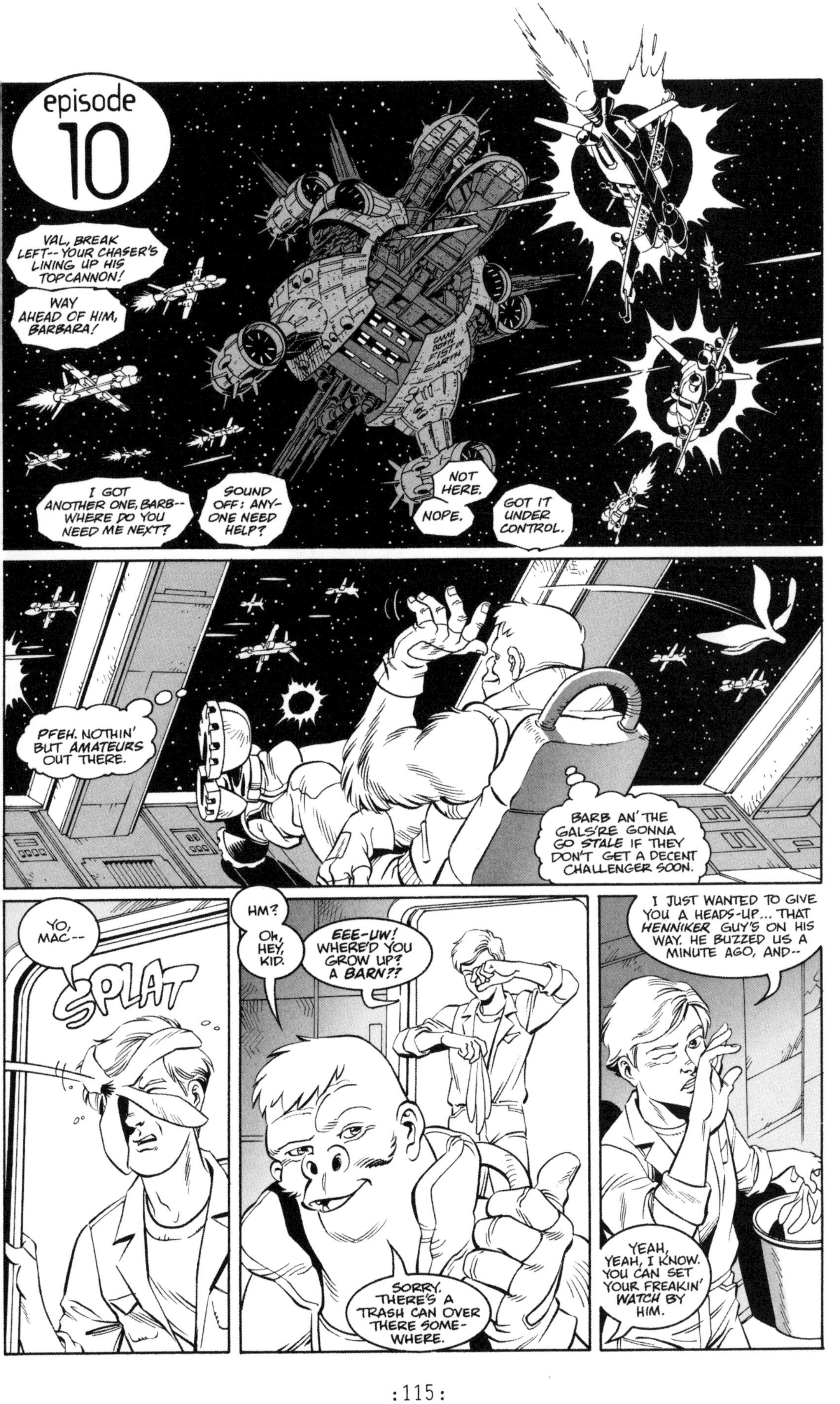
episode 10
VAL, BREAK LEFT-- YOUR CHASER'S LINING UP HIS TOPCANNON!
WAY AHEAD OF HIM, BARBARA!
I GOT ANOTHER ONE, BARB-- WHERE DO YOU NEED ME NEXT?
SOUND OFF: ANY-ONE NEED HELP?
NOT HERE.
NOPE.
GOT IT UNDER CONTROL.
PFEH. NOTHIN' BUT AMATEURS OUT THERE.
BARB AN' THE GALS'RE GONNA GO STALE IF THEY DON'T GET A DECENT CHALLENGER SOON.
YO, MAC--
SPLAT
HM?
OH, HEY, KID.
EEE-UW! WHERE'D YOU GROW UP? A BARN??
SORRY. THERE'S A TRASH CAN OVER THERE SOME-WHERE.
I JUST WANTED TO GIVE YOU A HEADS-UP... THAT HENNIKER GUY'S ON HIS WAY. HE BUZZED US A MINUTE AGO, AND--
YEAH, YEAH, I KNOW. YOU CAN SET YOUR FREAKIN' WATCH BY HIM.

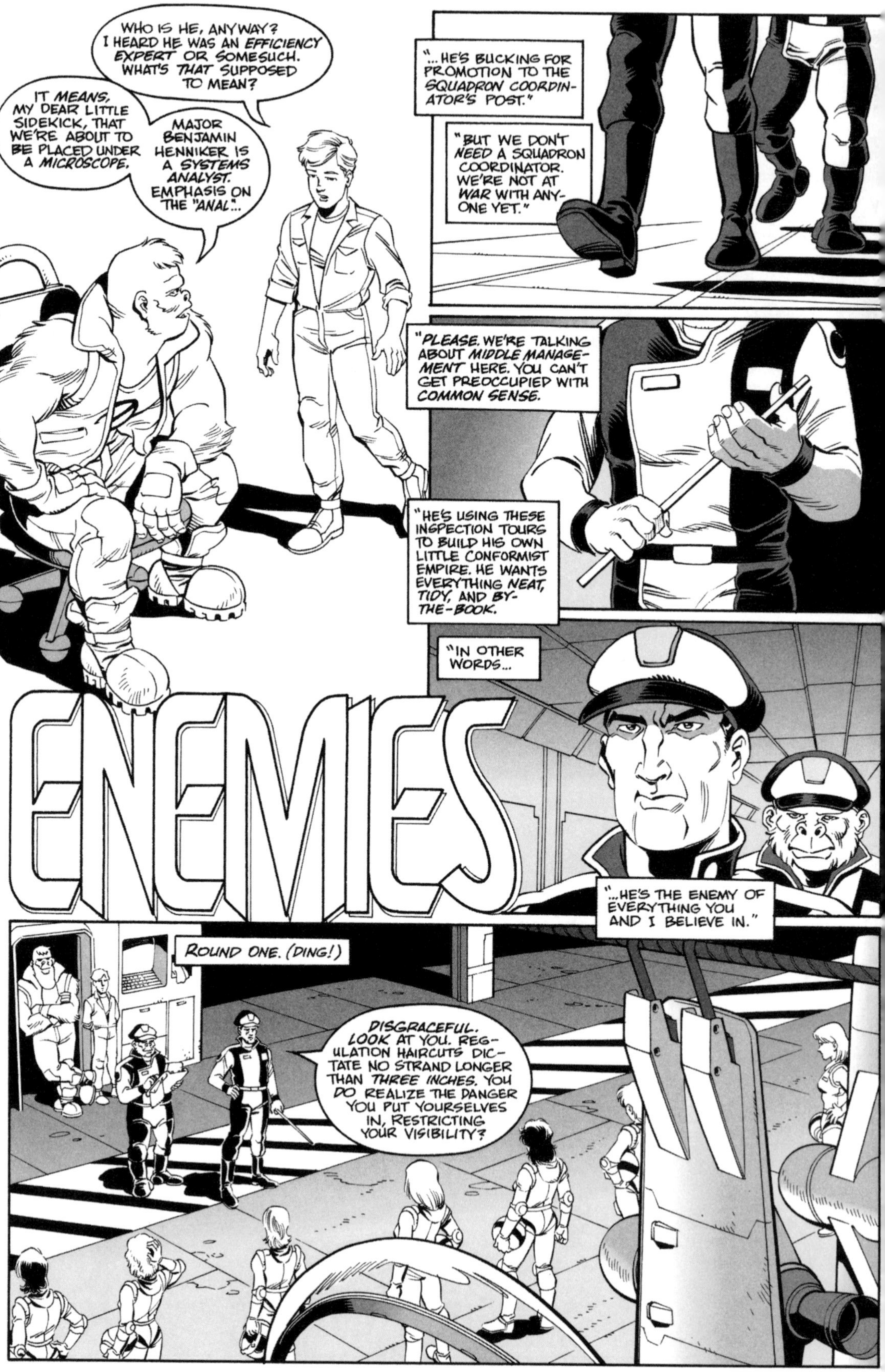

WHO IS HE, ANYWAY? I HEARD HE WAS AN EFFICIENCY EXPERT OR SOMESUCH. WHAT'S THAT SUPPOSED TO MEAN?
IT MEANS, MY DEAR LITTLE SIDEKICK, THAT WE'RE ABOUT TO BE PLACED UNDER A MICROSCOPE.
MAJOR BENJAMIN HENNIKER IS A SYSTEMS ANALYST. EMPHASIS ON THE "ANAL"...
"...HE'S BUCKING FOR PROMOTION TO THE SQUADRON COORDINATOR'S POST."
"BUT WE DON'T NEED A SQUADRON COORDINATOR. WE'RE NOT AT WAR WITH ANYONE YET."
"PLEASE. WE'RE TALKING ABOUT MIDDLE MANAGEMENT HERE. YOU CAN'T GET PREOCCUPIED WITH COMMON SENSE.
"HE'S USING THESE INSPECTION TOURS TO BUILD HIS OWN LITTLE CONFORMIST EMPIRE. HE WANTS EVERYTHING NEAT, TIDY, AND BY-THE-BOOK.
"IN OTHER WORDS...
ENEMIES
"...HE'S THE ENEMY OF EVERYTHING YOU AND I BELIEVE IN."
ROUND ONE. (DING!)
DISGRACEFUL. LOOK AT YOU. REGULATION HAIRCUTS DICTATE NO STRAND LONGER THAN THREE INCHES. YOU DO REALIZE THE DANGER YOU PUT YOURSELVES IN, RESTRICTING YOUR VISIBILITY?

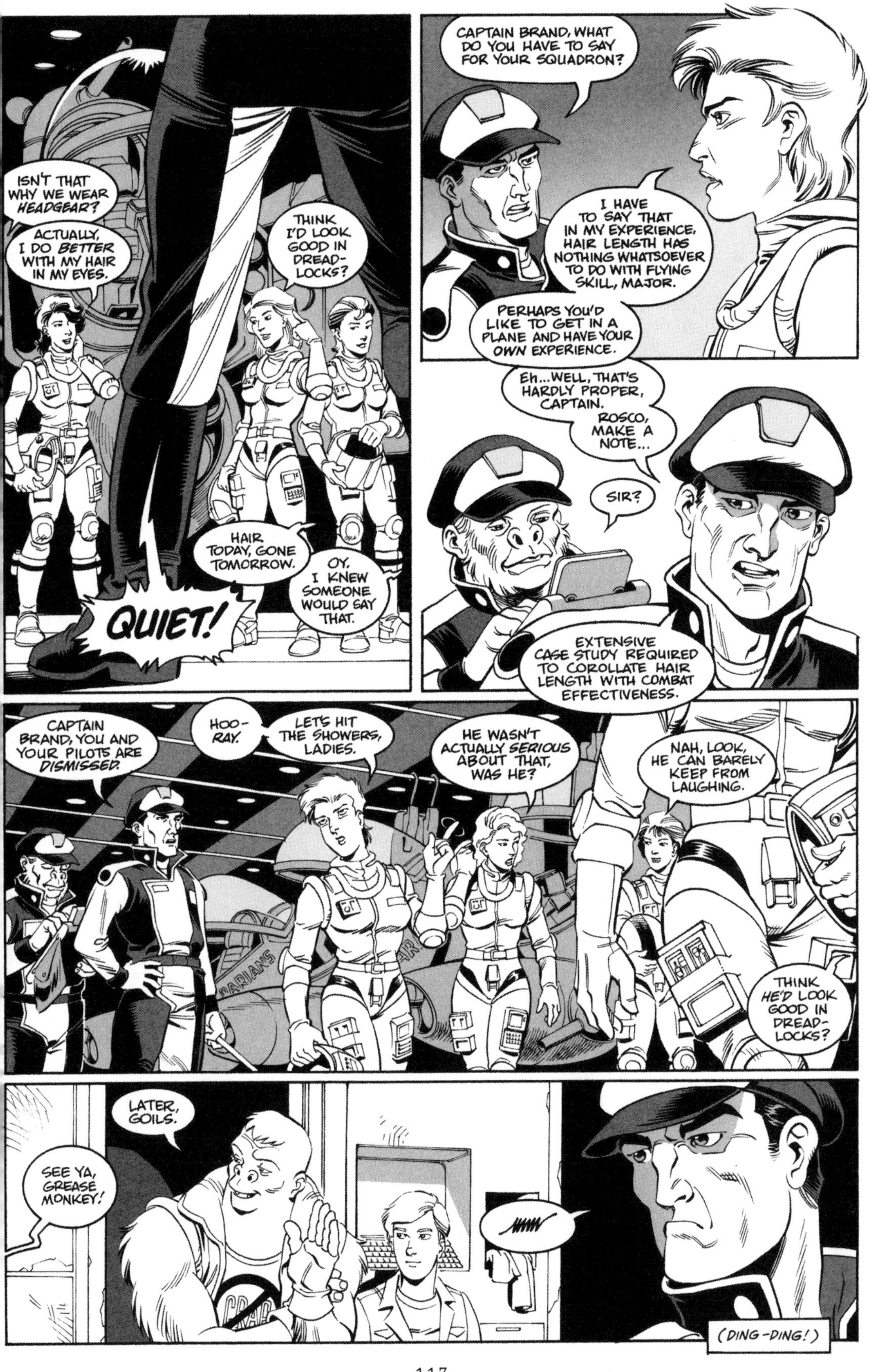
ISN'T THAT WHY WE WEAR HEADGEAR?
ACTUALLY, I DO BETTER WITH MY HAIR IN MY EYES.
THINK I'D LOOK GOOD IN DREAD-LOCKS?
HAIR TODAY, GONE TOMORROW.
OY, I KNEW SOMEONE WOULD SAY THAT.
QUIET!
CAPTAIN BRAND, WHAT DO YOU HAVE TO SAY FOR YOUR SQUADRON?
I HAVE TO SAY THAT IN MY EXPERIENCE, HAIR LENGTH HAS NOTHING WHATSOEVER TO DO WITH FLYING SKILL, MAJOR.
PERHAPS YOU'D LIKE TO GET IN A PLANE AND HAVE YOUR OWN EXPERIENCE.
Eh...WELL, THAT'S HARDLY PROPER, CAPTAIN.
ROSCO, MAKE A NOTE...
SIR?
EXTENSIVE CASE STUDY REQUIRED TO COROLLATE HAIR LENGTH WITH COMBAT EFFECTIVENESS.
CAPTAIN BRAND, YOU AND YOUR PILOTS ARE DISMISSED.
HOO-RAY.
LET'S HIT THE SHOWERS, LADIES.
HE WASN'T ACTUALLY SERIOUS ABOUT THAT, WAS HE?
NAH, LOOK, HE CAN BARELY KEEP FROM LAUGHING.
THINK HE'D LOOK GOOD IN DREAD-LOCKS?
LATER, GOILS.
SEE YA, GREASE MONKEY!
(DING-DING!)

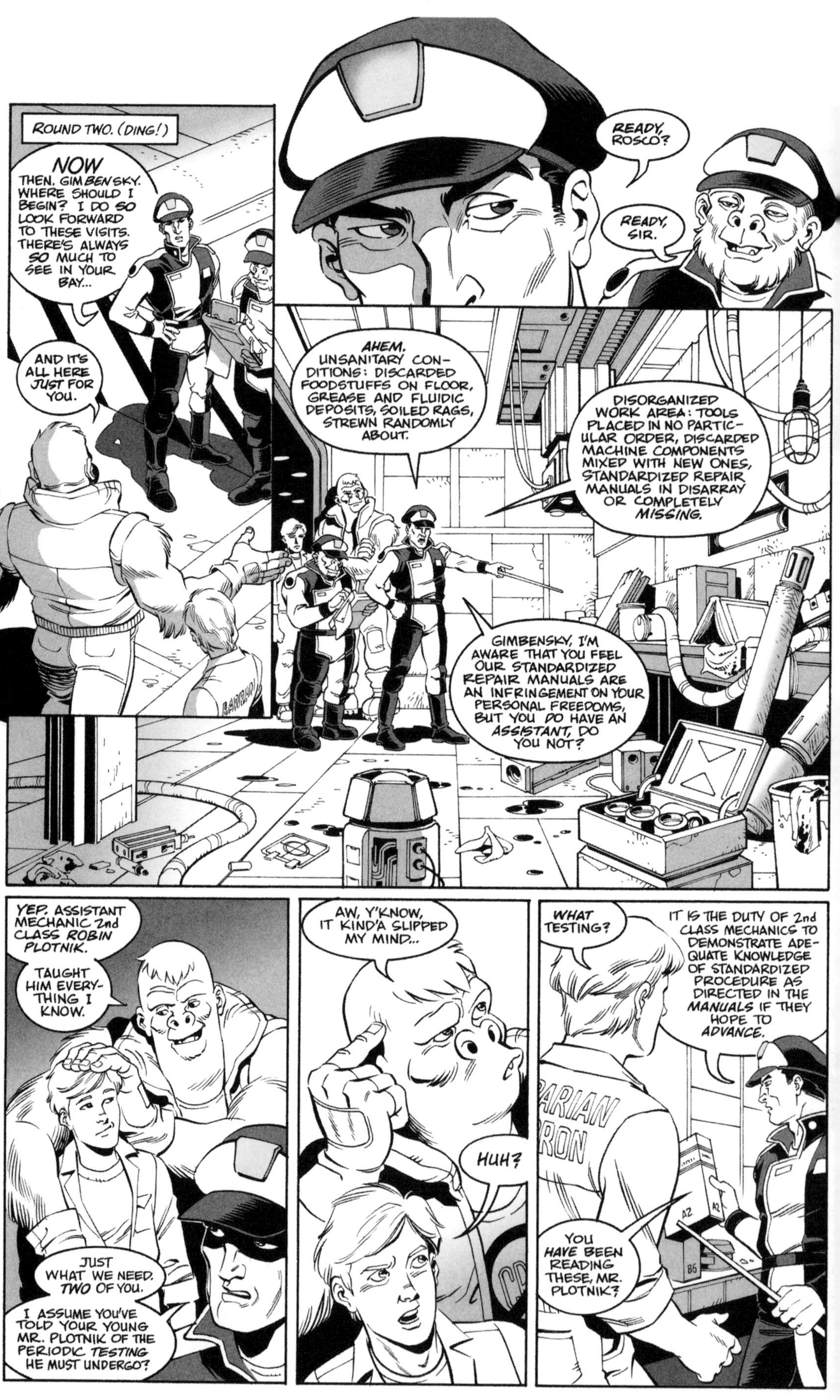

ROUND TWO. (DING!)
NOW THEN. GIMBENSKY. WHERE SHOULD I BEGIN? I DO SO LOOK FORWARD TO THESE VISITS. THERE'S ALWAYS SO MUCH TO SEE IN YOUR BAY...
AND IT'S ALL HERE JUST FOR YOU.
READY, ROSCO?
READY, SIR.
AHEM. UNSANITARY CONDITIONS: DISCARDED FOODSTUFFS ON FLOOR, GREASE AND FLUIDIC DEPOSITS, SOILED RAGS, STREWN RANDOMLY ABOUT.
DISORGANIZED WORK AREA: TOOLS PLACED IN NO PARTICULAR ORDER, DISCARDED MACHINE COMPONENTS MIXED WITH NEW ONES, STANDARDIZED REPAIR MANUALS IN DISARRAY OR COMPLETELY MISSING.
GIMBENSKY, I'M AWARE THAT YOU FEEL OUR STANDARDIZED REPAIR MANUALS ARE AN INFRINGEMENT ON YOUR PERSONAL FREEDOMS, BUT YOU DO HAVE AN ASSISTANT, DO YOU NOT?
YEP. ASSISTANT MECHANIC 2nd CLASS ROBIN PLOTNIK.
TAUGHT HIM EVERYTHING I KNOW.
JUST WHAT WE NEED. TWO OF YOU.
I ASSUME YOU'VE TOLD YOUR YOUNG MR. PLOTNIK OF THE PERIODIC TESTING HE MUST UNDERGO?
AW, Y'KNOW, IT KIND'A SLIPPED MY MIND...
HUH?
WHAT TESTING?
IT IS THE DUTY OF 2nd CLASS MECHANICS TO DEMONSTRATE ADEQUATE KNOWLEDGE OF STANDARDIZED PROCEDURE AS DIRECTED IN THE MANUALS IF THEY HOPE TO ADVANCE.
YOU HAVE BEEN READING THESE, MR. PLOTNIK?

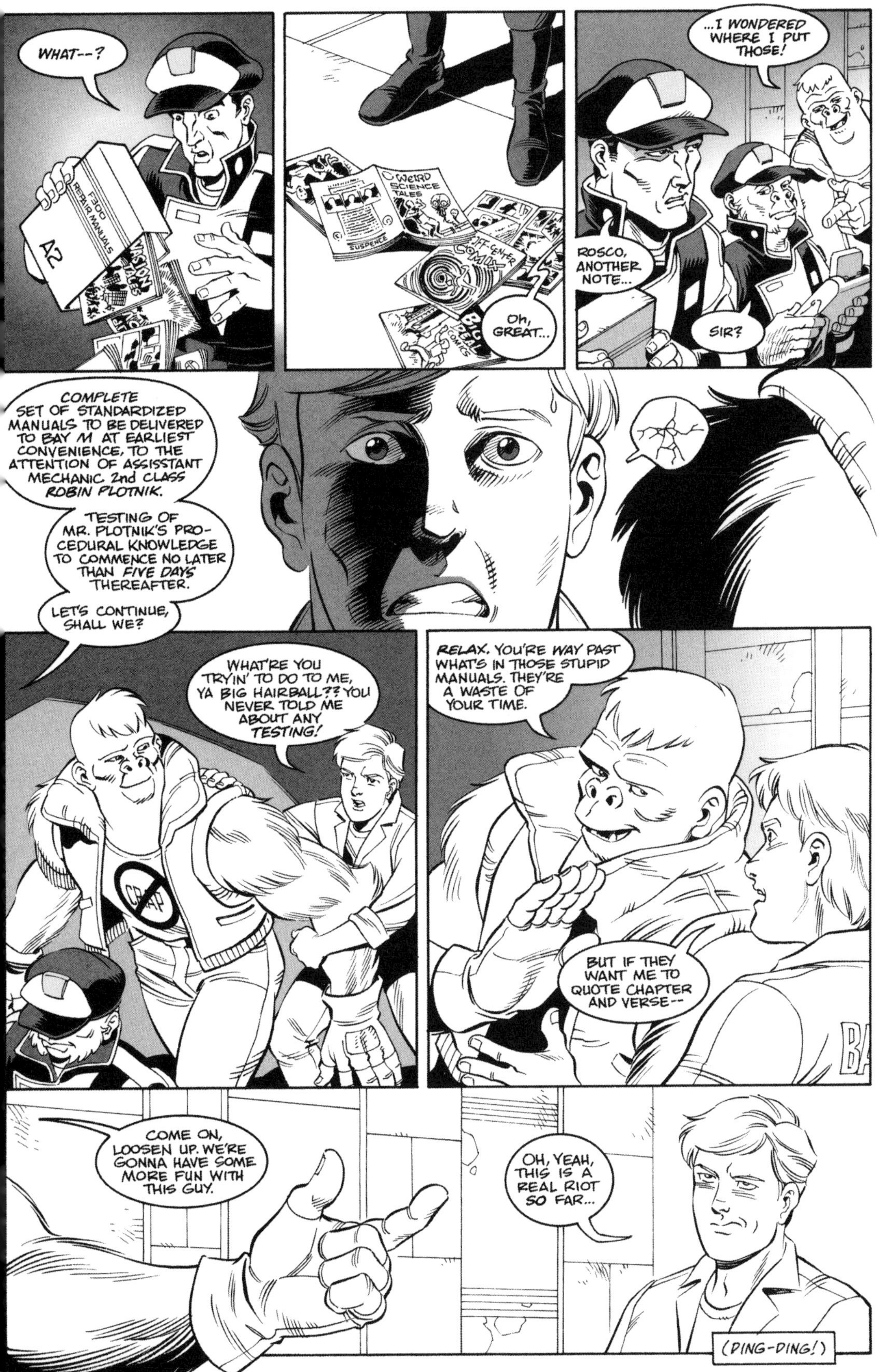
WHAT--?
F300 REPAIR MANUALS
A2
WEIRD SCIENCE TALES
SUSPENCE
OFF-CENTER COMIX
BIG REAL COMICS
OH, GREAT...
...I WONDERED WHERE I PUT THOSE!
ROSCO, ANOTHER NOTE...
SIR?
COMPLETE SET OF STANDARDIZED MANUALS TO BE DELIVERED TO BAY M AT EARLIEST CONVENIENCE, TO THE ATTENTION OF ASSISTANT MECHANIC 2nd CLASS ROBIN PLOTNIK.
TESTING OF MR. PLOTNIK'S PROCEDURAL KNOWLEDGE TO COMMENCE NO LATER THAN FIVE DAYS THEREAFTER.
LET'S CONTINUE, SHALL WE?
WHAT'RE YOU TRYIN' TO DO TO ME, YA BIG HAIRBALL?? YOU NEVER TOLD ME ABOUT ANY TESTING!
RELAX. YOU'RE WAY PAST WHAT'S IN THOSE STUPID MANUALS. THEY'RE A WASTE OF YOUR TIME.
BUT IF THEY WANT ME TO QUOTE CHAPTER AND VERSE--
COME ON, LOOSEN UP. WE'RE GONNA HAVE SOME MORE FUN WITH THIS GUY.
OH, YEAH, THIS IS A REAL RIOT SO FAR...
(DING-DING!)

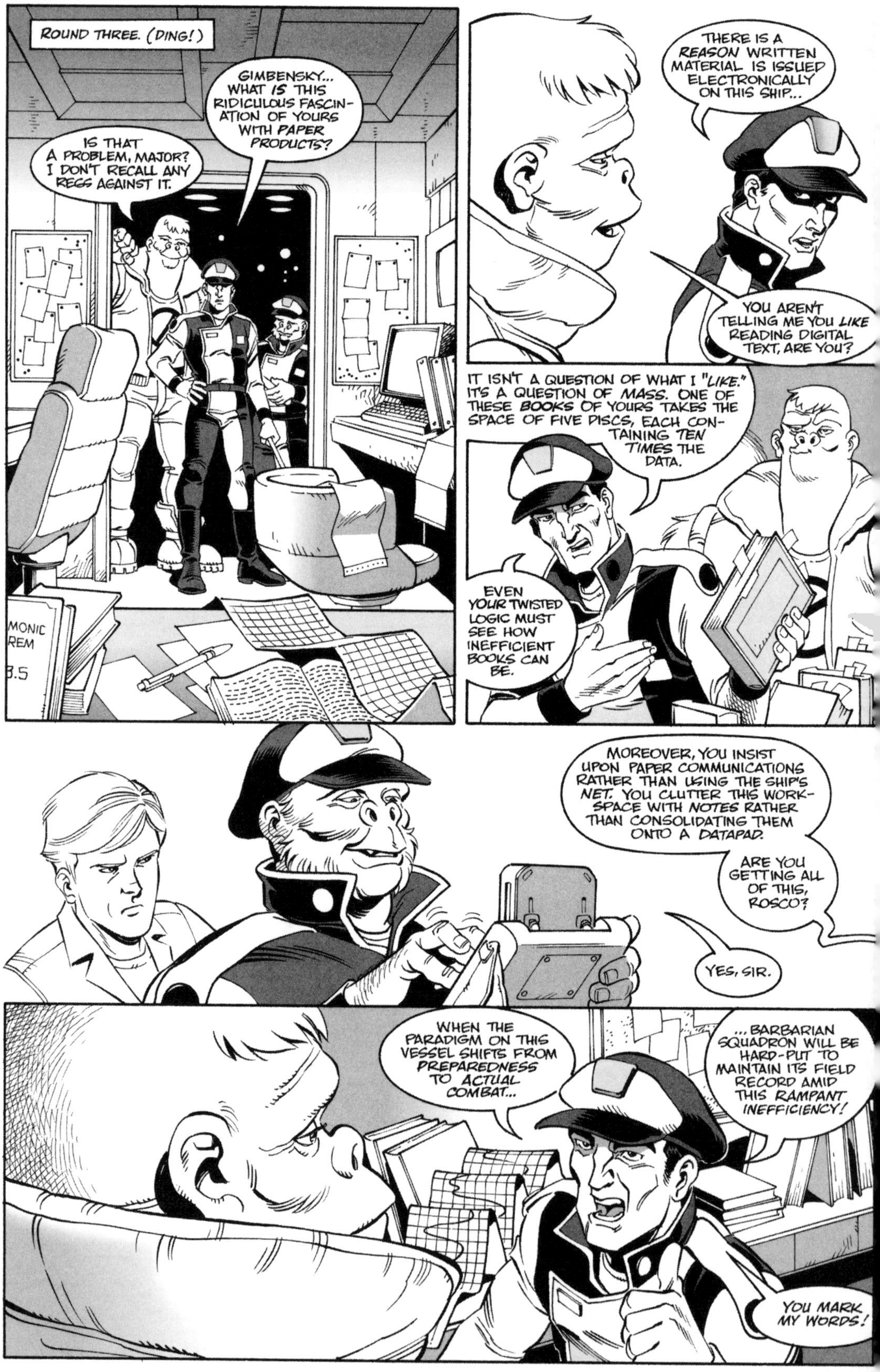
ROUND THREE. (DING!)
GIMBENSKY... WHAT IS THIS RIDICULOUS FASCINATION OF YOURS WITH PAPER PRODUCTS?
IS THAT A PROBLEM, MAJOR? I DON'T RECALL ANY REGS AGAINST IT.
MONIC REM
THERE IS A REASON WRITTEN MATERIAL IS ISSUED ELECTRONICALLY ON THIS SHIP...
YOU AREN'T TELLING ME YOU LIKE READING DIGITAL TEXT, ARE YOU?
IT ISN'T A QUESTION OF WHAT I "LIKE." IT'S A QUESTION OF MASS. ONE OF THESE BOOKS OF YOURS TAKES THE SPACE OF FIVE DISCS, EACH CONTAINING TEN TIMES THE DATA.
EVEN YOUR TWISTED LOGIC MUST SEE HOW INEFFICIENT BOOKS CAN BE.
MOREOVER, YOU INSIST UPON PAPER COMMUNICATIONS RATHER THAN USING THE SHIP'S NET. YOU CLUTTER THIS WORKSPACE WITH NOTES RATHER THAN CONSOLIDATING THEM ONTO A DATAPAD.
ARE YOU GETTING ALL OF THIS, ROSCO?
YES, SIR.
WHEN THE PARADIGM ON THIS VESSEL SHIFTS FROM PREPAREDNESS TO ACTUAL COMBAT...
...BARBARIAN SQUADRON WILL BE HARD-PUT TO MAINTAIN ITS FIELD RECORD AMID THIS RAMPANT INEFFICIENCY!
YOU MARK MY WORDS!

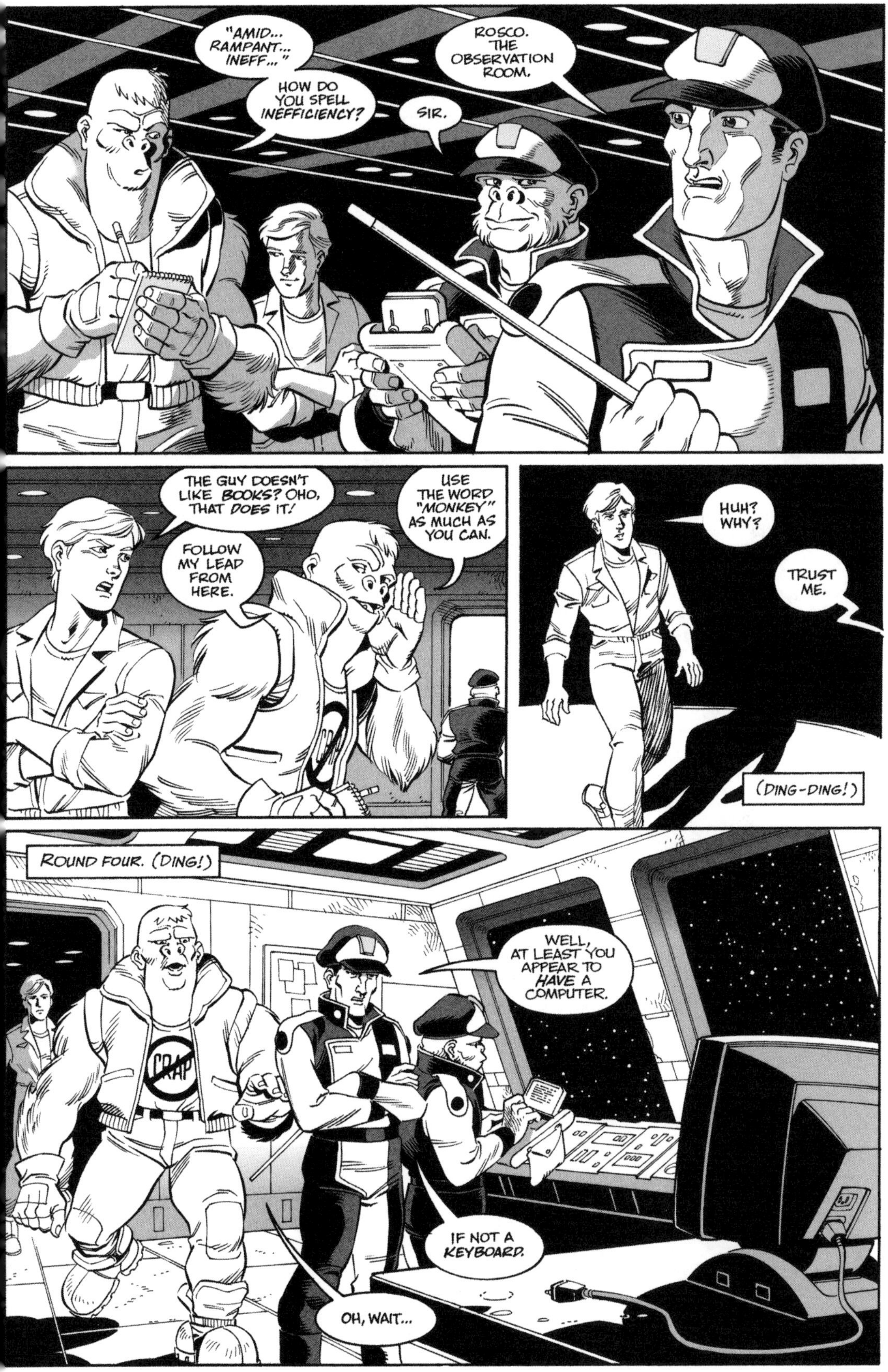
"AMID... RAMPANT... INEFF..."
HOW DO YOU SPELL INEFFICIENCY?
ROSCO. THE OBSERVATION ROOM.
SIR.
THE GUY DOESN'T LIKE BOOKS? OHO, THAT DOES IT!
FOLLOW MY LEAD FROM HERE.
USE THE WORD "MONKEY" AS MUCH AS YOU CAN.
HUH? WHY?
TRUST ME.
(DING-DING!)
ROUND FOUR. (DING!)
CRAP
WELL, AT LEAST YOU APPEAR TO HAVE A COMPUTER.
IF NOT A KEYBOARD.
OH, WAIT...

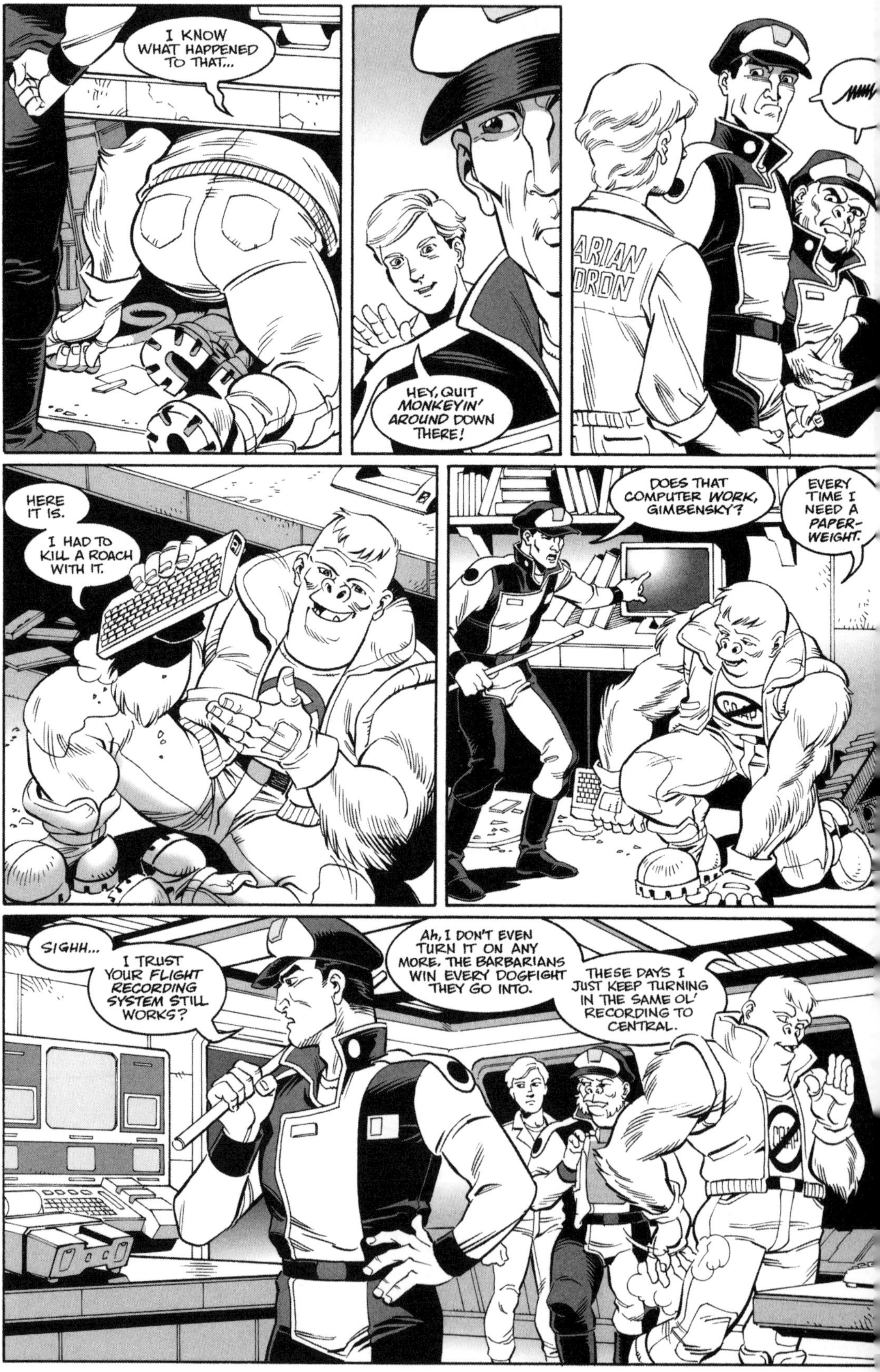
I KNOW WHAT HAPPENED TO THAT...
HEY, QUIT MONKEYIN' AROUND DOWN THERE!
ARIAN DRON
HERE IT IS.
I HAD TO KILL A ROACH WITH IT.
DOES THAT COMPUTER WORK, GIMBENSKY?
EVERY TIME I NEED A PAPER-WEIGHT.
SIGHH...
I TRUST YOUR FLIGHT RECORDING SYSTEM STILL WORKS?
Ah, I DON'T EVEN TURN IT ON ANY MORE. THE BARBARIANS WIN EVERY DOGFIGHT THEY GO INTO.
THESE DAYS I JUST KEEP TURNING IN THE SAME OL' RECORDING TO CENTRAL.

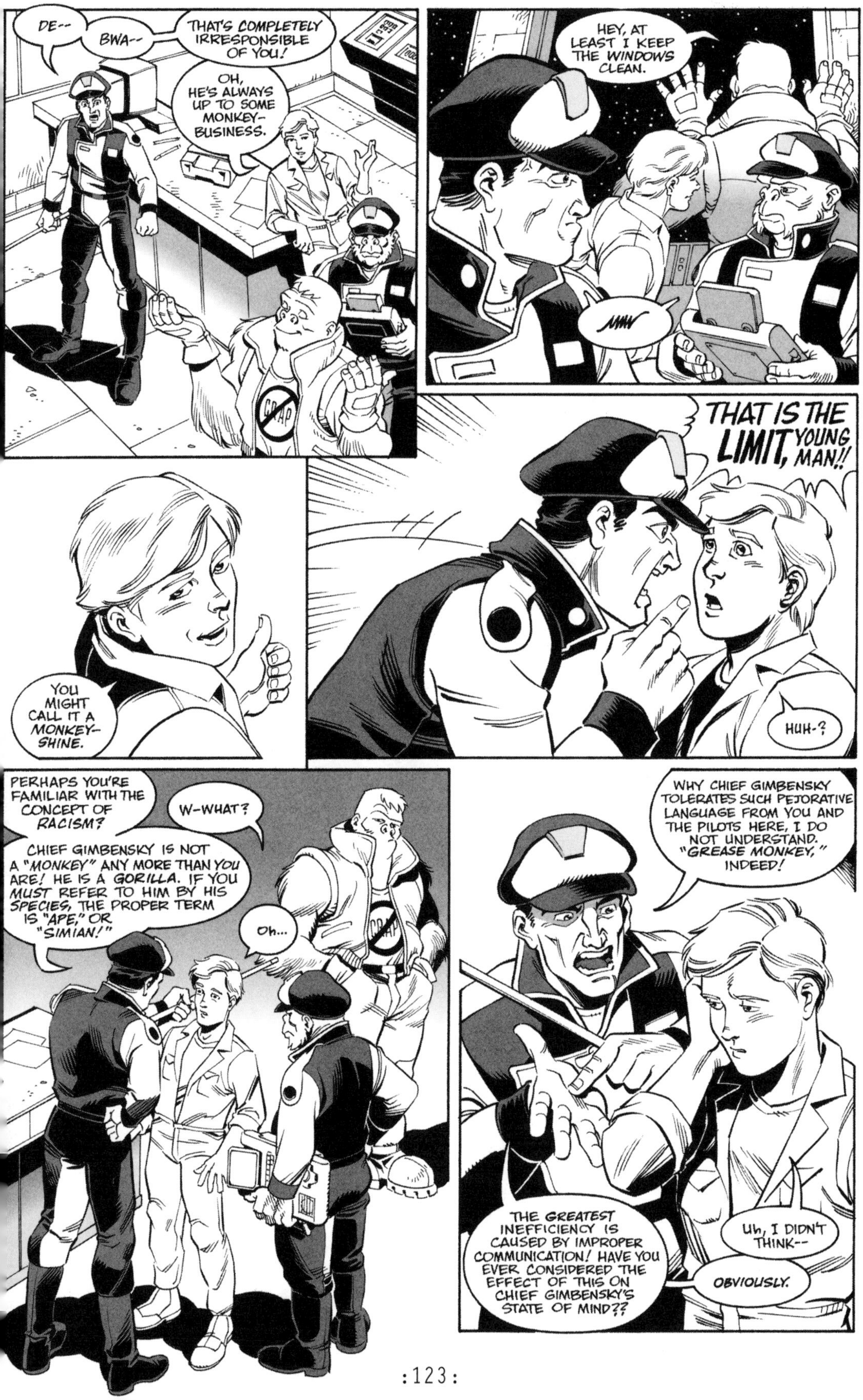
DE--
BWA--
THAT'S COMPLETELY IRRESPONSIBLE OF YOU!
OH, HE'S ALWAYS UP TO SOME MONKEY-BUSINESS.
HEY, AT LEAST I KEEP THE WINDOWS CLEAN.
MNW
YOU MIGHT CALL IT A MONKEY-SHINE.
THAT IS THE LIMIT, YOUNG MAN!!
HUH-?
PERHAPS YOU'RE FAMILIAR WITH THE CONCEPT OF RACISM?
W-WHAT?
CHIEF GIMBENSKY IS NOT A "MONKEY" ANY MORE THAN YOU ARE! HE IS A GORILLA. IF YOU MUST REFER TO HIM BY HIS SPECIES, THE PROPER TERM IS "APE," OR "SIMIAN!"
Oh...
WHY CHIEF GIMBENSKY TOLERATES SUCH PEJORATIVE LANGUAGE FROM YOU AND THE PILOTS HERE, I DO NOT UNDERSTAND. "GREASE MONKEY," INDEED!
THE GREATEST INEFFICIENCY IS CAUSED BY IMPROPER COMMUNICATION! HAVE YOU EVER CONSIDERED THE EFFECT OF THIS ON CHIEF GIMBENSKY'S STATE OF MIND??
Uh, I DIDN'T THINK--
OBVIOUSLY.

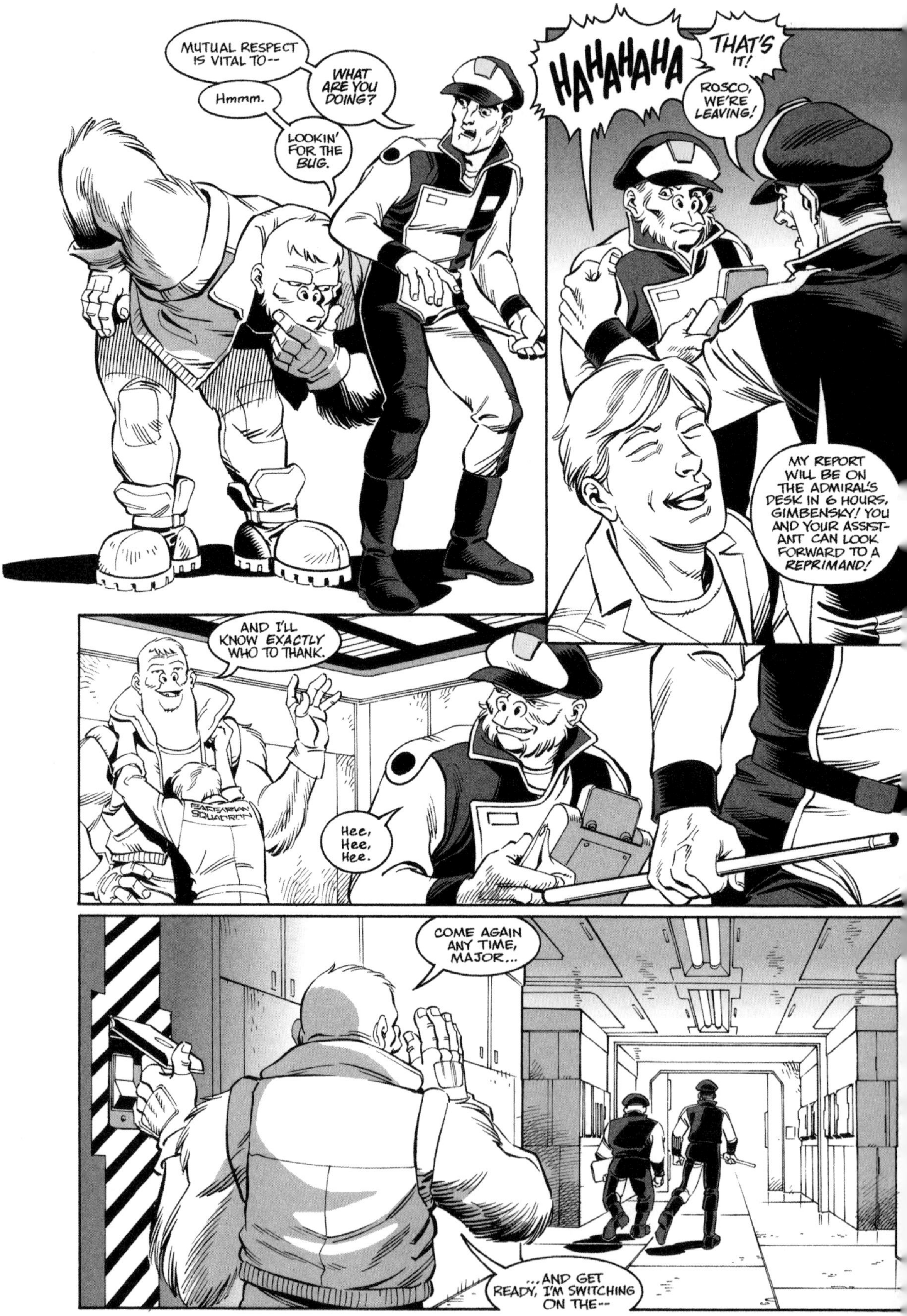
MUTUAL RESPECT IS VITAL TO--
WHAT ARE YOU DOING?
Hmmm.
LOOKIN' FOR THE BUG.
HAHAHAHA
THAT'S IT!
ROSCO, WE'RE LEAVING!
MY REPORT WILL BE ON THE ADMIRAL'S DESK IN 6 HOURS, GIMBENSKY! YOU AND YOUR ASSIST-ANT CAN LOOK FORWARD TO A REPRIMAND!
AND I'LL KNOW EXACTLY WHO TO THANK.
BARBARIAN SQUADRON
Hee, Hee, Hee.
COME AGAIN ANY TIME, MAJOR...
...AND GET READY, I'M SWITCHING ON THE--

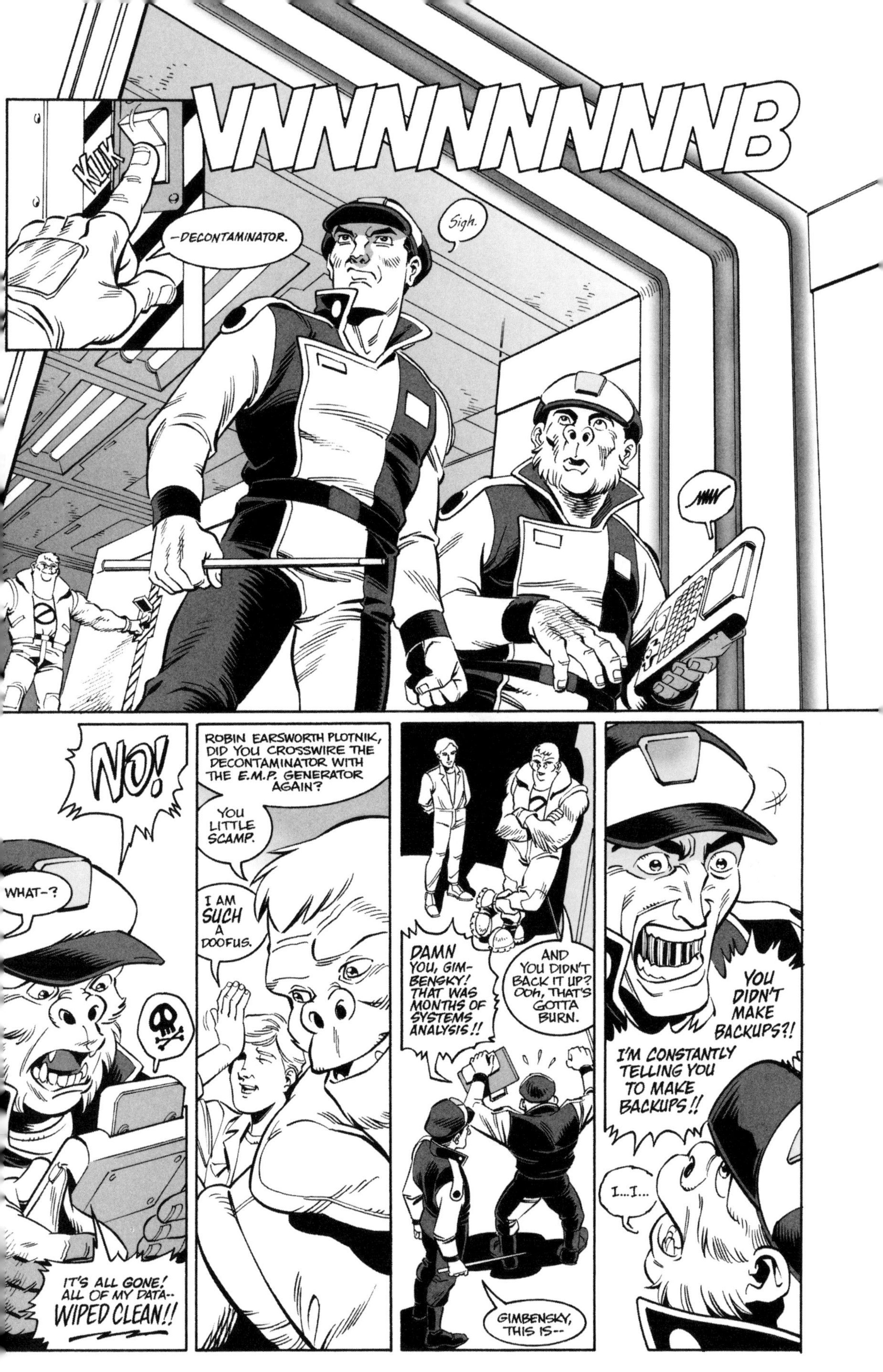
VNNNNNNNNNB
KLIK
-DECONTAMINATOR.
Sigh.
NO!
WHAT-?
IT'S ALL GONE! ALL OF MY DATA-- WIPED CLEAN!!
ROBIN EARSWORTH PLOTNIK, DID YOU CROSSWIRE THE DECONTAMINATOR WITH THE E.M.P. GENERATOR AGAIN?
YOU LITTLE SCAMP.
I AM SUCH A DOOFUS.
DAMN YOU, GIMBENSKY! THAT WAS MONTHS OF SYSTEMS ANALYSIS!!
AND YOU DIDN'T BACK IT UP? Ooh, THAT'S GOTTA BURN.
GIMBENSKY, THIS IS--
YOU DIDN'T MAKE BACKUPS?!
I'M CONSTANTLY TELLING YOU TO MAKE BACKUPS!!
I...I...

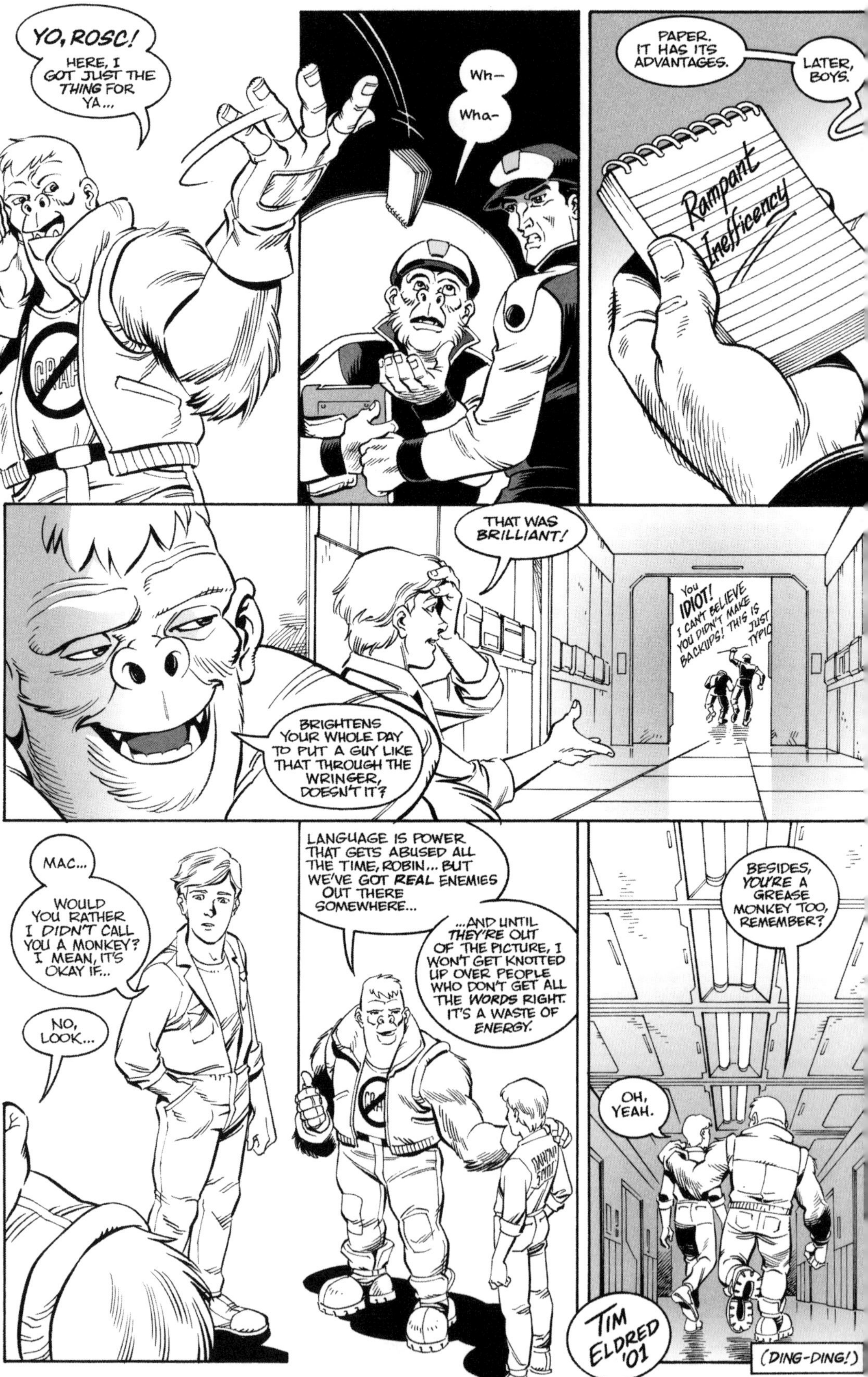
YO, ROSC!
HERE, I GOT JUST THE THING FOR YA...
Wh—
Wha-
PAPER. IT HAS ITS ADVANTAGES.
LATER, BOYS.
Rampant Inefficency
THAT WAS BRILLIANT!
You IDIOT! I CAN'T BELIEVE YOU DIDN'T MAKE BACKUPS! THIS IS JUST TYPIC
BRIGHTENS YOUR WHOLE DAY TO PUT A GUY LIKE THAT THROUGH THE WRINGER, DOESN'T IT?
MAC...
WOULD YOU RATHER I DIDN'T CALL YOU A MONKEY? I MEAN, IT'S OKAY IF...
NO, LOOK...
LANGUAGE IS POWER THAT GETS ABUSED ALL THE TIME, ROBIN... BUT WE'VE GOT REAL ENEMIES OUT THERE SOMEWHERE...
...AND UNTIL THEY'RE OUT OF THE PICTURE, I WON'T GET KNOTTED UP OVER PEOPLE WHO DON'T GET ALL THE WORDS RIGHT. IT'S A WASTE OF ENERGY.
BESIDES, YOU'RE A GREASE MONKEY TOO, REMEMBER?
OH, YEAH.
TIM ELDRED '01
(DING-DING!)

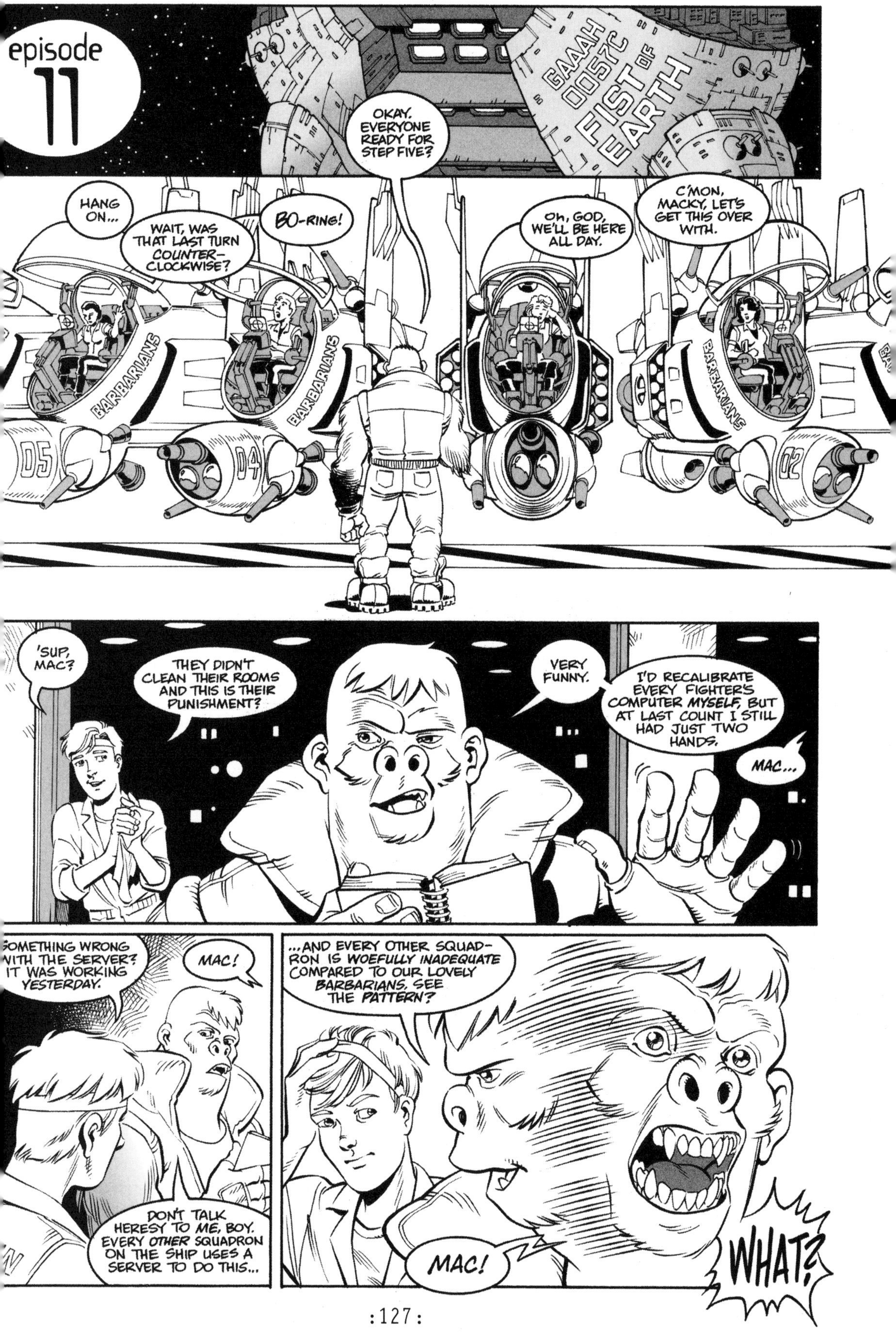
episode 11
GAAAH 0057C
FIST OF EARTH
OKAY. EVERYONE READY FOR STEP FIVE?
HANG ON...
WAIT, WAS THAT LAST TURN COUNTER-CLOCKWISE?
BO-RING!
Oh, GOD, WE'LL BE HERE ALL DAY.
C'MON, MACKY, LET'S GET THIS OVER WITH.
BARBARIANS
05
04
02
'SUP, MAC?
THEY DIDN'T CLEAN THEIR ROOMS AND THIS IS THEIR PUNISHMENT?
VERY FUNNY.
I'D RECALIBRATE EVERY FIGHTER'S COMPUTER MYSELF, BUT AT LAST COUNT I STILL HAD JUST TWO HANDS.
MAC...
SOMETHING WRONG WITH THE SERVER? IT WAS WORKING YESTERDAY.
MAC!
DON'T TALK HERESY TO ME, BOY. EVERY OTHER SQUADRON ON THE SHIP USES A SERVER TO DO THIS...
...AND EVERY OTHER SQUADRON IS WOEFULLY INADEQUATE COMPARED TO OUR LOVELY BARBARIANS. SEE THE PATTERN?
MAC!
WHAT?

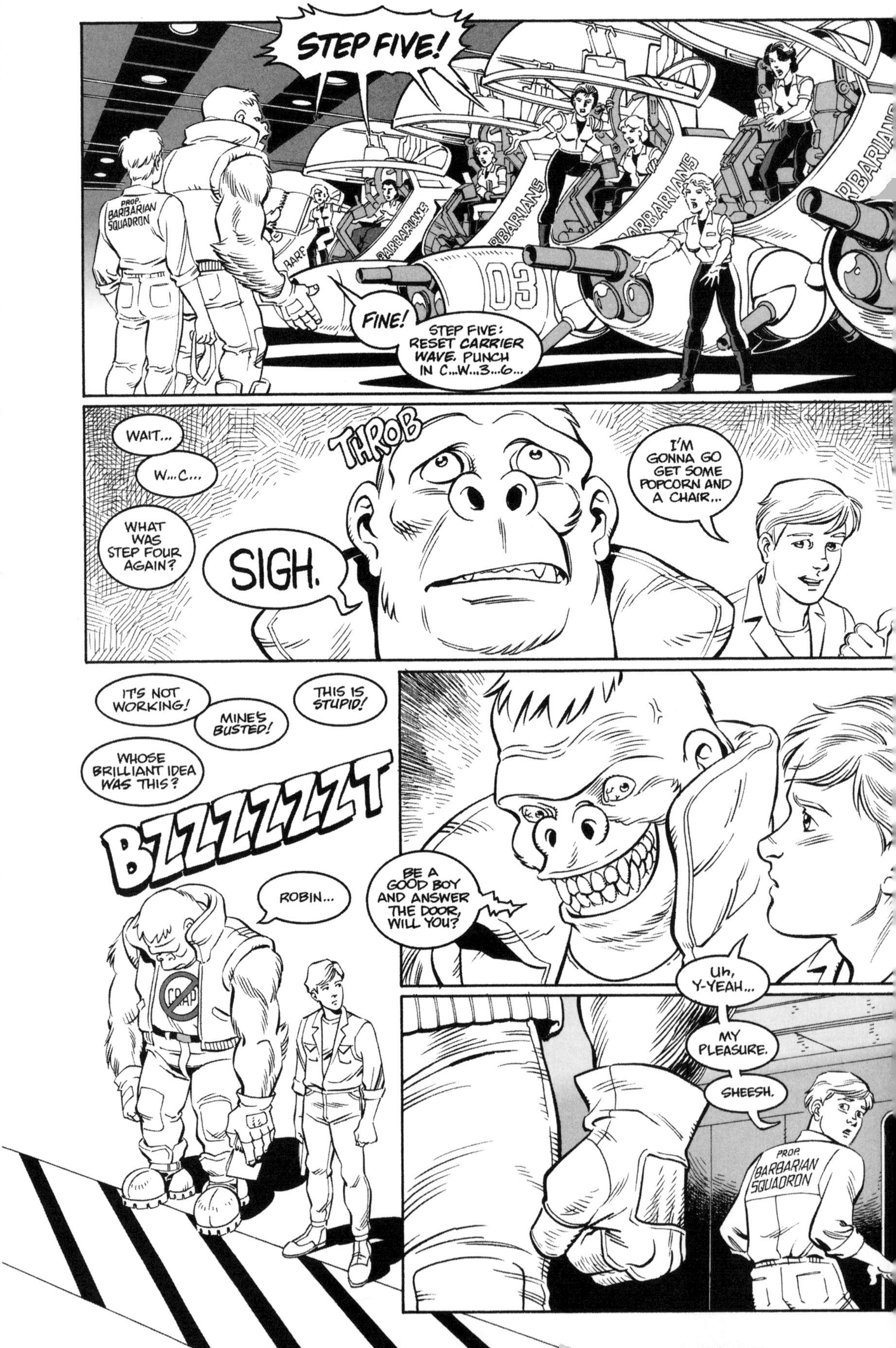
STEP FIVE!
PROP. BARBARIAN SQUADRON
BARBARIANS
03
FINE!
STEP FIVE: RESET CARRIER WAVE. PUNCH IN C...W...3...6...
WAIT...
W...C...
WHAT WAS STEP FOUR AGAIN?
THROB
SIGH.
I'M GONNA GO GET SOME POPCORN AND A CHAIR...
IT'S NOT WORKING!
MINE'S BUSTED!
THIS IS STUPID!
WHOSE BRILLIANT IDEA WAS THIS?
BZZZZZZZT
ROBIN...
BE A GOOD BOY AND ANSWER THE DOOR, WILL YOU?
Uh, Y-YEAH...
MY PLEASURE.
SHEESH.
PROP. BARBARIAN SQUADRON

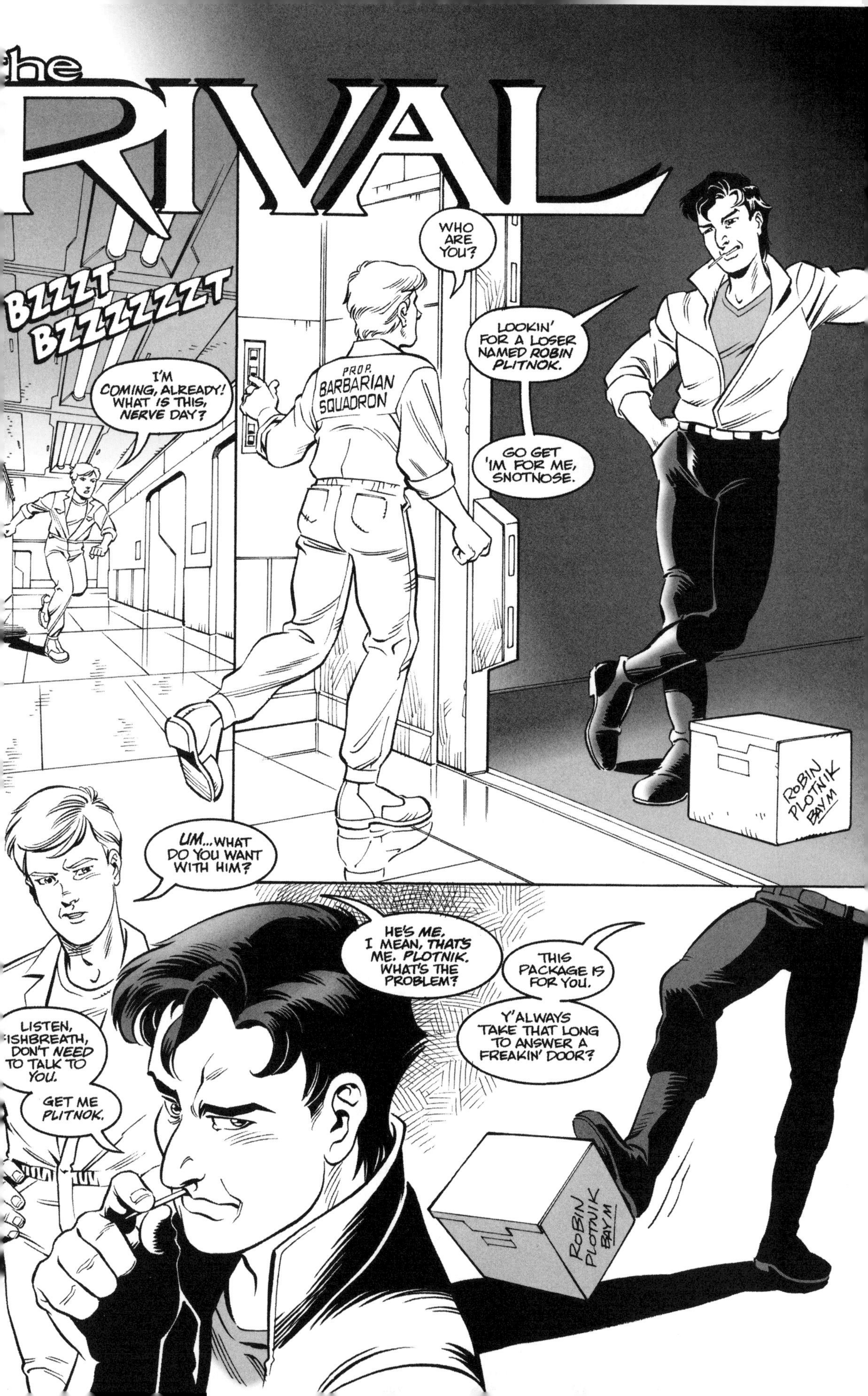

he RIVAL
BZZZZT BZZZZZZZT
I'M COMING, ALREADY! WHAT IS THIS, NERVE DAY?
PROP. BARBARIAN SQUADRON
WHO ARE YOU?
LOOKIN' FOR A LOSER NAMED ROBIN PLITNOK.
GO GET 'IM FOR ME, SNOTNOSE.
ROBIN PLOTNIK BAY M
UM... WHAT DO YOU WANT WITH HIM?
LISTEN, FISHBREATH, DON'T NEED TO TALK TO YOU.
GET ME PLITNOK.
HE'S ME. I MEAN, THAT'S ME. PLOTNIK. WHAT'S THE PROBLEM?
THIS PACKAGE IS FOR YOU.
Y'ALWAYS TAKE THAT LONG TO ANSWER A FREAKIN' DOOR?
ROBIN PLOTNIK BAY M

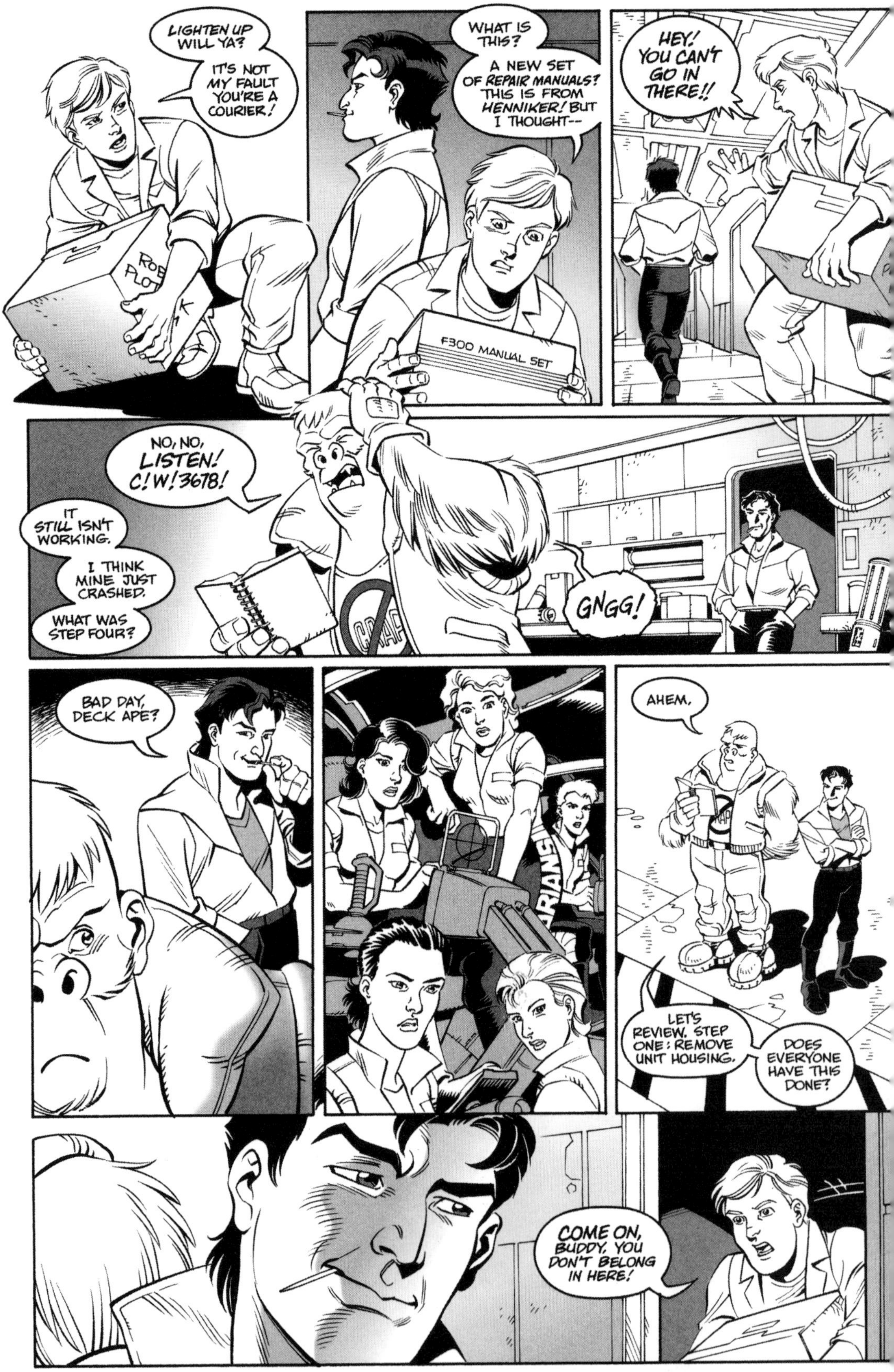
LIGHTEN UP WILL YA?
IT'S NOT MY FAULT YOU'RE A COURIER!
ROB PLOT
WHAT IS THIS?
A NEW SET OF REPAIR MANUALS? THIS IS FROM HENNIKER! BUT I THOUGHT--
F300 MANUAL SET
HEY! YOU CAN'T GO IN THERE!!
NO, NO, LISTEN! C!W!3678!
IT STILL ISN'T WORKING.
I THINK MINE JUST CRASHED.
WHAT WAS STEP FOUR?
GNGG!
BAD DAY, DECK APE?
AHEM.
LET'S REVIEW. STEP ONE: REMOVE UNIT HOUSING.
DOES EVERYONE HAVE THIS DONE?
COME ON, BUDDY. YOU DON'T BELONG IN HERE!

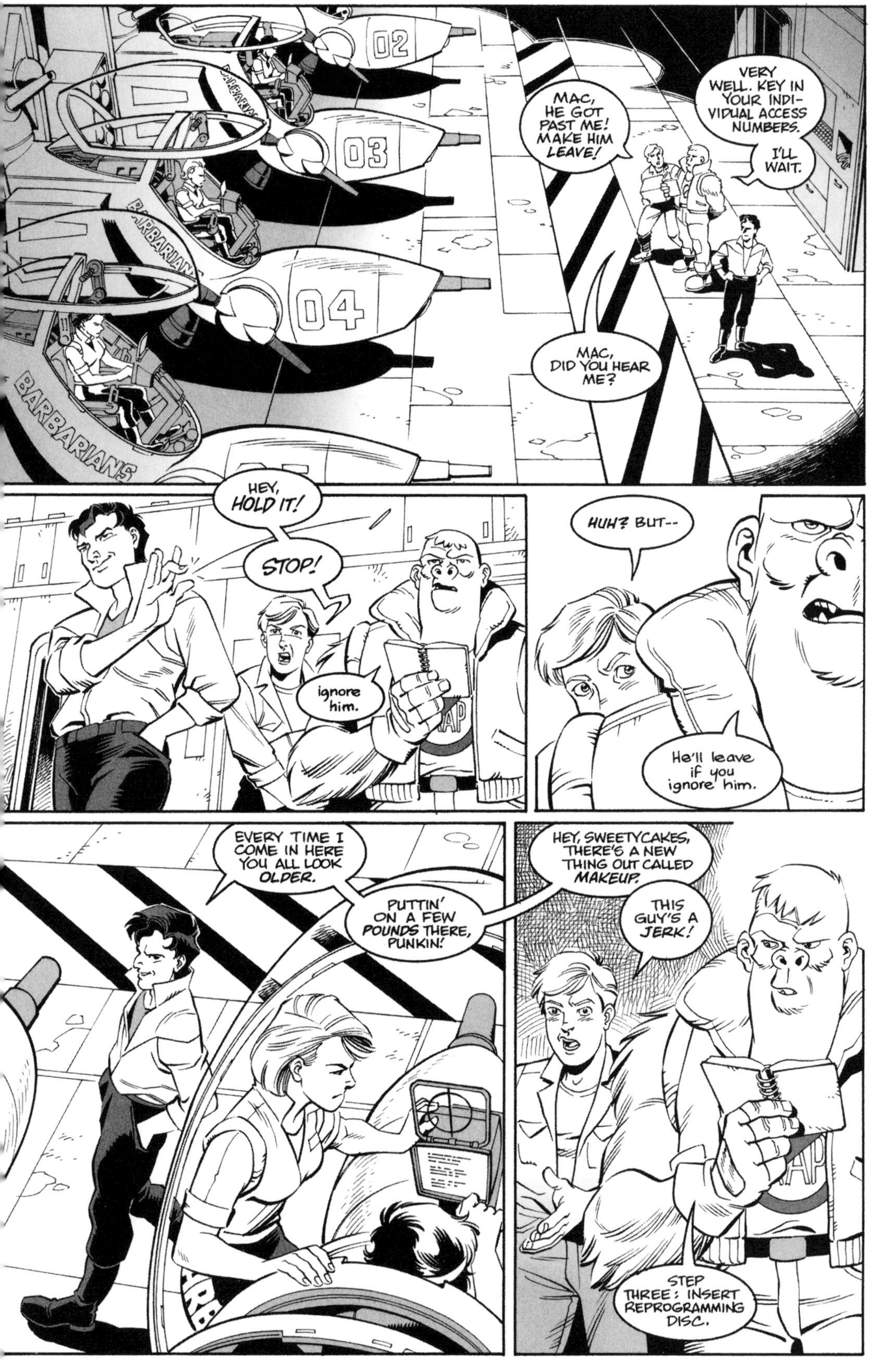
02
03
04
BARBARIANS
MAC, HE GOT PAST ME! MAKE HIM LEAVE!
VERY WELL. KEY IN YOUR INDIVIDUAL ACCESS NUMBERS.
I'LL WAIT.
MAC, DID YOU HEAR ME?
HEY, HOLD IT!
STOP!
ignore him.
HUH? BUT--
He'll leave if you ignore him.
EVERY TIME I COME IN HERE YOU ALL LOOK OLDER.
PUTTIN' ON A FEW POUNDS THERE, PUNKIN!
HEY, SWEETYCAKES, THERE'S A NEW THING OUT CALLED MAKEUP.
THIS GUY'S A JERK!
STEP THREE: INSERT REPROGRAMMING DISC.

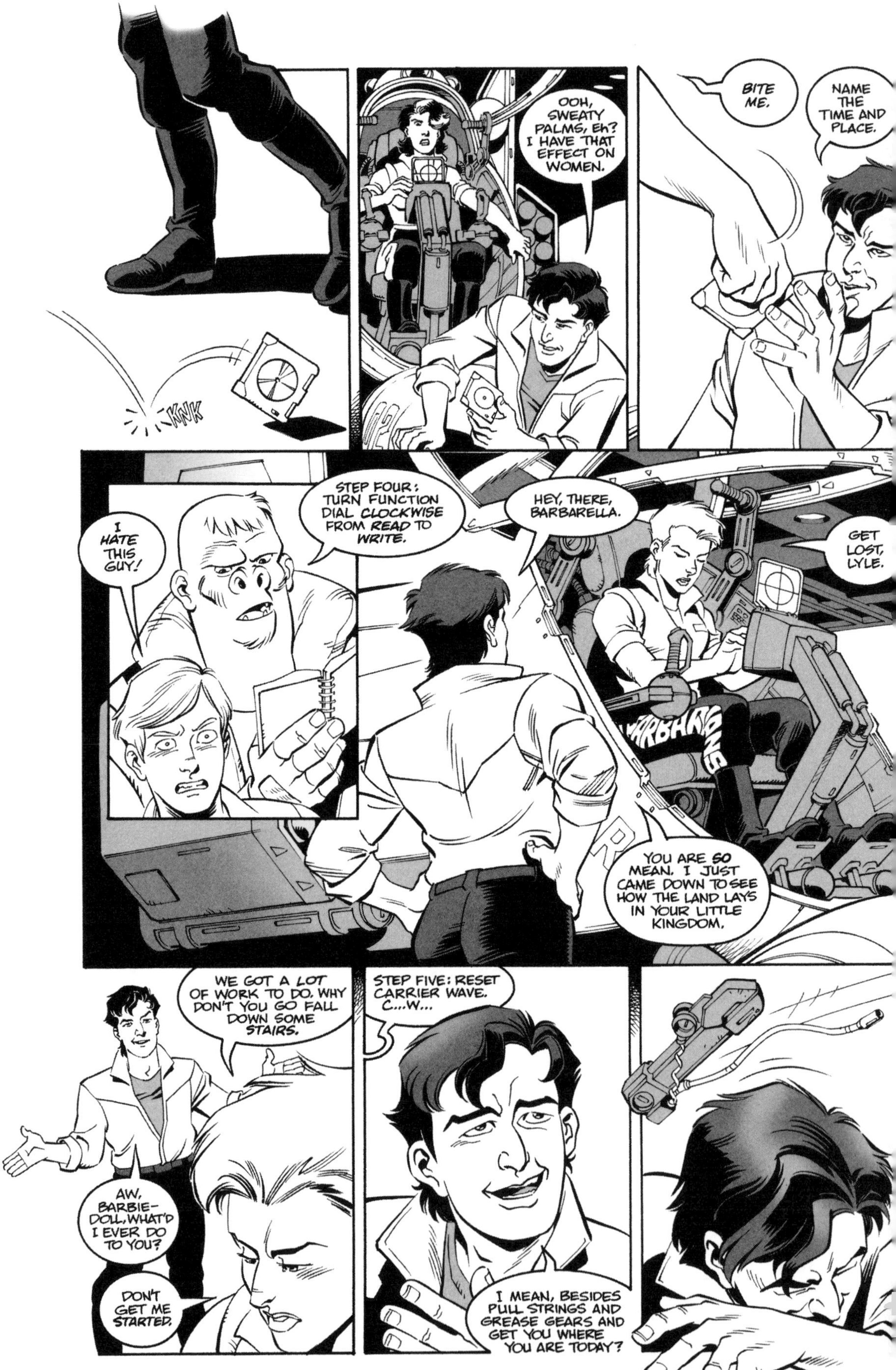
KNK
OOH, SWEATY PALMS, Eh? I HAVE THAT EFFECT ON WOMEN.
BITE ME.
NAME THE TIME AND PLACE.
I HATE THIS GUY!
STEP FOUR: TURN FUNCTION DIAL CLOCKWISE FROM READ TO WRITE.
HEY, THERE, BARBARELLA.
GET LOST, LYLE.
YOU ARE SO MEAN. I JUST CAME DOWN TO SEE HOW THE LAND LAYS IN YOUR LITTLE KINGDOM.
WE GOT A LOT OF WORK TO DO. WHY DON'T YOU GO FALL DOWN SOME STAIRS.
AW, BARBIE-DOLL, WHAT'D I EVER DO TO YOU?
DON'T GET ME STARTED.
STEP FIVE: RESET CARRIER WAVE. C...W...
I MEAN, BESIDES PULL STRINGS AND GREASE GEARS AND GET YOU WHERE YOU ARE TODAY?

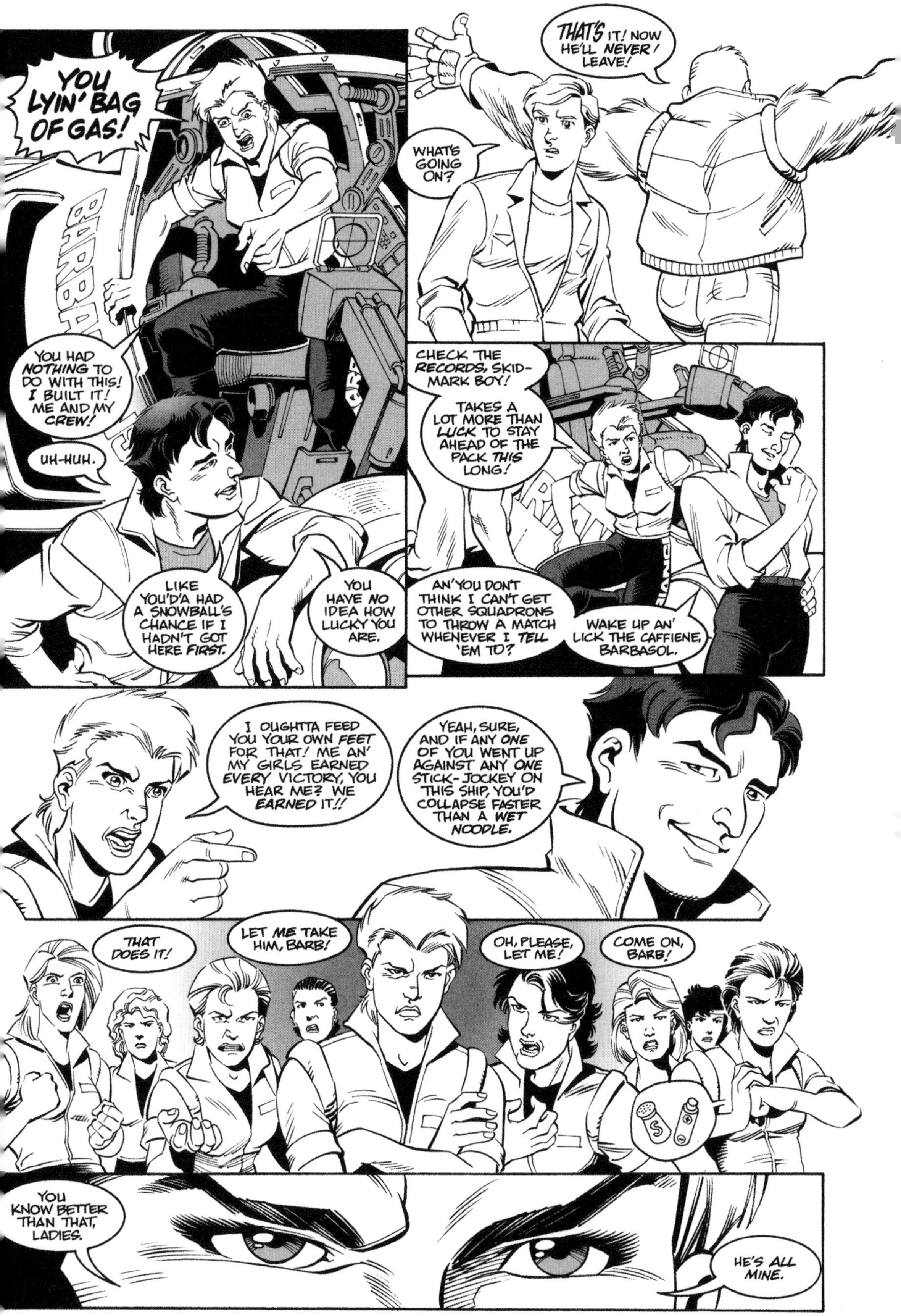
YOU LYIN' BAG OF GAS!
YOU HAD NOTHING TO DO WITH THIS! I BUILT IT! ME AND MY CREW!
UH-HUH.
LIKE YOU'D'A HAD A SNOWBALL'S CHANCE IF I HADN'T GOT HERE FIRST.
YOU HAVE NO IDEA HOW LUCKY YOU ARE.
THAT'S IT! NOW HE'LL NEVER LEAVE!
WHAT'S GOING ON?
CHECK THE RECORDS, SKID-MARK BOY!
TAKES A LOT MORE THAN LUCK TO STAY AHEAD OF THE PACK THIS LONG!
AN' YOU DON'T THINK I CAN'T GET OTHER SQUADRONS TO THROW A MATCH WHENEVER I TELL 'EM TO?
WAKE UP AN' LICK THE CAFFIENE, BARBASOL.
I OUGHTTA FEED YOU YOUR OWN FEET FOR THAT! ME AN' MY GIRLS EARNED EVERY VICTORY, YOU HEAR ME? WE EARNED IT!!
YEAH, SURE, AND IF ANY ONE OF YOU WENT UP AGAINST ANY ONE STICK-JOCKEY ON THIS SHIP, YOU'D COLLAPSE FASTER THAN A WET NOODLE.
THAT DOES IT!
LET ME TAKE HIM, BARB!
OH, PLEASE, LET ME!
COME ON, BARB!
YOU KNOW BETTER THAN THAT, LADIES.
HE'S ALL MINE.

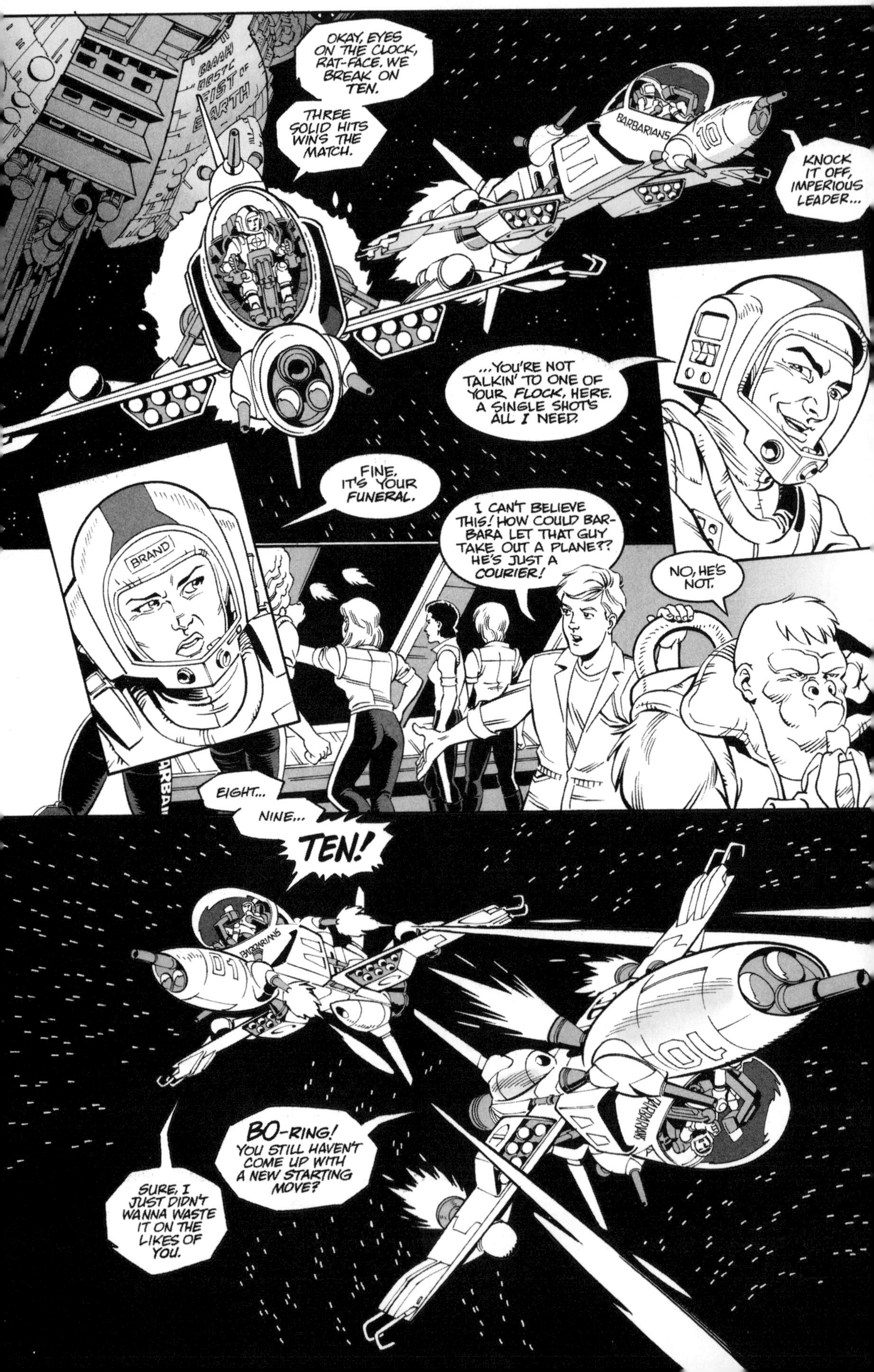
BAAAH OOSTC FIST OF EARTH
OKAY, EYES ON THE CLOCK, RAT-FACE. WE BREAK ON TEN.
THREE SOLID HITS WINS THE MATCH.
BARBARIANS
10
KNOCK IT OFF, IMPERIOUS LEADER...
...YOU'RE NOT TALKIN' TO ONE OF YOUR FLOCK, HERE. A SINGLE SHOT'S ALL I NEED.
FINE, IT'S YOUR FUNERAL.
BRAND
I CAN'T BELIEVE THIS! HOW COULD BARBARA LET THAT GUY TAKE OUT A PLANE?? HE'S JUST A COURIER!
NO, HE'S NOT.
EIGHT...
NINE...
TEN!
BARBARIANS
BO-RING! YOU STILL HAVEN'T COME UP WITH A NEW STARTING MOVE?
SURE, I JUST DIDN'T WANNA WASTE IT ON THE LIKES OF YOU.

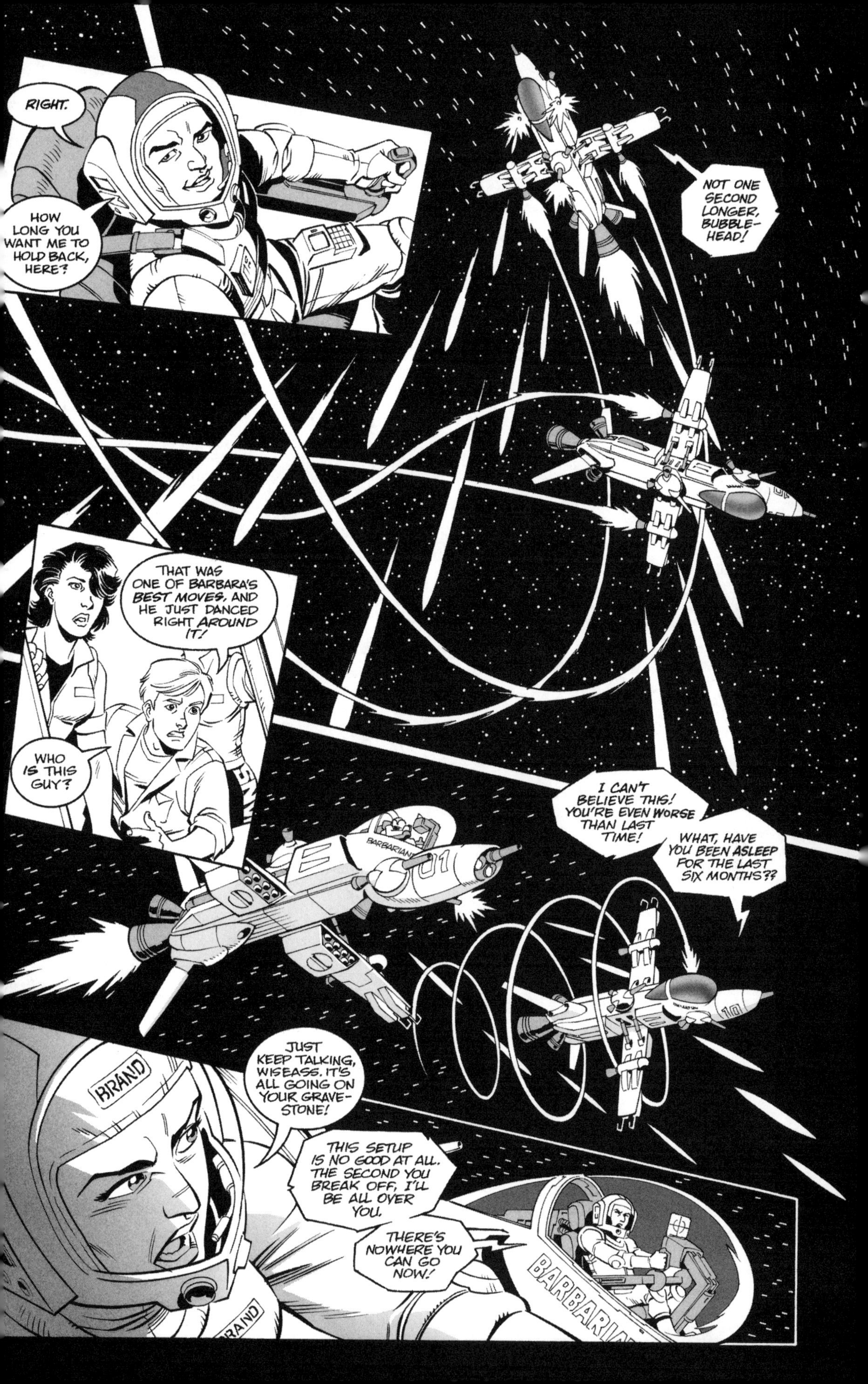
RIGHT.
HOW LONG YOU WANT ME TO HOLD BACK, HERE?
NOT ONE SECOND LONGER, BUBBLE-HEAD!
THAT WAS ONE OF BARBARA'S BEST MOVES, AND HE JUST DANCED RIGHT AROUND IT!
WHO IS THIS GUY?
BARBARIAN
I CAN'T BELIEVE THIS! YOU'RE EVEN WORSE THAN LAST TIME!
WHAT, HAVE YOU BEEN ASLEEP FOR THE LAST SIX MONTHS??
BRAND
JUST KEEP TALKING, WISEASS. IT'S ALL GOING ON YOUR GRAVE-STONE!
THIS SETUP IS NO GOOD AT ALL. THE SECOND YOU BREAK OFF, I'LL BE ALL OVER YOU.
THERE'S NOWHERE YOU CAN GO NOW!
BARBARIAN
BRAND

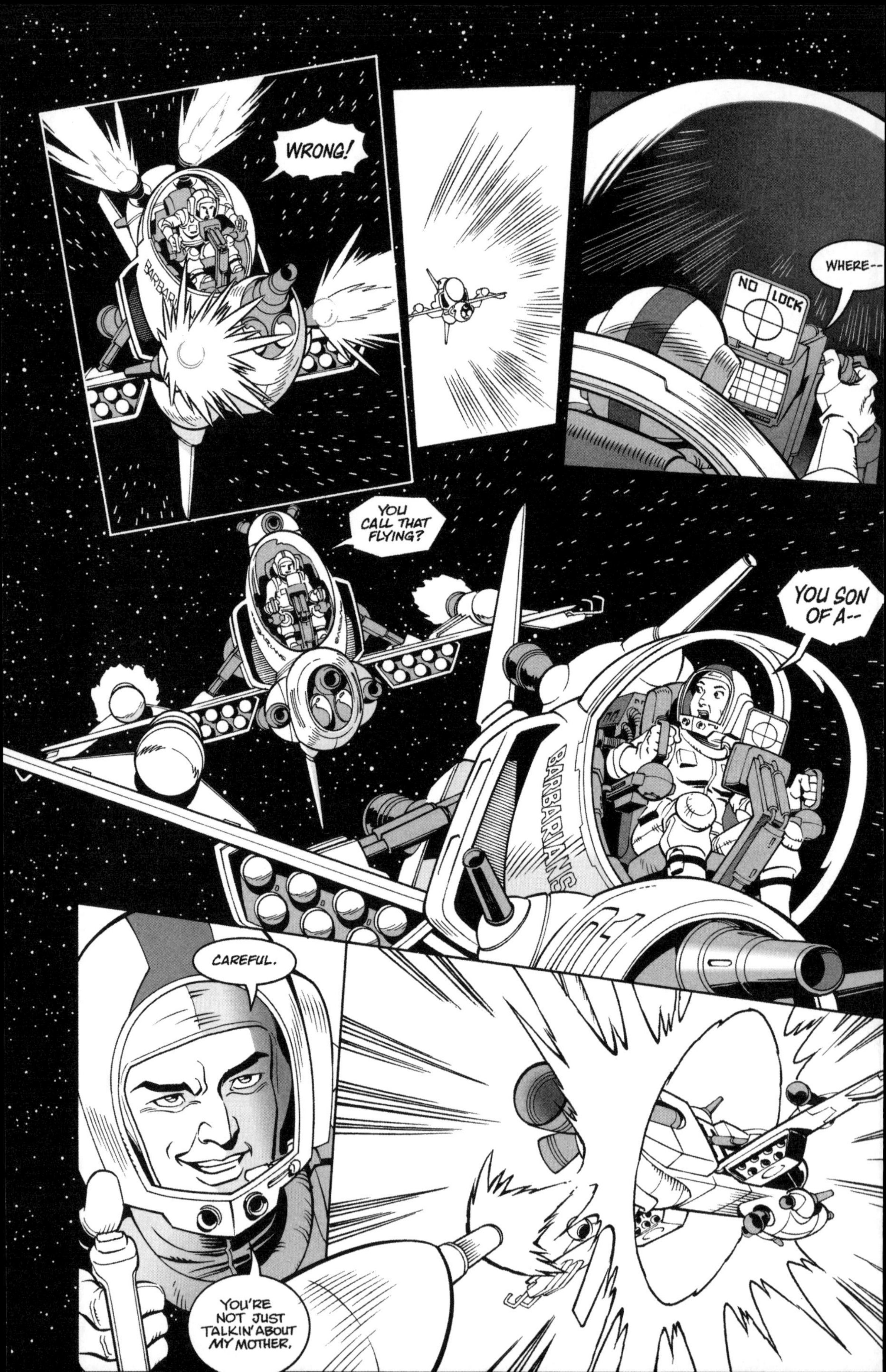
WRONG!
WHERE--
NO LOCK
YOU CALL THAT FLYING?
YOU SON OF A--
BARBARIANS
CAREFUL.
YOU'RE NOT JUST TALKIN' ABOUT MY MOTHER.

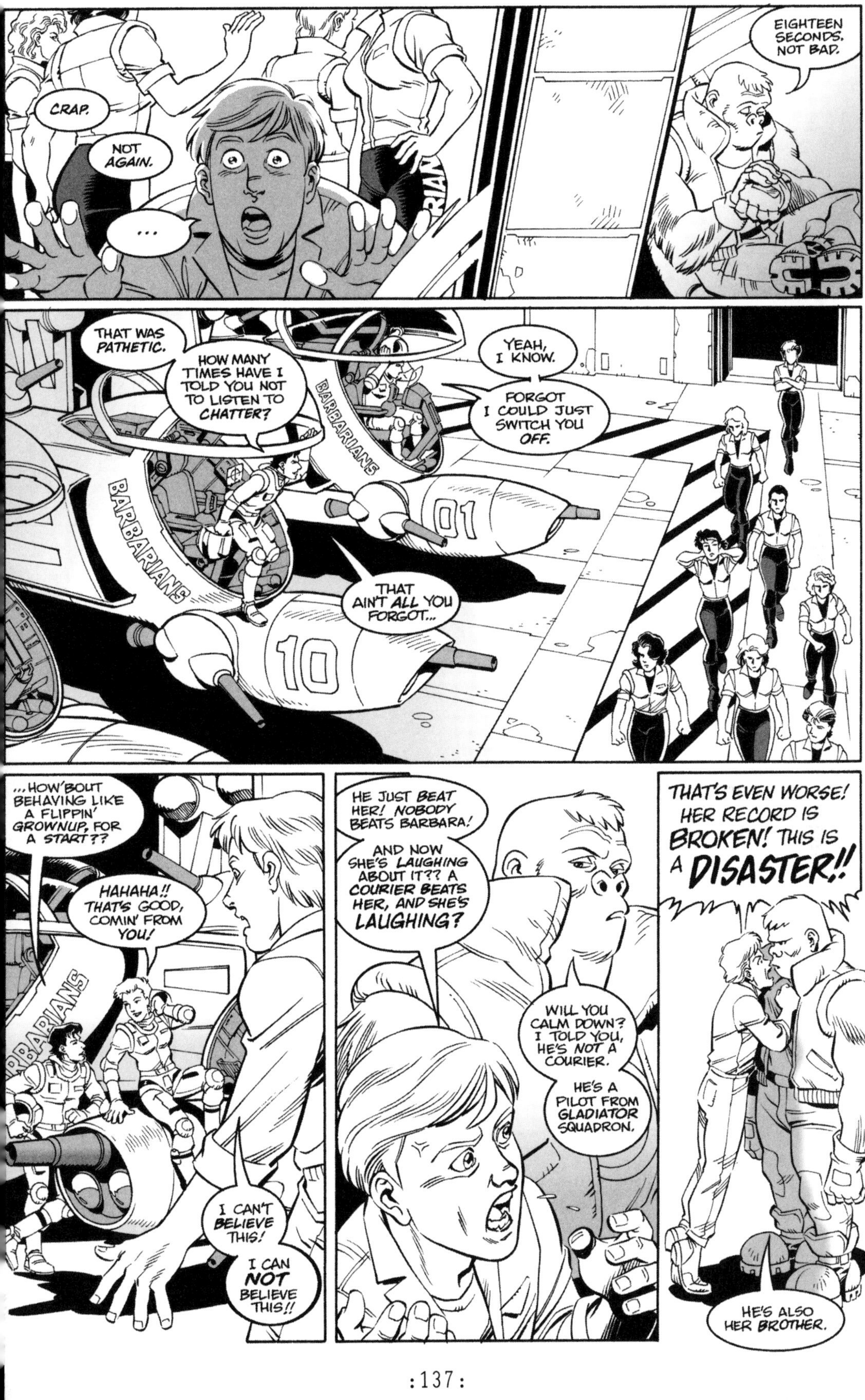
CRAP.
NOT AGAIN.
...
EIGHTEEN SECONDS. NOT BAD.
THAT WAS PATHETIC.
HOW MANY TIMES HAVE I TOLD YOU NOT TO LISTEN TO CHATTER?
YEAH, I KNOW.
FORGOT I COULD JUST SWITCH YOU OFF.
THAT AIN'T ALL YOU FORGOT...
BARBARIANS
01
10
...HOW'BOUT BEHAVING LIKE A FLIPPIN' GROWNUP, FOR A START??
HAHAHA!! THAT'S GOOD, COMIN' FROM YOU!
I CAN'T BELIEVE THIS!
I CAN NOT BELIEVE THIS!!
HE JUST BEAT HER! NOBODY BEATS BARBARA!
AND NOW SHE'S LAUGHING ABOUT IT?? A COURIER BEATS HER, AND SHE'S LAUGHING?
WILL YOU CALM DOWN? I TOLD YOU, HE'S NOT A COURIER.
HE'S A PILOT FROM GLADIATOR SQUADRON.
THAT'S EVEN WORSE! HER RECORD IS BROKEN! THIS IS A DISASTER!!
HE'S ALSO HER BROTHER.

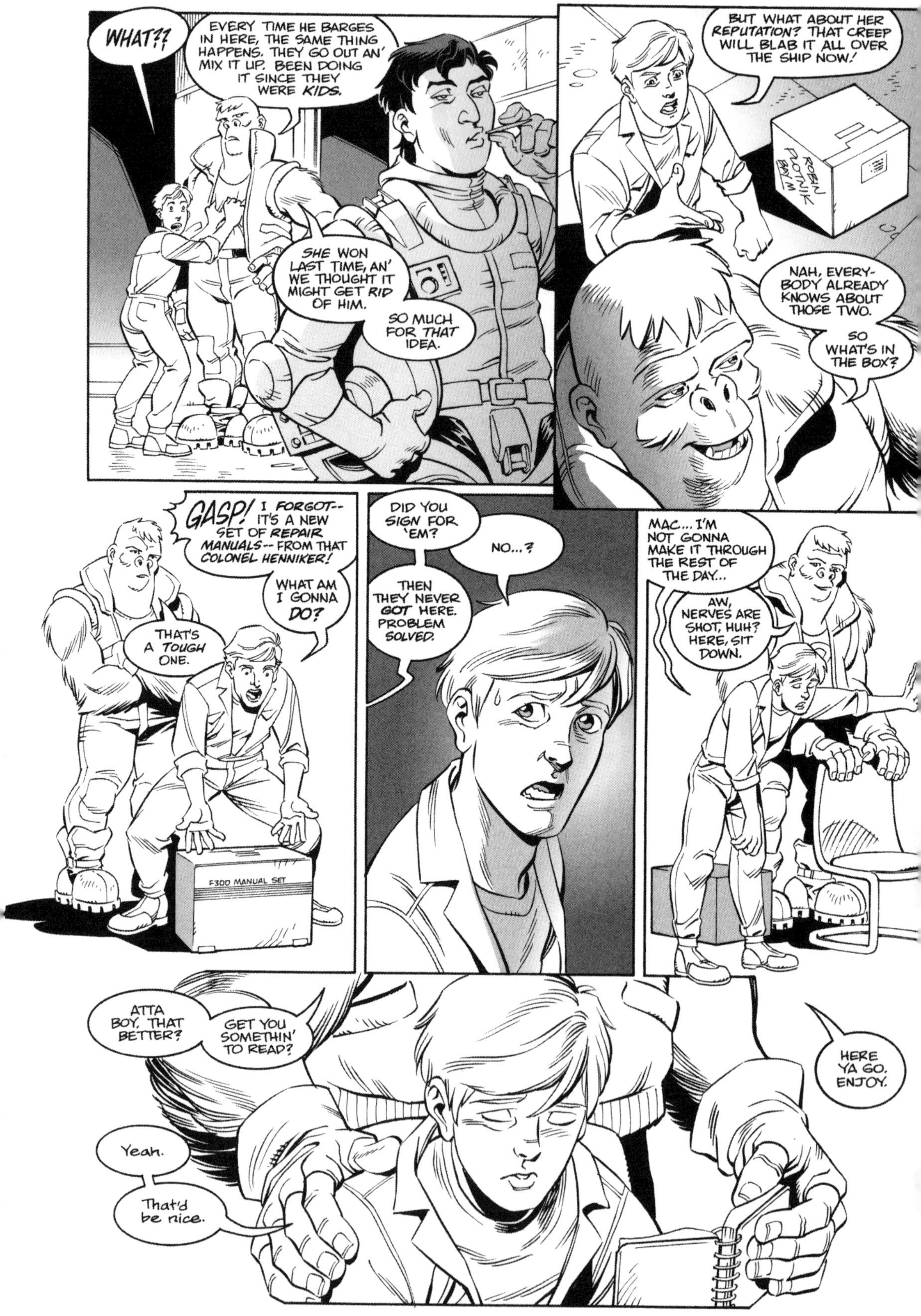
WHAT??
EVERY TIME HE BARGES IN HERE, THE SAME THING HAPPENS. THEY GO OUT AN' MIX IT UP. BEEN DOING IT SINCE THEY WERE KIDS.
SHE WON LAST TIME, AN' WE THOUGHT IT MIGHT GET RID OF HIM.
SO MUCH FOR THAT IDEA.
BUT WHAT ABOUT HER REPUTATION? THAT CREEP WILL BLAB IT ALL OVER THE SHIP NOW!
ROBIN PLOTNIK BAY M
NAH, EVERY-BODY ALREADY KNOWS ABOUT THOSE TWO.
SO WHAT'S IN THE BOX?
GASP! I FORGOT-- IT'S A NEW SET OF REPAIR MANUALS-- FROM THAT COLONEL HENNIKER!
WHAT AM I GONNA DO?
THAT'S A TOUGH ONE.
F300 MANUAL SET
DID YOU SIGN FOR 'EM?
NO...?
THEN THEY NEVER GOT HERE. PROBLEM SOLVED.
MAC... I'M NOT GONNA MAKE IT THROUGH THE REST OF THE DAY...
AW, NERVES ARE SHOT, HUH? HERE, SIT DOWN.
ATTA BOY, THAT BETTER?
GET YOU SOMETHIN' TO READ?
HERE YA GO. ENJOY.
Yeah.
That'd be nice.

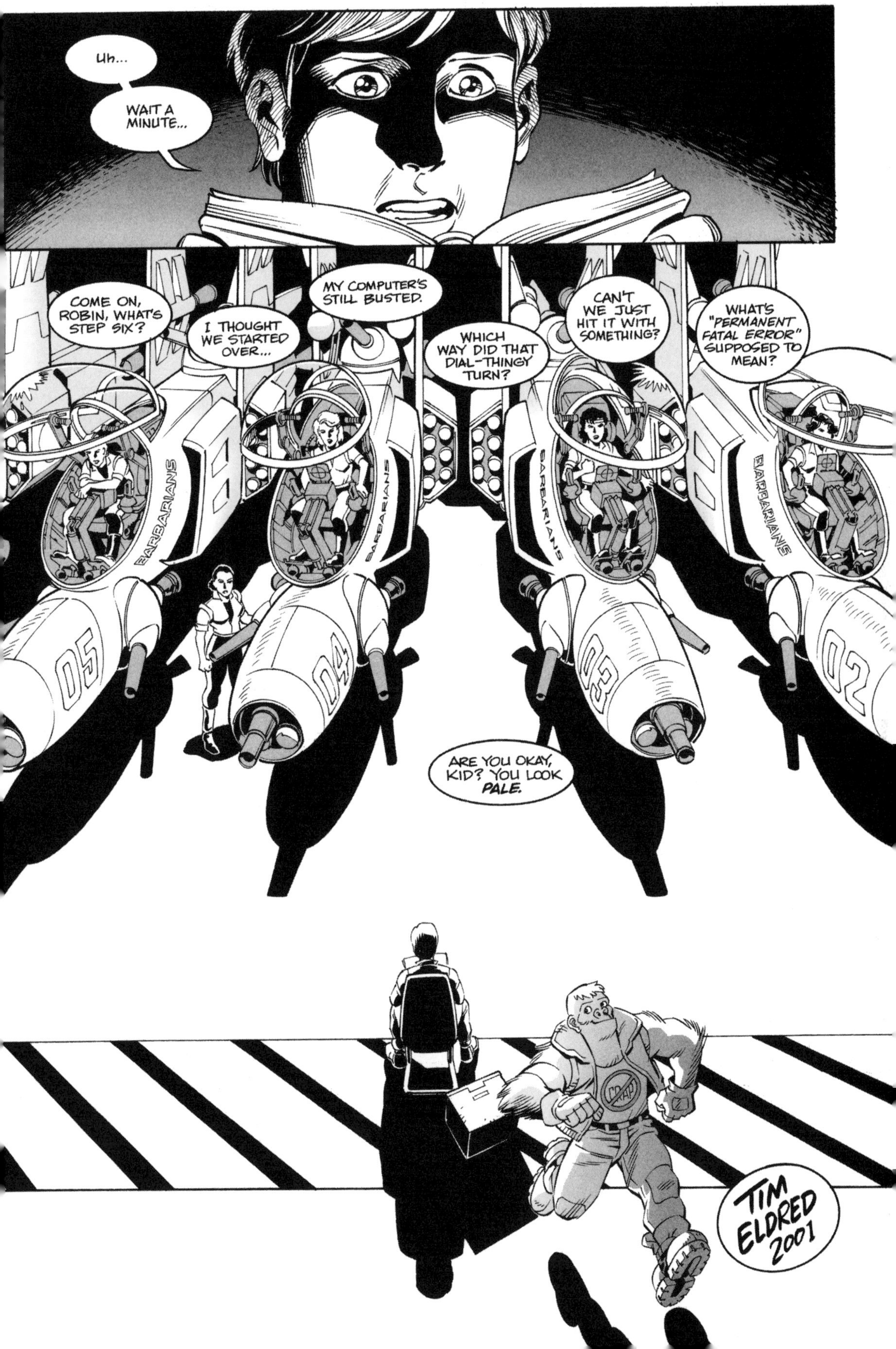
Uh...
WAIT A MINUTE...
COME ON, ROBIN, WHAT'S STEP SIX?
I THOUGHT WE STARTED OVER...
MY COMPUTER'S STILL BUSTED.
WHICH WAY DID THAT DIAL-THINGY TURN?
CAN'T WE JUST HIT IT WITH SOMETHING?
WHAT'S "PERMANENT FATAL ERROR" SUPPOSED TO MEAN?
BARBARIANS
05
04
03
02
ARE YOU OKAY, KID? YOU LOOK PALE.
TIM ELDRED 2001

F300 SPACE SUPERIORITY FIGHTER

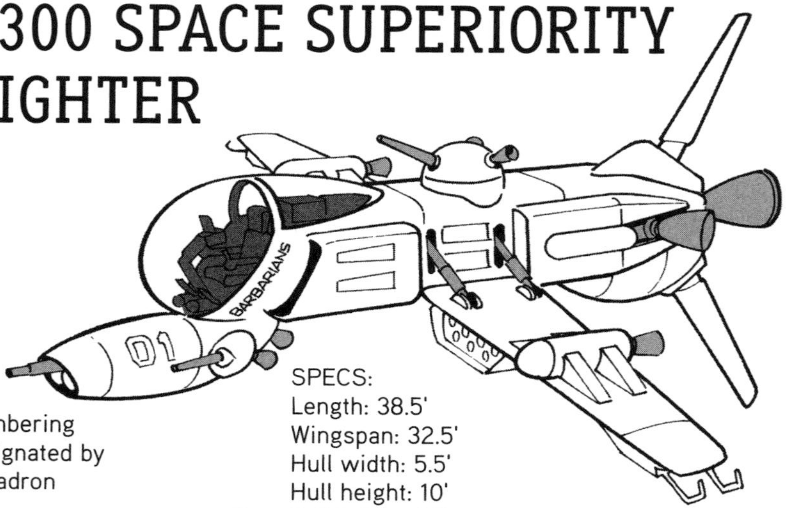

BARBARIANS
01

Numbering designated by squadron

SPECS:
Length: 38.5'
Wingspan: 32.5'
Hull width: 5.5'
Hull height: 10'
Full height: 23'
Missile racks: 2
Beam cannon: 4
Verniers: 10

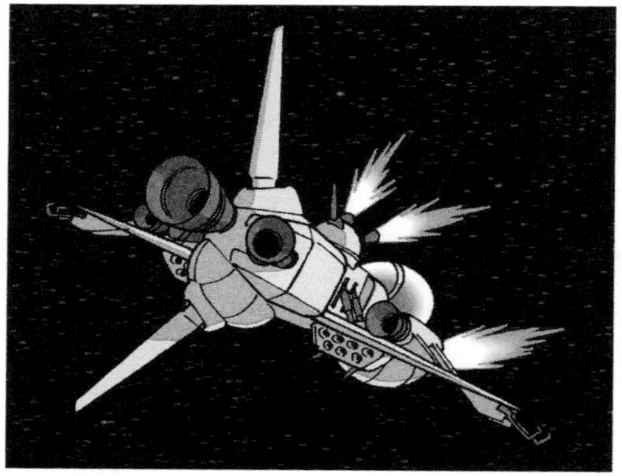

Verniers firing for instant braking in flight.

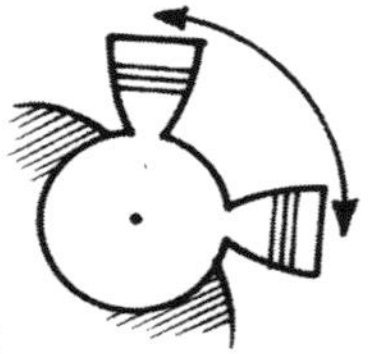

Variable verniers are positioned at key points for maximum turning and braking capacity.

Cockpit detail at right: life support sytem located behind pilot

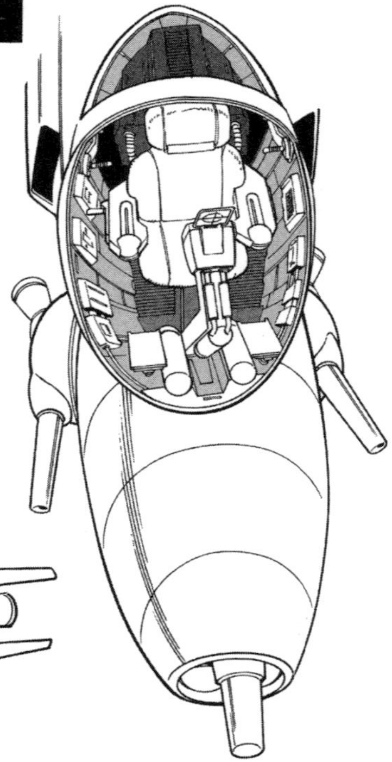

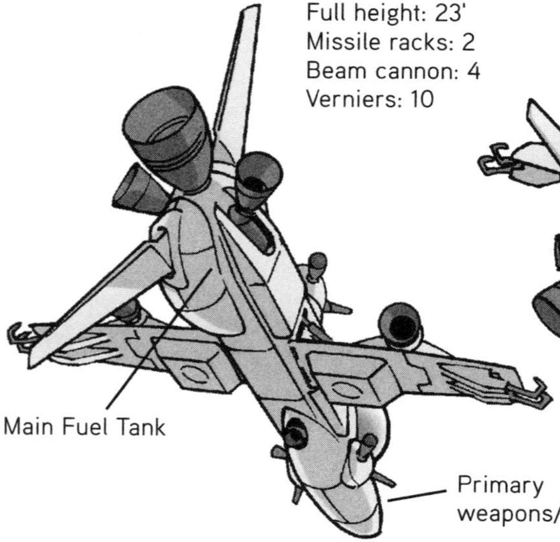

Main Fuel Tank

Primary weapons/sensor pod

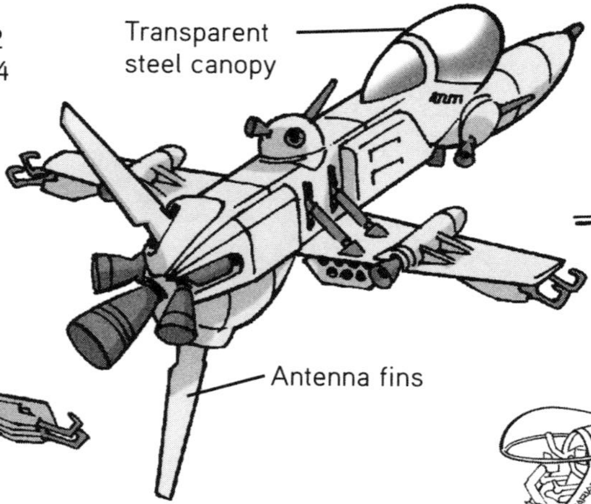

Transparent steel canopy

Antenna fins

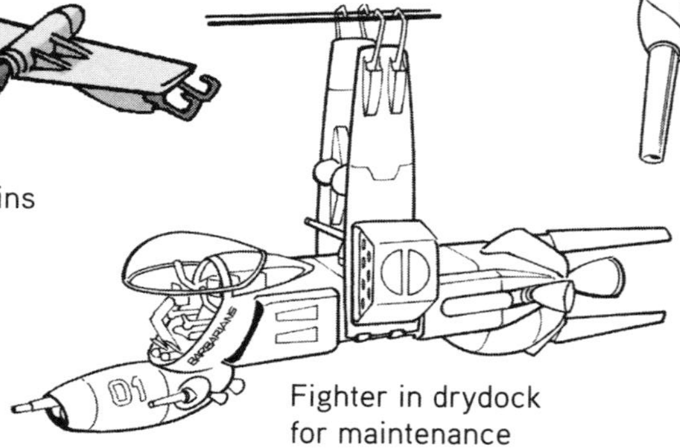

BARBARIANS
01

Fighter in drydock for maintenance

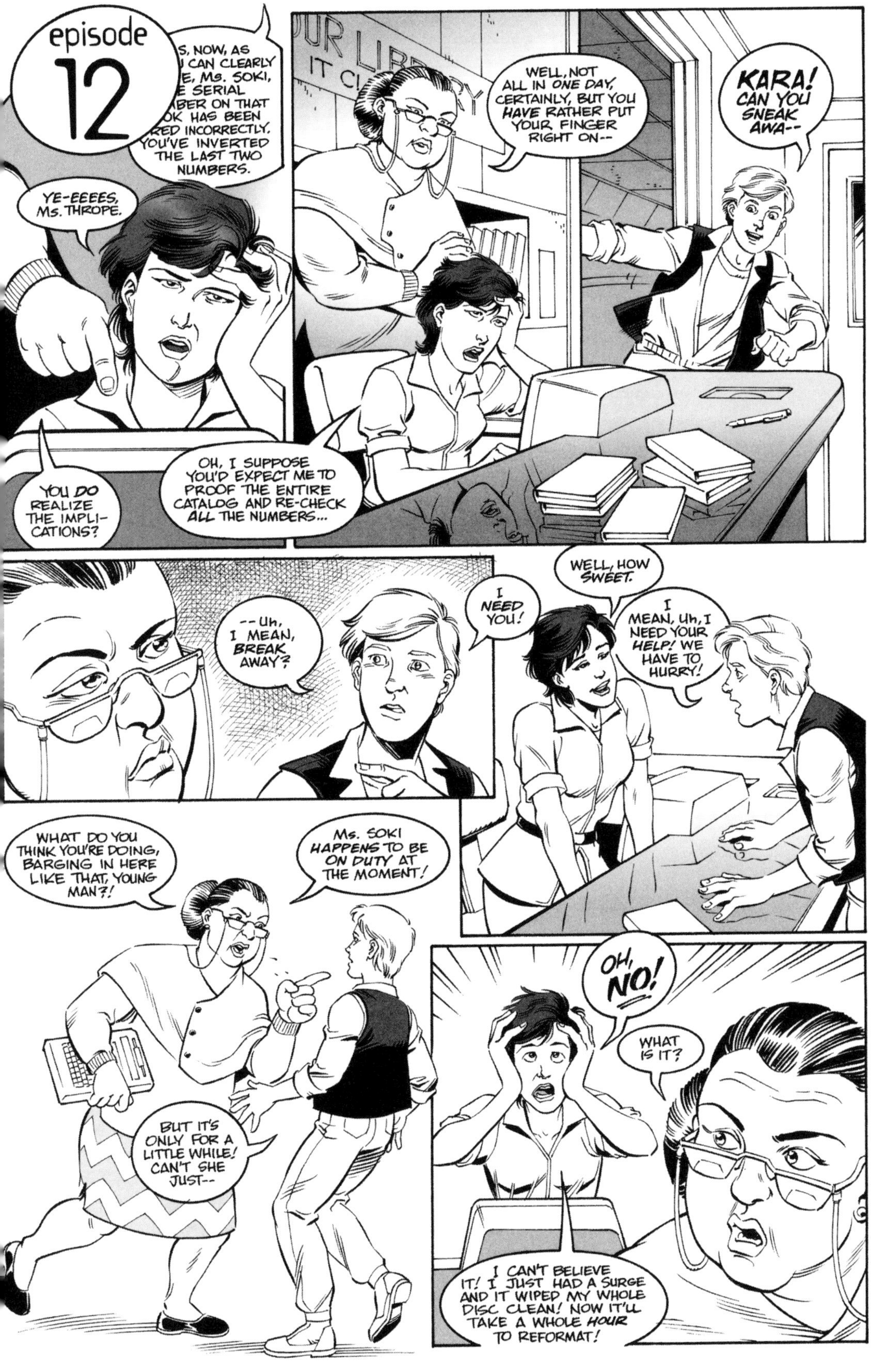
episode 12
S, NOW, AS U CAN CLEARLY E, Ms. SOKI, E SERIAL BER ON THAT OK HAS BEEN RED INCORRECTLY. YOU'VE INVERTED THE LAST TWO NUMBERS.
YE-EEEES, Ms. THROPE.
YOU DO REALIZE THE IMPLI-CATIONS?
OH, I SUPPOSE YOU'D EXPECT ME TO PROOF THE ENTIRE CATALOG AND RE-CHECK ALL THE NUMBERS...
WELL, NOT ALL IN ONE DAY, CERTAINLY, BUT YOU HAVE RATHER PUT YOUR FINGER RIGHT ON--
KARA! CAN YOU SNEAK AWA--
--Uh, I MEAN, BREAK AWAY?
I NEED YOU!
WELL, HOW SWEET.
I MEAN, Uh, I NEED YOUR HELP! WE HAVE TO HURRY!
WHAT DO YOU THINK YOU'RE DOING, BARGING IN HERE LIKE THAT, YOUNG MAN?!
Ms. SOKI HAPPENS TO BE ON DUTY AT THE MOMENT!
BUT IT'S ONLY FOR A LITTLE WHILE! CAN'T SHE JUST--
OH, NO!
WHAT IS IT?
I CAN'T BELIEVE IT! I JUST HAD A SURGE AND IT WIPED MY WHOLE DISC CLEAN! NOW IT'LL TAKE A WHOLE HOUR TO REFORMAT!

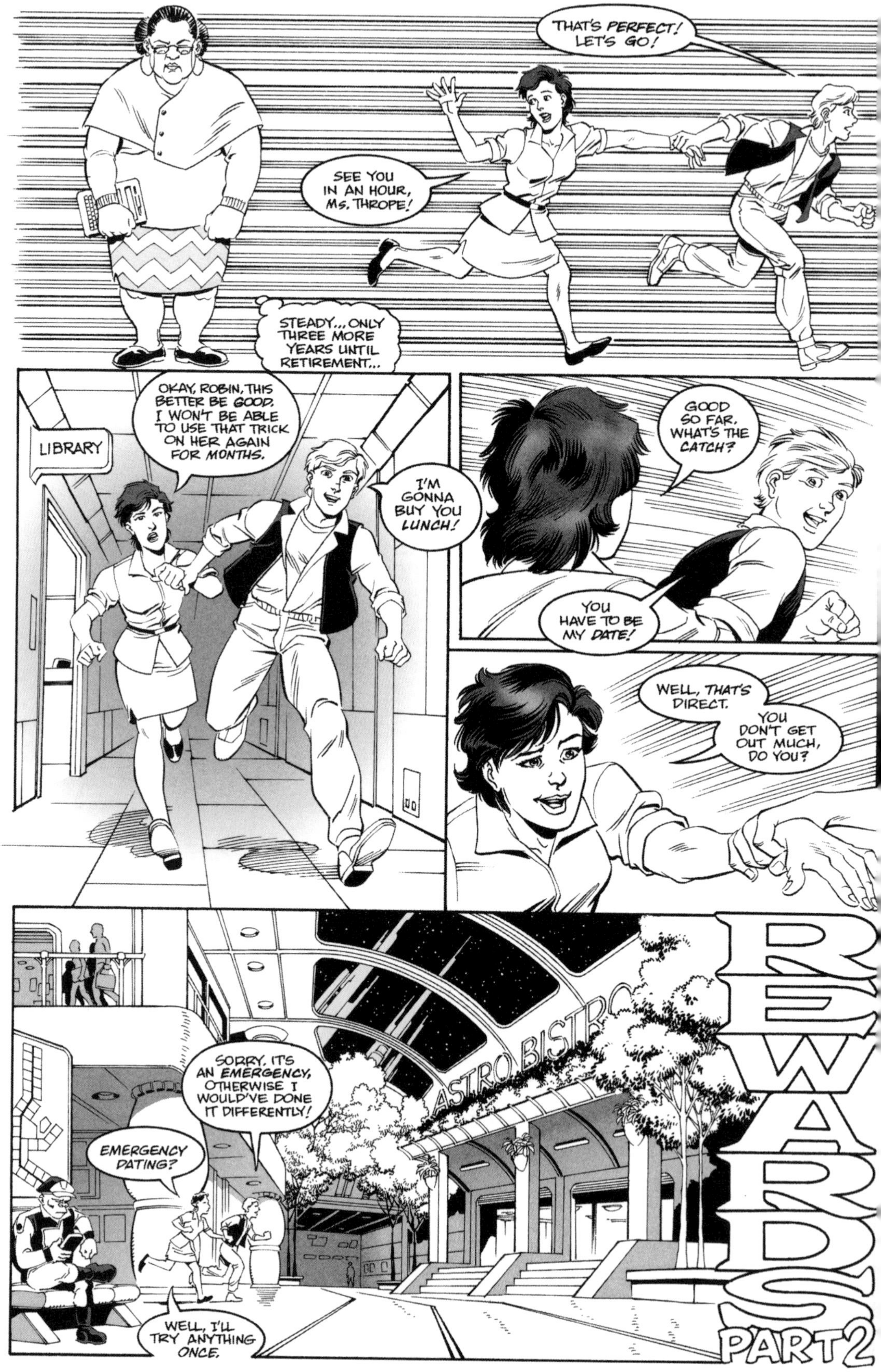
THAT'S PERFECT! LET'S GO!
SEE YOU IN AN HOUR, MS. THROPE!
STEADY... ONLY THREE MORE YEARS UNTIL RETIREMENT...
LIBRARY
OKAY, ROBIN, THIS BETTER BE GOOD. I WON'T BE ABLE TO USE THAT TRICK ON HER AGAIN FOR MONTHS.
I'M GONNA BUY YOU LUNCH!
GOOD SO FAR. WHAT'S THE CATCH?
YOU HAVE TO BE MY DATE!
WELL, THAT'S DIRECT.
YOU DON'T GET OUT MUCH, DO YOU?
ASTRO BISTRO
SORRY, IT'S AN EMERGENCY, OTHERWISE I WOULD'VE DONE IT DIFFERENTLY!
EMERGENCY DATING?
WELL, I'LL TRY ANYTHING ONCE.
REWARDS PART 2

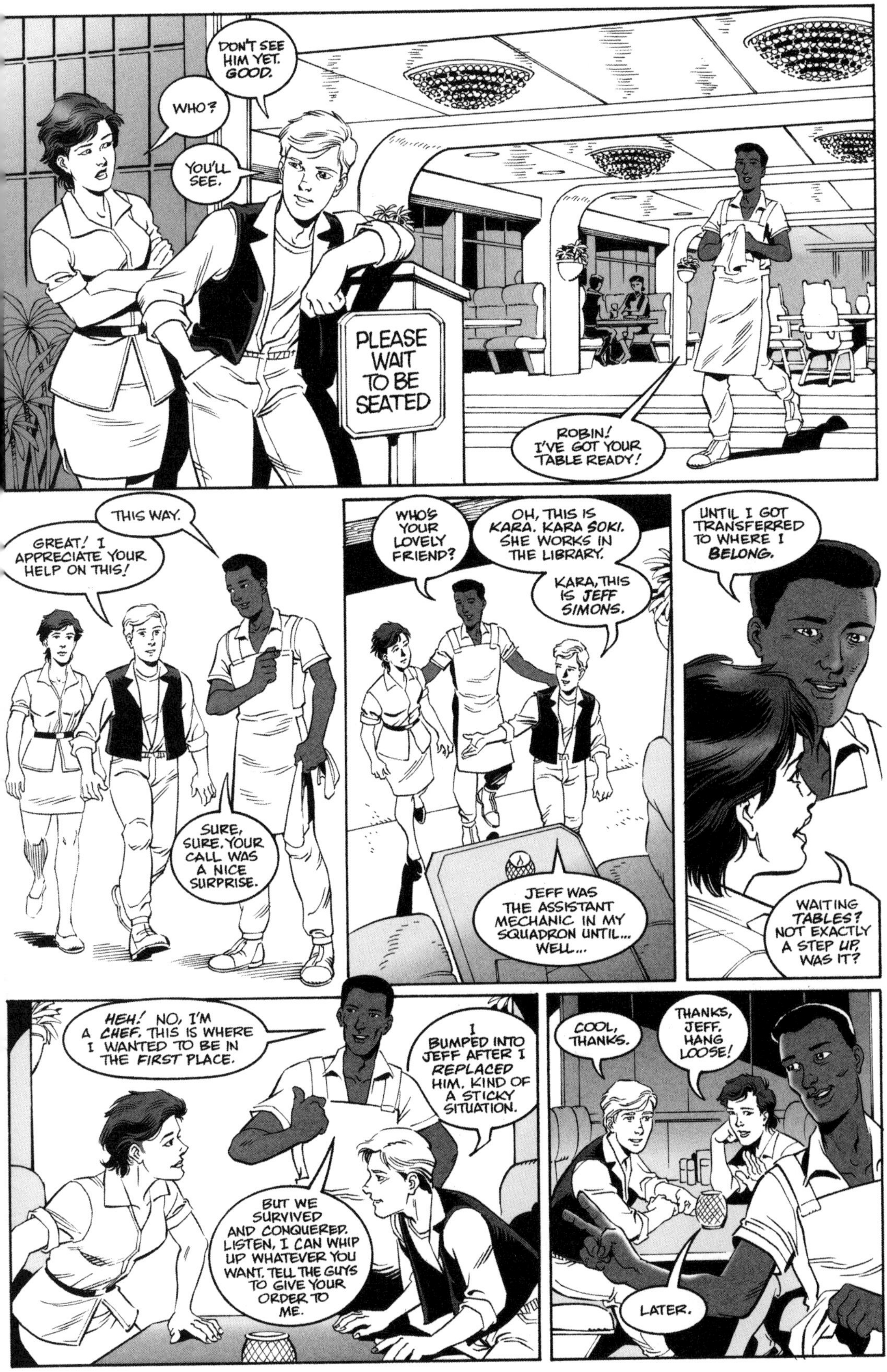
DON'T SEE HIM YET. GOOD.
WHO?
YOU'LL SEE.
PLEASE WAIT TO BE SEATED
ROBIN! I'VE GOT YOUR TABLE READY!
THIS WAY.
GREAT! I APPRECIATE YOUR HELP ON THIS!
SURE, SURE. YOUR CALL WAS A NICE SURPRISE.
WHO'S YOUR LOVELY FRIEND?
OH, THIS IS KARA. KARA SOKI. SHE WORKS IN THE LIBRARY.
KARA, THIS IS JEFF SIMONS.
JEFF WAS THE ASSISTANT MECHANIC IN MY SQUADRON UNTIL... WELL...
UNTIL I GOT TRANSFERRED TO WHERE I BELONG.
WAITING TABLES? NOT EXACTLY A STEP UP, WAS IT?
HEH! NO, I'M A CHEF. THIS IS WHERE I WANTED TO BE IN THE FIRST PLACE.
I BUMPED INTO JEFF AFTER I REPLACED HIM. KIND OF A STICKY SITUATION.
BUT WE SURVIVED AND CONQUERED. LISTEN, I CAN WHIP UP WHATEVER YOU WANT. TELL THE GUYS TO GIVE YOUR ORDER TO ME.
COOL, THANKS.
THANKS, JEFF. HANG LOOSE!
LATER.

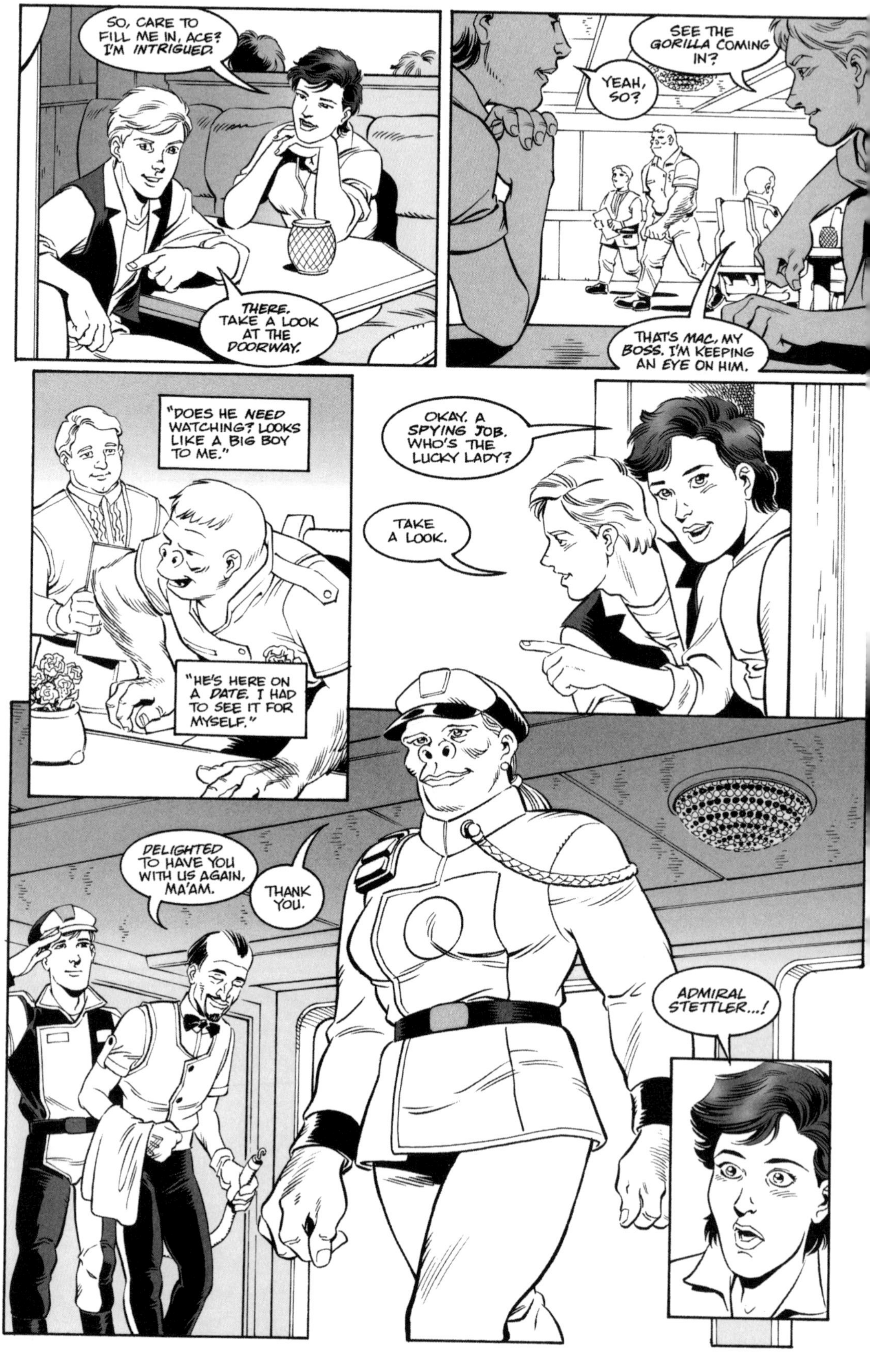
SO, CARE TO FILL ME IN, ACE? I'M INTRIGUED.
THERE. TAKE A LOOK AT THE DOORWAY.
SEE THE GORILLA COMING IN?
YEAH, SO?
THAT'S MAC, MY BOSS. I'M KEEPING AN EYE ON HIM.
"DOES HE NEED WATCHING? LOOKS LIKE A BIG BOY TO ME."
"HE'S HERE ON A DATE. I HAD TO SEE IT FOR MYSELF."
OKAY. A SPYING JOB. WHO'S THE LUCKY LADY?
TAKE A LOOK.
DELIGHTED TO HAVE YOU WITH US AGAIN, MA'AM.
THANK YOU.
ADMIRAL STETTLER...!

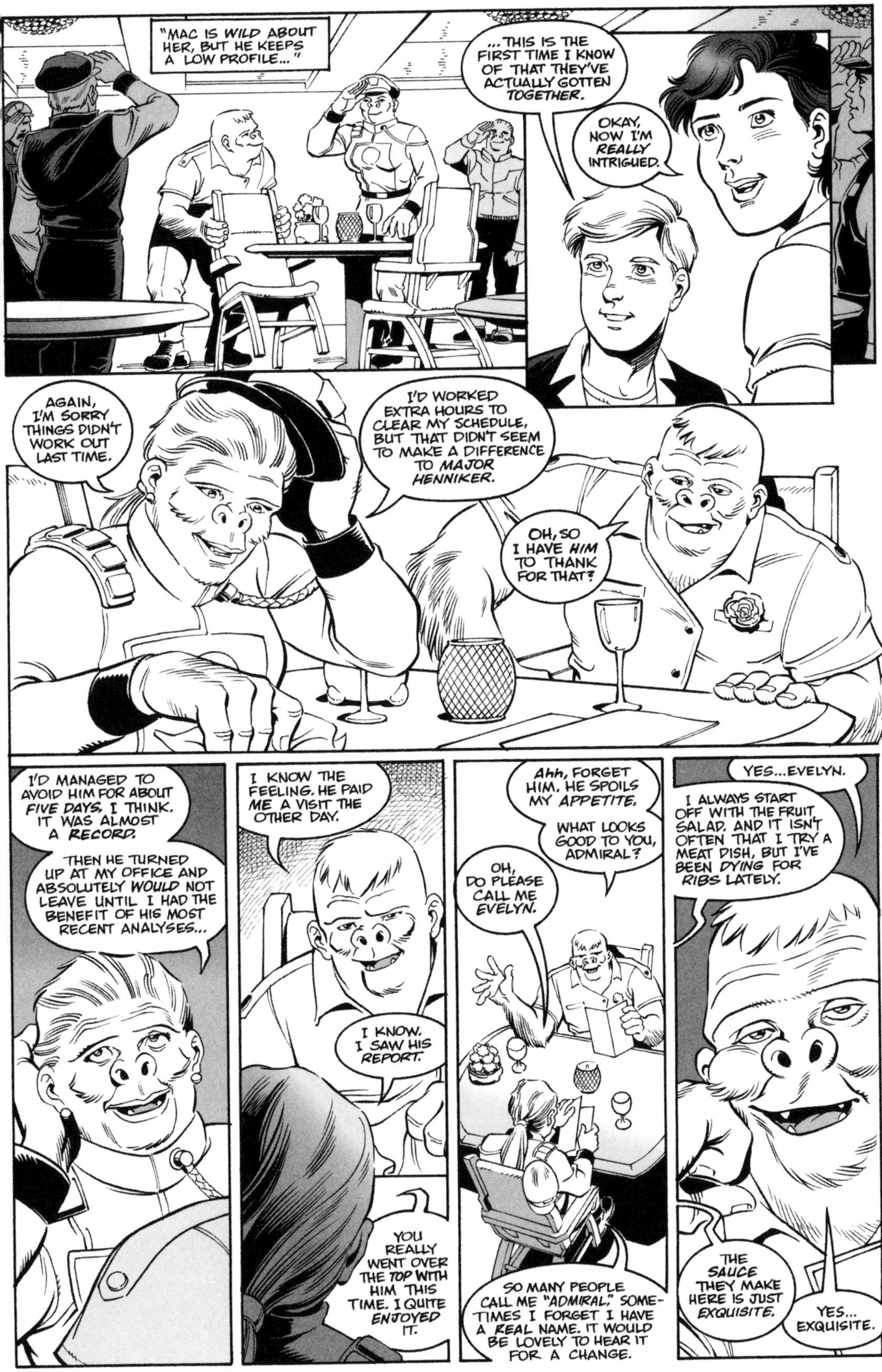
"MAC IS WILD ABOUT HER, BUT HE KEEPS A LOW PROFILE..."
...THIS IS THE FIRST TIME I KNOW OF THAT THEY'VE ACTUALLY GOTTEN TOGETHER.
OKAY, NOW I'M REALLY INTRIGUED.
AGAIN, I'M SORRY THINGS DIDN'T WORK OUT LAST TIME.
I'D WORKED EXTRA HOURS TO CLEAR MY SCHEDULE, BUT THAT DIDN'T SEEM TO MAKE A DIFFERENCE TO MAJOR HENNIKER.
OH, SO I HAVE HIM TO THANK FOR THAT?
I'D MANAGED TO AVOID HIM FOR ABOUT FIVE DAYS, I THINK. IT WAS ALMOST A RECORD.
THEN HE TURNED UP AT MY OFFICE AND ABSOLUTELY WOULD NOT LEAVE UNTIL I HAD THE BENEFIT OF HIS MOST RECENT ANALYSES...
I KNOW THE FEELING. HE PAID ME A VISIT THE OTHER DAY.
I KNOW. I SAW HIS REPORT.
YOU REALLY WENT OVER THE TOP WITH HIM THIS TIME. I QUITE ENJOYED IT.
Ahh, FORGET HIM. HE SPOILS MY APPETITE.
WHAT LOOKS GOOD TO YOU, ADMIRAL?
OH, DO PLEASE CALL ME EVELYN.
SO MANY PEOPLE CALL ME "ADMIRAL," SOMETIMES I FORGET I HAVE A REAL NAME. IT WOULD BE LOVELY TO HEAR IT FOR A CHANGE.
YES...EVELYN.
I ALWAYS START OFF WITH THE FRUIT SALAD, AND IT ISN'T OFTEN THAT I TRY A MEAT DISH, BUT I'VE BEEN DYING FOR RIBS LATELY.
THE SAUCE THEY MAKE HERE IS JUST EXQUISITE.
YES... EXQUISITE.

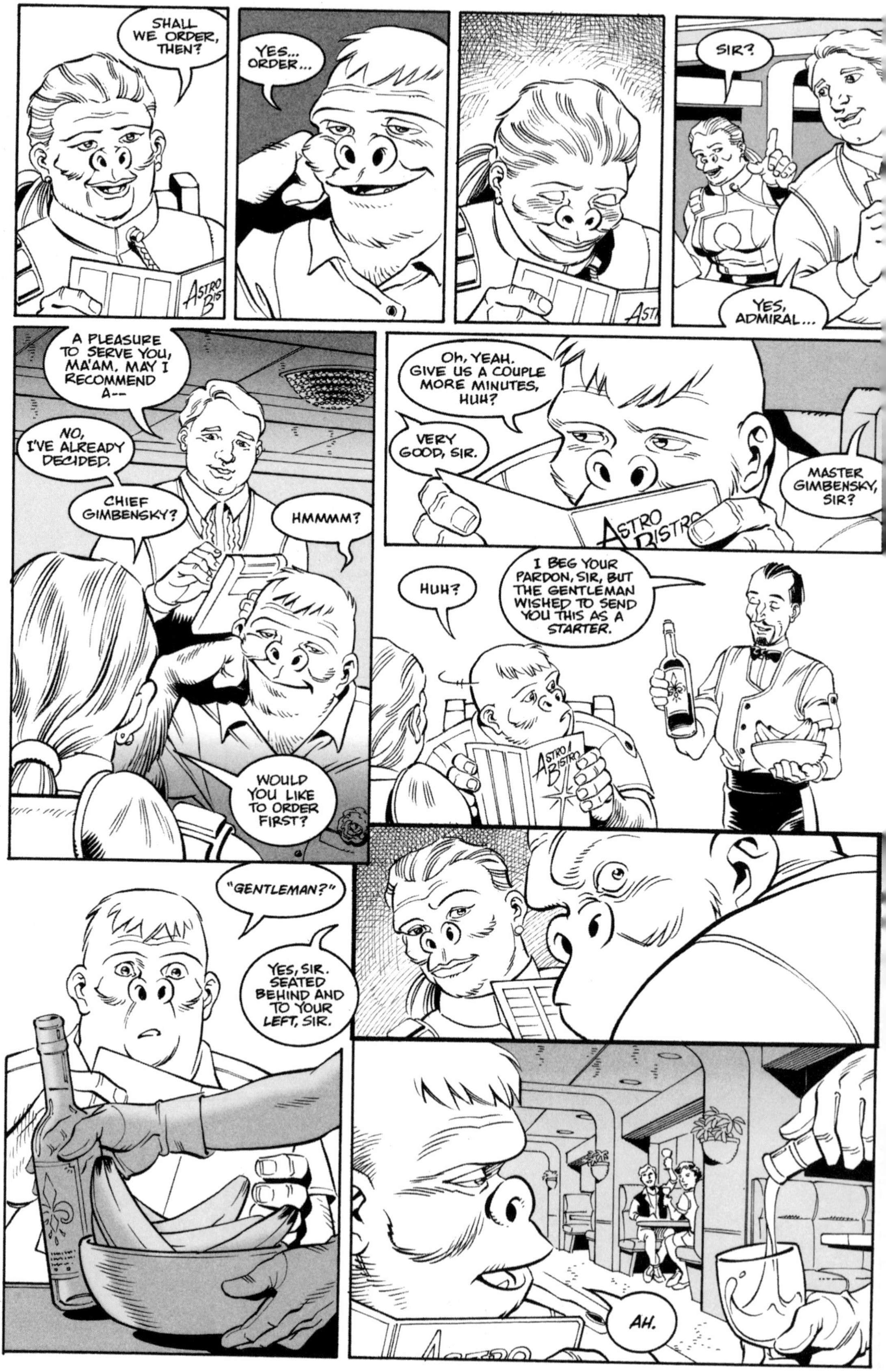
SHALL WE ORDER, THEN?
YES... ORDER...
SIR?
YES, ADMIRAL...
A PLEASURE TO SERVE YOU, MA'AM. MAY I RECOMMEND A--
NO, I'VE ALREADY DECIDED.
CHIEF GIMBENSKY?
HMMMM?
WOULD YOU LIKE TO ORDER FIRST?
OH, YEAH. GIVE US A COUPLE MORE MINUTES, HUH?
VERY GOOD, SIR.
MASTER GIMBENSKY, SIR?
HUH?
I BEG YOUR PARDON, SIR, BUT THE GENTLEMAN WISHED TO SEND YOU THIS AS A STARTER.
"GENTLEMAN?"
YES, SIR. SEATED BEHIND AND TO YOUR LEFT, SIR.
AH.

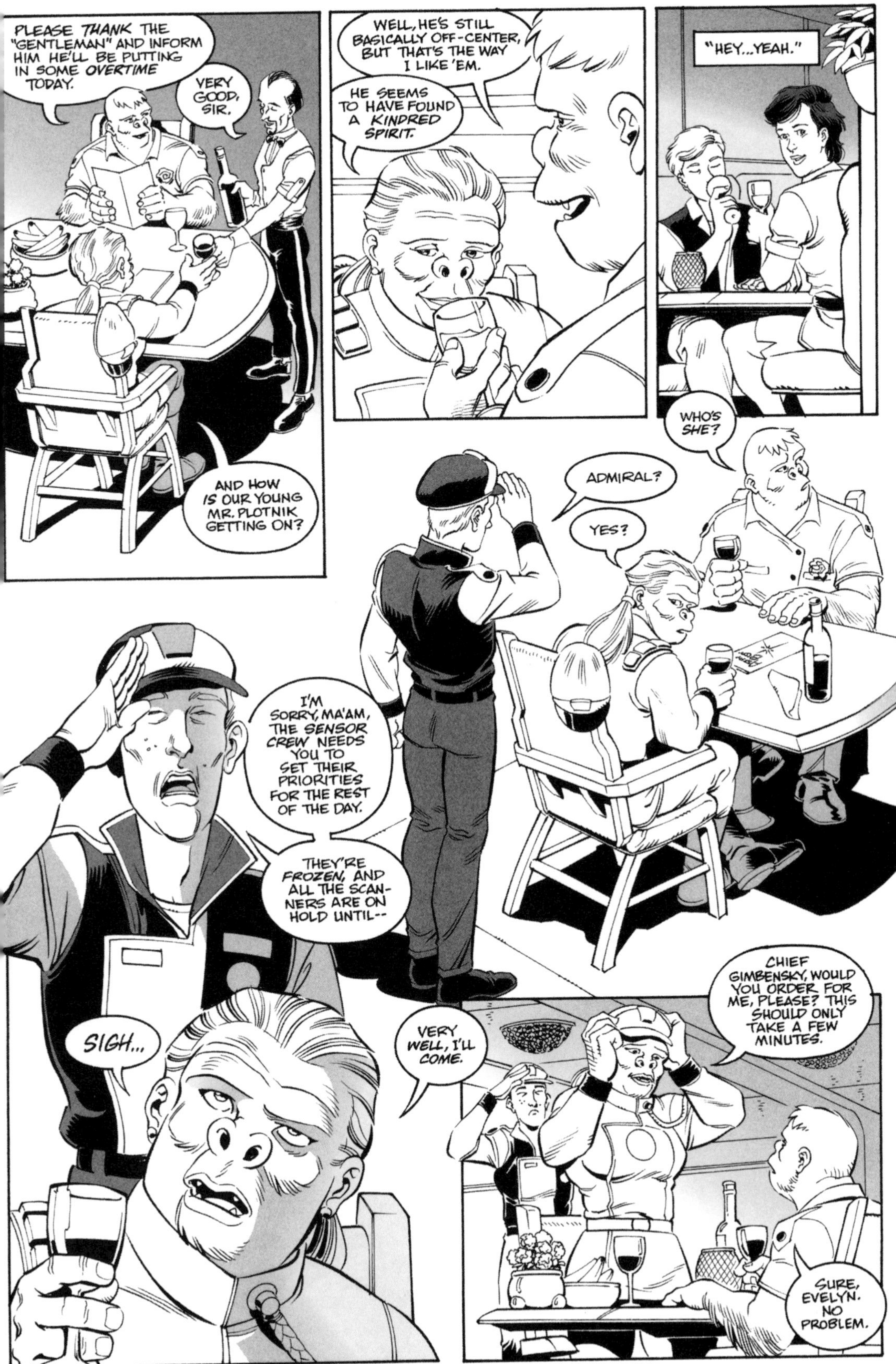
PLEASE THANK THE "GENTLEMAN" AND INFORM HIM HE'LL BE PUTTING IN SOME OVERTIME TODAY.
VERY GOOD, SIR.
AND HOW IS OUR YOUNG MR. PLOTNIK GETTING ON?
WELL, HE'S STILL BASICALLY OFF-CENTER, BUT THAT'S THE WAY I LIKE 'EM.
HE SEEMS TO HAVE FOUND A KINDRED SPIRIT.
"HEY...YEAH."
WHO'S SHE?
ADMIRAL?
YES?
I'M SORRY, MA'AM, THE SENSOR CREW NEEDS YOU TO SET THEIR PRIORITIES FOR THE REST OF THE DAY.
THEY'RE FROZEN, AND ALL THE SCANNERS ARE ON HOLD UNTIL--
SIGH...
VERY WELL, I'LL COME.
CHIEF GIMBENSKY, WOULD YOU ORDER FOR ME, PLEASE? THIS SHOULD ONLY TAKE A FEW MINUTES.
SURE, EVELYN. NO PROBLEM.

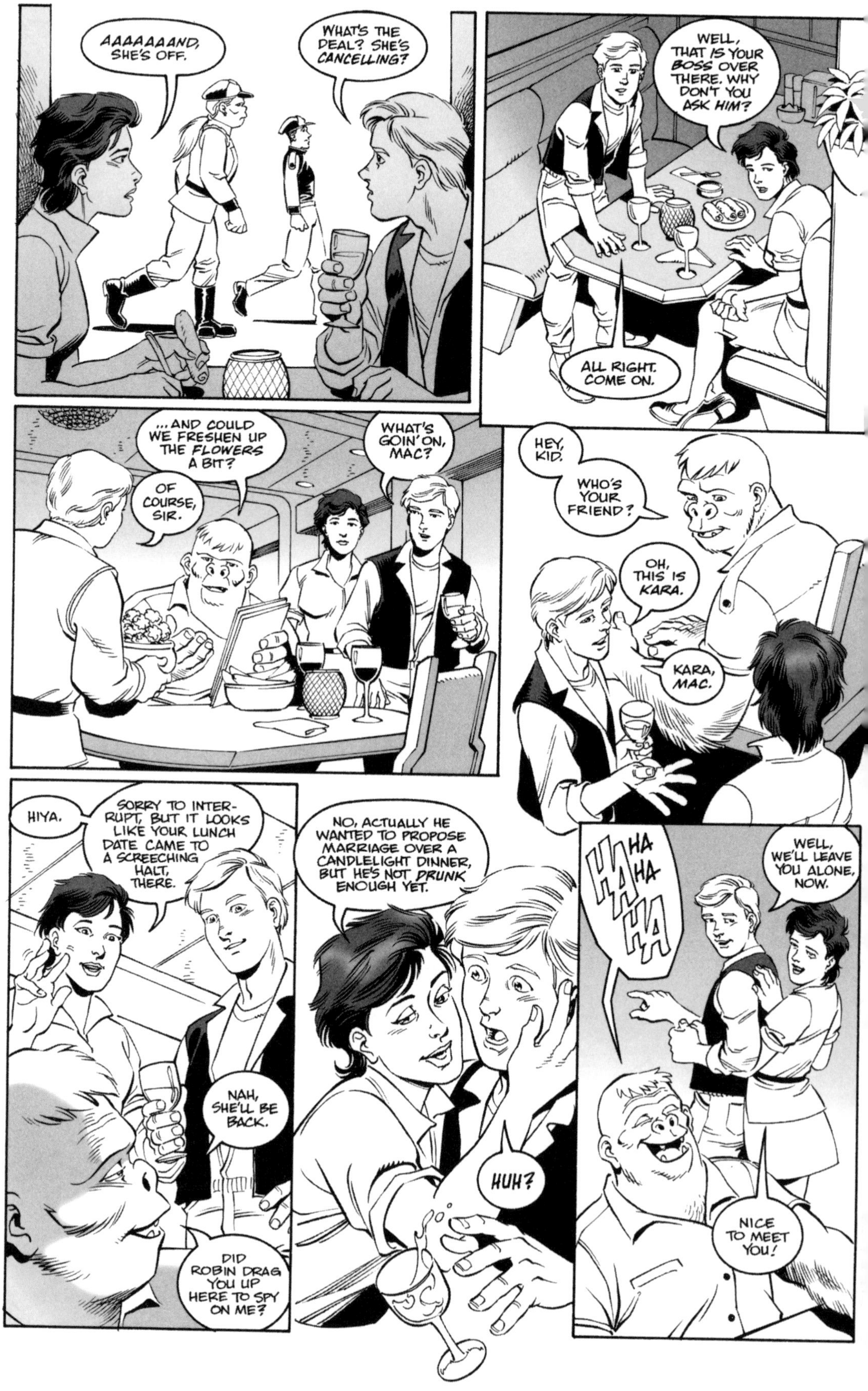

AAAAAAAND, SHE'S OFF.
WHAT'S THE DEAL? SHE'S CANCELLING?
WELL, THAT IS YOUR BOSS OVER THERE. WHY DON'T YOU ASK HIM?
ALL RIGHT. COME ON.
...AND COULD WE FRESHEN UP THE FLOWERS A BIT?
OF COURSE, SIR.
WHAT'S GOIN' ON, MAC?
HEY, KID.
WHO'S YOUR FRIEND?
OH, THIS IS KARA.
KARA, MAC.
HIYA.
SORRY TO INTER-RUPT, BUT IT LOOKS LIKE YOUR LUNCH DATE CAME TO A SCREECHING HALT, THERE.
NAH, SHE'LL BE BACK.
DID ROBIN DRAG YOU UP HERE TO SPY ON ME?
NO, ACTUALLY HE WANTED TO PROPOSE MARRIAGE OVER A CANDLELIGHT DINNER, BUT HE'S NOT DRUNK ENOUGH YET.
HUH?
HA HA HA HA HA
WELL, WE'LL LEAVE YOU ALONE, NOW.
NICE TO MEET YOU!

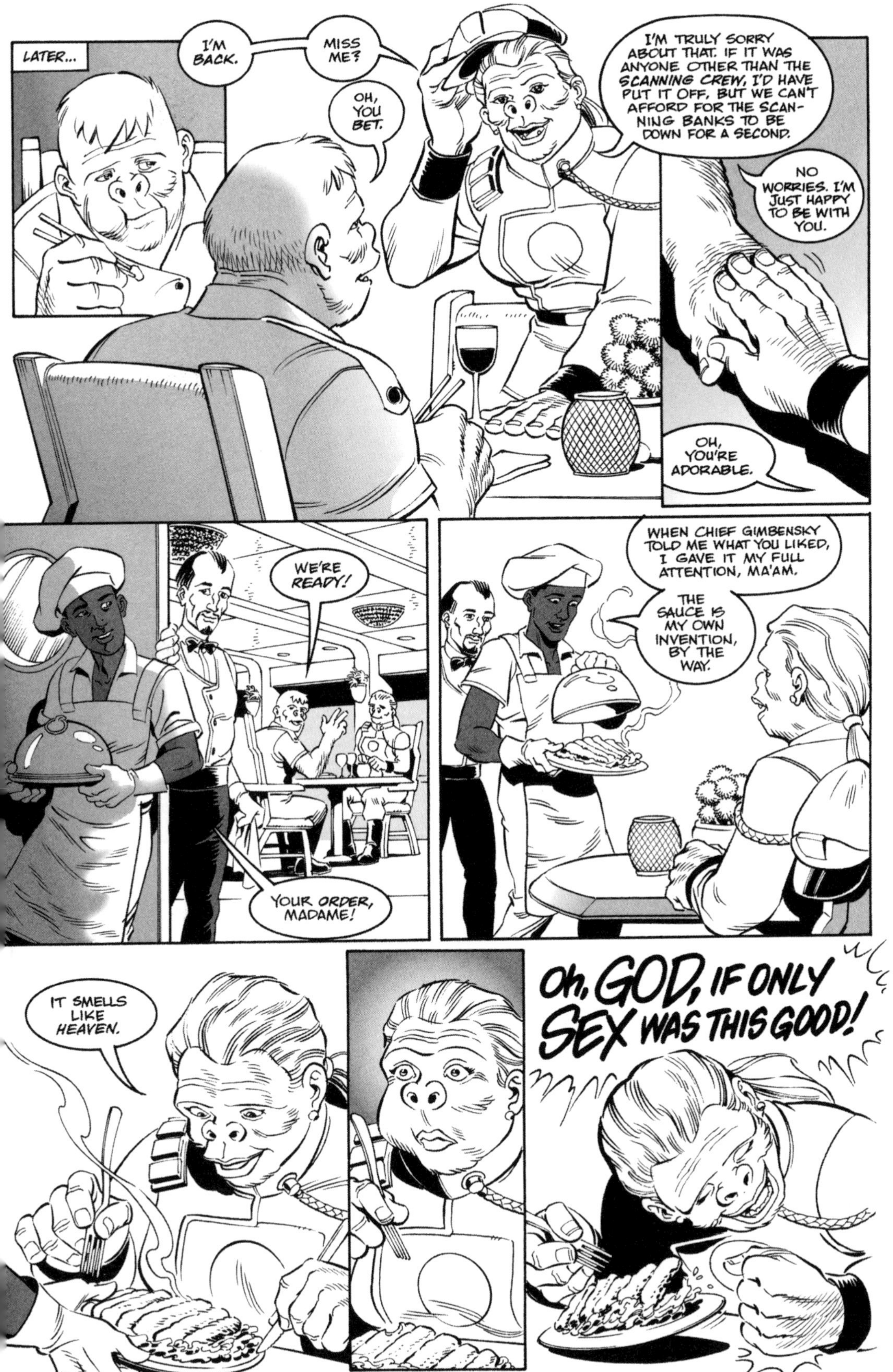
LATER...
I'M BACK.
MISS ME?
OH, YOU BET.
I'M TRULY SORRY ABOUT THAT. IF IT WAS ANYONE OTHER THAN THE SCANNING CREW, I'D HAVE PUT IT OFF, BUT WE CAN'T AFFORD FOR THE SCANNING BANKS TO BE DOWN FOR A SECOND.
NO WORRIES. I'M JUST HAPPY TO BE WITH YOU.
OH, YOU'RE ADORABLE.
WE'RE READY!
YOUR ORDER, MADAME!
WHEN CHIEF GIMBENSKY TOLD ME WHAT YOU LIKED, I GAVE IT MY FULL ATTENTION, MA'AM.
THE SAUCE IS MY OWN INVENTION, BY THE WAY.
IT SMELLS LIKE HEAVEN.
Oh, GOD, IF ONLY SEX WAS THIS GOOD!

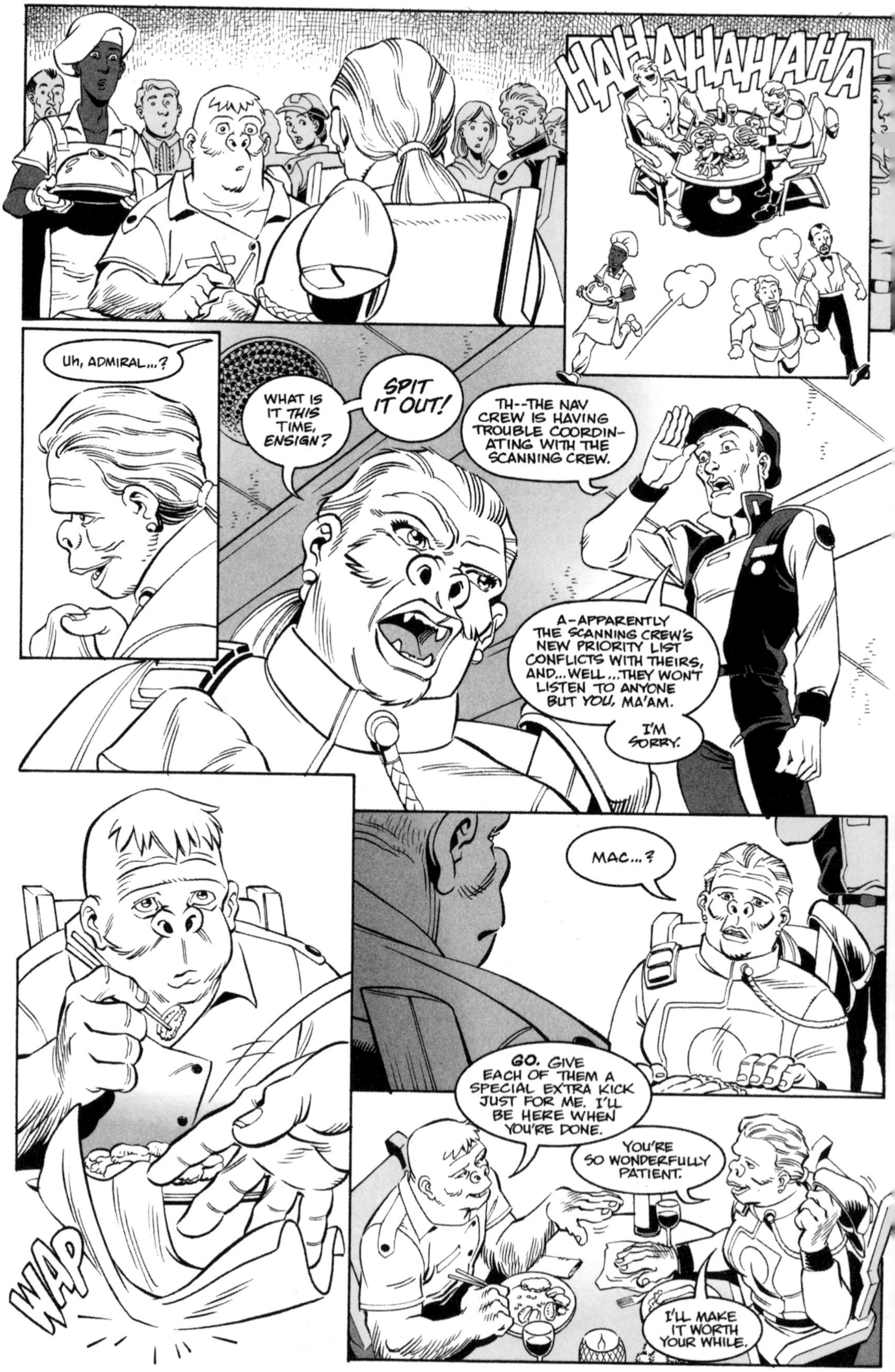
HAHAHAHAHAHA
Uh, ADMIRAL...?
WHAT IS IT THIS TIME, ENSIGN?
SPIT IT OUT!
TH--THE NAV CREW IS HAVING TROUBLE COORDINATING WITH THE SCANNING CREW.
A-APPARENTLY THE SCANNING CREW'S NEW PRIORITY LIST CONFLICTS WITH THEIRS, AND...WELL...THEY WON'T LISTEN TO ANYONE BUT YOU, MA'AM.
I'M SORRY.
WAP
MAC...?
GO. GIVE EACH OF THEM A SPECIAL EXTRA KICK JUST FOR ME. I'LL BE HERE WHEN YOU'RE DONE.
YOU'RE SO WONDERFULLY PATIENT.
I'LL MAKE IT WORTH YOUR WHILE.

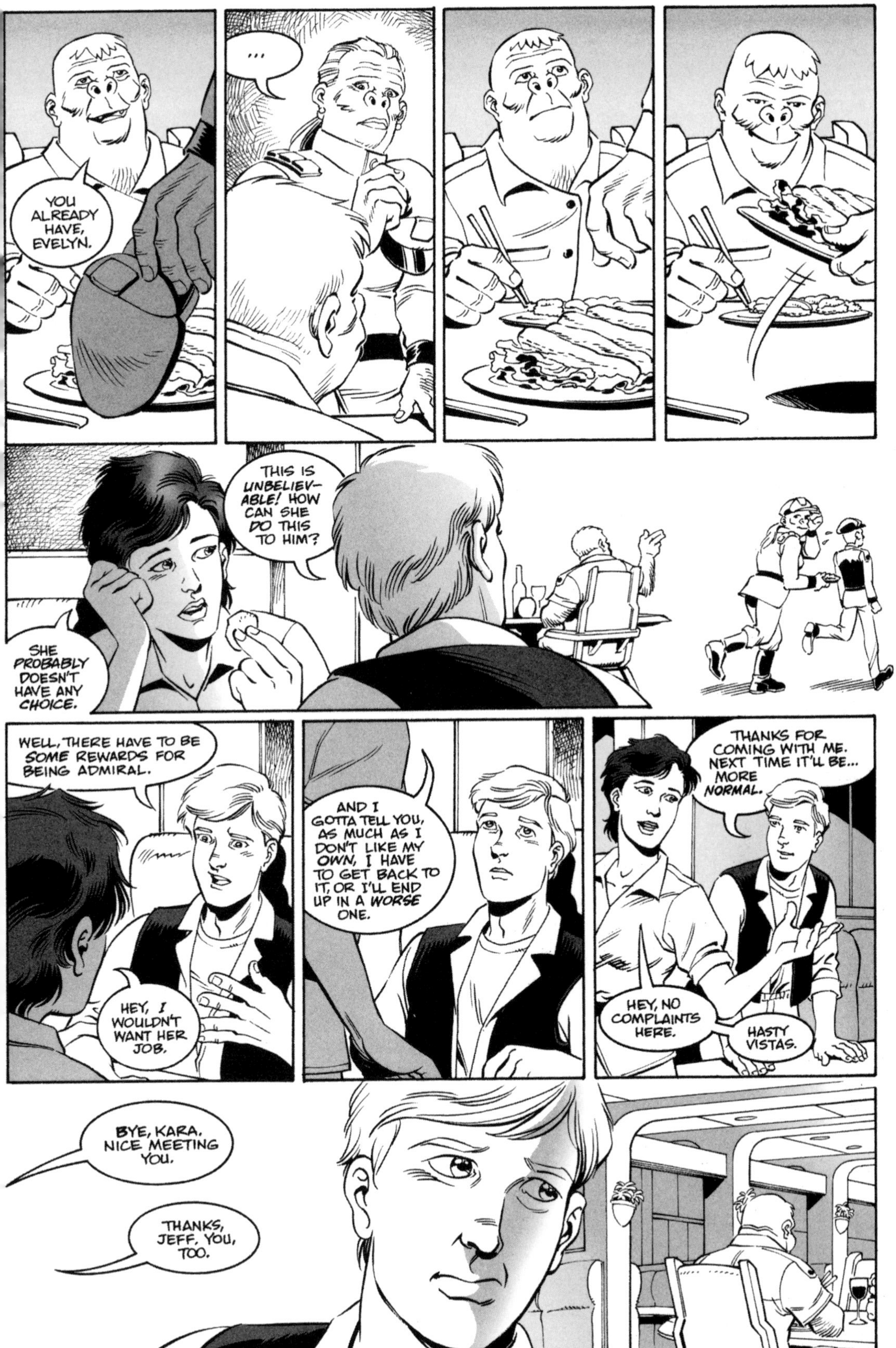
YOU ALREADY HAVE, EVELYN.
...
THIS IS UNBELIEVABLE! HOW CAN SHE DO THIS TO HIM?
SHE PROBABLY DOESN'T HAVE ANY CHOICE.
WELL, THERE HAVE TO BE SOME REWARDS FOR BEING ADMIRAL.
HEY, I WOULDN'T WANT HER JOB.
AND I GOTTA TELL YOU, AS MUCH AS I DON'T LIKE MY OWN, I HAVE TO GET BACK TO IT, OR I'LL END UP IN A WORSE ONE.
THANKS FOR COMING WITH ME. NEXT TIME IT'LL BE... MORE NORMAL.
HEY, NO COMPLAINTS HERE.
HASTY VISTAS.
BYE, KARA. NICE MEETING YOU.
THANKS, JEFF. YOU, TOO.

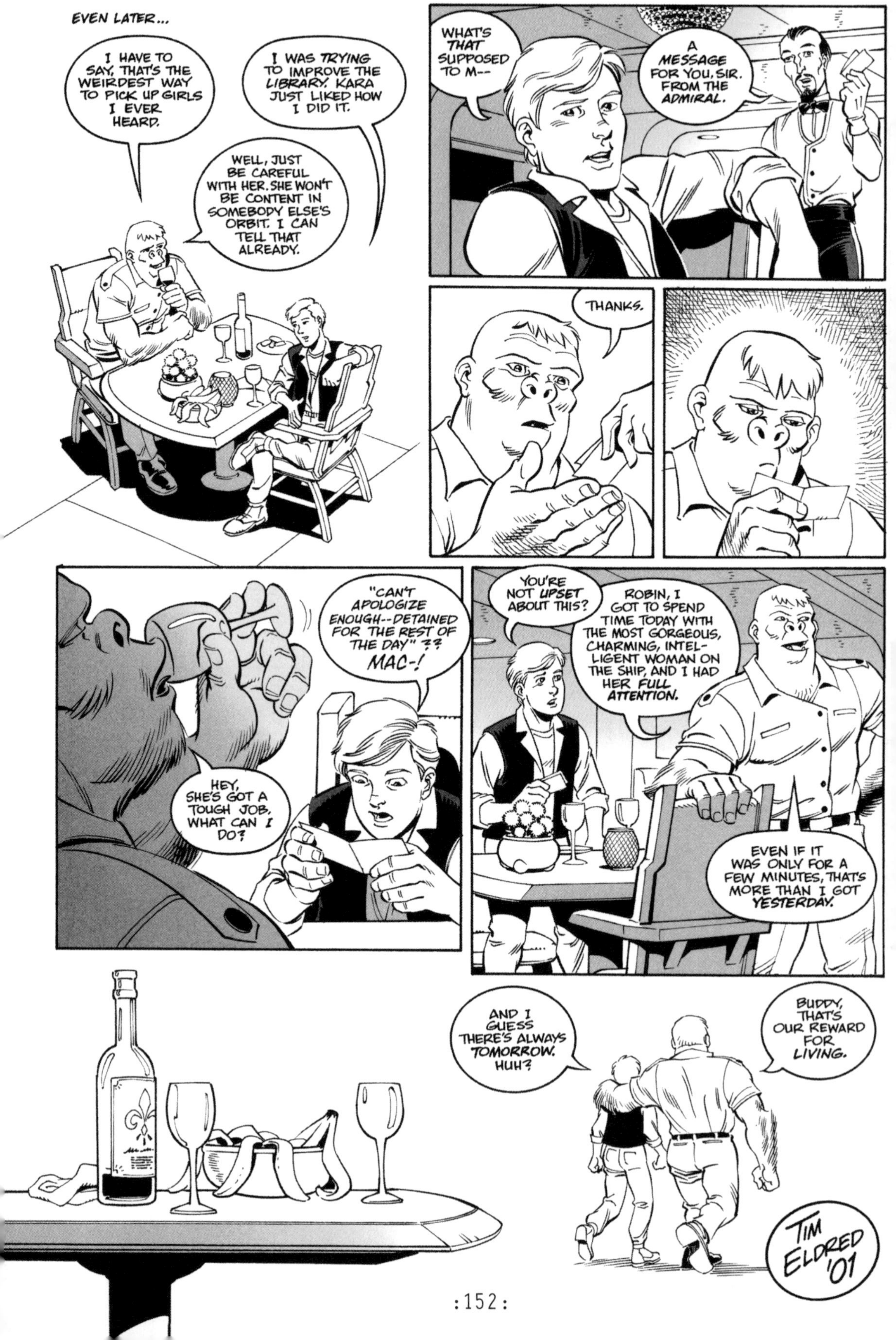
EVEN LATER...
I HAVE TO SAY, THAT'S THE WEIRDEST WAY TO PICK UP GIRLS I EVER HEARD.
I WAS TRYING TO IMPROVE THE LIBRARY. KARA JUST LIKED HOW I DID IT.
WELL, JUST BE CAREFUL WITH HER. SHE WON'T BE CONTENT IN SOMEBODY ELSE'S ORBIT. I CAN TELL THAT ALREADY.
WHAT'S THAT SUPPOSED TO M--
A MESSAGE FOR YOU, SIR. FROM THE ADMIRAL.
THANKS.
"CAN'T APOLOGIZE ENOUGH--DETAINED FOR THE REST OF THE DAY" ?? MAC-!
HEY, SHE'S GOT A TOUGH JOB. WHAT CAN I DO?
YOU'RE NOT UPSET ABOUT THIS?
ROBIN, I GOT TO SPEND TIME TODAY WITH THE MOST GORGEOUS, CHARMING, INTEL-LIGENT WOMAN ON THE SHIP, AND I HAD HER FULL ATTENTION.
EVEN IF IT WAS ONLY FOR A FEW MINUTES, THAT'S MORE THAN I GOT YESTERDAY.
AND I GUESS THERE'S ALWAYS TOMORROW. HUH?
BUDDY, THAT'S OUR REWARD FOR LIVING.
TIM ELDRED '01

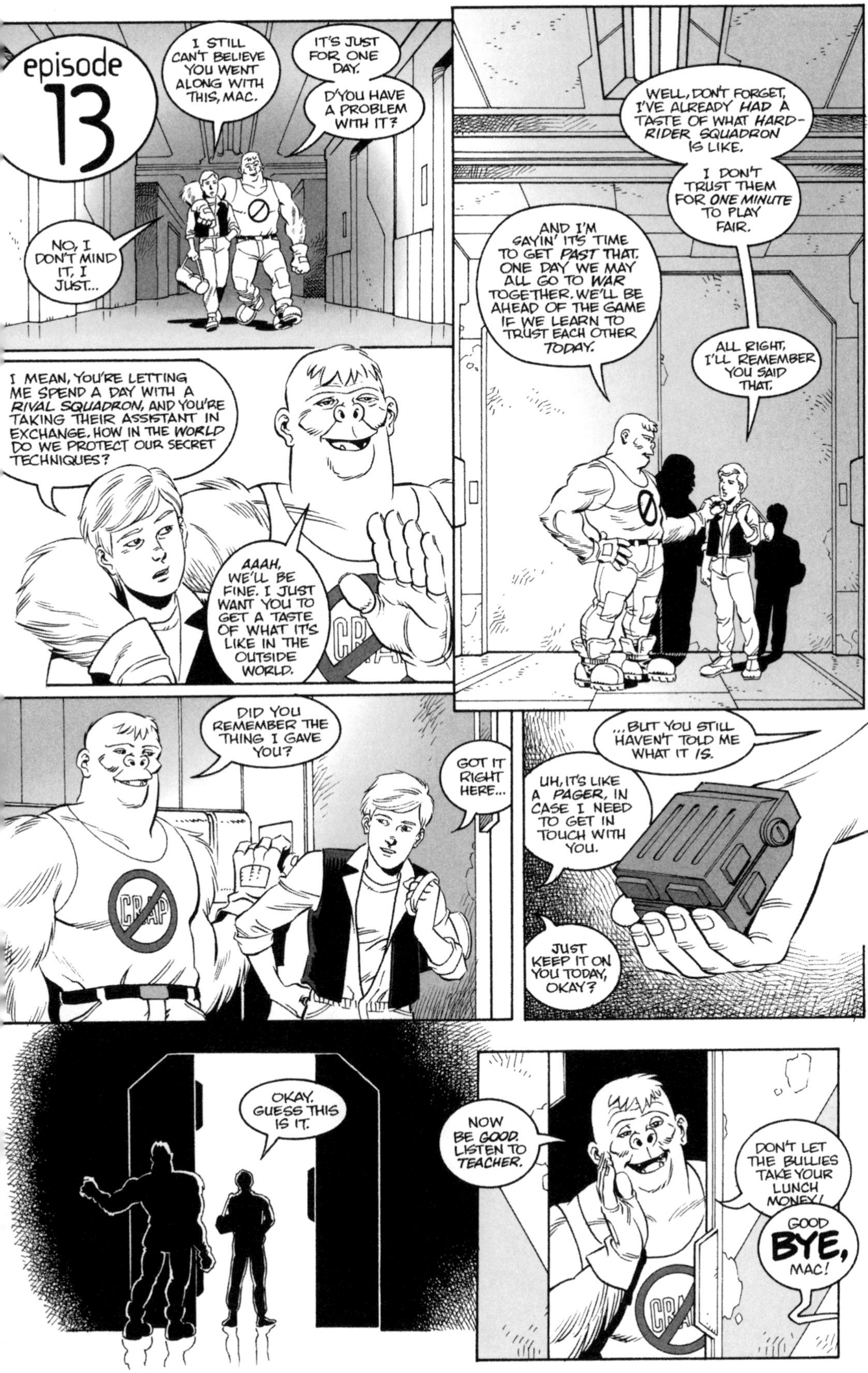
episode 13
I STILL CAN'T BELIEVE YOU WENT ALONG WITH THIS, MAC.
IT'S JUST FOR ONE DAY.
D'YOU HAVE A PROBLEM WITH IT?
NO, I DON'T MIND IT, I JUST...
I MEAN, YOU'RE LETTING ME SPEND A DAY WITH A RIVAL SQUADRON, AND YOU'RE TAKING THEIR ASSISTANT IN EXCHANGE. HOW IN THE WORLD DO WE PROTECT OUR SECRET TECHNIQUES?
AAAH, WE'LL BE FINE. I JUST WANT YOU TO GET A TASTE OF WHAT IT'S LIKE IN THE OUTSIDE WORLD.
WELL, DON'T FORGET, I'VE ALREADY HAD A TASTE OF WHAT HARD-RIDER SQUADRON IS LIKE.
I DON'T TRUST THEM FOR ONE MINUTE TO PLAY FAIR.
AND I'M SAYIN' IT'S TIME TO GET PAST THAT. ONE DAY WE MAY ALL GO TO WAR TOGETHER. WE'LL BE AHEAD OF THE GAME IF WE LEARN TO TRUST EACH OTHER TODAY.
ALL RIGHT, I'LL REMEMBER YOU SAID THAT.
DID YOU REMEMBER THE THING I GAVE YOU?
GOT IT RIGHT HERE...
...BUT YOU STILL HAVEN'T TOLD ME WHAT IT IS.
UH, IT'S LIKE A PAGER, IN CASE I NEED TO GET IN TOUCH WITH YOU.
JUST KEEP IT ON YOU TODAY, OKAY?
OKAY. GUESS THIS IS IT.
NOW BE GOOD. LISTEN TO TEACHER.
DON'T LET THE BULLIES TAKE YOUR LUNCH MONEY!
GOOD BYE, MAC!

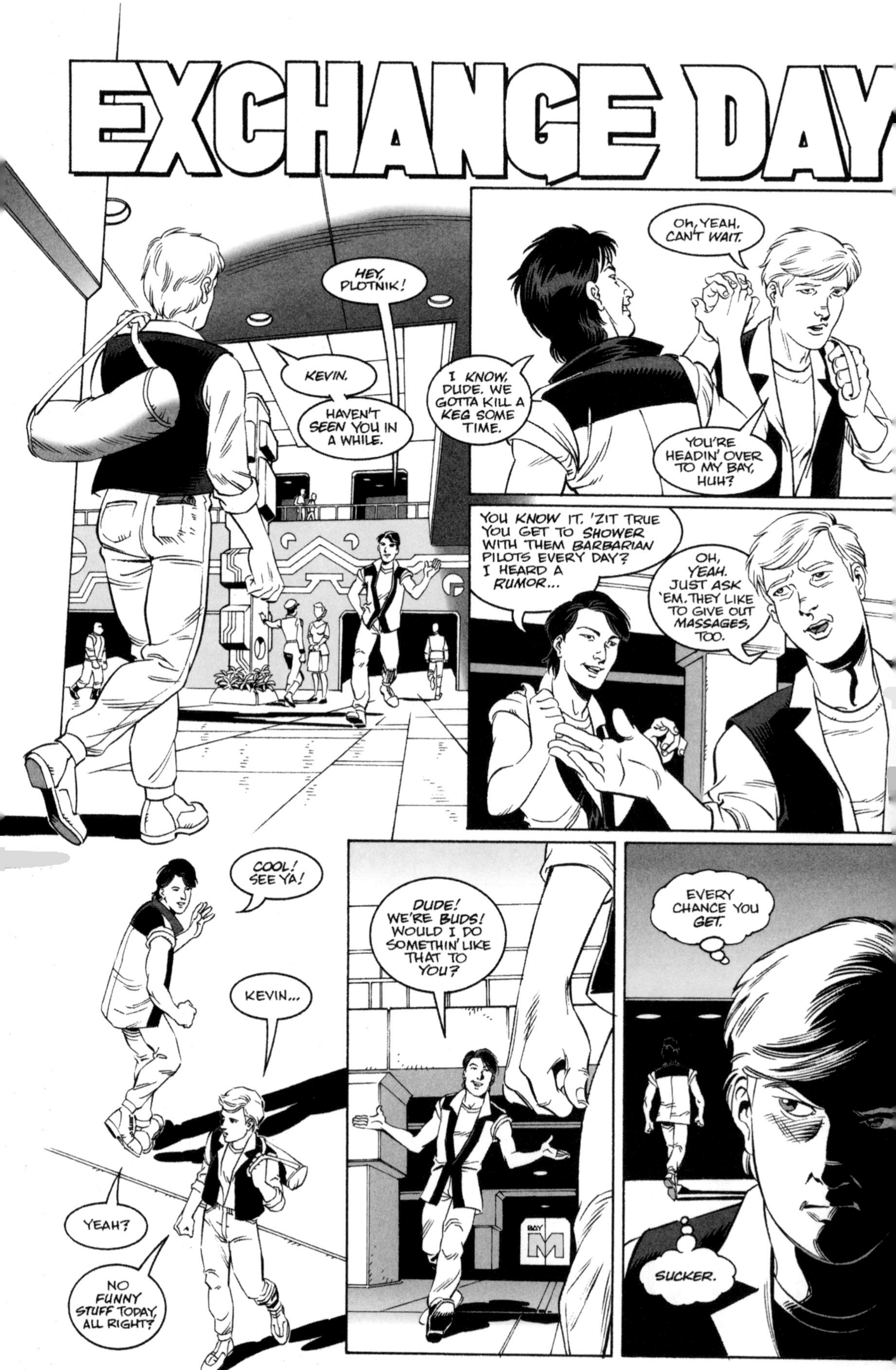
EXCHANGE DAY
HEY, PLOTNIK!
KEVIN.
HAVEN'T SEEN YOU IN A WHILE.
I KNOW, DUDE. WE GOTTA KILL A KEG SOME TIME.
OH, YEAH, CAN'T WAIT.
YOU'RE HEADIN' OVER TO MY BAY, HUH?
YOU KNOW IT. 'ZIT TRUE YOU GET TO SHOWER WITH THEM BARBARIAN PILOTS EVERY DAY? I HEARD A RUMOR...
OH, YEAH. JUST ASK 'EM. THEY LIKE TO GIVE OUT MASSAGES, TOO.
COOL! SEE YA!
KEVIN...
YEAH?
NO FUNNY STUFF TODAY, ALL RIGHT?
DUDE! WE'RE BUDS! WOULD I DO SOMETHIN' LIKE THAT TO YOU?
BAY M
EVERY CHANCE YOU GET.
SUCKER.

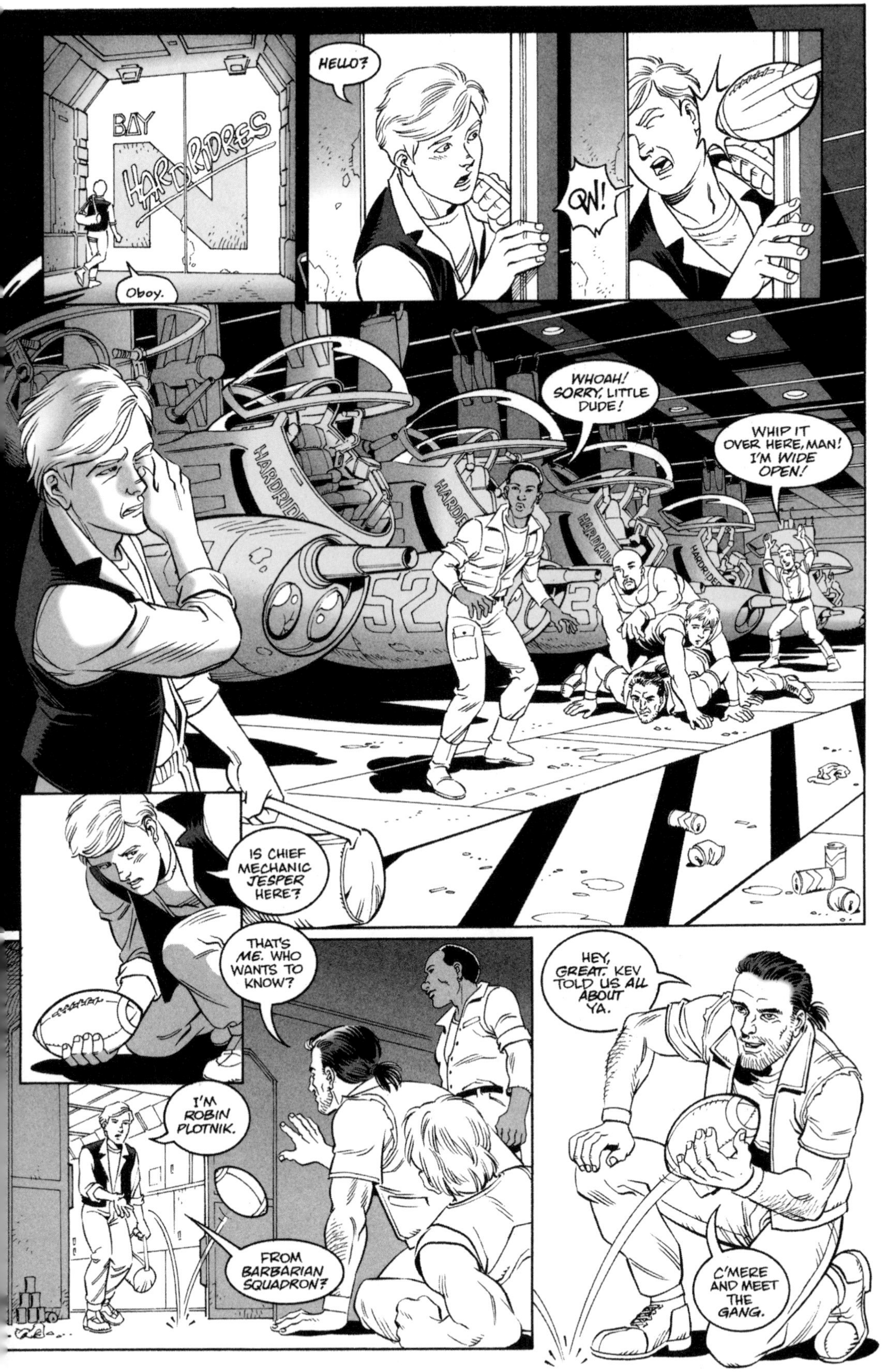
BAY
HARDRIDRES
Oboy.
HELLO?
OW!
WHOAH! SORRY, LITTLE DUDE!
WHIP IT OVER HERE, MAN! I'M WIDE OPEN!
IS CHIEF MECHANIC JESPER HERE?
THAT'S ME. WHO WANTS TO KNOW?
I'M ROBIN PLOTNIK.
FROM BARBARIAN SQUADRON?
HEY, GREAT. KEV TOLD US ALL ABOUT YA.
C'MERE AND MEET THE GANG.

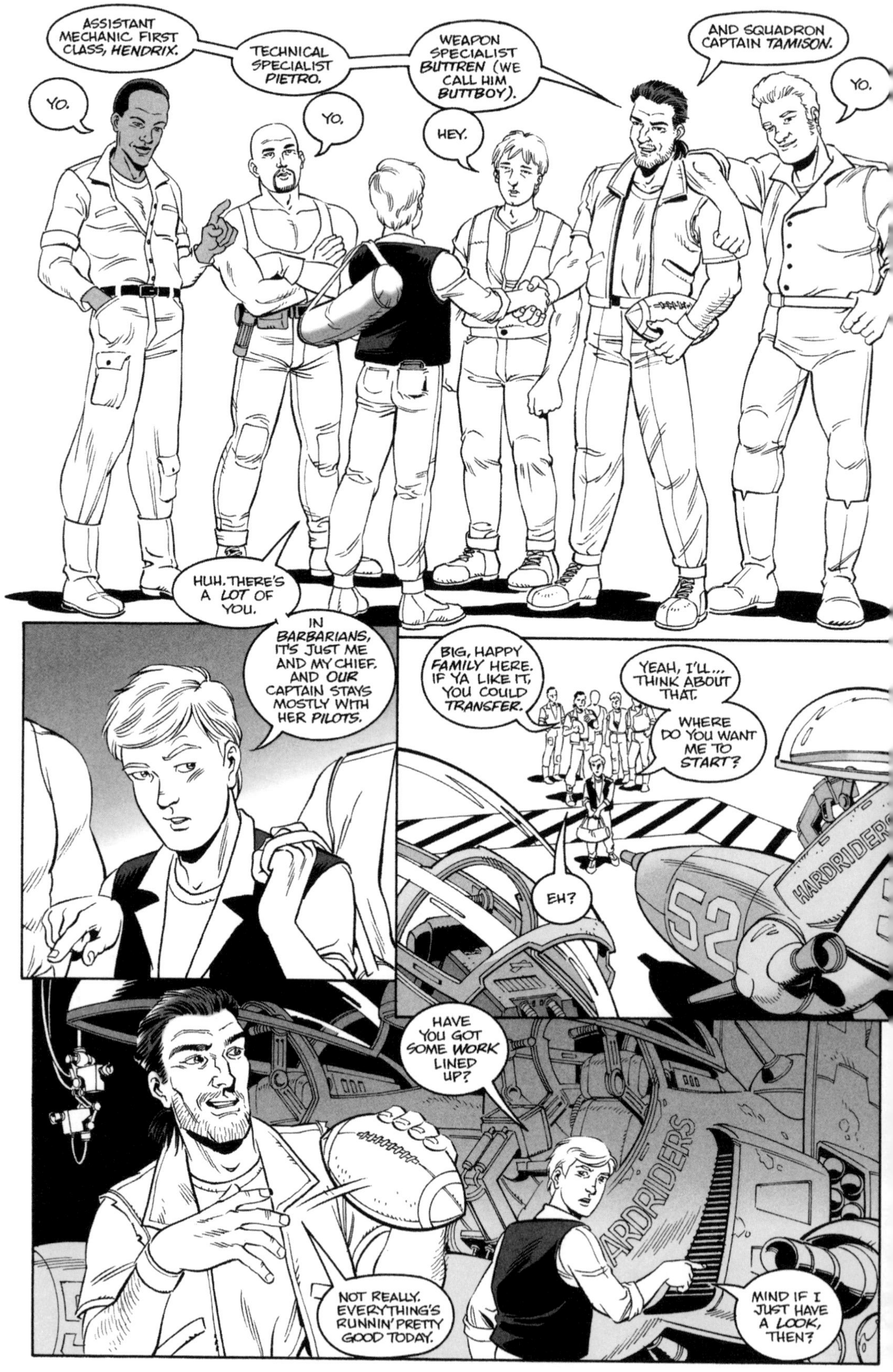
ASSISTANT MECHANIC FIRST CLASS, HENDRIX.
YO.
TECHNICAL SPECIALIST PIETRO.
YO.
WEAPON SPECIALIST BUTTREN (WE CALL HIM BUTTBOY).
HEY.
AND SQUADRON CAPTAIN TAMISON.
YO.
HUH. THERE'S A LOT OF YOU.
IN BARBARIANS, IT'S JUST ME AND MY CHIEF. AND OUR CAPTAIN STAYS MOSTLY WITH HER PILOTS.
BIG, HAPPY FAMILY HERE. IF YA LIKE IT, YOU COULD TRANSFER.
EH?
YEAH, I'LL... THINK ABOUT THAT.
WHERE DO YOU WANT ME TO START?
HARDRIDERS
52
HAVE YOU GOT SOME WORK LINED UP?
HARDRIDERS
NOT REALLY. EVERYTHING'S RUNNIN' PRETTY GOOD TODAY.
MIND IF I JUST HAVE A LOOK, THEN?

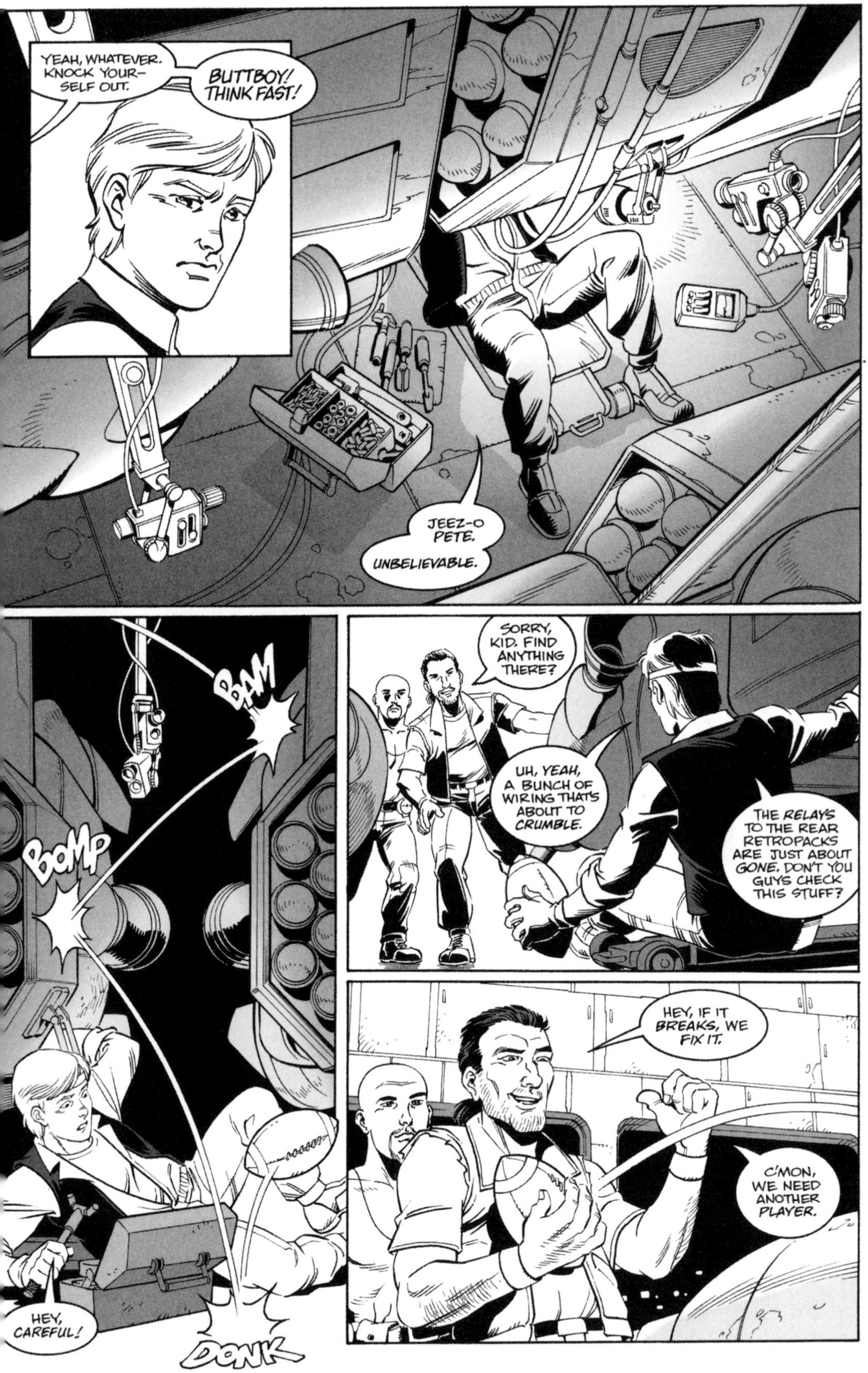
YEAH, WHATEVER. KNOCK YOURSELF OUT.
BUTTBOY! THINK FAST!
JEEZ-O PETE.
UNBELIEVABLE.
BAM
BOMP
HEY, CAREFUL!
DONK
SORRY, KID. FIND ANYTHING THERE?
UH, YEAH, A BUNCH OF WIRING THAT'S ABOUT TO CRUMBLE.
THE RELAYS TO THE REAR RETROPACKS ARE JUST ABOUT GONE. DON'T YOU GUYS CHECK THIS STUFF?
HEY, IF IT BREAKS, WE FIX IT.
C'MON, WE NEED ANOTHER PLAYER.

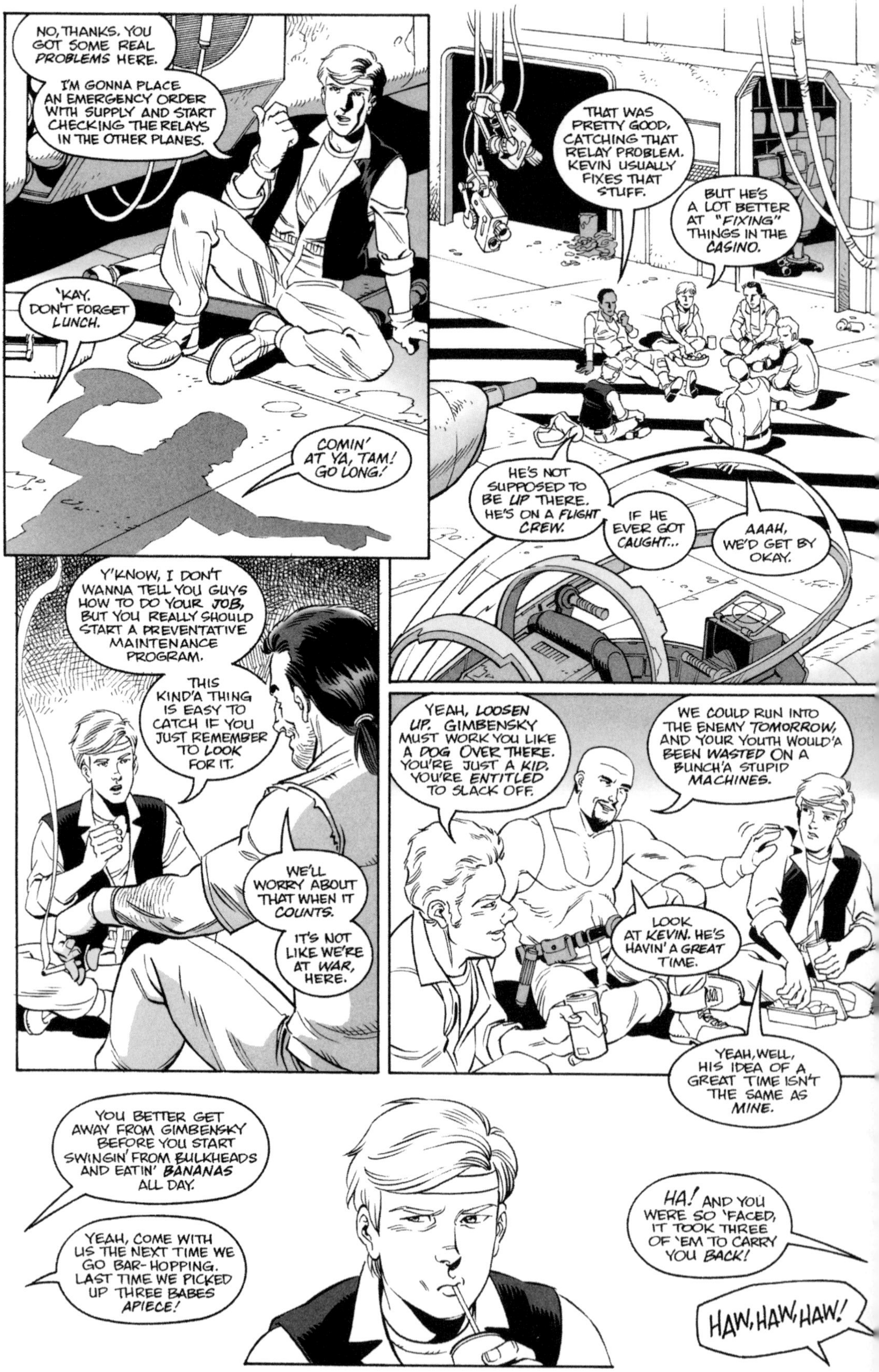
NO, THANKS. YOU GOT SOME REAL PROBLEMS HERE.
I'M GONNA PLACE AN EMERGENCY ORDER WITH SUPPLY AND START CHECKING THE RELAYS IN THE OTHER PLANES.
'KAY. DON'T FORGET LUNCH.
COMIN' AT YA, TAM! GO LONG!
THAT WAS PRETTY GOOD, CATCHING THAT RELAY PROBLEM. KEVIN USUALLY FIXES THAT STUFF.
BUT HE'S A LOT BETTER AT "FIXING" THINGS IN THE CASINO.
HE'S NOT SUPPOSED TO BE UP THERE. HE'S ON A FLIGHT CREW.
IF HE EVER GOT CAUGHT...
AAAH, WE'D GET BY OKAY.
Y'KNOW, I DON'T WANNA TELL YOU GUYS HOW TO DO YOUR JOB, BUT YOU REALLY SHOULD START A PREVENTATIVE MAINTENANCE PROGRAM.
THIS KIND'A THING IS EASY TO CATCH IF YOU JUST REMEMBER TO LOOK FOR IT.
WE'LL WORRY ABOUT THAT WHEN IT COUNTS.
IT'S NOT LIKE WE'RE AT WAR, HERE.
YEAH, LOOSEN UP. GIMBENSKY MUST WORK YOU LIKE A DOG OVER THERE. YOU'RE JUST A KID. YOU'RE ENTITLED TO SLACK OFF.
WE COULD RUN INTO THE ENEMY TOMORROW, AND YOUR YOUTH WOULD'A BEEN WASTED ON A BUNCH'A STUPID MACHINES.
LOOK AT KEVIN. HE'S HAVIN' A GREAT TIME.
YEAH, WELL, HIS IDEA OF A GREAT TIME ISN'T THE SAME AS MINE.
YOU BETTER GET AWAY FROM GIMBENSKY BEFORE YOU START SWINGIN' FROM BULKHEADS AND EATIN' BANANAS ALL DAY.
YEAH, COME WITH US THE NEXT TIME WE GO BAR-HOPPING. LAST TIME WE PICKED UP THREE BABES APIECE!
HA! AND YOU WERE SO 'FACED, IT TOOK THREE OF 'EM TO CARRY YOU BACK!
HAW, HAW, HAW!

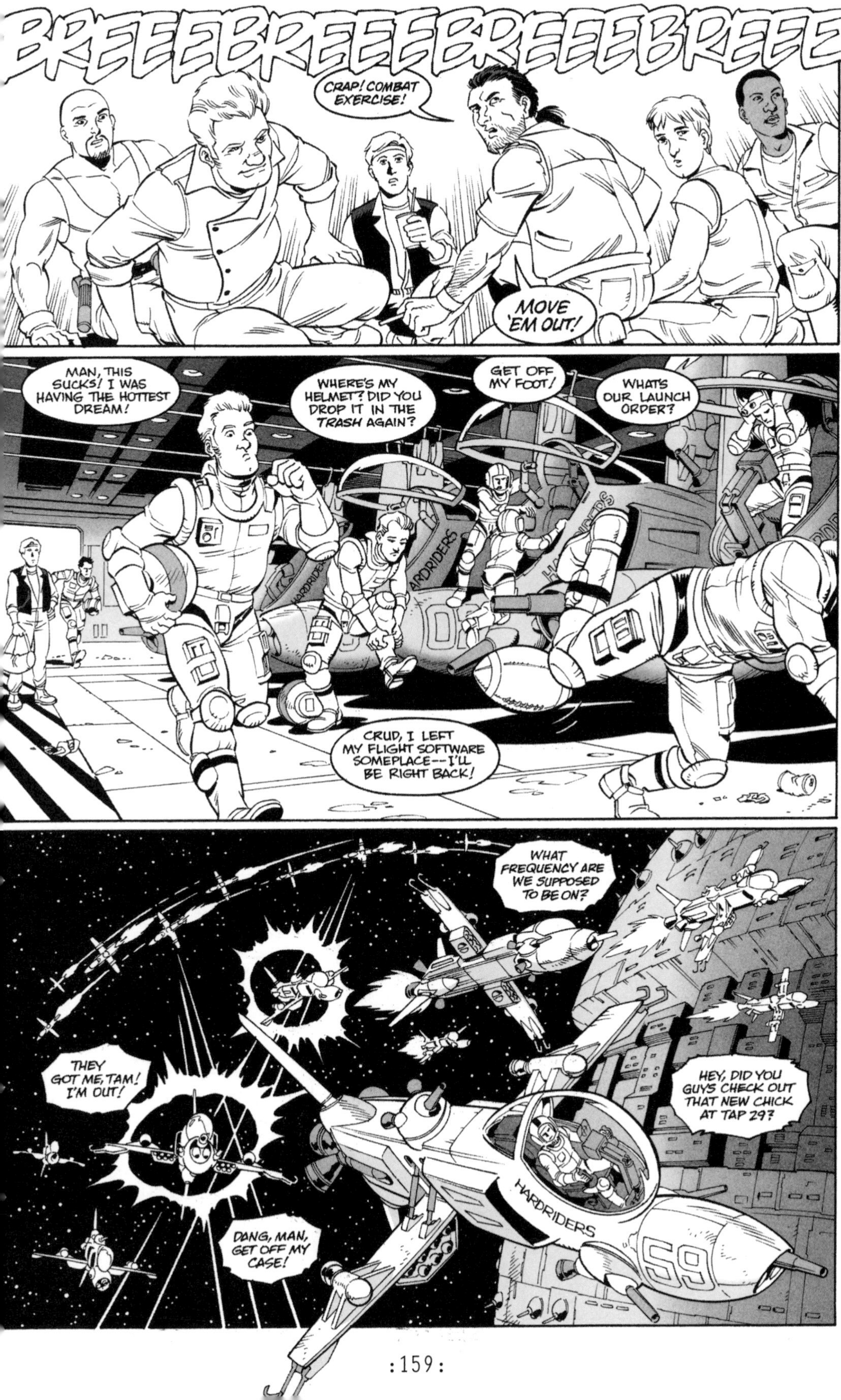
BREEEBREEEEBREEEEBREEE
CRAP! COMBAT EXERCISE!
MOVE 'EM OUT!
MAN, THIS SUCKS! I WAS HAVING THE HOTTEST DREAM!
WHERE'S MY HELMET? DID YOU DROP IT IN THE TRASH AGAIN?
GET OFF MY FOOT!
WHAT'S OUR LAUNCH ORDER?
HARDRIDERS
CRUD, I LEFT MY FLIGHT SOFTWARE SOMEPLACE--I'LL BE RIGHT BACK!
WHAT FREQUENCY ARE WE SUPPOSED TO BE ON?
THEY GOT ME, TAM! I'M OUT!
HEY, DID YOU GUYS CHECK OUT THAT NEW CHICK AT TAP 29?
DANG, MAN, GET OFF MY CASE!
HARDRIDERS
59

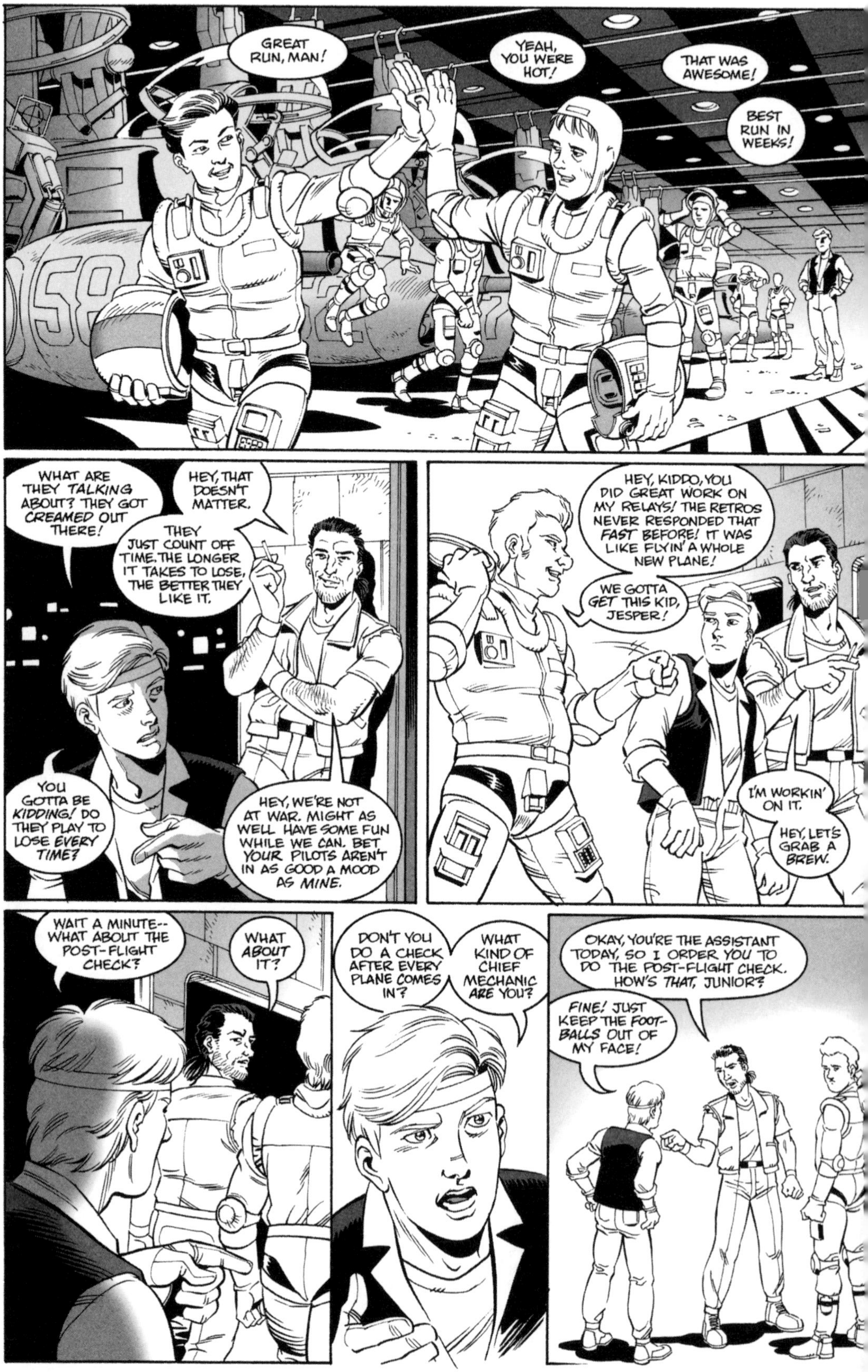
GREAT RUN, MAN!
YEAH, YOU WERE HOT!
THAT WAS AWESOME!
BEST RUN IN WEEKS!
WHAT ARE THEY TALKING ABOUT? THEY GOT CREAMED OUT THERE!
HEY, THAT DOESN'T MATTER.
THEY JUST COUNT OFF TIME. THE LONGER IT TAKES TO LOSE, THE BETTER THEY LIKE IT.
YOU GOTTA BE KIDDING! DO THEY PLAY TO LOSE EVERY TIME?
HEY, WE'RE NOT AT WAR. MIGHT AS WELL HAVE SOME FUN WHILE WE CAN. BET YOUR PILOTS AREN'T IN AS GOOD A MOOD AS MINE.
HEY, KIDDO, YOU DID GREAT WORK ON MY RELAYS! THE RETROS NEVER RESPONDED THAT FAST BEFORE! IT WAS LIKE FLYIN' A WHOLE NEW PLANE!
WE GOTTA GET THIS KID, JESPER!
I'M WORKIN' ON IT.
HEY, LET'S GRAB A BREW.
WAIT A MINUTE-- WHAT ABOUT THE POST-FLIGHT CHECK?
WHAT ABOUT IT?
DON'T YOU DO A CHECK AFTER EVERY PLANE COMES IN?
WHAT KIND OF CHIEF MECHANIC ARE YOU?
OKAY, YOU'RE THE ASSISTANT TODAY, SO I ORDER YOU TO DO THE POST-FLIGHT CHECK. HOW'S THAT, JUNIOR?
FINE! JUST KEEP THE FOOT-BALLS OUT OF MY FACE!

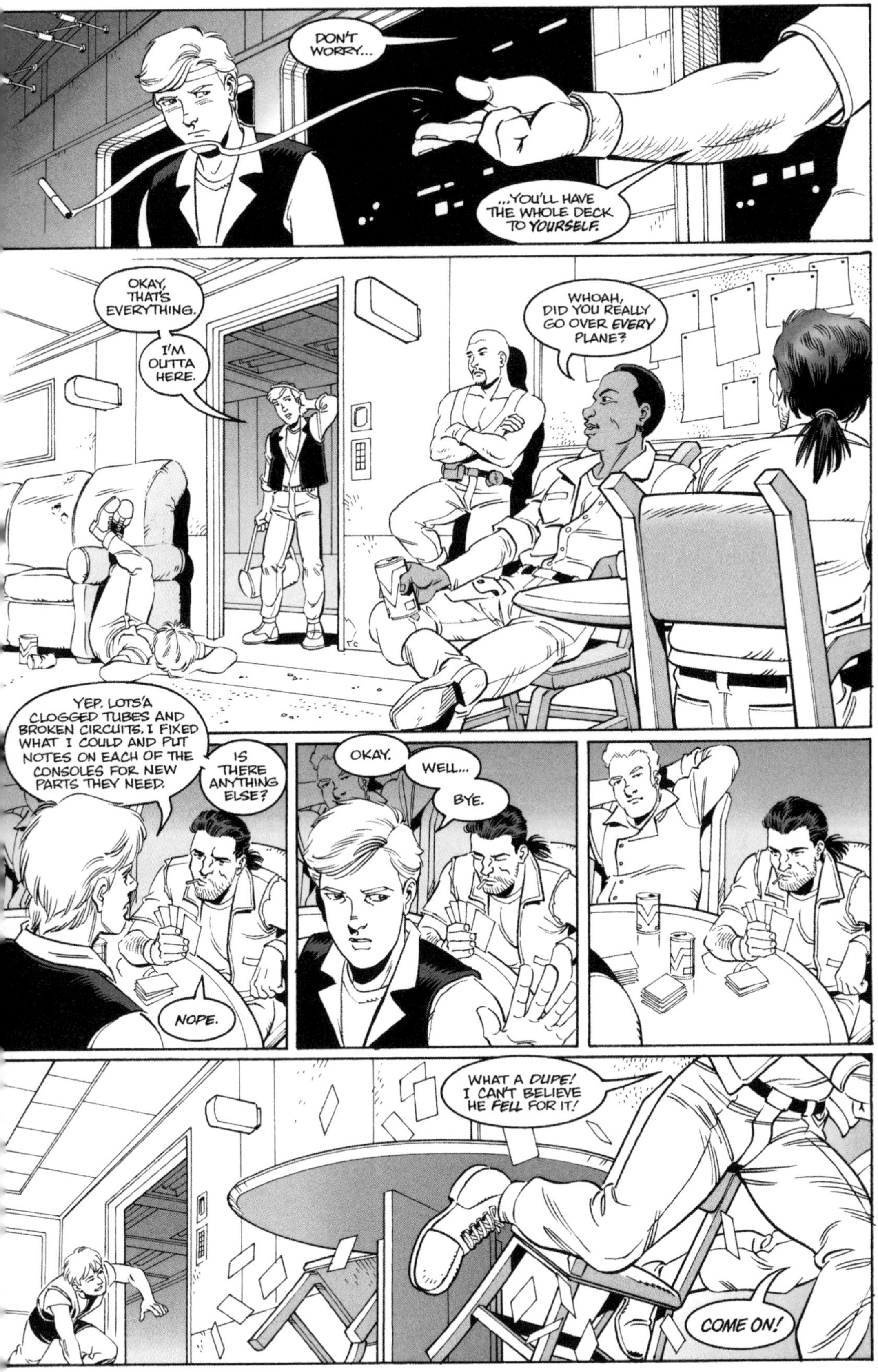
DON'T WORRY...
...YOU'LL HAVE THE WHOLE DECK TO YOURSELF.
OKAY, THAT'S EVERYTHING.
I'M OUTTA HERE.
WHOAH, DID YOU REALLY GO OVER EVERY PLANE?
YEP. LOTS'A CLOGGED TUBES AND BROKEN CIRCUITS. I FIXED WHAT I COULD AND PUT NOTES ON EACH OF THE CONSOLES FOR NEW PARTS THEY NEED.
IS THERE ANYTHING ELSE?
NOPE.
OKAY.
WELL...
BYE.
WHAT A DUPE! I CAN'T BELIEVE HE FELL FOR IT!
COME ON!

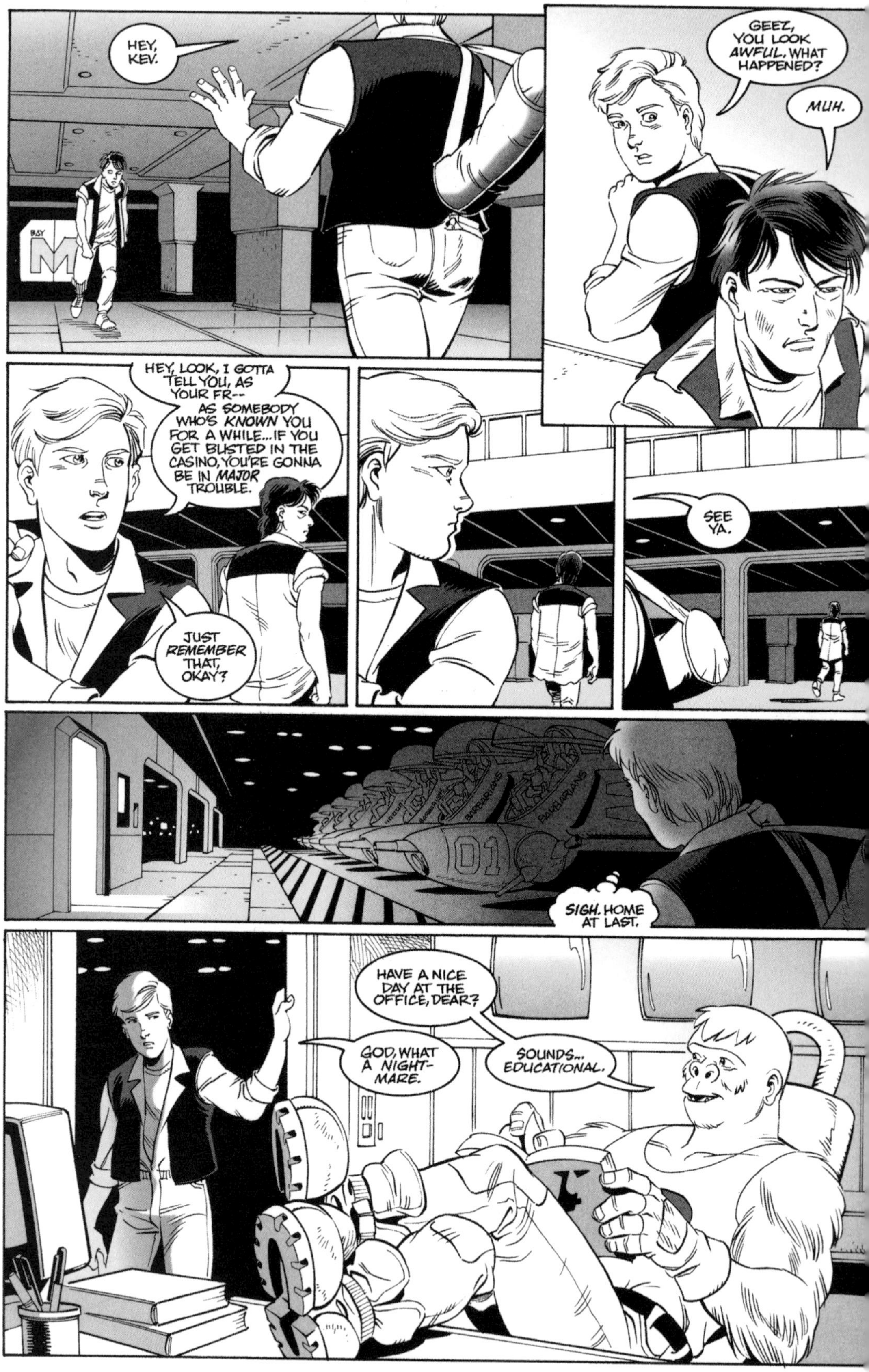
HEY, KEV.
GEEZ, YOU LOOK AWFUL. WHAT HAPPENED?
MUH.
HEY, LOOK, I GOTTA TELL YOU, AS YOUR FR-- AS SOMEBODY WHO'S KNOWN YOU FOR A WHILE... IF YOU GET BUSTED IN THE CASINO, YOU'RE GONNA BE IN MAJOR TROUBLE.
JUST REMEMBER THAT, OKAY?
SEE YA.
SIGH. HOME AT LAST.
HAVE A NICE DAY AT THE OFFICE, DEAR?
GOD, WHAT A NIGHT-MARE.
SOUNDS... EDUCATIONAL.

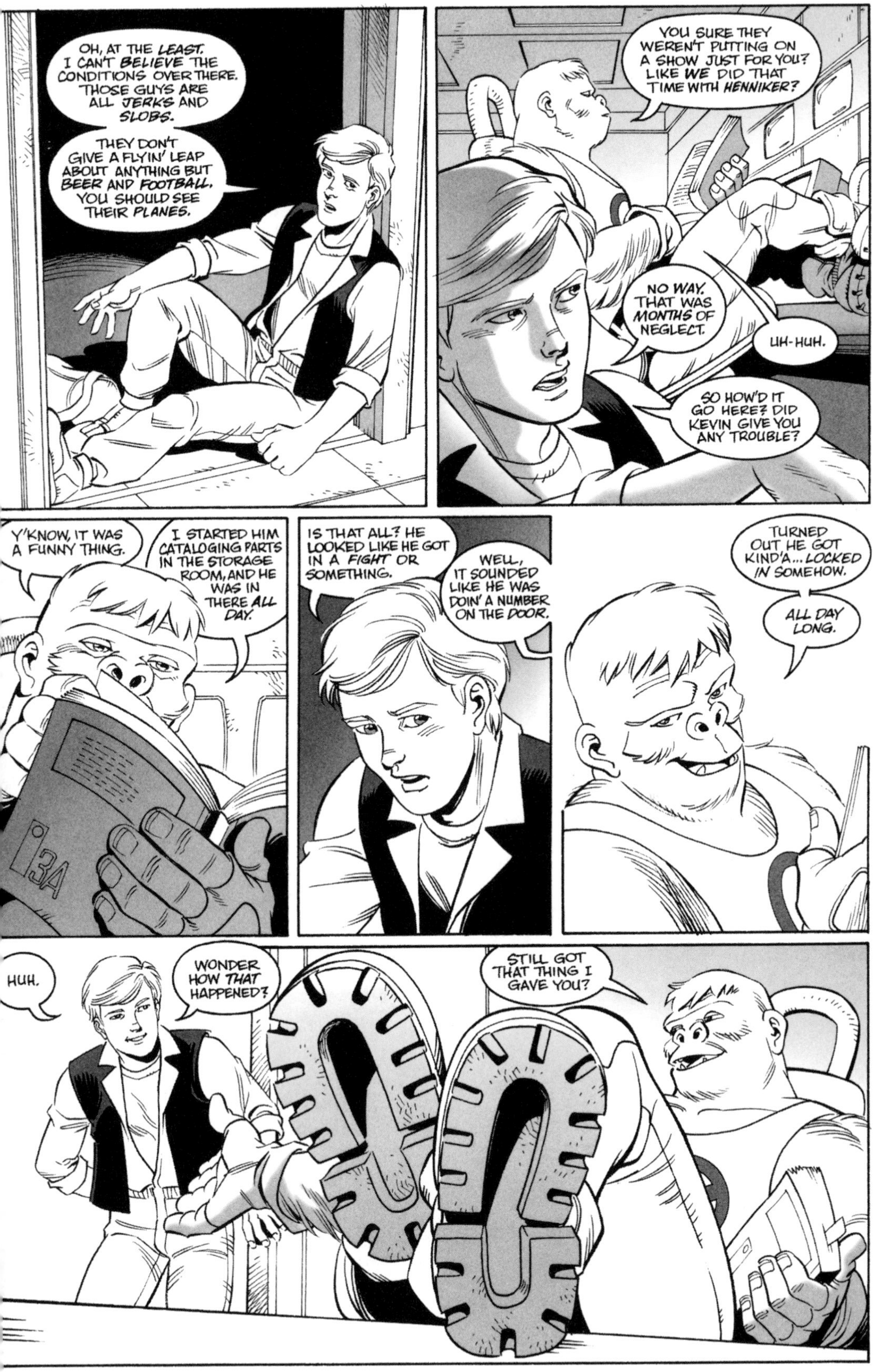

OH, AT THE LEAST. I CAN'T BELIEVE THE CONDITIONS OVER THERE. THOSE GUYS ARE ALL JERKS AND SLOBS.
THEY DON'T GIVE A FLYIN' LEAP ABOUT ANYTHING BUT BEER AND FOOTBALL. YOU SHOULD SEE THEIR PLANES.
YOU SURE THEY WEREN'T PUTTING ON A SHOW JUST FOR YOU? LIKE WE DID THAT TIME WITH HENNIKER?
NO WAY. THAT WAS MONTHS OF NEGLECT.
UH-HUH.
SO HOW'D IT GO HERE? DID KEVIN GIVE YOU ANY TROUBLE?
Y'KNOW, IT WAS A FUNNY THING.
I STARTED HIM CATALOGING PARTS IN THE STORAGE ROOM, AND HE WAS IN THERE ALL DAY.
3A
IS THAT ALL? HE LOOKED LIKE HE GOT IN A FIGHT OR SOMETHING.
WELL, IT SOUNDED LIKE HE WAS DOIN' A NUMBER ON THE DOOR.
TURNED OUT HE GOT KIND'A... LOCKED IN SOMEHOW.
ALL DAY LONG.
HUH.
WONDER HOW THAT HAPPENED?
STILL GOT THAT THING I GAVE YOU?

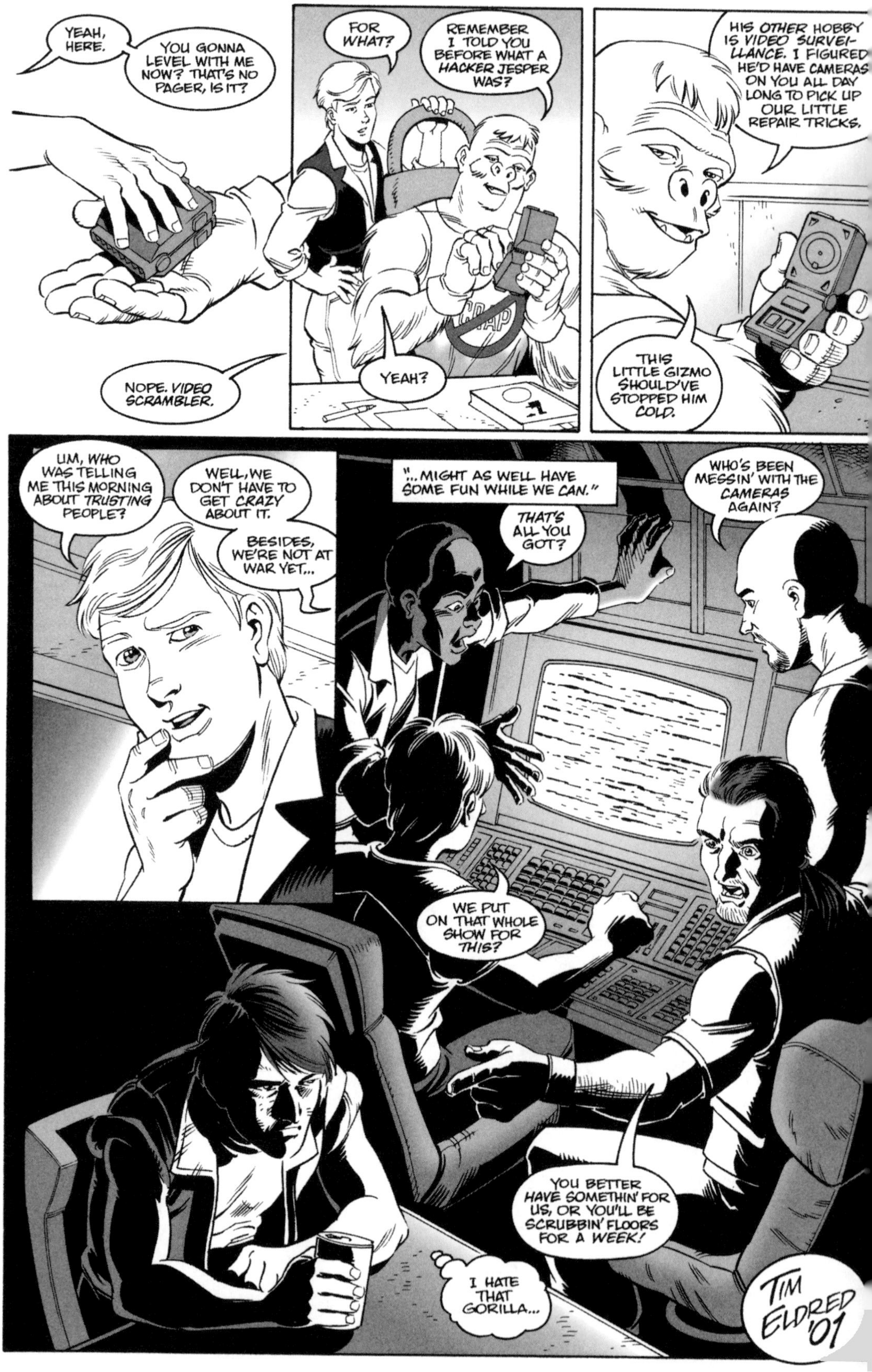
YEAH, HERE.
YOU GONNA LEVEL WITH ME NOW? THAT'S NO PAGER, IS IT?
NOPE. *VIDEO SCRAMBLER.*
FOR *WHAT?*
REMEMBER I TOLD YOU BEFORE WHAT A *HACKER* JESPER WAS?
YEAH?
HIS *OTHER* HOBBY IS *VIDEO SURVEILLANCE.* I FIGURED HE'D HAVE CAMERAS ON YOU ALL DAY LONG TO PICK UP OUR LITTLE REPAIR TRICKS.
THIS LITTLE GIZMO SHOULD'VE STOPPED HIM COLD.
UM, WHO WAS TELLING ME THIS MORNING ABOUT *TRUSTING* PEOPLE?
WELL, WE DON'T HAVE TO GET *CRAZY* ABOUT IT.
BESIDES, WE'RE NOT AT WAR YET...
"...MIGHT AS WELL HAVE SOME FUN WHILE WE *CAN.*"
THAT'S ALL YOU GOT?
WHO'S BEEN MESSIN' WITH THE *CAMERAS* AGAIN?
WE PUT ON THAT WHOLE SHOW FOR *THIS?*
YOU BETTER HAVE SOMETHIN' FOR US, OR YOU'LL BE SCRUBBIN' FLOORS FOR A *WEEK!*
I HATE THAT GORILLA...
TIM ELDRED '01

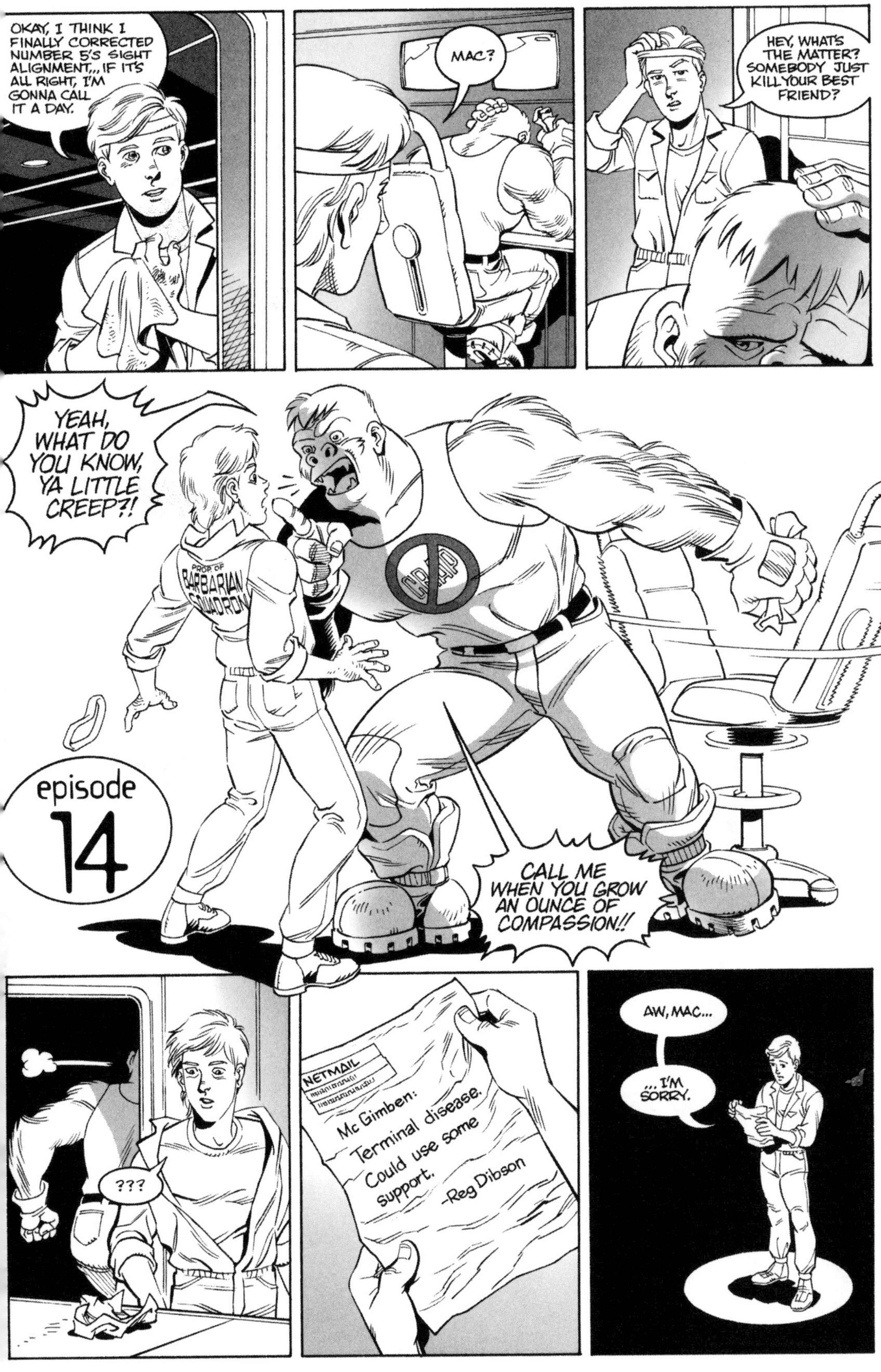
OKAY, I THINK I FINALLY CORRECTED NUMBER 5'S SIGHT ALIGNMENT,,, IF IT'S ALL RIGHT, I'M GONNA CALL IT A DAY.
MAC?
HEY, WHAT'S THE MATTER? SOMEBODY JUST KILL YOUR BEST FRIEND?
YEAH, WHAT DO YOU KNOW, YA LITTLE CREEP?!
PROP. OF BARBARIAN SQUADRON
CRAP
episode 14
CALL ME WHEN YOU GROW AN OUNCE OF COMPASSION!!
???
NETMAIL
McGimben:
Terminal disease.
Could use some support.
-Reg Dibson
AW, MAC...
... I'M SORRY.

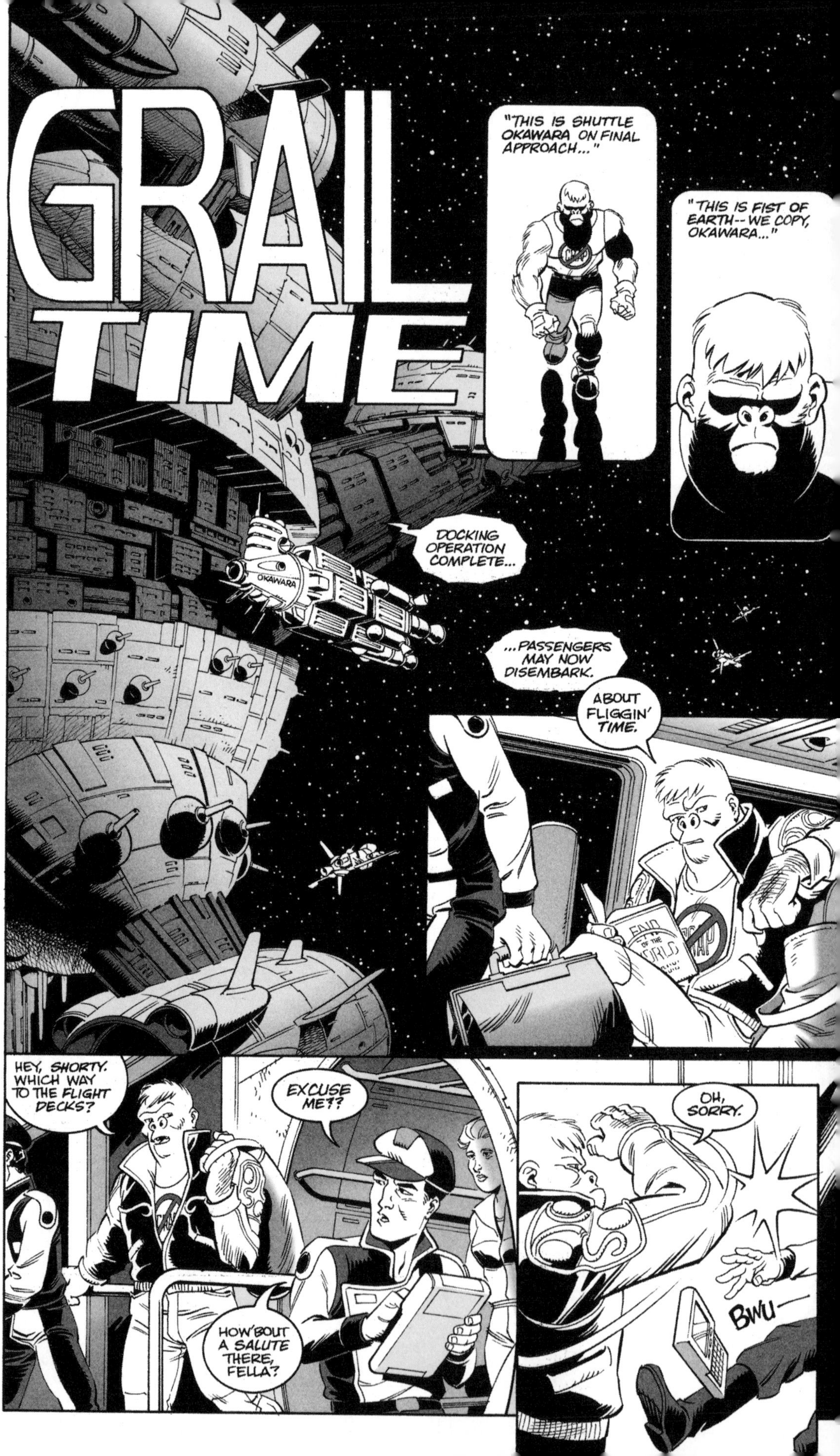
GRAIL TIME
"THIS IS SHUTTLE OKAWARA ON FINAL APPROACH..."
"THIS IS FIST OF EARTH-- WE COPY, OKAWARA..."
OKAWARA
DOCKING OPERATION COMPLETE...
...PASSENGERS MAY NOW DISEMBARK.
ABOUT FLIGGIN' TIME.
HEY, SHORTY. WHICH WAY TO THE FLIGHT DECKS?
EXCUSE ME??
HOW'BOUT A SALUTE THERE, FELLA?
OH, SORRY.
BWU--

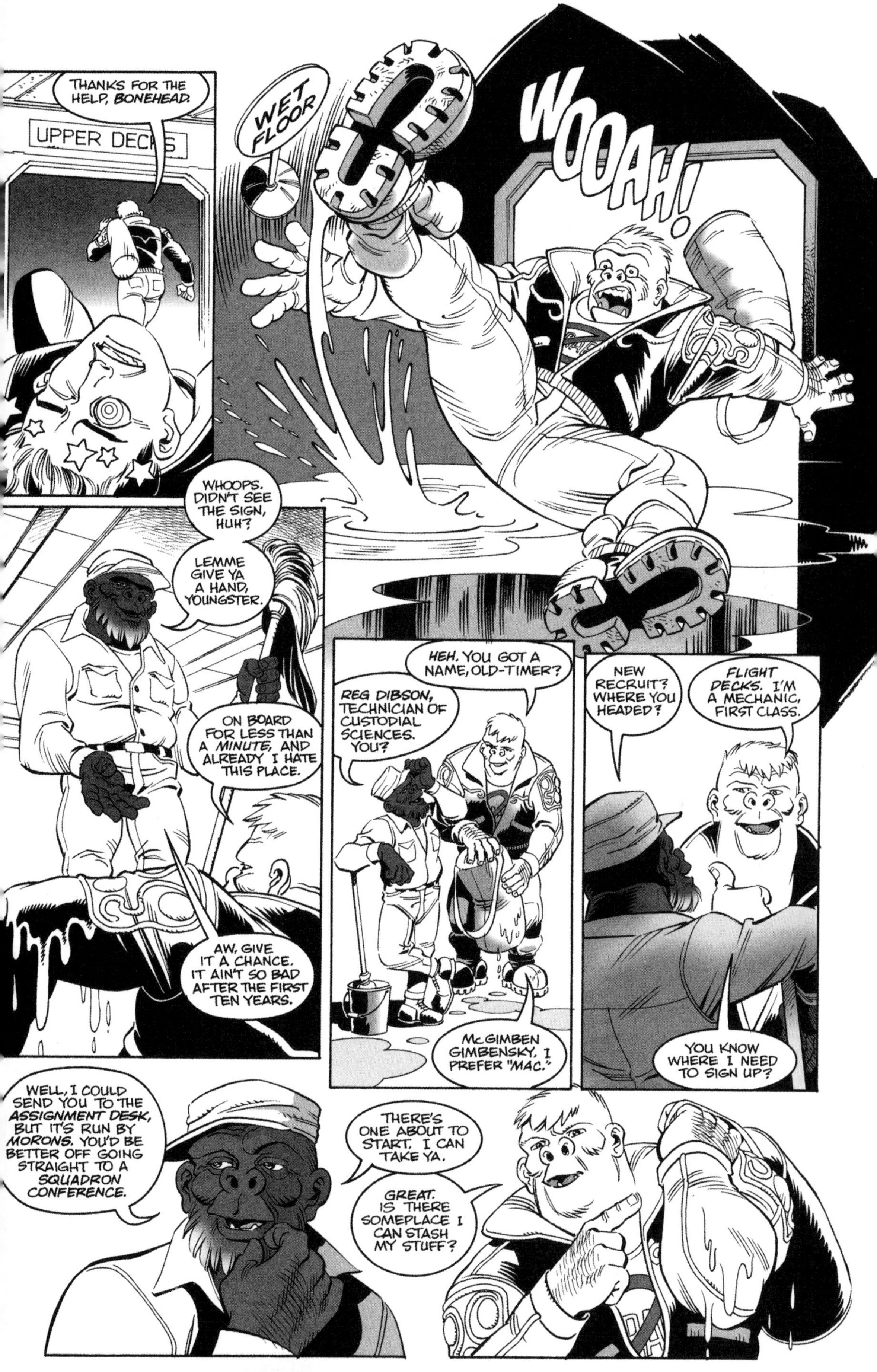
THANKS FOR THE HELP, *BONEHEAD.*
UPPER DECKS
WET FLOOR
WOOAH!
WHOOPS. DIDN'T SEE THE SIGN, HUH?
LEMME GIVE YA A HAND, YOUNGSTER.
ON BOARD FOR LESS THAN A *MINUTE,* AND ALREADY I HATE THIS PLACE.
AW, GIVE IT A CHANCE. IT AIN'T SO BAD AFTER THE FIRST TEN YEARS.
HEH. YOU GOT A NAME, OLD-TIMER?
REG DIBSON, TECHNICIAN OF CUSTODIAL SCIENCES. YOU?
McGIMBEN GIMBENSKY. I PREFER "*MAC.*"
NEW RECRUIT? WHERE YOU HEADED?
FLIGHT DECKS. I'M A MECHANIC, FIRST CLASS.
YOU KNOW WHERE I NEED TO SIGN UP?
WELL, I COULD SEND YOU TO THE *ASSIGNMENT DESK,* BUT IT'S RUN BY *MORONS.* YOU'D BE BETTER OFF GOING STRAIGHT TO A *SQUADRON CONFERENCE.*
THERE'S ONE ABOUT TO START. I CAN TAKE YA.
GREAT. IS THERE SOMEPLACE I CAN STASH MY STUFF?

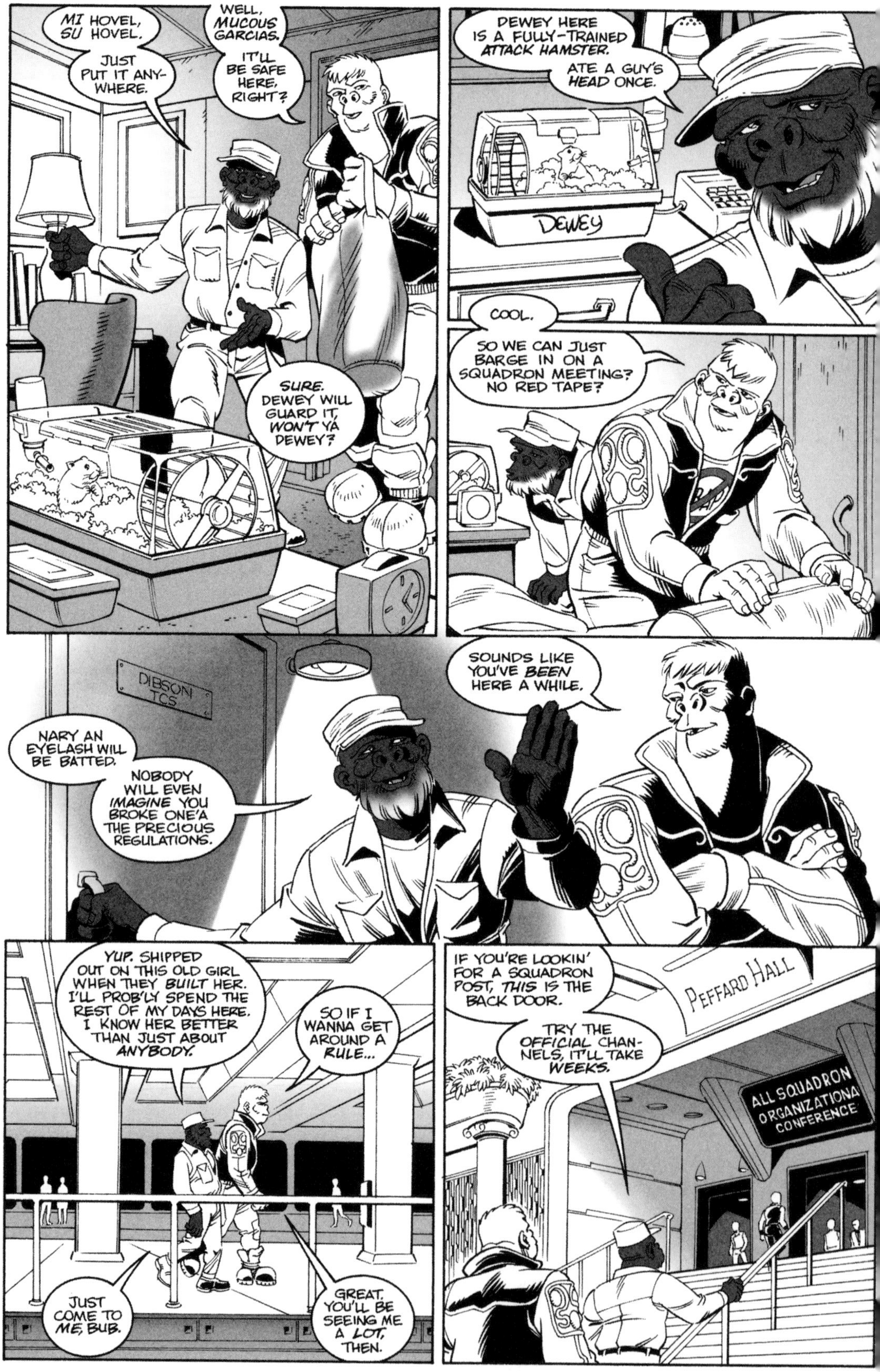
MI HOVEL, SU HOVEL.
WELL, MUCOUS GARCIAS.
JUST PUT IT ANY-WHERE.
IT'LL BE SAFE HERE, RIGHT?
SURE. DEWEY WILL GUARD IT, WON'T YA DEWEY?
DEWEY HERE IS A FULLY-TRAINED ATTACK HAMSTER.
ATE A GUY'S HEAD ONCE.
DEWEY
COOL.
SO WE CAN JUST BARGE IN ON A SQUADRON MEETING? NO RED TAPE?
DIBSON TCS
NARY AN EYELASH WILL BE BATTED.
NOBODY WILL EVEN IMAGINE YOU BROKE ONE'A THE PRECIOUS REGULATIONS.
SOUNDS LIKE YOU'VE BEEN HERE A WHILE.
YUP. SHIPPED OUT ON THIS OLD GIRL WHEN THEY BUILT HER. I'LL PROB'LY SPEND THE REST OF MY DAYS HERE. I KNOW HER BETTER THAN JUST ABOUT ANYBODY.
SO IF I WANNA GET AROUND A RULE...
JUST COME TO ME, BUB.
GREAT. YOU'LL BE SEEING ME A LOT, THEN.
IF YOU'RE LOOKIN' FOR A SQUADRON POST, THIS IS THE BACK DOOR.
PEFFARD HALL
TRY THE OFFICIAL CHAN-NELS, IT'LL TAKE WEEKS.
ALL SQUADRON ORGANIZATIONAL CONFERENCE

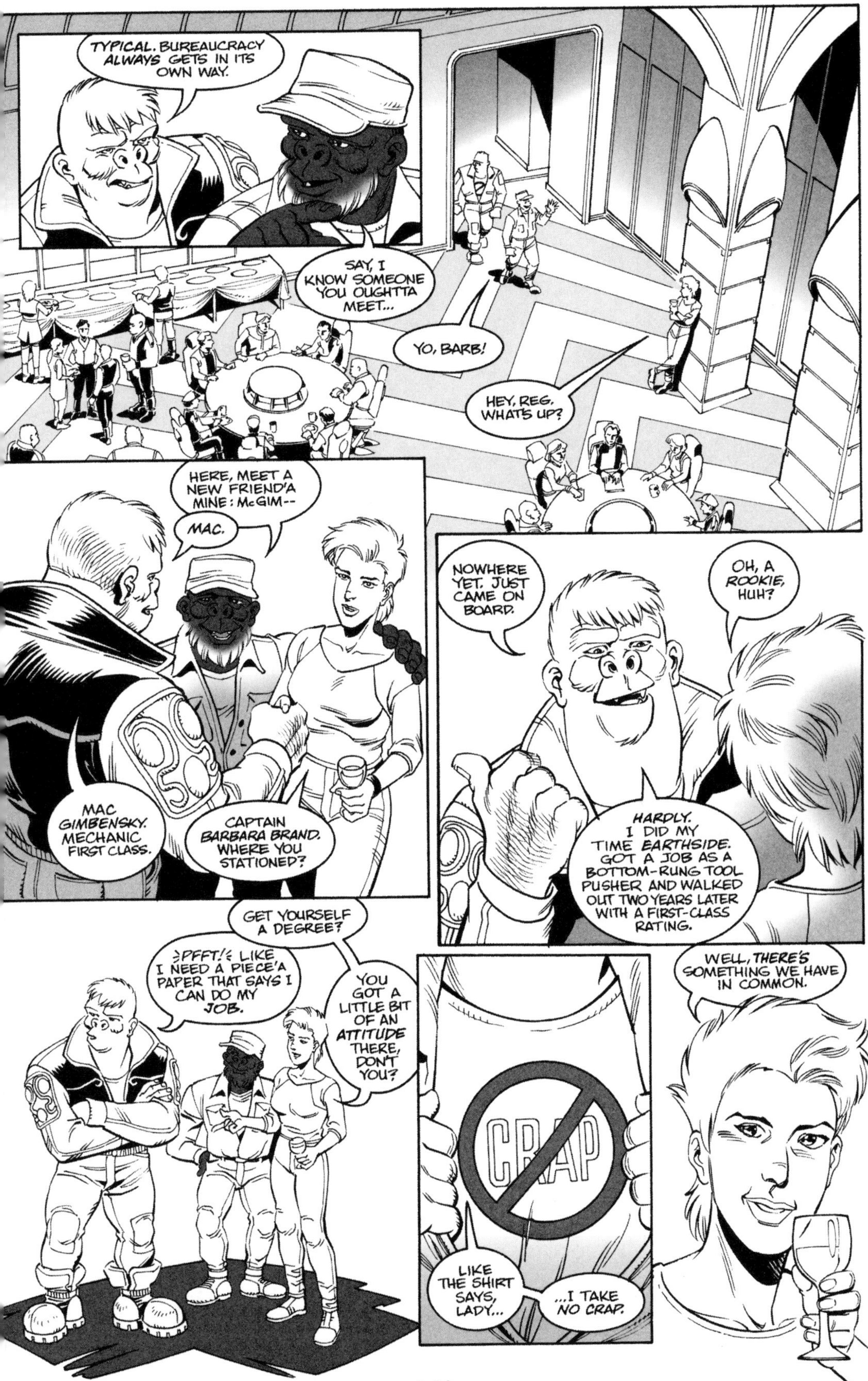
TYPICAL. BUREAUCRACY ALWAYS GETS IN ITS OWN WAY.
SAY, I KNOW SOMEONE YOU OUGHTTA MEET...
YO, BARB!
HEY, REG. WHAT'S UP?
HERE, MEET A NEW FRIEND'A MINE: McGIM--
MAC.
MAC GIMBENSKY. MECHANIC FIRST CLASS.
CAPTAIN BARBARA BRAND. WHERE YOU STATIONED?
NOWHERE YET. JUST CAME ON BOARD.
OH, A ROOKIE, HUH?
HARDLY. I DID MY TIME EARTHSIDE. GOT A JOB AS A BOTTOM-RUNG TOOL PUSHER AND WALKED OUT TWO YEARS LATER WITH A FIRST-CLASS RATING.
GET YOURSELF A DEGREE?
PFFT! LIKE I NEED A PIECE'A PAPER THAT SAYS I CAN DO MY JOB.
YOU GOT A LITTLE BIT OF AN ATTITUDE THERE, DON'T YOU?
CRAP
LIKE THE SHIRT SAYS, LADY...
...I TAKE NO CRAP.
WELL, THERE'S SOMETHING WE HAVE IN COMMON.

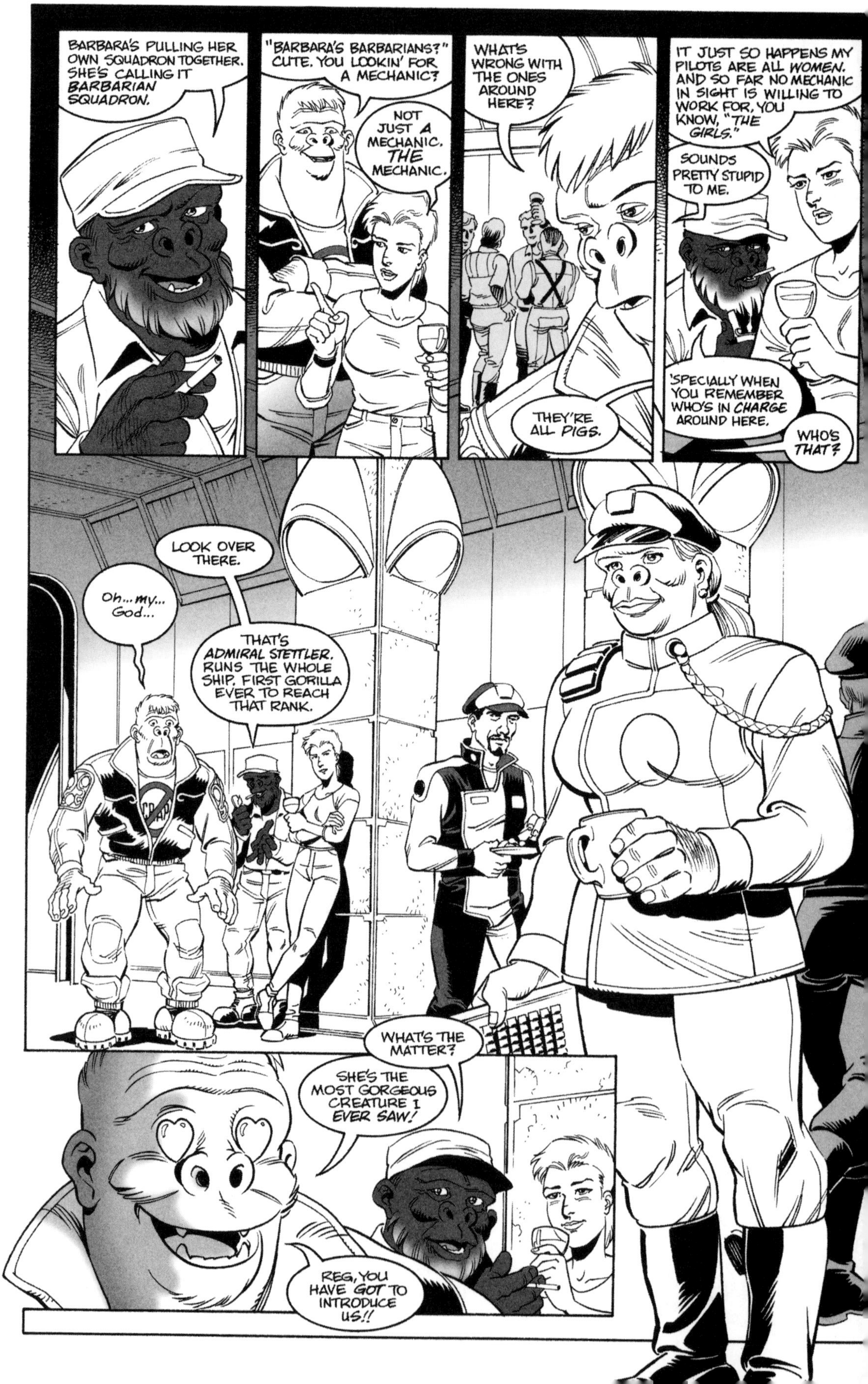
BARBARA'S PULLING HER OWN SQUADRON TOGETHER. SHE'S CALLING IT BARBARIAN SQUADRON.
"BARBARA'S BARBARIANS?" CUTE. YOU LOOKIN' FOR A MECHANIC?
NOT JUST A MECHANIC. THE MECHANIC.
WHAT'S WRONG WITH THE ONES AROUND HERE?
THEY'RE ALL PIGS.
IT JUST SO HAPPENS MY PILOTS ARE ALL WOMEN. AND SO FAR NO MECHANIC IN SIGHT IS WILLING TO WORK FOR, YOU KNOW, "THE GIRLS."
SOUNDS PRETTY STUPID TO ME.
'SPECIALLY WHEN YOU REMEMBER WHO'S IN CHARGE AROUND HERE.
WHO'S THAT?
LOOK OVER THERE.
Oh... my... God...
THAT'S ADMIRAL STETTLER. RUNS THE WHOLE SHIP. FIRST GORILLA EVER TO REACH THAT RANK.
WHAT'S THE MATTER?
SHE'S THE MOST GORGEOUS CREATURE I EVER SAW!
REG, YOU HAVE GOT TO INTRODUCE US!!

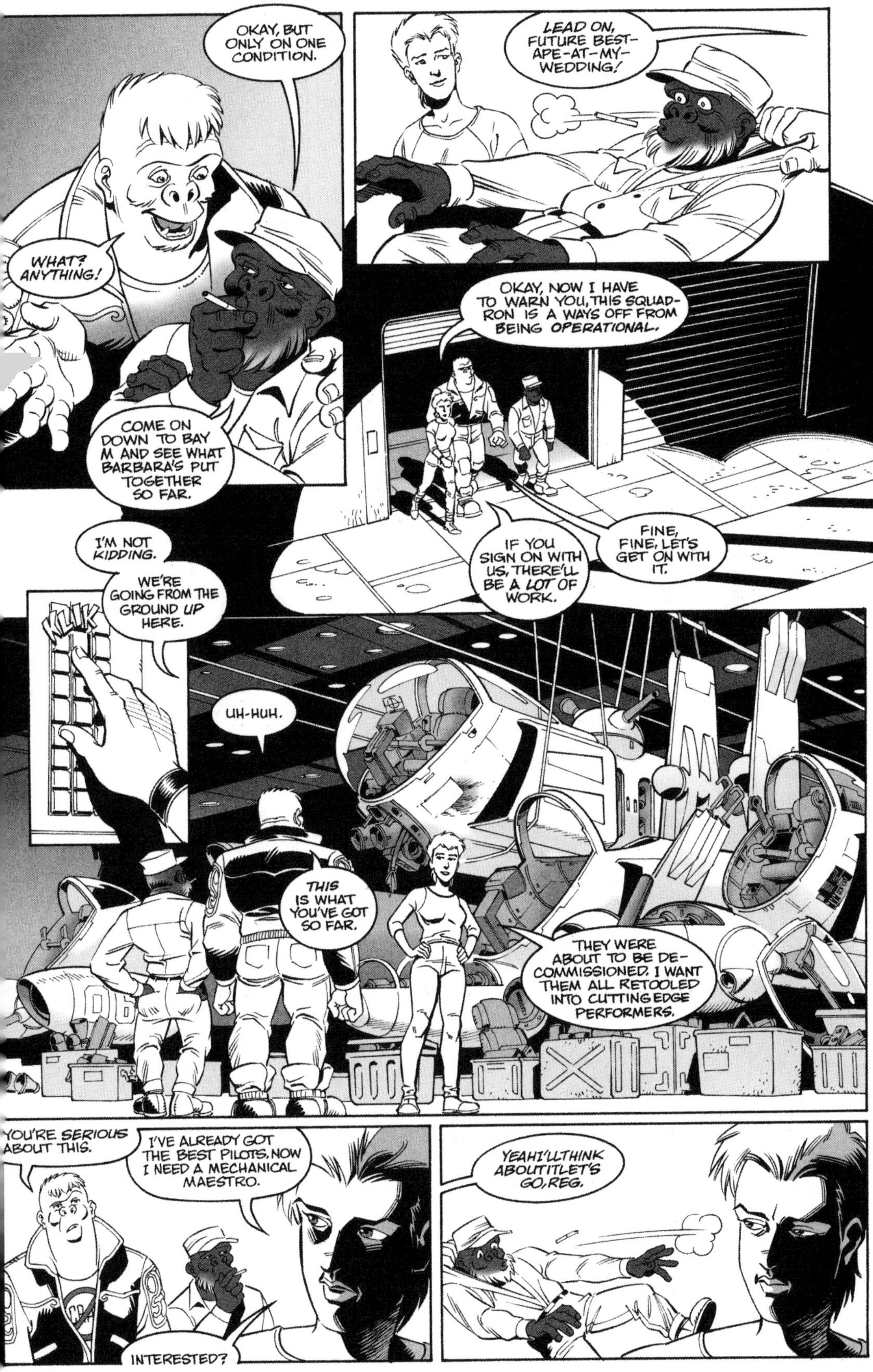
OKAY, BUT ONLY ON ONE CONDITION.
WHAT? ANYTHING!
COME ON DOWN TO BAY M AND SEE WHAT BARBARA'S PUT TOGETHER SO FAR.
LEAD ON, FUTURE BEST-APE-AT-MY-WEDDING!
OKAY, NOW I HAVE TO WARN YOU, THIS SQUADRON IS A WAYS OFF FROM BEING OPERATIONAL.
IF YOU SIGN ON WITH US, THERE'LL BE A LOT OF WORK.
FINE, FINE, LET'S GET ON WITH IT.
I'M NOT KIDDING.
WE'RE GOING FROM THE GROUND UP HERE.
KLIK
UH-HUH.
THIS IS WHAT YOU'VE GOT SO FAR.
THEY WERE ABOUT TO BE DECOMMISSIONED. I WANT THEM ALL RETOOLED INTO CUTTING EDGE PERFORMERS.
YOU'RE SERIOUS ABOUT THIS.
I'VE ALREADY GOT THE BEST PILOTS. NOW I NEED A MECHANICAL MAESTRO.
INTERESTED?
YEAHI'LLTHINK ABOUTITLET'S GO,REG.

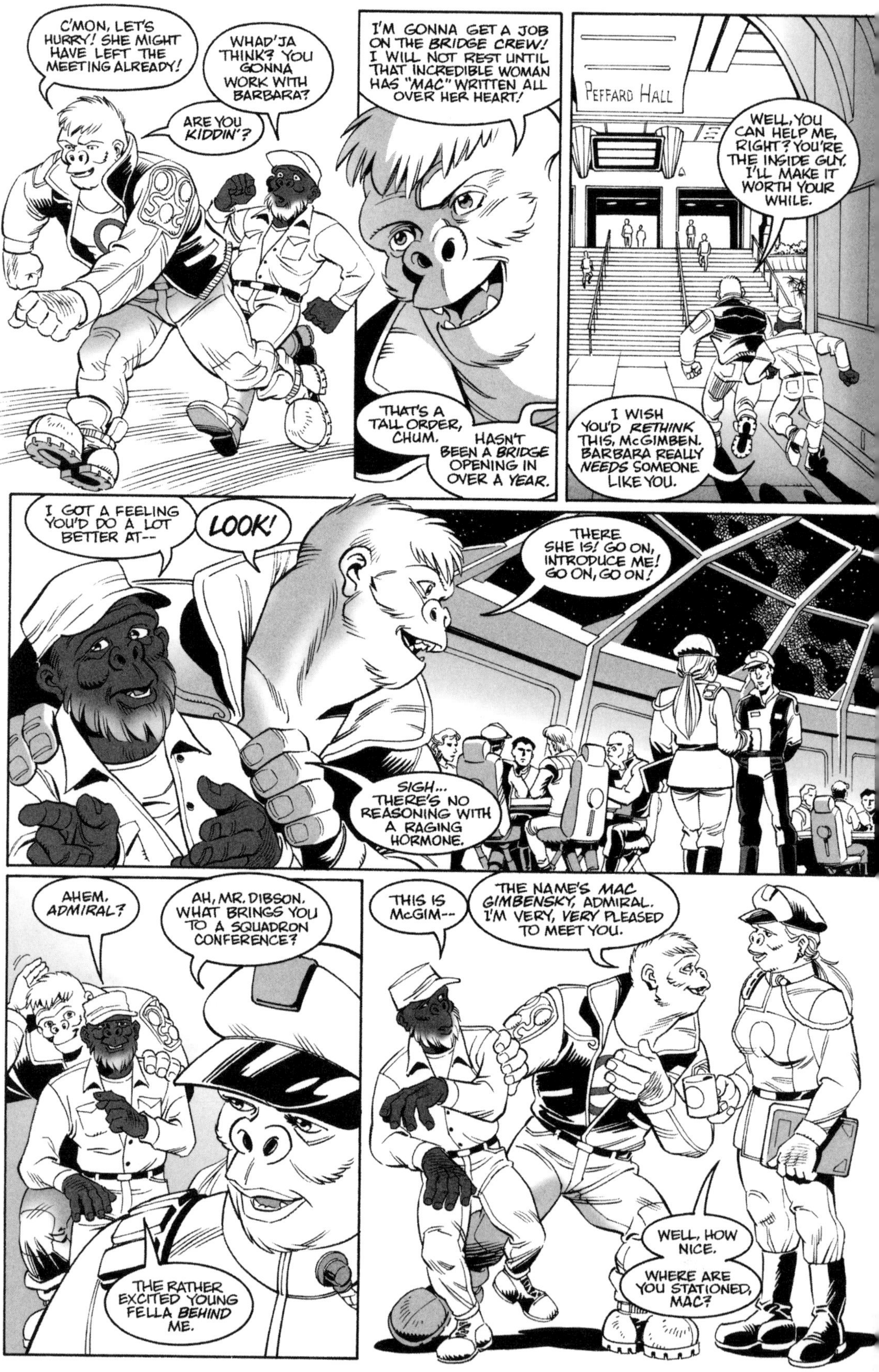
C'MON, LET'S HURRY! SHE MIGHT HAVE LEFT THE MEETING ALREADY!
WHAD'JA THINK? YOU GONNA WORK WITH BARBARA?
ARE YOU KIDDIN'?
I'M GONNA GET A JOB ON THE BRIDGE CREW! I WILL NOT REST UNTIL THAT INCREDIBLE WOMAN HAS "MAC" WRITTEN ALL OVER HER HEART!
THAT'S A TALL ORDER, CHUM.
HASN'T BEEN A BRIDGE OPENING IN OVER A YEAR.
PEFFARD HALL
WELL, YOU CAN HELP ME, RIGHT? YOU'RE THE INSIDE GUY. I'LL MAKE IT WORTH YOUR WHILE.
I WISH YOU'D RETHINK THIS, McGIMBEN. BARBARA REALLY NEEDS SOMEONE LIKE YOU.
I GOT A FEELING YOU'D DO A LOT BETTER AT--
LOOK!
THERE SHE IS! GO ON, INTRODUCE ME! GO ON, GO ON!
SIGH... THERE'S NO REASONING WITH A RAGING HORMONE.
AHEM, ADMIRAL?
AH, MR. DIBSON. WHAT BRINGS YOU TO A SQUADRON CONFERENCE?
THE RATHER EXCITED YOUNG FELLA BEHIND ME.
THIS IS McGIM--
THE NAME'S MAC GIMBENSKY, ADMIRAL. I'M VERY, VERY PLEASED TO MEET YOU.
WELL, HOW NICE.
WHERE ARE YOU STATIONED, MAC?

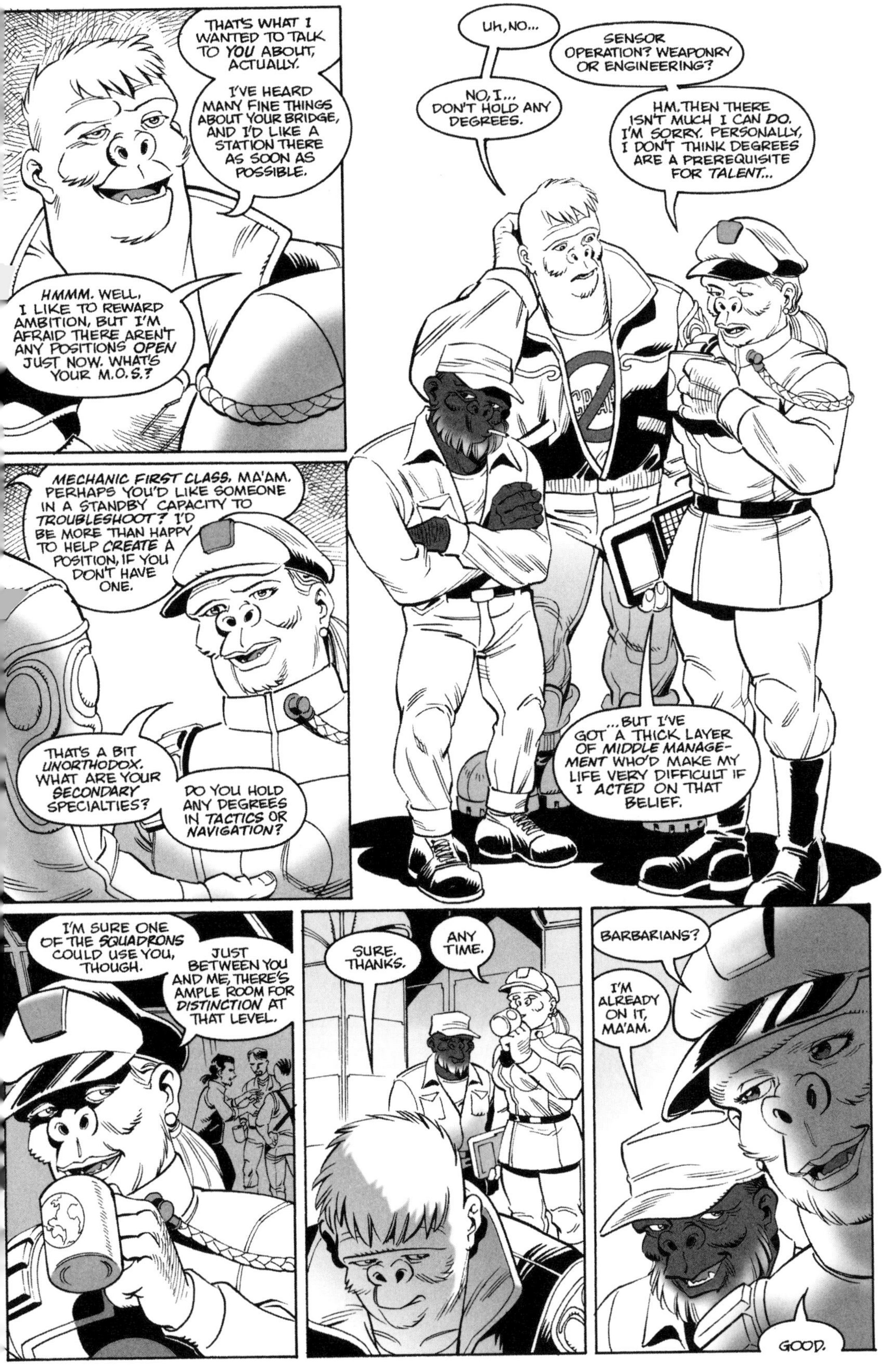
THAT'S WHAT I WANTED TO TALK TO YOU ABOUT, ACTUALLY.
I'VE HEARD MANY FINE THINGS ABOUT YOUR BRIDGE, AND I'D LIKE A STATION THERE AS SOON AS POSSIBLE.
HMMM. WELL, I LIKE TO REWARD AMBITION, BUT I'M AFRAID THERE AREN'T ANY POSITIONS OPEN JUST NOW. WHAT'S YOUR M.O.S.?
MECHANIC FIRST CLASS, MA'AM. PERHAPS YOU'D LIKE SOMEONE IN A STANDBY CAPACITY TO TROUBLESHOOT? I'D BE MORE THAN HAPPY TO HELP CREATE A POSITION, IF YOU DON'T HAVE ONE.
THAT'S A BIT UNORTHODOX. WHAT ARE YOUR SECONDARY SPECIALTIES?
DO YOU HOLD ANY DEGREES IN TACTICS OR NAVIGATION?
Uh, NO...
SENSOR OPERATION? WEAPONRY OR ENGINEERING?
NO, I... DON'T HOLD ANY DEGREES.
HM. THEN THERE ISN'T MUCH I CAN DO. I'M SORRY. PERSONALLY, I DON'T THINK DEGREES ARE A PREREQUISITE FOR TALENT...
...BUT I'VE GOT A THICK LAYER OF MIDDLE MANAGEMENT WHO'D MAKE MY LIFE VERY DIFFICULT IF I ACTED ON THAT BELIEF.
I'M SURE ONE OF THE SQUADRONS COULD USE YOU, THOUGH.
JUST BETWEEN YOU AND ME, THERE'S AMPLE ROOM FOR DISTINCTION AT THAT LEVEL.
SURE. THANKS.
ANY TIME.
BARBARIANS?
I'M ALREADY ON IT, MA'AM.
GOOD.

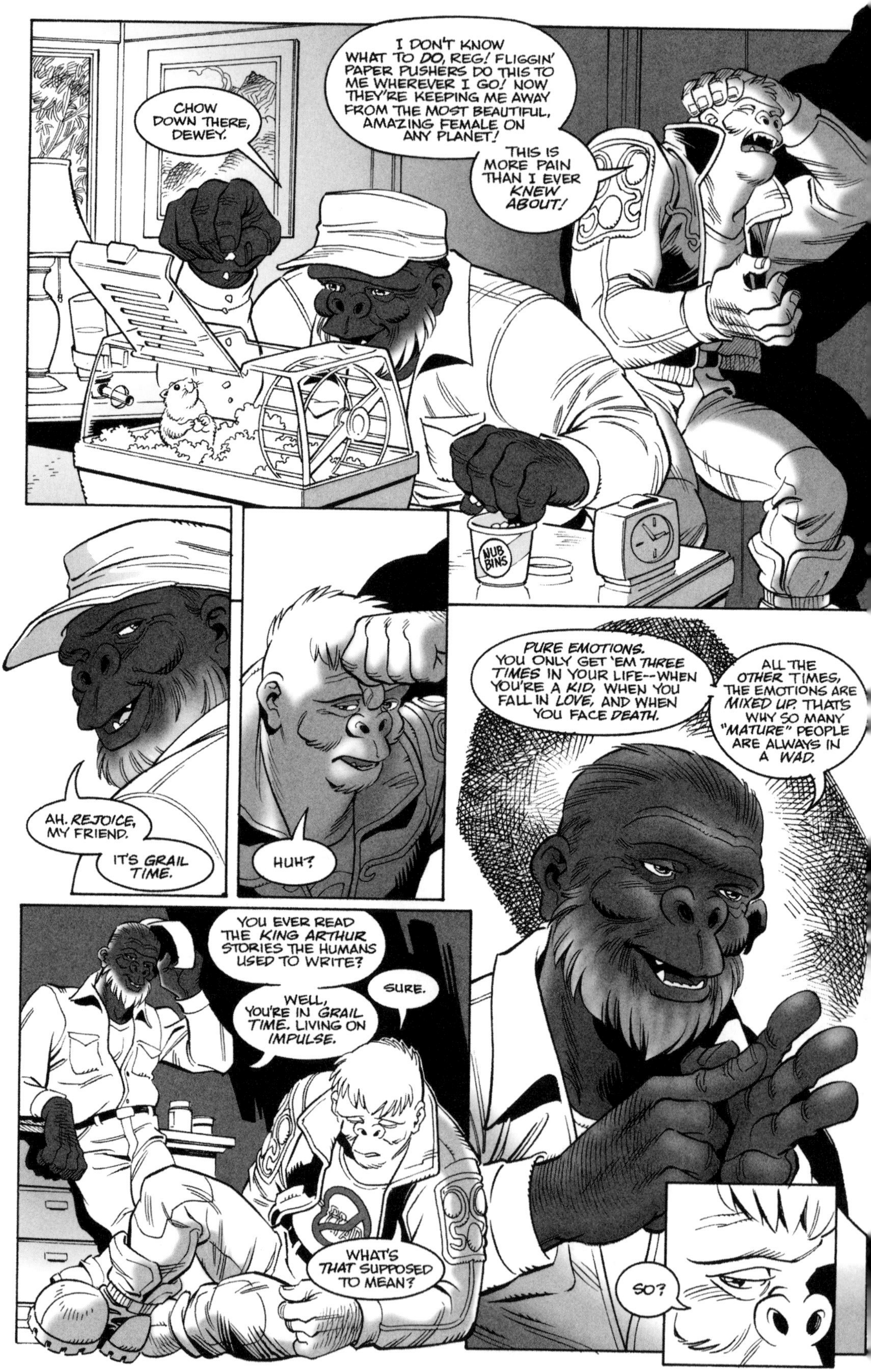
CHOW DOWN THERE, DEWEY.
I DON'T KNOW WHAT TO DO, REG! FLIGGIN' PAPER PUSHERS DO THIS TO ME WHEREVER I GO! NOW THEY'RE KEEPING ME AWAY FROM THE MOST BEAUTIFUL, AMAZING FEMALE ON ANY PLANET!
THIS IS MORE PAIN THAN I EVER KNEW ABOUT!
NUB BINS
AH. REJOICE, MY FRIEND.
IT'S GRAIL TIME.
HUH?
PURE EMOTIONS. YOU ONLY GET 'EM THREE TIMES IN YOUR LIFE--WHEN YOU'RE A KID, WHEN YOU FALL IN LOVE, AND WHEN YOU FACE DEATH.
ALL THE OTHER TIMES, THE EMOTIONS ARE MIXED UP. THAT'S WHY SO MANY "MATURE" PEOPLE ARE ALWAYS IN A WAD.
YOU EVER READ THE KING ARTHUR STORIES THE HUMANS USED TO WRITE?
SURE.
WELL, YOU'RE IN GRAIL TIME. LIVING ON IMPULSE.
WHAT'S THAT SUPPOSED TO MEAN?
SO?

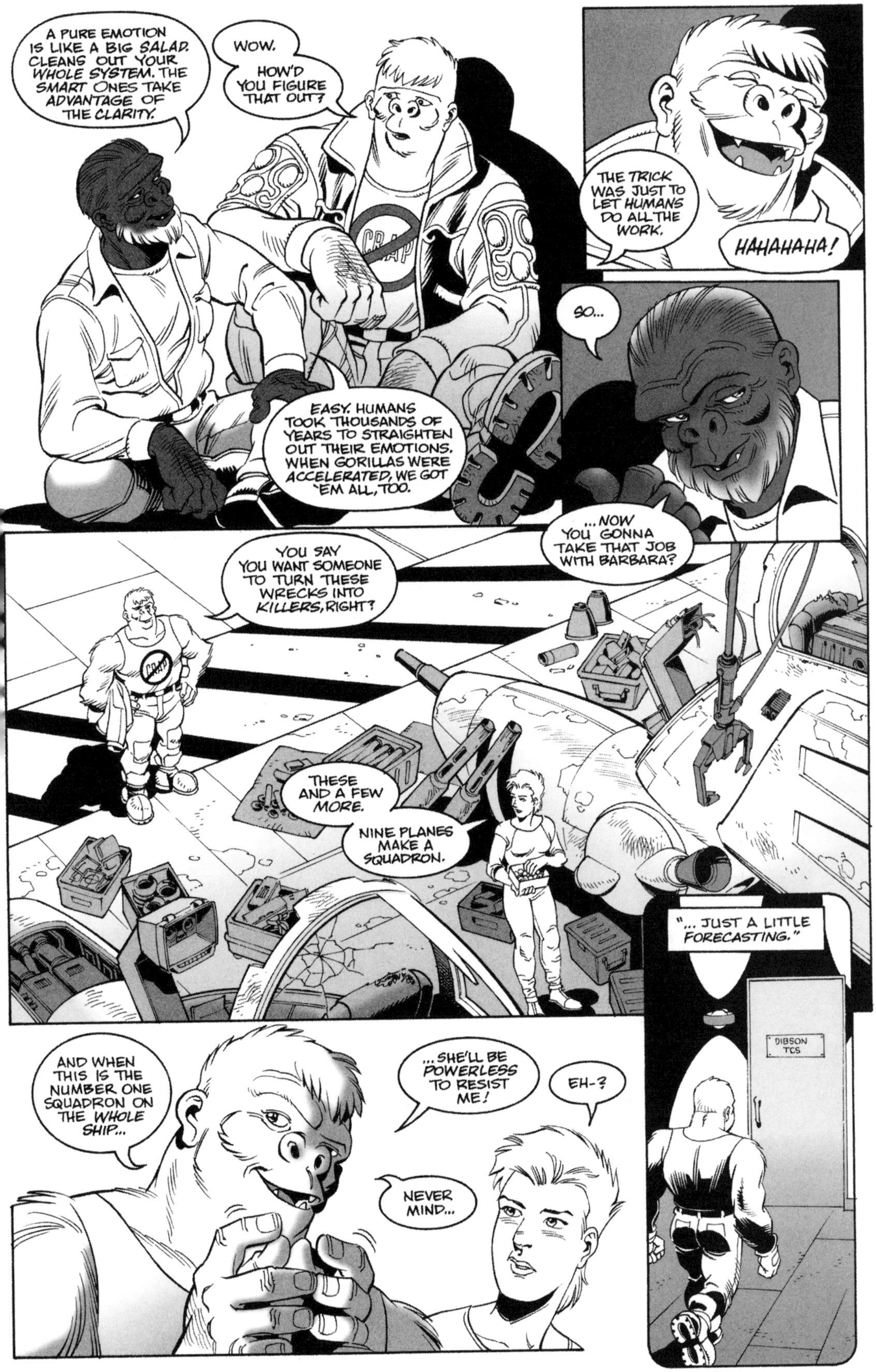
A PURE EMOTION IS LIKE A BIG SALAD. CLEANS OUT YOUR WHOLE SYSTEM. THE SMART ONES TAKE ADVANTAGE OF THE CLARITY.
WOW.
HOW'D YOU FIGURE THAT OUT?
EASY. HUMANS TOOK THOUSANDS OF YEARS TO STRAIGHTEN OUT THEIR EMOTIONS. WHEN GORILLAS WERE ACCELERATED, WE GOT 'EM ALL, TOO.
THE TRICK WAS JUST TO LET HUMANS DO ALL THE WORK.
HAHAHAHA!
SO...
...NOW YOU GONNA TAKE THAT JOB WITH BARBARA?
YOU SAY YOU WANT SOMEONE TO TURN THESE WRECKS INTO KILLERS, RIGHT?
THESE AND A FEW MORE.
NINE PLANES MAKE A SQUADRON.
"... JUST A LITTLE FORECASTING."
DIBSON TCS
AND WHEN THIS IS THE NUMBER ONE SQUADRON ON THE WHOLE SHIP...
...SHE'LL BE POWERLESS TO RESIST ME!
EH-?
NEVER MIND...

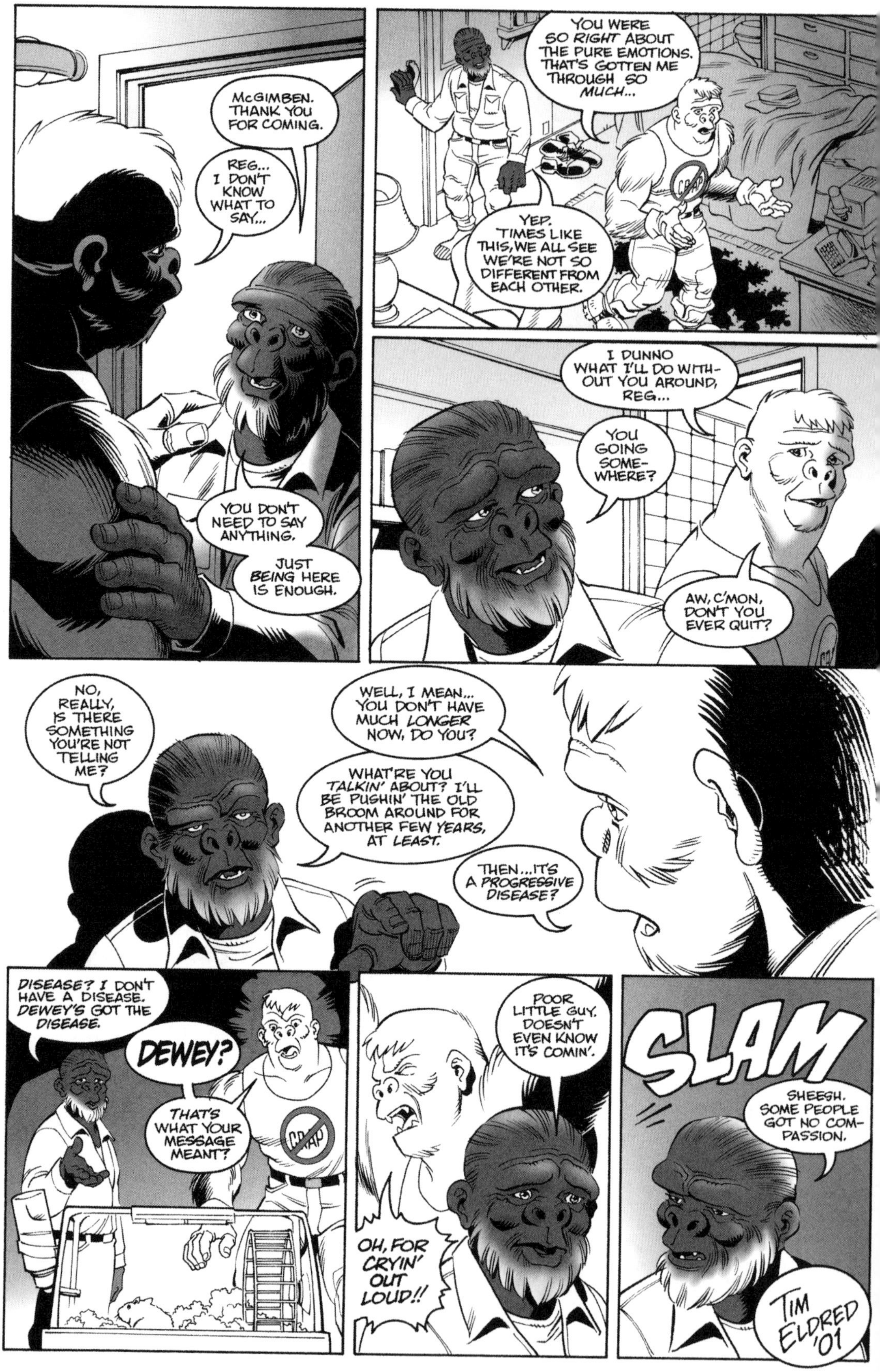
McGIMBEN. THANK YOU FOR COMING.
REG... I DON'T KNOW WHAT TO SAY...
YOU DON'T NEED TO SAY ANYTHING.
JUST BEING HERE IS ENOUGH.
YOU WERE SO RIGHT ABOUT THE PURE EMOTIONS. THAT'S GOTTEN ME THROUGH SO MUCH...
YEP. TIMES LIKE THIS, WE ALL SEE WE'RE NOT SO DIFFERENT FROM EACH OTHER.
I DUNNO WHAT I'LL DO WITH-OUT YOU AROUND, REG...
YOU GOING SOME-WHERE?
AW, C'MON, DON'T YOU EVER QUIT?
NO, REALLY, IS THERE SOMETHING YOU'RE NOT TELLING ME?
WELL, I MEAN... YOU DON'T HAVE MUCH LONGER NOW, DO YOU?
WHAT'RE YOU TALKIN' ABOUT? I'LL BE PUSHIN' THE OLD BROOM AROUND FOR ANOTHER FEW YEARS, AT LEAST.
THEN... IT'S A PROGRESSIVE DISEASE?
DISEASE? I DON'T HAVE A DISEASE. DEWEY'S GOT THE DISEASE.
DEWEY?
THAT'S WHAT YOUR MESSAGE MEANT?
POOR LITTLE GUY. DOESN'T EVEN KNOW IT'S COMIN'.
OH, FOR CRYIN' OUT LOUD!!
SLAM
SHEESH. SOME PEOPLE GOT NO COM-PASSION.
TIM ELDRED '01

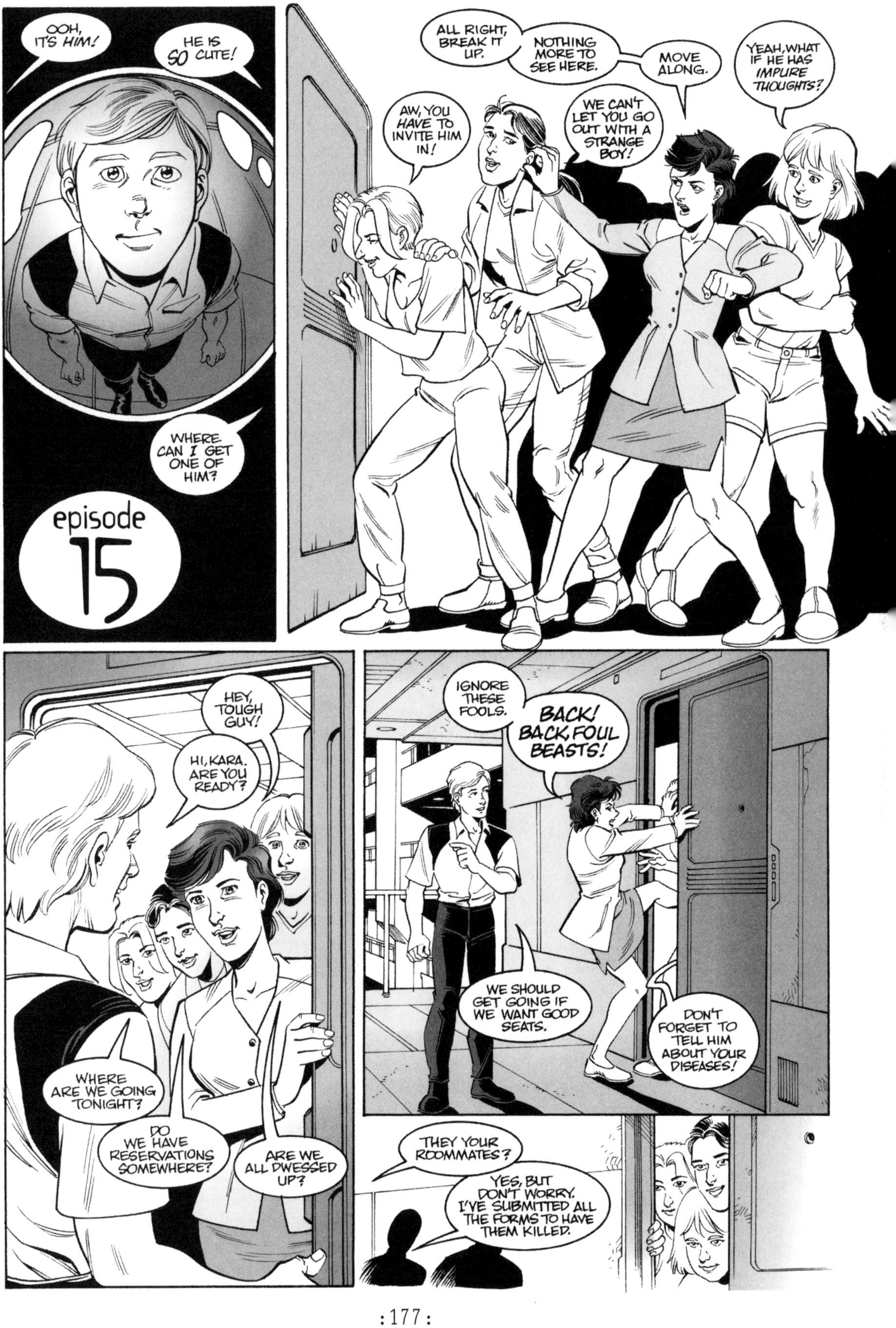
OOH, IT'S HIM!
HE IS SO CUTE!
WHERE CAN I GET ONE OF HIM?
episode 15
ALL RIGHT, BREAK IT UP.
NOTHING MORE TO SEE HERE.
MOVE ALONG.
YEAH, WHAT IF HE HAS IMPURE THOUGHTS?
AW, YOU HAVE TO INVITE HIM IN!
WE CAN'T LET YOU GO OUT WITH A STRANGE BOY!
HEY, TOUGH GUY!
HI, KARA. ARE YOU READY?
WHERE ARE WE GOING TONIGHT?
DO WE HAVE RESERVATIONS SOMEWHERE?
ARE WE ALL DWESSED UP?
IGNORE THESE FOOLS.
BACK! BACK, FOUL BEASTS!
WE SHOULD GET GOING IF WE WANT GOOD SEATS.
DON'T FORGET TO TELL HIM ABOUT YOUR DISEASES!
THEY YOUR ROOMMATES?
YES, BUT DON'T WORRY. I'VE SUBMITTED ALL THE FORMS TO HAVE THEM KILLED.

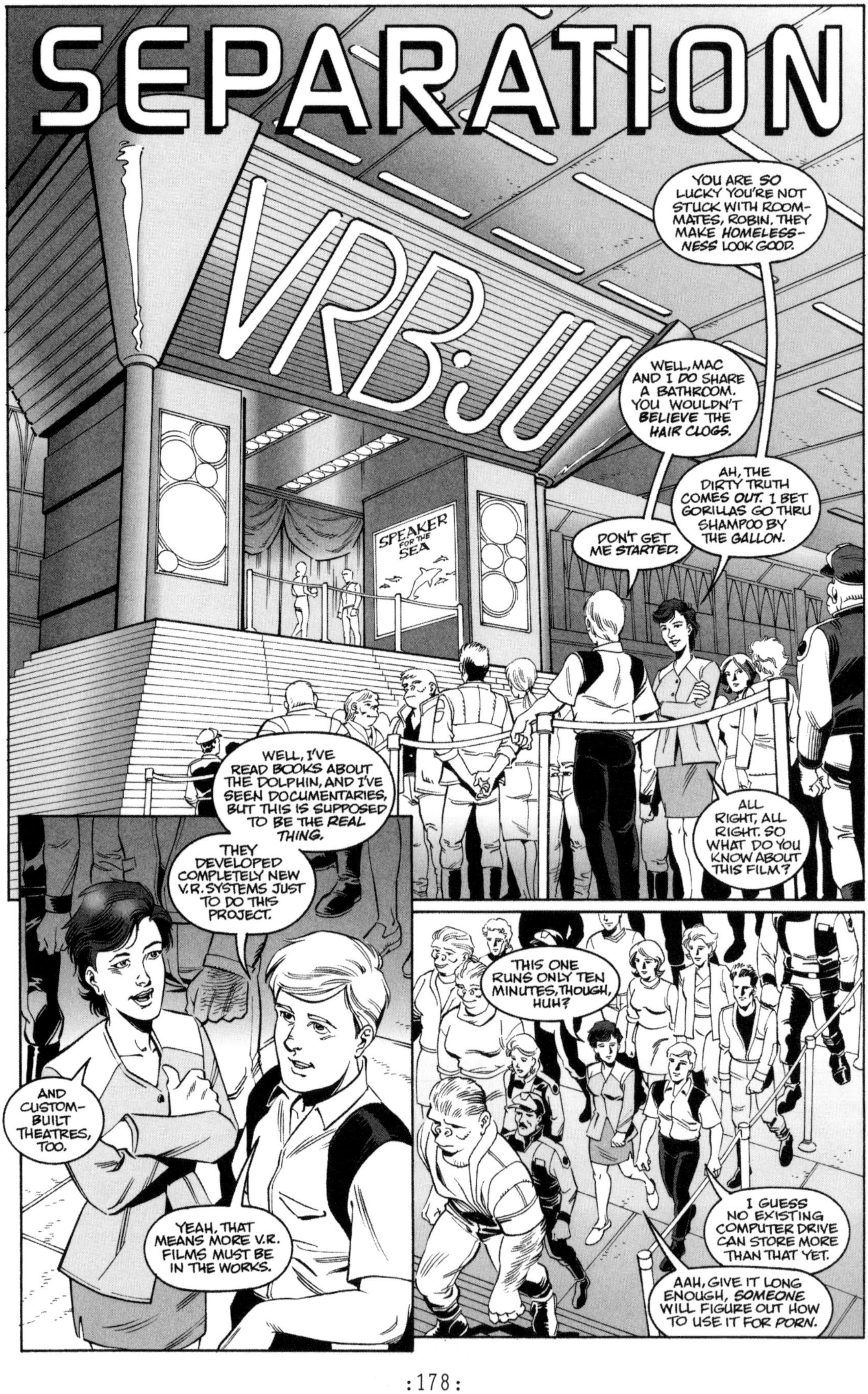
SEPARATION
VRBIJU
SPEAKER FOR THE SEA
YOU ARE SO LUCKY YOU'RE NOT STUCK WITH ROOM-MATES, ROBIN. THEY MAKE HOMELESS-NESS LOOK GOOD.
WELL, MAC AND I DO SHARE A BATHROOM. YOU WOULDN'T BELIEVE THE HAIR CLOGS.
AH, THE DIRTY TRUTH COMES OUT. I BET GORILLAS GO THRU SHAMPOO BY THE GALLON.
DON'T GET ME STARTED.
ALL RIGHT, ALL RIGHT. SO WHAT DO YOU KNOW ABOUT THIS FILM?
WELL, I'VE READ BOOKS ABOUT THE DOLPHIN, AND I'VE SEEN DOCUMENTARIES, BUT THIS IS SUPPOSED TO BE THE REAL THING.
THEY DEVELOPED COMPLETELY NEW V.R. SYSTEMS JUST TO DO THIS PROJECT.
AND CUSTOM-BUILT THEATRES, TOO.
YEAH, THAT MEANS MORE V.R. FILMS MUST BE IN THE WORKS.
THIS ONE RUNS ONLY TEN MINUTES, THOUGH, HUH?
I GUESS NO EXISTING COMPUTER DRIVE CAN STORE MORE THAN THAT YET.
AAH, GIVE IT LONG ENOUGH, SOMEONE WILL FIGURE OUT HOW TO USE IT FOR PORN.

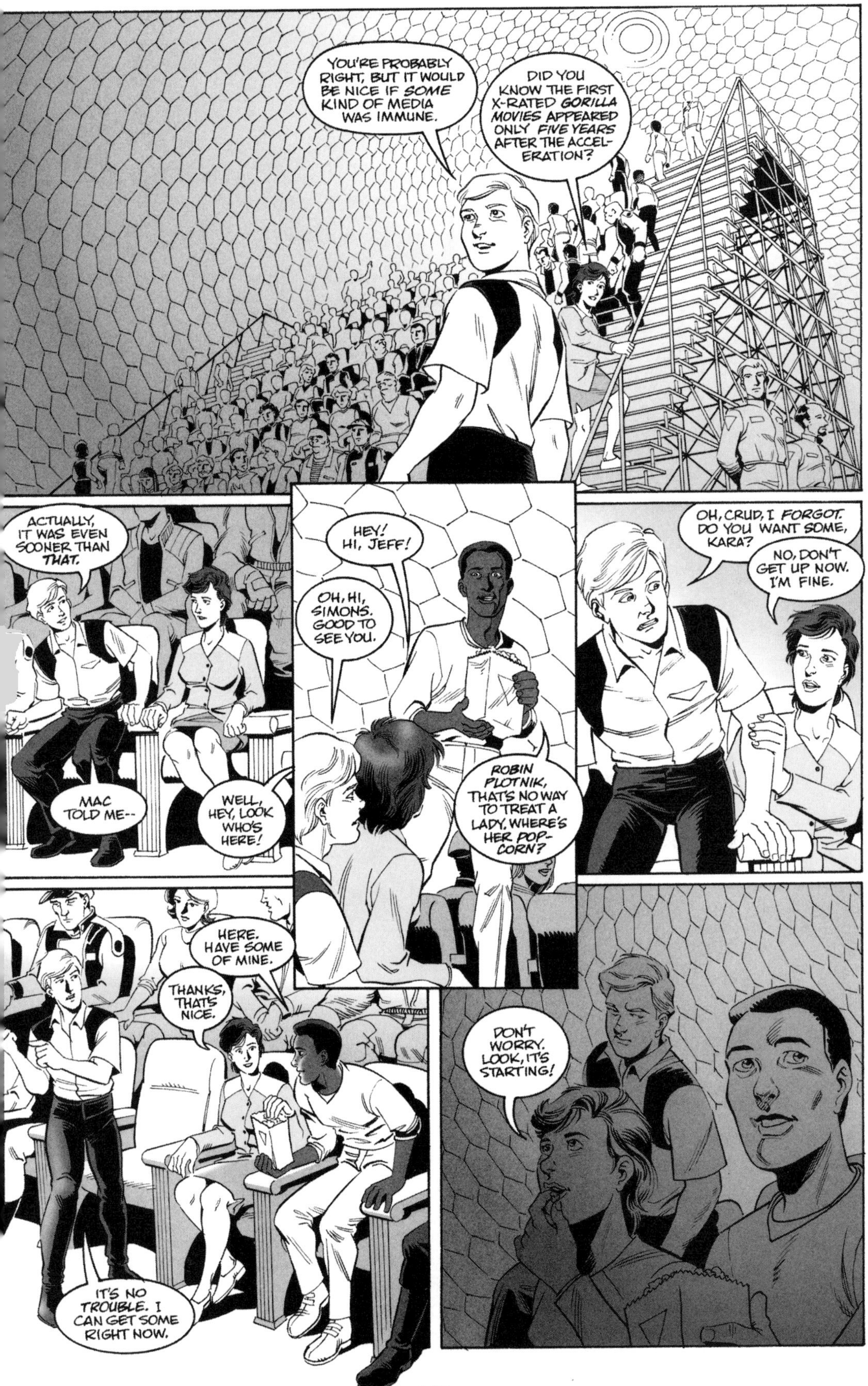
YOU'RE PROBABLY RIGHT, BUT IT WOULD BE NICE IF SOME KIND OF MEDIA WAS IMMUNE.
DID YOU KNOW THE FIRST X-RATED GORILLA MOVIES APPEARED ONLY FIVE YEARS AFTER THE ACCELERATION?
ACTUALLY, IT WAS EVEN SOONER THAN THAT.
MAC TOLD ME--
WELL, HEY, LOOK WHO'S HERE!
HEY! HI, JEFF!
OH, HI, SIMONS. GOOD TO SEE YOU.
ROBIN PLOTNIK, THAT'S NO WAY TO TREAT A LADY. WHERE'S HER POPCORN?
OH, CRUD, I FORGOT. DO YOU WANT SOME, KARA?
NO, DON'T GET UP NOW. I'M FINE.
HERE. HAVE SOME OF MINE.
THANKS, THAT'S NICE.
IT'S NO TROUBLE. I CAN GET SOME RIGHT NOW.
DON'T WORRY. LOOK, IT'S STARTING!

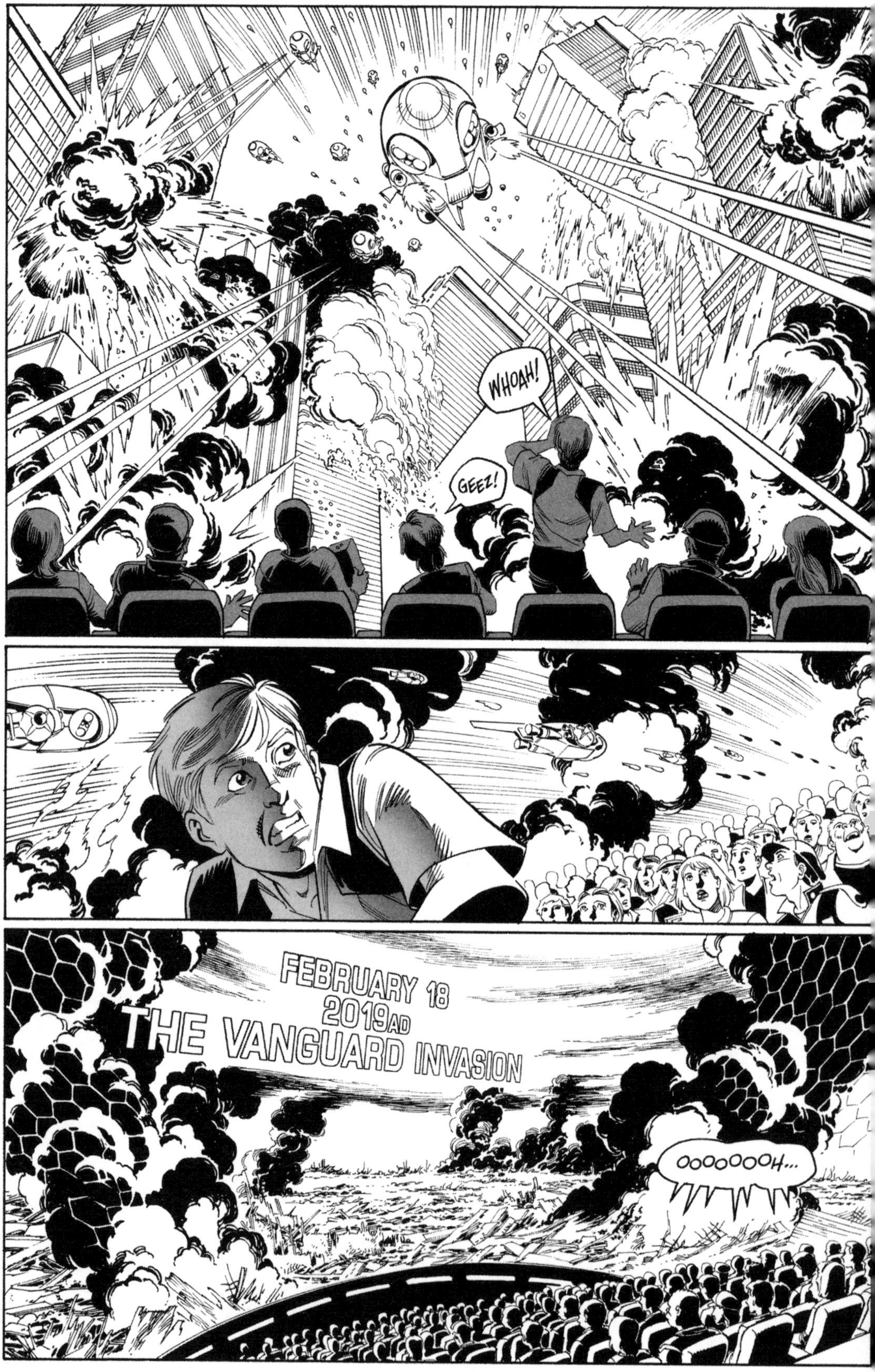
WHOAH!
GEEZ!
FEBRUARY 18
2019AD
THE VANGUARD INVASION
OOOOOOOH...

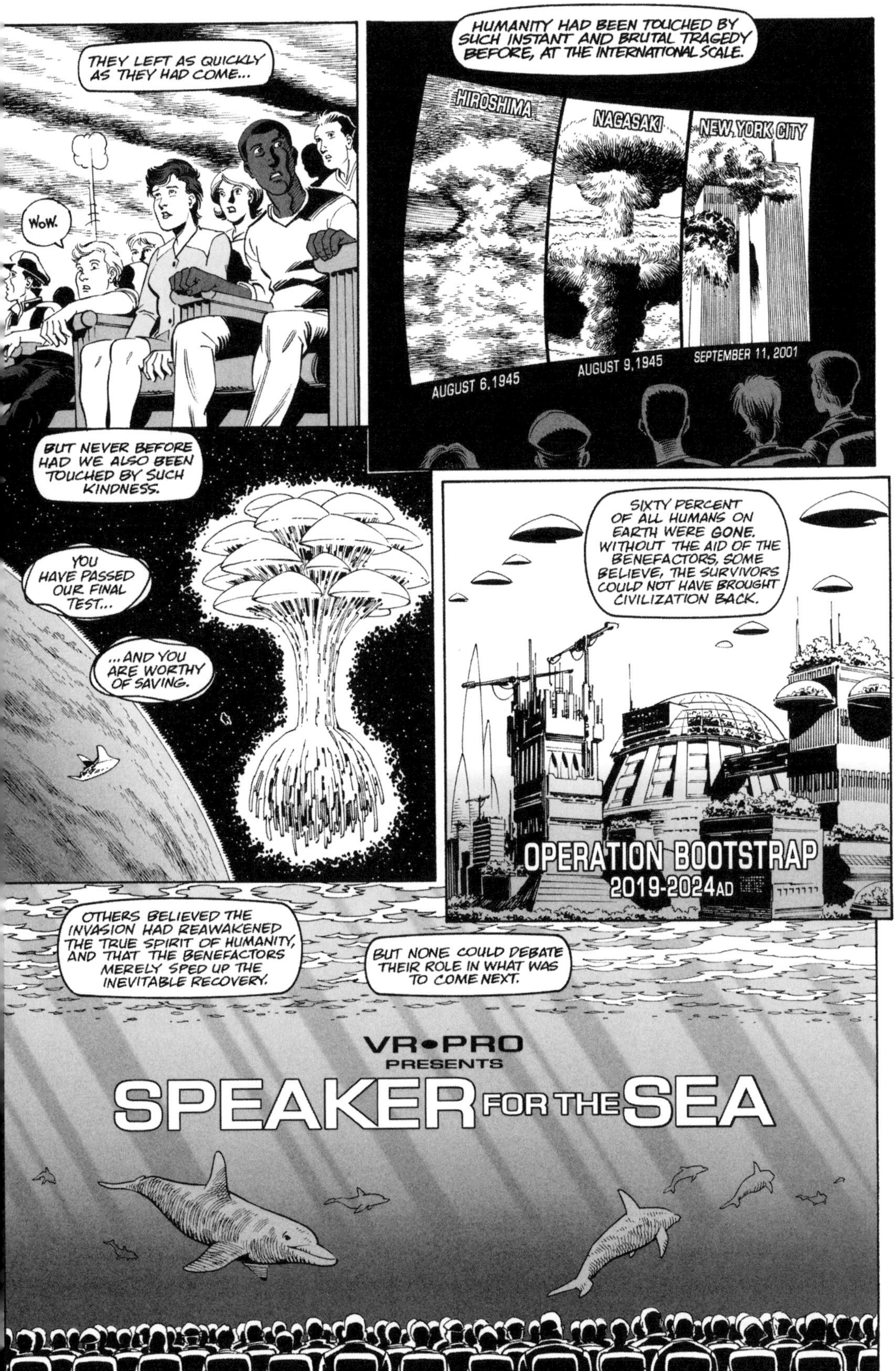
THEY LEFT AS QUICKLY AS THEY HAD COME...
WOW.
HUMANITY HAD BEEN TOUCHED BY SUCH INSTANT AND BRUTAL TRAGEDY BEFORE, AT THE INTERNATIONAL SCALE.
HIROSHIMA
NAGASAKI
NEW YORK CITY
AUGUST 6, 1945
AUGUST 9, 1945
SEPTEMBER 11, 2001
BUT NEVER BEFORE HAD WE ALSO BEEN TOUCHED BY SUCH KINDNESS.
YOU HAVE PASSED OUR FINAL TEST...
...AND YOU ARE WORTHY OF SAVING.
SIXTY PERCENT OF ALL HUMANS ON EARTH WERE GONE. WITHOUT THE AID OF THE BENEFACTORS, SOME BELIEVE, THE SURVIVORS COULD NOT HAVE BROUGHT CIVILIZATION BACK.
OPERATION BOOTSTRAP
2019-2024AD
OTHERS BELIEVED THE INVASION HAD REAWAKENED THE TRUE SPIRIT OF HUMANITY, AND THAT THE BENEFACTORS MERELY SPED UP THE INEVITABLE RECOVERY.
BUT NONE COULD DEBATE THEIR ROLE IN WHAT WAS TO COME NEXT.
VR•PRO
PRESENTS
SPEAKER FOR THE SEA

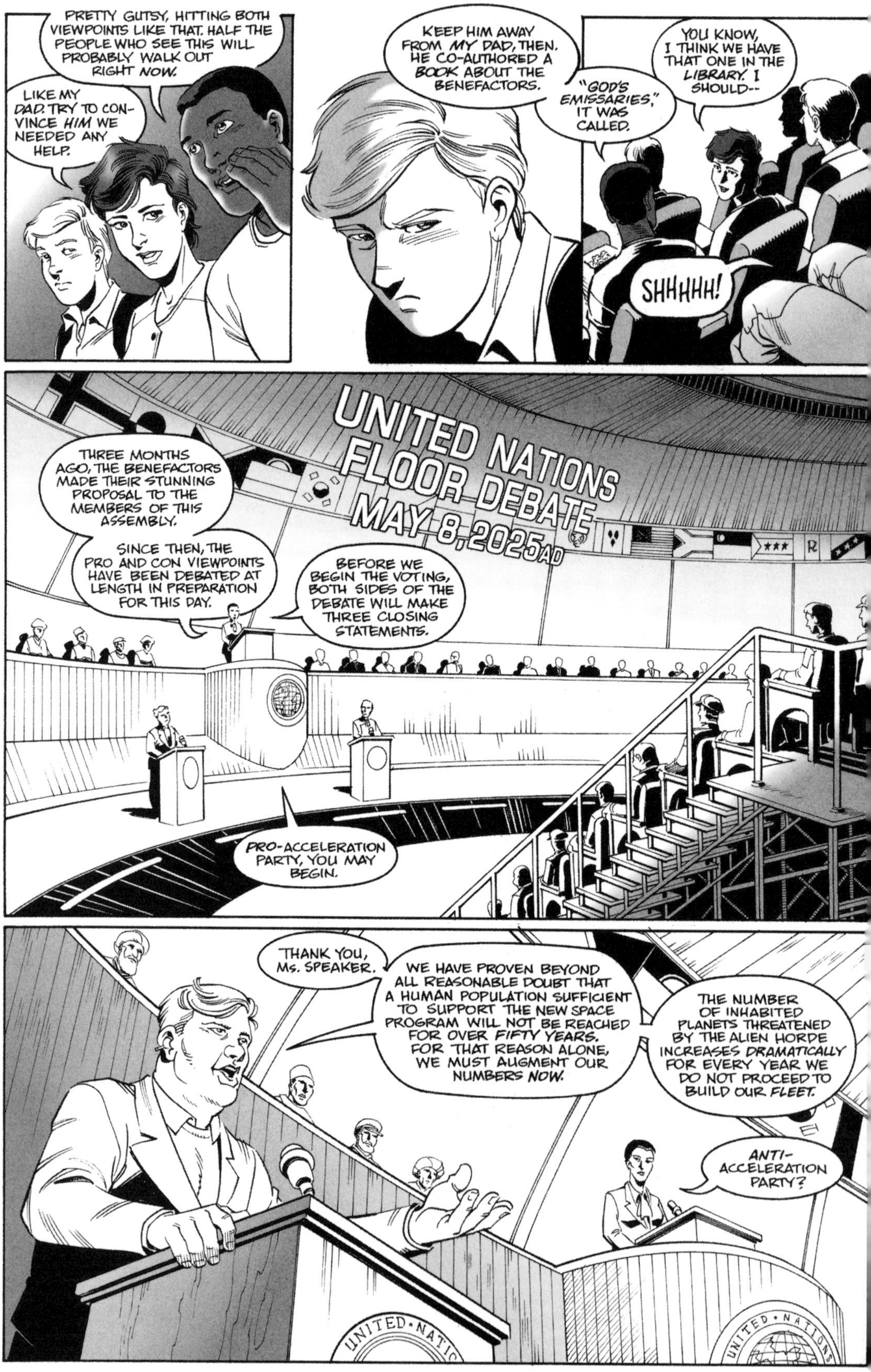
PRETTY GUTSY, HITTING BOTH VIEWPOINTS LIKE THAT. HALF THE PEOPLE WHO SEE THIS WILL PROBABLY WALK OUT RIGHT NOW.
LIKE MY DAD. TRY TO CONVINCE HIM WE NEEDED ANY HELP.
KEEP HIM AWAY FROM MY DAD, THEN. HE CO-AUTHORED A BOOK ABOUT THE BENEFACTORS.
"GOD'S EMISSARIES," IT WAS CALLED.
YOU KNOW, I THINK WE HAVE THAT ONE IN THE LIBRARY. I SHOULD--
SHHHHH!
UNITED NATIONS FLOOR DEBATE MAY 8, 2025 AD
THREE MONTHS AGO, THE BENEFACTORS MADE THEIR STUNNING PROPOSAL TO THE MEMBERS OF THIS ASSEMBLY.
SINCE THEN, THE PRO AND CON VIEWPOINTS HAVE BEEN DEBATED AT LENGTH IN PREPARATION FOR THIS DAY.
BEFORE WE BEGIN THE VOTING, BOTH SIDES OF THE DEBATE WILL MAKE THREE CLOSING STATEMENTS.
PRO-ACCELERATION PARTY, YOU MAY BEGIN.
THANK YOU, Ms. SPEAKER.
WE HAVE PROVEN BEYOND ALL REASONABLE DOUBT THAT A HUMAN POPULATION SUFFICIENT TO SUPPORT THE NEW SPACE PROGRAM WILL NOT BE REACHED FOR OVER FIFTY YEARS. FOR THAT REASON ALONE, WE MUST AUGMENT OUR NUMBERS NOW.
THE NUMBER OF INHABITED PLANETS THREATENED BY THE ALIEN HORDE INCREASES DRAMATICALLY FOR EVERY YEAR WE DO NOT PROCEED TO BUILD OUR FLEET.
ANTI-ACCELERATION PARTY?
UNITED NATIONS

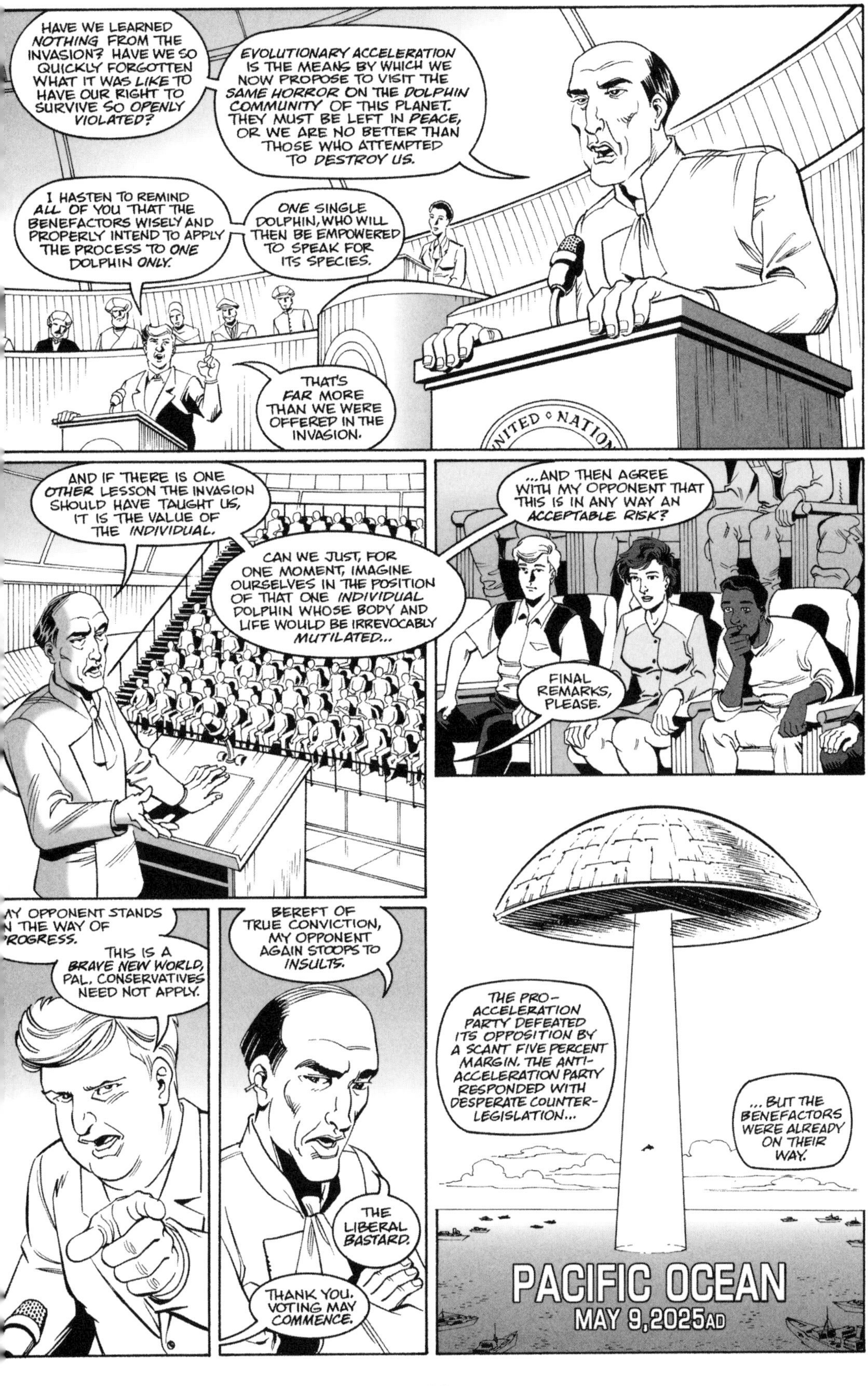
HAVE WE LEARNED NOTHING FROM THE INVASION? HAVE WE SO QUICKLY FORGOTTEN WHAT IT WAS LIKE TO HAVE OUR RIGHT TO SURVIVE SO OPENLY VIOLATED?
EVOLUTIONARY ACCELERATION IS THE MEANS BY WHICH WE NOW PROPOSE TO VISIT THE SAME HORROR ON THE DOLPHIN COMMUNITY OF THIS PLANET. THEY MUST BE LEFT IN PEACE, OR WE ARE NO BETTER THAN THOSE WHO ATTEMPTED TO DESTROY US.
I HASTEN TO REMIND ALL OF YOU THAT THE BENEFACTORS WISELY AND PROPERLY INTEND TO APPLY THE PROCESS TO ONE DOLPHIN ONLY.
ONE SINGLE DOLPHIN, WHO WILL THEN BE EMPOWERED TO SPEAK FOR ITS SPECIES.
THAT'S FAR MORE THAN WE WERE OFFERED IN THE INVASION.
UNITED NATIONS
AND IF THERE IS ONE OTHER LESSON THE INVASION SHOULD HAVE TAUGHT US, IT IS THE VALUE OF THE INDIVIDUAL.
CAN WE JUST, FOR ONE MOMENT, IMAGINE OURSELVES IN THE POSITION OF THAT ONE INDIVIDUAL DOLPHIN WHOSE BODY AND LIFE WOULD BE IRREVOCABLY MUTILATED...
...AND THEN AGREE WITH MY OPPONENT THAT THIS IS IN ANY WAY AN ACCEPTABLE RISK?
FINAL REMARKS, PLEASE.
MY OPPONENT STANDS IN THE WAY OF PROGRESS.
THIS IS A BRAVE NEW WORLD, PAL. CONSERVATIVES NEED NOT APPLY.
BEREFT OF TRUE CONVICTION, MY OPPONENT AGAIN STOOPS TO INSULTS.
THE LIBERAL BASTARD.
THANK YOU. VOTING MAY COMMENCE.
THE PRO-ACCELERATION PARTY DEFEATED ITS OPPOSITION BY A SCANT FIVE PERCENT MARGIN. THE ANTI-ACCELERATION PARTY RESPONDED WITH DESPERATE COUNTER-LEGISLATION...
...BUT THE BENEFACTORS WERE ALREADY ON THEIR WAY.
PACIFIC OCEAN
MAY 9, 2025AD

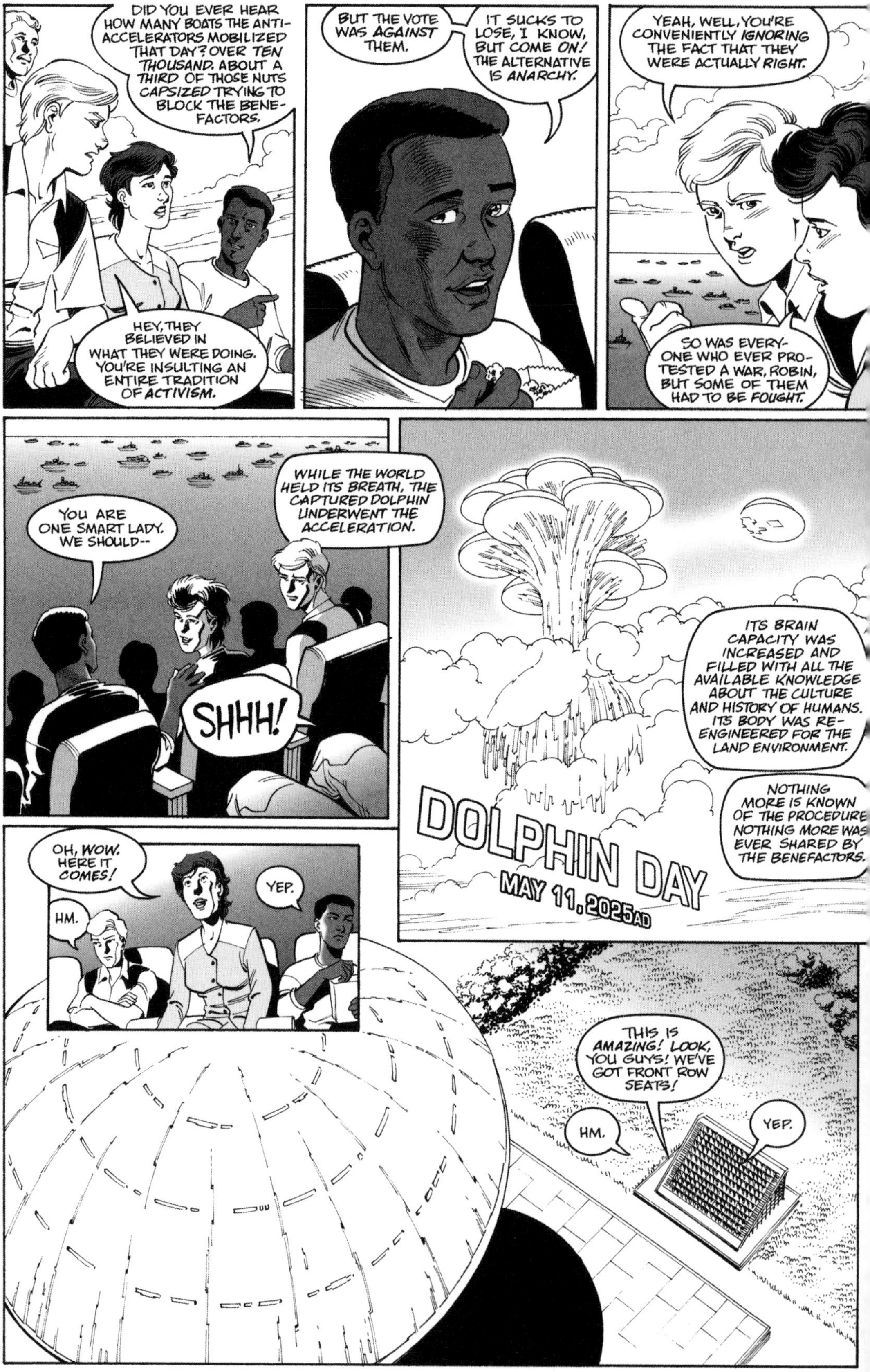
DID YOU EVER HEAR HOW MANY BOATS THE ANTI-ACCELERATORS MOBILIZED THAT DAY? OVER TEN THOUSAND. ABOUT A THIRD OF THOSE NUTS CAPSIZED TRYING TO BLOCK THE BENE-FACTORS.
HEY, THEY BELIEVED IN WHAT THEY WERE DOING. YOU'RE INSULTING AN ENTIRE TRADITION OF ACTIVISM.
BUT THE VOTE WAS AGAINST THEM.
IT SUCKS TO LOSE, I KNOW, BUT COME ON! THE ALTERNATIVE IS ANARCHY.
YEAH, WELL, YOU'RE CONVENIENTLY IGNORING THE FACT THAT THEY WERE ACTUALLY RIGHT.
SO WAS EVERY-ONE WHO EVER PRO-TESTED A WAR, ROBIN, BUT SOME OF THEM HAD TO BE FOUGHT.
YOU ARE ONE SMART LADY. WE SHOULD--
WHILE THE WORLD HELD ITS BREATH, THE CAPTURED DOLPHIN UNDERWENT THE ACCELERATION.
SHHH!
ITS BRAIN CAPACITY WAS INCREASED AND FILLED WITH ALL THE AVAILABLE KNOWLEDGE ABOUT THE CULTURE AND HISTORY OF HUMANS. ITS BODY WAS RE-ENGINEERED FOR THE LAND ENVIRONMENT.
NOTHING MORE IS KNOWN OF THE PROCEDURE NOTHING MORE WAS EVER SHARED BY THE BENEFACTORS.
DOLPHIN DAY
MAY 11, 2025AD
OH, WOW. HERE IT COMES!
YEP.
HM.
THIS IS AMAZING! LOOK, YOU GUYS! WE'VE GOT FRONT ROW SEATS!
HM.
YEP.

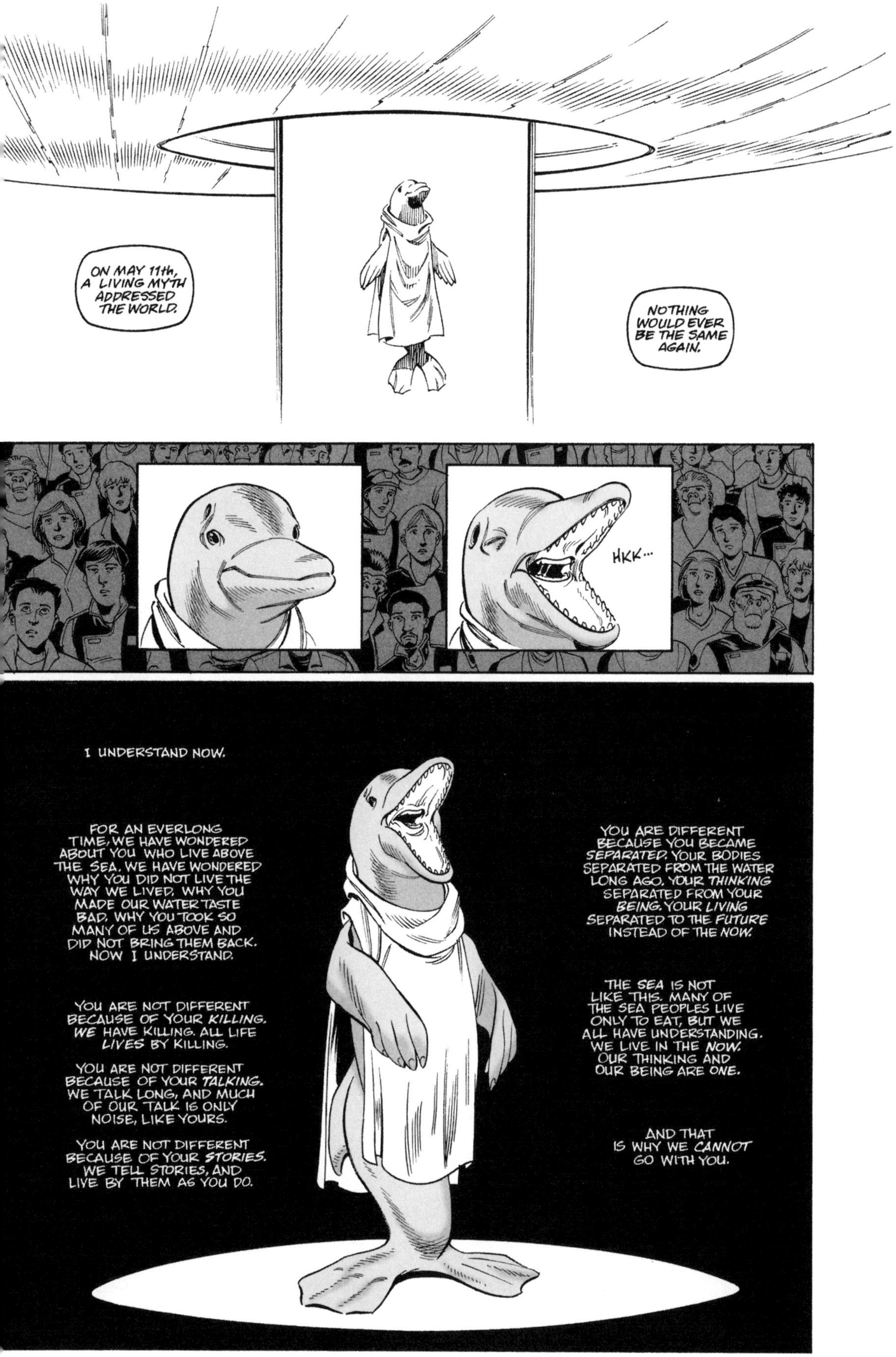
ON MAY 11th, A LIVING MYTH ADDRESSED THE WORLD.
NOTHING WOULD EVER BE THE SAME AGAIN.
HKK...
I UNDERSTAND NOW.
FOR AN EVERLONG TIME, WE HAVE WONDERED ABOUT YOU WHO LIVE ABOVE THE SEA. WE HAVE WONDERED WHY YOU DID NOT LIVE THE WAY WE LIVED. WHY YOU MADE OUR WATER TASTE BAD. WHY YOU TOOK SO MANY OF US ABOVE AND DID NOT BRING THEM BACK. NOW I UNDERSTAND.
YOU ARE NOT DIFFERENT BECAUSE OF YOUR *KILLING*. *WE* HAVE KILLING. ALL LIFE *LIVES* BY KILLING.
YOU ARE NOT DIFFERENT BECAUSE OF YOUR *TALKING*. WE TALK LONG, AND MUCH OF OUR TALK IS ONLY NOISE, LIKE YOURS.
YOU ARE NOT DIFFERENT BECAUSE OF YOUR *STORIES*. WE TELL STORIES, AND LIVE BY THEM AS YOU DO.
YOU ARE DIFFERENT BECAUSE YOU BECAME *SEPARATED*. YOUR BODIES SEPARATED FROM THE WATER LONG AGO. YOUR *THINKING* SEPARATED FROM YOUR *BEING*. YOUR *LIVING* SEPARATED TO THE *FUTURE* INSTEAD OF THE *NOW*.
THE *SEA* IS NOT LIKE THIS. MANY OF THE SEA PEOPLES LIVE ONLY TO EAT, BUT WE ALL HAVE UNDERSTANDING. WE LIVE IN THE *NOW*. OUR THINKING AND OUR BEING ARE *ONE*.
AND THAT IS WHY WE *CANNOT* GO WITH YOU.

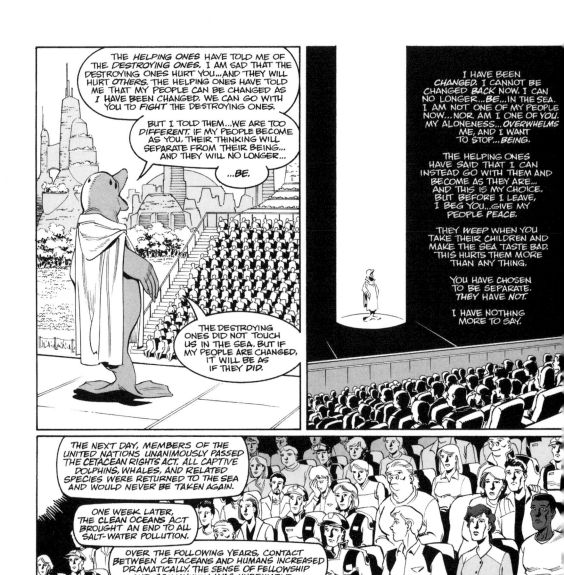

THE *HELPING ONES* HAVE TOLD ME OF THE *DESTROYING ONES.* I AM SAD THAT THE DESTROYING ONES HURT YOU...AND THEY WILL HURT *OTHERS.* THE HELPING ONES HAVE TOLD ME THAT MY PEOPLE CAN BE CHANGED AS I HAVE BEEN CHANGED. WE CAN GO WITH YOU TO *FIGHT* THE DESTROYING ONES.

BUT I TOLD THEM...WE ARE TOO *DIFFERENT.* IF MY PEOPLE BECOME AS YOU, THEIR THINKING WILL SEPARATE FROM THEIR BEING... AND THEY WILL NO LONGER...

...BE.

THE DESTROYING ONES DID NOT TOUCH US IN THE SEA. BUT IF MY PEOPLE ARE CHANGED, IT WILL BE AS IF THEY DID.

I HAVE BEEN *CHANGED.* I CANNOT BE CHANGED *BACK* NOW. I CAN NO LONGER...BE...IN THE SEA. I AM NOT ONE OF MY PEOPLE NOW...NOR AM I ONE OF YOU. MY ALONENESS...*OVERWHELMS* ME, AND I WANT TO STOP...*BEING.*

THE HELPING ONES HAVE SAID THAT I CAN INSTEAD GO WITH THEM AND BECOME AS THEY ARE... AND THIS IS MY CHOICE. BUT BEFORE I LEAVE, I BEG YOU...GIVE MY PEOPLE PEACE.

THEY *WEEP* WHEN YOU TAKE THEIR CHILDREN AND MAKE THE SEA TASTE BAD. THIS HURTS THEM MORE THAN ANY THING.

YOU HAVE CHOSEN TO BE SEPARATE. THEY HAVE *NOT.*

I HAVE NOTHING MORE TO SAY.

THE NEXT DAY, MEMBERS OF THE UNITED NATIONS UNANIMOUSLY PASSED THE CETACEAN RIGHTS ACT. ALL CAPTIVE DOLPHINS, WHALES, AND RELATED SPECIES WERE RETURNED TO THE SEA AND WOULD NEVER BE TAKEN AGAIN.

ONE WEEK LATER, THE CLEAN OCEANS ACT BROUGHT AN END TO ALL SALT-WATER POLLUTION.

OVER THE FOLLOWING YEARS, CONTACT BETWEEN CETACEANS AND HUMANS INCREASED DRAMATICALLY. THE SENSE OF FELLOWSHIP AND COMMUNION WAS UNDENIABLE.

AND NOW EYES TURNED FROM THE OCEAN...TO THE JUNGLE.

THE END

COMING SOON
THE STORY OF ISHMAEL

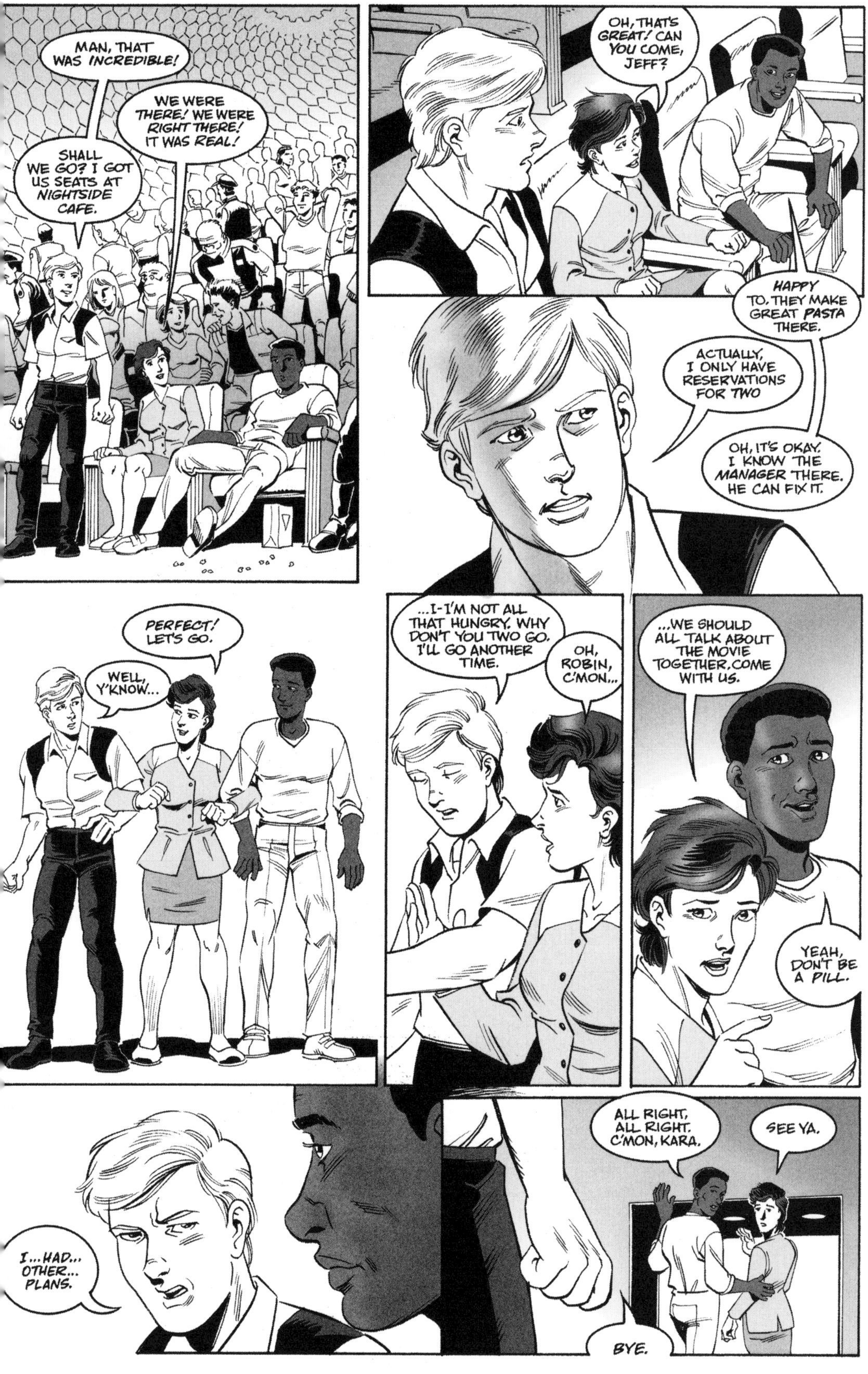
MAN, THAT WAS INCREDIBLE!
WE WERE THERE! WE WERE RIGHT THERE! IT WAS REAL!
SHALL WE GO? I GOT US SEATS AT NIGHTSIDE CAFE.
OH, THAT'S GREAT! CAN YOU COME, JEFF?
HAPPY TO. THEY MAKE GREAT PASTA THERE.
ACTUALLY, I ONLY HAVE RESERVATIONS FOR TWO
OH, IT'S OKAY. I KNOW THE MANAGER THERE. HE CAN FIX IT.
PERFECT! LET'S GO.
WELL, Y'KNOW...
...I-I'M NOT ALL THAT HUNGRY. WHY DON'T YOU TWO GO. I'LL GO ANOTHER TIME.
OH, ROBIN, C'MON...
...WE SHOULD ALL TALK ABOUT THE MOVIE TOGETHER. COME WITH US.
YEAH, DON'T BE A PILL.
I... HAD... OTHER... PLANS.
ALL RIGHT, ALL RIGHT. C'MON, KARA.
SEE YA.
BYE.

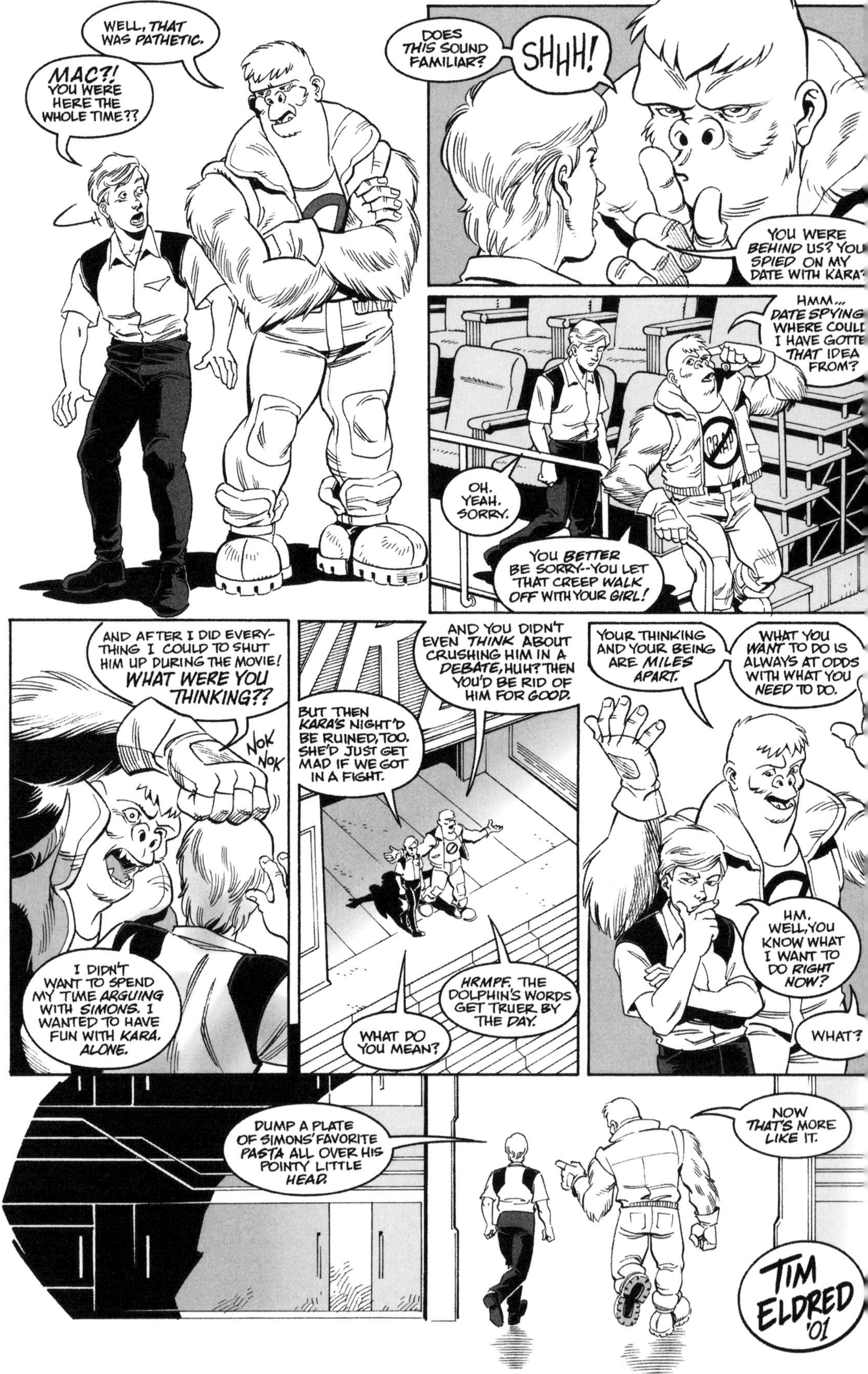
WELL, THAT WAS PATHETIC.
MAC?! YOU WERE HERE THE WHOLE TIME??
DOES THIS SOUND FAMILIAR?
SHHH!
YOU WERE BEHIND US? YOU SPIED ON MY DATE WITH KARA?
HMM... DATE SPYING WHERE COUL I HAVE GOTTE THAT IDEA FROM?
OH. YEAH. SORRY.
YOU BETTER BE SORRY--YOU LET THAT CREEP WALK OFF WITH YOUR GIRL!
AND AFTER I DID EVERYTHING I COULD TO SHUT HIM UP DURING THE MOVIE! WHAT WERE YOU THINKING??
NOK NOK
I DIDN'T WANT TO SPEND MY TIME ARGUING WITH SIMONS. I WANTED TO HAVE FUN WITH KARA. ALONE.
AND YOU DIDN'T EVEN THINK ABOUT CRUSHING HIM IN A DEBATE, HUH? THEN YOU'D BE RID OF HIM FOR GOOD.
BUT THEN KARA'S NIGHT'D BE RUINED, TOO. SHE'D JUST GET MAD IF WE GOT IN A FIGHT.
HRMPF. THE DOLPHIN'S WORDS GET TRUER BY THE DAY.
WHAT DO YOU MEAN?
YOUR THINKING AND YOUR BEING ARE MILES APART.
WHAT YOU WANT TO DO IS ALWAYS AT ODDS WITH WHAT YOU NEED TO DO.
HM. WELL, YOU KNOW WHAT I WANT TO DO RIGHT NOW?
WHAT?
DUMP A PLATE OF SIMONS' FAVORITE PASTA ALL OVER HIS POINTY LITTLE HEAD.
NOW THAT'S MORE LIKE IT.
TIM ELDRED '01

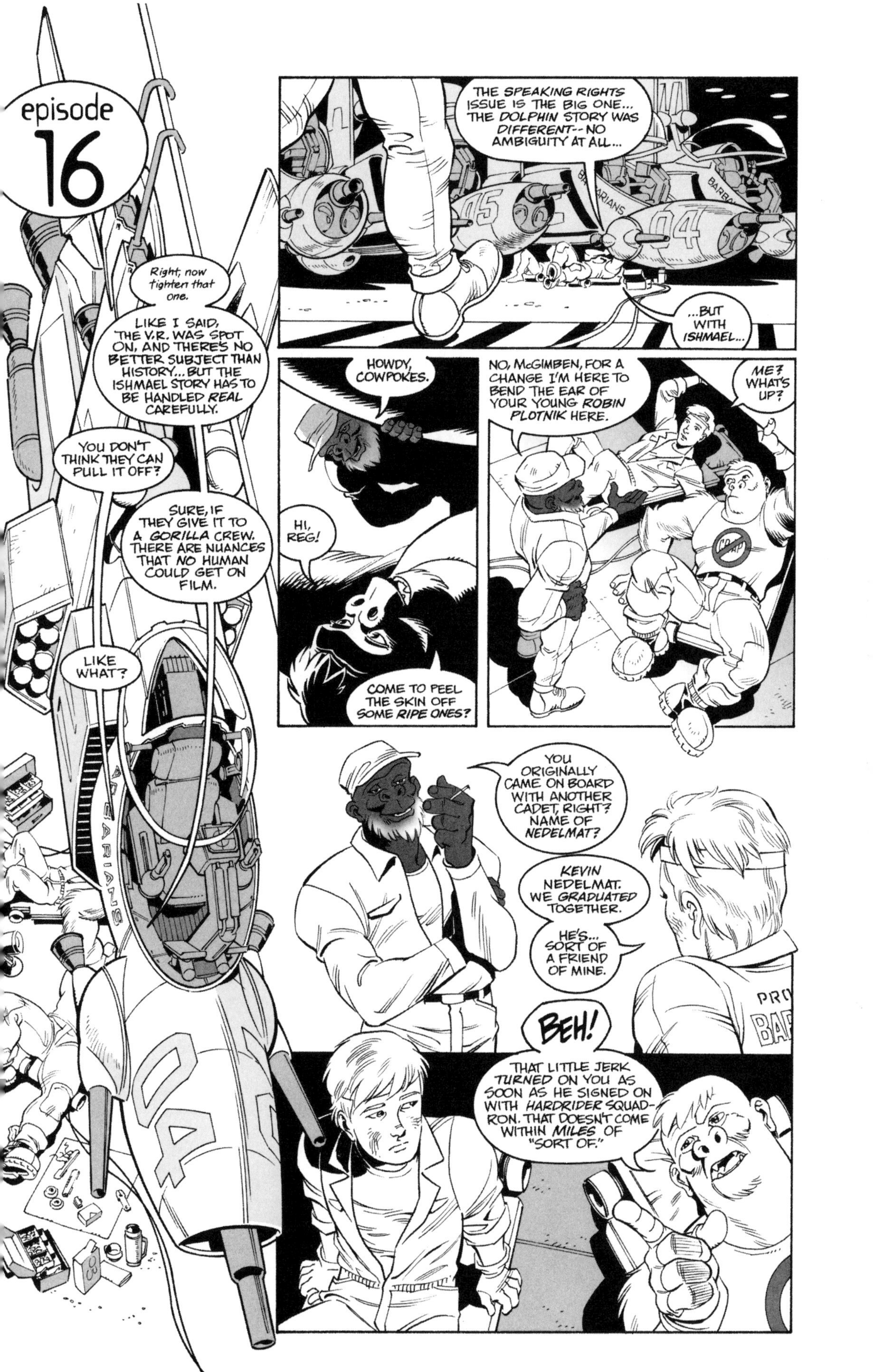
episode
16
THE SPEAKING RIGHTS ISSUE IS THE BIG ONE... THE DOLPHIN STORY WAS DIFFERENT-- NO AMBIGUITY AT ALL...
...BUT WITH ISHMAEL...
Right, now tighten that one.
LIKE I SAID, THE V.R. WAS SPOT ON, AND THERE'S NO BETTER SUBJECT THAN HISTORY... BUT THE ISHMAEL STORY HAS TO BE HANDLED REAL CAREFULLY.
YOU DON'T THINK THEY CAN PULL IT OFF?
SURE, IF THEY GIVE IT TO A GORILLA CREW. THERE ARE NUANCES THAT NO HUMAN COULD GET ON FILM.
LIKE WHAT?
HOWDY, COWPOKES.
HI, REG!
COME TO PEEL THE SKIN OFF SOME RIPE ONES?
NO, McGIMBEN, FOR A CHANGE I'M HERE TO BEND THE EAR OF YOUR YOUNG ROBIN PLOTNIK HERE.
ME? WHAT'S UP?
YOU ORIGINALLY CAME ON BOARD WITH ANOTHER CADET, RIGHT? NAME OF NEDELMAT?
KEVIN NEDELMAT. WE GRADUATED TOGETHER.
HE'S... SORT OF A FRIEND OF MINE.
BEH!
THAT LITTLE JERK TURNED ON YOU AS SOON AS HE SIGNED ON WITH HARDRIDER SQUADRON. THAT DOESN'T COME WITHIN MILES OF "SORT OF."

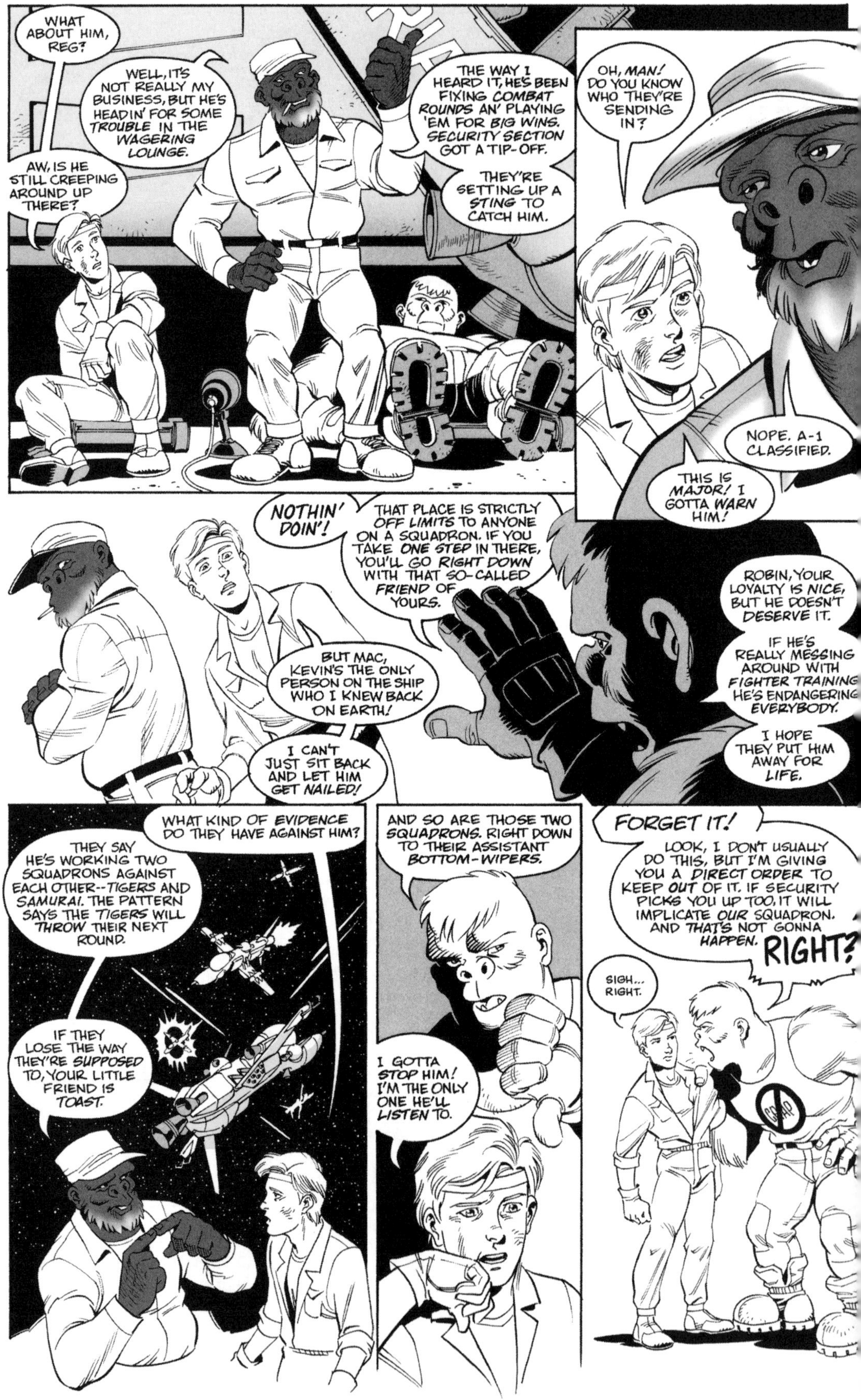

WHAT ABOUT HIM, REG?
WELL, IT'S NOT REALLY MY BUSINESS, BUT HE'S HEADIN' FOR SOME TROUBLE IN THE WAGERING LOUNGE.
AW, IS HE STILL CREEPING AROUND UP THERE?
THE WAY I HEARD IT, HE'S BEEN FIXING COMBAT ROUNDS AN' PLAYING 'EM FOR BIG WINS. SECURITY SECTION GOT A TIP-OFF.
THEY'RE SETTING UP A STING TO CATCH HIM.
OH, MAN! DO YOU KNOW WHO THEY'RE SENDING IN?
NOPE. A-1 CLASSIFIED.
THIS IS MAJOR! I GOTTA WARN HIM!
NOTHIN' DOIN'!
THAT PLACE IS STRICTLY OFF LIMITS TO ANYONE ON A SQUADRON. IF YOU TAKE ONE STEP IN THERE, YOU'LL GO RIGHT DOWN WITH THAT SO-CALLED FRIEND OF YOURS.
BUT MAC, KEVIN'S THE ONLY PERSON ON THE SHIP WHO I KNEW BACK ON EARTH!
I CAN'T JUST SIT BACK AND LET HIM GET NAILED!
ROBIN, YOUR LOYALTY IS NICE, BUT HE DOESN'T DESERVE IT.
IF HE'S REALLY MESSING AROUND WITH FIGHTER TRAINING HE'S ENDANGERING EVERYBODY.
I HOPE THEY PUT HIM AWAY FOR LIFE.
WHAT KIND OF EVIDENCE DO THEY HAVE AGAINST HIM?
THEY SAY HE'S WORKING TWO SQUADRONS AGAINST EACH OTHER--TIGERS AND SAMURAI. THE PATTERN SAYS THE TIGERS WILL THROW THEIR NEXT ROUND.
IF THEY LOSE THE WAY THEY'RE SUPPOSED TO, YOUR LITTLE FRIEND IS TOAST.
AND SO ARE THOSE TWO SQUADRONS. RIGHT DOWN TO THEIR ASSISTANT BOTTOM-WIPERS.
I GOTTA STOP HIM! I'M THE ONLY ONE HE'LL LISTEN TO.
FORGET IT!
LOOK, I DON'T USUALLY DO THIS, BUT I'M GIVING YOU A DIRECT ORDER TO KEEP OUT OF IT. IF SECURITY PICKS YOU UP TOO, IT WILL IMPLICATE OUR SQUADRON. AND THAT'S NOT GONNA HAPPEN. RIGHT?
SIGH... RIGHT.

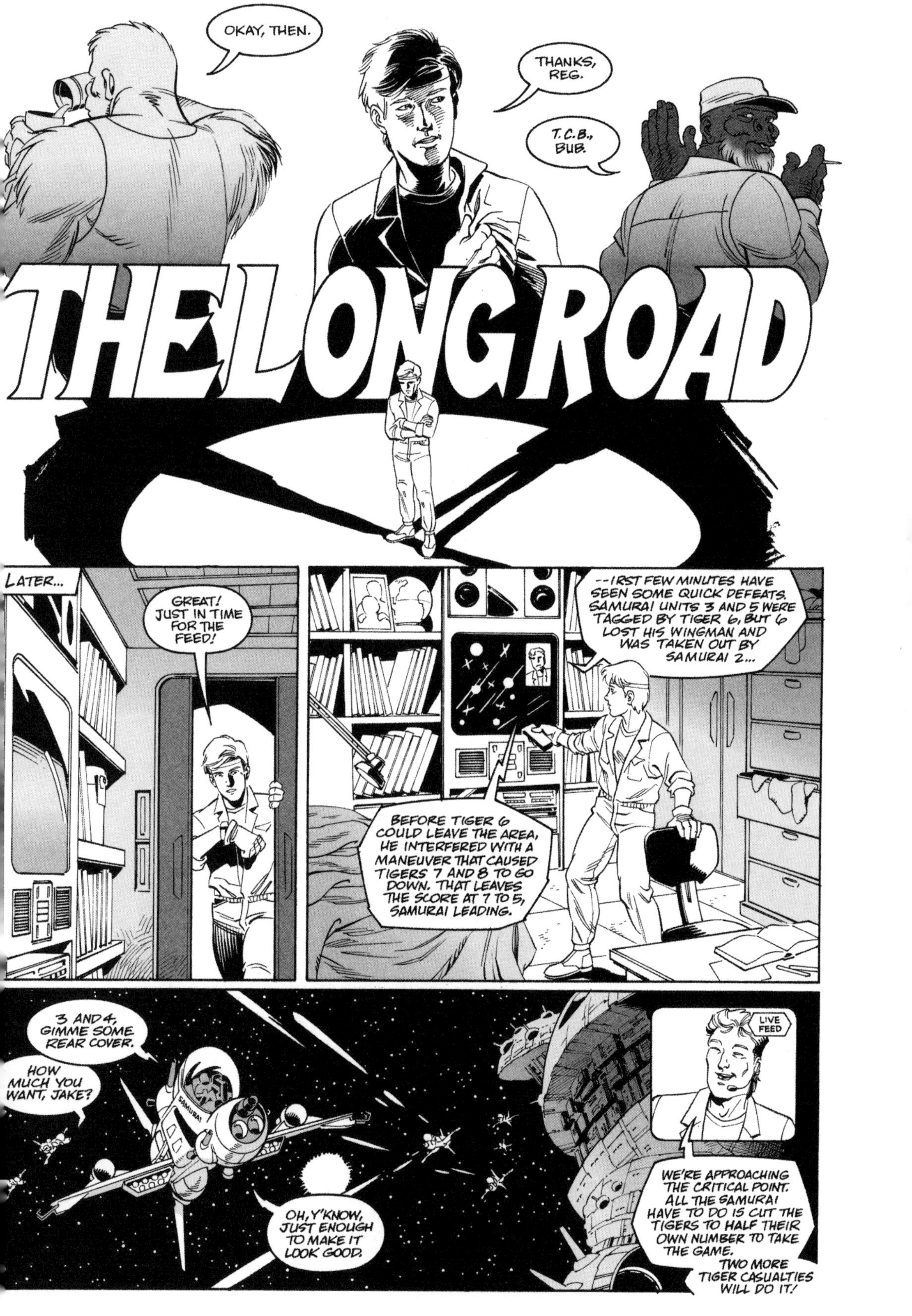
OKAY, THEN.
THANKS, REG.
T.C.B., BUB.
THE LONG ROAD
LATER...
GREAT! JUST IN TIME FOR THE FEED!
--IRST FEW MINUTES HAVE SEEN SOME QUICK DEFEATS. SAMURAI UNITS 3 AND 5 WERE TAGGED BY TIGER 6, BUT 6 LOST HIS WINGMAN AND WAS TAKEN OUT BY SAMURAI 2...
BEFORE TIGER 6 COULD LEAVE THE AREA, HE INTERFERED WITH A MANEUVER THAT CAUSED TIGERS 7 AND 8 TO GO DOWN. THAT LEAVES THE SCORE AT 7 TO 5, SAMURAI LEADING.
3 AND 4, GIMME SOME REAR COVER.
HOW MUCH YOU WANT, JAKE?
OH, Y'KNOW, JUST ENOUGH TO MAKE IT LOOK GOOD.
LIVE FEED
WE'RE APPROACHING THE CRITICAL POINT. ALL THE SAMURAI HAVE TO DO IS CUT THE TIGERS TO HALF THEIR OWN NUMBER TO TAKE THE GAME.
TWO MORE TIGER CASUALTIES WILL DO IT!

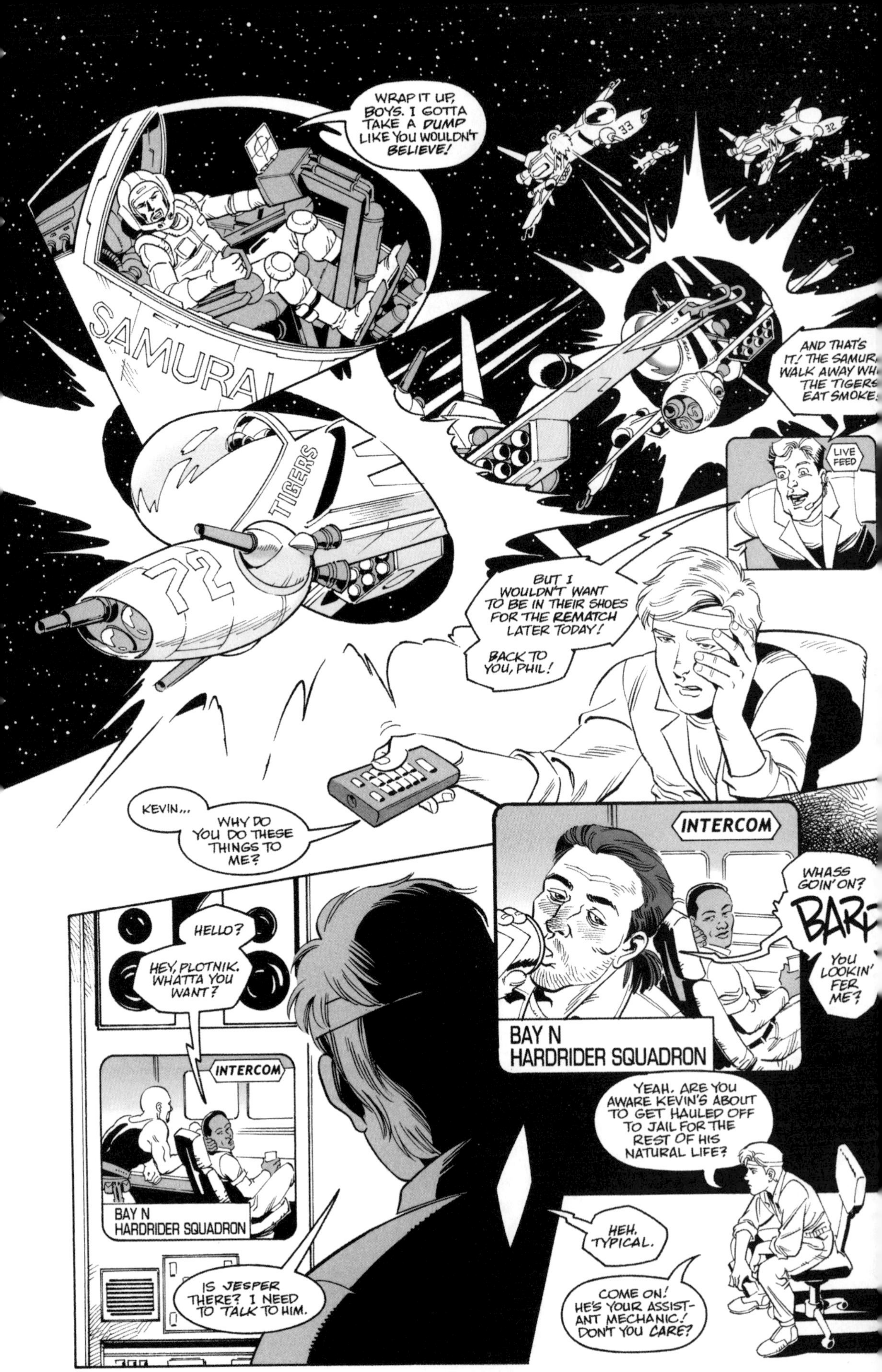
WRAP IT UP, BOYS. I GOTTA TAKE A DUMP LIKE YOU WOULDN'T BELIEVE!
SAMURAI
AND THAT'S IT! THE SAMURA WALK AWAY WH THE TIGERS EAT SMOKE
LIVE FEED
TIGERS
72
BUT I WOULDN'T WANT TO BE IN THEIR SHOES FOR THE REMATCH LATER TODAY!
BACK TO YOU, PHIL!
KEVIN... WHY DO YOU DO THESE THINGS TO ME?
INTERCOM
WHASS GOIN' ON?
BAR
YOU LOOKIN' FER ME?
BAY N HARDRIDER SQUADRON
HELLO?
HEY, PLOTNIK. WHATTA YOU WANT?
INTERCOM
BAY N HARDRIDER SQUADRON
YEAH. ARE YOU AWARE KEVIN'S ABOUT TO GET HAULED OFF TO JAIL FOR THE REST OF HIS NATURAL LIFE?
HEH. TYPICAL.
IS JESPER THERE? I NEED TO TALK TO HIM.
COME ON! HE'S YOUR ASSISTANT MECHANIC! DON'T YOU CARE?

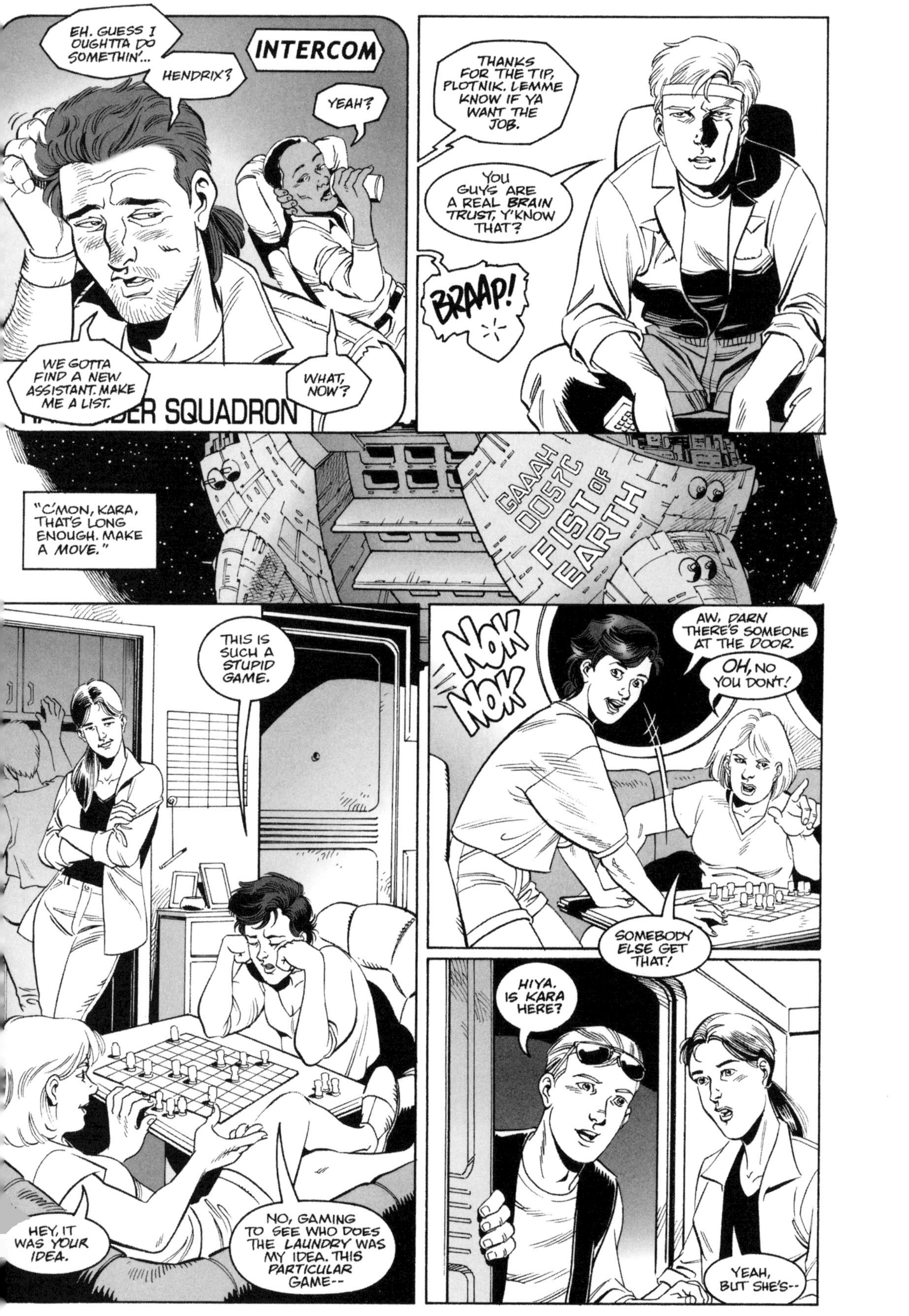
EH. GUESS I OUGHTTA DO SOMETHIN'...
INTERCOM
HENDRIX?
YEAH?
WE GOTTA FIND A NEW ASSISTANT. MAKE ME A LIST.
WHAT, NOW?
THANKS FOR THE TIP, PLOTNIK. LEMME KNOW IF YA WANT THE JOB.
YOU GUYS ARE A REAL BRAIN TRUST, Y'KNOW THAT?
BRAAP!
"C'MON, KARA, THAT'S LONG ENOUGH. MAKE A MOVE."
GAAAH
005?C
FIST of EARTH
THIS IS SUCH A STUPID GAME.
HEY, IT WAS YOUR IDEA.
NO, GAMING TO SEE WHO DOES THE LAUNDRY WAS MY IDEA. THIS PARTICULAR GAME--
NOK NOK
AW, DARN THERE'S SOMEONE AT THE DOOR.
OH, NO YOU DON'T!
SOMEBODY ELSE GET THAT!
HIYA. IS KARA HERE?
YEAH, BUT SHE'S--

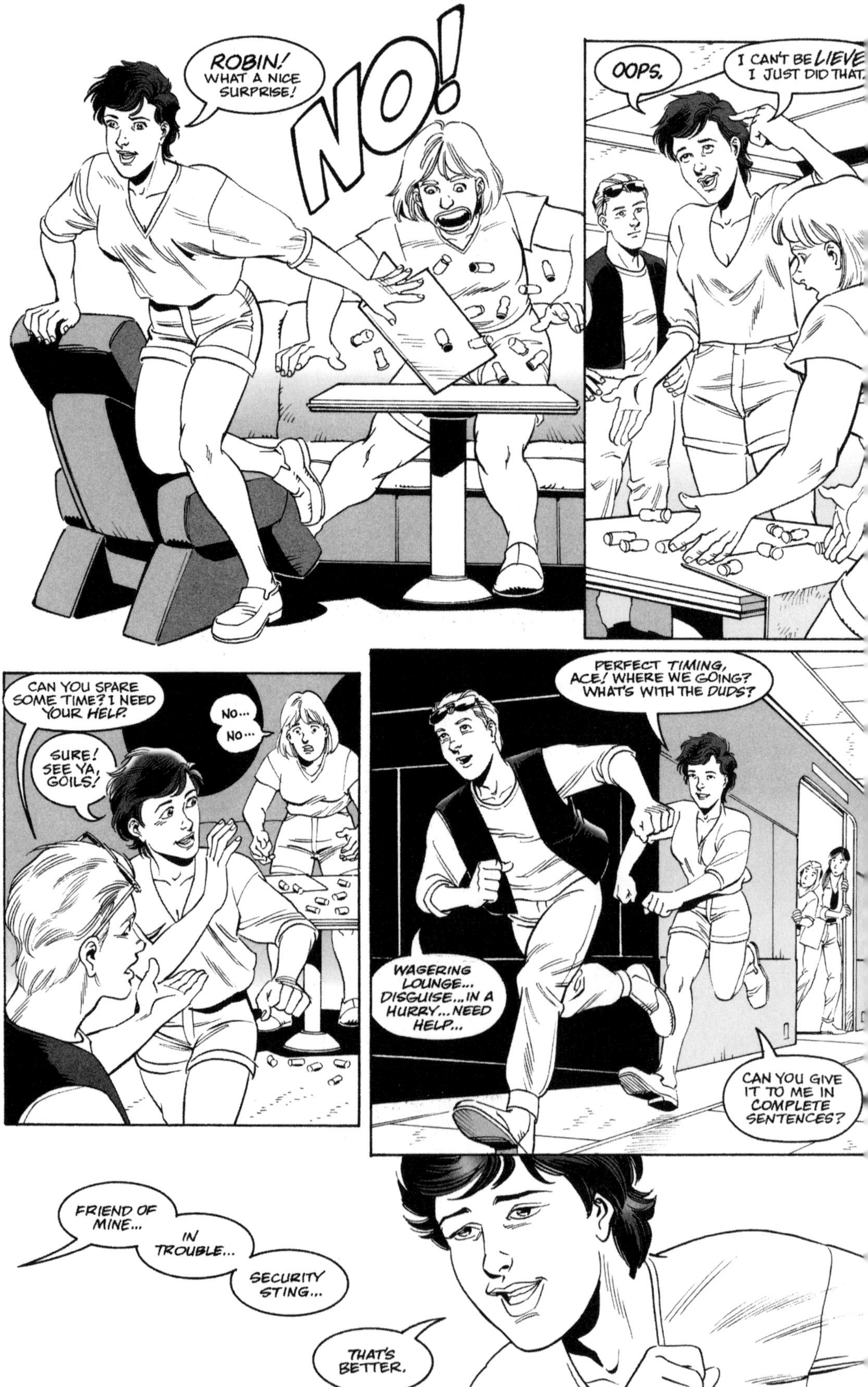
ROBIN! WHAT A NICE SURPRISE!
NO!
OOPS.
I CAN'T BELIEVE I JUST DID THAT.
CAN YOU SPARE SOME TIME? I NEED YOUR HELP.
NO... NO...
SURE! SEE YA, GOILS!
PERFECT TIMING, ACE! WHERE WE GOING? WHAT'S WITH THE DUDS?
WAGERING LOUNGE... DISGUISE... IN A HURRY... NEED HELP...
CAN YOU GIVE IT TO ME IN COMPLETE SENTENCES?
FRIEND OF MINE...
IN TROUBLE...
SECURITY STING...
THAT'S BETTER.

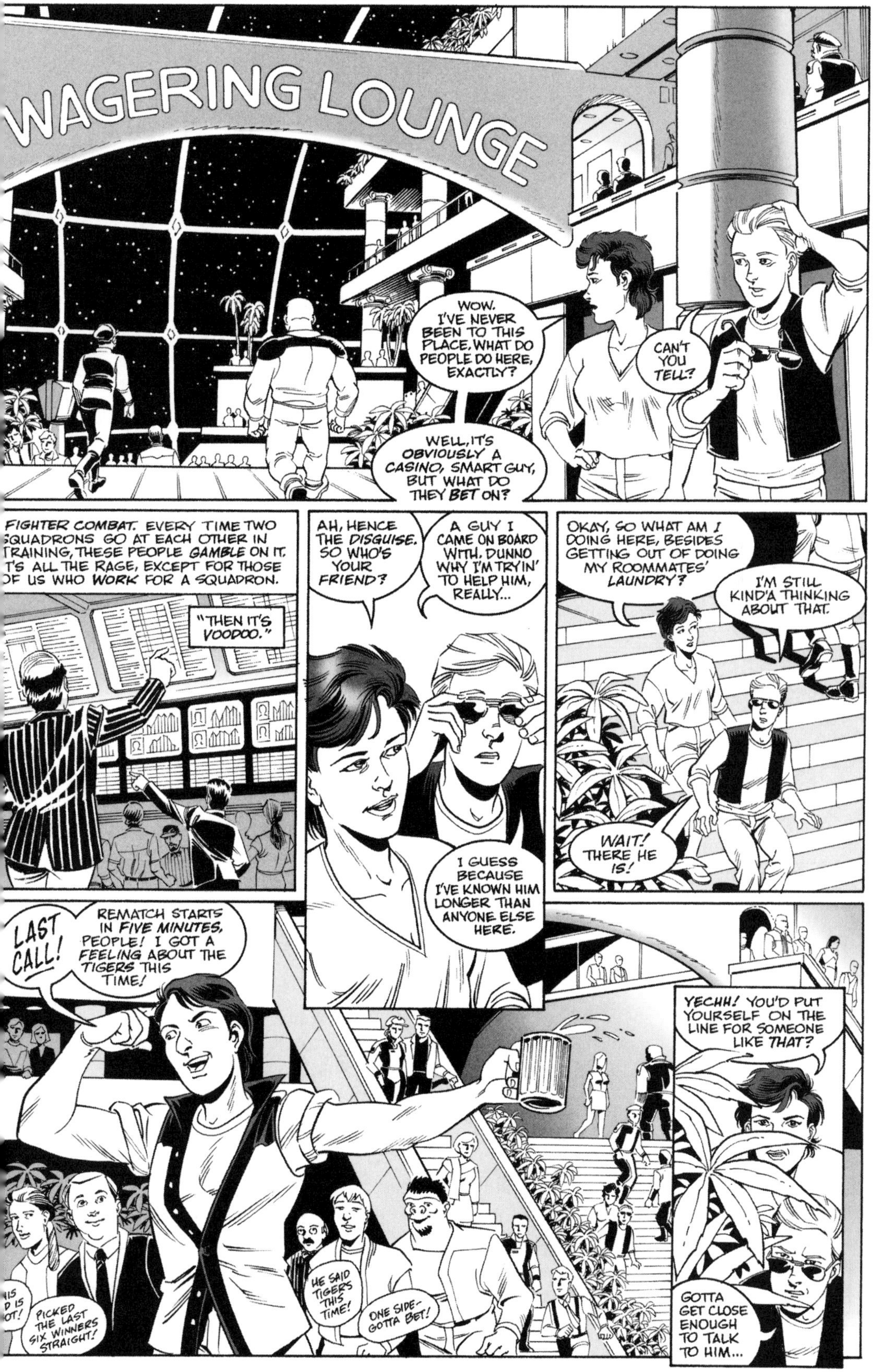
WAGERING LOUNGE
WOW. I'VE NEVER BEEN TO THIS PLACE. WHAT DO PEOPLE DO HERE, EXACTLY?
CAN'T YOU TELL?
WELL, IT'S OBVIOUSLY A CASINO, SMART GUY, BUT WHAT DO THEY BET ON?
FIGHTER COMBAT. EVERY TIME TWO SQUADRONS GO AT EACH OTHER IN TRAINING, THESE PEOPLE GAMBLE ON IT. IT'S ALL THE RAGE, EXCEPT FOR THOSE OF US WHO WORK FOR A SQUADRON.
"THEN IT'S VOODOO."
AH, HENCE THE DISGUISE. SO WHO'S YOUR FRIEND?
A GUY I CAME ON BOARD WITH. DUNNO WHY I'M TRYIN' TO HELP HIM, REALLY...
I GUESS BECAUSE I'VE KNOWN HIM LONGER THAN ANYONE ELSE HERE.
OKAY, SO WHAT AM I DOING HERE, BESIDES GETTING OUT OF DOING MY ROOMMATES' LAUNDRY?
I'M STILL KIND'A THINKING ABOUT THAT.
WAIT! THERE HE IS!
LAST CALL!
REMATCH STARTS IN FIVE MINUTES, PEOPLE! I GOT A FEELING ABOUT THE TIGERS THIS TIME!
PICKED THE LAST SIX WINNERS STRAIGHT!
HE SAID TIGERS THIS TIME!
ONE SIDE- GOTTA BET!
YECHH! YOU'D PUT YOURSELF ON THE LINE FOR SOMEONE LIKE THAT?
GOTTA GET CLOSE ENOUGH TO TALK TO HIM...

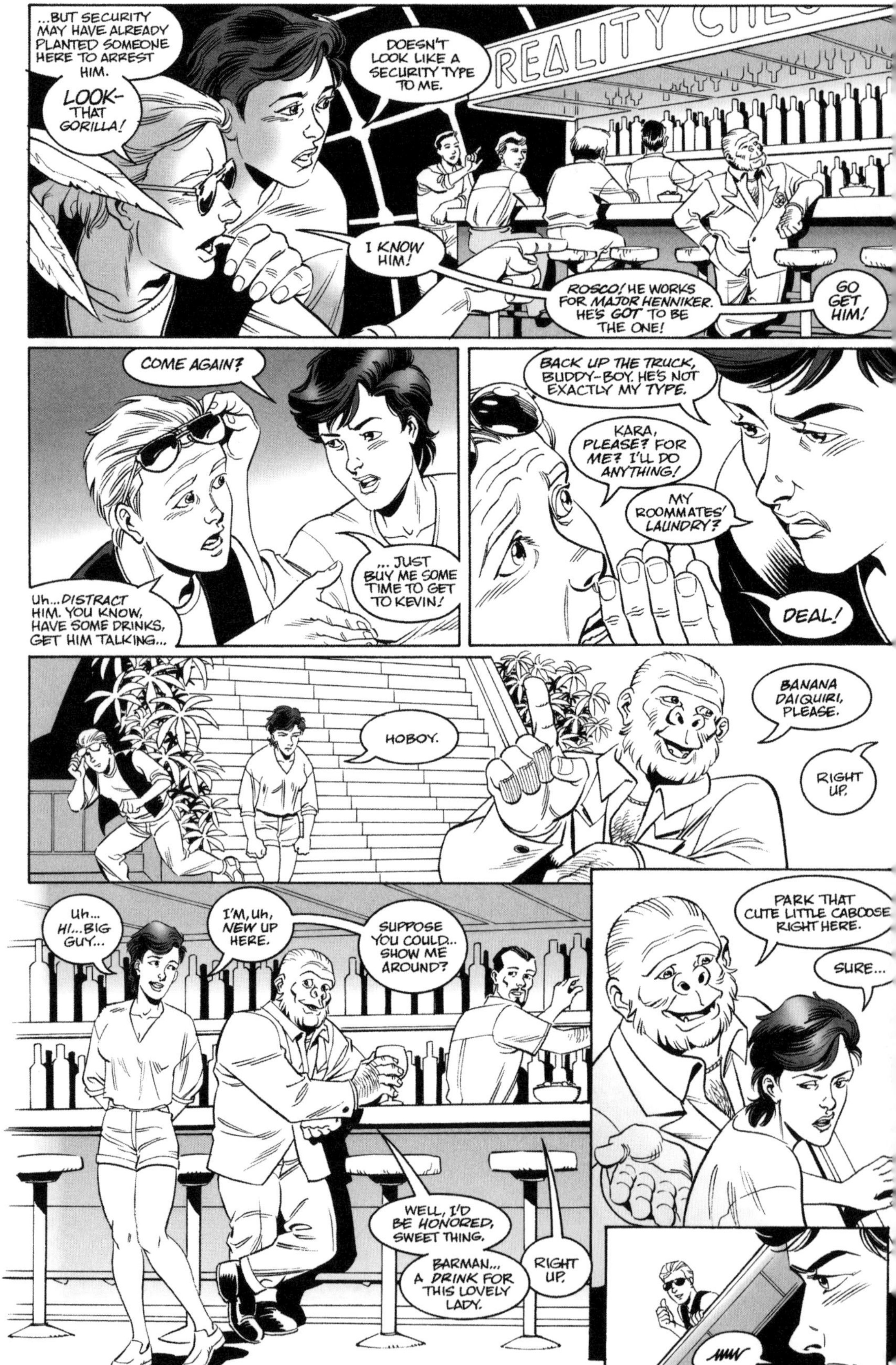
...BUT SECURITY MAY HAVE ALREADY PLANTED SOMEONE HERE TO ARREST HIM.
LOOK- THAT GORILLA!
DOESN'T LOOK LIKE A SECURITY TYPE TO ME.
REALITY CHEC
I KNOW HIM!
ROSCO! HE WORKS FOR MAJOR HENNIKER. HE'S GOT TO BE THE ONE!
GO GET HIM!
COME AGAIN?
Uh...DISTRACT HIM. YOU KNOW, HAVE SOME DRINKS, GET HIM TALKING...
...JUST BUY ME SOME TIME TO GET TO KEVIN!
BACK UP THE TRUCK, BUDDY-BOY. HE'S NOT EXACTLY MY TYPE.
KARA, PLEASE? FOR ME? I'LL DO ANYTHING!
MY ROOMMATES' LAUNDRY?
DEAL!
HOBOY.
BANANA DAIQUIRI, PLEASE.
RIGHT UP.
Uh... HI...BIG GUY...
I'M, Uh, NEW UP HERE.
SUPPOSE YOU COULD... SHOW ME AROUND?
WELL, I'D BE HONORED, SWEET THING.
BARMAN... A DRINK FOR THIS LOVELY LADY.
RIGHT UP.
PARK THAT CUTE LITTLE CABOOSE RIGHT HERE.
SURE...
MMM

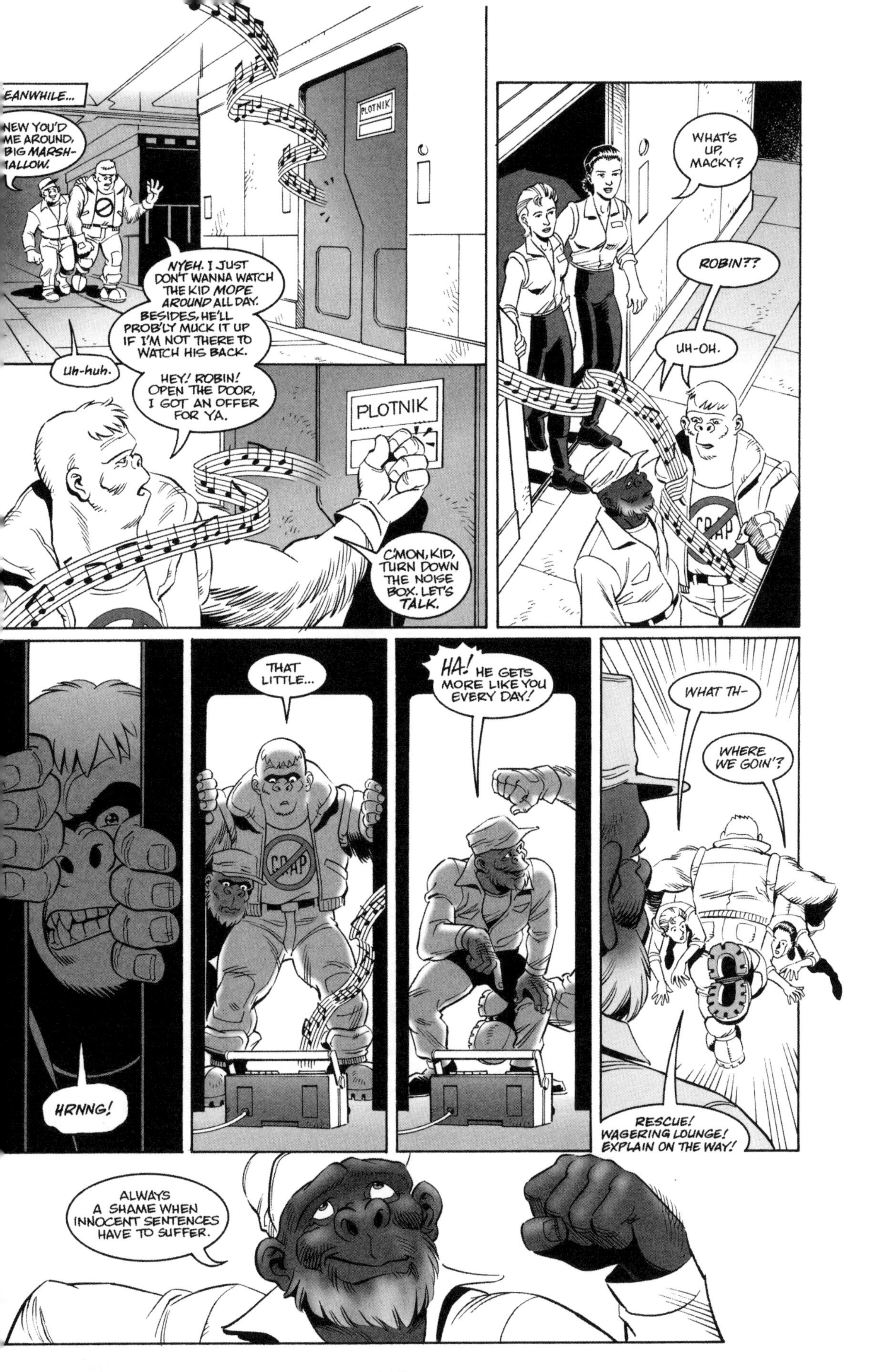
EANWHILE...
NEW YOU'D ME AROUND, BIG MARSH-MALLOW.
NYEH. I JUST DON'T WANNA WATCH THE KID MOPE AROUND ALL DAY. BESIDES, HE'LL PROB'LY MUCK IT UP IF I'M NOT THERE TO WATCH HIS BACK.
Uh-huh.
HEY! ROBIN! OPEN THE DOOR, I GOT AN OFFER FOR YA.
PLOTNIK
C'MON, KID, TURN DOWN THE NOISE BOX. LET'S TALK.
WHAT'S UP, MACKY?
ROBIN??
UH-OH.
HRNNG!
THAT LITTLE...
HA! HE GETS MORE LIKE YOU EVERY DAY!
WHAT TH-
WHERE WE GOIN'?
RESCUE! WAGERING LOUNGE! EXPLAIN ON THE WAY!
ALWAYS A SHAME WHEN INNOCENT SENTENCES HAVE TO SUFFER.

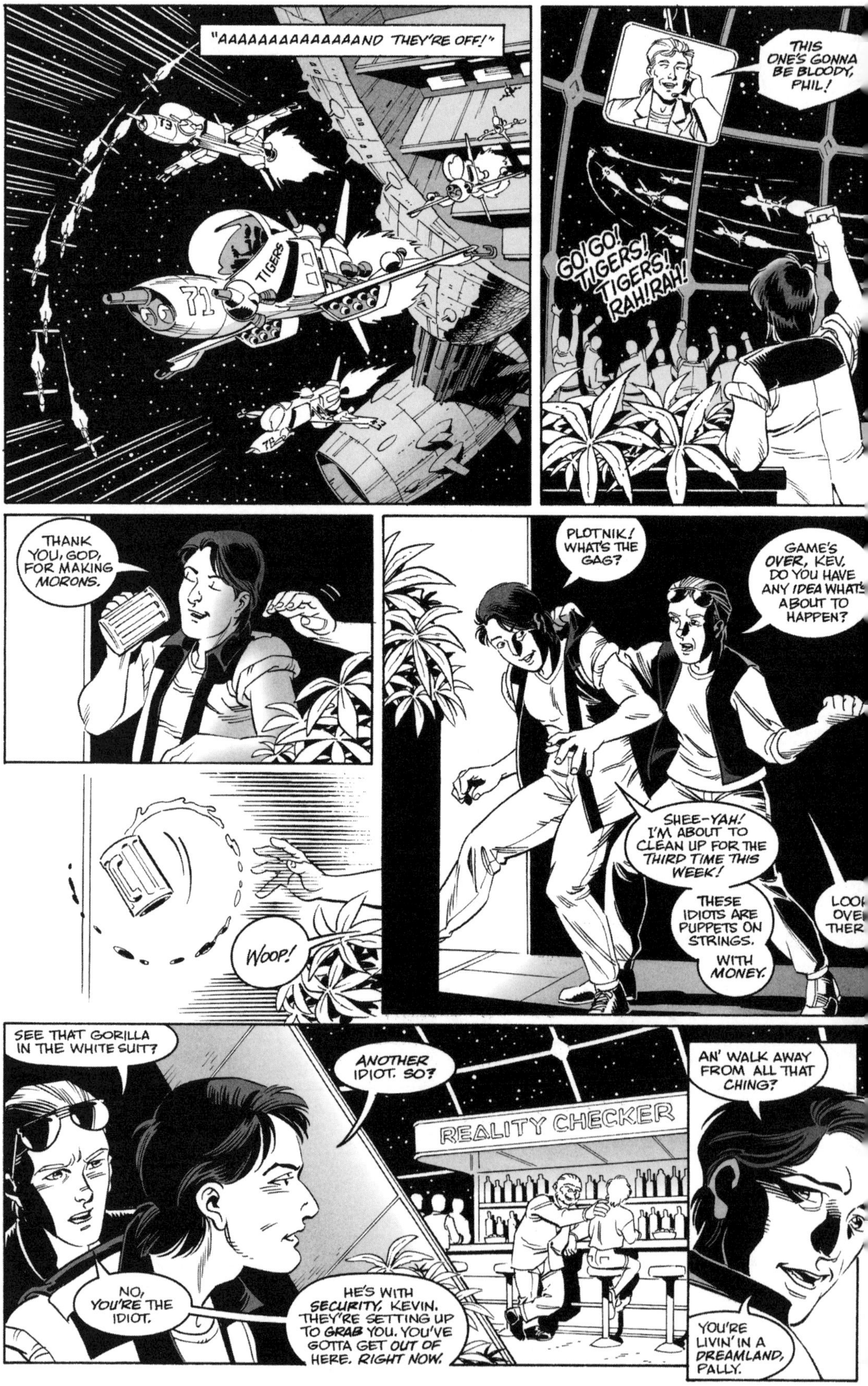

"AAAAAAAAAAAAAAND THEY'RE OFF!"
TIGERS
71
THIS ONE'S GONNA BE BLOODY, PHIL!
GO! GO! TIGERS! TIGERS! RAH! RAH!
THANK YOU, GOD, FOR MAKING MORONS.
WOOP!
PLOTNIK! WHAT'S THE GAG?
GAME'S OVER, KEV. DO YOU HAVE ANY IDEA WHAT'S ABOUT TO HAPPEN?
SHEE-YAH! I'M ABOUT TO CLEAN UP FOR THE THIRD TIME THIS WEEK!
THESE IDIOTS ARE PUPPETS ON STRINGS.
WITH MONEY.
SEE THAT GORILLA IN THE WHITE SUIT?
ANOTHER IDIOT. SO?
NO, YOU'RE THE IDIOT.
HE'S WITH SECURITY, KEVIN. THEY'RE SETTING UP TO GRAB YOU. YOU'VE GOTTA GET OUT OF HERE. RIGHT NOW.
REALITY CHECKER
AN' WALK AWAY FROM ALL THAT CHING?
YOU'RE LIVIN' IN A DREAMLAND, PALLY.

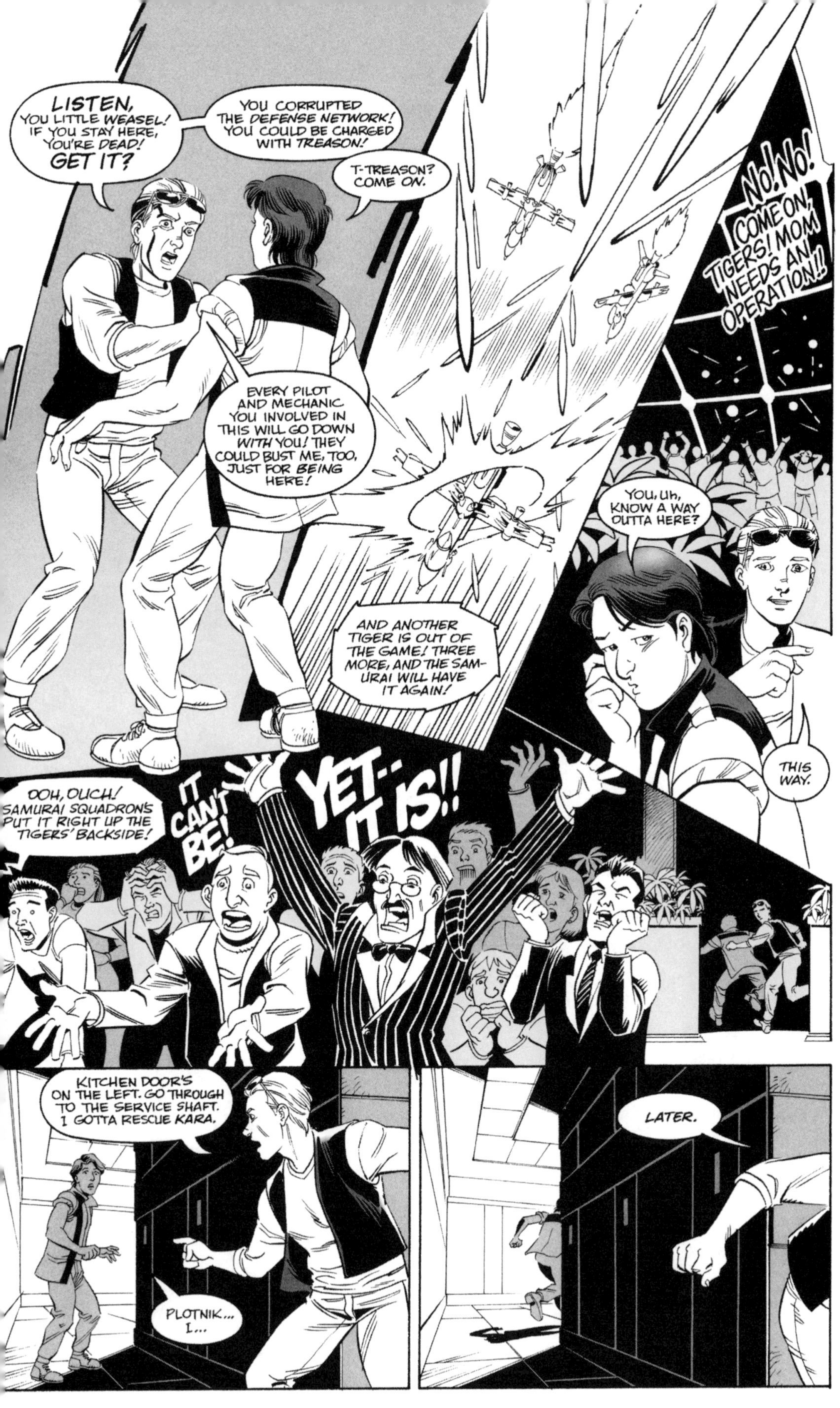
LISTEN, YOU LITTLE WEASEL! IF YOU STAY HERE, YOU'RE DEAD! GET IT?
YOU CORRUPTED THE DEFENSE NETWORK! YOU COULD BE CHARGED WITH TREASON!
T-TREASON? COME ON.
No! No! COME ON, TIGERS! MOM NEEDS AN OPERATION!!
EVERY PILOT AND MECHANIC YOU INVOLVED IN THIS WILL GO DOWN WITH YOU! THEY COULD BUST ME, TOO, JUST FOR BEING HERE!
YOU, UH, KNOW A WAY OUTTA HERE?
AND ANOTHER TIGER IS OUT OF THE GAME! THREE MORE, AND THE SAMURAI WILL HAVE IT AGAIN!
THIS WAY.
OOH, OUCH! SAMURAI SQUADRON'S PUT IT RIGHT UP THE TIGERS' BACKSIDE!
IT CAN'T BE!
YET-- IT IS!!
KITCHEN DOOR'S ON THE LEFT. GO THROUGH TO THE SERVICE SHAFT. I GOTTA RESCUE KARA.
PLOTNIK... I...
LATER.

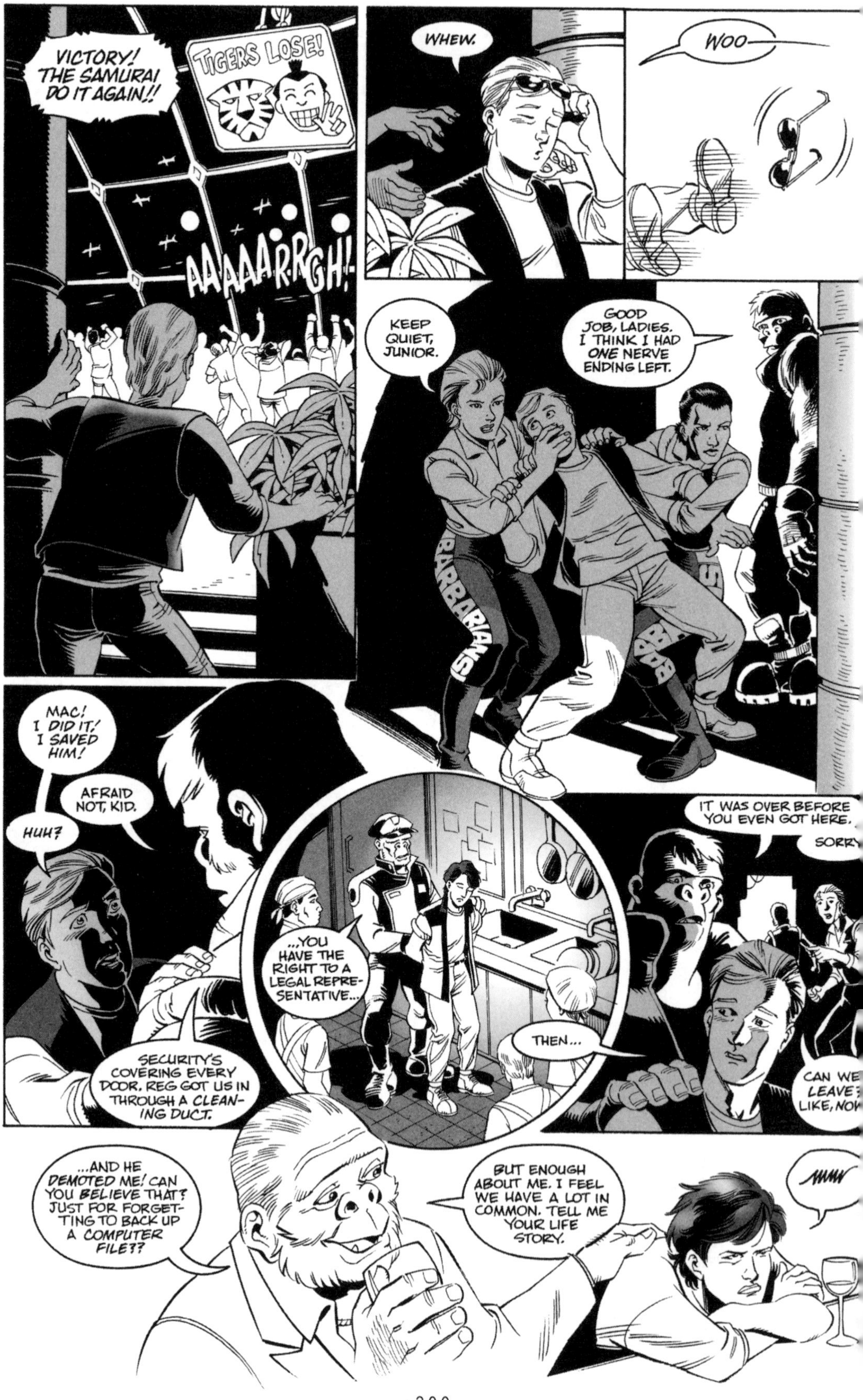
VICTORY! THE SAMURAI DO IT AGAIN!!
TIGERS LOSE!
AAAAARRGH!
WHEW.
WOO—
KEEP QUIET, JUNIOR.
GOOD JOB, LADIES. I THINK I HAD ONE NERVE ENDING LEFT.
SORRY
BARBARIANS
MAC! I DID IT! I SAVED HIM!
AFRAID NOT, KID.
HUH?
SECURITY'S COVERING EVERY DOOR. REG GOT US IN THROUGH A CLEANING DUCT.
...YOU HAVE THE RIGHT TO A LEGAL REPRESENTATIVE...
THEN...
IT WAS OVER BEFORE YOU EVEN GOT HERE.
SORRY
CAN WE LEAVE LIKE, NOW
...AND HE DEMOTED ME! CAN YOU BELIEVE THAT? JUST FOR FORGETTING TO BACK UP A COMPUTER FILE??
BUT ENOUGH ABOUT ME. I FEEL WE HAVE A LOT IN COMMON. TELL ME YOUR LIFE STORY.

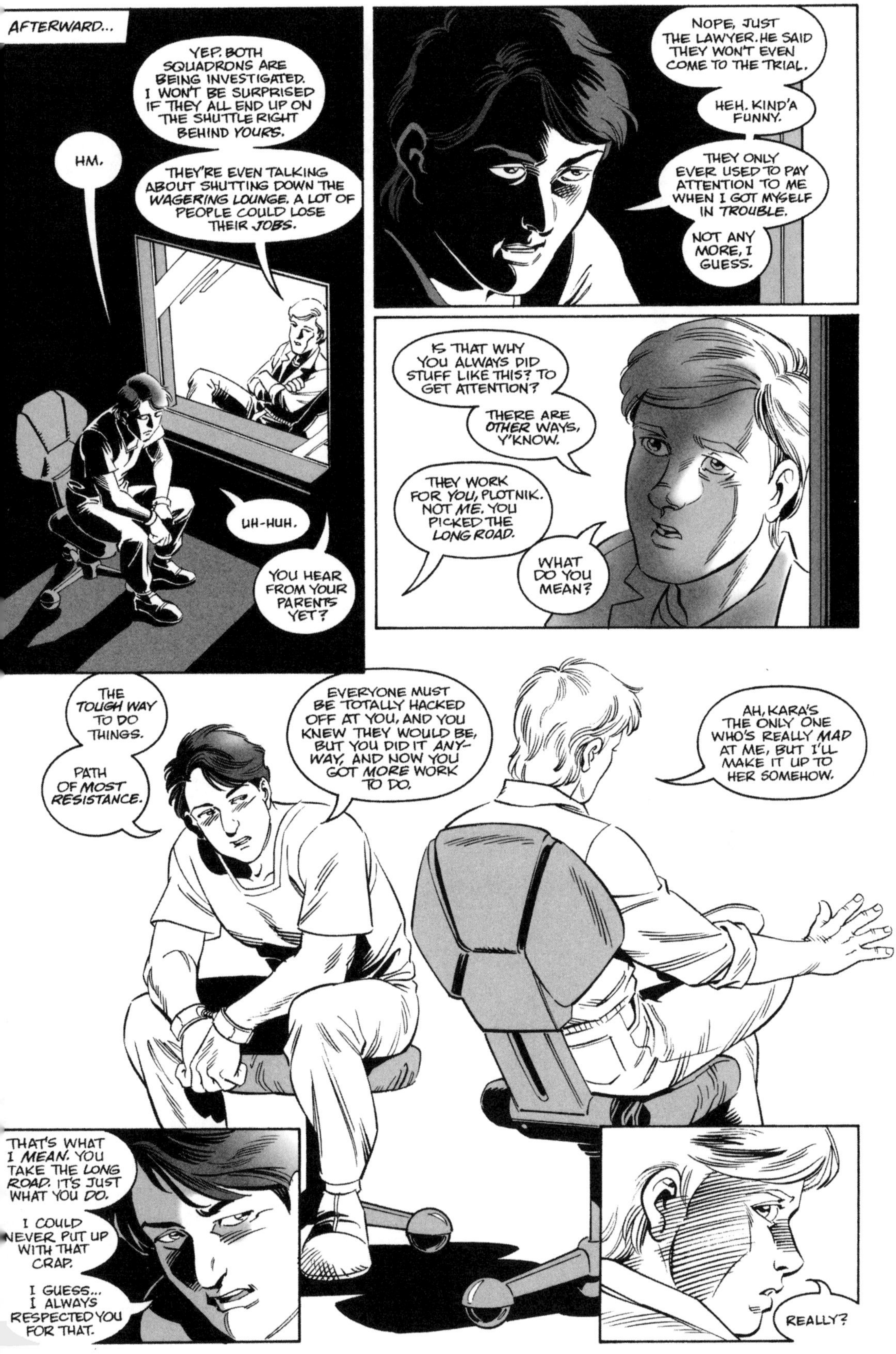
AFTERWARD...
YEP. BOTH SQUADRONS ARE BEING INVESTIGATED. I WON'T BE SURPRISED IF THEY ALL END UP ON THE SHUTTLE RIGHT BEHIND YOURS.
HM.
THEY'RE EVEN TALKING ABOUT SHUTTING DOWN THE WAGERING LOUNGE. A LOT OF PEOPLE COULD LOSE THEIR JOBS.
UH-HUH.
YOU HEAR FROM YOUR PARENTS YET?
NOPE, JUST THE LAWYER. HE SAID THEY WON'T EVEN COME TO THE TRIAL.
HEH. KIND'A FUNNY.
THEY ONLY EVER USED TO PAY ATTENTION TO ME WHEN I GOT MYSELF IN TROUBLE.
NOT ANY MORE, I GUESS.
IS THAT WHY YOU ALWAYS DID STUFF LIKE THIS? TO GET ATTENTION?
THERE ARE OTHER WAYS, Y'KNOW.
THEY WORK FOR YOU, PLOTNIK. NOT ME. YOU PICKED THE LONG ROAD.
WHAT DO YOU MEAN?
THE TOUGH WAY TO DO THINGS.
PATH OF MOST RESISTANCE.
EVERYONE MUST BE TOTALLY HACKED OFF AT YOU, AND YOU KNEW THEY WOULD BE, BUT YOU DID IT ANY-WAY, AND NOW YOU GOT MORE WORK TO DO.
AH, KARA'S THE ONLY ONE WHO'S REALLY MAD AT ME, BUT I'LL MAKE IT UP TO HER SOMEHOW.
THAT'S WHAT I MEAN. YOU TAKE THE LONG ROAD. IT'S JUST WHAT YOU DO.
I COULD NEVER PUT UP WITH THAT CRAP.
I GUESS... I ALWAYS RESPECTED YOU FOR THAT.
REALLY?

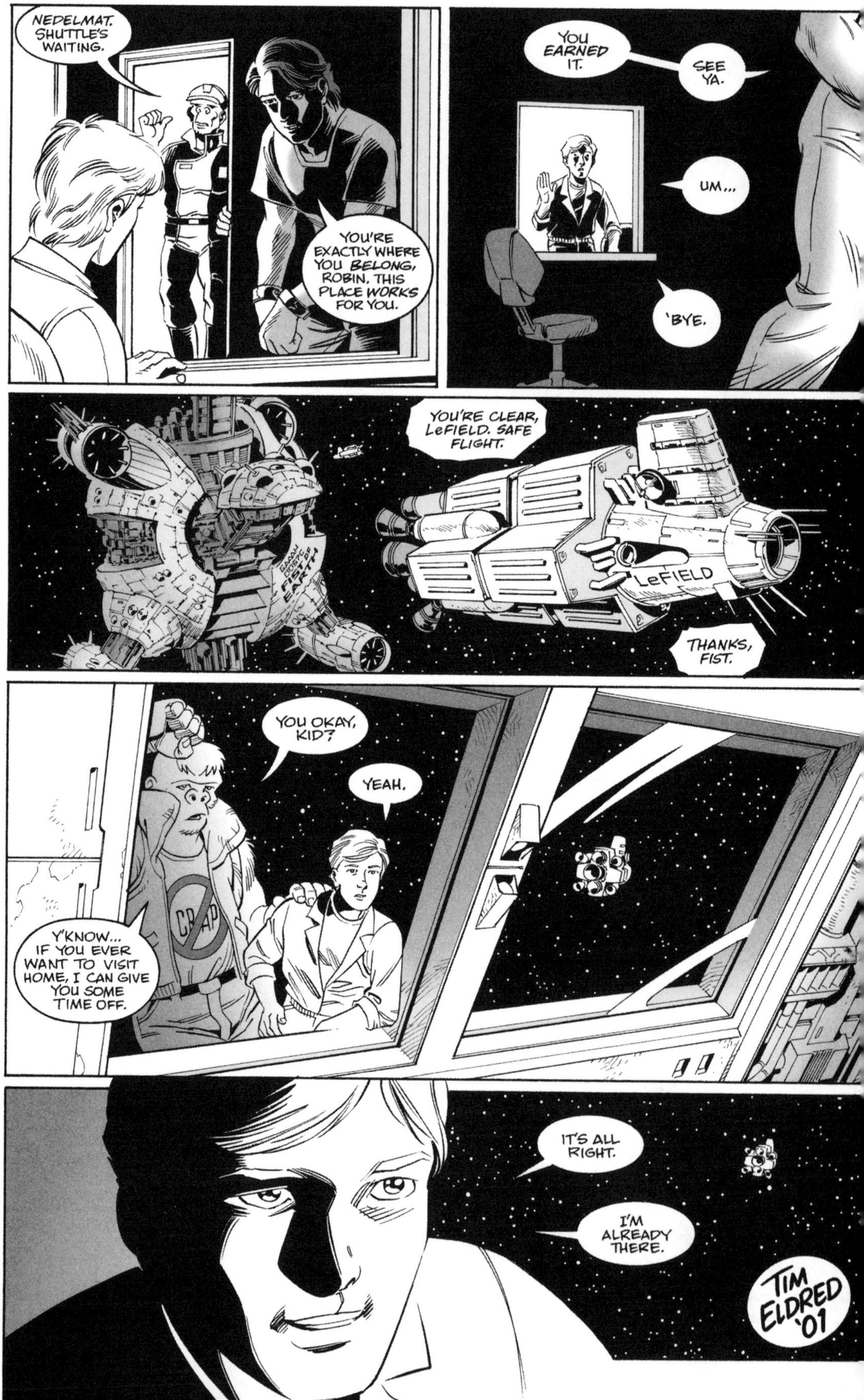
NEDELMAT. SHUTTLE'S WAITING.
YOU'RE EXACTLY WHERE YOU BELONG, ROBIN. THIS PLACE WORKS FOR YOU.
YOU EARNED IT.
SEE YA.
UM...
'BYE.
YOU'RE CLEAR, LeFIELD. SAFE FLIGHT.
LeFIELD
THANKS, FIST.
YOU OKAY, KID?
YEAH.
Y'KNOW... IF YOU EVER WANT TO VISIT HOME, I CAN GIVE YOU SOME TIME OFF.
CRAP
IT'S ALL RIGHT.
I'M ALREADY THERE.
TIM ELDRED '01

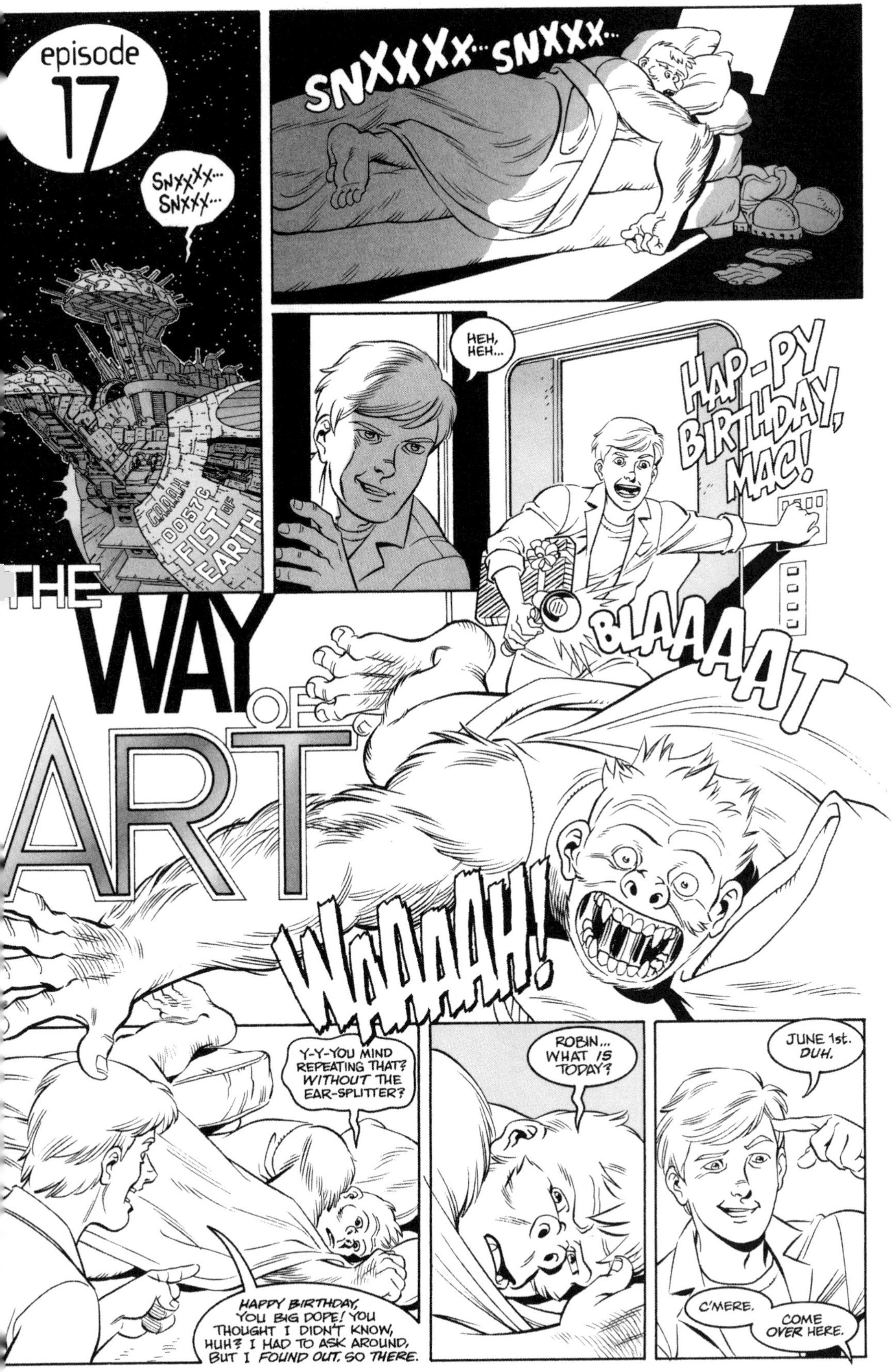
episode
17
THE WAY OF ART
SNXXXX... SNXXX...
SNXXXx... SNXXX...
SNXXX...
CCCCH
0057C
FIST OF EARTH
HEH, HEH...
HAP-PY BIRTHDAY, MAC!
BLAAAAAT
WAAAAH!
Y-Y-YOU MIND REPEATING THAT? WITHOUT THE EAR-SPLITTER?
HAPPY BIRTHDAY, YOU BIG DOPE! YOU THOUGHT I DIDN'T KNOW, HUH? I HAD TO ASK AROUND, BUT I FOUND OUT, SO THERE.
ROBIN... WHAT IS TODAY?
JUNE 1st. DUH.
C'MERE.
COME OVER HERE.

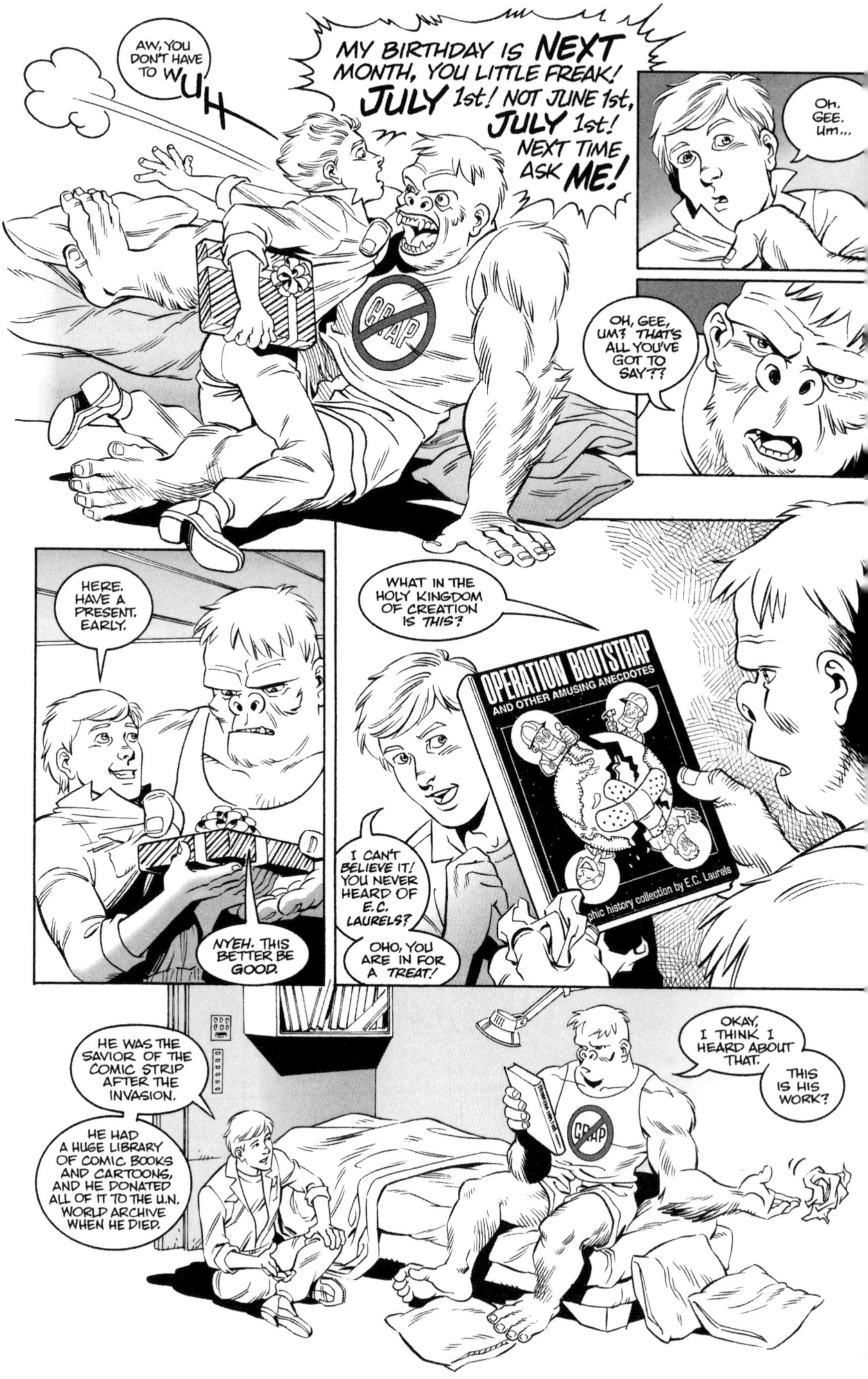
AW, YOU DON'T HAVE TO W
UH
MY BIRTHDAY IS NEXT MONTH, YOU LITTLE FREAK! JULY 1st! NOT JUNE 1st, JULY 1st! NEXT TIME ASK ME!
CRAP
Oh. GEE. Um...
OH, GEE, UM? THAT'S ALL YOU'VE GOT TO SAY??
HERE. HAVE A PRESENT. EARLY.
NYEH. THIS BETTER BE GOOD.
WHAT IN THE HOLY KINGDOM OF CREATION IS THIS?
OPERATION BOOTSTRAP
AND OTHER AMUSING ANECDOTES
phic history collection by E.C. Laurels
I CAN'T BELIEVE IT! YOU NEVER HEARD OF E.C. LAURELS?
OHO, YOU ARE IN FOR A TREAT!
HE WAS THE SAVIOR OF THE COMIC STRIP AFTER THE INVASION.
HE HAD A HUGE LIBRARY OF COMIC BOOKS AND CARTOONS, AND HE DONATED ALL OF IT TO THE U.N. WORLD ARCHIVE WHEN HE DIED.
OKAY, I THINK I HEARD ABOUT THAT.
THIS IS HIS WORK?

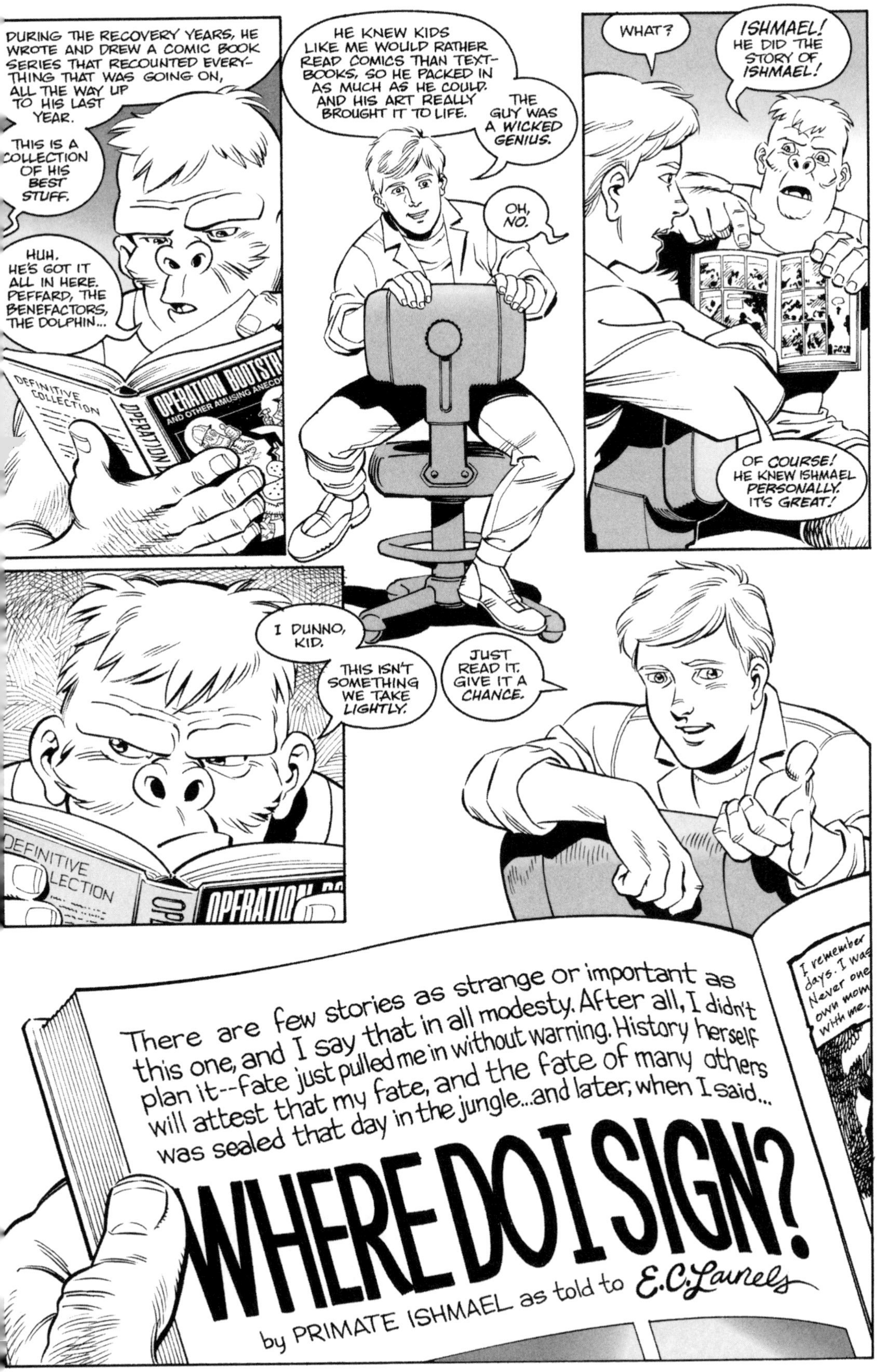
DURING THE RECOVERY YEARS, HE WROTE AND DREW A COMIC BOOK SERIES THAT RECOUNTED EVERYTHING THAT WAS GOING ON, ALL THE WAY UP TO HIS LAST YEAR.
THIS IS A COLLECTION OF HIS BEST STUFF.
HUH. HE'S GOT IT ALL IN HERE. PEFFARD, THE BENEFACTORS, THE DOLPHIN...
DEFINITIVE COLLECTION
HE KNEW KIDS LIKE ME WOULD RATHER READ COMICS THAN TEXTBOOKS, SO HE PACKED IN AS MUCH AS HE COULD. AND HIS ART REALLY BROUGHT IT TO LIFE.
THE GUY WAS A *WICKED* GENIUS.
OH, *NO.*
WHAT?
ISHMAEL! HE DID THE STORY OF *ISHMAEL!*
OF *COURSE!* HE KNEW ISHMAEL *PERSONALLY.* IT'S *GREAT!*
I DUNNO, KID.
THIS ISN'T SOMETHING WE TAKE *LIGHTLY.*
JUST READ IT. GIVE IT A *CHANCE.*
DEFINITIVE COLLECTION
There are few stories as strange or important as this one, and I say that in all modesty. After all, I didn't plan it--fate just pulled me in without warning. History herself will attest that my fate, and the fate of many others was sealed that day in the jungle...and later, when I said...
WHERE DO I SIGN?
by PRIMATE ISHMAEL as told to E.C. Laurels

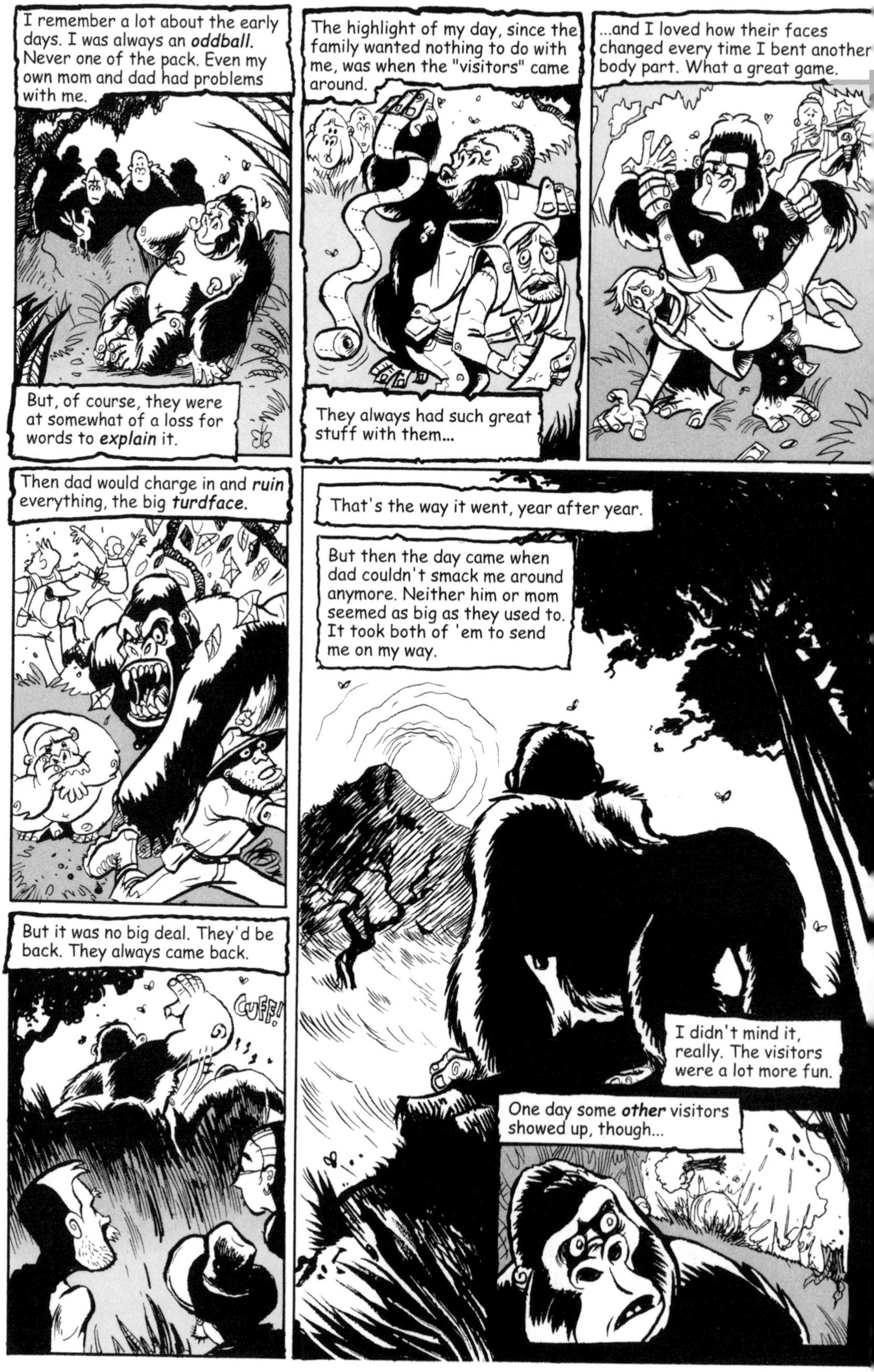
I remember a lot about the early days. I was always an ***oddball.*** Never one of the pack. Even my own mom and dad had problems with me.
But, of course, they were at somewhat of a loss for words to ***explain*** it.
The highlight of my day, since the family wanted nothing to do with me, was when the "visitors" came around.
They always had such great stuff with them...
...and I loved how their faces changed every time I bent another body part. What a great game.
Then dad would charge in and ***ruin*** everything, the big ***turdface.***
But it was no big deal. They'd be back. They always came back.
CUFF!
That's the way it went, year after year.
But then the day came when dad couldn't smack me around anymore. Neither him or mom seemed as big as they used to. It took both of 'em to send me on my way.
I didn't mind it, really. The visitors were a lot more fun.
One day some ***other*** visitors showed up, though...

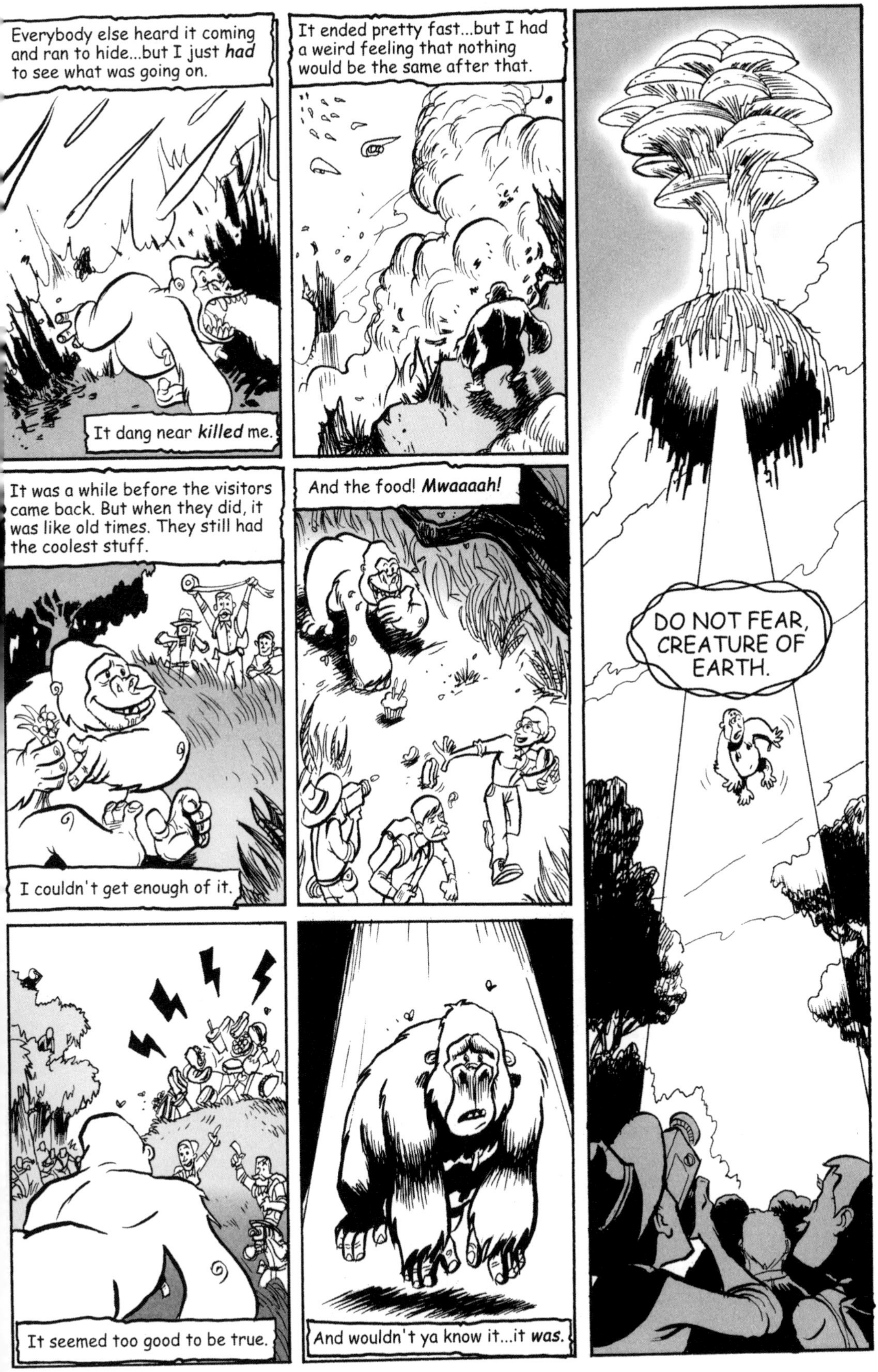
Everybody else heard it coming and ran to hide...but I just *had* to see what was going on.
It dang near *killed* me.
It ended pretty fast...but I had a weird feeling that nothing would be the same after that.
DO NOT FEAR, CREATURE OF EARTH.
It was a while before the visitors came back. But when they did, it was like old times. They still had the coolest stuff.
I couldn't get enough of it.
And the food! *Mwaaaah!*
It seemed too good to be true.
And wouldn't ya know it...it *was*.

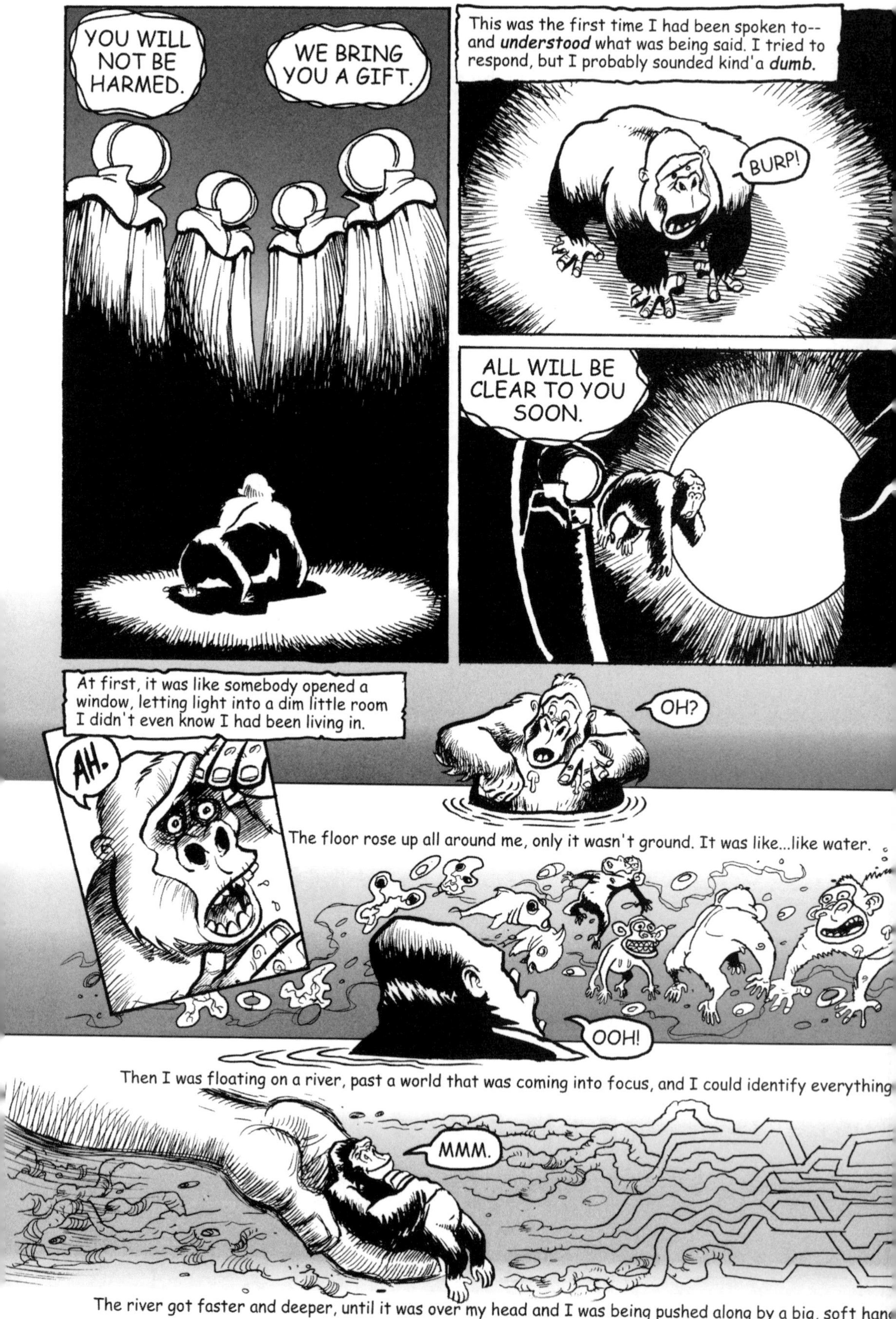
YOU WILL NOT BE HARMED.
WE BRING YOU A GIFT.
This was the first time I had been spoken to--and *understood* what was being said. I tried to respond, but I probably sounded kind'a *dumb.*
BURP!
ALL WILL BE CLEAR TO YOU SOON.
At first, it was like somebody opened a window, letting light into a dim little room I didn't even know I had been living in.
AH.
OH?
The floor rose up all around me, only it wasn't ground. It was like...like water.
OOH!
Then I was floating on a river, past a world that was coming into focus, and I could identify everything
MMM.
The river got faster and deeper, until it was over my head and I was being pushed along by a big, soft hand

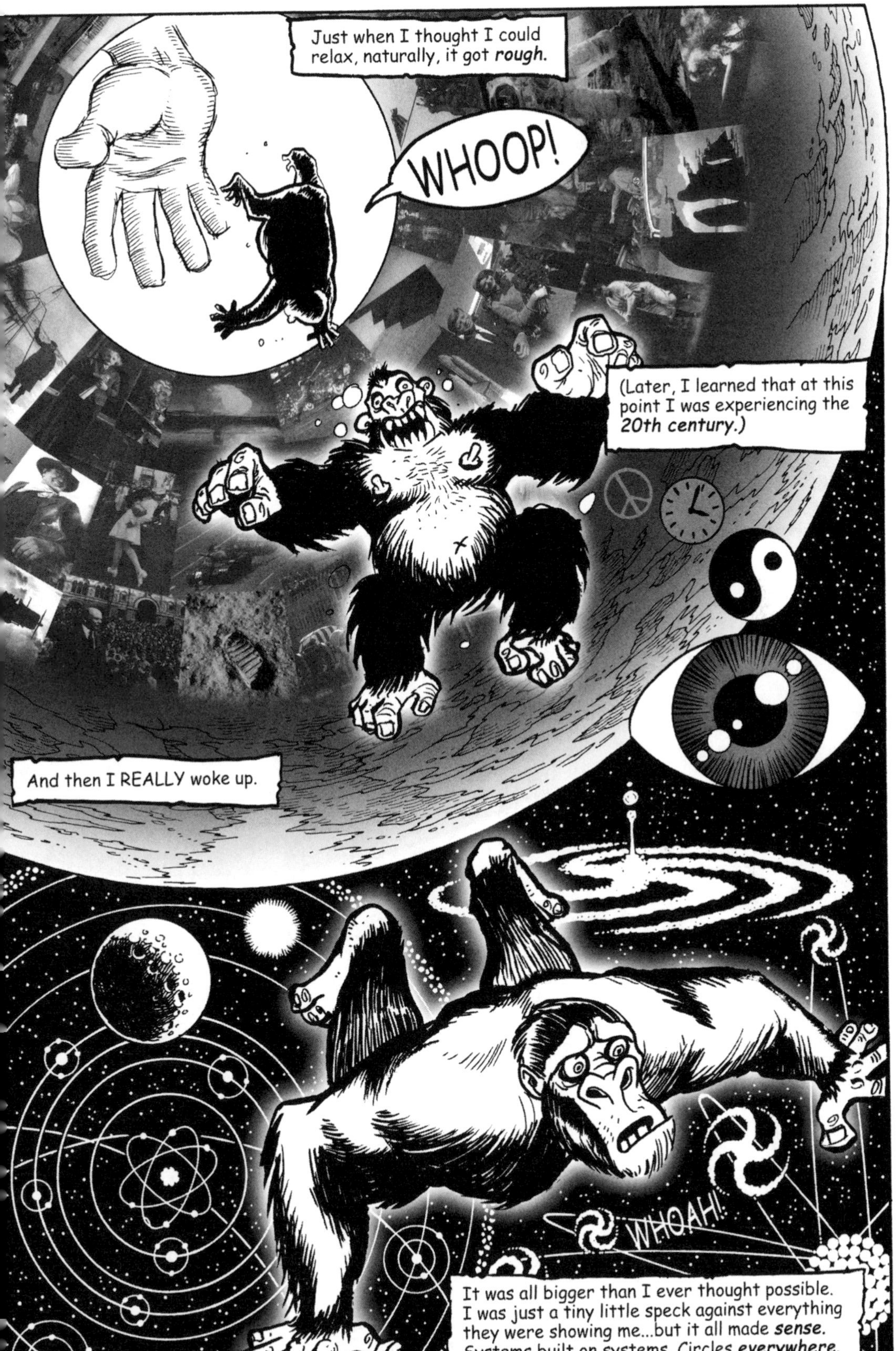
Just when I thought I could relax, naturally, it got *rough*.
WHOOP!
(Later, I learned that at this point I was experiencing the *20th century.*)
And then I REALLY woke up.
WHOAH!
It was all bigger than I ever thought possible. I was just a tiny little speck against everything they were showing me...but it all made *sense*. Systems built on systems. Circles *everywhere*.

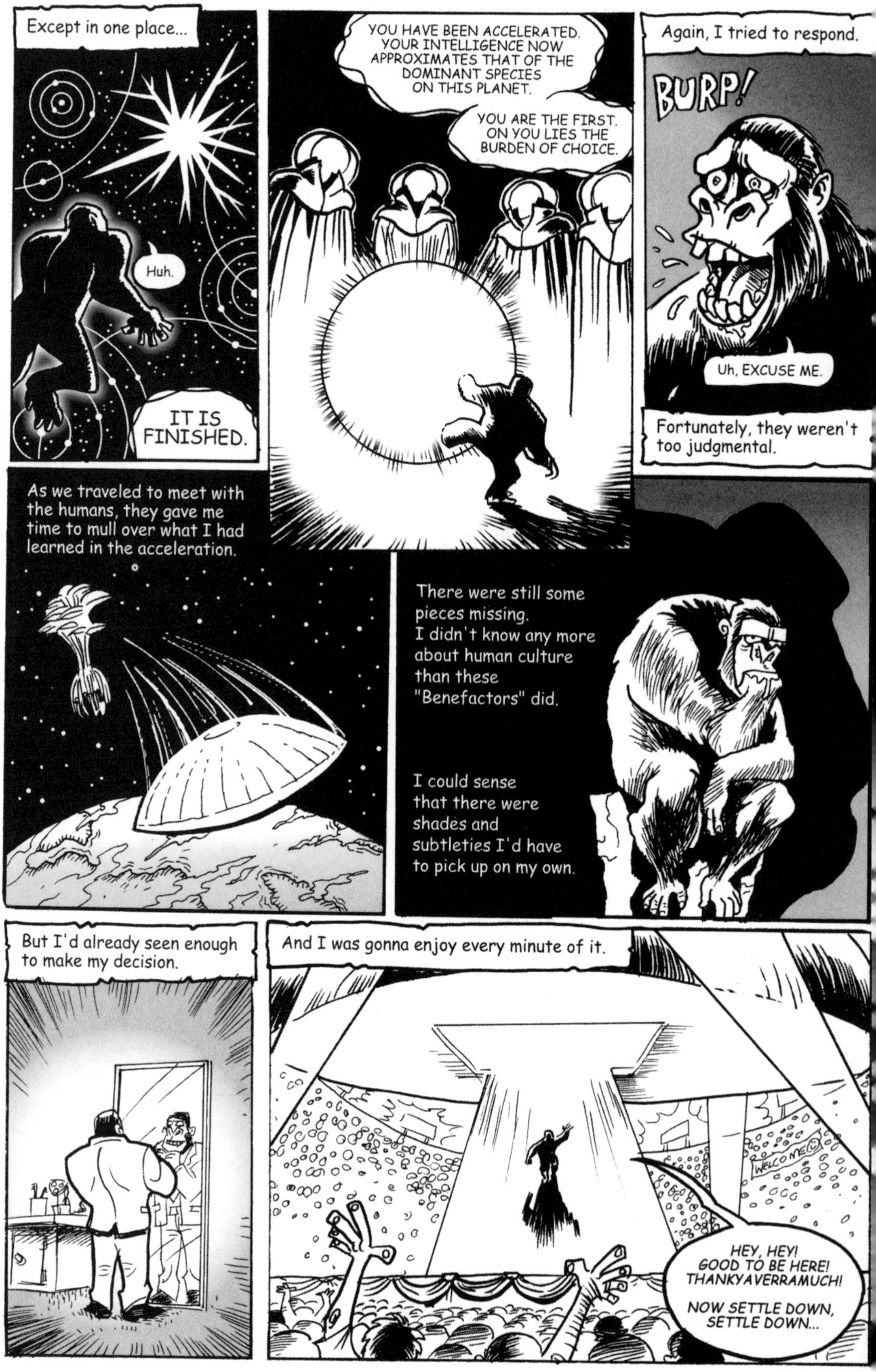

Except in one place...
Huh.
IT IS FINISHED.
YOU HAVE BEEN ACCELERATED. YOUR INTELLIGENCE NOW APPROXIMATES THAT OF THE DOMINANT SPECIES ON THIS PLANET.
YOU ARE THE FIRST. ON YOU LIES THE BURDEN OF CHOICE.
Again, I tried to respond.
BURP!
Uh, EXCUSE ME.
Fortunately, they weren't too judgmental.
As we traveled to meet with the humans, they gave me time to mull over what I had learned in the acceleration.
There were still some pieces missing.
I didn't know any more about human culture than these "Benefactors" did.
I could sense that there were shades and subtleties I'd have to pick up on my own.
But I'd already seen enough to make my decision.
And I was gonna enjoy every minute of it.
WELCOME
HEY, HEY! GOOD TO BE HERE! THANKYAVERRAMUCH!
NOW SETTLE DOWN, SETTLE DOWN...

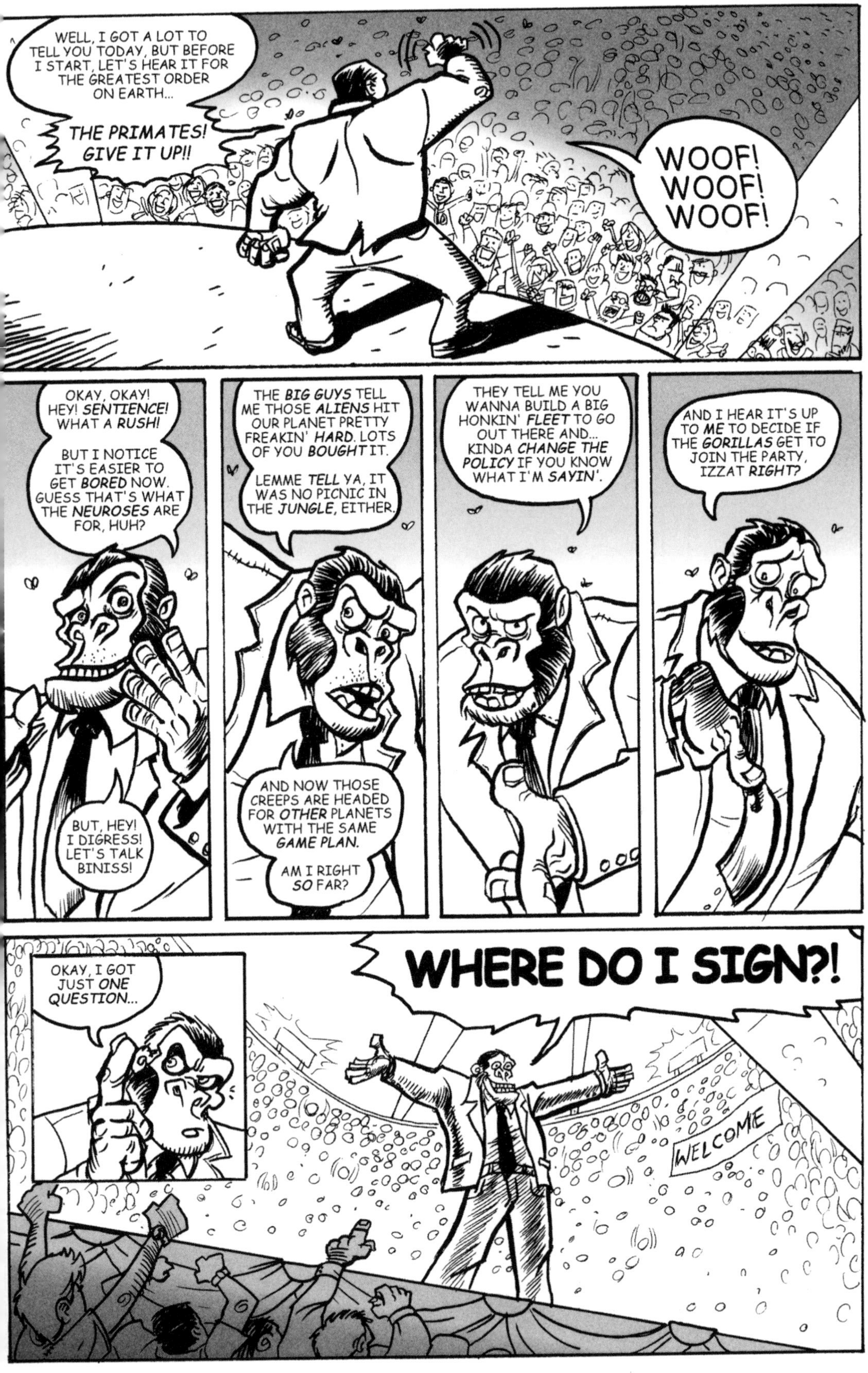

WELL, I GOT A LOT TO TELL YOU TODAY, BUT BEFORE I START, LET'S HEAR IT FOR THE GREATEST ORDER ON EARTH...
THE PRIMATES! GIVE IT UP!!
WOOF! WOOF! WOOF!
OKAY, OKAY! HEY! SENTIENCE! WHAT A RUSH!
BUT I NOTICE IT'S EASIER TO GET BORED NOW. GUESS THAT'S WHAT THE NEUROSES ARE FOR, HUH?
BUT, HEY! I DIGRESS! LET'S TALK BINISS!
THE BIG GUYS TELL ME THOSE ALIENS HIT OUR PLANET PRETTY FREAKIN' HARD. LOTS OF YOU BOUGHT IT.
LEMME TELL YA, IT WAS NO PICNIC IN THE JUNGLE, EITHER.
AND NOW THOSE CREEPS ARE HEADED FOR OTHER PLANETS WITH THE SAME GAME PLAN.
AM I RIGHT SO FAR?
THEY TELL ME YOU WANNA BUILD A BIG HONKIN' FLEET TO GO OUT THERE AND... KINDA CHANGE THE POLICY IF YOU KNOW WHAT I'M SAYIN'.
AND I HEAR IT'S UP TO ME TO DECIDE IF THE GORILLAS GET TO JOIN THE PARTY, IZZAT RIGHT?
OKAY, I GOT JUST ONE QUESTION...
WHERE DO I SIGN?!
WELCOME

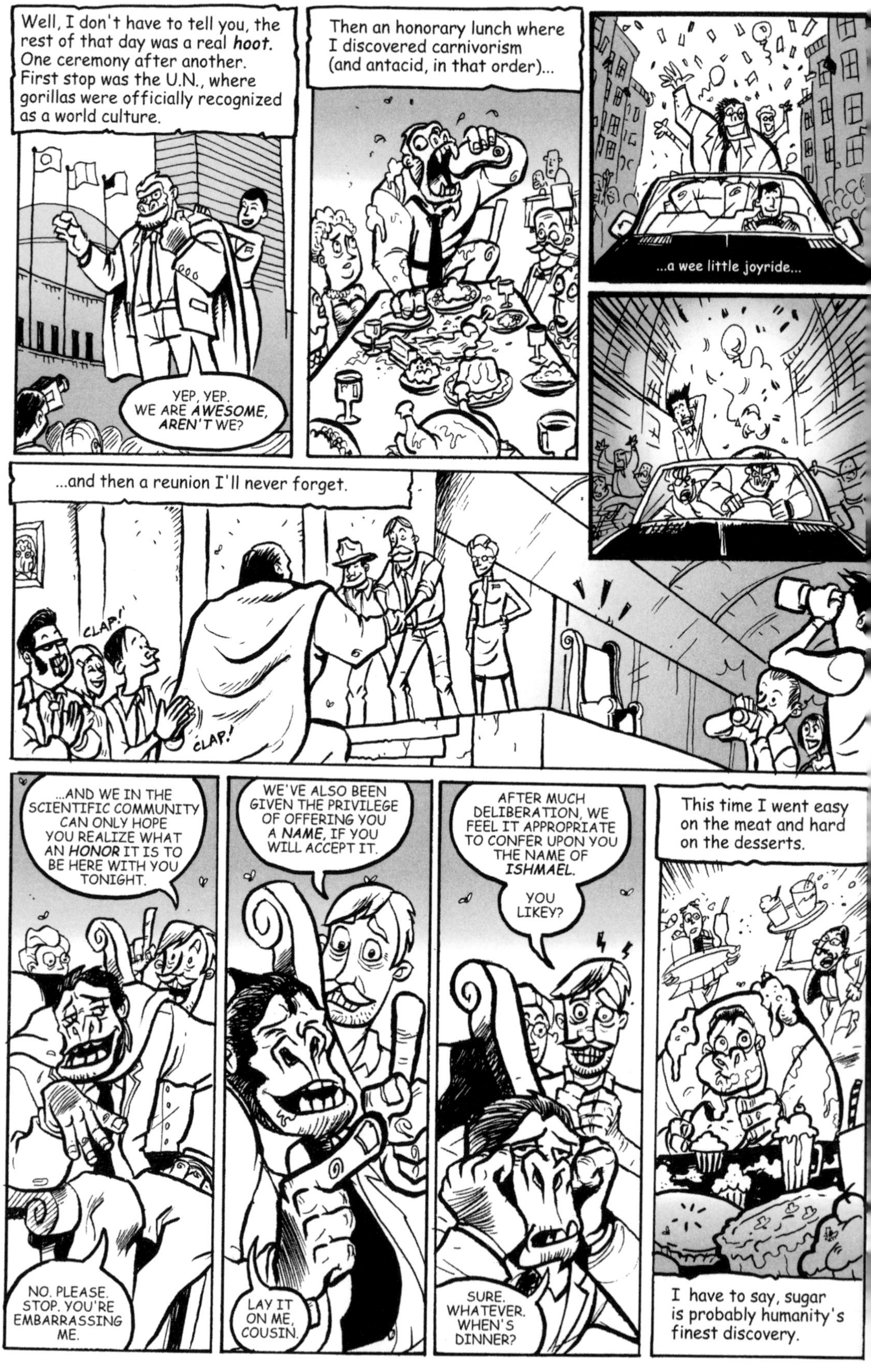
Well, I don't have to tell you, the rest of that day was a real **hoot.** One ceremony after another. First stop was the U.N., where gorillas were officially recognized as a world culture.
YEP, YEP. WE ARE ***AWESOME, AREN'T*** WE?
Then an honorary lunch where I discovered carnivorism (and antacid, in that order)...
...a wee little joyride...
...and then a reunion I'll never forget.
CLAP!
CLAP!
...AND WE IN THE SCIENTIFIC COMMUNITY CAN ONLY HOPE YOU REALIZE WHAT AN ***HONOR*** IT IS TO BE HERE WITH YOU TONIGHT.
NO. PLEASE. STOP. YOU'RE EMBARRASSING ME.
WE'VE ALSO BEEN GIVEN THE PRIVILEGE OF OFFERING YOU A ***NAME,*** IF YOU WILL ACCEPT IT.
LAY IT ON ME, COUSIN.
AFTER MUCH DELIBERATION, WE FEEL IT APPROPRIATE TO CONFER UPON YOU THE NAME OF ***ISHMAEL.***
YOU LIKEY?
SURE. WHATEVER. WHEN'S DINNER?
This time I went easy on the meat and hard on the desserts.
I have to say, sugar is probably humanity's finest discovery.

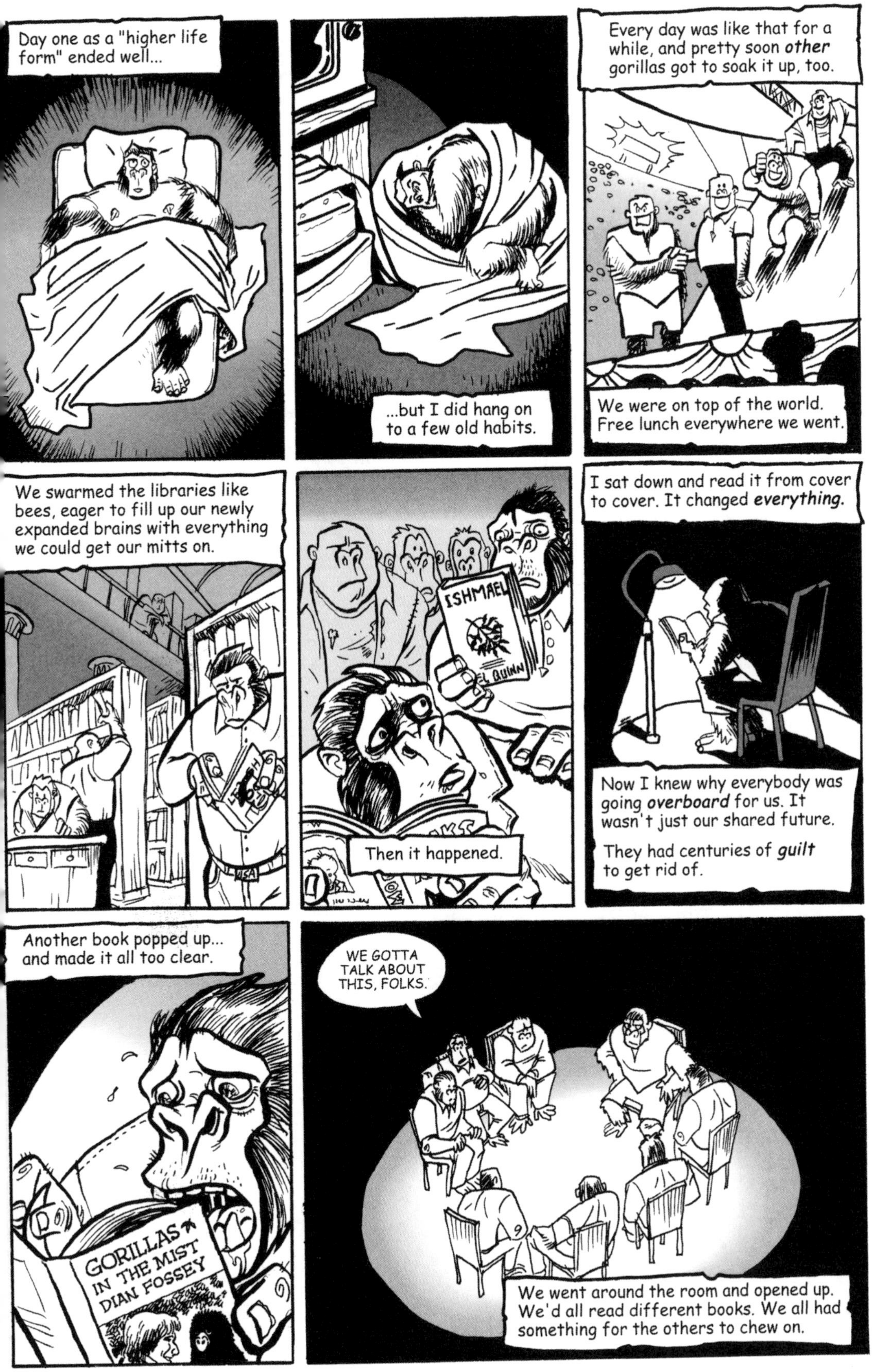

Day one as a "higher life form" ended well...
...but I did hang on to a few old habits.
Every day was like that for a while, and pretty soon *other* gorillas got to soak it up, too.
We were on top of the world. Free lunch everywhere we went.
We swarmed the libraries like bees, eager to fill up our newly expanded brains with everything we could get our mitts on.
ISHMAEL
Then it happened.
I sat down and read it from cover to cover. It changed *everything.*
Now I knew why everybody was going *overboard* for us. It wasn't just our shared future.
They had centuries of *guilt* to get rid of.
Another book popped up... and made it all too clear.
GORILLAS IN THE MIST
DIAN FOSSEY
WE GOTTA TALK ABOUT THIS, FOLKS.
We went around the room and opened up. We'd all read different books. We all had something for the others to chew on.

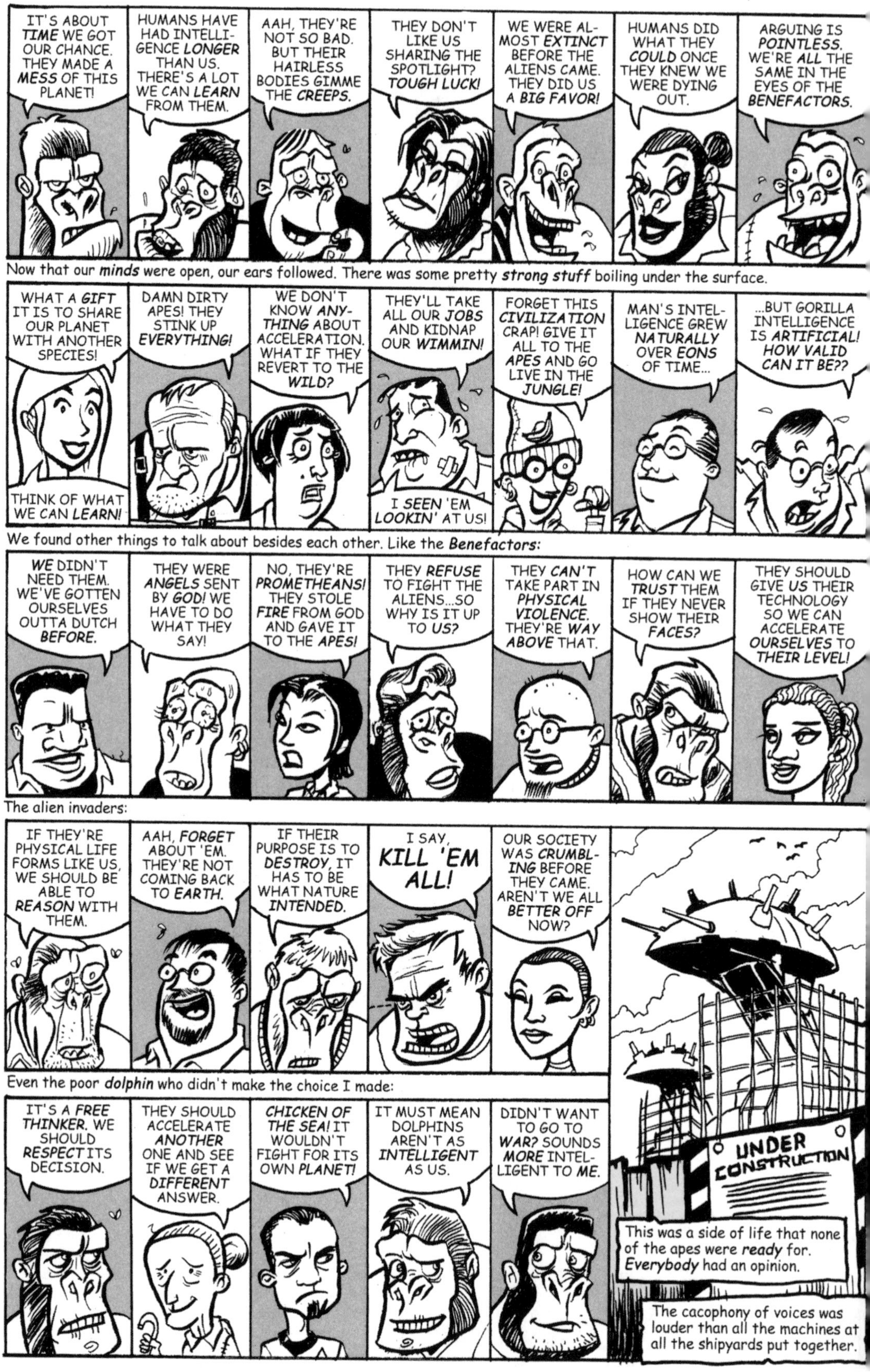
IT'S ABOUT TIME WE GOT OUR CHANCE. THEY MADE A MESS OF THIS PLANET!
HUMANS HAVE HAD INTELLIGENCE LONGER THAN US. THERE'S A LOT WE CAN LEARN FROM THEM.
AAH, THEY'RE NOT SO BAD. BUT THEIR HAIRLESS BODIES GIMME THE CREEPS.
THEY DON'T LIKE US SHARING THE SPOTLIGHT? TOUGH LUCK!
WE WERE ALMOST EXTINCT BEFORE THE ALIENS CAME. THEY DID US A BIG FAVOR!
HUMANS DID WHAT THEY COULD ONCE THEY KNEW WE WERE DYING OUT.
ARGUING IS POINTLESS. WE'RE ALL THE SAME IN THE EYES OF THE BENEFACTORS.
Now that our minds were open, our ears followed. There was some pretty strong stuff boiling under the surface.
WHAT A GIFT IT IS TO SHARE OUR PLANET WITH ANOTHER SPECIES!
THINK OF WHAT WE CAN LEARN!
DAMN DIRTY APES! THEY STINK UP EVERYTHING!
WE DON'T KNOW ANYTHING ABOUT ACCELERATION. WHAT IF THEY REVERT TO THE WILD?
THEY'LL TAKE ALL OUR JOBS AND KIDNAP OUR WIMMIN!
I SEEN 'EM LOOKIN' AT US!
FORGET THIS CIVILIZATION CRAP! GIVE IT ALL TO THE APES AND GO LIVE IN THE JUNGLE!
MAN'S INTELLIGENCE GREW NATURALLY OVER EONS OF TIME...
...BUT GORILLA INTELLIGENCE IS ARTIFICIAL! HOW VALID CAN IT BE??
We found other things to talk about besides each other. Like the Benefactors:
WE DIDN'T NEED THEM. WE'VE GOTTEN OURSELVES OUTTA DUTCH BEFORE.
THEY WERE ANGELS SENT BY GOD! WE HAVE TO DO WHAT THEY SAY!
NO, THEY'RE PROMETHEANS! THEY STOLE FIRE FROM GOD AND GAVE IT TO THE APES!
THEY REFUSE TO FIGHT THE ALIENS...SO WHY IS IT UP TO US?
THEY CAN'T TAKE PART IN PHYSICAL VIOLENCE. THEY'RE WAY ABOVE THAT.
HOW CAN WE TRUST THEM IF THEY NEVER SHOW THEIR FACES?
THEY SHOULD GIVE US THEIR TECHNOLOGY SO WE CAN ACCELERATE OURSELVES TO THEIR LEVEL!
The alien invaders:
IF THEY'RE PHYSICAL LIFE FORMS LIKE US, WE SHOULD BE ABLE TO REASON WITH THEM.
AAH, FORGET ABOUT 'EM. THEY'RE NOT COMING BACK TO EARTH.
IF THEIR PURPOSE IS TO DESTROY, IT HAS TO BE WHAT NATURE INTENDED.
I SAY, KILL 'EM ALL!
OUR SOCIETY WAS CRUMBLING BEFORE THEY CAME. AREN'T WE ALL BETTER OFF NOW?
Even the poor dolphin who didn't make the choice I made:
IT'S A FREE THINKER. WE SHOULD RESPECT ITS DECISION.
THEY SHOULD ACCELERATE ANOTHER ONE AND SEE IF WE GET A DIFFERENT ANSWER.
CHICKEN OF THE SEA! IT WOULDN'T FIGHT FOR ITS OWN PLANET!
IT MUST MEAN DOLPHINS AREN'T AS INTELLIGENT AS US.
DIDN'T WANT TO GO TO WAR? SOUNDS MORE INTELLIGENT TO ME.
UNDER CONSTRUCTION
This was a side of life that none of the apes were ready for. Everybody had an opinion.
The cacophony of voices was louder than all the machines at all the shipyards put together.

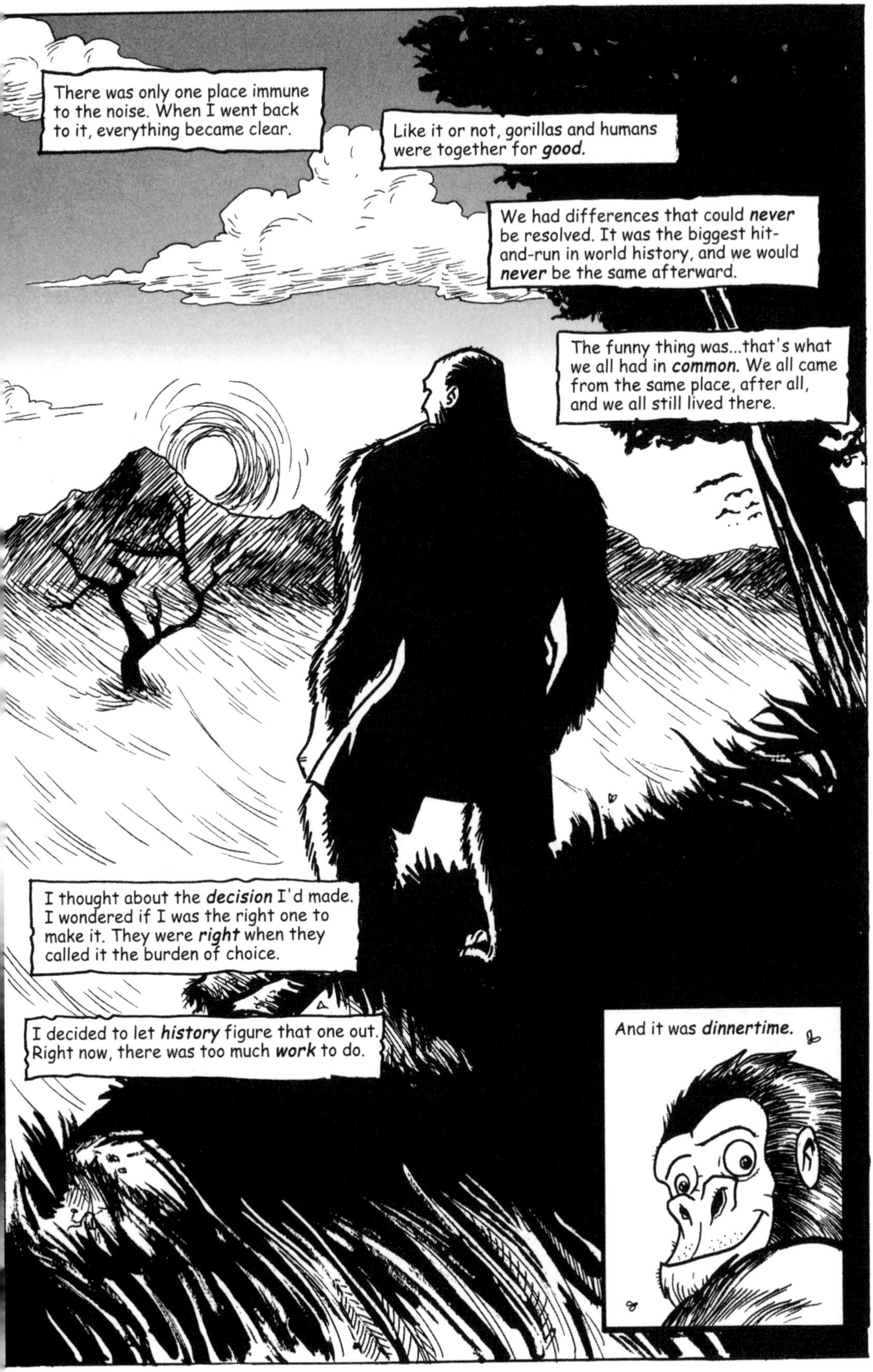
There was only one place immune to the noise. When I went back to it, everything became clear.
Like it or not, gorillas and humans were together for ***good.***
We had differences that could ***never*** be resolved. It was the biggest hit-and-run in world history, and we would ***never*** be the same afterward.
The funny thing was...that's what we all had in ***common.*** We all came from the same place, after all, and we all still lived there.
I thought about the ***decision*** I'd made. I wondered if I was the right one to make it. They were ***right*** when they called it the burden of choice.
I decided to let ***history*** figure that one out. Right now, there was too much ***work*** to do.
And it was ***dinnertime.***

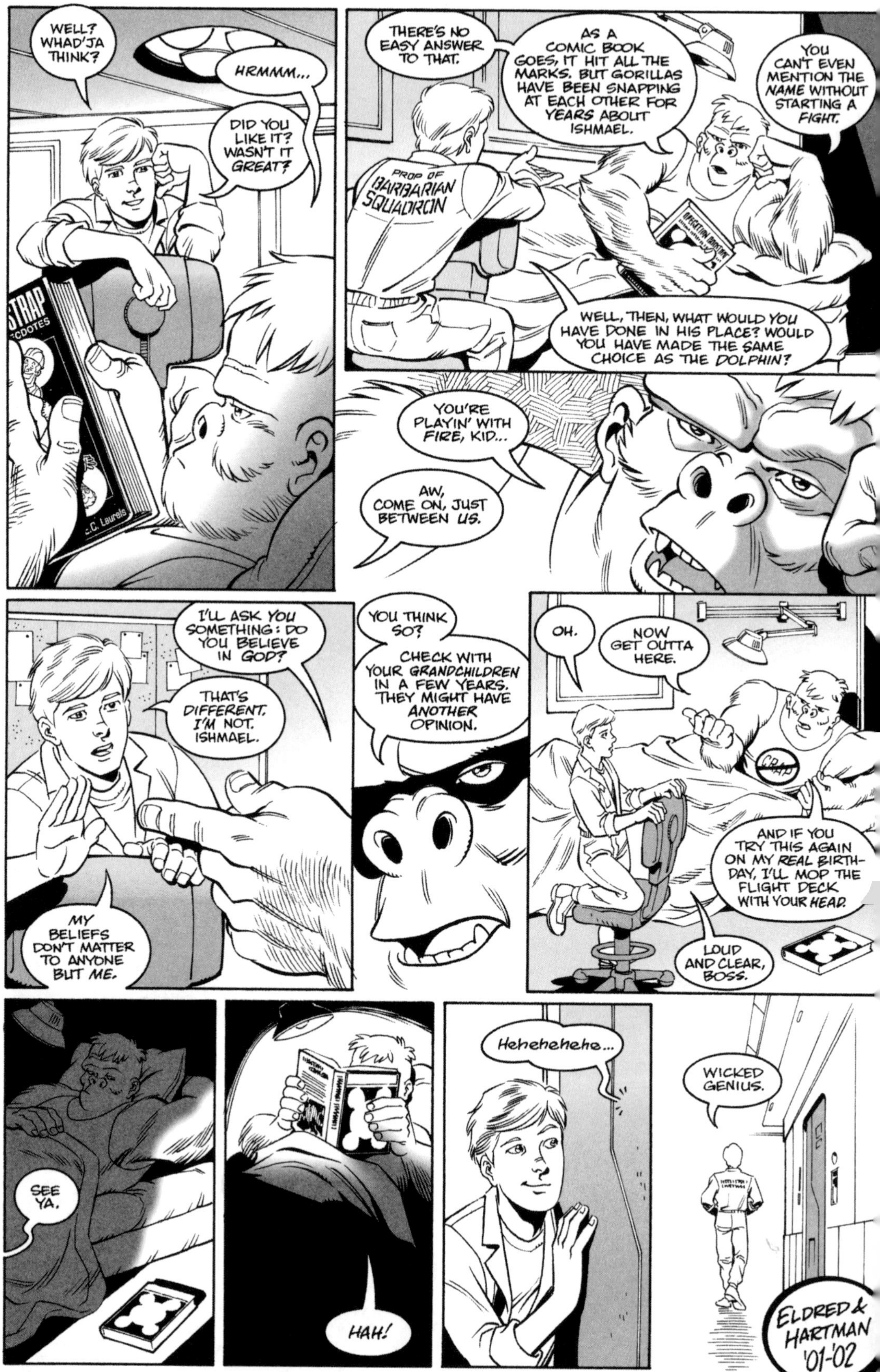
WELL? WHAD'JA THINK?
HRMMM...
DID YOU LIKE IT? WASN'T IT GREAT?
THERE'S NO EASY ANSWER TO THAT.
PROP OF BARBARIAN SQUADRON
AS A COMIC BOOK GOES, IT HIT ALL THE MARKS. BUT GORILLAS HAVE BEEN SNAPPING AT EACH OTHER FOR YEARS ABOUT ISHMAEL.
YOU CAN'T EVEN MENTION THE NAME WITHOUT STARTING A FIGHT.
WELL, THEN, WHAT WOULD YOU HAVE DONE IN HIS PLACE? WOULD YOU HAVE MADE THE SAME CHOICE AS THE DOLPHIN?
YOU'RE PLAYIN' WITH FIRE, KID...
AW, COME ON, JUST BETWEEN US.
I'LL ASK YOU SOMETHING: DO YOU BELIEVE IN GOD?
THAT'S DIFFERENT. I'M NOT ISHMAEL.
MY BELIEFS DON'T MATTER TO ANYONE BUT ME.
YOU THINK SO?
CHECK WITH YOUR GRANDCHILDREN IN A FEW YEARS. THEY MIGHT HAVE ANOTHER OPINION.
OH.
NOW GET OUTTA HERE.
AND IF YOU TRY THIS AGAIN ON MY REAL BIRTHDAY, I'LL MOP THE FLIGHT DECK WITH YOUR HEAD.
LOUD AND CLEAR, BOSS.
SEE YA.
HAH!
Hehehehehe...
WICKED GENIUS.
ELDRED & HARTMAN '01-'02

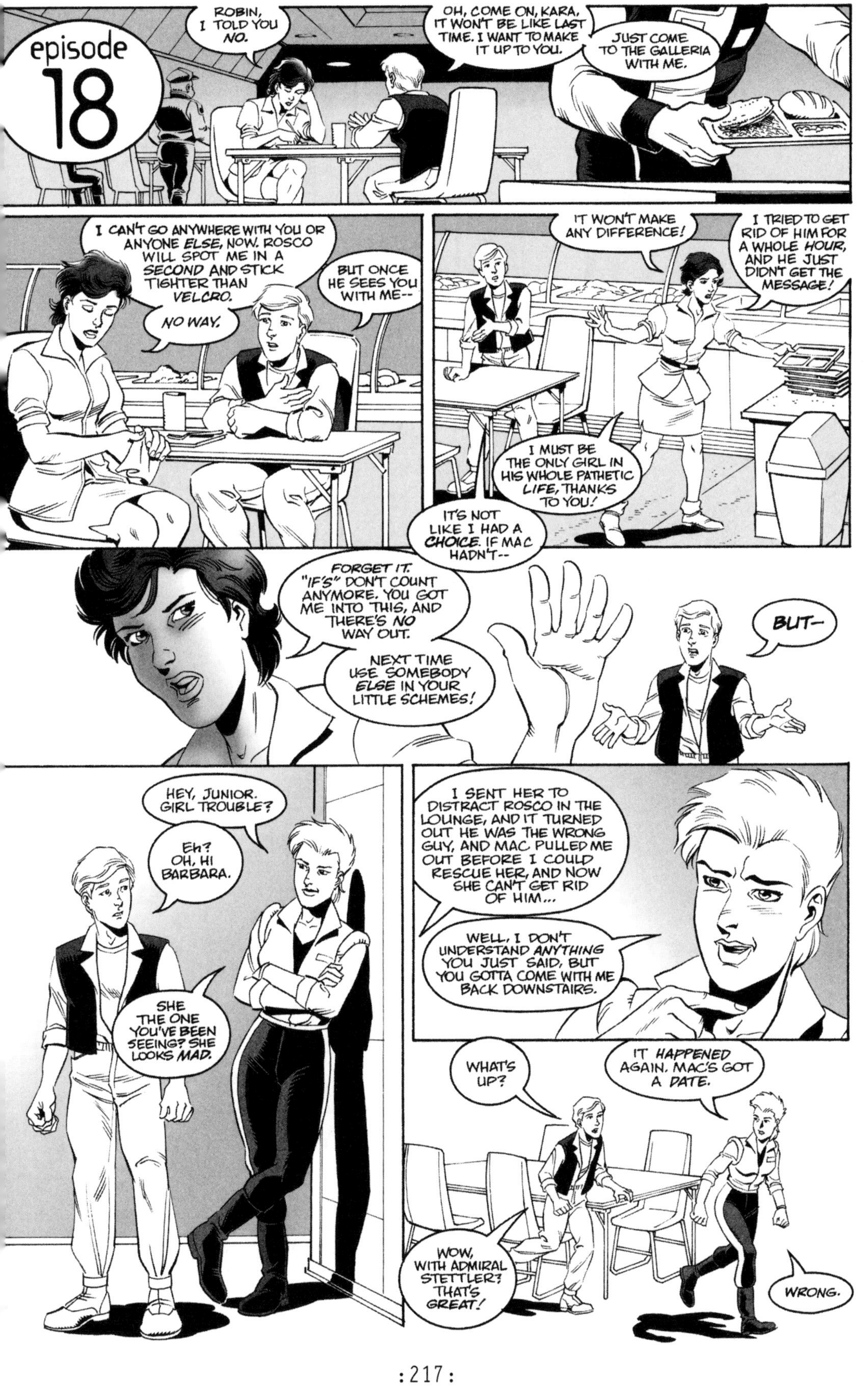
episode 18
ROBIN, I TOLD YOU NO.
OH, COME ON, KARA, IT WON'T BE LIKE LAST TIME. I WANT TO MAKE IT UP TO YOU.
JUST COME TO THE GALLERIA WITH ME.
I CAN'T GO ANYWHERE WITH YOU OR ANYONE ELSE, NOW. ROSCO WILL SPOT ME IN A SECOND AND STICK TIGHTER THAN VELCRO.
BUT ONCE HE SEES YOU WITH ME--
NO WAY.
IT WON'T MAKE ANY DIFFERENCE!
I TRIED TO GET RID OF HIM FOR A WHOLE HOUR, AND HE JUST DIDN'T GET THE MESSAGE!
I MUST BE THE ONLY GIRL IN HIS WHOLE PATHETIC LIFE, THANKS TO YOU!
IT'S NOT LIKE I HAD A CHOICE. IF MAC HADN'T--
FORGET IT. "IF'S" DON'T COUNT ANYMORE. YOU GOT ME INTO THIS, AND THERE'S NO WAY OUT.
NEXT TIME USE SOMEBODY ELSE IN YOUR LITTLE SCHEMES!
BUT-
HEY, JUNIOR. GIRL TROUBLE?
Eh? OH, HI BARBARA.
SHE THE ONE YOU'VE BEEN SEEING? SHE LOOKS MAD.
I SENT HER TO DISTRACT ROSCO IN THE LOUNGE, AND IT TURNED OUT HE WAS THE WRONG GUY, AND MAC PULLED ME OUT BEFORE I COULD RESCUE HER, AND NOW SHE CAN'T GET RID OF HIM...
WELL, I DON'T UNDERSTAND ANYTHING YOU JUST SAID, BUT YOU GOTTA COME WITH ME BACK DOWNSTAIRS.
WHAT'S UP?
IT HAPPENED AGAIN. MAC'S GOT A DATE.
WOW, WITH ADMIRAL STETTLER? THAT'S GREAT!
WRONG.

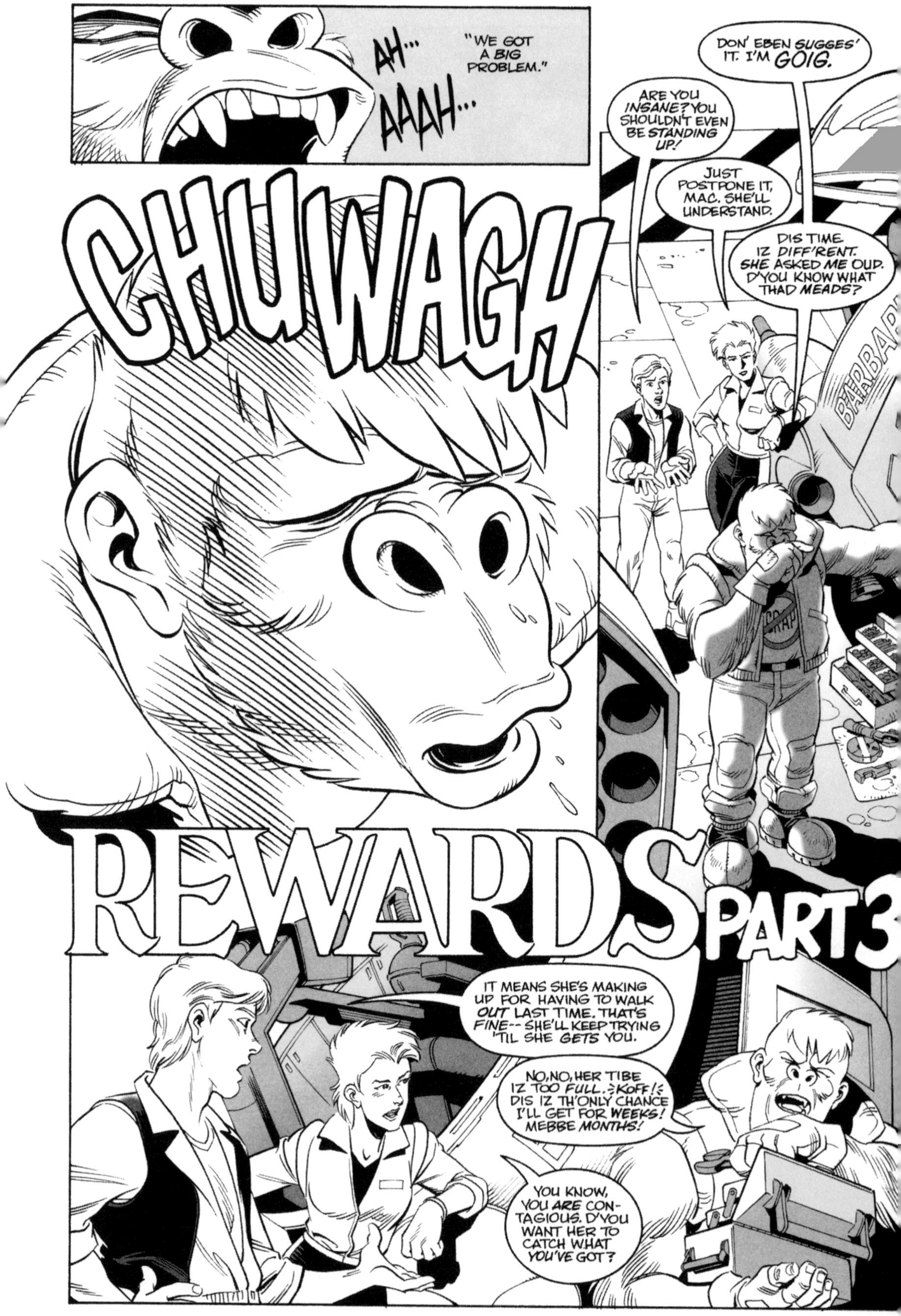
AH... AAAH...
"WE GOT A BIG PROBLEM."
CHUWAGH
ARE YOU INSANE? YOU SHOULDN'T EVEN BE STANDING UP!
DON' EBEN SUGGES' IT. I'M GOIG.
JUST POSTPONE IT, MAC. SHE'LL UNDERSTAND.
DIS TIME IZ DIFF'RENT. SHE ASKED ME OUD. D'YOU KNOW WHAT THAD MEADS?
BARBAR
REWARDS PART 3
IT MEANS SHE'S MAKING UP FOR HAVING TO WALK OUT LAST TIME. THAT'S FINE-- SHE'LL KEEP TRYING 'TIL SHE GETS YOU.
NO, NO, HER TIBE IZ TOO FULL. KOFF! DIS IZ TH'ONLY CHANCE I'LL GET FOR WEEKS! MEBBE MONTHS!
YOU KNOW, YOU ARE CONTAGIOUS. D'YOU WANT HER TO CATCH WHAT YOU'VE GOT?

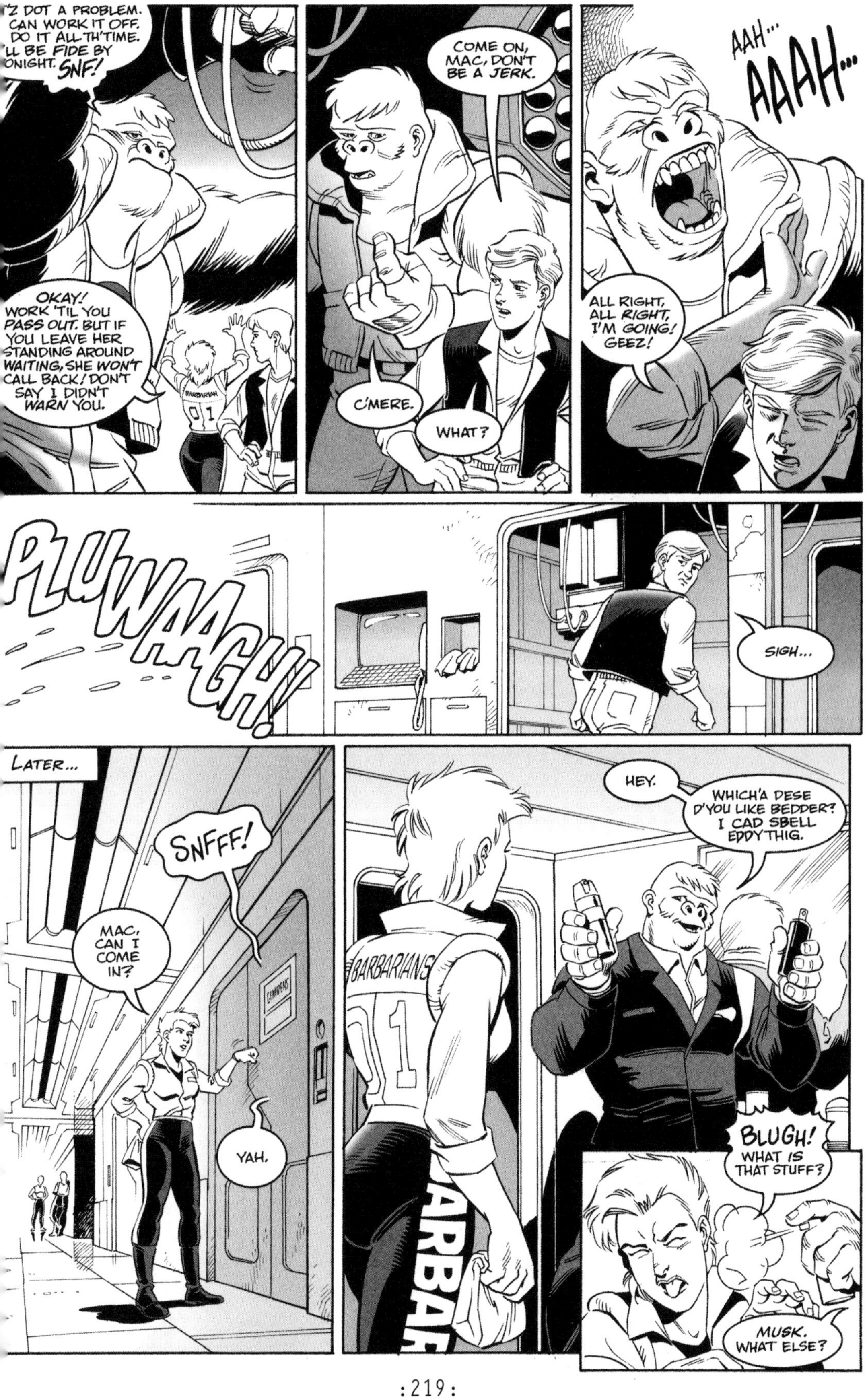
'Z DOT A PROBLEM. CAN WORK IT OFF. DO IT ALL TH'TIME. 'LL BE FIDE BY ONIGHT. SNF!
OKAY! WORK 'TIL YOU PASS OUT. BUT IF YOU LEAVE HER STANDING AROUND WAITING, SHE WON'T CALL BACK! DON'T SAY I DIDN'T WARN YOU.
COME ON, MAC, DON'T BE A JERK.
C'MERE.
WHAT?
AAH... AAAH...
ALL RIGHT, ALL RIGHT, I'M GOING! GEEZ!
PLUWAAGH!
SIGH...
LATER...
SNFFF!
MAC, CAN I COME IN?
YAH.
HEY.
WHICH'A DESE D'YOU LIKE BEDDER? I CAD SBELL EDDYTHIG.
BLUGH! WHAT IS THAT STUFF?
MUSK. WHAT ELSE?

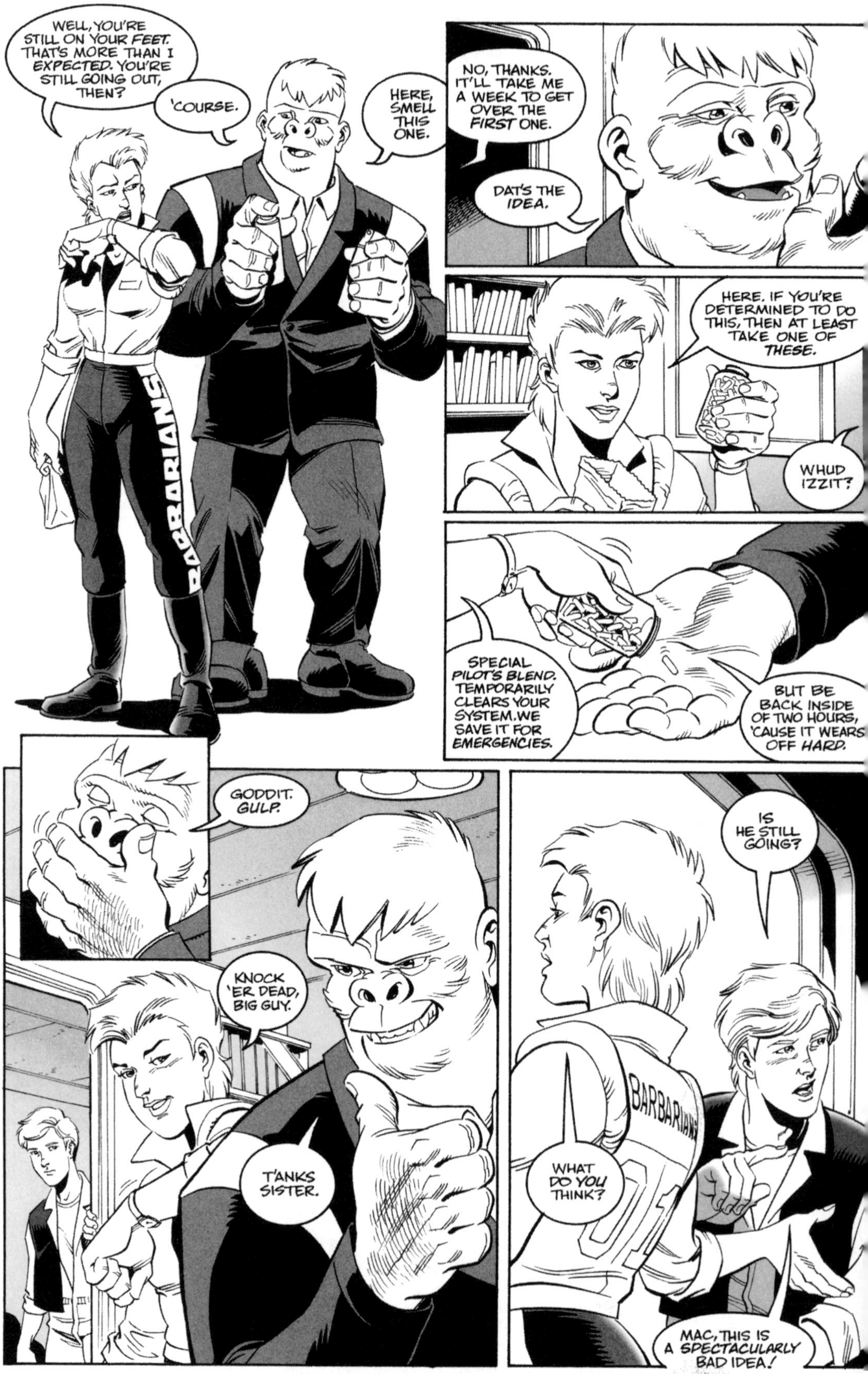
WELL, YOU'RE STILL ON YOUR FEET. THAT'S MORE THAN I EXPECTED. YOU'RE STILL GOING OUT, THEN?
'COURSE.
HERE, SMELL THIS ONE.
NO, THANKS. IT'LL TAKE ME A WEEK TO GET OVER THE FIRST ONE.
DAT'S THE IDEA.
HERE. IF YOU'RE DETERMINED TO DO THIS, THEN AT LEAST TAKE ONE OF THESE.
WHUD IZZIT?
SPECIAL PILOT'S BLEND. TEMPORARILY CLEARS YOUR SYSTEM. WE SAVE IT FOR EMERGENCIES.
BUT BE BACK INSIDE OF TWO HOURS, 'CAUSE IT WEARS OFF HARD.
GODDIT. GULP.
KNOCK 'ER DEAD, BIG GUY.
T'ANKS SISTER.
IS HE STILL GOING?
WHAT DO YOU THINK?
MAC, THIS IS A SPECTACULARLY BAD IDEA!
BARBARIANS

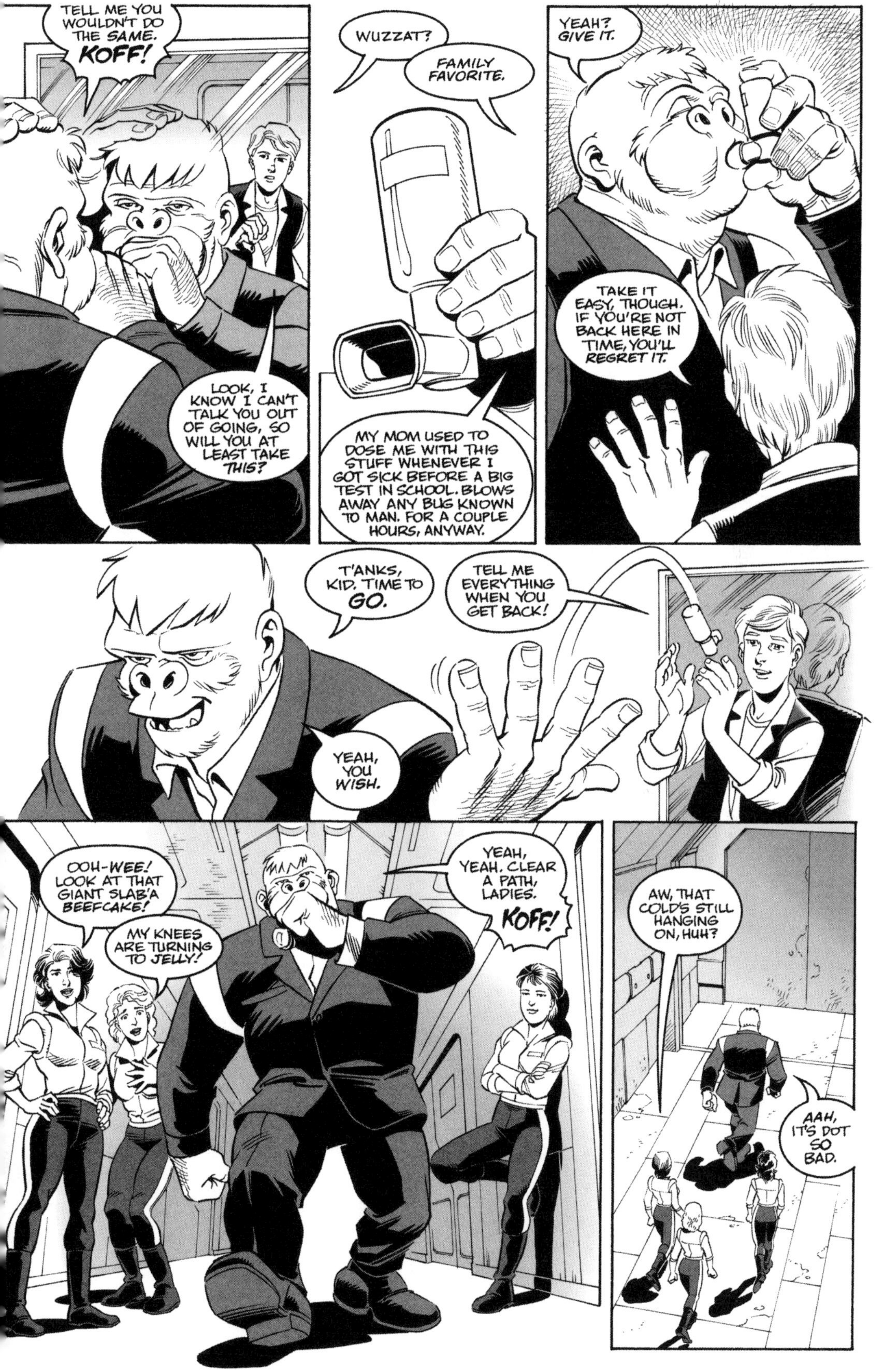
TELL ME YOU WOULDN'T DO THE SAME. KOFF!
LOOK, I KNOW I CAN'T TALK YOU OUT OF GOING, SO WILL YOU AT LEAST TAKE THIS?
WUZZAT?
FAMILY FAVORITE.
MY MOM USED TO DOSE ME WITH THIS STUFF WHENEVER I GOT SICK BEFORE A BIG TEST IN SCHOOL. BLOWS AWAY ANY BUG KNOWN TO MAN. FOR A COUPLE HOURS, ANYWAY.
YEAH? GIVE IT.
TAKE IT EASY, THOUGH. IF YOU'RE NOT BACK HERE IN TIME, YOU'LL REGRET IT.
T'ANKS, KID. TIME TO GO.
TELL ME EVERYTHING WHEN YOU GET BACK!
YEAH, YOU WISH.
OOH-WEE! LOOK AT THAT GIANT SLAB'A BEEFCAKE!
MY KNEES ARE TURNING TO JELLY!
YEAH, YEAH. CLEAR A PATH, LADIES. KOFF!
AW, THAT COLD'S STILL HANGING ON, HUH?
AAH, IT'S DOT SO BAD.

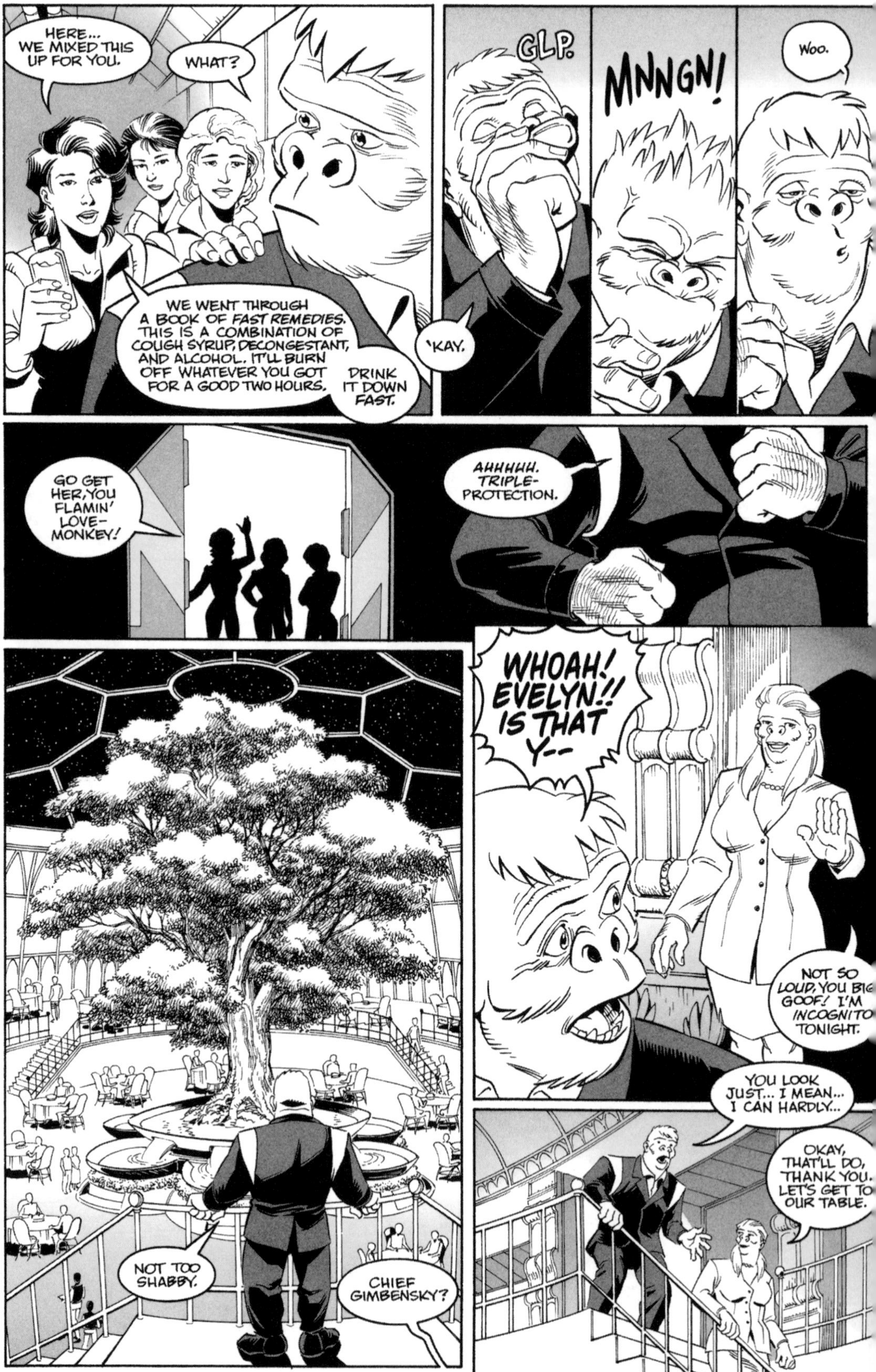
HERE... WE MIXED THIS UP FOR YOU.
WHAT?
WE WENT THROUGH A BOOK OF FAST REMEDIES. THIS IS A COMBINATION OF COUGH SYRUP, DECONGESTANT, AND ALCOHOL. IT'LL BURN OFF WHATEVER YOU GOT FOR A GOOD TWO HOURS.
DRINK IT DOWN FAST.
'KAY.
GLP.
MNNGN!
WOO.
GO GET HER, YOU FLAMIN' LOVE-MONKEY!
AHHHHH. TRIPLE-PROTECTION.
NOT TOO SHABBY.
CHIEF GIMBENSKY?
WHOAH! EVELYN!! IS THAT Y--
NOT SO LOUD, YOU BIG GOOF! I'M INCOGNITO TONIGHT.
YOU LOOK JUST... I MEAN... I CAN HARDLY...
OKAY, THAT'LL DO, THANK YOU. LET'S GET TO OUR TABLE.

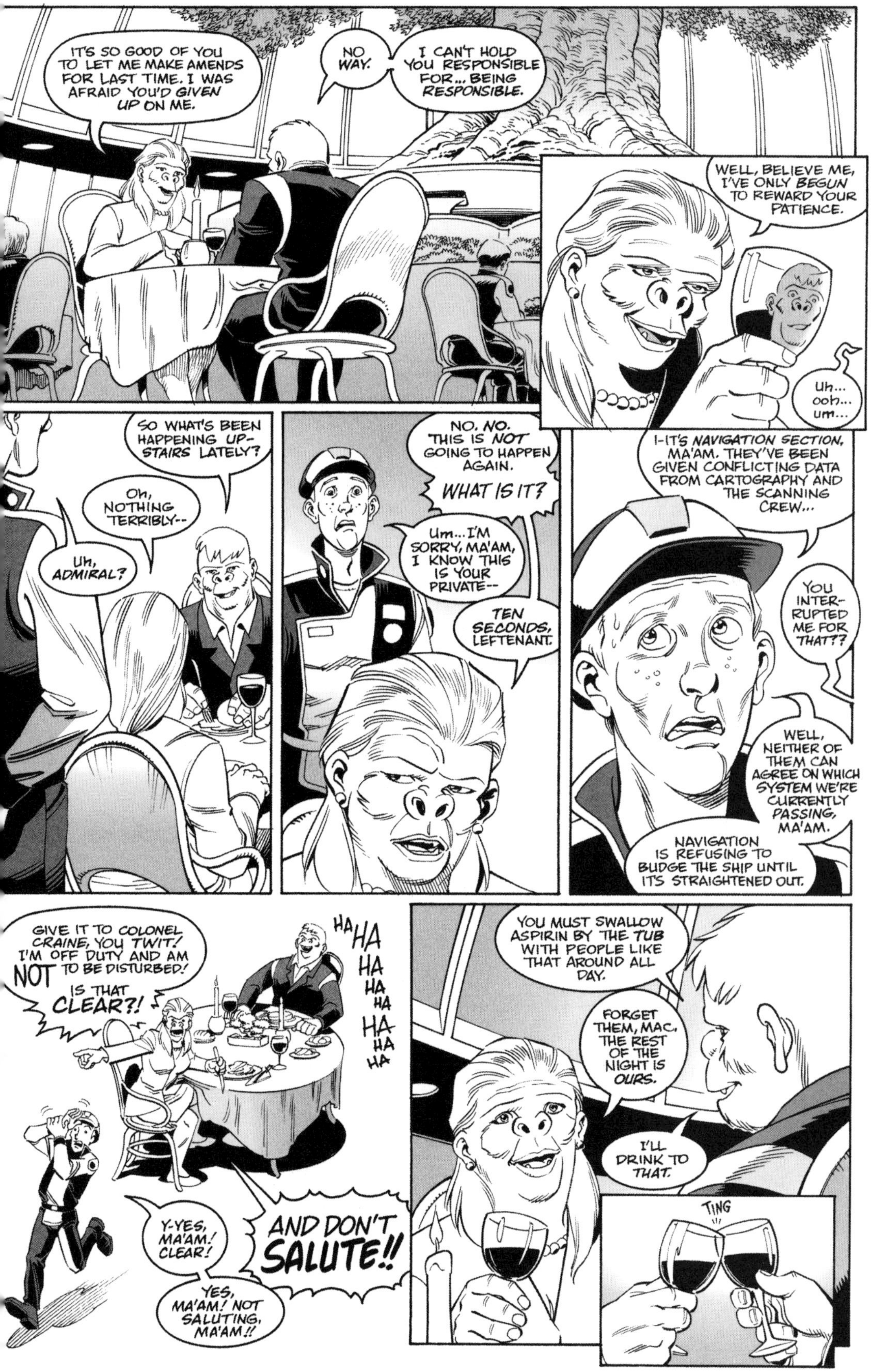
IT'S SO GOOD OF YOU TO LET ME MAKE AMENDS FOR LAST TIME. I WAS AFRAID YOU'D GIVEN UP ON ME.
NO WAY.
I CAN'T HOLD YOU RESPONSIBLE FOR... BEING RESPONSIBLE.
WELL, BELIEVE ME, I'VE ONLY BEGUN TO REWARD YOUR PATIENCE.
Uh... ooh... um...
SO WHAT'S BEEN HAPPENING UPSTAIRS LATELY?
Oh, NOTHING TERRIBLY--
Uh, ADMIRAL?
NO. NO. THIS IS NOT GOING TO HAPPEN AGAIN.
WHAT IS IT?
Um... I'M SORRY, MA'AM, I KNOW THIS IS YOUR PRIVATE--
TEN SECONDS, LEFTENANT.
I-IT'S NAVIGATION SECTION, MA'AM. THEY'VE BEEN GIVEN CONFLICTING DATA FROM CARTOGRAPHY AND THE SCANNING CREW...
YOU INTERRUPTED ME FOR THAT??
WELL, NEITHER OF THEM CAN AGREE ON WHICH SYSTEM WE'RE CURRENTLY PASSING, MA'AM.
NAVIGATION IS REFUSING TO BUDGE THE SHIP UNTIL IT'S STRAIGHTENED OUT.
GIVE IT TO COLONEL CRAINE, YOU TWIT! I'M OFF DUTY AND AM NOT TO BE DISTURBED!
IS THAT CLEAR?!
HA HA HA HA HA HA HA HA HA
Y-YES, MA'AM! CLEAR!
AND DON'T SALUTE!!
YES, MA'AM! NOT SALUTING, MA'AM!!
YOU MUST SWALLOW ASPIRIN BY THE TUB WITH PEOPLE LIKE THAT AROUND ALL DAY.
FORGET THEM, MAC, THE REST OF THE NIGHT IS OURS.
I'LL DRINK TO THAT.
TING

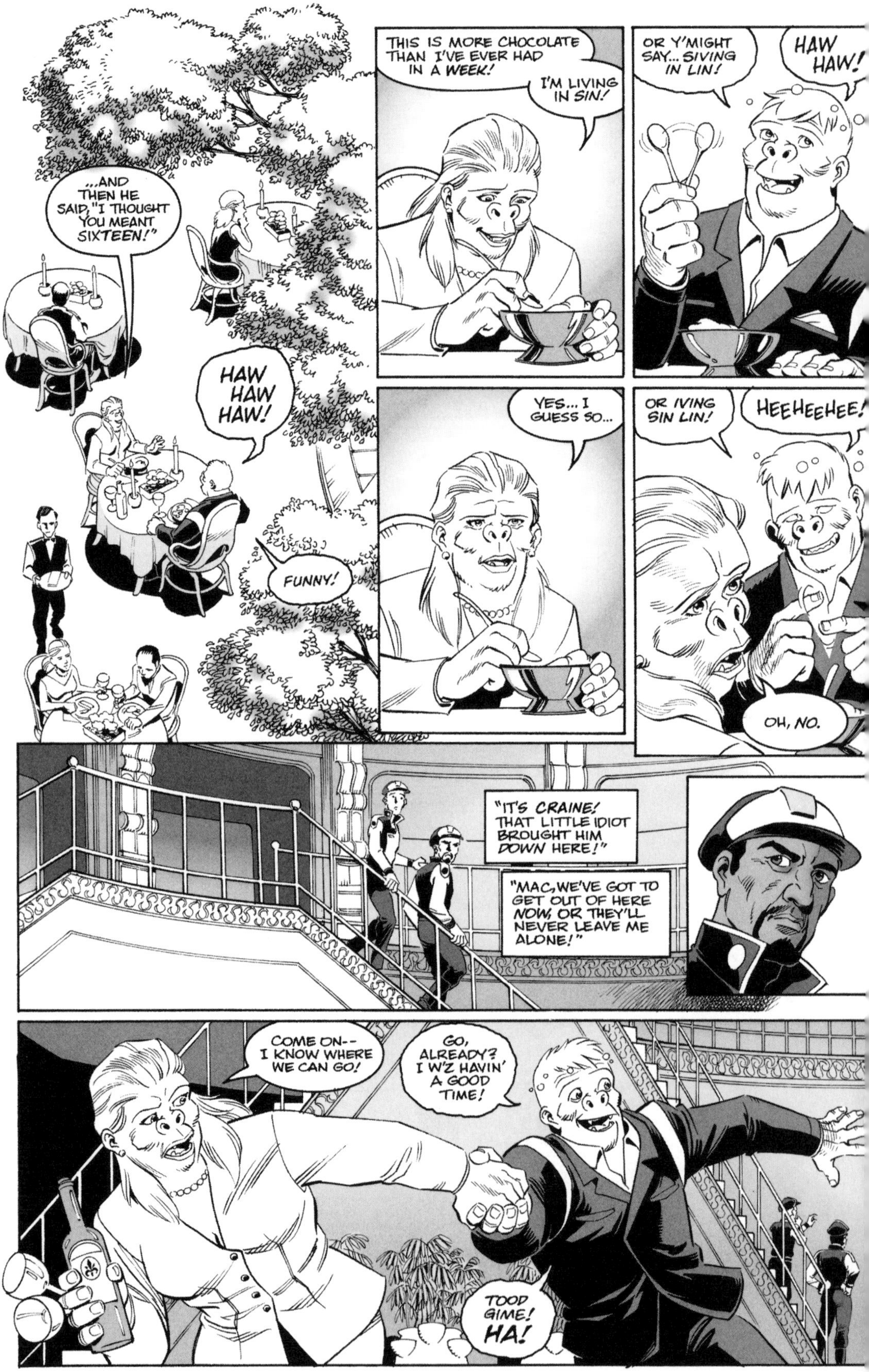
...AND THEN HE SAID, "I THOUGHT YOU MEANT SIXTEEN!"
HAW HAW HAW!
FUNNY!
THIS IS MORE CHOCOLATE THAN I'VE EVER HAD IN A WEEK!
I'M LIVING IN SIN!
OR Y'MIGHT SAY... SIVING IN LIN!
HAW HAW!
YES... I GUESS SO...
OR IVING SIN LIN!
HEEHEEHEE!
OH, NO.
"IT'S CRAINE! THAT LITTLE IDIOT BROUGHT HIM DOWN HERE!"
"MAC, WE'VE GOT TO GET OUT OF HERE NOW, OR THEY'LL NEVER LEAVE ME ALONE!"
COME ON-- I KNOW WHERE WE CAN GO!
GO, ALREADY? I W'Z HAVIN' A GOOD TIME!
TOOD GIME! HA!

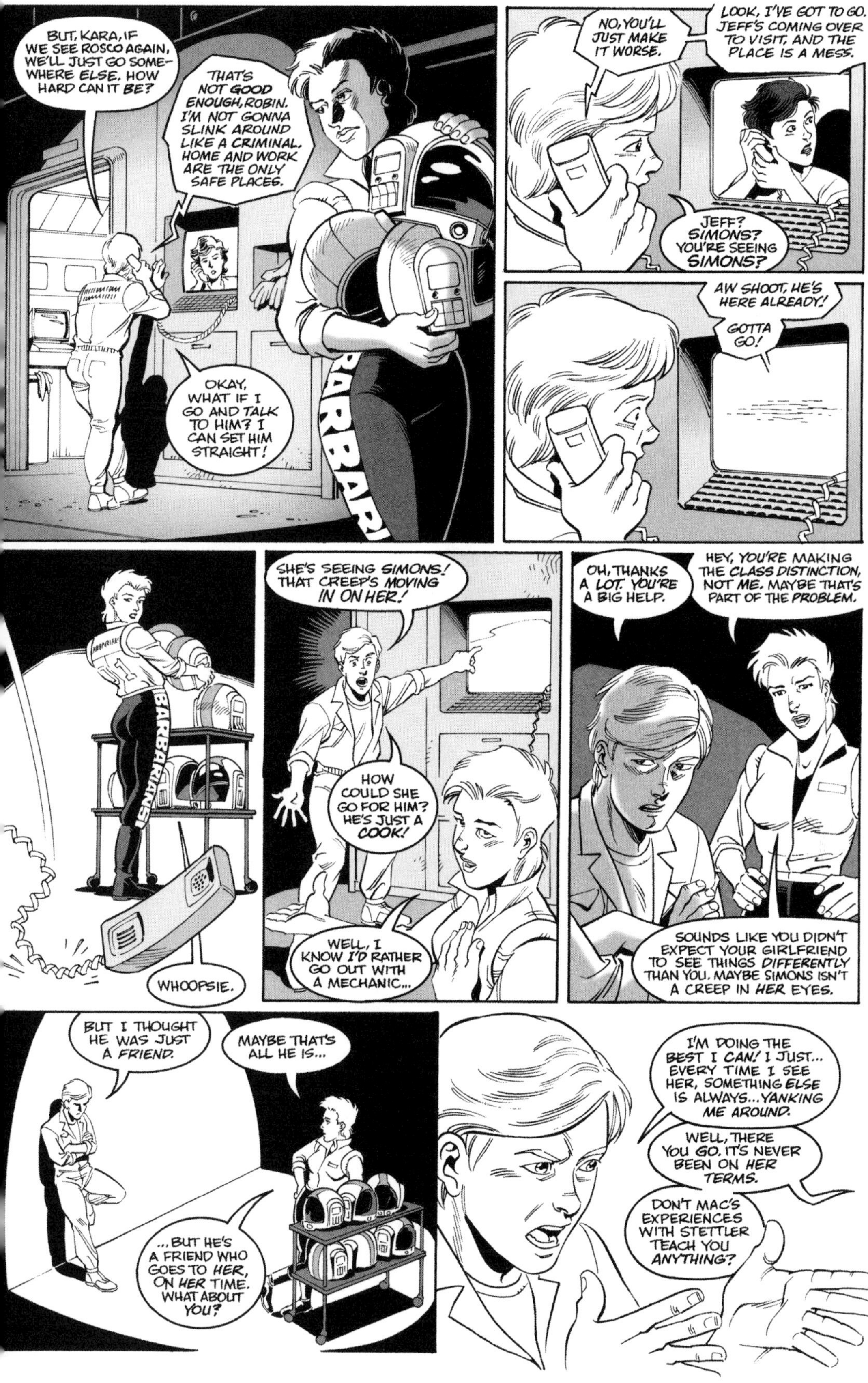

BUT, KARA, IF WE SEE ROSCO AGAIN, WE'LL JUST GO SOMEWHERE ELSE. HOW HARD CAN IT BE?
THAT'S NOT GOOD ENOUGH, ROBIN. I'M NOT GONNA SLINK AROUND LIKE A CRIMINAL. HOME AND WORK ARE THE ONLY SAFE PLACES.
OKAY, WHAT IF I GO AND TALK TO HIM? I CAN SET HIM STRAIGHT!
BARBARIANS
NO, YOU'LL JUST MAKE IT WORSE.
LOOK, I'VE GOT TO GO. JEFF'S COMING OVER TO VISIT, AND THE PLACE IS A MESS.
JEFF? SIMONS? YOU'RE SEEING SIMONS?
AW SHOOT, HE'S HERE ALREADY!
GOTTA GO!
WHOOPSIE.
SHE'S SEEING SIMONS! THAT CREEP'S MOVING IN ON HER!
HOW COULD SHE GO FOR HIM? HE'S JUST A COOK!
WELL, I KNOW I'D RATHER GO OUT WITH A MECHANIC...
OH, THANKS A LOT. YOU'RE A BIG HELP.
HEY, YOU'RE MAKING THE CLASS DISTINCTION, NOT ME. MAYBE THAT'S PART OF THE PROBLEM.
SOUNDS LIKE YOU DIDN'T EXPECT YOUR GIRLFRIEND TO SEE THINGS DIFFERENTLY THAN YOU. MAYBE SIMONS ISN'T A CREEP IN HER EYES.
BUT I THOUGHT HE WAS JUST A FRIEND.
MAYBE THAT'S ALL HE IS...
...BUT HE'S A FRIEND WHO GOES TO HER, ON HER TIME. WHAT ABOUT YOU?
I'M DOING THE BEST I CAN! I JUST... EVERY TIME I SEE HER, SOMETHING ELSE IS ALWAYS...YANKING ME AROUND.
WELL, THERE YOU GO. IT'S NEVER BEEN ON HER TERMS.
DON'T MAC'S EXPERIENCES WITH STETTLER TEACH YOU ANYTHING?

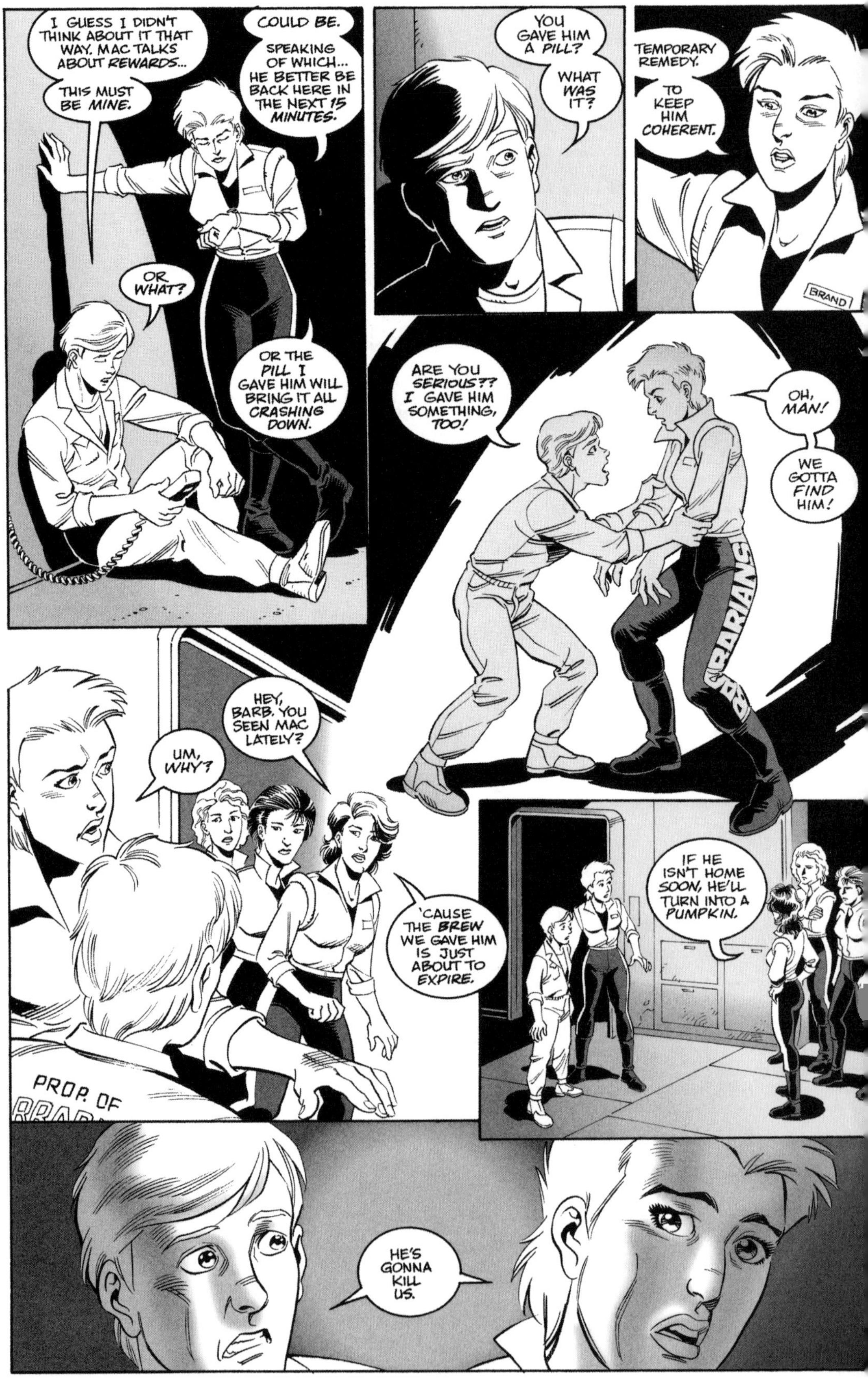
I GUESS I DIDN'T THINK ABOUT IT THAT WAY. MAC TALKS ABOUT REWARDS...
THIS MUST BE MINE.
COULD BE.
SPEAKING OF WHICH... HE BETTER BE BACK HERE IN THE NEXT 15 MINUTES.
OR WHAT?
OR THE PILL I GAVE HIM WILL BRING IT ALL CRASHING DOWN.
YOU GAVE HIM A PILL?
WHAT WAS IT?
TEMPORARY REMEDY.
TO KEEP HIM COHERENT.
BRAND
ARE YOU SERIOUS?? I GAVE HIM SOMETHING, TOO!
OH, MAN!
WE GOTTA FIND HIM!
BARBARIANS
HEY, BARB. YOU SEEN MAC LATELY?
UM, WHY?
'CAUSE THE BREW WE GAVE HIM IS JUST ABOUT TO EXPIRE.
IF HE ISN'T HOME SOON, HE'LL TURN INTO A PUMPKIN.
PROP. OF
HE'S GONNA KILL US.

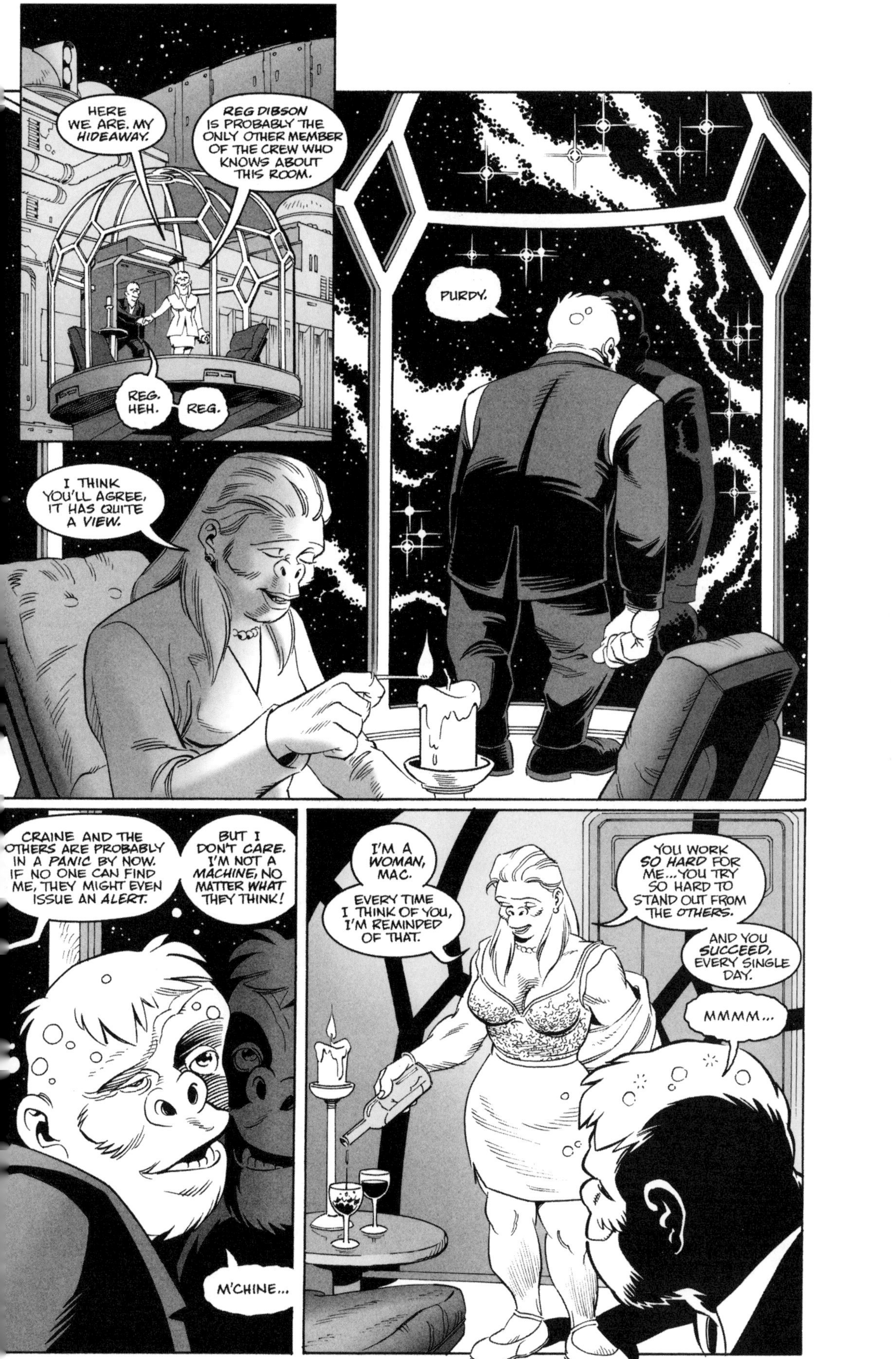
HERE WE ARE. MY *HIDEAWAY.*
REG DIBSON IS PROBABLY THE ONLY OTHER MEMBER OF THE CREW WHO KNOWS ABOUT THIS ROOM.
REG. HEH.
REG.
PURDY.
I THINK YOU'LL AGREE, IT HAS QUITE A *VIEW.*
CRAINE AND THE OTHERS ARE PROBABLY IN A *PANIC* BY NOW. IF NO ONE CAN FIND ME, THEY MIGHT EVEN ISSUE AN *ALERT.*
BUT I DON'T *CARE.* I'M NOT A *MACHINE,* NO MATTER *WHAT* THEY THINK!
M'CHINE...
I'M A *WOMAN,* MAC.
EVERY TIME I THINK OF YOU, I'M REMINDED OF THAT.
YOU WORK *SO HARD* FOR ME... YOU TRY SO HARD TO STAND OUT FROM THE *OTHERS.*
AND YOU *SUCCEED,* EVERY SINGLE DAY.
MMMM...

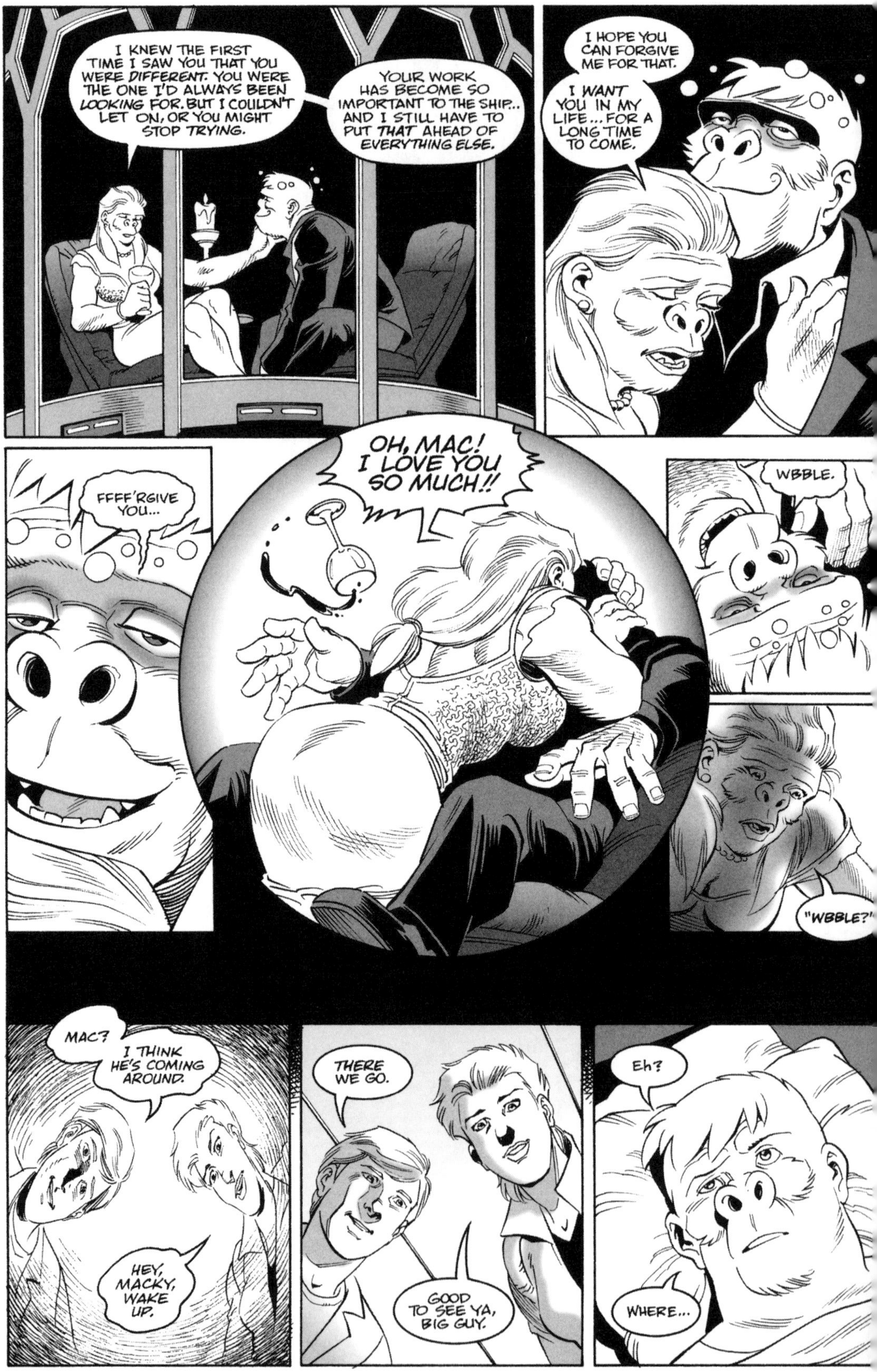

I KNEW THE FIRST TIME I SAW YOU THAT YOU WERE *DIFFERENT*. YOU WERE THE ONE I'D ALWAYS BEEN *LOOKING* FOR. BUT I COULDN'T LET ON, OR YOU MIGHT STOP *TRYING*.
YOUR WORK HAS BECOME SO IMPORTANT TO THE SHIP... AND I STILL HAVE TO PUT *THAT* AHEAD OF EVERYTHING ELSE.
I HOPE YOU CAN FORGIVE ME FOR THAT.
I *WANT* YOU IN MY LIFE... FOR A LONG TIME TO COME.
FFFF'RGIVE YOU...
OH, MAC! I LOVE YOU SO MUCH!!
WBBLE.
"WBBLE?"
MAC?
I THINK HE'S COMING AROUND.
HEY, MACKY, WAKE UP.
THERE WE GO.
GOOD TO SEE YA, BIG GUY.
Eh?
WHERE...

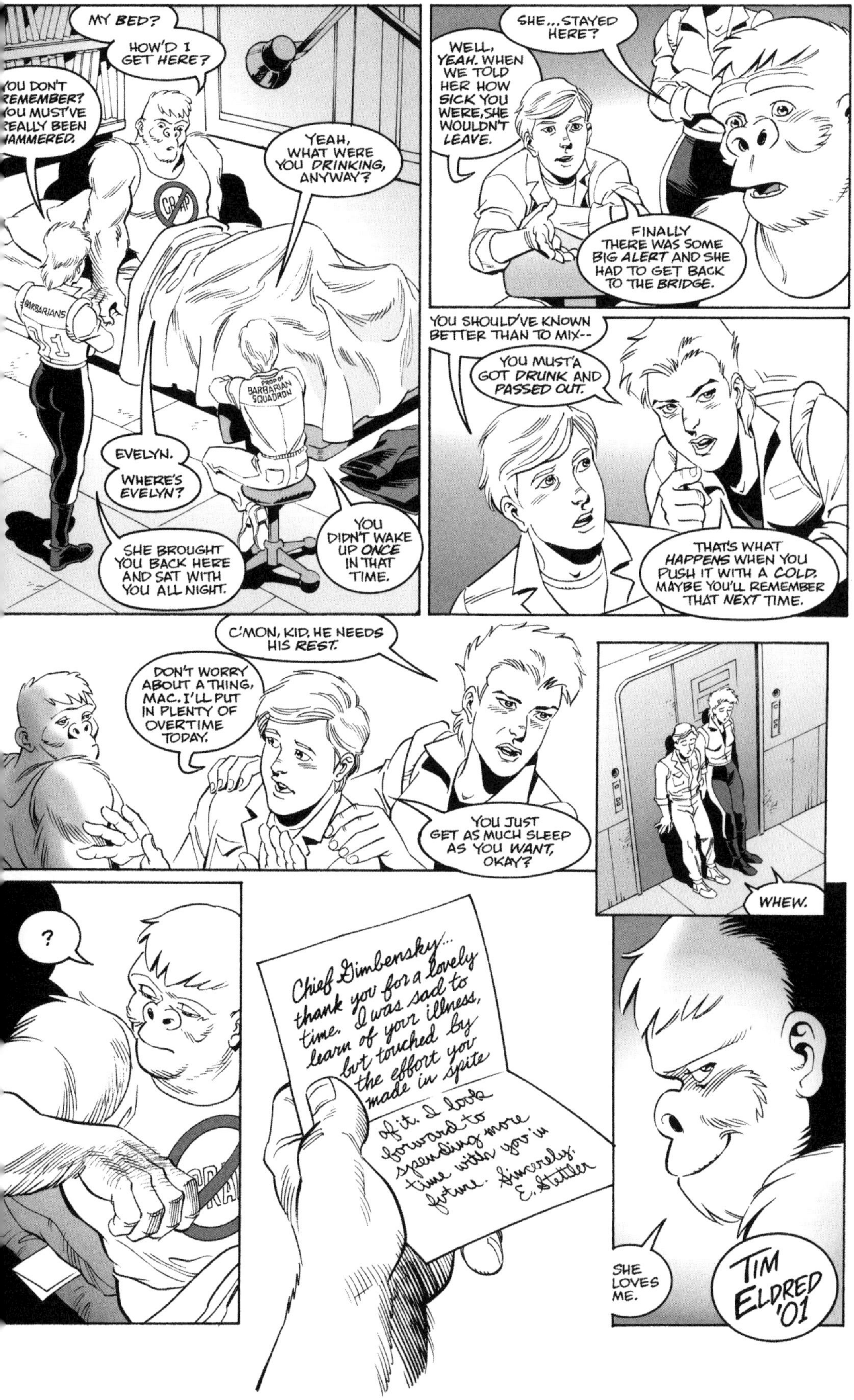
MY BED?
HOW'D I GET HERE?
YOU DON'T REMEMBER? YOU MUST'VE REALLY BEEN HAMMERED.
YEAH, WHAT WERE YOU DRINKING, ANYWAY?
BARBARIANS
PROP OF BARBARIAN SQUADRON
EVELYN.
WHERE'S EVELYN?
SHE BROUGHT YOU BACK HERE AND SAT WITH YOU ALL NIGHT.
YOU DIDN'T WAKE UP ONCE IN THAT TIME.
SHE...STAYED HERE?
WELL, YEAH. WHEN WE TOLD HER HOW SICK YOU WERE, SHE WOULDN'T LEAVE.
FINALLY THERE WAS SOME BIG ALERT AND SHE HAD TO GET BACK TO THE BRIDGE.
YOU SHOULD'VE KNOWN BETTER THAN TO MIX--
YOU MUST'A GOT DRUNK AND PASSED OUT.
THAT'S WHAT HAPPENS WHEN YOU PUSH IT WITH A COLD. MAYBE YOU'LL REMEMBER THAT NEXT TIME.
C'MON, KID, HE NEEDS HIS REST.
DON'T WORRY ABOUT A THING, MAC. I'LL PUT IN PLENTY OF OVERTIME TODAY.
YOU JUST GET AS MUCH SLEEP AS YOU WANT, OKAY?
WHEW.
?
Chief Gimbensky... thank you for a lovely time. I was sad to learn of your illness, but touched by the effort you made in spite of it. I look forward to spending more time with you in future. Sincerely, E. Stettler
SHE LOVES ME.
TIM ELDRED '01

BAY M LAYOUT

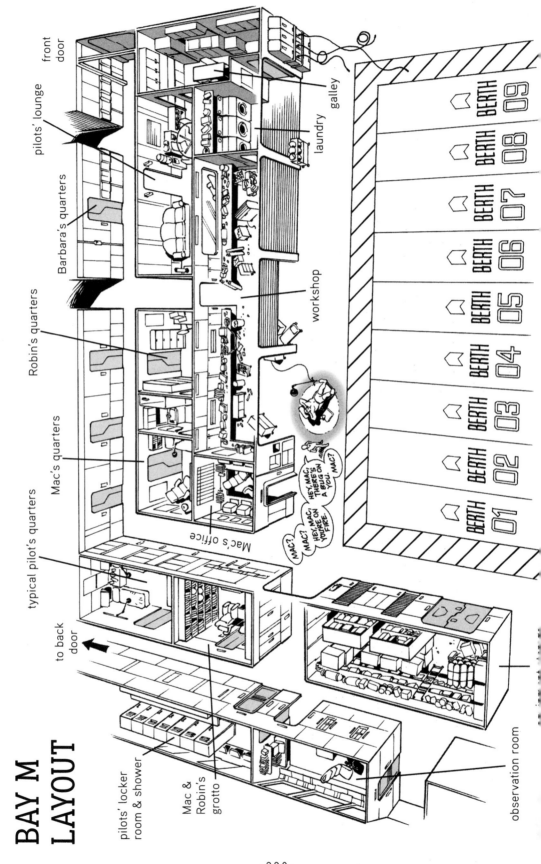

front door

pilots' lounge

Barbara's quarters

Robin's quarters

Mac's quarters

typical pilot's quarters

to back door

pilots' locker room & shower

Mac & Robin's grotto

galley

laundry

workshop

Mac's office

observation room

MAC?

MAC? HEY, MAC, YOU'RE ON FIRE.

HEY, MAC, THERE'S A BUG ON YOU.

MAC?

BERTH 01

BERTH 02

BERTH 03

BERTH 04

BERTH 05

BERTH 06

BERTH 07

BERTH 08

BERTH 09

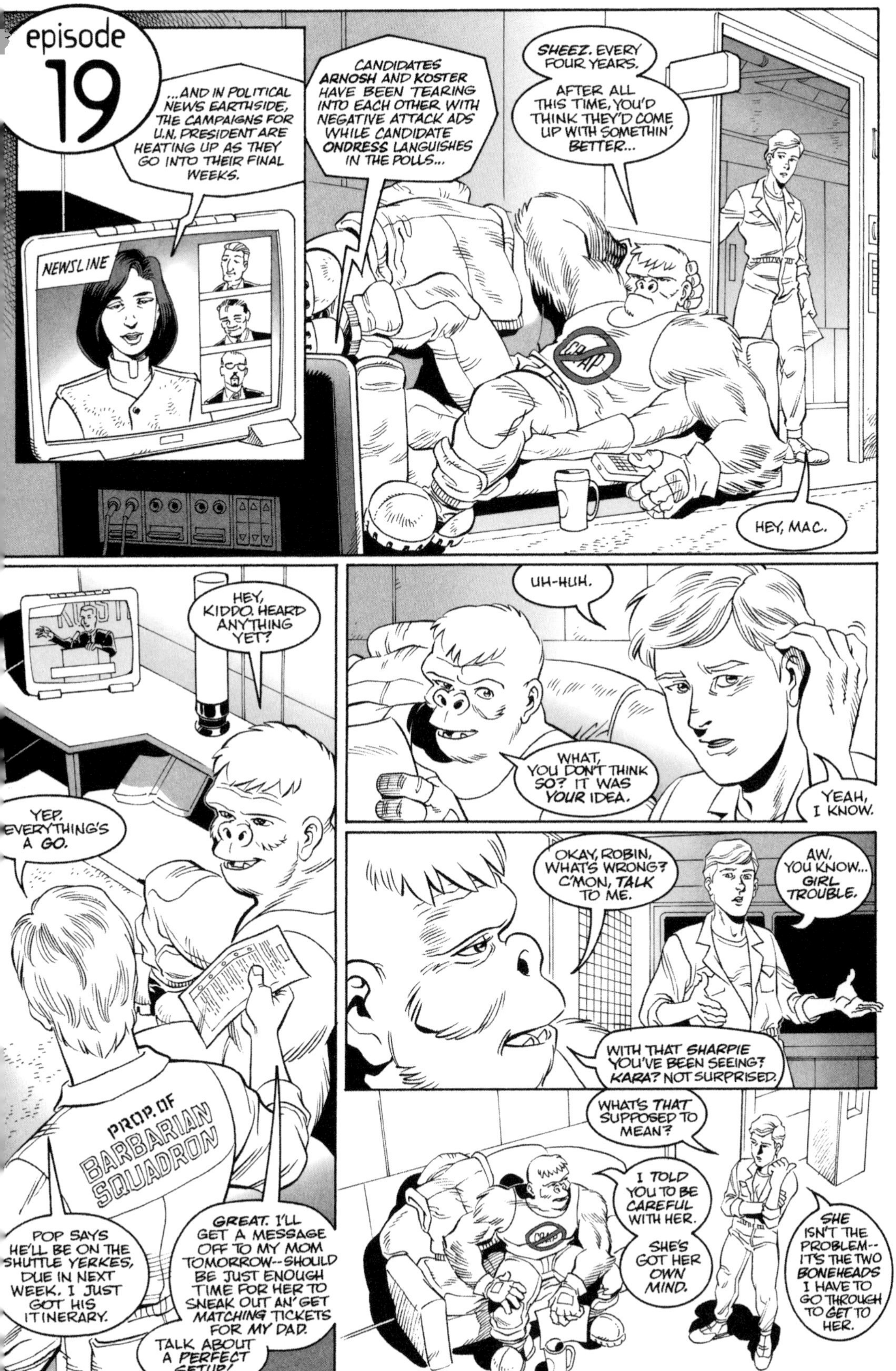
episode 19
...AND IN POLITICAL NEWS EARTHSIDE, THE CAMPAIGNS FOR U.N. PRESIDENT ARE HEATING UP AS THEY GO INTO THEIR FINAL WEEKS.
NEWSLINE
CANDIDATES ARNOSH AND KOSTER HAVE BEEN TEARING INTO EACH OTHER WITH NEGATIVE ATTACK ADS WHILE CANDIDATE ONDRESS LANGUISHES IN THE POLLS...
SHEEZ. EVERY FOUR YEARS.
AFTER ALL THIS TIME, YOU'D THINK THEY'D COME UP WITH SOMETHIN' BETTER...
HEY, MAC.
HEY, KIDDO. HEARD ANYTHING YET?
YEP. EVERYTHING'S A GO.
PROP. OF BARBARIAN SQUADRON
POP SAYS HE'LL BE ON THE SHUTTLE YERKES, DUE IN NEXT WEEK. I JUST GOT HIS ITINERARY.
GREAT. I'LL GET A MESSAGE OFF TO MY MOM TOMORROW--SHOULD BE JUST ENOUGH TIME FOR HER TO SNEAK OUT AN' GET MATCHING TICKETS FOR MY DAD.
TALK ABOUT A PERFECT SETUP!
UH-HUH.
WHAT, YOU DON'T THINK SO? IT WAS YOUR IDEA.
YEAH, I KNOW.
OKAY, ROBIN, WHAT'S WRONG? C'MON, TALK TO ME.
AW, YOU KNOW... GIRL TROUBLE.
WITH THAT SHARPIE YOU'VE BEEN SEEING? KARA? NOT SURPRISED.
WHAT'S THAT SUPPOSED TO MEAN?
I TOLD YOU TO BE CAREFUL WITH HER.
SHE'S GOT HER OWN MIND.
SHE ISN'T THE PROBLEM--IT'S THE TWO BONEHEADS I HAVE TO GO THROUGH TO GET TO HER.

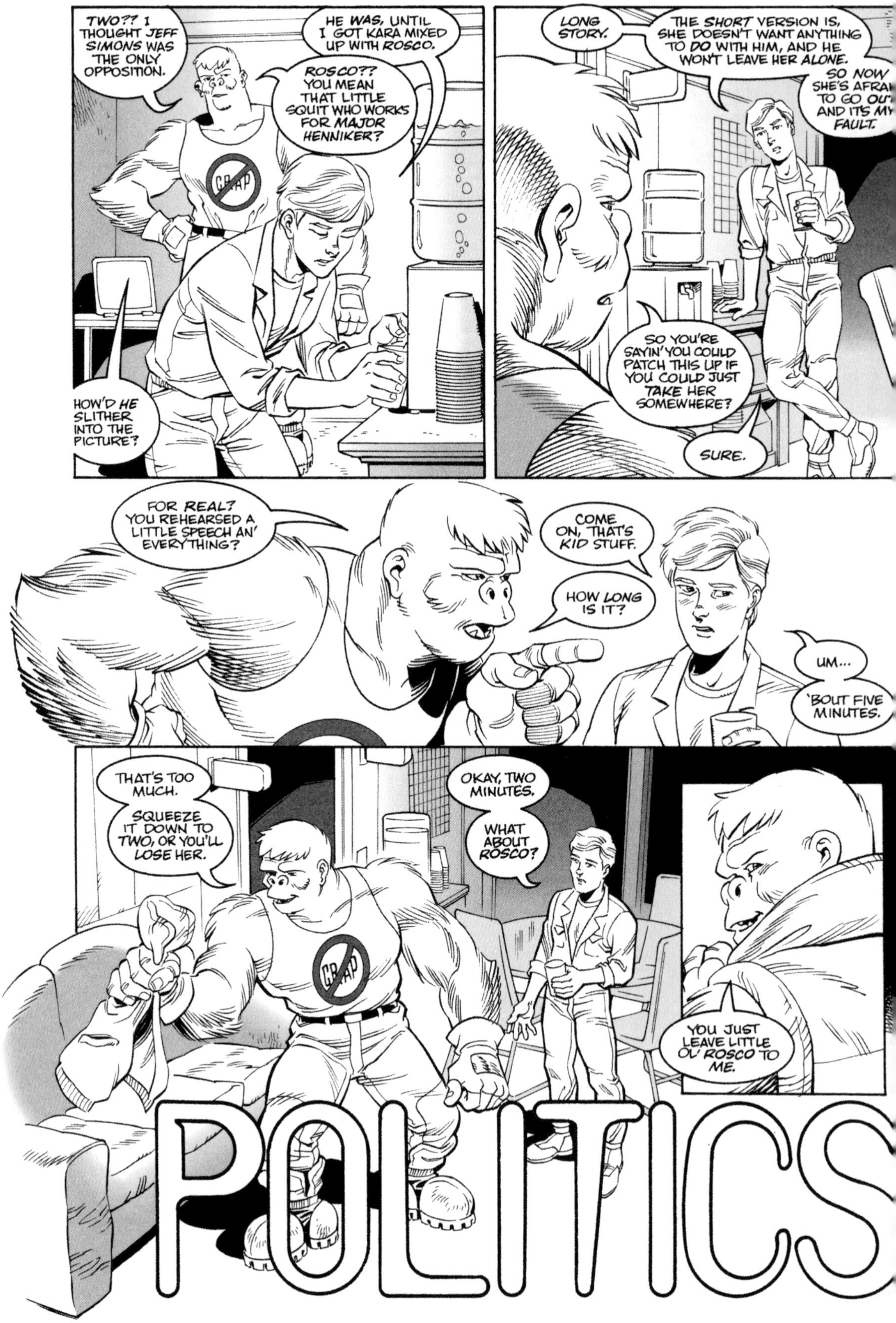

TWO?? I THOUGHT JEFF SIMONS WAS THE ONLY OPPOSITION.
HE WAS, UNTIL I GOT KARA MIXED UP WITH ROSCO.
ROSCO?? YOU MEAN THAT LITTLE SQUIT WHO WORKS FOR MAJOR HENNIKER?
HOW'D HE SLITHER INTO THE PICTURE?
LONG STORY.
THE SHORT VERSION IS, SHE DOESN'T WANT ANYTHING TO DO WITH HIM, AND HE WON'T LEAVE HER ALONE.
SO NOW SHE'S AFRAI TO GO OU AND IT'S MY FAULT.
SO YOU'RE SAYIN' YOU COULD PATCH THIS UP IF YOU COULD JUST TAKE HER SOMEWHERE?
SURE.
FOR REAL? YOU REHEARSED A LITTLE SPEECH AN' EVERYTHING?
COME ON, THAT'S KID STUFF.
HOW LONG IS IT?
UM...
'BOUT FIVE MINUTES.
THAT'S TOO MUCH.
SQUEEZE IT DOWN TO TWO, OR YOU'LL LOSE HER.
OKAY, TWO MINUTES.
WHAT ABOUT ROSCO?
YOU JUST LEAVE LITTLE OL' ROSCO TO ME.
POLITICS

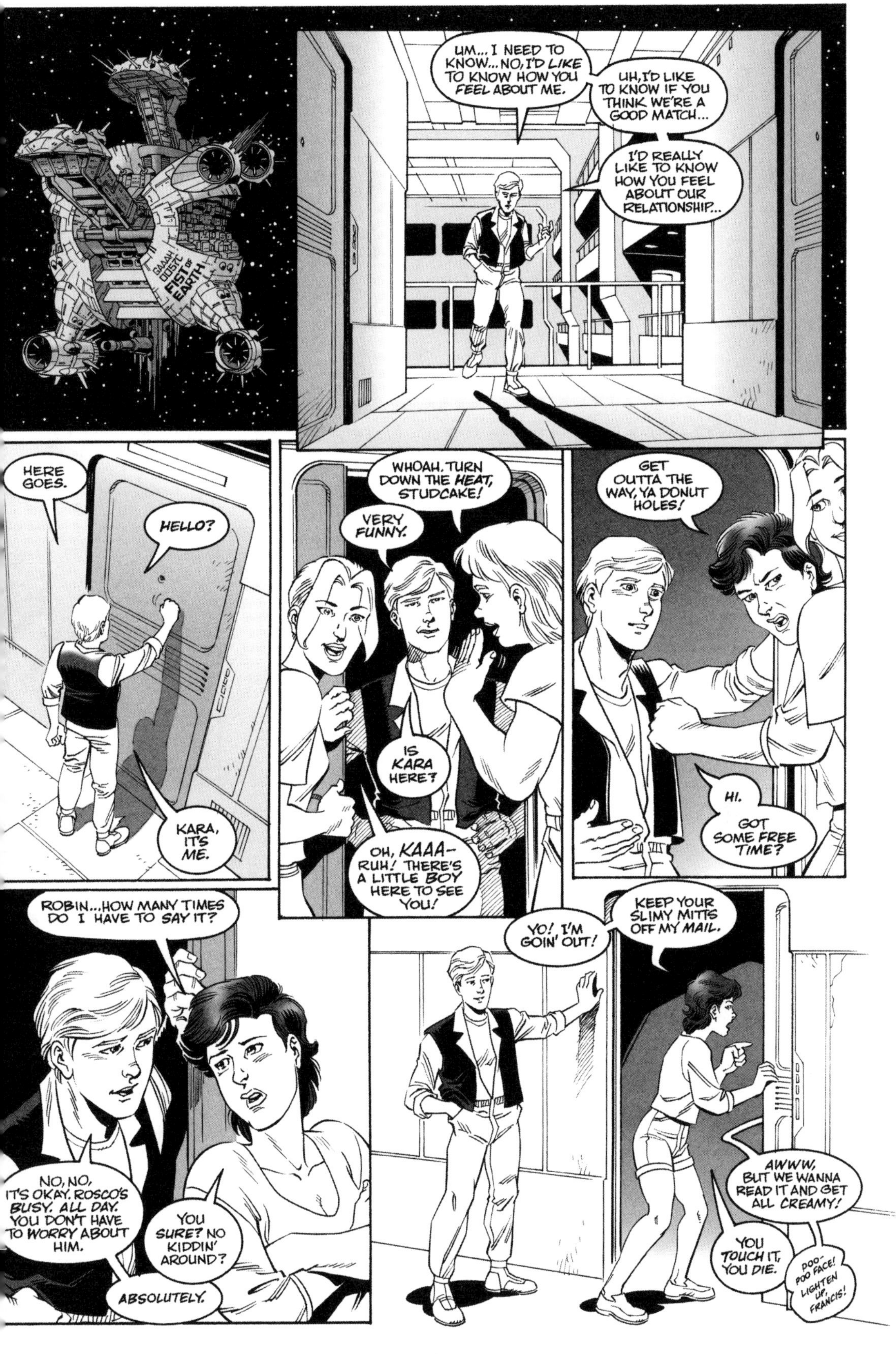
GAAAH! OOSTC FIST OF EARTH
UM... I NEED TO KNOW... NO, I'D LIKE TO KNOW HOW YOU FEEL ABOUT ME.
UH, I'D LIKE TO KNOW IF YOU THINK WE'RE A GOOD MATCH...
I'D REALLY LIKE TO KNOW HOW YOU FEEL ABOUT OUR RELATIONSHIP...
HERE GOES.
HELLO?
KARA, IT'S ME.
WHOAH. TURN DOWN THE HEAT, STUDCAKE!
VERY FUNNY.
IS KARA HERE?
OH, KAAA-RUH! THERE'S A LITTLE BOY HERE TO SEE YOU!
GET OUTTA THE WAY, YA DONUT HOLES!
HI.
GOT SOME FREE TIME?
ROBIN...HOW MANY TIMES DO I HAVE TO SAY IT?
NO, NO, IT'S OKAY. ROSCO'S BUSY. ALL DAY. YOU DON'T HAVE TO WORRY ABOUT HIM.
YOU SURE? NO KIDDIN' AROUND?
ABSOLUTELY.
YO! I'M GOIN' OUT!
KEEP YOUR SLIMY MITTS OFF MY MAIL.
AWWW, BUT WE WANNA READ IT AND GET ALL CREAMY!
YOU TOUCH IT, YOU DIE.
POO-POO FACE! LIGHTEN UP, FRANCIS!

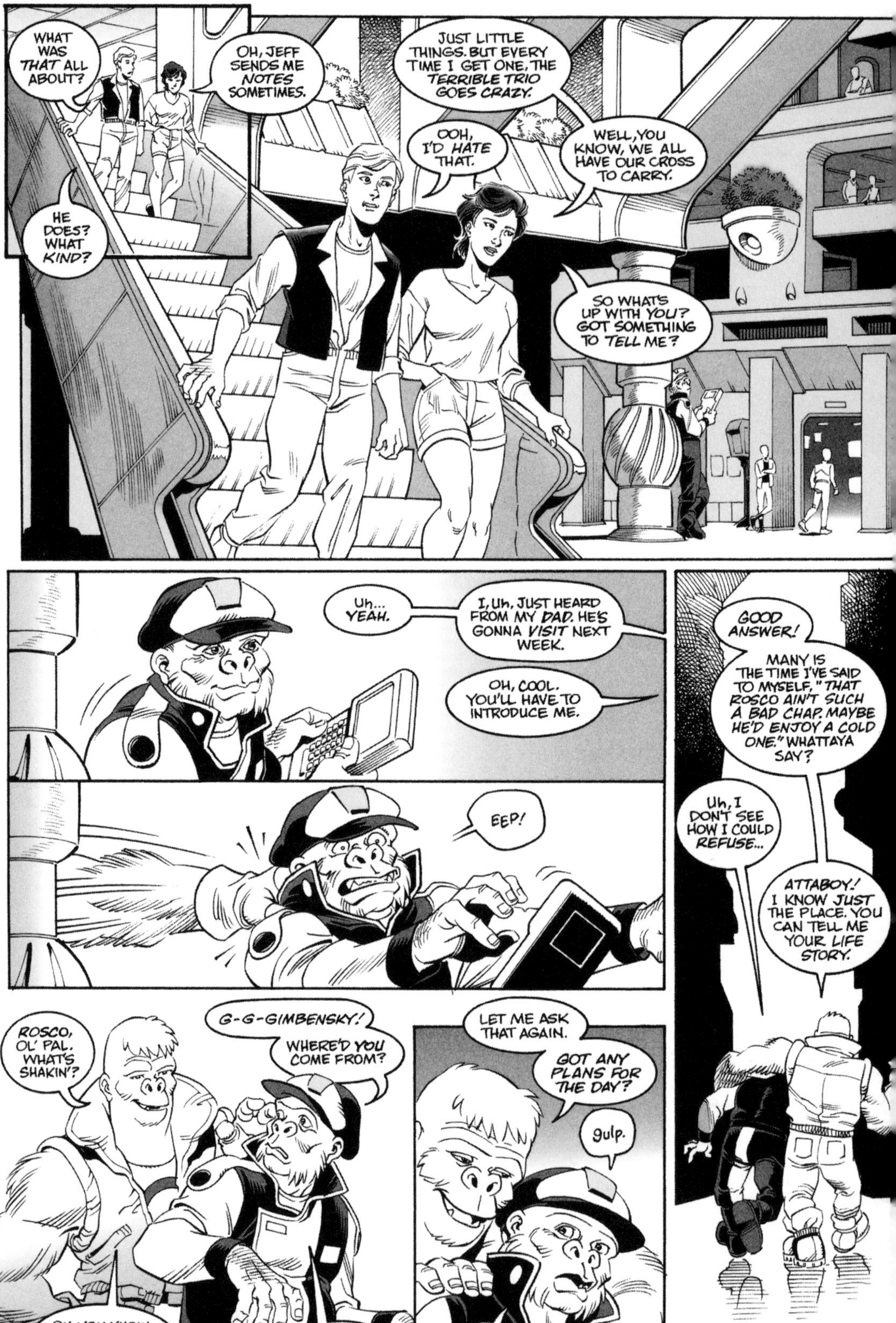
WHAT WAS THAT ALL ABOUT?
OH, JEFF SENDS ME NOTES SOMETIMES.
HE DOES? WHAT KIND?
JUST LITTLE THINGS. BUT EVERY TIME I GET ONE, THE TERRIBLE TRIO GOES CRAZY.
OOH, I'D HATE THAT.
WELL, YOU KNOW, WE ALL HAVE OUR CROSS TO CARRY.
SO WHAT'S UP WITH YOU? GOT SOMETHING TO TELL ME?
Uh... YEAH.
I, Uh, JUST HEARD FROM MY DAD. HE'S GONNA VISIT NEXT WEEK.
OH, COOL. YOU'LL HAVE TO INTRODUCE ME.
EEP!
ROSCO, OL' PAL. WHAT'S SHAKIN'?
G-G-GIMBENSKY!
WHERE'D YOU COME FROM?
OH, YOU KNOW ME. BAD PENNY. GOT ANY PLANS FOR THE DAY?
ACTUALLY, YES, I WAS ABOUT TO--
LET ME ASK THAT AGAIN.
GOT ANY PLANS FOR THE DAY?
gulp.
NOPE, TOTALLY FREE.
GOOD ANSWER!
MANY IS THE TIME I'VE SAID TO MYSELF, "THAT ROSCO AIN'T SUCH A BAD CHAP. MAYBE HE'D ENJOY A COLD ONE." WHATTAYA SAY?
Uh, I DON'T SEE HOW I COULD REFUSE...
ATTABOY! I KNOW JUST THE PLACE. YOU CAN TELL ME YOUR LIFE STORY.

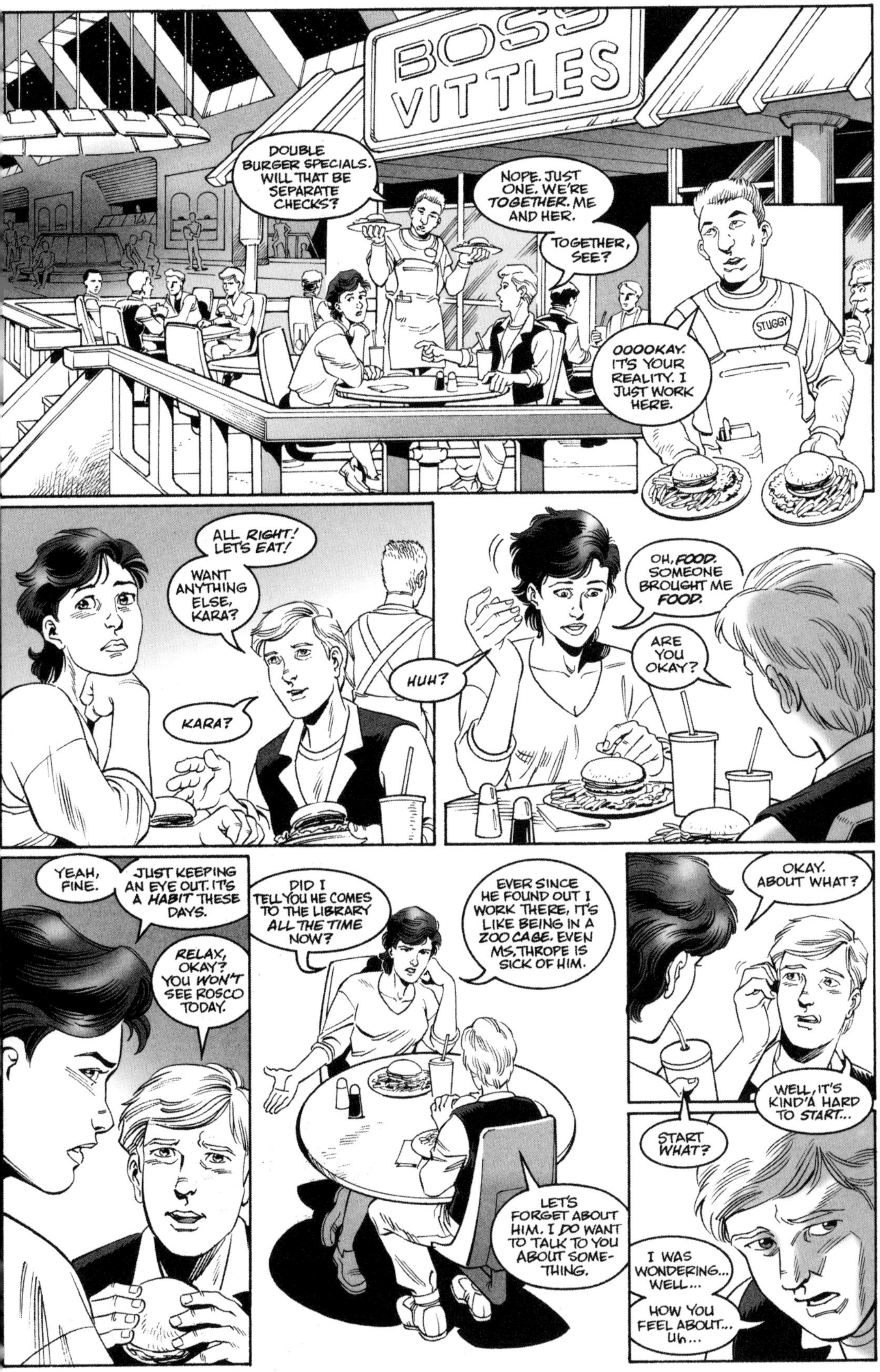
BOSS VITTLES
DOUBLE BURGER SPECIALS. WILL THAT BE SEPARATE CHECKS?
NOPE. JUST ONE. WE'RE TOGETHER. ME AND HER.
TOGETHER, SEE?
OOOOKAY. IT'S YOUR REALITY. I JUST WORK HERE.
STUGGY
ALL RIGHT! LET'S EAT!
WANT ANYTHING ELSE, KARA?
KARA?
HUH?
OH, FOOD. SOMEONE BROUGHT ME FOOD.
ARE YOU OKAY?
YEAH, FINE.
JUST KEEPING AN EYE OUT. IT'S A HABIT THESE DAYS.
RELAX, OKAY? YOU WON'T SEE ROSCO TODAY.
DID I TELL YOU HE COMES TO THE LIBRARY ALL THE TIME NOW?
EVER SINCE HE FOUND OUT I WORK THERE, IT'S LIKE BEING IN A ZOO CAGE. EVEN MS. THROPE IS SICK OF HIM.
LET'S FORGET ABOUT HIM. I DO WANT TO TALK TO YOU ABOUT SOME-THING.
OKAY. ABOUT WHAT?
WELL, IT'S KIND'A HARD TO START...
START WHAT?
I WAS WONDERING... WELL...
HOW YOU FEEL ABOUT... Uh...

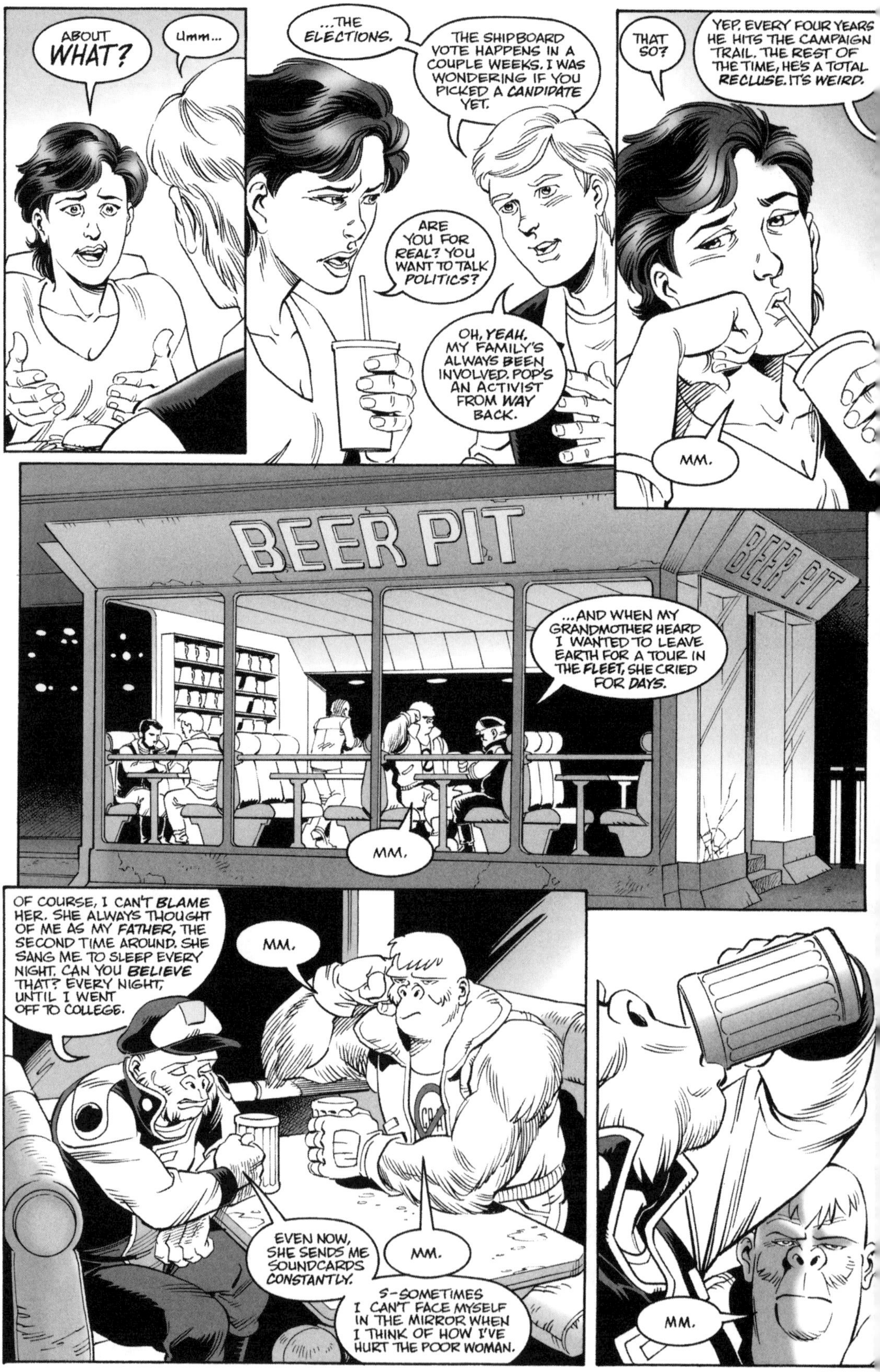
ABOUT WHAT?
Umm...
...THE ELECTIONS.
THE SHIPBOARD VOTE HAPPENS IN A COUPLE WEEKS. I WAS WONDERING IF YOU PICKED A CANDIDATE YET.
ARE YOU FOR REAL? YOU WANT TO TALK POLITICS?
OH, YEAH. MY FAMILY'S ALWAYS BEEN INVOLVED. POP'S AN ACTIVIST FROM WAY BACK.
THAT SO?
YEP, EVERY FOUR YEARS HE HITS THE CAMPAIGN TRAIL. THE REST OF THE TIME, HE'S A TOTAL RECLUSE. IT'S WEIRD.
MM.
BEER PIT
BEER PIT
...AND WHEN MY GRANDMOTHER HEARD I WANTED TO LEAVE EARTH FOR A TOUR IN THE FLEET, SHE CRIED FOR DAYS.
MM.
OF COURSE, I CAN'T BLAME HER. SHE ALWAYS THOUGHT OF ME AS MY FATHER, THE SECOND TIME AROUND. SHE SANG ME TO SLEEP EVERY NIGHT. CAN YOU BELIEVE THAT? EVERY NIGHT, UNTIL I WENT OFF TO COLLEGE.
MM.
EVEN NOW, SHE SENDS ME SOUNDCARDS CONSTANTLY.
MM.
S-SOMETIMES I CAN'T FACE MYSELF IN THE MIRROR WHEN I THINK OF HOW I'VE HURT THE POOR WOMAN.
MM.

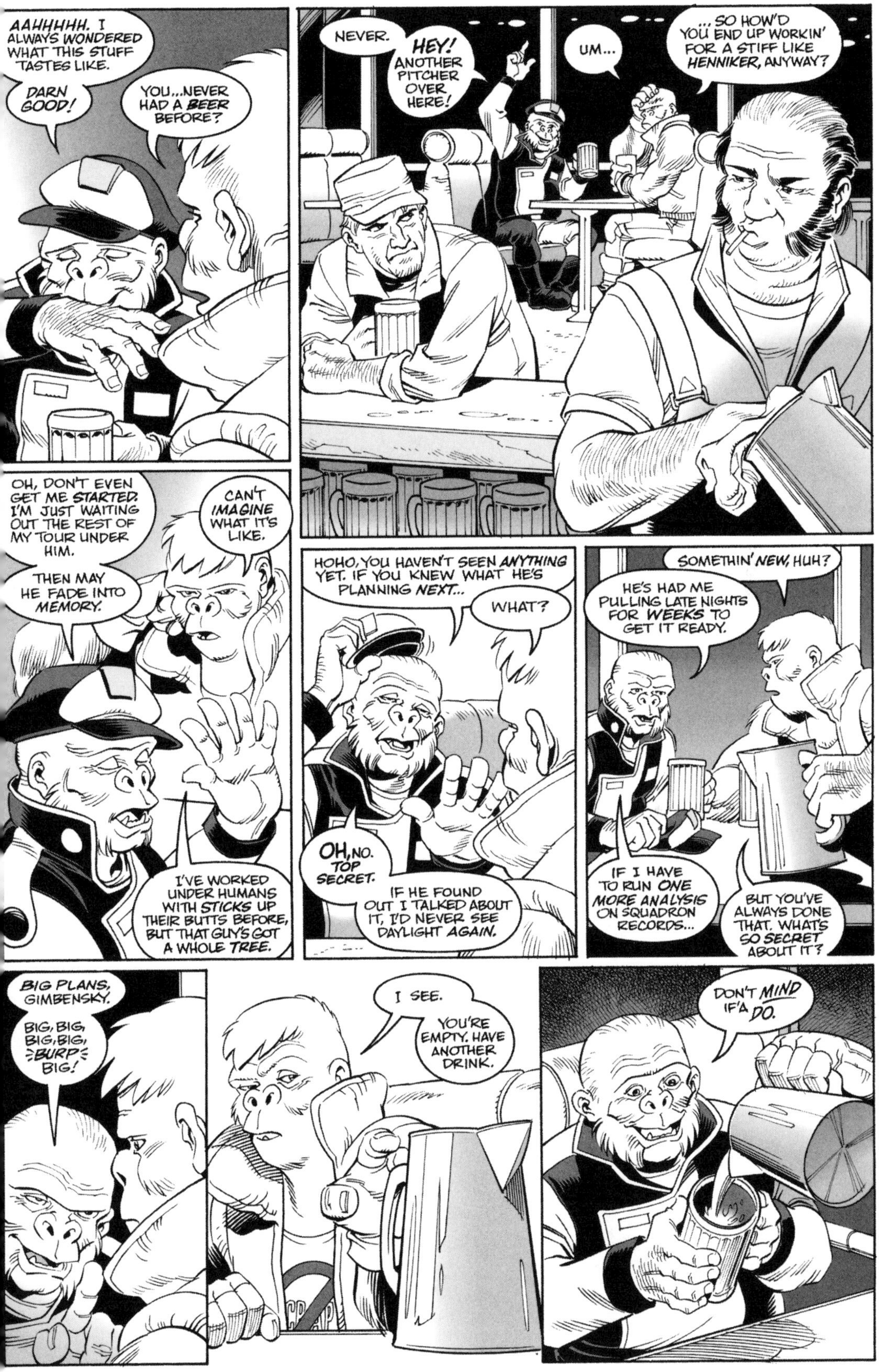
AAHHHHH. I ALWAYS WONDERED WHAT THIS STUFF TASTES LIKE.
DARN GOOD!
YOU...NEVER HAD A BEER BEFORE?
NEVER.
HEY! ANOTHER PITCHER OVER HERE!
UM...
...SO HOW'D YOU END UP WORKIN' FOR A STIFF LIKE HENNIKER, ANYWAY?
OH, DON'T EVEN GET ME STARTED. I'M JUST WAITING OUT THE REST OF MY TOUR UNDER HIM.
CAN'T IMAGINE WHAT IT'S LIKE.
THEN MAY HE FADE INTO MEMORY.
I'VE WORKED UNDER HUMANS WITH STICKS UP THEIR BUTTS BEFORE, BUT THAT GUY'S GOT A WHOLE TREE.
HOHO, YOU HAVEN'T SEEN ANYTHING YET. IF YOU KNEW WHAT HE'S PLANNING NEXT...
WHAT?
OH, NO. TOP SECRET.
IF HE FOUND OUT I TALKED ABOUT IT, I'D NEVER SEE DAYLIGHT AGAIN.
SOMETHIN' NEW, HUH?
HE'S HAD ME PULLING LATE NIGHTS FOR WEEKS TO GET IT READY.
IF I HAVE TO RUN ONE MORE ANALYSIS ON SQUADRON RECORDS...
BUT YOU'VE ALWAYS DONE THAT. WHAT'S SO SECRET ABOUT IT?
BIG PLANS, GIMBENSKY.
BIG, BIG, BIG, BIG, BURP BIG!
I SEE.
YOU'RE EMPTY. HAVE ANOTHER DRINK.
DON'T MIND IF A DO.

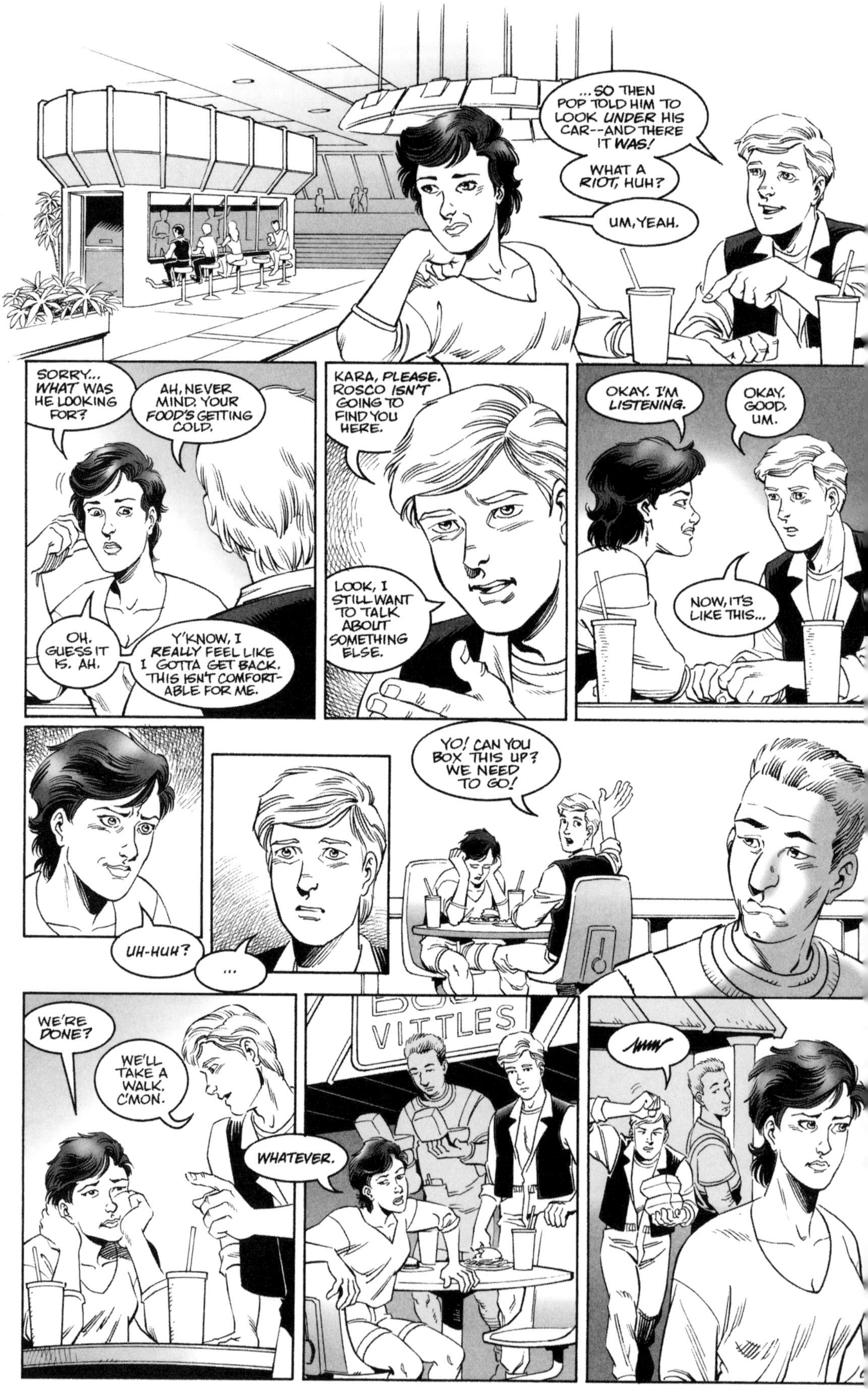
...SO THEN POP TOLD HIM TO LOOK UNDER HIS CAR--AND THERE IT WAS!
WHAT A RIOT, HUH?
UM, YEAH.
SORRY... WHAT WAS HE LOOKING FOR?
AH, NEVER MIND. YOUR FOOD'S GETTING COLD.
OH. GUESS IT IS. AH.
Y'KNOW, I REALLY FEEL LIKE I GOTTA GET BACK. THIS ISN'T COMFORTABLE FOR ME.
KARA, PLEASE. ROSCO ISN'T GOING TO FIND YOU HERE.
LOOK, I STILL WANT TO TALK ABOUT SOMETHING ELSE.
OKAY. I'M LISTENING.
OKAY. GOOD. UM.
NOW, IT'S LIKE THIS...
UH-HUH?
...
YO! CAN YOU BOX THIS UP? WE NEED TO GO!
WE'RE DONE?
WE'LL TAKE A WALK. C'MON.
WHATEVER.
VITTLES

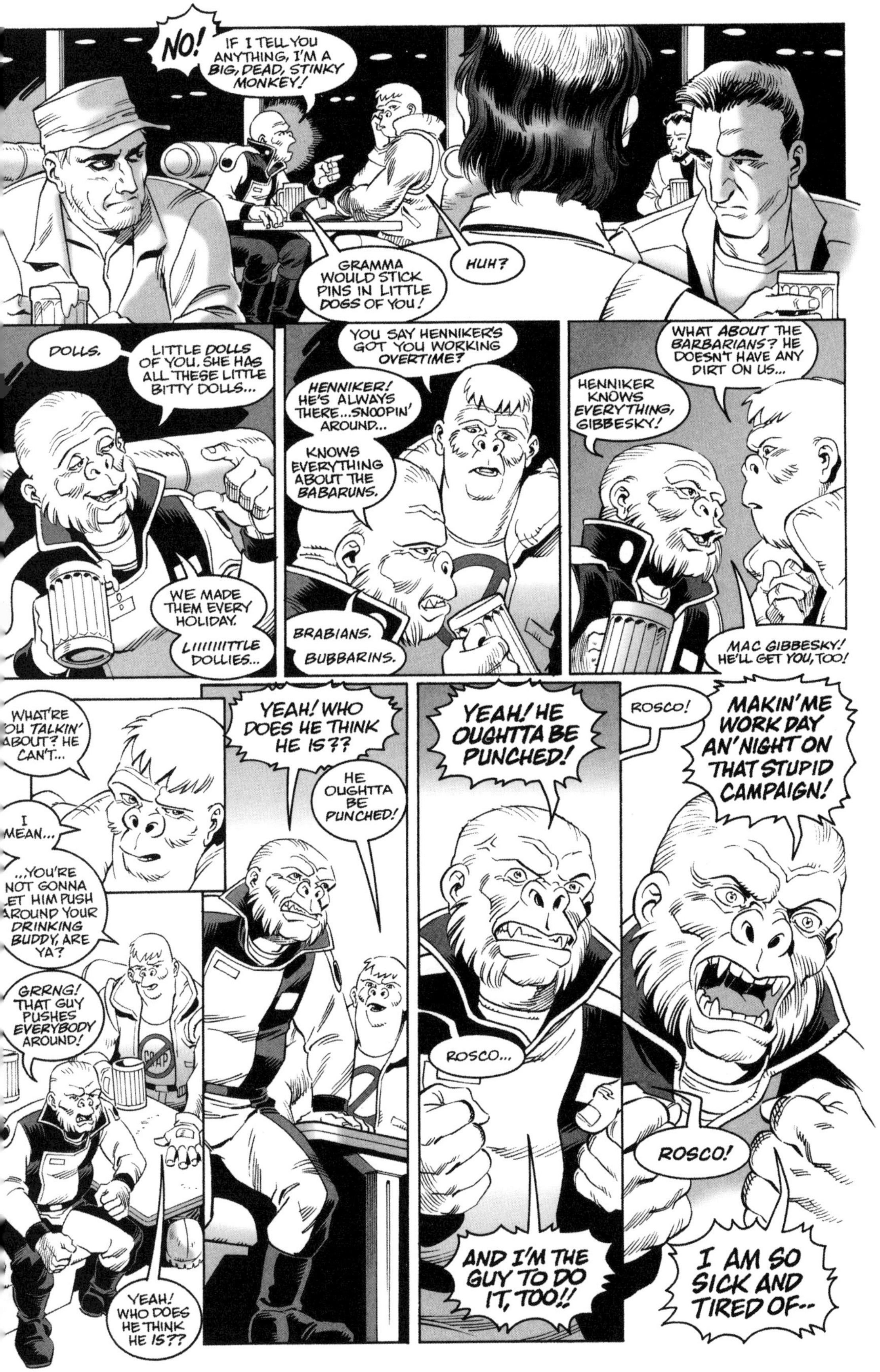
NO!
IF I TELL YOU ANYTHING, I'M A BIG, DEAD, STINKY MONKEY!
GRAMMA WOULD STICK PINS IN LITTLE DOGS OF YOU!
HUH?
DOLLS.
LITTLE DOLLS OF YOU. SHE HAS ALL THESE LITTLE BITTY DOLLS...
WE MADE THEM EVERY HOLIDAY.
LIIIIIIITTLE DOLLIES...
YOU SAY HENNIKER'S GOT YOU WORKING OVERTIME?
HENNIKER! HE'S ALWAYS THERE...SNOOPIN' AROUND...
KNOWS EVERYTHING ABOUT THE BABARUNS.
BRABIANS.
BUBBARINS.
WHAT ABOUT THE BARBARIANS? HE DOESN'T HAVE ANY DIRT ON US...
HENNIKER KNOWS EVERYTHING, GIBBESKY!
MAC GIBBESKY! HE'LL GET YOU, TOO!
WHAT'RE YOU TALKIN' ABOUT? HE CAN'T...
I MEAN...
...YOU'RE NOT GONNA LET HIM PUSH AROUND YOUR DRINKING BUDDY, ARE YA?
GRRNG! THAT GUY PUSHES EVERYBODY AROUND!
YEAH! WHO DOES HE THINK HE IS??
YEAH! WHO DOES HE THINK HE IS??
HE OUGHTTA BE PUNCHED!
YEAH! HE OUGHTTA BE PUNCHED!
ROSCO...
AND I'M THE GUY TO DO IT, TOO!!
ROSCO!
MAKIN' ME WORK DAY AN' NIGHT ON THAT STUPID CAMPAIGN!
ROSCO!
I AM SO SICK AND TIRED OF--

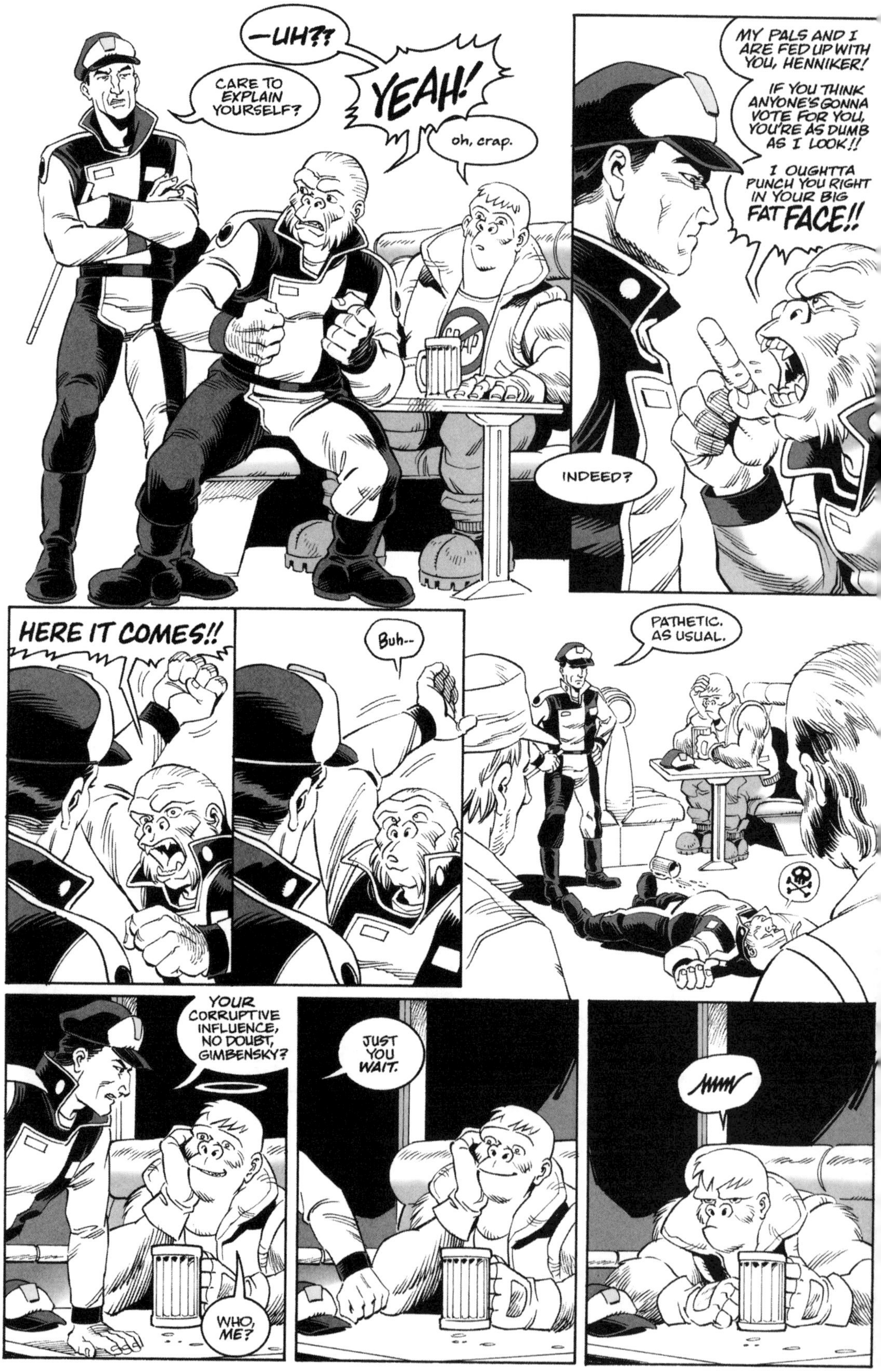
CARE TO EXPLAIN YOURSELF?
—UH??
YEAH!
oh, crap.
MY PALS AND I ARE FED UP WITH YOU, HENNIKER!
IF YOU THINK ANYONE'S GONNA VOTE FOR YOU, YOU'RE AS DUMB AS I LOOK!!
I OUGHTTA PUNCH YOU RIGHT IN YOUR BIG FAT FACE!!
INDEED?
HERE IT COMES!!
Buh--
PATHETIC. AS USUAL.
YOUR CORRUPTIVE INFLUENCE, NO DOUBT, GIMBENSKY?
WHO, ME?
JUST YOU WAIT.

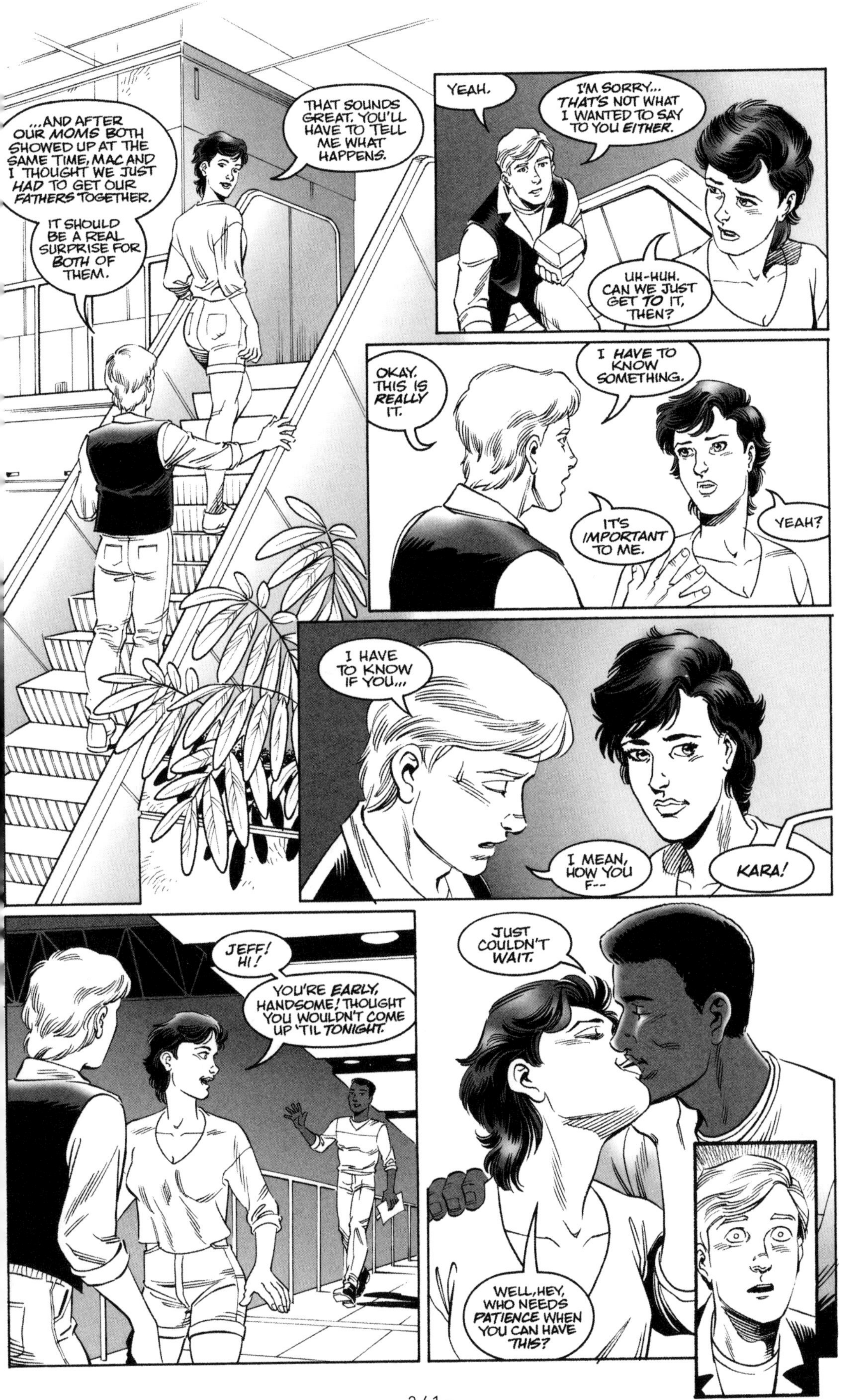
...AND AFTER OUR MOMS BOTH SHOWED UP AT THE SAME TIME, MAC AND I THOUGHT WE JUST HAD TO GET OUR FATHERS TOGETHER.
IT SHOULD BE A REAL SURPRISE FOR BOTH OF THEM.
THAT SOUNDS GREAT. YOU'LL HAVE TO TELL ME WHAT HAPPENS.
YEAH.
I'M SORRY... THAT'S NOT WHAT I WANTED TO SAY TO YOU EITHER.
UH-HUH. CAN WE JUST GET TO IT, THEN?
OKAY. THIS IS REALLY IT.
I HAVE TO KNOW SOMETHING.
YEAH?
IT'S IMPORTANT TO ME.
I HAVE TO KNOW IF YOU...
I MEAN, HOW YOU F--
KARA!
JEFF! HI!
YOU'RE EARLY, HANDSOME! THOUGHT YOU WOULDN'T COME UP 'TIL TONIGHT.
JUST COULDN'T WAIT.
WELL, HEY, WHO NEEDS PATIENCE WHEN YOU CAN HAVE THIS?

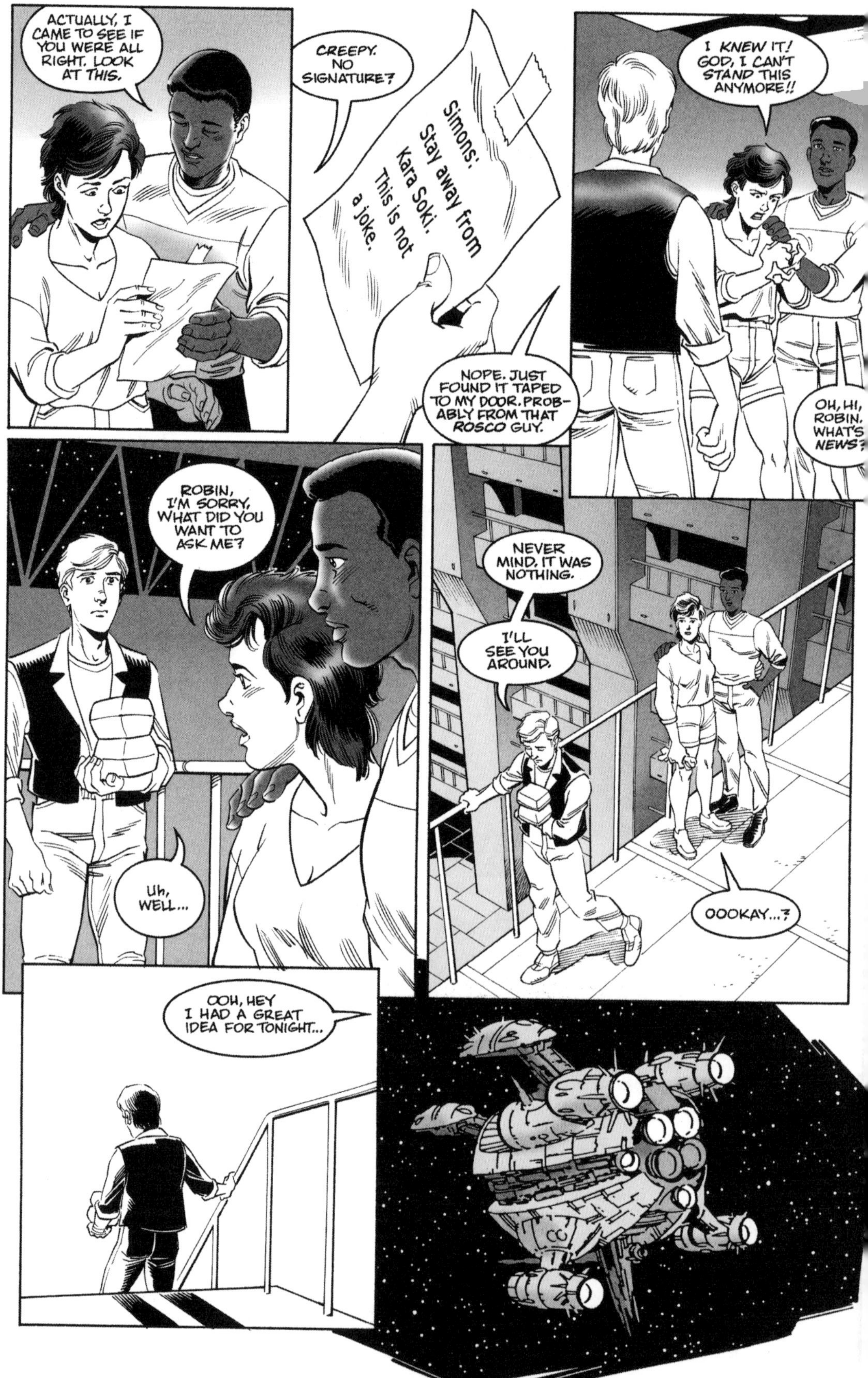
ACTUALLY, I CAME TO SEE IF YOU WERE ALL RIGHT. LOOK AT THIS.
CREEPY. NO SIGNATURE?
Simons: Stay away from Kara Soki. This is not a joke.
NOPE. JUST FOUND IT TAPED TO MY DOOR. PROBABLY FROM THAT ROSCO GUY.
I KNEW IT! GOD, I CAN'T STAND THIS ANYMORE!!
OH, HI, ROBIN. WHAT'S NEWS?
ROBIN, I'M SORRY, WHAT DID YOU WANT TO ASK ME?
Uh, WELL...
NEVER MIND. IT WAS NOTHING.
I'LL SEE YOU AROUND.
OOOKAY...?
OOH, HEY I HAD A GREAT IDEA FOR TONIGHT...

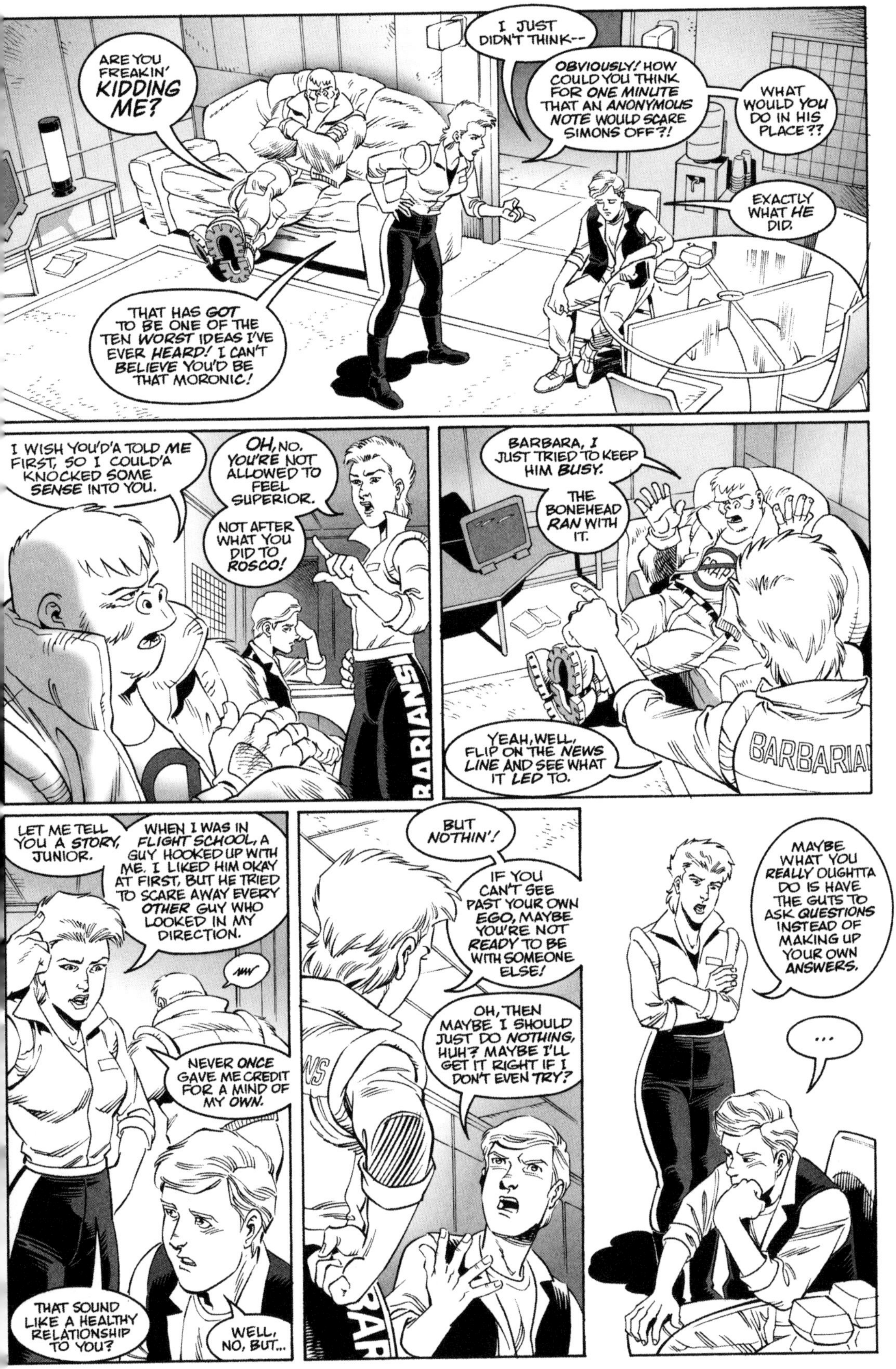
ARE YOU FREAKIN' KIDDING ME?
I JUST DIDN'T THINK--
OBVIOUSLY! HOW COULD YOU THINK FOR ONE MINUTE THAT AN ANONYMOUS NOTE WOULD SCARE SIMONS OFF?!
WHAT WOULD YOU DO IN HIS PLACE??
EXACTLY WHAT HE DID.
THAT HAS GOT TO BE ONE OF THE TEN WORST IDEAS I'VE EVER HEARD! I CAN'T BELIEVE YOU'D BE THAT MORONIC!
I WISH YOU'D'A TOLD ME FIRST, SO I COULD'A KNOCKED SOME SENSE INTO YOU.
OH, NO. YOU'RE NOT ALLOWED TO FEEL SUPERIOR.
NOT AFTER WHAT YOU DID TO ROSCO!
BARBARIANS
BARBARA, I JUST TRIED TO KEEP HIM BUSY.
THE BONEHEAD RAN WITH IT.
YEAH, WELL, FLIP ON THE NEWS LINE AND SEE WHAT IT LED TO.
BARBARIAI
LET ME TELL YOU A STORY, JUNIOR.
WHEN I WAS IN FLIGHT SCHOOL, A GUY HOOKED UP WITH ME. I LIKED HIM OKAY AT FIRST, BUT HE TRIED TO SCARE AWAY EVERY OTHER GUY WHO LOOKED IN MY DIRECTION.
NEVER ONCE GAVE ME CREDIT FOR A MIND OF MY OWN.
THAT SOUND LIKE A HEALTHY RELATIONSHIP TO YOU?
WELL, NO, BUT...
BUT NOTHIN'!
IF YOU CAN'T SEE PAST YOUR OWN EGO, MAYBE YOU'RE NOT READY TO BE WITH SOMEONE ELSE!
OH, THEN MAYBE I SHOULD JUST DO NOTHING, HUH? MAYBE I'LL GET IT RIGHT IF I DON'T EVEN TRY?
MAYBE WHAT YOU REALLY OUGHTTA DO IS HAVE THE GUTS TO ASK QUESTIONS INSTEAD OF MAKING UP YOUR OWN ANSWERS.
...

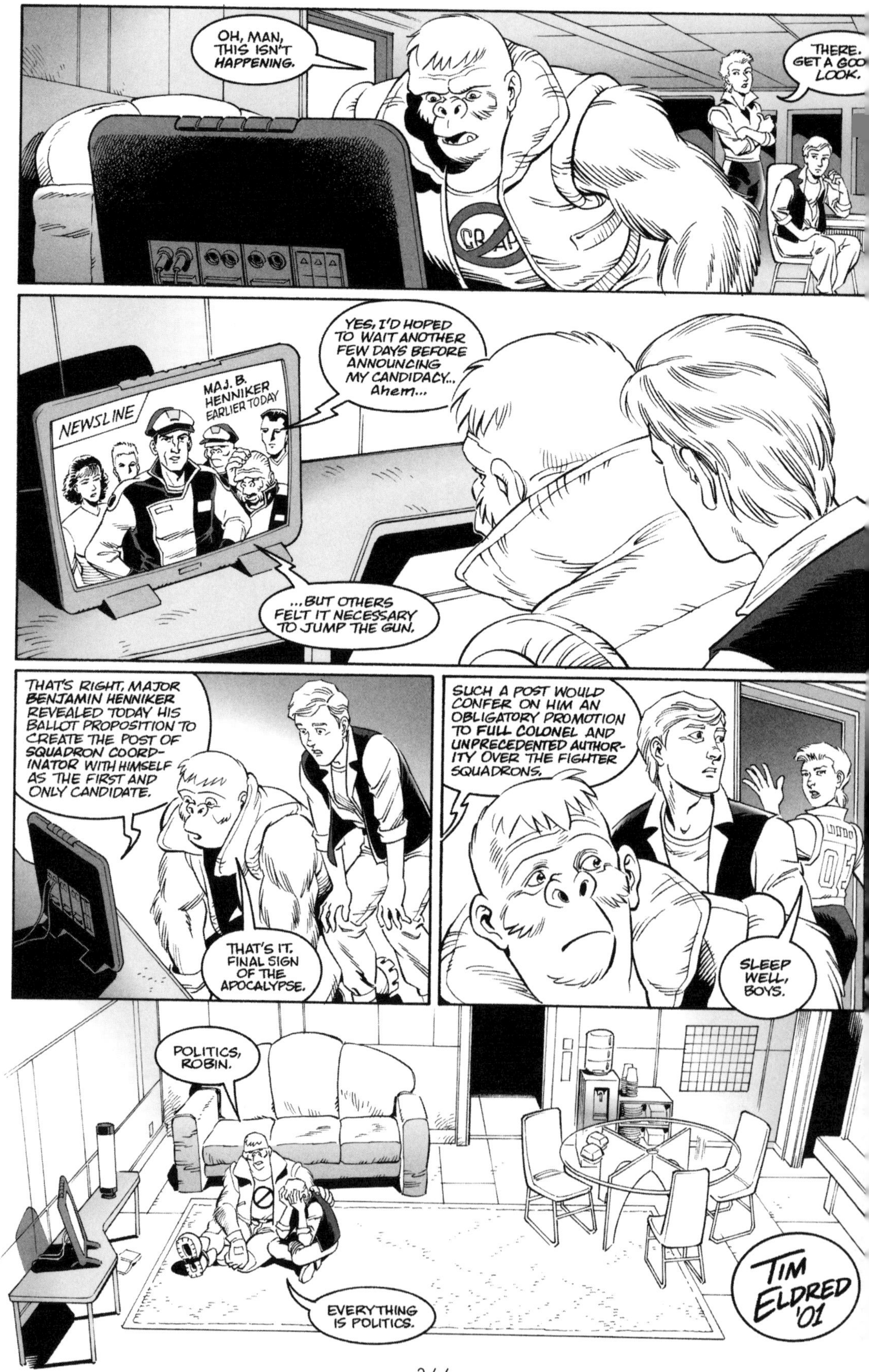
OH, MAN, THIS ISN'T HAPPENING.
THERE. GET A GOO LOOK.
YES, I'D HOPED TO WAIT ANOTHER FEW DAYS BEFORE ANNOUNCING MY CANDIDACY... Ahem...
NEWSLINE
MAJ. B. HENNIKER EARLIER TODAY
...BUT OTHERS FELT IT NECESSARY TO JUMP THE GUN.
THAT'S RIGHT, MAJOR BENJAMIN HENNIKER REVEALED TODAY HIS BALLOT PROPOSITION TO CREATE THE POST OF SQUADRON COORD-INATOR WITH HIMSELF AS THE FIRST AND ONLY CANDIDATE.
THAT'S IT. FINAL SIGN OF THE APOCALYPSE.
SUCH A POST WOULD CONFER ON HIM AN OBLIGATORY PROMOTION TO FULL COLONEL AND UNPRECEDENTED AUTHOR-ITY OVER THE FIGHTER SQUADRONS.
SLEEP WELL, BOYS.
POLITICS, ROBIN.
EVERYTHING IS POLITICS.
TIM ELDRED '01

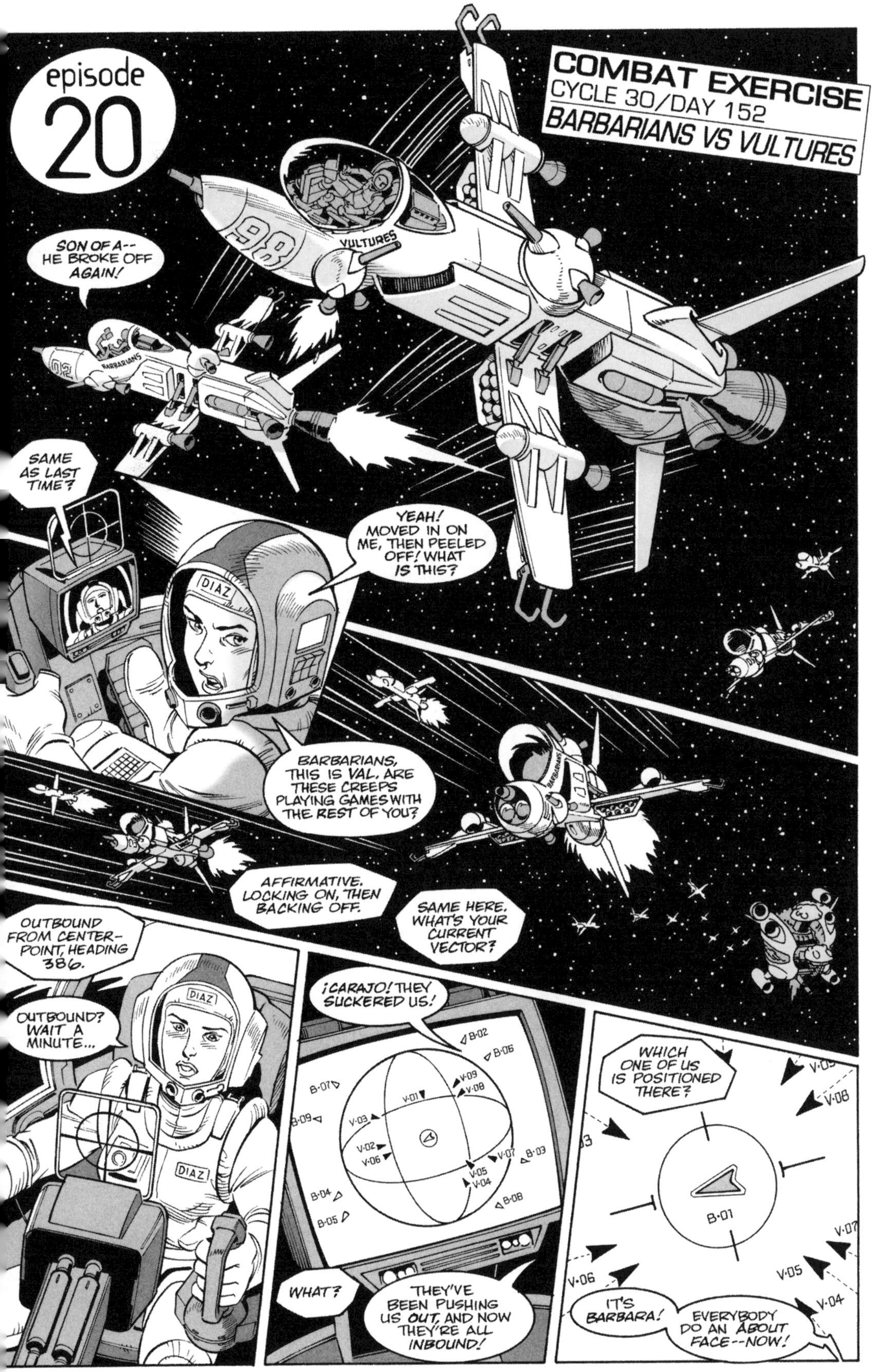
episode 20
COMBAT EXERCISE
CYCLE 30/DAY 152
BARBARIANS VS VULTURES
SON OF A-- HE BROKE OFF AGAIN!
SAME AS LAST TIME?
YEAH! MOVED IN ON ME, THEN PEELED OFF! WHAT IS THIS?
BARBARIANS, THIS IS VAL. ARE THESE CREEPS PLAYING GAMES WITH THE REST OF YOU?
AFFIRMATIVE. LOCKING ON, THEN BACKING OFF.
SAME HERE. WHAT'S YOUR CURRENT VECTOR?
OUTBOUND FROM CENTER-POINT, HEADING 386.
OUTBOUND? WAIT A MINUTE...
¡CARAJO! THEY SUCKERED US!
WHAT?
THEY'VE BEEN PUSHING US OUT, AND NOW THEY'RE ALL INBOUND!
WHICH ONE OF US IS POSITIONED THERE?
IT'S BARBARA!
EVERYBODY DO AN ABOUT FACE--NOW!

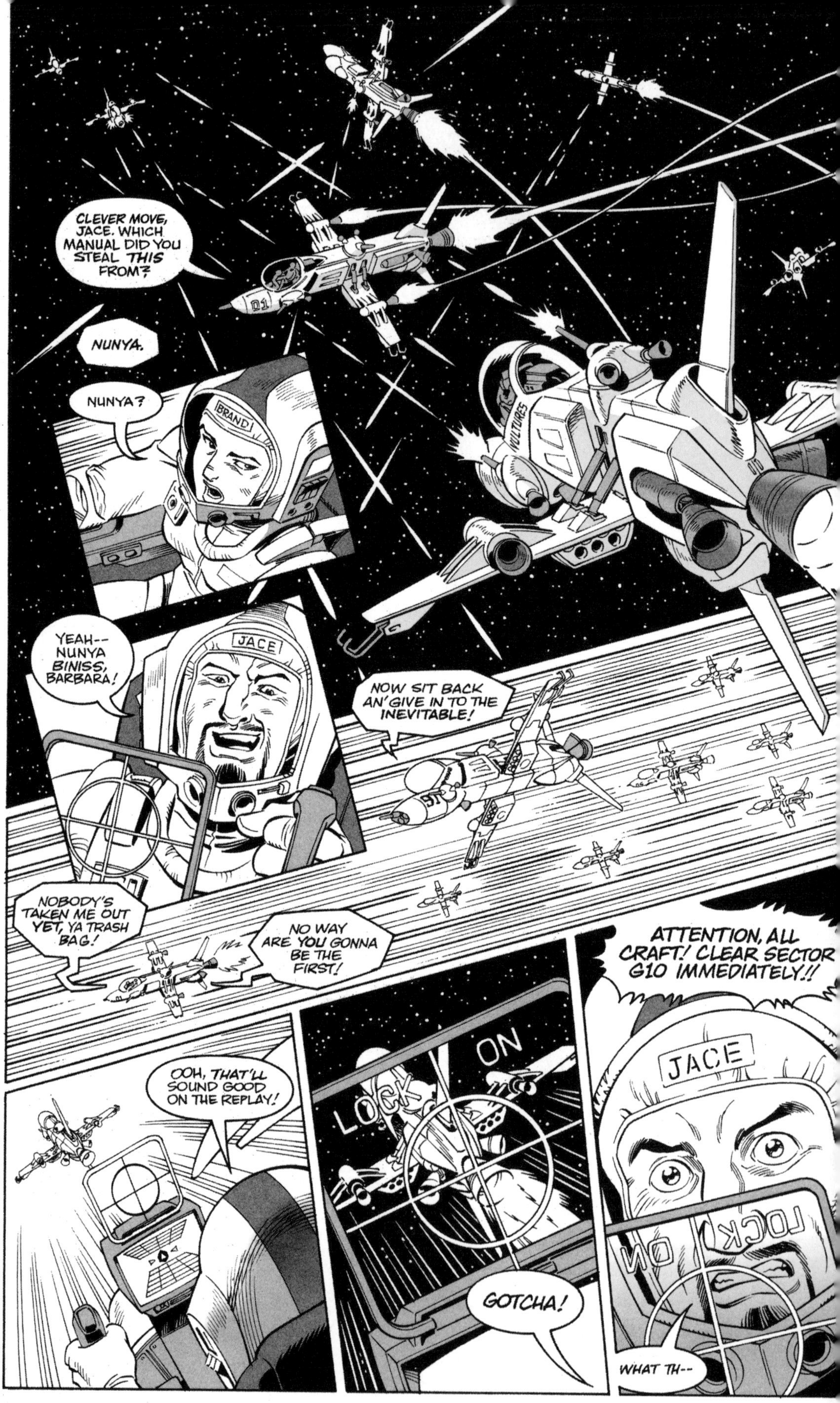
CLEVER MOVE, JACE. WHICH MANUAL DID YOU STEAL THIS FROM?
NUNYA.
NUNYA?
BRAND
YEAH-- NUNYA BINISS, BARBARA!
JACE
NOW SIT BACK AN' GIVE IN TO THE INEVITABLE!
NOBODY'S TAKEN ME OUT YET, YA TRASH BAG!
NO WAY ARE YOU GONNA BE THE FIRST!
ATTENTION, ALL CRAFT! CLEAR SECTOR G10 IMMEDIATELY!!
OOH, THAT'LL SOUND GOOD ON THE REPLAY!
LOCK ON
GOTCHA!
JACE
WHAT TH--

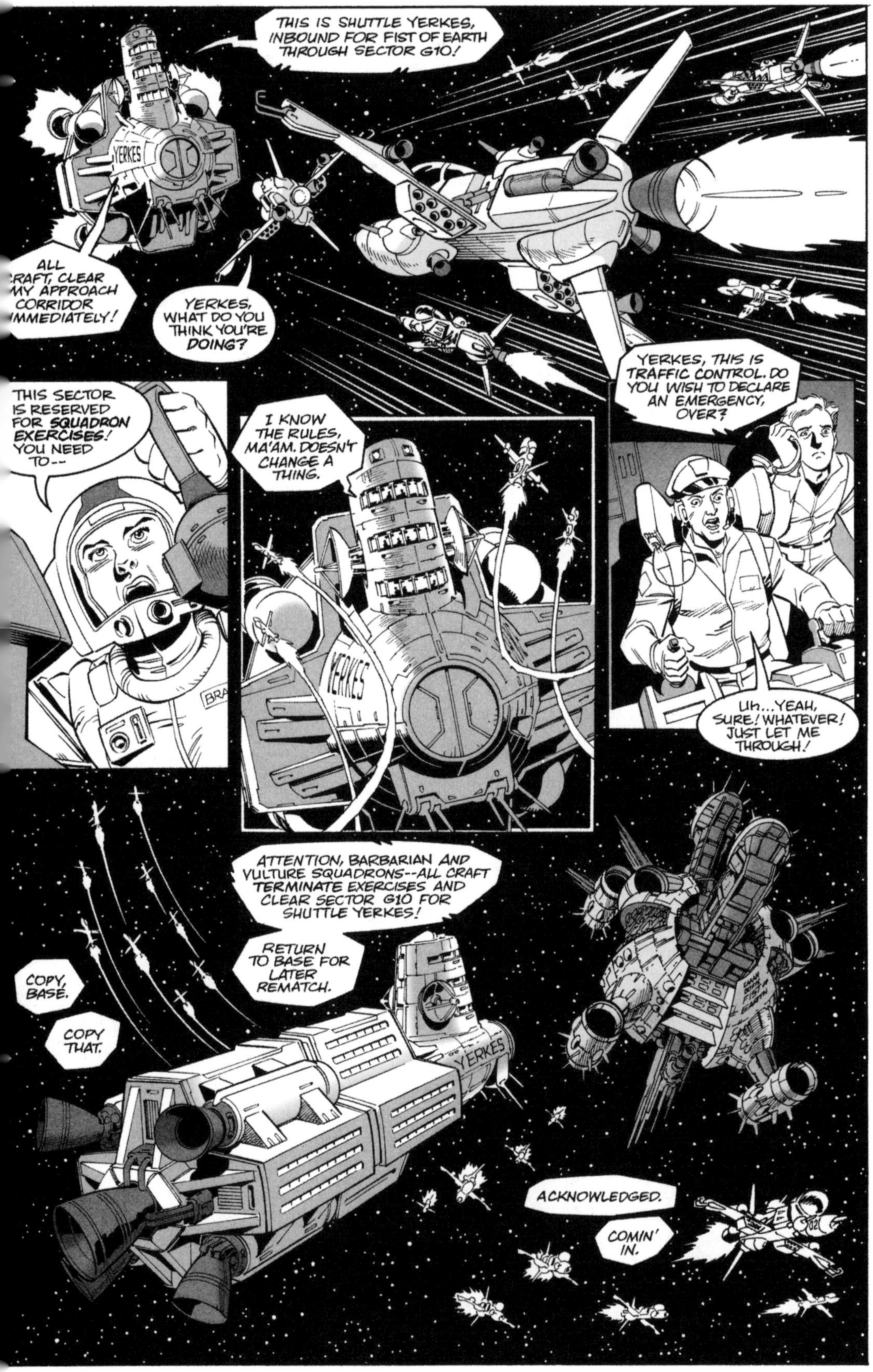
THIS IS SHUTTLE YERKES, INBOUND FOR FIST OF EARTH THROUGH SECTOR G10!
ALL CRAFT, CLEAR MY APPROACH CORRIDOR IMMEDIATELY!
YERKES, WHAT DO YOU THINK YOU'RE DOING?
YERKES, THIS IS TRAFFIC CONTROL. DO YOU WISH TO DECLARE AN EMERGENCY, OVER?
THIS SECTOR IS RESERVED FOR SQUADRON EXERCISES! YOU NEED TO--
I KNOW THE RULES, MA'AM. DOESN'T CHANGE A THING.
UH... YEAH, SURE! WHATEVER! JUST LET ME THROUGH!
ATTENTION, BARBARIAN AND VULTURE SQUADRONS--ALL CRAFT TERMINATE EXERCISES AND CLEAR SECTOR G10 FOR SHUTTLE YERKES!
RETURN TO BASE FOR LATER REMATCH.
COPY, BASE.
COPY THAT.
ACKNOWLEDGED.
COMIN' IN.

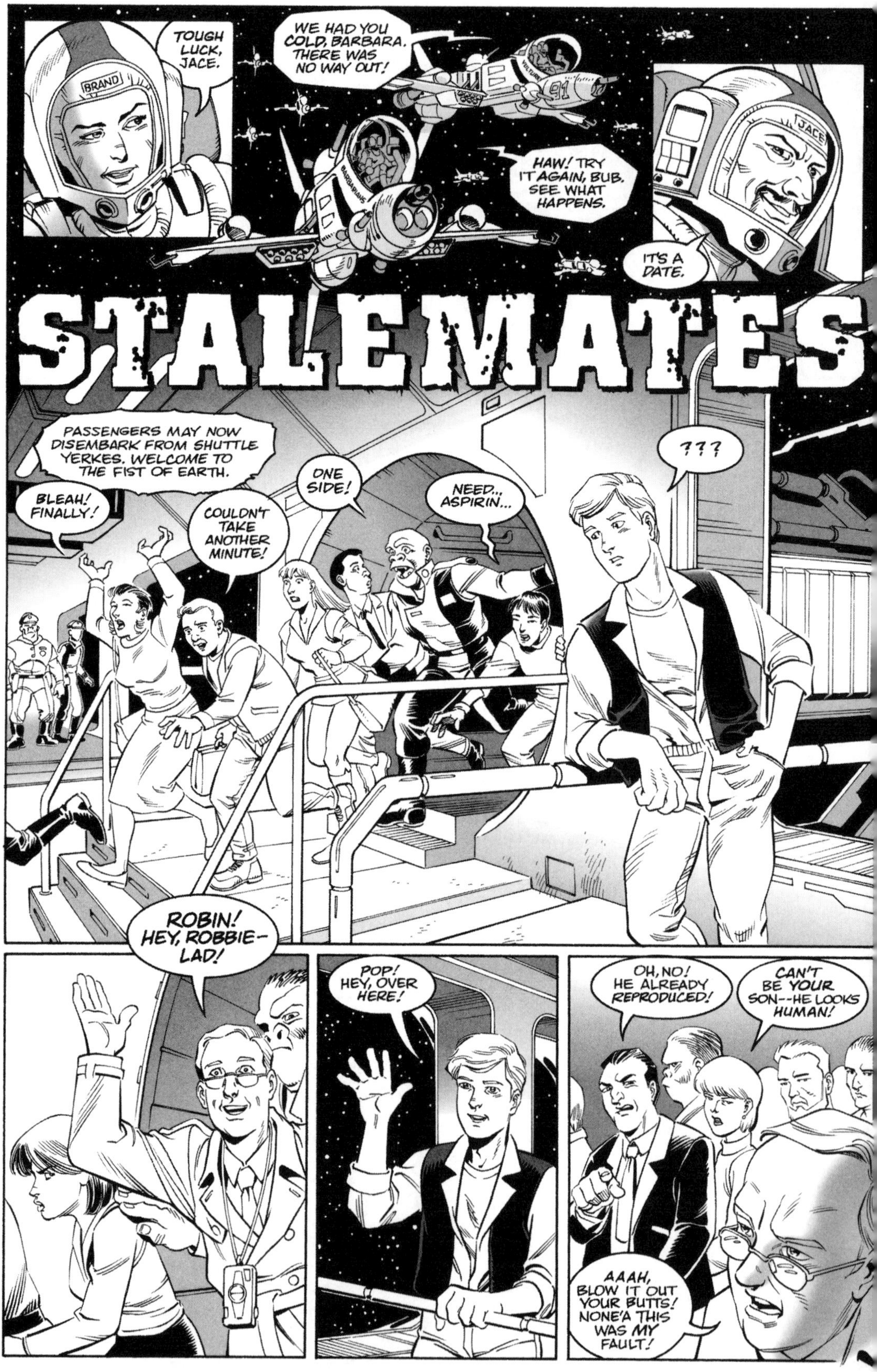
TOUGH LUCK, JACE.
WE HAD YOU COLD, BARBARA. THERE WAS NO WAY OUT!
HAW! TRY IT AGAIN, BUB. SEE WHAT HAPPENS.
IT'S A DATE.
STALEMATES
PASSENGERS MAY NOW DISEMBARK FROM SHUTTLE YERKES. WELCOME TO THE FIST OF EARTH.
BLEAH! FINALLY!
COULDN'T TAKE ANOTHER MINUTE!
ONE SIDE!
NEED... ASPIRIN...
???
ROBIN! HEY, ROBBIE-LAD!
POP! HEY, OVER HERE!
OH, NO! HE ALREADY REPRODUCED!
CAN'T BE YOUR SON--HE LOOKS HUMAN!
AAAH, BLOW IT OUT YOUR BUTTS! NONE'A THIS WAS MY FAULT!

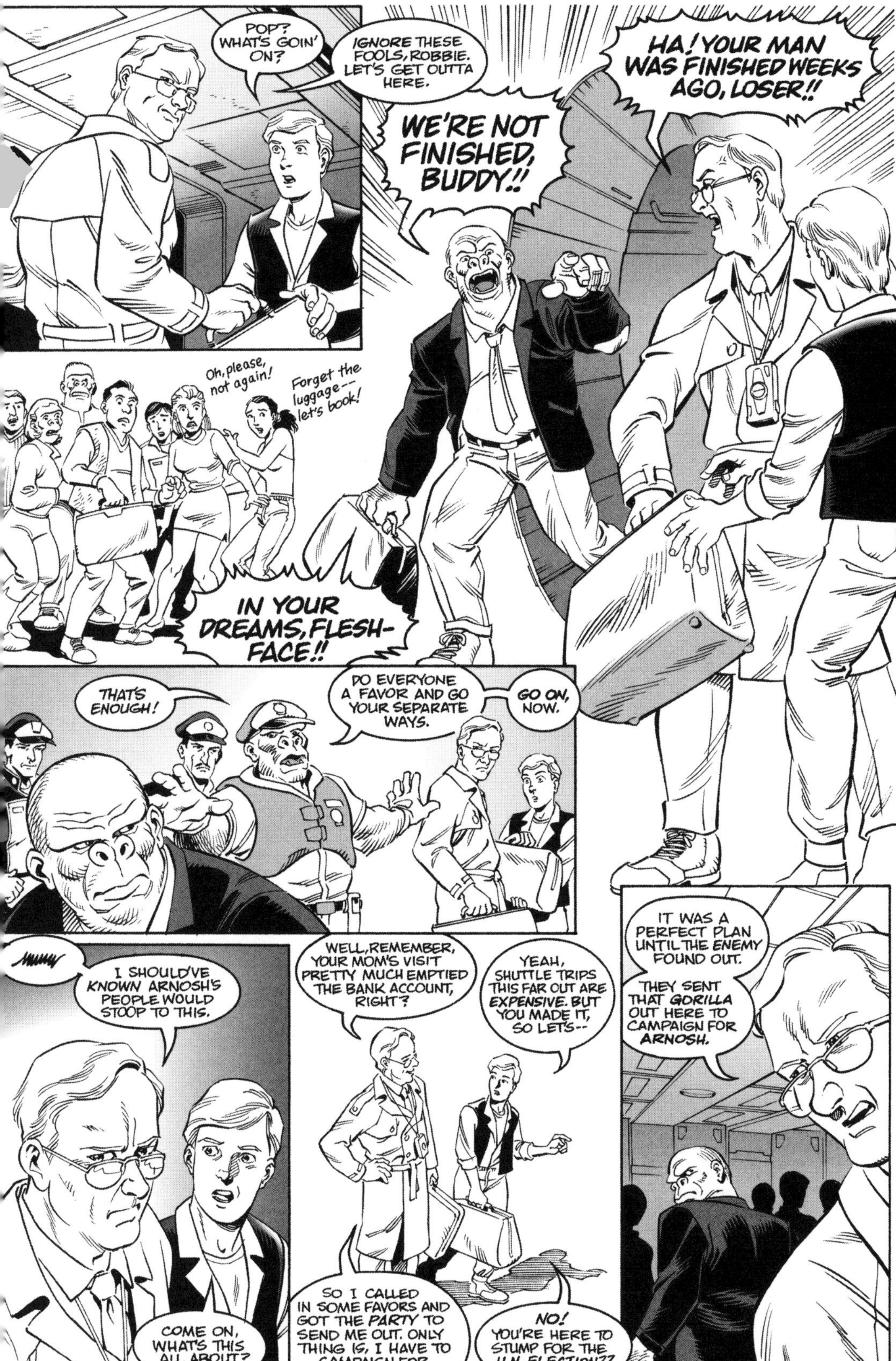
POP? WHAT'S GOIN' ON?
IGNORE THESE FOOLS, ROBBIE. LET'S GET OUTTA HERE.
WE'RE NOT FINISHED, BUDDY!!
HA! YOUR MAN WAS FINISHED WEEKS AGO, LOSER!!
Oh, please, not again!
Forget the luggage--- let's book!
IN YOUR DREAMS, FLESH-FACE!!
THAT'S ENOUGH!
DO EVERYONE A FAVOR AND GO YOUR SEPARATE WAYS.
GO ON, NOW.
I SHOULD'VE KNOWN ARNOSH'S PEOPLE WOULD STOOP TO THIS.
COME ON, WHAT'S THIS ALL ABOUT?
WELL, REMEMBER, YOUR MOM'S VISIT PRETTY MUCH EMPTIED THE BANK ACCOUNT, RIGHT?
YEAH, SHUTTLE TRIPS THIS FAR OUT ARE EXPENSIVE. BUT YOU MADE IT, SO LET'S--
SO I CALLED IN SOME FAVORS AND GOT THE PARTY TO SEND ME OUT. ONLY THING IS, I HAVE TO CAMPAIGN FOR KOSTER WHILE I'M HERE.
NO! YOU'RE HERE TO STUMP FOR THE U.N. ELECTION??
IT WAS A PERFECT PLAN UNTIL THE ENEMY FOUND OUT.
THEY SENT THAT GORILLA OUT HERE TO CAMPAIGN FOR ARNOSH.

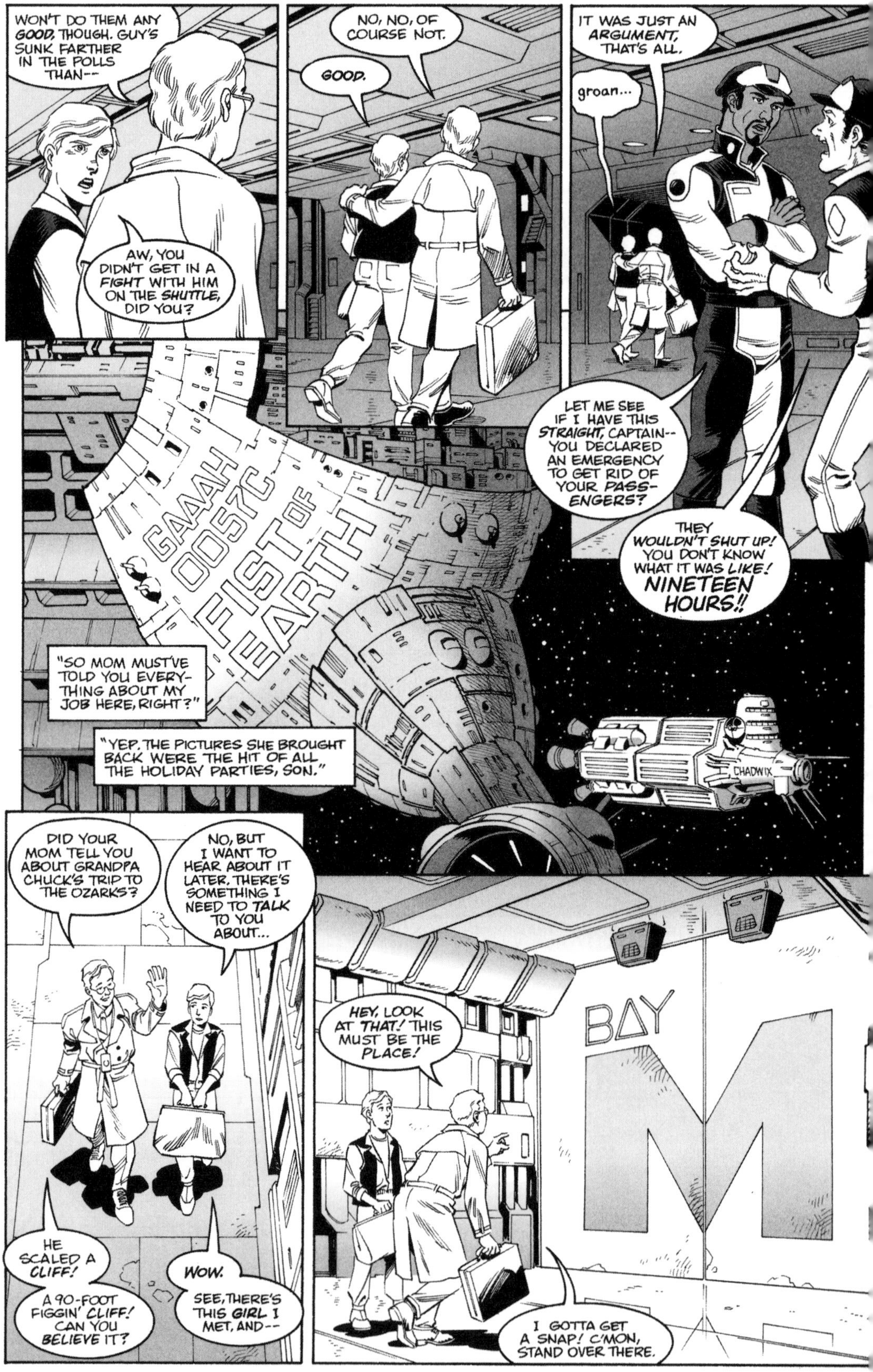
WON'T DO THEM ANY GOOD, THOUGH. GUY'S SUNK FARTHER IN THE POLLS THAN--
AW, YOU DIDN'T GET IN A FIGHT WITH HIM ON THE SHUTTLE, DID YOU?
NO, NO, OF COURSE NOT.
GOOD.
IT WAS JUST AN ARGUMENT, THAT'S ALL.
groan...
LET ME SEE IF I HAVE THIS STRAIGHT, CAPTAIN-- YOU DECLARED AN EMERGENCY TO GET RID OF YOUR PASSENGERS?
THEY WOULDN'T SHUT UP! YOU DON'T KNOW WHAT IT WAS LIKE! NINETEEN HOURS!!
GAAAH
005YC
FIST OF EARTH
"SO MOM MUST'VE TOLD YOU EVERYTHING ABOUT MY JOB HERE, RIGHT?"
"YEP. THE PICTURES SHE BROUGHT BACK WERE THE HIT OF ALL THE HOLIDAY PARTIES, SON."
CHADWIX
DID YOUR MOM TELL YOU ABOUT GRANDPA CHUCK'S TRIP TO THE OZARKS?
NO, BUT I WANT TO HEAR ABOUT IT LATER. THERE'S SOMETHING I NEED TO TALK TO YOU ABOUT...
HE SCALED A CLIFF!
A 90-FOOT FIGGIN' CLIFF! CAN YOU BELIEVE IT?
WOW.
SEE, THERE'S THIS GIRL I MET, AND--
HEY, LOOK AT THAT! THIS MUST BE THE PLACE!
BAY
M
I GOTTA GET A SNAP! C'MON, STAND OVER THERE.

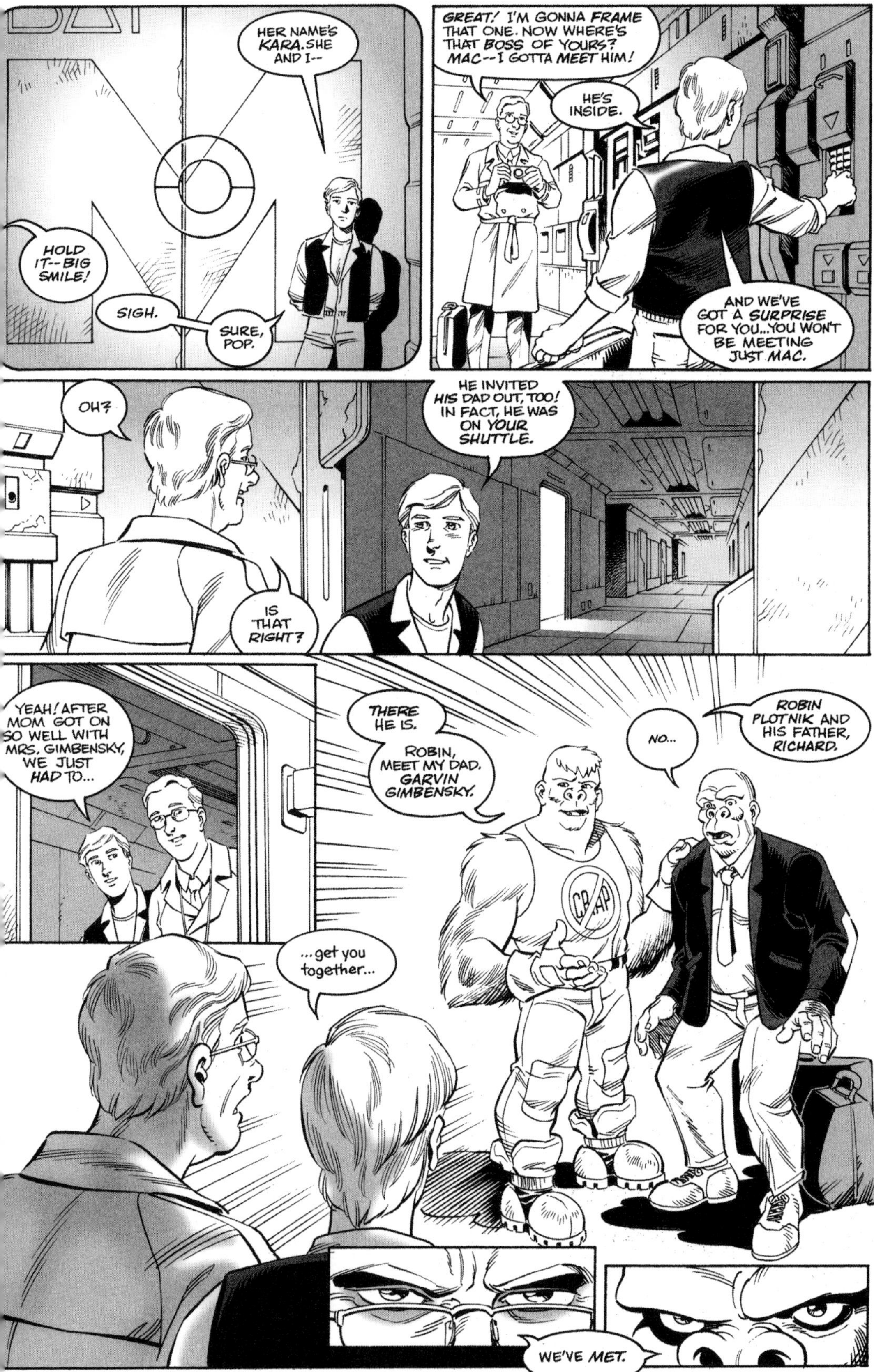
HER NAME'S KARA. SHE AND I--
HOLD IT--BIG SMILE!
SIGH.
SURE, POP.
GREAT! I'M GONNA FRAME THAT ONE. NOW WHERE'S THAT BOSS OF YOURS? MAC--I GOTTA MEET HIM!
HE'S INSIDE.
AND WE'VE GOT A SURPRISE FOR YOU...YOU WON'T BE MEETING JUST MAC.
OH?
HE INVITED HIS DAD OUT, TOO! IN FACT, HE WAS ON YOUR SHUTTLE.
IS THAT RIGHT?
YEAH! AFTER MOM GOT ON SO WELL WITH MRS. GIMBENSKY, WE JUST HAD TO...
...get you together...
THERE HE IS.
ROBIN, MEET MY DAD. GARVIN GIMBENSKY.
NO...
ROBIN PLOTNIK AND HIS FATHER, RICHARD.
CRAP
WE'VE MET.

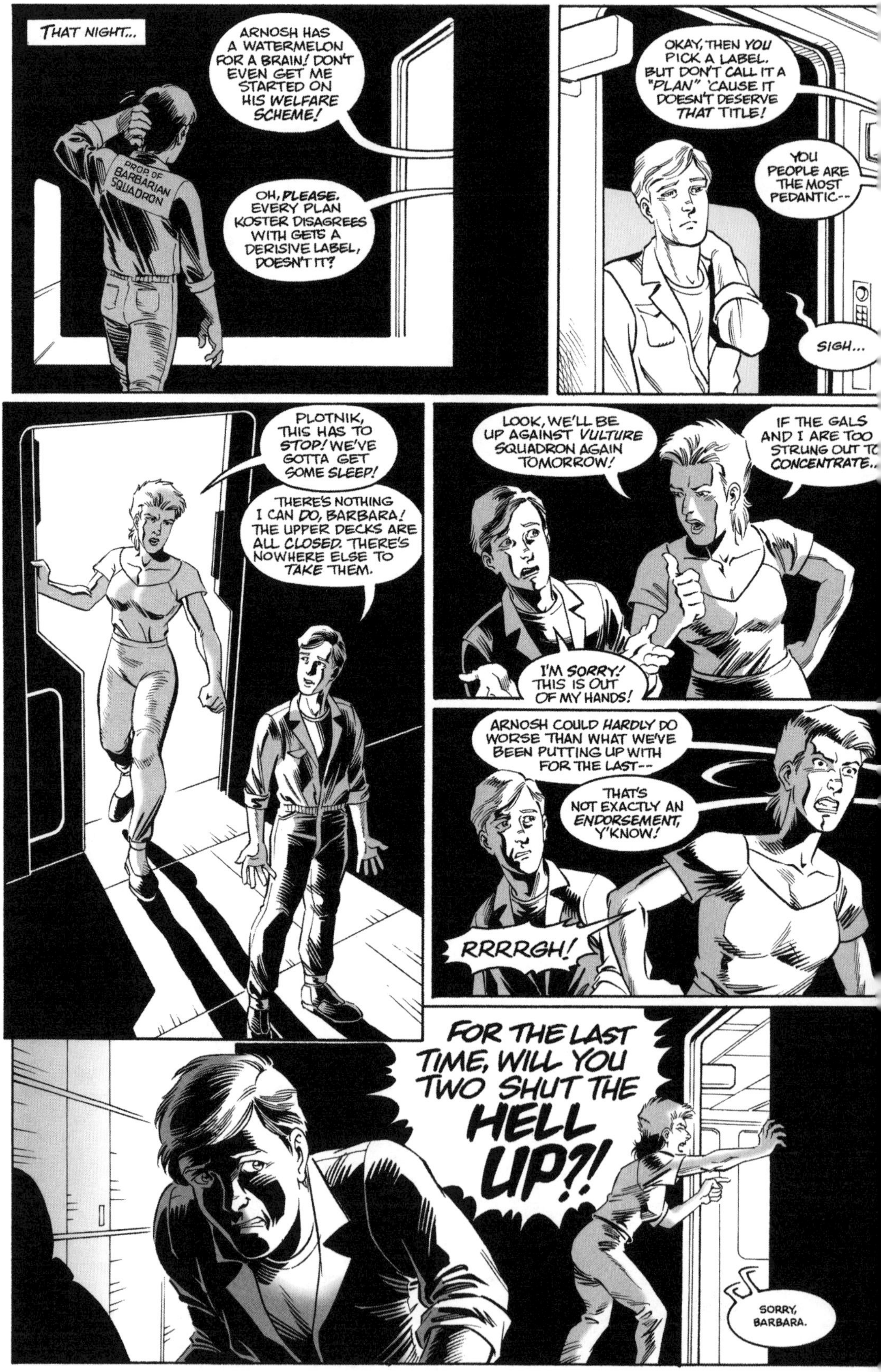
THAT NIGHT...
ARNOSH HAS A WATERMELON FOR A BRAIN! DON'T EVEN GET ME STARTED ON HIS WELFARE SCHEME!
PROP OF BARBARIAN SQUADRON
OH, PLEASE. EVERY PLAN KOSTER DISAGREES WITH GETS A DERISIVE LABEL, DOESN'T IT?
OKAY, THEN YOU PICK A LABEL. BUT DON'T CALL IT A "PLAN" 'CAUSE IT DOESN'T DESERVE THAT TITLE!
YOU PEOPLE ARE THE MOST PEDANTIC--
SIGH...
PLOTNIK, THIS HAS TO STOP! WE'VE GOTTA GET SOME SLEEP!
THERE'S NOTHING I CAN DO, BARBARA! THE UPPER DECKS ARE ALL CLOSED. THERE'S NOWHERE ELSE TO TAKE THEM.
LOOK, WE'LL BE UP AGAINST VULTURE SQUADRON AGAIN TOMORROW!
IF THE GALS AND I ARE TOO STRUNG OUT TO CONCENTRATE...
I'M SORRY! THIS IS OUT OF MY HANDS!
ARNOSH COULD HARDLY DO WORSE THAN WHAT WE'VE BEEN PUTTING UP WITH FOR THE LAST--
THAT'S NOT EXACTLY AN ENDORSEMENT, Y'KNOW!
RRRRGH!
FOR THE LAST TIME, WILL YOU TWO SHUT THE HELL UP?!
SORRY, BARBARA.

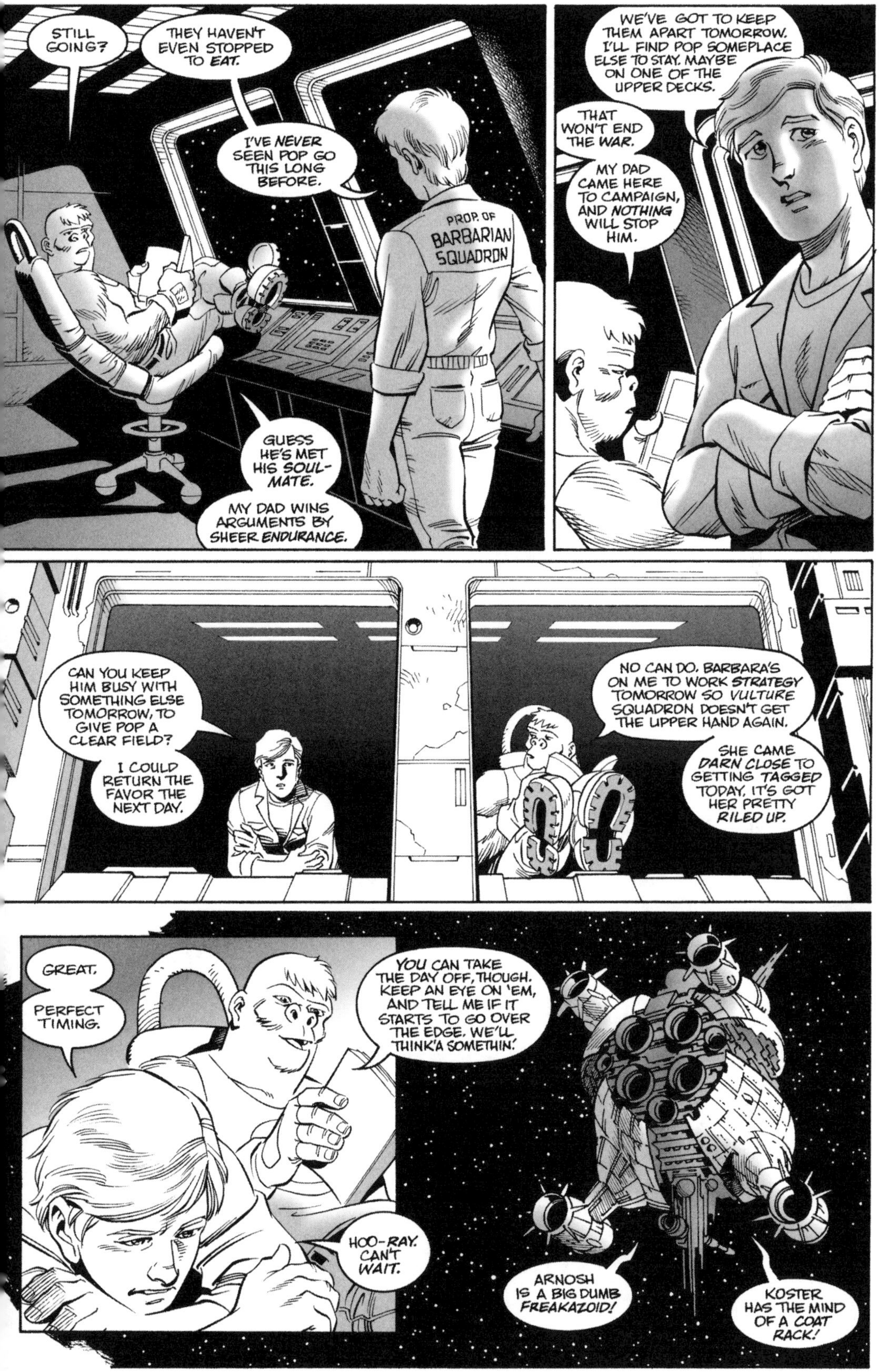
STILL GOING?
THEY HAVEN'T EVEN STOPPED TO EAT.
I'VE NEVER SEEN POP GO THIS LONG BEFORE.
PROP. OF BARBARIAN SQUADRON
GUESS HE'S MET HIS SOUL-MATE.
MY DAD WINS ARGUMENTS BY SHEER ENDURANCE.
WE'VE GOT TO KEEP THEM APART TOMORROW. I'LL FIND POP SOMEPLACE ELSE TO STAY. MAYBE ON ONE OF THE UPPER DECKS.
THAT WON'T END THE WAR.
MY DAD CAME HERE TO CAMPAIGN, AND NOTHING WILL STOP HIM.
CAN YOU KEEP HIM BUSY WITH SOMETHING ELSE TOMORROW, TO GIVE POP A CLEAR FIELD?
I COULD RETURN THE FAVOR THE NEXT DAY.
NO CAN DO. BARBARA'S ON ME TO WORK STRATEGY TOMORROW SO VULTURE SQUADRON DOESN'T GET THE UPPER HAND AGAIN.
SHE CAME DARN CLOSE TO GETTING TAGGED TODAY, IT'S GOT HER PRETTY RILED UP.
GREAT.
PERFECT TIMING.
YOU CAN TAKE THE DAY OFF, THOUGH. KEEP AN EYE ON 'EM, AND TELL ME IF IT STARTS TO GO OVER THE EDGE. WE'LL THINK'A SOMETHIN'.
HOO-RAY. CAN'T WAIT.
ARNOSH IS A BIG DUMB FREAKAZOID!
KOSTER HAS THE MIND OF A COAT RACK!

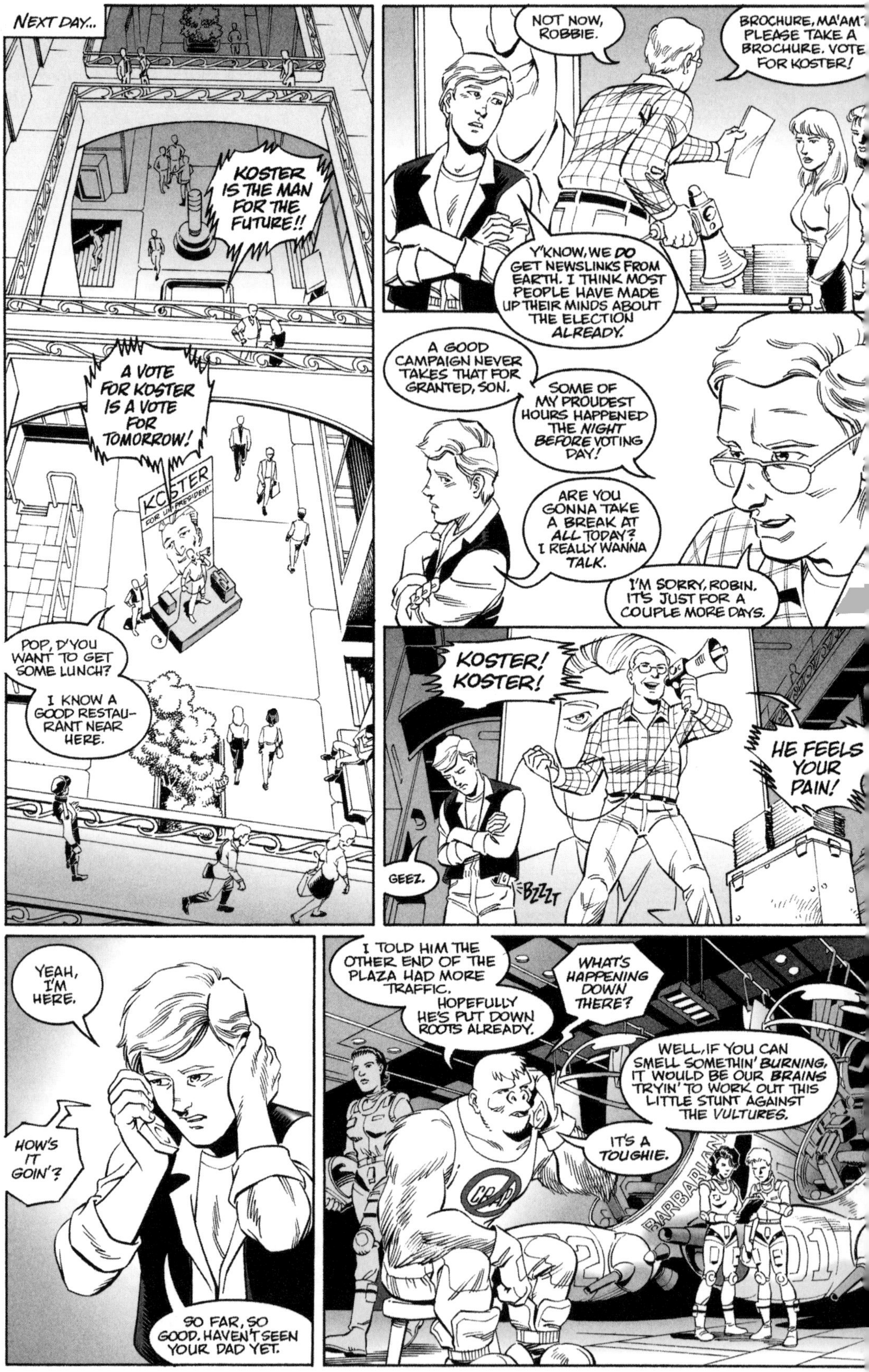
NEXT DAY...
KOSTER IS THE MAN FOR THE FUTURE!!
A VOTE FOR KOSTER IS A VOTE FOR TOMORROW!
KOSTER FOR UN PRESIDENT
POP, D'YOU WANT TO GET SOME LUNCH?
I KNOW A GOOD RESTAURANT NEAR HERE.
NOT NOW, ROBBIE.
BROCHURE, MA'AM? PLEASE TAKE A BROCHURE. VOTE FOR KOSTER!
Y'KNOW, WE DO GET NEWSLINKS FROM EARTH. I THINK MOST PEOPLE HAVE MADE UP THEIR MINDS ABOUT THE ELECTION ALREADY.
A GOOD CAMPAIGN NEVER TAKES THAT FOR GRANTED, SON.
SOME OF MY PROUDEST HOURS HAPPENED THE NIGHT BEFORE VOTING DAY!
ARE YOU GONNA TAKE A BREAK AT ALL TODAY? I REALLY WANNA TALK.
I'M SORRY, ROBIN. IT'S JUST FOR A COUPLE MORE DAYS.
KOSTER! KOSTER!
HE FEELS YOUR PAIN!
GEEZ.
BZZZT
YEAH, I'M HERE.
HOW'S IT GOIN'?
SO FAR, SO GOOD. HAVEN'T SEEN YOUR DAD YET.
I TOLD HIM THE OTHER END OF THE PLAZA HAD MORE TRAFFIC.
HOPEFULLY HE'S PUT DOWN ROOTS ALREADY.
WHAT'S HAPPENING DOWN THERE?
WELL, IF YOU CAN SMELL SOMETHIN' BURNING, IT WOULD BE OUR BRAINS TRYIN' TO WORK OUT THIS LITTLE STUNT AGAINST THE VULTURES.
IT'S A TOUGHIE.
BARBARIAN

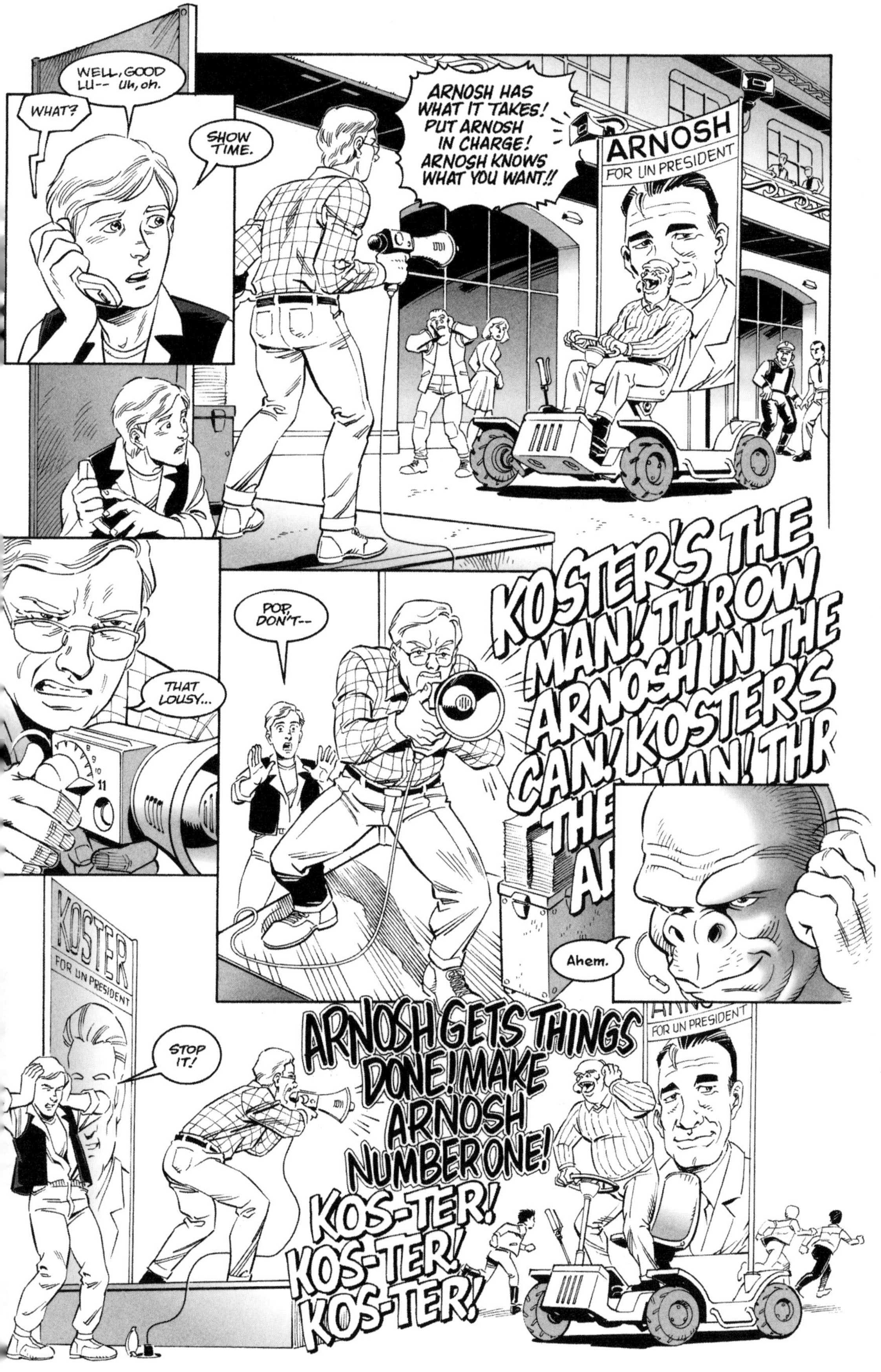
WELL, GOOD LU-- Uh, oh.
WHAT?
SHOW TIME.
ARNOSH HAS WHAT IT TAKES! PUT ARNOSH IN CHARGE! ARNOSH KNOWS WHAT YOU WANT!!
ARNOSH
FOR UN PRESIDENT
THAT LOUSY...
POP, DON'T--
KOSTER'S THE MAN! THROW ARNOSH IN THE CAN! KOSTER'S THE MAN! THR
Ahem.
KOSTER
FOR UN PRESIDENT
STOP IT!
ARNOSH GETS THINGS DONE! MAKE ARNOSH NUMBER ONE!
KOS-TER! KOS-TER! KOS-TER!
FOR UN PRESIDENT

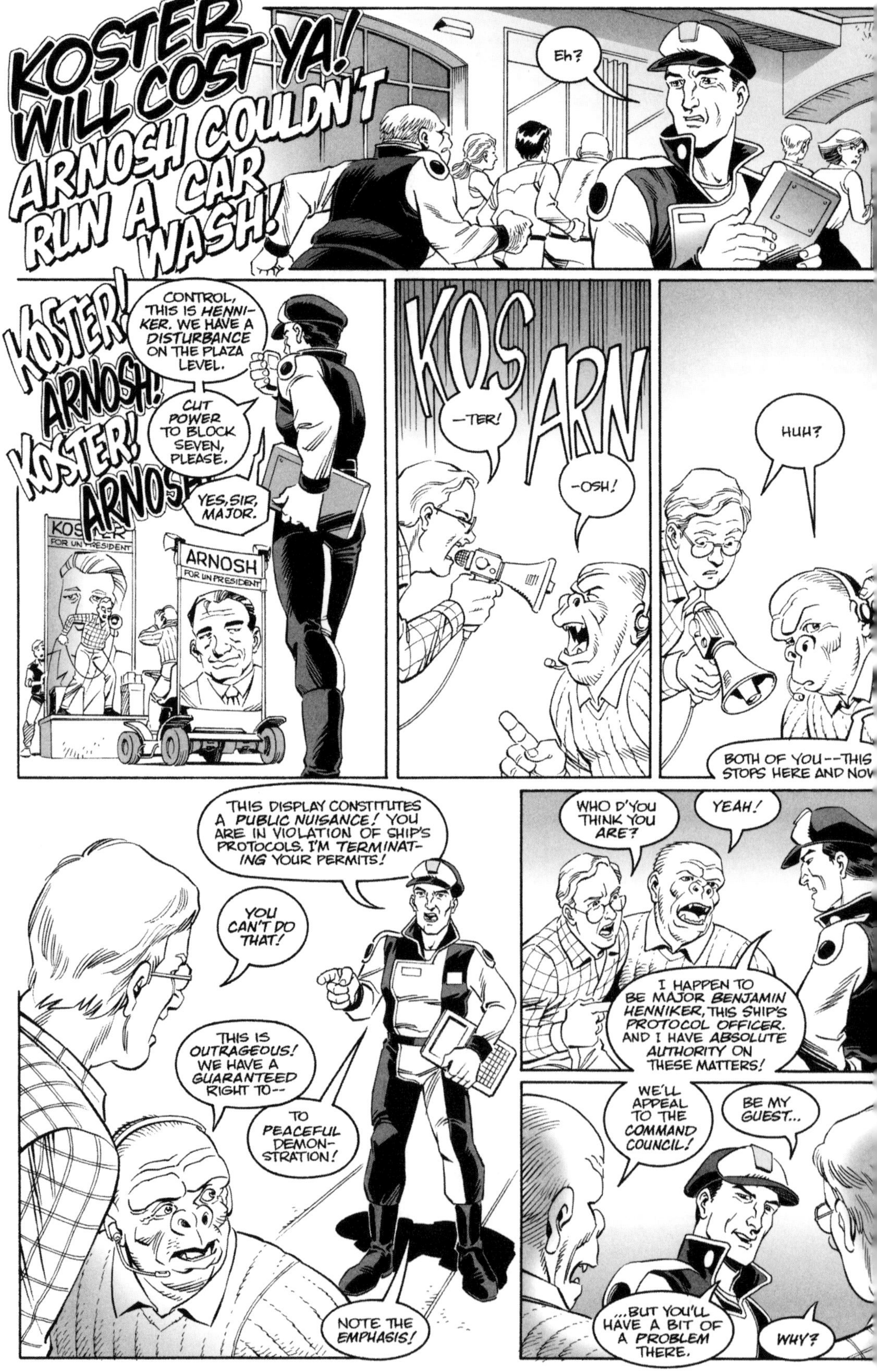
KOSTER WILL COST YA!
ARNOSH COULDN'T RUN A CAR WASH!
Eh?
KOSTER! ARNOSH! KOSTER! ARNOSH!
CONTROL, THIS IS HENNIKER. WE HAVE A DISTURBANCE ON THE PLAZA LEVEL.
CUT POWER TO BLOCK SEVEN, PLEASE.
YES, SIR, MAJOR.
ARNOSH FOR UN PRESIDENT
FOR UN PRESIDENT
KOS
ARN
—TER!
-OSH!
HUH?
BOTH OF YOU--THIS STOPS HERE AND NOW
THIS DISPLAY CONSTITUTES A PUBLIC NUISANCE! YOU ARE IN VIOLATION OF SHIP'S PROTOCOLS. I'M TERMINATING YOUR PERMITS!
YOU CAN'T DO THAT!
THIS IS OUTRAGEOUS! WE HAVE A GUARANTEED RIGHT TO--
TO PEACEFUL DEMONSTRATION!
NOTE THE EMPHASIS!
WHO D'YOU THINK YOU ARE?
YEAH!
I HAPPEN TO BE MAJOR BENJAMIN HENNIKER, THIS SHIP'S PROTOCOL OFFICER. AND I HAVE ABSOLUTE AUTHORITY ON THESE MATTERS!
WE'LL APPEAL TO THE COMMAND COUNCIL!
BE MY GUEST...
...BUT YOU'LL HAVE A BIT OF A PROBLEM THERE.
WHY?

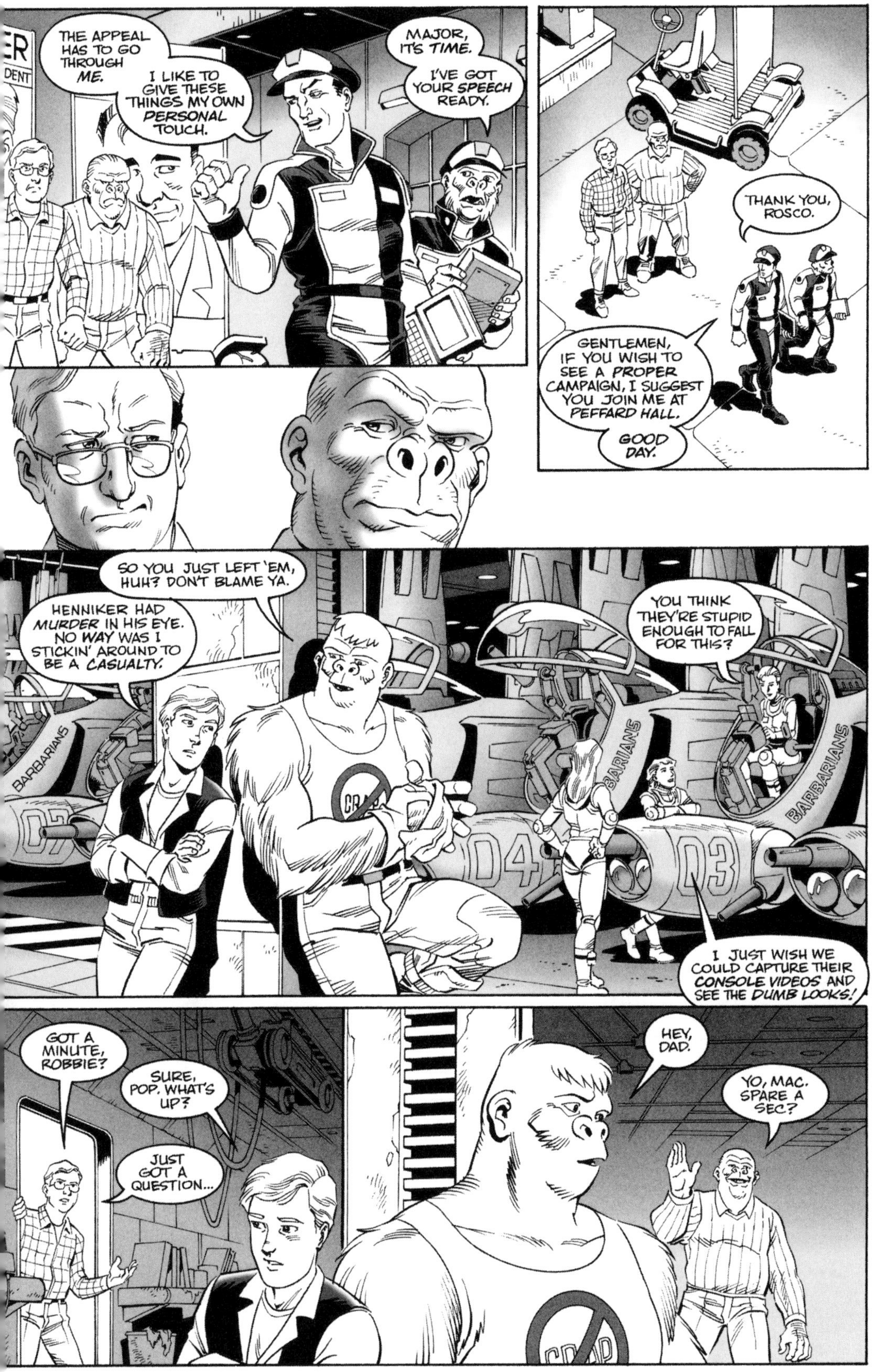
THE APPEAL HAS TO GO THROUGH *ME.*
I LIKE TO GIVE THESE THINGS MY OWN *PERSONAL* TOUCH.
MAJOR, IT'S *TIME.*
I'VE GOT YOUR *SPEECH* READY.
THANK YOU, ROSCO.
GENTLEMEN, IF YOU WISH TO SEE A *PROPER* CAMPAIGN, I SUGGEST YOU JOIN ME AT *PEFFARD HALL.*
GOOD DAY.
SO YOU JUST LEFT 'EM, HUH? DON'T BLAME YA.
HENNIKER HAD *MURDER* IN HIS EYE. NO *WAY* WAS I STICKIN' AROUND TO BE A *CASUALTY.*
YOU THINK THEY'RE STUPID ENOUGH TO FALL FOR THIS?
BARBARIANS
BARBARIANS
BARBARIANS
07
04
03
I JUST WISH WE COULD CAPTURE THEIR *CONSOLE VIDEOS* AND SEE THE *DUMB LOOKS!*
GOT A MINUTE, ROBBIE?
SURE, POP. WHAT'S UP?
JUST GOT A QUESTION...
HEY, DAD.
YO, MAC. SPARE A SEC?

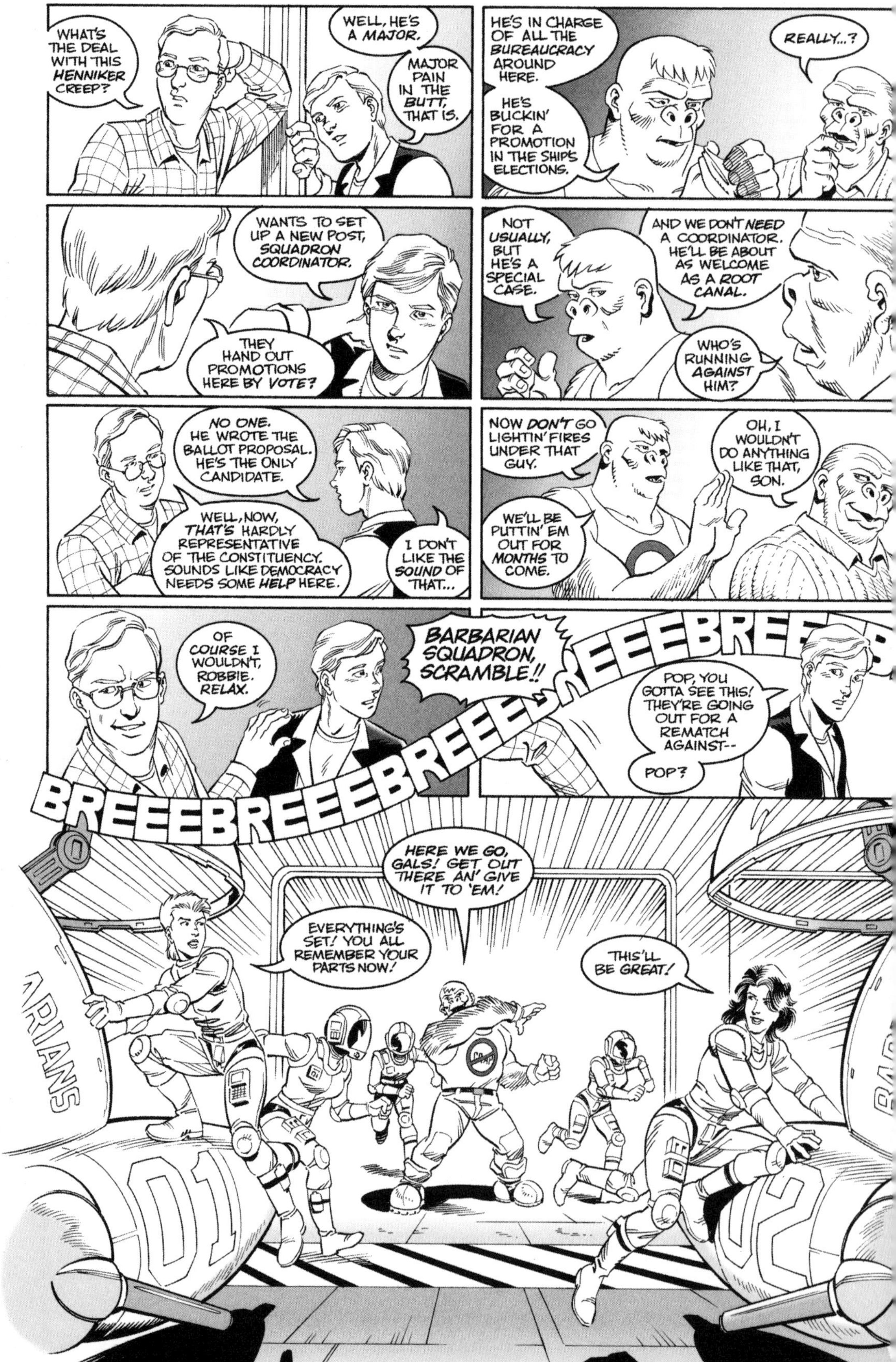
WHAT'S THE DEAL WITH THIS HENNIKER CREEP?
WELL, HE'S A MAJOR.
MAJOR PAIN IN THE BUTT, THAT IS.
HE'S IN CHARGE OF ALL THE BUREAUCRACY AROUND HERE.
HE'S BUCKIN' FOR A PROMOTION IN THE SHIP'S ELECTIONS.
REALLY...?
WANTS TO SET UP A NEW POST, SQUADRON COORDINATOR.
THEY HAND OUT PROMOTIONS HERE BY VOTE?
NOT USUALLY, BUT HE'S A SPECIAL CASE.
AND WE DON'T NEED A COORDINATOR. HE'LL BE ABOUT AS WELCOME AS A ROOT CANAL.
WHO'S RUNNING AGAINST HIM?
NO ONE. HE WROTE THE BALLOT PROPOSAL. HE'S THE ONLY CANDIDATE.
WELL, NOW, THAT'S HARDLY REPRESENTATIVE OF THE CONSTITUENCY. SOUNDS LIKE DEMOCRACY NEEDS SOME HELP HERE.
I DON'T LIKE THE SOUND OF THAT...
NOW DON'T GO LIGHTIN' FIRES UNDER THAT GUY.
WE'LL BE PUTTIN' EM OUT FOR MONTHS TO COME.
OH, I WOULDN'T DO ANYTHING LIKE THAT, SON.
OF COURSE I WOULDN'T, ROBBIE. RELAX.
BARBARIAN SQUADRON, SCRAMBLE!!
BREEEBREEEBREEEBREEEBREEEBREEEB
POP, YOU GOTTA SEE THIS! THEY'RE GOING OUT FOR A REMATCH AGAINST--
POP?
HERE WE GO, GALS! GET OUT THERE AN' GIVE IT TO 'EM!
EVERYTHING'S SET! YOU ALL REMEMBER YOUR PARTS NOW!
THIS'LL BE GREAT!
ARIANS
01
02

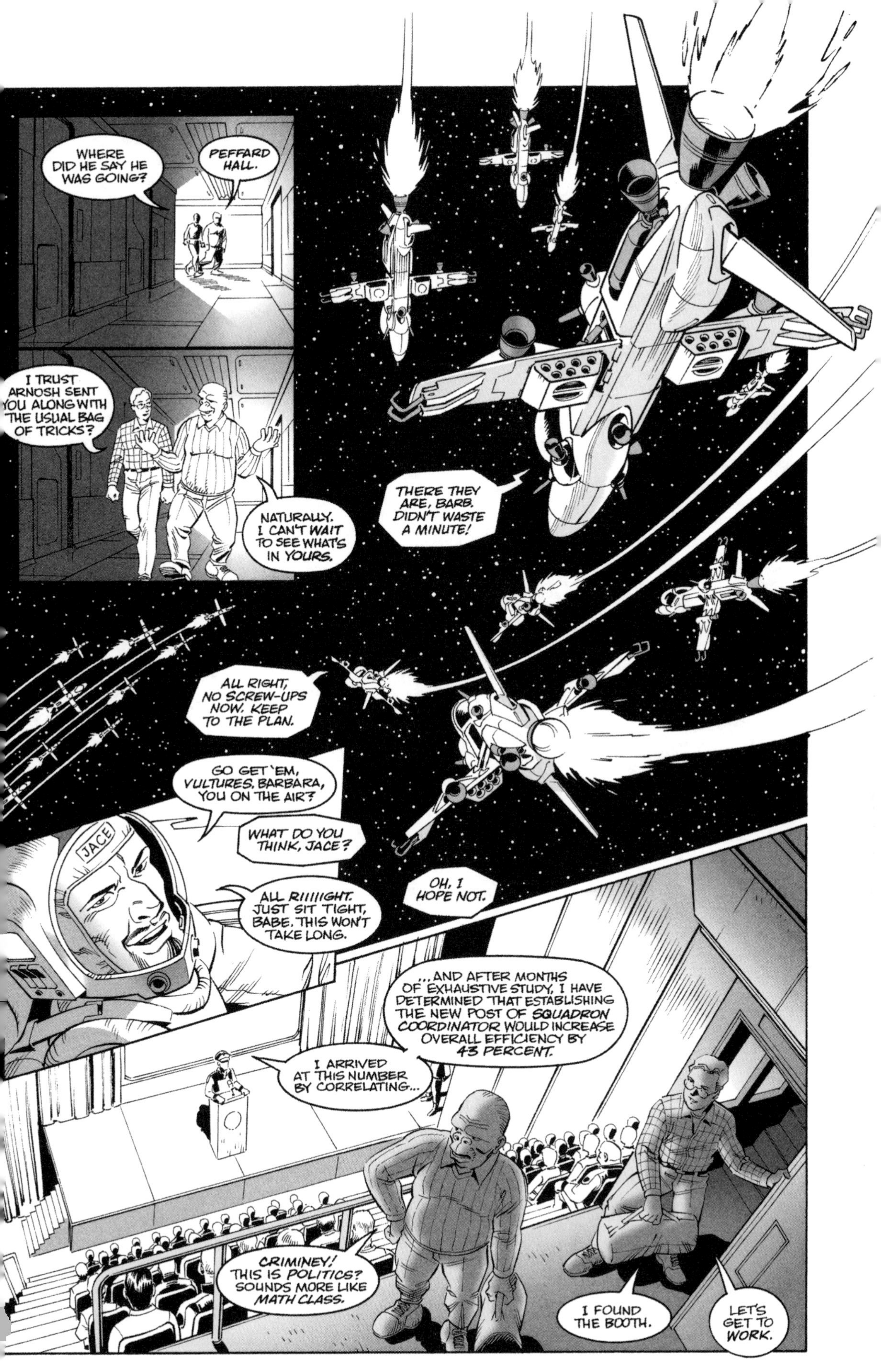

WHERE DID HE SAY HE WAS GOING?
PEFFARD HALL.
I TRUST ARNOSH SENT YOU ALONG WITH THE USUAL BAG OF TRICKS?
NATURALLY. I CAN'T WAIT TO SEE WHAT'S IN YOURS.
THERE THEY ARE, BARB. DIDN'T WASTE A MINUTE!
ALL RIGHT, NO SCREW-UPS NOW. KEEP TO THE PLAN.
GO GET 'EM, VULTURES. BARBARA, YOU ON THE AIR?
WHAT DO YOU THINK, JACE?
JACE
ALL RIIIIIGHT. JUST SIT TIGHT, BABE. THIS WON'T TAKE LONG.
OH, I HOPE NOT.
...AND AFTER MONTHS OF EXHAUSTIVE STUDY, I HAVE DETERMINED THAT ESTABLISHING THE NEW POST OF SQUADRON COORDINATOR WOULD INCREASE OVERALL EFFICIENCY BY 43 PERCENT.
I ARRIVED AT THIS NUMBER BY CORRELATING...
CRIMINEY! THIS IS POLITICS? SOUNDS MORE LIKE MATH CLASS.
I FOUND THE BOOTH.
LET'S GET TO WORK.

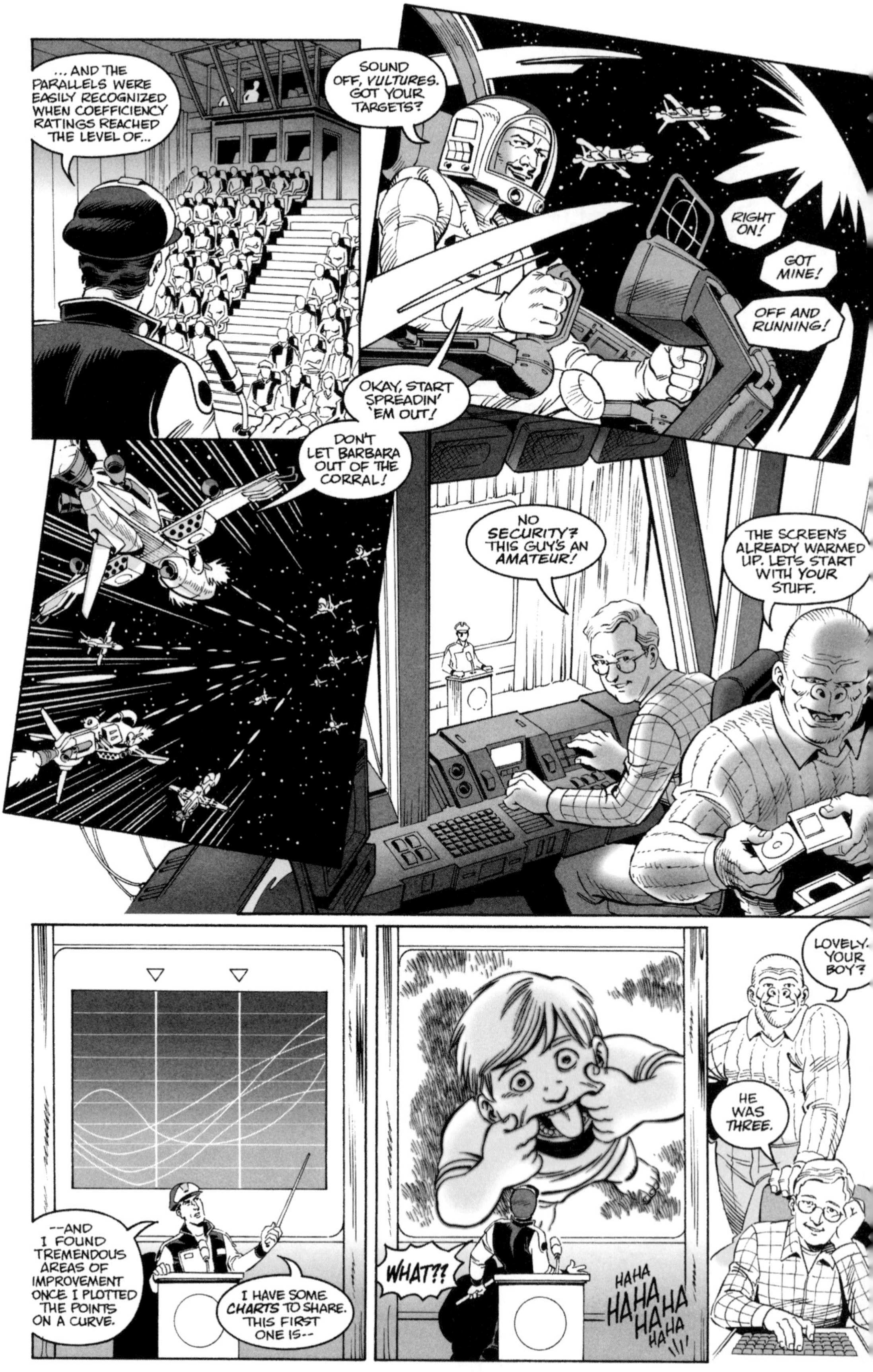
...AND THE PARALLELS WERE EASILY RECOGNIZED WHEN COEFFICIENCY RATINGS REACHED THE LEVEL OF...
SOUND OFF, VULTURES. GOT YOUR TARGETS?
RIGHT ON!
GOT MINE!
OFF AND RUNNING!
OKAY, START SPREADIN' 'EM OUT!
DON'T LET BARBARA OUT OF THE CORRAL!
NO SECURITY? THIS GUY'S AN AMATEUR!
THE SCREEN'S ALREADY WARMED UP. LET'S START WITH YOUR STUFF.
--AND I FOUND TREMENDOUS AREAS OF IMPROVEMENT ONCE I PLOTTED THE POINTS ON A CURVE.
I HAVE SOME CHARTS TO SHARE. THIS FIRST ONE IS--
WHAT?!
HAHA HAHA HAHA HAHA HAHA
LOVELY. YOUR BOY?
HE WAS THREE.

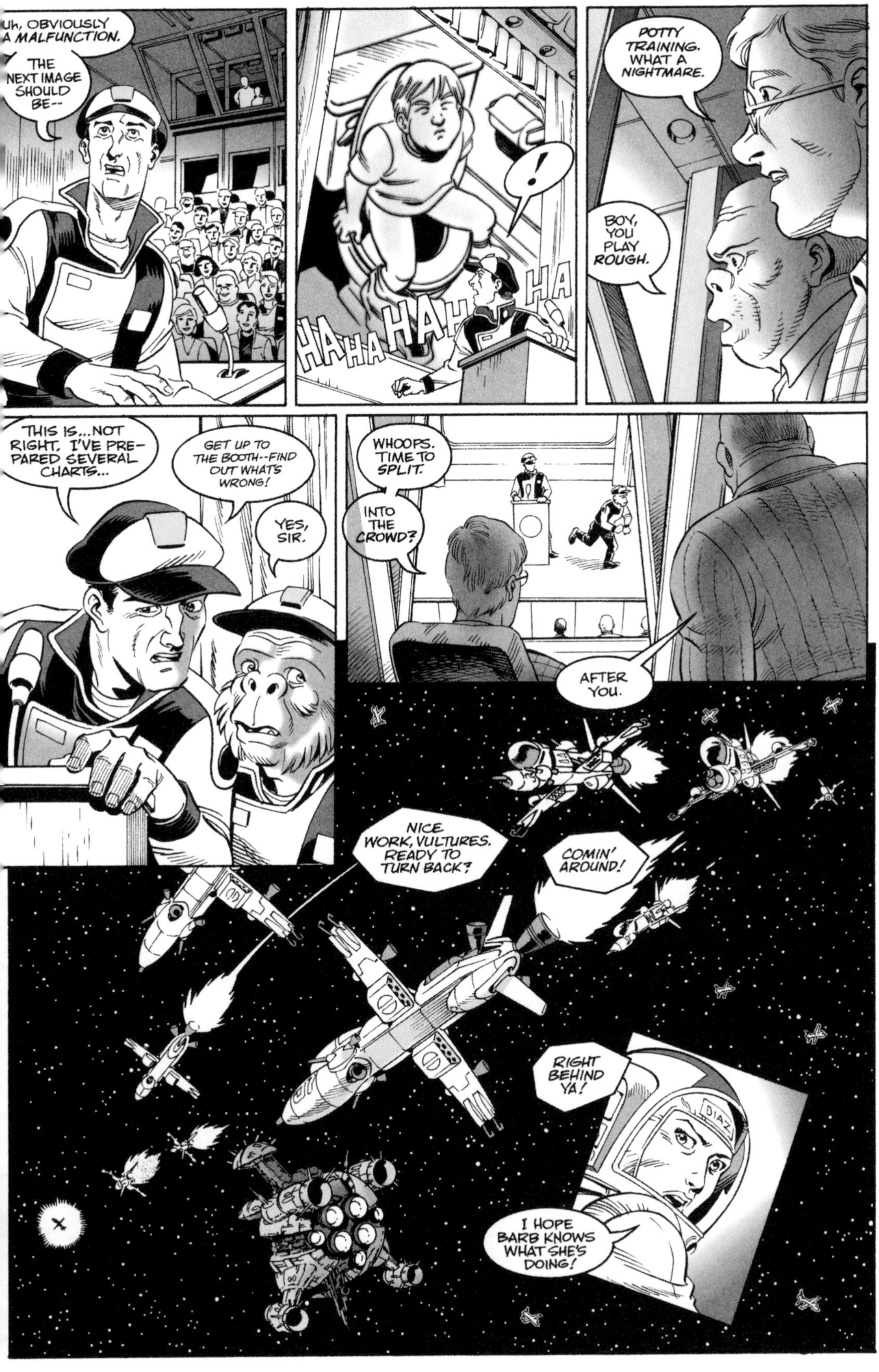
Uh, OBVIOUSLY A MALFUNCTION.
THE NEXT IMAGE SHOULD BE--
!
HAHAHAHAHAHA
POTTY TRAINING. WHAT A NIGHTMARE.
BOY, YOU PLAY ROUGH.
THIS IS...NOT RIGHT. I'VE PRE-PARED SEVERAL CHARTS...
GET UP TO THE BOOTH--FIND OUT WHAT'S WRONG!
YES, SIR.
WHOOPS. TIME TO SPLIT.
INTO THE CROWD?
AFTER YOU.
NICE WORK, VULTURES. READY TO TURN BACK?
COMIN' AROUND!
RIGHT BEHIND YA!
DIAZ
I HOPE BARB KNOWS WHAT SHE'S DOING!

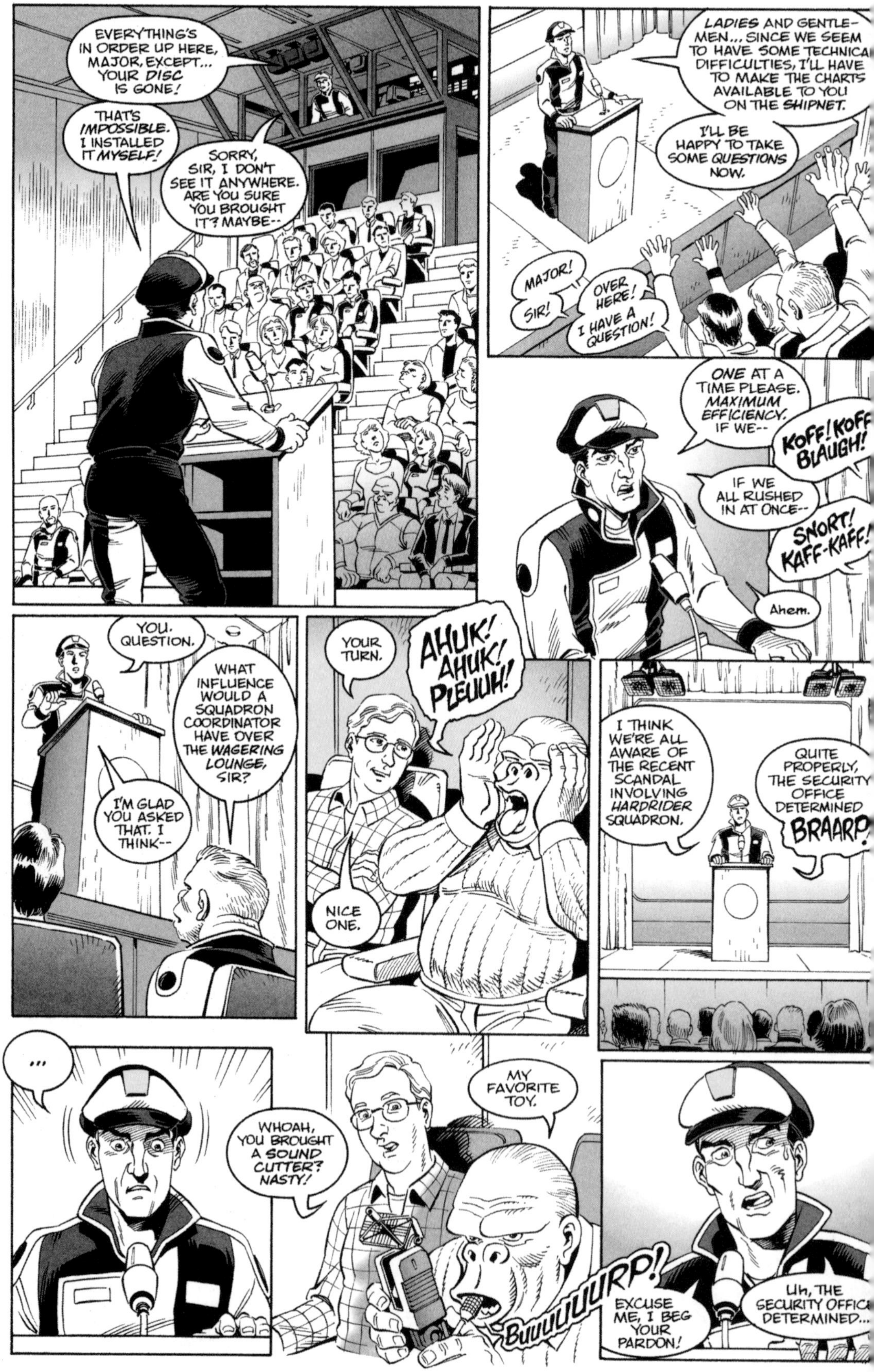
EVERYTHING'S IN ORDER UP HERE, MAJOR, EXCEPT... YOUR DISC IS GONE!
THAT'S IMPOSSIBLE. I INSTALLED IT MYSELF!
SORRY, SIR, I DON'T SEE IT ANYWHERE. ARE YOU SURE YOU BROUGHT IT? MAYBE--
LADIES AND GENTLEMEN... SINCE WE SEEM TO HAVE SOME TECHNICA DIFFICULTIES, I'LL HAVE TO MAKE THE CHARTS AVAILABLE TO YOU ON THE SHIPNET.
I'LL BE HAPPY TO TAKE SOME QUESTIONS NOW.
MAJOR!
SIR!
OVER HERE! I HAVE A QUESTION!
ONE AT A TIME PLEASE. MAXIMUM EFFICIENCY. IF WE--
KOFF! KOFF BLAUGH!
IF WE ALL RUSHED IN AT ONCE--
SNORT! KAFF-KAFF!
Ahem.
YOU. QUESTION.
WHAT INFLUENCE WOULD A SQUADRON COORDINATOR HAVE OVER THE WAGERING LOUNGE, SIR?
I'M GLAD YOU ASKED THAT. I THINK--
YOUR TURN.
AHUK! AHUK! PLEUUH!
NICE ONE.
I THINK WE'RE ALL AWARE OF THE RECENT SCANDAL INVOLVING HARDRIDER SQUADRON.
QUITE PROPERLY, THE SECURITY OFFICE DETERMINED
BRAARP.
...
WHOAH, YOU BROUGHT A SOUND CUTTER? NASTY!
MY FAVORITE TOY.
BUUUUUURP!
EXCUSE ME, I BEG YOUR PARDON!
Uh, THE SECURITY OFFIC DETERMINED...

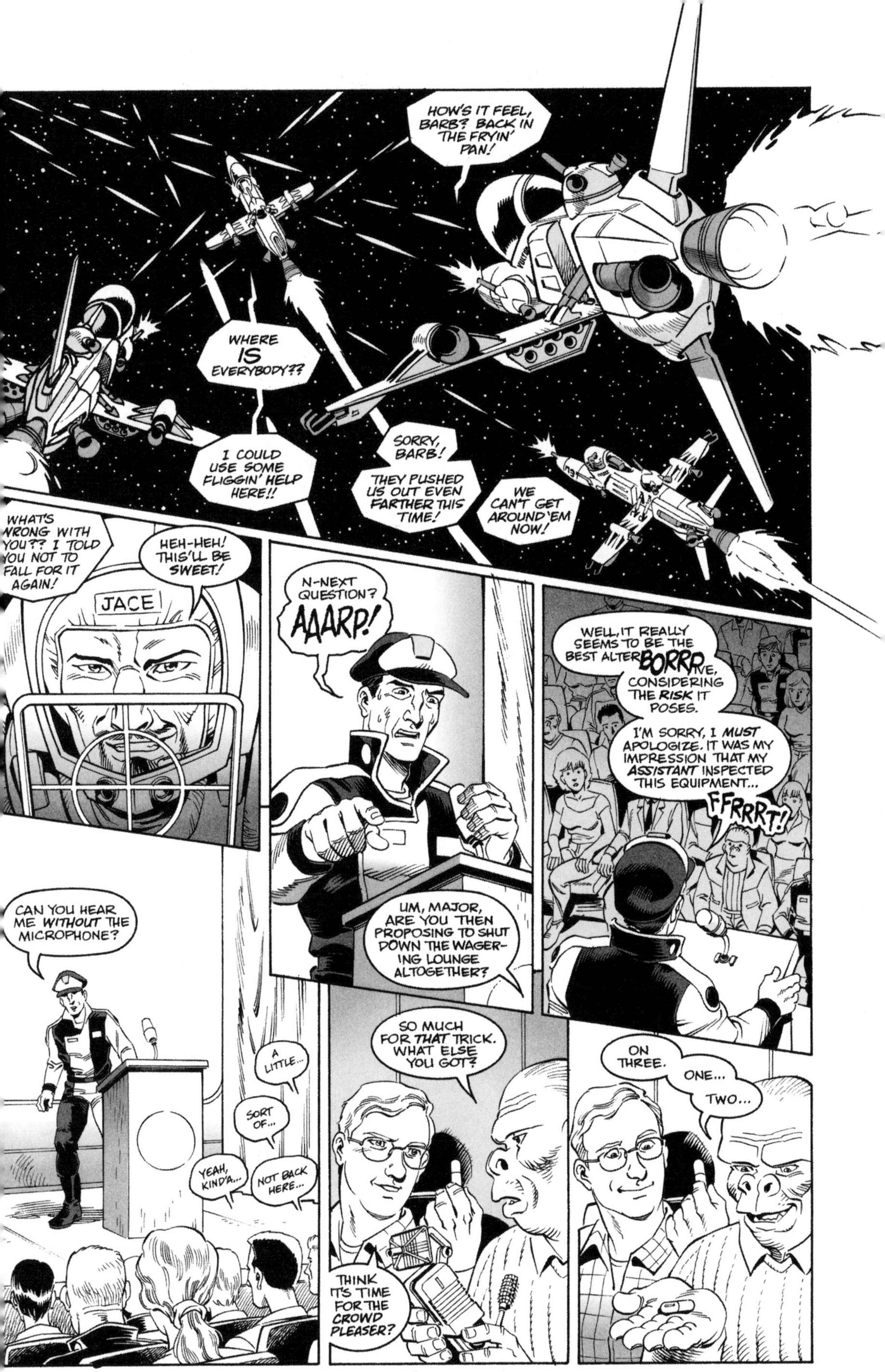
HOW'S IT FEEL, BARB? BACK IN THE FRYIN' PAN!
WHERE IS EVERYBODY??
I COULD USE SOME FLIGGIN' HELP HERE!!
SORRY, BARB!
THEY PUSHED US OUT EVEN FARTHER THIS TIME!
WE CAN'T GET AROUND 'EM NOW!
WHAT'S WRONG WITH YOU?? I TOLD YOU NOT TO FALL FOR IT AGAIN!
HEH-HEH! THIS'LL BE SWEET!
JACE
N-NEXT QUESTION? AAARP!
WELL, IT REALLY SEEMS TO BE THE BEST ALTERBORRRVE, CONSIDERING THE RISK IT POSES.
I'M SORRY, I MUST APOLOGIZE. IT WAS MY IMPRESSION THAT MY ASSISTANT INSPECTED THIS EQUIPMENT...
FFRRRT!
CAN YOU HEAR ME WITHOUT THE MICROPHONE?
A LITTLE...
SORT OF...
YEAH, KIND'A...
NOT BACK HERE...
UM, MAJOR, ARE YOU THEN PROPOSING TO SHUT DOWN THE WAGERING LOUNGE ALTOGETHER?
SO MUCH FOR THAT TRICK. WHAT ELSE YOU GOT?
THINK IT'S TIME FOR THE CROWD PLEASER?
ON THREE.
ONE...
TWO...

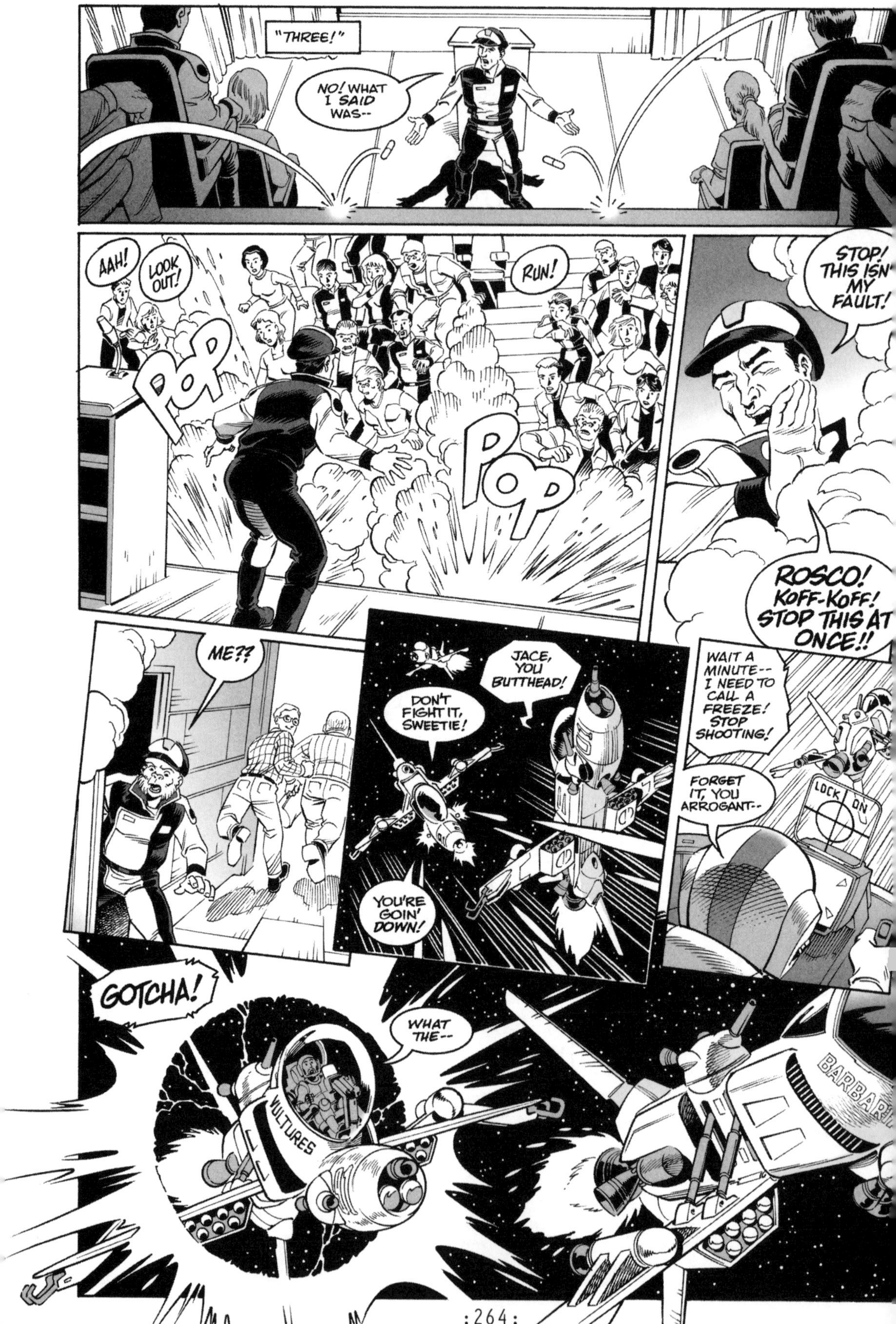
"THREE!"
NO! WHAT I SAID WAS--
AAH!
LOOK OUT!
RUN!
POP
POP
STOP! THIS ISN' MY FAULT!
ROSCO! KOFF-KOFF! STOP THIS AT ONCE!!
ME??
JACE, YOU BUTTHEAD!
DON'T FIGHT IT, SWEETIE!
YOU'RE GOIN' DOWN!
WAIT A MINUTE-- I NEED TO CALL A FREEZE! STOP SHOOTING!
FORGET IT, YOU ARROGANT--
LOCK ON
GOTCHA!
WHAT THE--
VULTURES
BARBAR

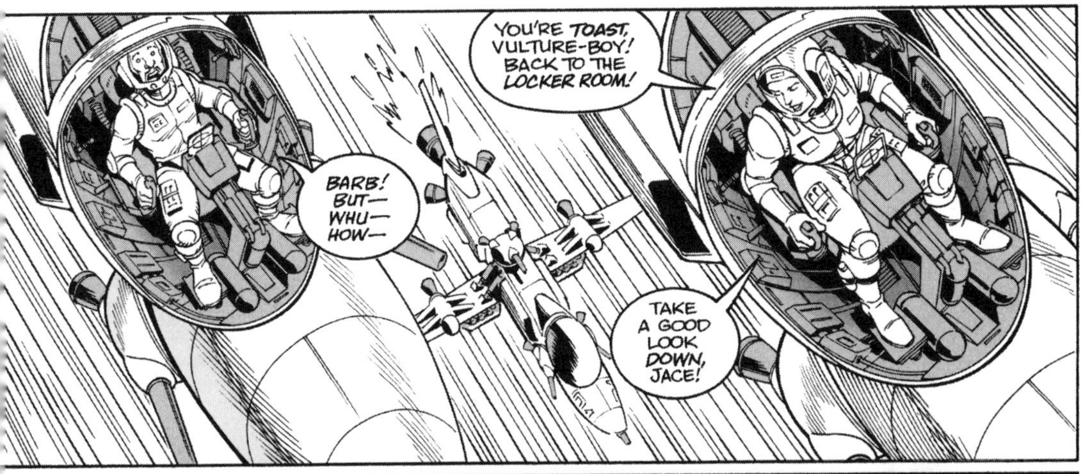
YOU'RE TOAST, VULTURE-BOY! BACK TO THE LOCKER ROOM!
BARB! BUT— WHU— HOW—
TAKE A GOOD LOOK DOWN, JACE!

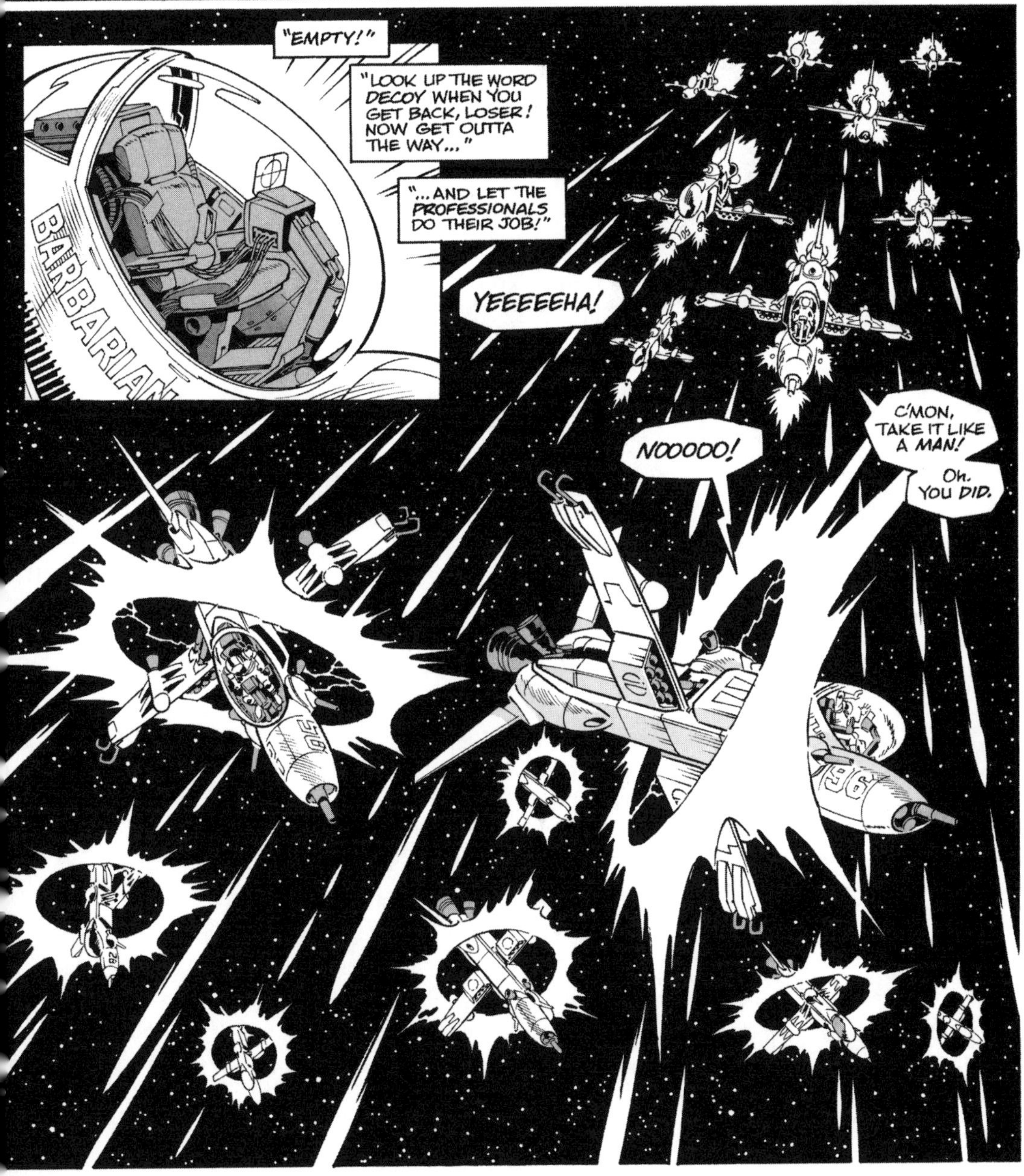
"EMPTY!"
"LOOK UP THE WORD DECOY WHEN YOU GET BACK, LOSER! NOW GET OUTTA THE WAY..."
"...AND LET THE PROFESSIONALS DO THEIR JOB!"
BARBARIAN
YEEEEEHA!
NOOOOO!
C'MON, TAKE IT LIKE A MAN!
Oh. You DID.

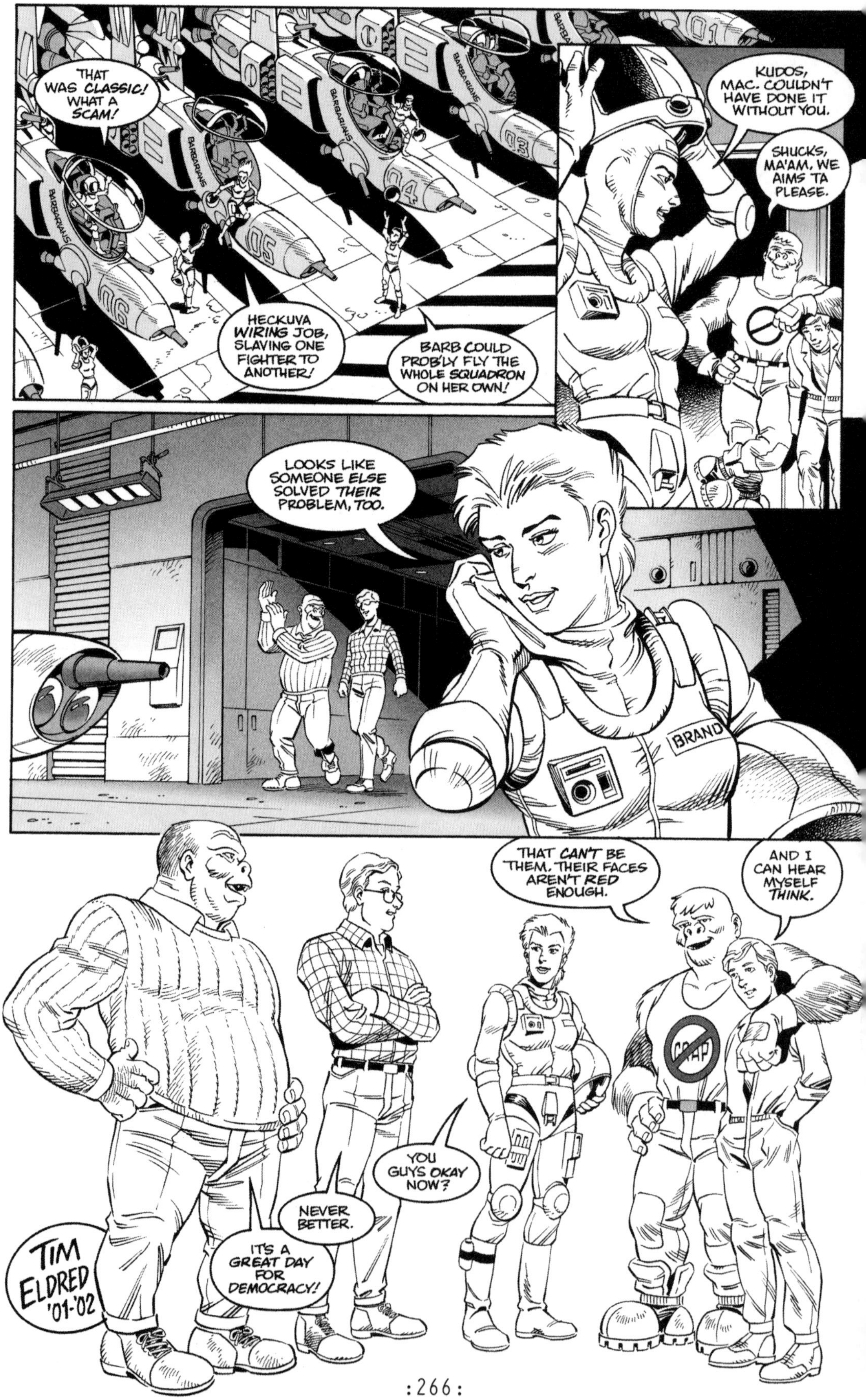
THAT WAS CLASSIC! WHAT A SCAM!
HECKUVA WIRING JOB, SLAVING ONE FIGHTER TO ANOTHER!
BARB COULD PROB'LY FLY THE WHOLE SQUADRON ON HER OWN!
KUDOS, MAC. COULDN'T HAVE DONE IT WITHOUT YOU.
SHUCKS, MA'AM, WE AIMS TA PLEASE.
LOOKS LIKE SOMEONE ELSE SOLVED THEIR PROBLEM, TOO.
BRAND
THAT CAN'T BE THEM. THEIR FACES AREN'T RED ENOUGH.
AND I CAN HEAR MYSELF THINK.
YOU GUYS OKAY NOW?
NEVER BETTER.
IT'S A GREAT DAY FOR DEMOCRACY!
TIM ELDRED '01-'02

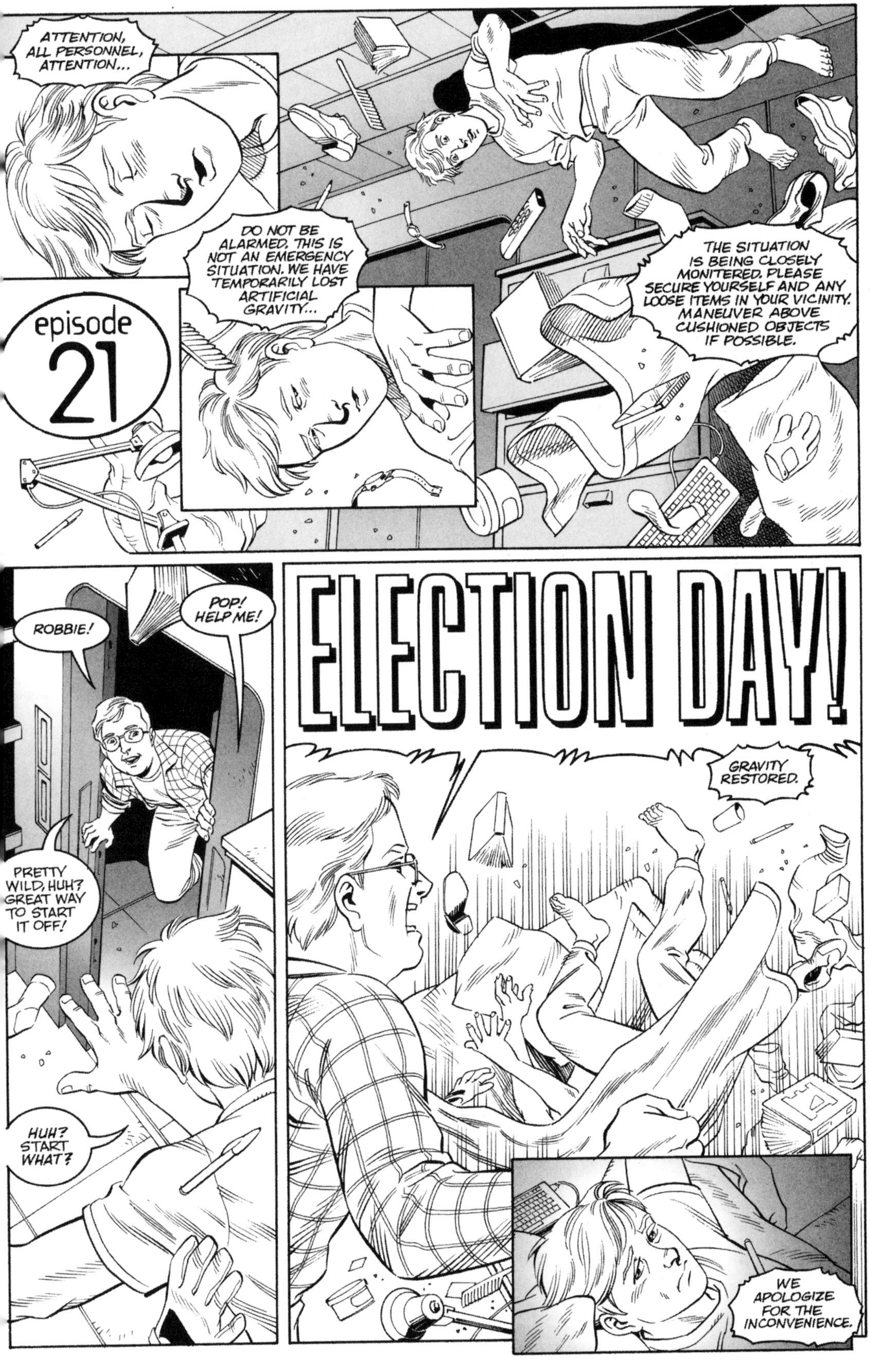
ATTENTION, ALL PERSONNEL, ATTENTION...
DO NOT BE ALARMED. THIS IS NOT AN EMERGENCY SITUATION. WE HAVE TEMPORARILY LOST ARTIFICIAL GRAVITY...
THE SITUATION IS BEING CLOSELY MONITERED. PLEASE SECURE YOURSELF AND ANY LOOSE ITEMS IN YOUR VICINITY. MANEUVER ABOVE CUSHIONED OBJECTS IF POSSIBLE.
episode 21
ROBBIE!
POP! HELP ME!
PRETTY WILD, HUH? GREAT WAY TO START IT OFF!
HUH? START WHAT?
ELECTION DAY!
GRAVITY RESTORED.
WE APOLOGIZE FOR THE INCONVENIENCE.

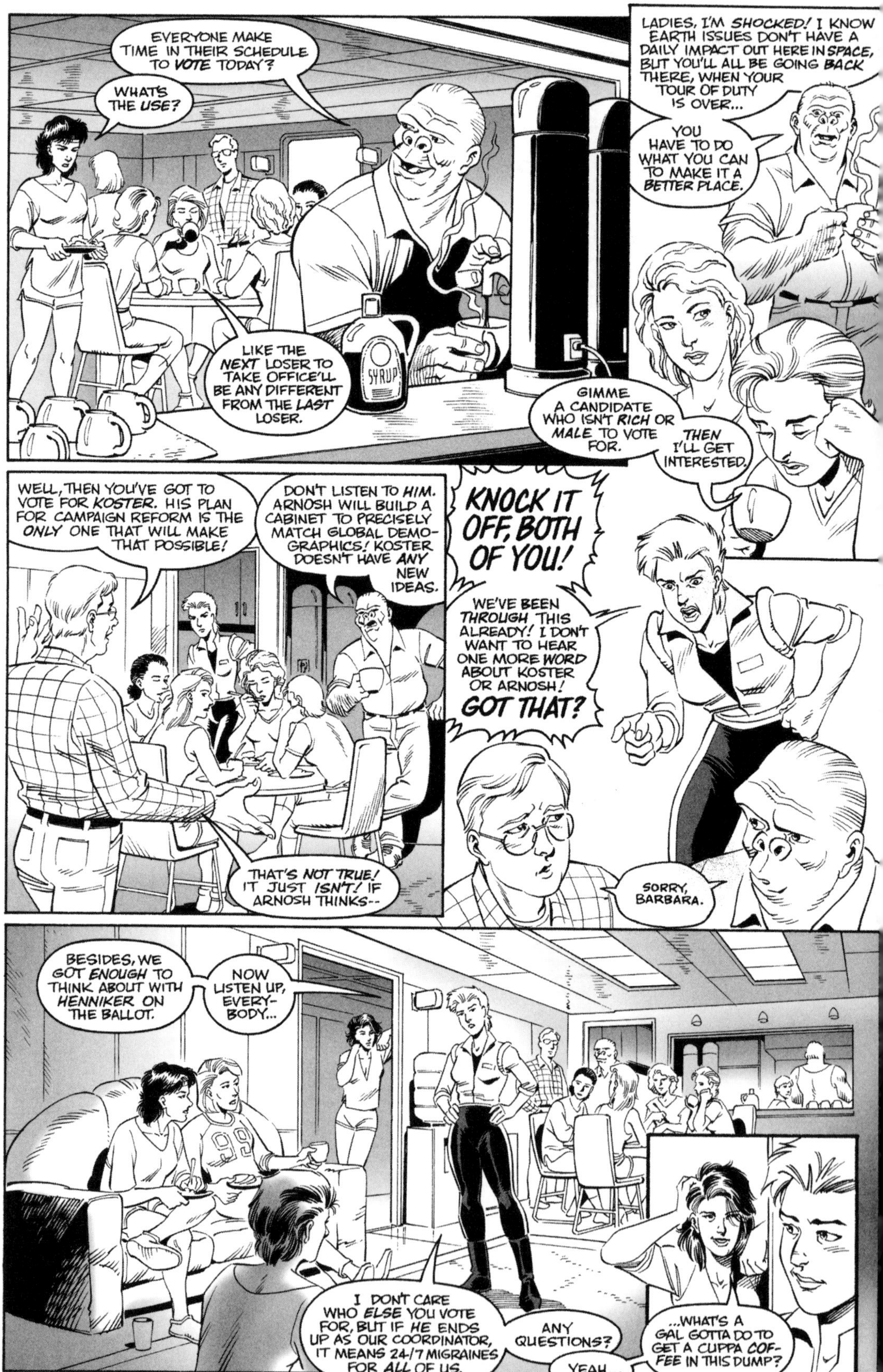
EVERYONE MAKE TIME IN THEIR SCHEDULE TO VOTE TODAY?
WHAT'S THE USE?
LIKE THE NEXT LOSER TO TAKE OFFICE'LL BE ANY DIFFERENT FROM THE LAST LOSER.
SYRUP
LADIES, I'M SHOCKED! I KNOW EARTH ISSUES DON'T HAVE A DAILY IMPACT OUT HERE IN SPACE, BUT YOU'LL ALL BE GOING BACK THERE, WHEN YOUR TOUR OF DUTY IS OVER...
YOU HAVE TO DO WHAT YOU CAN TO MAKE IT A BETTER PLACE.
GIMME A CANDIDATE WHO ISN'T RICH OR MALE TO VOTE FOR.
THEN I'LL GET INTERESTED.
WELL, THEN YOU'VE GOT TO VOTE FOR KOSTER. HIS PLAN FOR CAMPAIGN REFORM IS THE ONLY ONE THAT WILL MAKE THAT POSSIBLE!
DON'T LISTEN TO HIM. ARNOSH WILL BUILD A CABINET TO PRECISELY MATCH GLOBAL DEMOGRAPHICS! KOSTER DOESN'T HAVE ANY NEW IDEAS.
THAT'S NOT TRUE! IT JUST ISN'T! IF ARNOSH THINKS--
KNOCK IT OFF, BOTH OF YOU!
WE'VE BEEN THROUGH THIS ALREADY! I DON'T WANT TO HEAR ONE MORE WORD ABOUT KOSTER OR ARNOSH! GOT THAT?
SORRY, BARBARA.
BESIDES, WE GOT ENOUGH TO THINK ABOUT WITH HENNIKER ON THE BALLOT.
NOW LISTEN UP, EVERYBODY...
I DON'T CARE WHO ELSE YOU VOTE FOR, BUT IF HE ENDS UP AS OUR COORDINATOR, IT MEANS 24/7 MIGRAINES FOR ALL OF US.
ANY QUESTIONS?
YEAH...
...WHAT'S A GAL GOTTA DO TO GET A CUPPA COFFEE IN THIS DUMP?

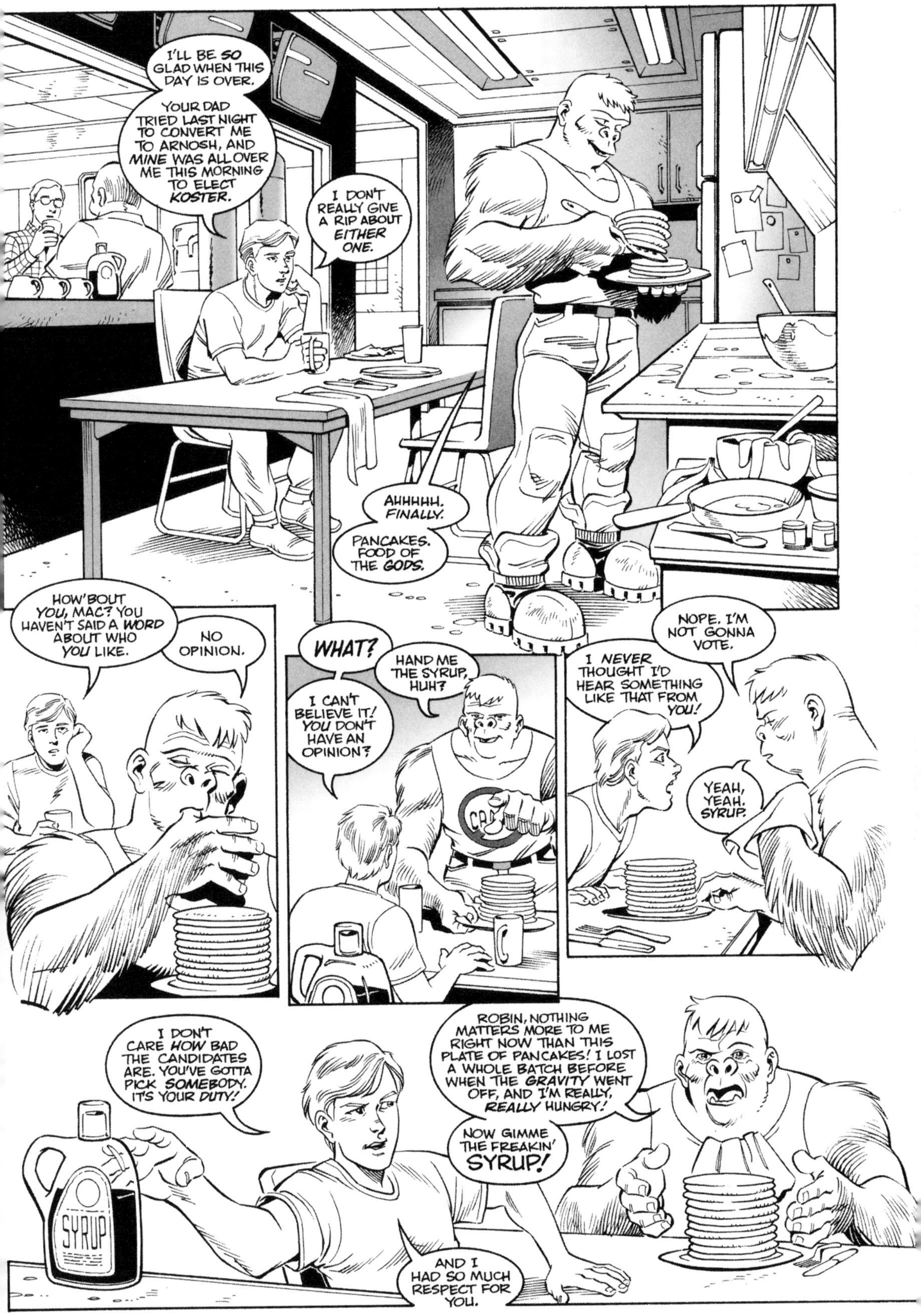
I'LL BE SO GLAD WHEN THIS DAY IS OVER.
YOUR DAD TRIED LAST NIGHT TO CONVERT ME TO ARNOSH, AND MINE WAS ALL OVER ME THIS MORNING TO ELECT KOSTER.
I DON'T REALLY GIVE A RIP ABOUT EITHER ONE.
AHHHHH. FINALLY.
PANCAKES. FOOD OF THE GODS.
HOW'BOUT YOU, MAC? YOU HAVEN'T SAID A WORD ABOUT WHO YOU LIKE.
NO OPINION.
WHAT?
I CAN'T BELIEVE IT! YOU DON'T HAVE AN OPINION?
HAND ME THE SYRUP, HUH?
NOPE. I'M NOT GONNA VOTE.
I NEVER THOUGHT I'D HEAR SOMETHING LIKE THAT FROM YOU!
YEAH, YEAH. SYRUP.
I DON'T CARE HOW BAD THE CANDIDATES ARE. YOU'VE GOTTA PICK SOMEBODY. IT'S YOUR DUTY!
ROBIN, NOTHING MATTERS MORE TO ME RIGHT NOW THAN THIS PLATE OF PANCAKES! I LOST A WHOLE BATCH BEFORE WHEN THE GRAVITY WENT OFF, AND I'M REALLY, REALLY HUNGRY!
NOW GIMME THE FREAKIN' SYRUP!
AND I HAD SO MUCH RESPECT FOR YOU.
SYRUP

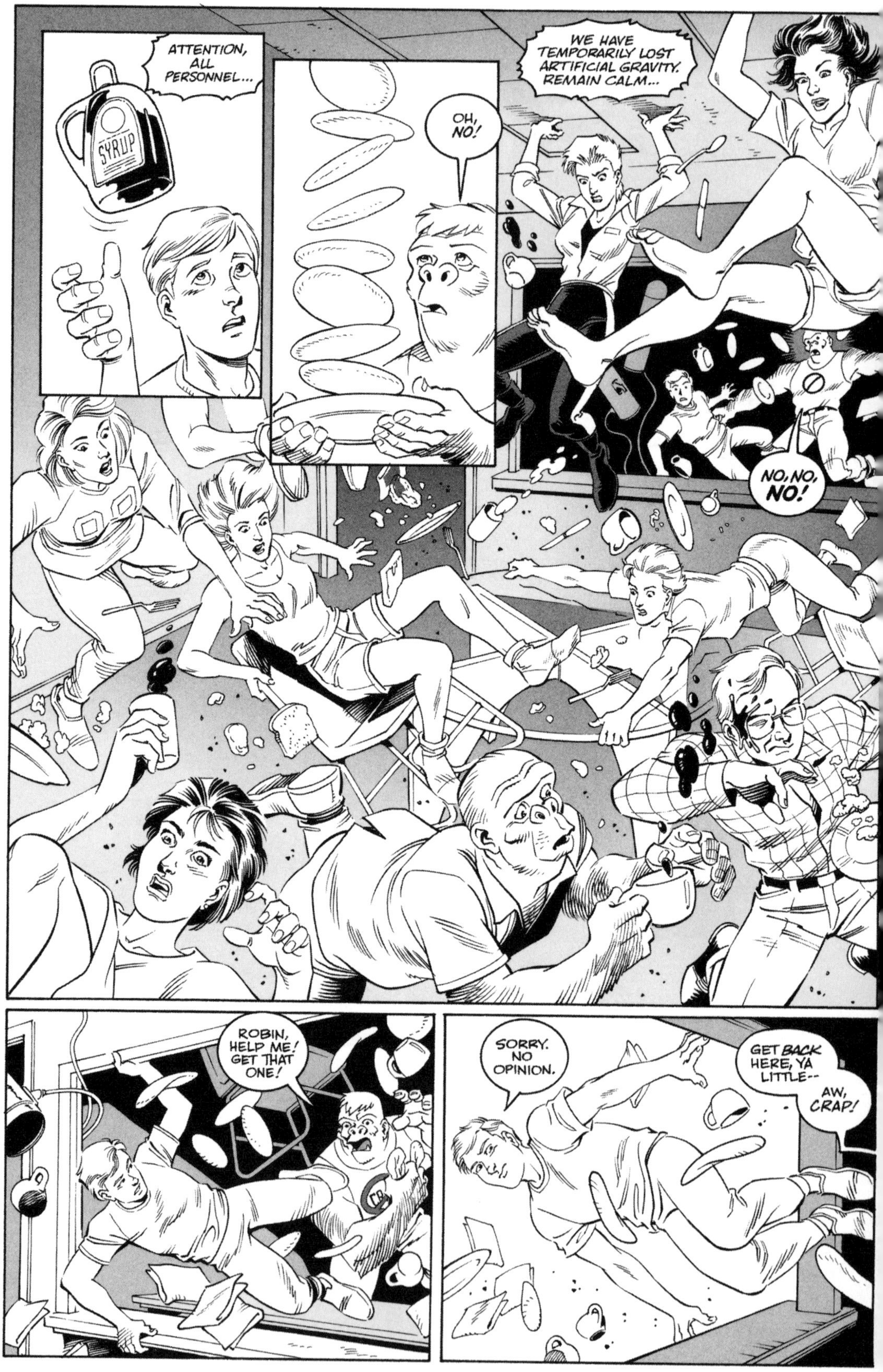
ATTENTION, ALL PERSONNEL...
SYRUP
OH, NO!
WE HAVE TEMPORARILY LOST ARTIFICIAL GRAVITY. REMAIN CALM...
NO, NO, NO!
ROBIN, HELP ME! GET THAT ONE!
SORRY. NO OPINION.
GET BACK HERE, YA LITTLE--
AW, CRAP!

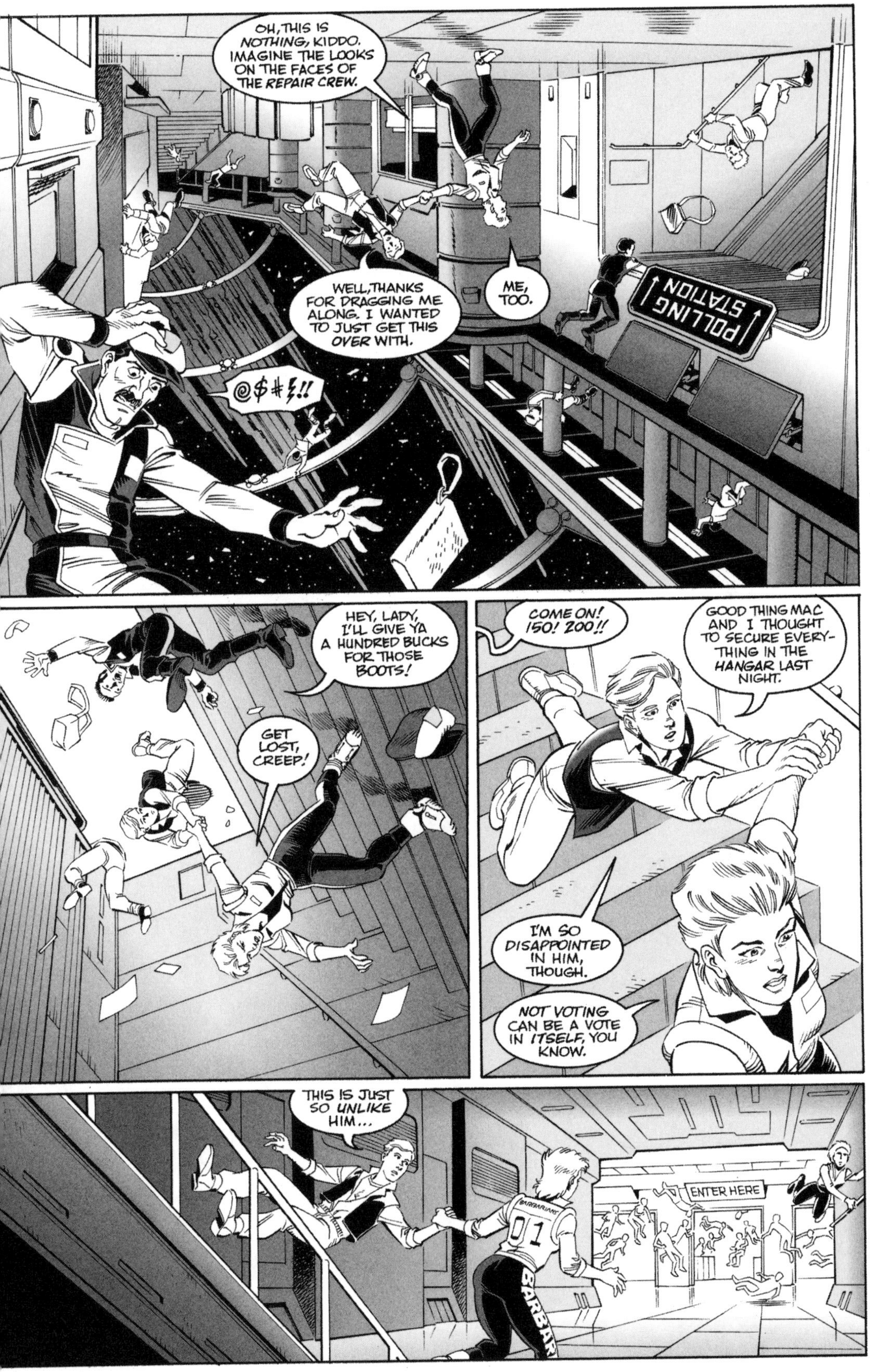

OH, THIS IS NOTHING, KIDDO. IMAGINE THE LOOKS ON THE FACES OF THE REPAIR CREW.
WELL, THANKS FOR DRAGGING ME ALONG. I WANTED TO JUST GET THIS OVER WITH.
ME, TOO.
POLLING STATION
@$#!!
HEY, LADY, I'LL GIVE YA A HUNDRED BUCKS FOR THOSE BOOTS!
GET LOST, CREEP!
COME ON! 150! 200!!
GOOD THING MAC AND I THOUGHT TO SECURE EVERYTHING IN THE HANGAR LAST NIGHT.
I'M SO DISAPPOINTED IN HIM, THOUGH.
NOT VOTING CAN BE A VOTE IN ITSELF, YOU KNOW.
THIS IS JUST SO UNLIKE HIM...
ENTER HERE

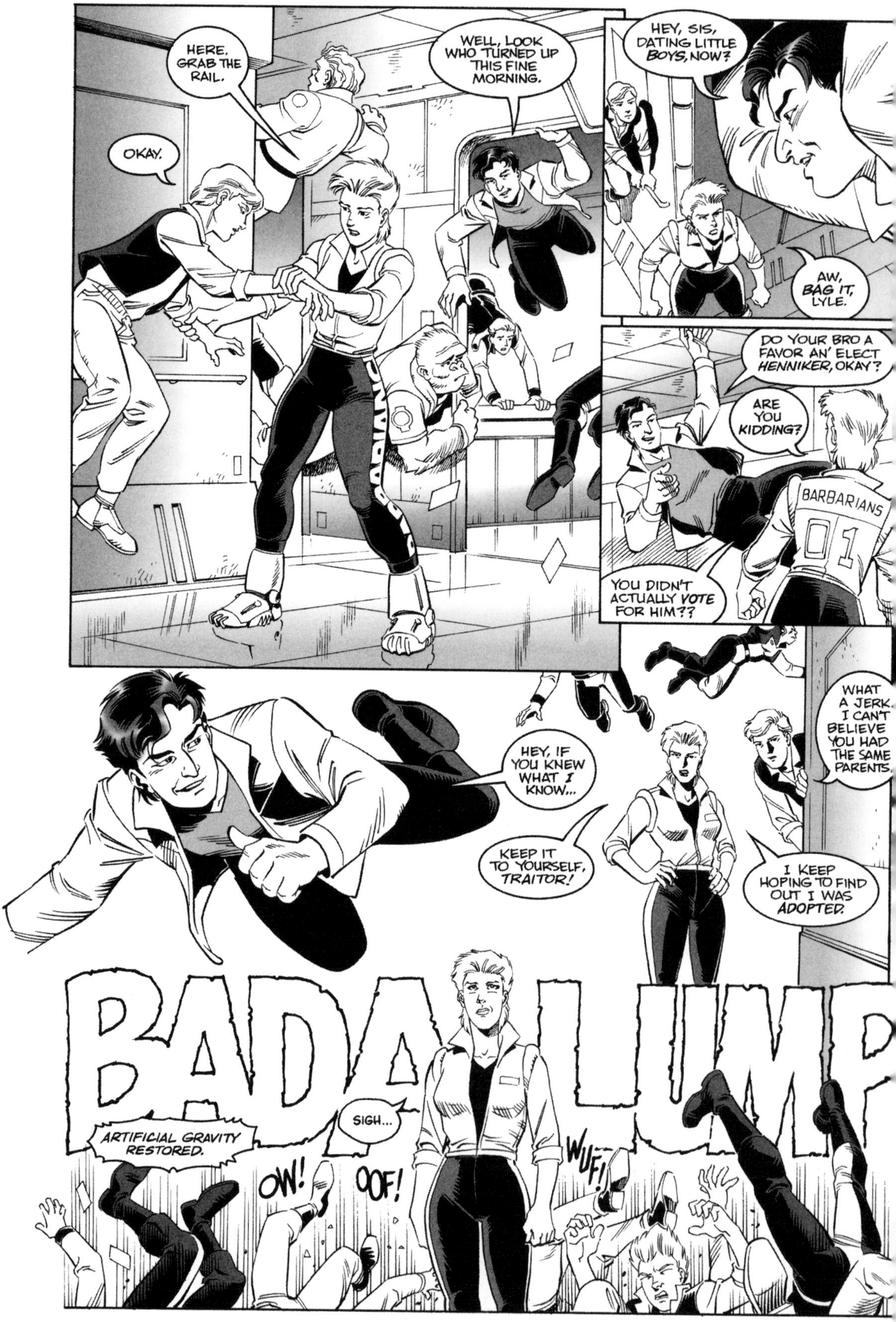

HERE. GRAB THE RAIL.
OKAY.
WELL, LOOK WHO TURNED UP THIS FINE MORNING.
HEY, SIS, DATING LITTLE BOYS, NOW?
AW, BAG IT, LYLE.
DO YOUR BRO A FAVOR AN' ELECT HENNIKER, OKAY?
ARE YOU KIDDING?
YOU DIDN'T ACTUALLY VOTE FOR HIM??
BARBARIANS
01
HEY, IF YOU KNEW WHAT I KNOW...
KEEP IT TO YOURSELF, TRAITOR!
WHAT A JERK. I CAN'T BELIEVE YOU HAD THE SAME PARENTS.
I KEEP HOPING TO FIND OUT I WAS ADOPTED.
BADALUMP
ARTIFICIAL GRAVITY RESTORED.
SIGH...
OW!
OOF!
WUF!

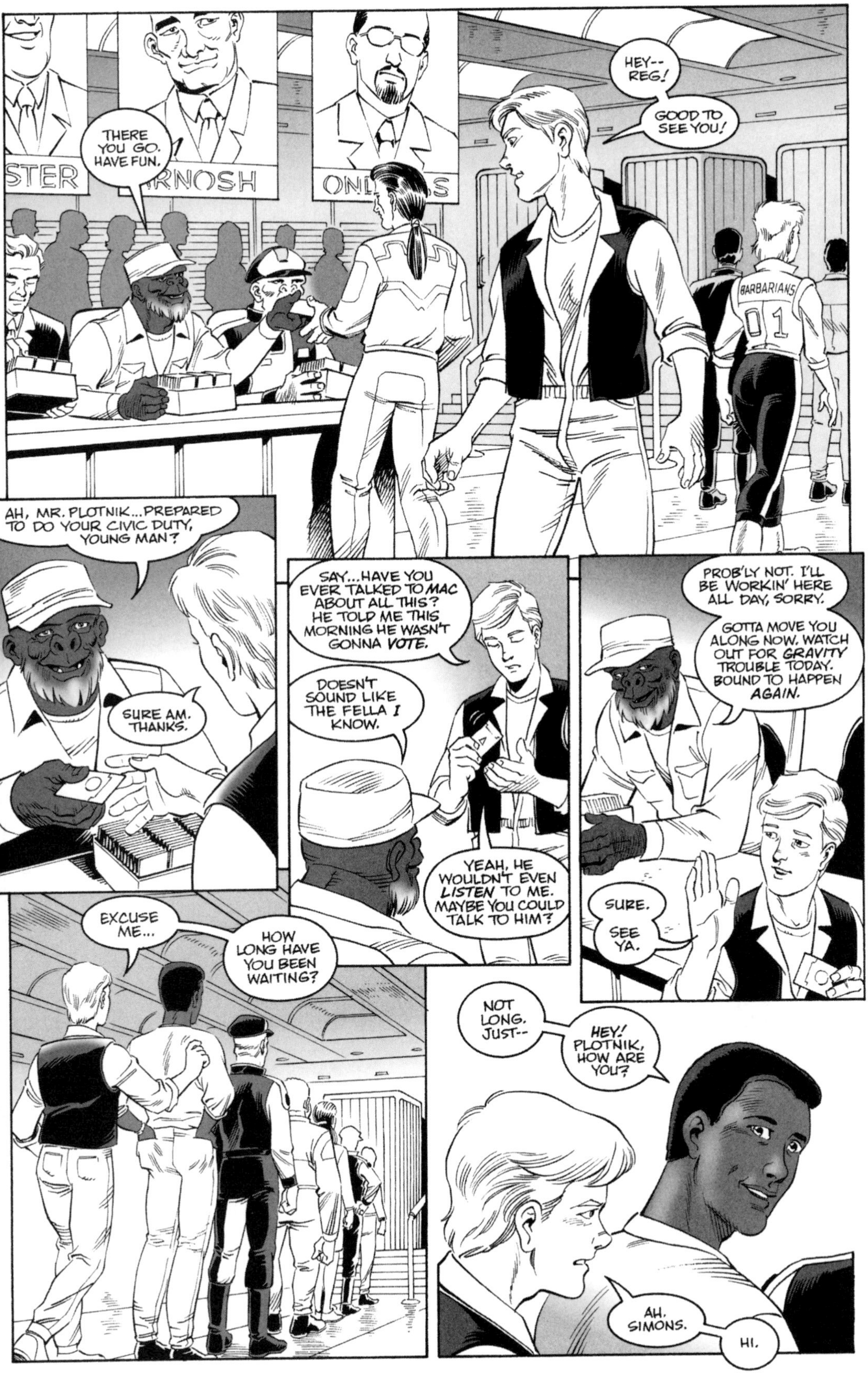
STER
RNOSH
ONL S
THERE YOU GO. HAVE FUN.
HEY-- REG!
GOOD TO SEE YOU!
BARBARIANS
01
AH, MR. PLOTNIK...PREPARED TO DO YOUR CIVIC DUTY, YOUNG MAN?
SURE AM. THANKS.
SAY...HAVE YOU EVER TALKED TO MAC ABOUT ALL THIS? HE TOLD ME THIS MORNING HE WASN'T GONNA VOTE.
DOESN'T SOUND LIKE THE FELLA I KNOW.
YEAH, HE WOULDN'T EVEN LISTEN TO ME. MAYBE YOU COULD TALK TO HIM?
PROB'LY NOT. I'LL BE WORKIN' HERE ALL DAY, SORRY.
GOTTA MOVE YOU ALONG NOW. WATCH OUT FOR GRAVITY TROUBLE TODAY. BOUND TO HAPPEN AGAIN.
SURE.
SEE YA.
EXCUSE ME...
HOW LONG HAVE YOU BEEN WAITING?
NOT LONG. JUST--
HEY! PLOTNIK, HOW ARE YOU?
AH. SIMONS.
HI.

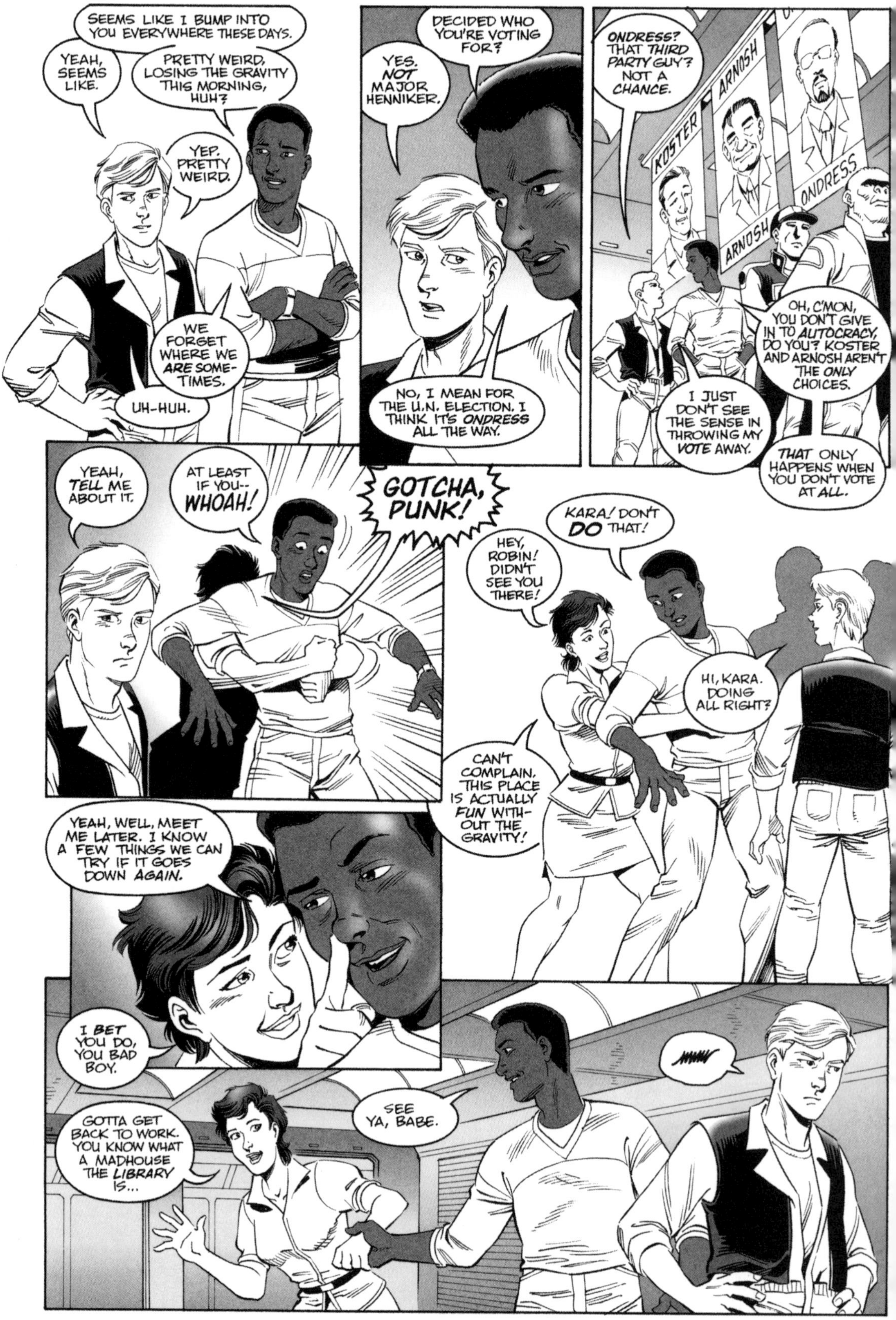
SEEMS LIKE I BUMP INTO YOU EVERYWHERE THESE DAYS.
YEAH, SEEMS LIKE.
PRETTY WEIRD, LOSING THE GRAVITY THIS MORNING, HUH?
YEP. PRETTY WEIRD.
WE FORGET WHERE WE ARE SOME-TIMES.
UH-HUH.
DECIDED WHO YOU'RE VOTING FOR?
YES. NOT MAJOR HENNIKER.
NO, I MEAN FOR THE U.N. ELECTION. I THINK IT'S ONDRESS ALL THE WAY.
ONDRESS? THAT THIRD PARTY GUY? NOT A CHANCE.
KOSTER
ARNOSH
ARNOSH
ONDRESS
OH, C'MON, YOU DON'T GIVE IN TO AUTOCRACY, DO YOU? KOSTER AND ARNOSH AREN'T THE ONLY CHOICES.
I JUST DON'T SEE THE SENSE IN THROWING MY VOTE AWAY.
THAT ONLY HAPPENS WHEN YOU DON'T VOTE AT ALL.
YEAH, TELL ME ABOUT IT.
AT LEAST IF YOU-- WHOAH!
GOTCHA, PUNK!
KARA! DON'T DO THAT!
HEY, ROBIN! DIDN'T SEE YOU THERE!
HI, KARA. DOING ALL RIGHT?
CAN'T COMPLAIN. THIS PLACE IS ACTUALLY FUN WITH-OUT THE GRAVITY!
YEAH, WELL, MEET ME LATER. I KNOW A FEW THINGS WE CAN TRY IF IT GOES DOWN AGAIN.
I BET YOU DO, YOU BAD BOY.
GOTTA GET BACK TO WORK. YOU KNOW WHAT A MADHOUSE THE LIBRARY IS...
SEE YA, BABE.

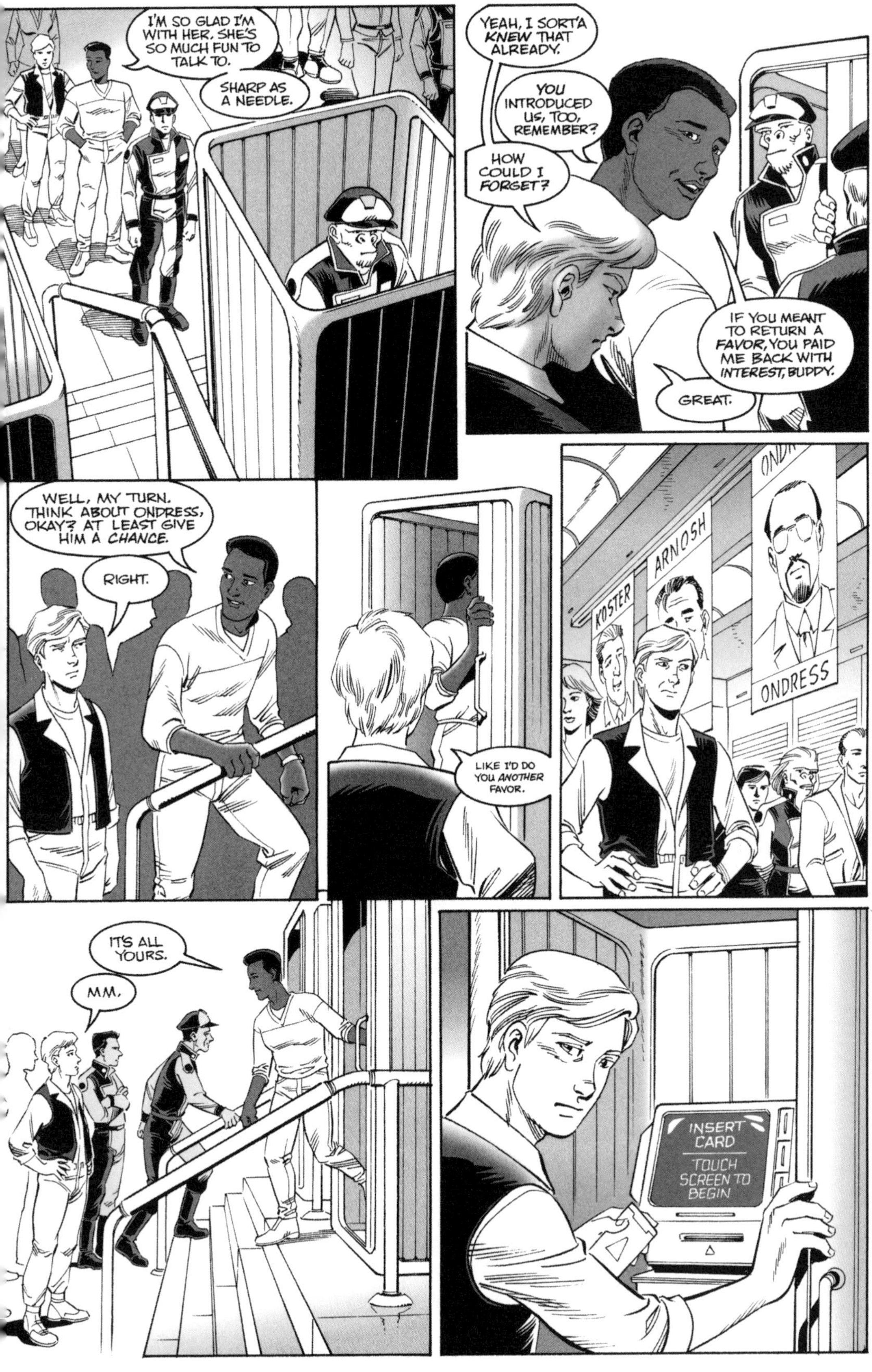
I'M SO GLAD I'M WITH HER. SHE'S SO MUCH FUN TO TALK TO.
SHARP AS A NEEDLE.
YEAH, I SORT'A KNEW THAT ALREADY.
YOU INTRODUCED US, TOO, REMEMBER?
HOW COULD I FORGET?
IF YOU MEANT TO RETURN A FAVOR, YOU PAID ME BACK WITH INTEREST, BUDDY.
GREAT.
WELL, MY TURN. THINK ABOUT ONDRESS, OKAY? AT LEAST GIVE HIM A CHANCE.
RIGHT.
LIKE I'D DO YOU ANOTHER FAVOR.
KOSTER
ARNOSH
ONDRESS
IT'S ALL YOURS.
MM.
INSERT CARD
TOUCH SCREEN TO BEGIN

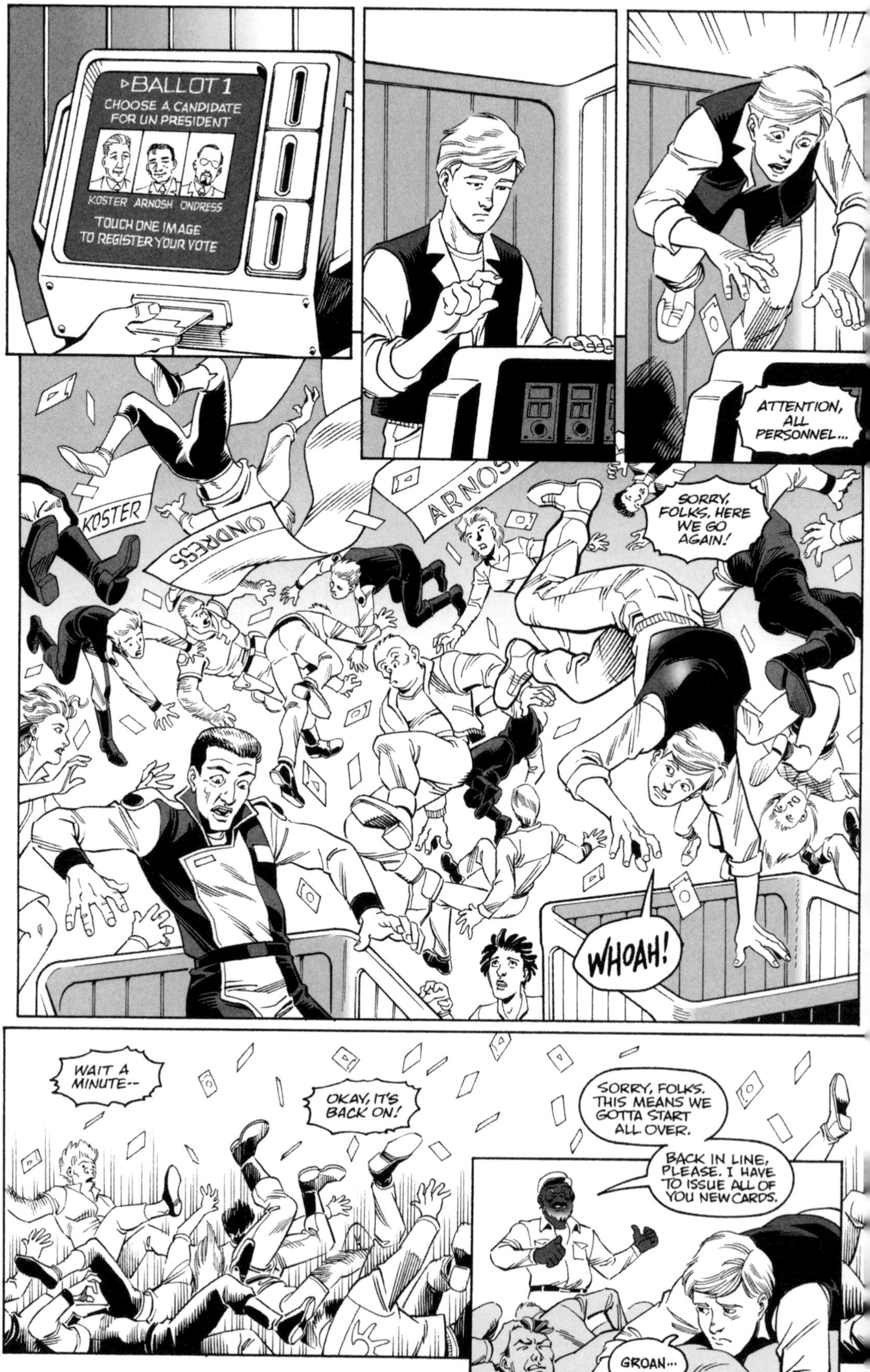
BALLOT 1
CHOOSE A CANDIDATE FOR UN PRESIDENT
KOSTER ARNOSH ONDRESS
TOUCH ONE IMAGE TO REGISTER YOUR VOTE
ATTENTION, ALL PERSONNEL...
KOSTER
ONDRESS
ARNOSH
SORRY, FOLKS. HERE WE GO AGAIN!
WHOAH!
WAIT A MINUTE--
OKAY, IT'S BACK ON!
SORRY, FOLKS. THIS MEANS WE GOTTA START ALL OVER.
BACK IN LINE, PLEASE. I HAVE TO ISSUE ALL OF YOU NEW CARDS.
GROAN...

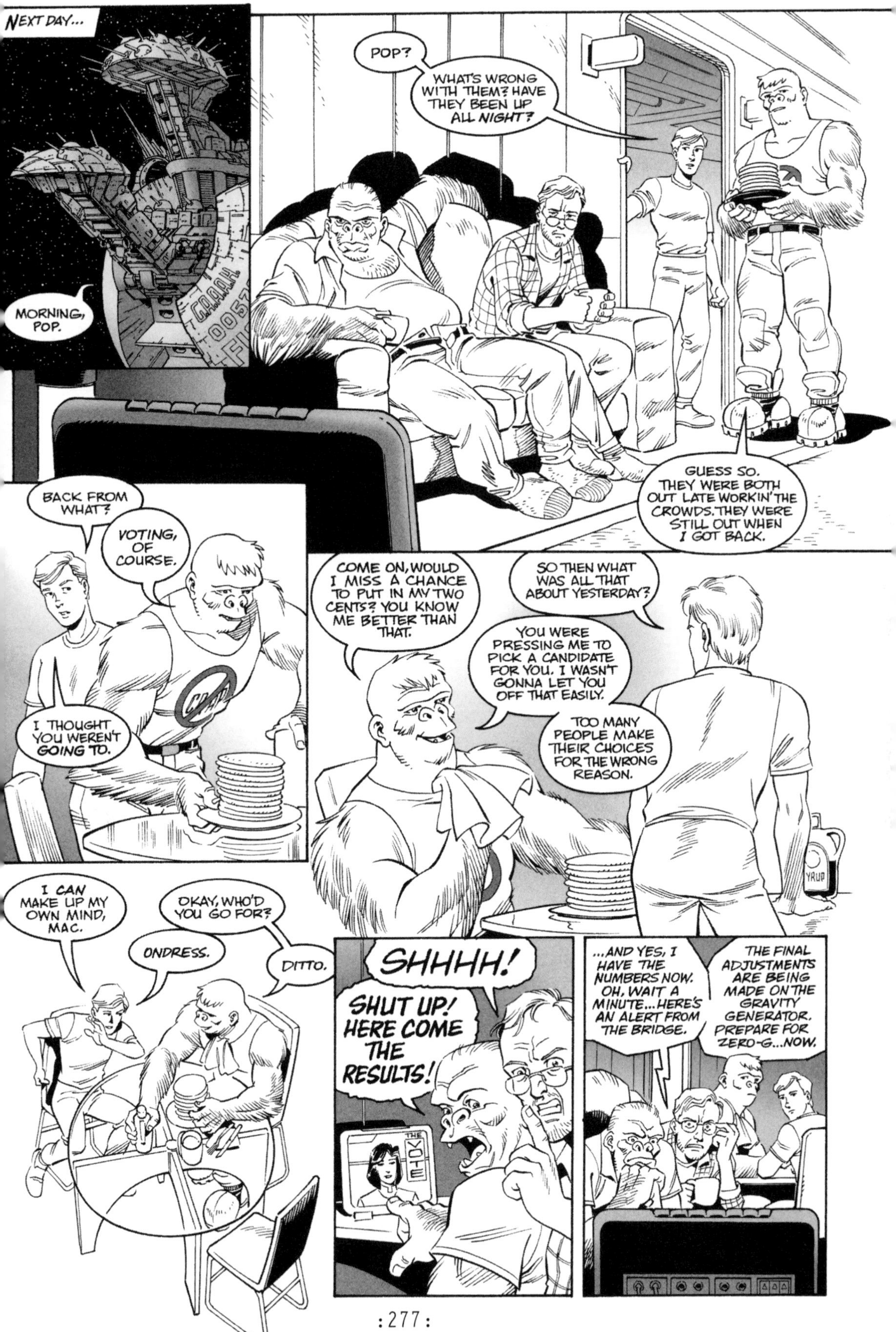
NEXT DAY...
MORNING, POP.
POP?
WHAT'S WRONG WITH THEM? HAVE THEY BEEN UP ALL NIGHT?
GUESS SO. THEY WERE BOTH OUT LATE WORKIN' THE CROWDS. THEY WERE STILL OUT WHEN I GOT BACK.
BACK FROM WHAT?
VOTING, OF COURSE.
I THOUGHT YOU WEREN'T GOING TO.
COME ON, WOULD I MISS A CHANCE TO PUT IN MY TWO CENTS? YOU KNOW ME BETTER THAN THAT.
SO THEN WHAT WAS ALL THAT ABOUT YESTERDAY?
YOU WERE PRESSING ME TO PICK A CANDIDATE FOR YOU. I WASN'T GONNA LET YOU OFF THAT EASILY.
TOO MANY PEOPLE MAKE THEIR CHOICES FOR THE WRONG REASON.
I CAN MAKE UP MY OWN MIND, MAC.
OKAY, WHO'D YOU GO FOR?
ONDRESS.
DITTO.
SHHHH!
SHUT UP! HERE COME THE RESULTS!
THE VOTE
...AND YES, I HAVE THE NUMBERS NOW. OH, WAIT A MINUTE...HERE'S AN ALERT FROM THE BRIDGE.
THE FINAL ADJUSTMENTS ARE BEING MADE ON THE GRAVITY GENERATOR. PREPARE FOR ZERO-G...NOW.

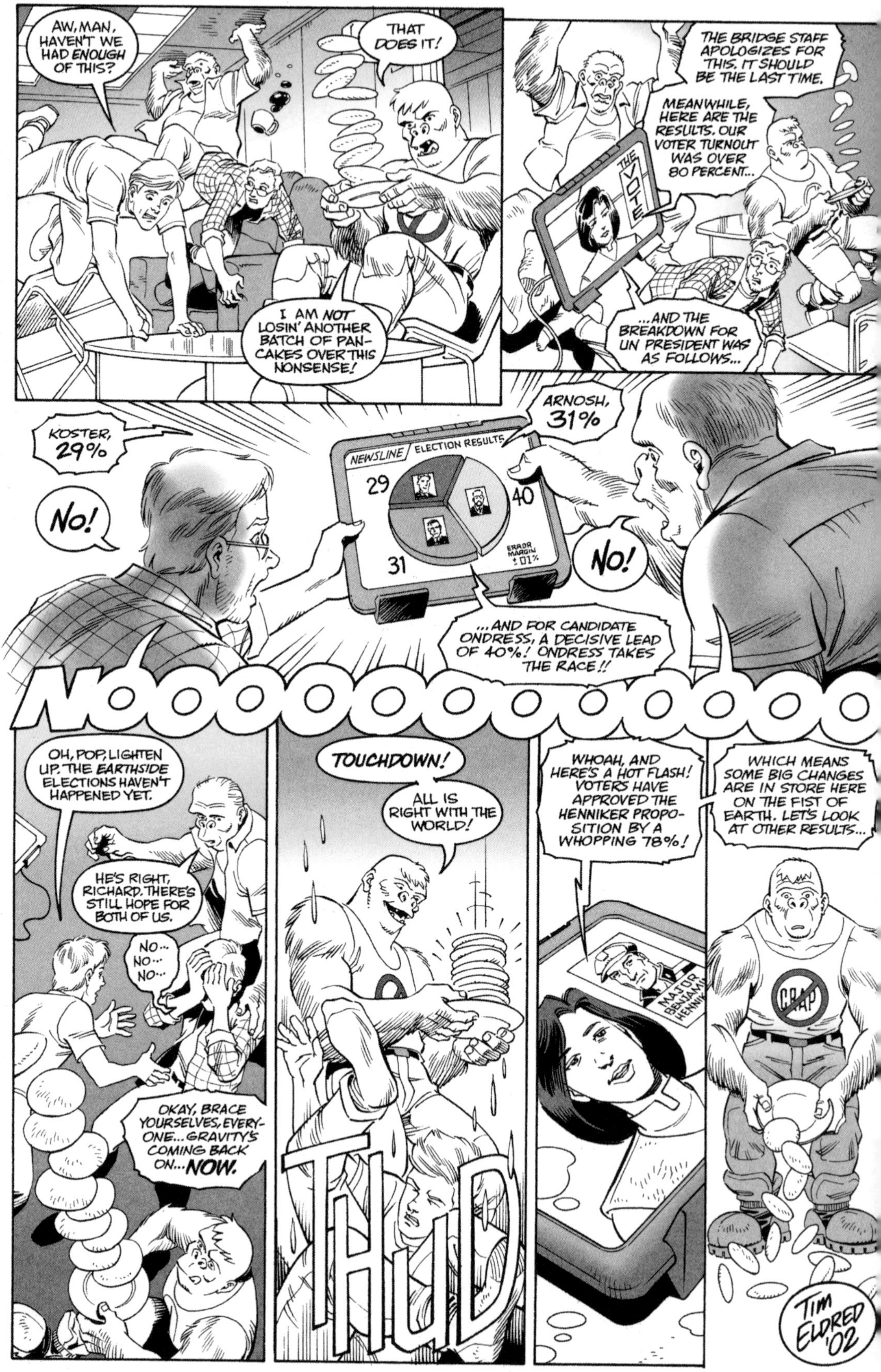
AW, MAN, HAVEN'T WE HAD ENOUGH OF THIS?
THAT DOES IT!
I AM NOT LOSIN' ANOTHER BATCH OF PANCAKES OVER THIS NONSENSE!
THE BRIDGE STAFF APOLOGIZES FOR THIS. IT SHOULD BE THE LAST TIME.
MEANWHILE, HERE ARE THE RESULTS. OUR VOTER TURNOUT WAS OVER 80 PERCENT...
THE VOTE
...AND THE BREAKDOWN FOR UN PRESIDENT WAS AS FOLLOWS...
KOSTER, 29%
No!
NEWSLINE
ELECTION RESULTS
29
40
31
ERROR MARGIN ±.01%
ARNOSH, 31%
No!
...AND FOR CANDIDATE ONDRESS, A DECISIVE LEAD OF 40%! ONDRESS TAKES THE RACE!!
NOOOOOOOOOOOOO
OH, POP, LIGHTEN UP. THE EARTHSIDE ELECTIONS HAVEN'T HAPPENED YET.
HE'S RIGHT, RICHARD. THERE'S STILL HOPE FOR BOTH OF US.
NO... NO... NO...
OKAY, BRACE YOURSELVES, EVERYONE... GRAVITY'S COMING BACK ON... NOW.
TOUCHDOWN!
ALL IS RIGHT WITH THE WORLD!
THUD
WHOAH, AND HERE'S A HOT FLASH! VOTERS HAVE APPROVED THE HENNIKER PROPOSITION BY A WHOPPING 78%!
WHICH MEANS SOME BIG CHANGES ARE IN STORE HERE ON THE FIST OF EARTH. LET'S LOOK AT OTHER RESULTS...
CRAP
TIM ELDRED '02

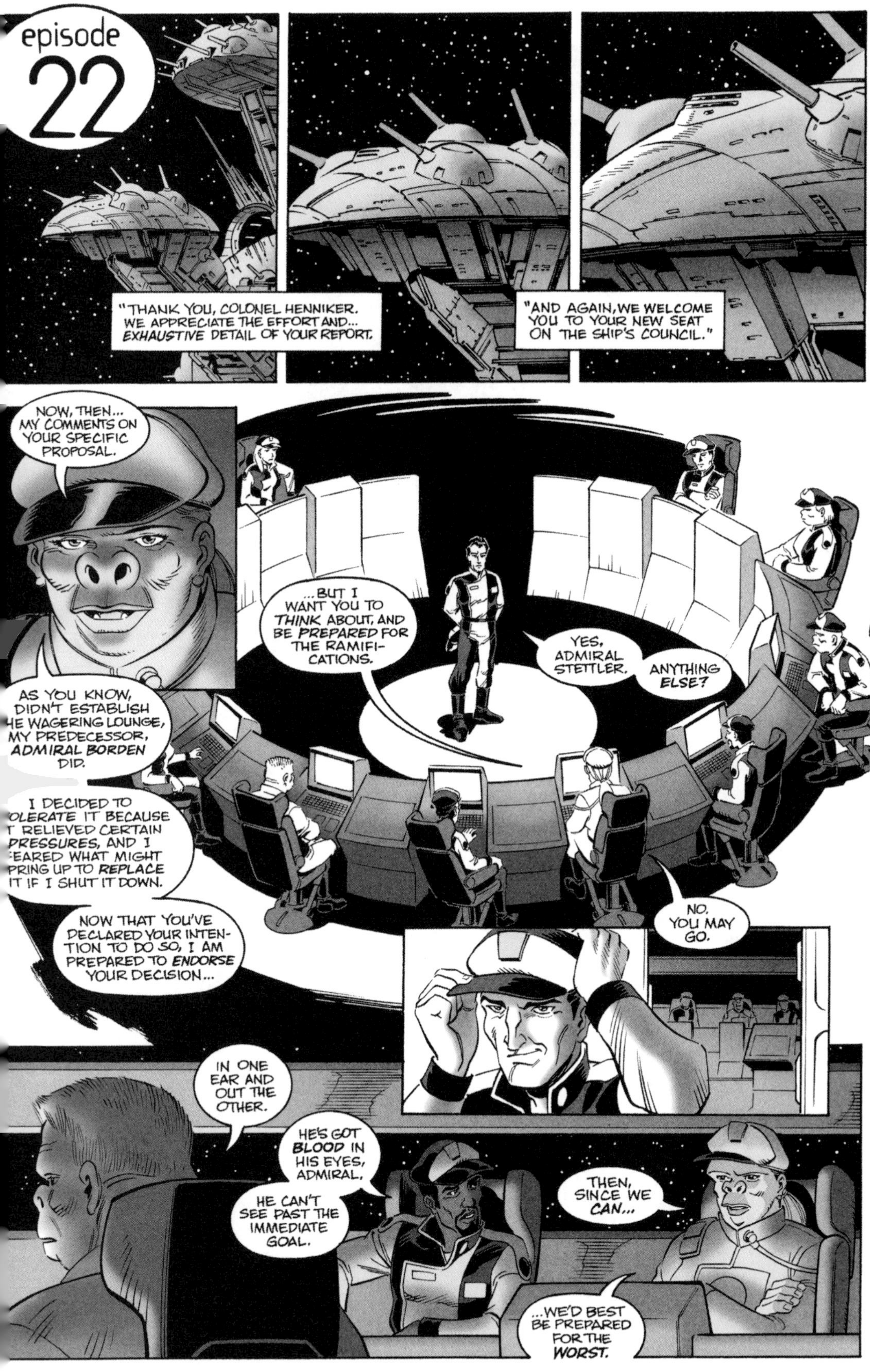
episode 22
"THANK YOU, COLONEL HENNIKER. WE APPRECIATE THE EFFORT AND... EXHAUSTIVE DETAIL OF YOUR REPORT.
"AND AGAIN, WE WELCOME YOU TO YOUR NEW SEAT ON THE SHIP'S COUNCIL."
NOW, THEN... MY COMMENTS ON YOUR SPECIFIC PROPOSAL.
AS YOU KNOW, DIDN'T ESTABLISH HE WAGERING LOUNGE, MY PREDECESSOR, ADMIRAL BORDEN DID.
I DECIDED TO OLERATE IT BECAUSE T RELIEVED CERTAIN PRESSURES, AND I EARED WHAT MIGHT PRING UP TO REPLACE IT IF I SHUT IT DOWN.
NOW THAT YOU'VE DECLARED YOUR INTENTION TO DO SO, I AM PREPARED TO ENDORSE YOUR DECISION...
...BUT I WANT YOU TO THINK ABOUT, AND BE PREPARED FOR THE RAMIFICATIONS.
YES, ADMIRAL STETTLER.
ANYTHING ELSE?
NO. YOU MAY GO.
IN ONE EAR AND OUT THE OTHER.
HE'S GOT BLOOD IN HIS EYES, ADMIRAL.
HE CAN'T SEE PAST THE IMMEDIATE GOAL.
THEN, SINCE WE CAN...
...WE'D BEST BE PREPARED FOR THE WORST.

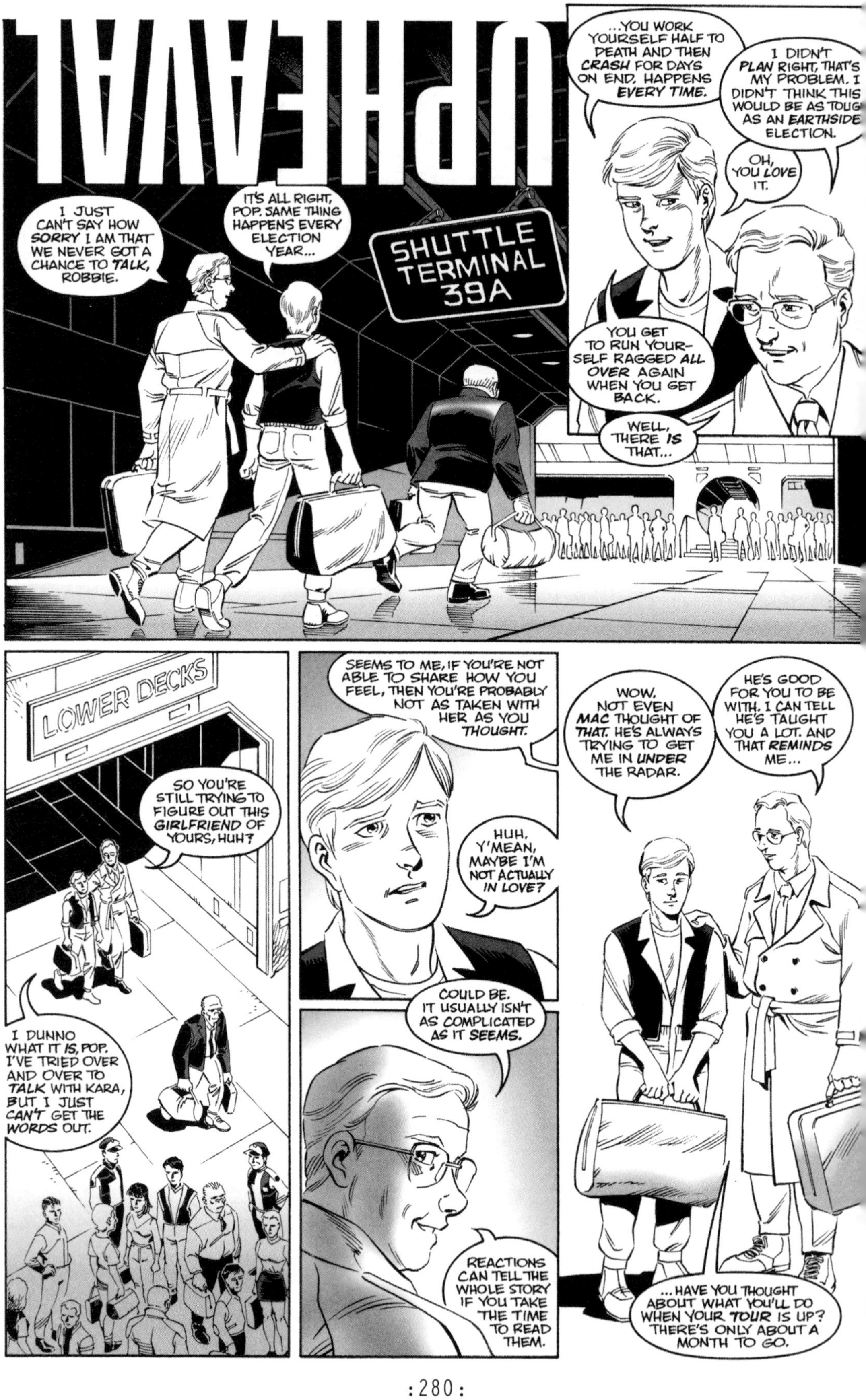
UPHEAVAL
I JUST CAN'T SAY HOW SORRY I AM THAT WE NEVER GOT A CHANCE TO TALK, ROBBIE.
IT'S ALL RIGHT, POP. SAME THING HAPPENS EVERY ELECTION YEAR...
SHUTTLE TERMINAL 39A
...YOU WORK YOURSELF HALF TO DEATH AND THEN CRASH FOR DAYS ON END. HAPPENS EVERY TIME.
I DIDN'T PLAN RIGHT, THAT'S MY PROBLEM. I DIDN'T THINK THIS WOULD BE AS TOUG AS AN EARTHSIDE ELECTION.
OH, YOU LOVE IT.
YOU GET TO RUN YOURSELF RAGGED ALL OVER AGAIN WHEN YOU GET BACK.
WELL, THERE IS THAT...
LOWER DECKS
SO YOU'RE STILL TRYING TO FIGURE OUT THIS GIRLFRIEND OF YOURS, HUH?
I DUNNO WHAT IT IS, POP. I'VE TRIED OVER AND OVER TO TALK WITH KARA, BUT I JUST CAN'T GET THE WORDS OUT.
SEEMS TO ME, IF YOU'RE NOT ABLE TO SHARE HOW YOU FEEL, THEN YOU'RE PROBABLY NOT AS TAKEN WITH HER AS YOU THOUGHT.
HUH. Y'MEAN, MAYBE I'M NOT ACTUALLY IN LOVE?
COULD BE. IT USUALLY ISN'T AS COMPLICATED AS IT SEEMS.
REACTIONS CAN TELL THE WHOLE STORY IF YOU TAKE THE TIME TO READ THEM.
WOW. NOT EVEN MAC THOUGHT OF THAT. HE'S ALWAYS TRYING TO GET ME IN UNDER THE RADAR.
HE'S GOOD FOR YOU TO BE WITH. I CAN TELL HE'S TAUGHT YOU A LOT. AND THAT REMINDS ME...
...HAVE YOU THOUGHT ABOUT WHAT YOU'LL DO WHEN YOUR TOUR IS UP? THERE'S ONLY ABOUT A MONTH TO GO.

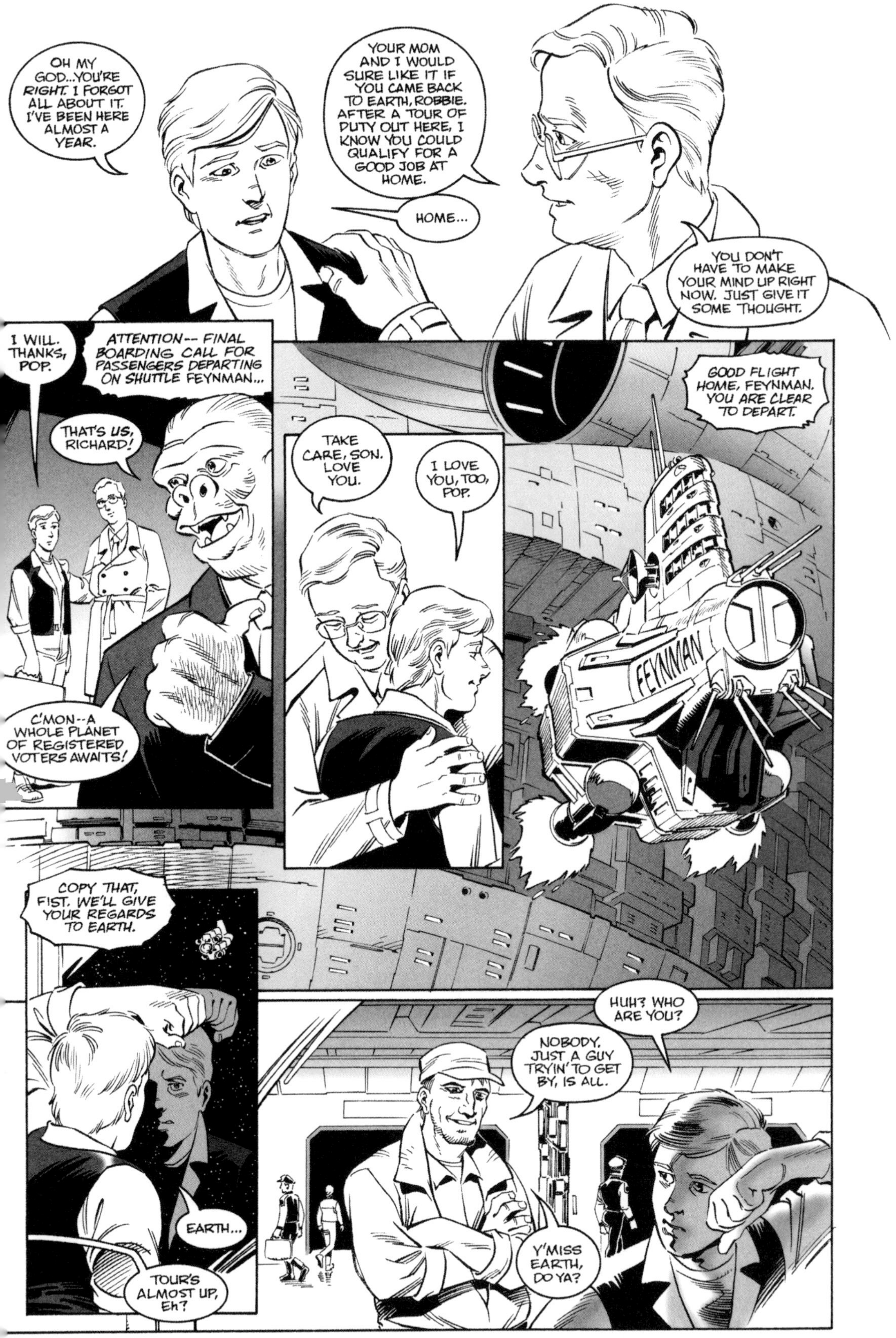
OH MY GOD...YOU'RE RIGHT. I FORGOT ALL ABOUT IT. I'VE BEEN HERE ALMOST A YEAR.
YOUR MOM AND I WOULD SURE LIKE IT IF YOU CAME BACK TO EARTH, ROBBIE. AFTER A TOUR OF DUTY OUT HERE, I KNOW YOU COULD QUALIFY FOR A GOOD JOB AT HOME.
HOME...
YOU DON'T HAVE TO MAKE YOUR MIND UP RIGHT NOW. JUST GIVE IT SOME THOUGHT.
I WILL. THANKS, POP.
ATTENTION-- FINAL BOARDING CALL FOR PASSENGERS DEPARTING ON SHUTTLE FEYNMAN...
THAT'S US, RICHARD!
C'MON--A WHOLE PLANET OF REGISTERED VOTERS AWAITS!
TAKE CARE, SON. LOVE YOU.
I LOVE YOU, TOO, POP.
GOOD FLIGHT HOME, FEYNMAN. YOU ARE CLEAR TO DEPART.
FEYNMAN
COPY THAT, FIST. WE'LL GIVE YOUR REGARDS TO EARTH.
EARTH...
TOUR'S ALMOST UP, Eh?
HUH? WHO ARE YOU?
NOBODY. JUST A GUY TRYIN' TO GET BY, IS ALL.
Y'MISS EARTH, DO YA?

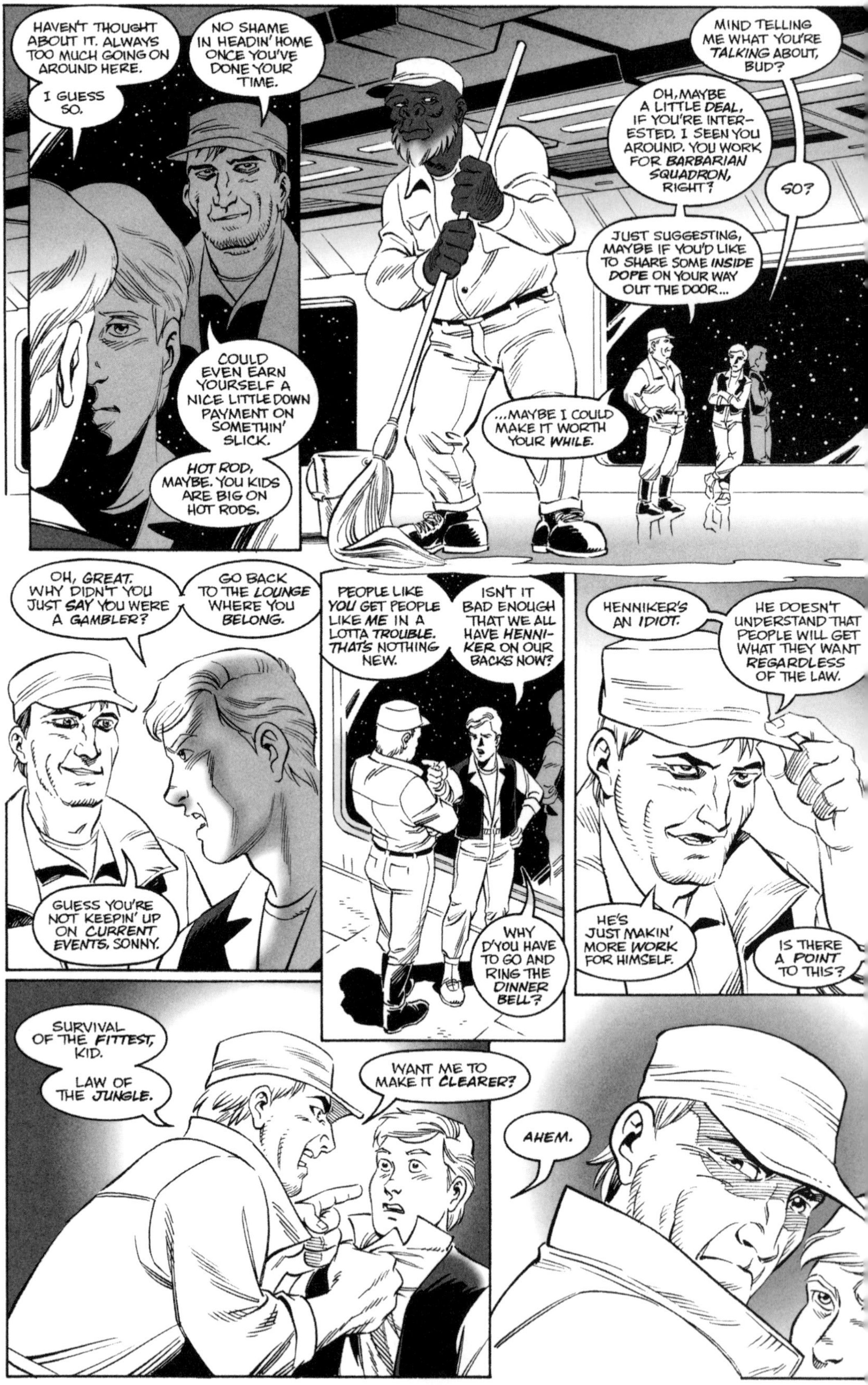
HAVEN'T THOUGHT ABOUT IT. ALWAYS TOO MUCH GOING ON AROUND HERE.
I GUESS SO.
NO SHAME IN HEADIN' HOME ONCE YOU'VE DONE YOUR TIME.
COULD EVEN EARN YOURSELF A NICE LITTLE DOWN PAYMENT ON SOMETHIN' SLICK.
HOT ROD, MAYBE. YOU KIDS ARE BIG ON HOT RODS.
MIND TELLING ME WHAT YOU'RE TALKING ABOUT, BUD?
OH, MAYBE A LITTLE DEAL, IF YOU'RE INTERESTED. I SEEN YOU AROUND. YOU WORK FOR BARBARIAN SQUADRON, RIGHT?
SO?
JUST SUGGESTING, MAYBE IF YOU'D LIKE TO SHARE SOME INSIDE DOPE ON YOUR WAY OUT THE DOOR...
...MAYBE I COULD MAKE IT WORTH YOUR WHILE.
OH, GREAT. WHY DIDN'T YOU JUST SAY YOU WERE A GAMBLER?
GO BACK TO THE LOUNGE WHERE YOU BELONG.
GUESS YOU'RE NOT KEEPIN' UP ON CURRENT EVENTS, SONNY.
PEOPLE LIKE YOU GET PEOPLE LIKE ME IN A LOTTA TROUBLE. THAT'S NOTHING NEW.
ISN'T IT BAD ENOUGH THAT WE ALL HAVE HENNIKER ON OUR BACKS NOW?
WHY D'YOU HAVE TO GO AND RING THE DINNER BELL?
HENNIKER'S AN IDIOT.
HE DOESN'T UNDERSTAND THAT PEOPLE WILL GET WHAT THEY WANT REGARDLESS OF THE LAW.
HE'S JUST MAKIN' MORE WORK FOR HIMSELF.
IS THERE A POINT TO THIS?
SURVIVAL OF THE FITTEST, KID.
LAW OF THE JUNGLE.
WANT ME TO MAKE IT CLEARER?
AHEM.

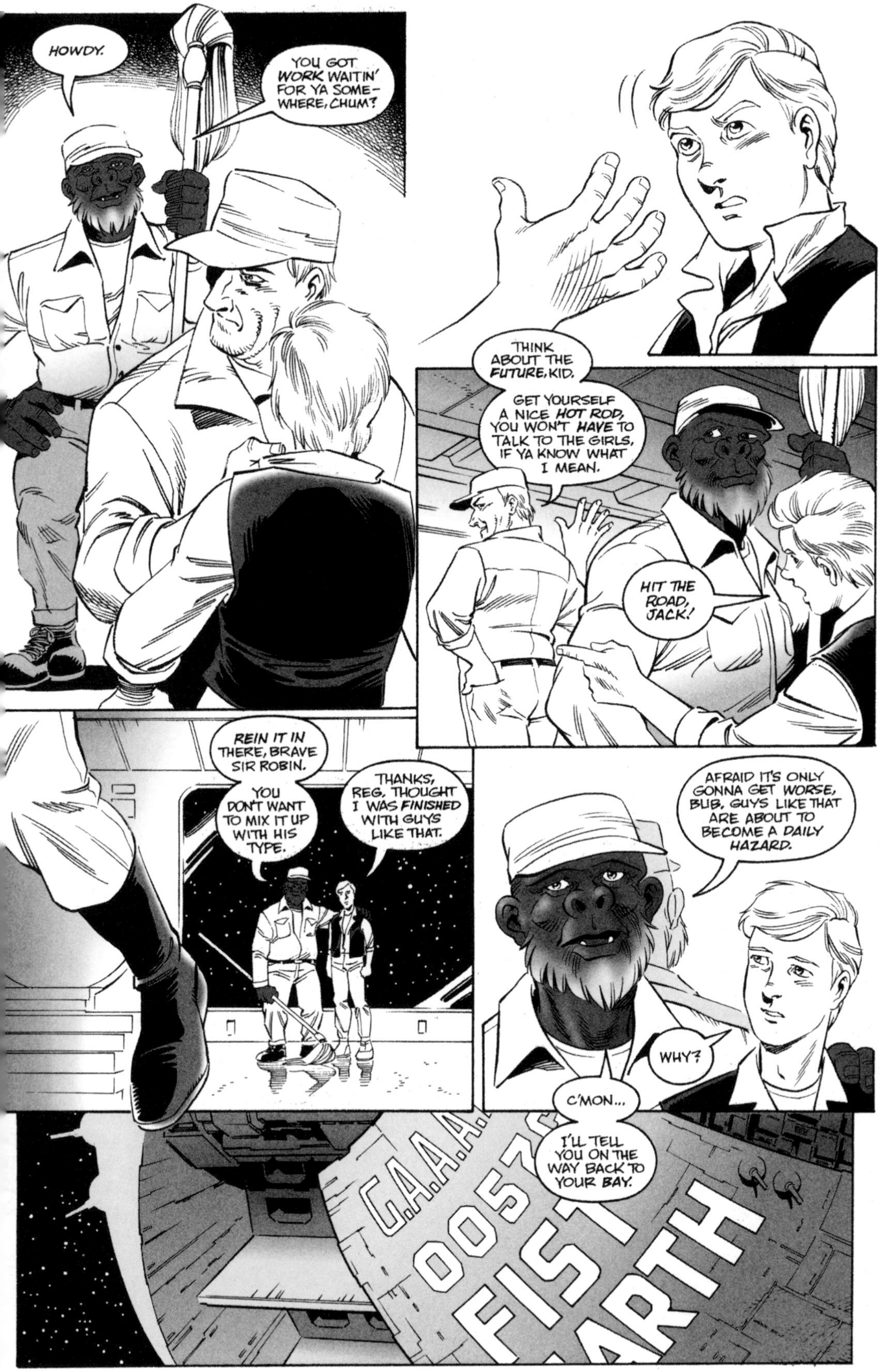
HOWDY.
YOU GOT WORK WAITIN' FOR YA SOME-WHERE, CHUM?
THINK ABOUT THE FUTURE, KID.
GET YOURSELF A NICE HOT ROD, YOU WON'T HAVE TO TALK TO THE GIRLS, IF YA KNOW WHAT I MEAN.
HIT THE ROAD, JACK!
REIN IT IN THERE, BRAVE SIR ROBIN.
YOU DON'T WANT TO MIX IT UP WITH HIS TYPE.
THANKS, REG. THOUGHT I WAS FINISHED WITH GUYS LIKE THAT.
AFRAID IT'S ONLY GONNA GET WORSE, BUB. GUYS LIKE THAT ARE ABOUT TO BECOME A DAILY HAZARD.
WHY?
C'MON...
I'LL TELL YOU ON THE WAY BACK TO YOUR BAY.

MUCH AS I HATE TO SAY IT, MAC, I'M GONNA HAVE TO PUT LIMITS ON WHICH AREAS OF THE SHIP YOU AND ROBIN CAN VISIT.

THE LAST THING WE NEED IS--

I KNOW, I KNOW. I DON'T NEED ANOTHER BUILDING TO FALL ON ME, HERE.

I'LL HAVE TO CLAMP DOWN ON MY *PILOTS,* TOO. MIGHT EVEN HAVE TO SCREEN THE *GUYS* THEY GO OUT WITH.

LIKE I NEED *THAT* ON MY BACK, TOO!

MAN, I'D LIKE TO PLANT MY BOOT THREE FEET UP HENNIKER'S REAR END!

HEY, MAC. BARBARA. JUST HEARD THE NEWS.

GOODY. WELCOME TO HAPPY CAMP.

WELL, *I* WON'T MISS THE WAGERING LOUNGE AT *ALL.* IT CAUSED ME NOTHING BUT *HEAD-ACHES.* I NEVER UNDER-STOOD WHAT A *CASINO* WAS DOING ON A BATTLESHIP ANYWAY.

WANT ME TO TELL HIM?

YOU'RE THE BOSS, BARB.

IT WAS SET UP A WHILE BACK, AFTER THE SQUADRONS FIRST STARTED *COMBAT TRAINING* AGAINST EACH OTHER.

NONCOMS WERE GAMBLING ON *WINNERS,* AND TO KEEP IT FROM GETTING OUT OF HAND, OL' ADMIRAL BORDEN *LEGALIZED* IT.

TURNED OUT TO BE EXACTLY THE RIGHT *RELIEF VALVE.*

SQUADRON	RANK
A 79/0	
SQUADRON	RANK
BARBARIANS	A 96/0
CRUSADERS	C 72/24
GLADIATORS	D 67/29
HARDRIDERS	F 54/42
SAMURAI	E 57/39
TIGERS	B 76/20
VULTURES	G 51/45

ADRON	RANK
BARIANS	A 79/0
SADERS	F 25/5
DIATORS	B 67/
HARDRIDERS	D 51
SAMURAI	E 46
TIGERS	C
URES	

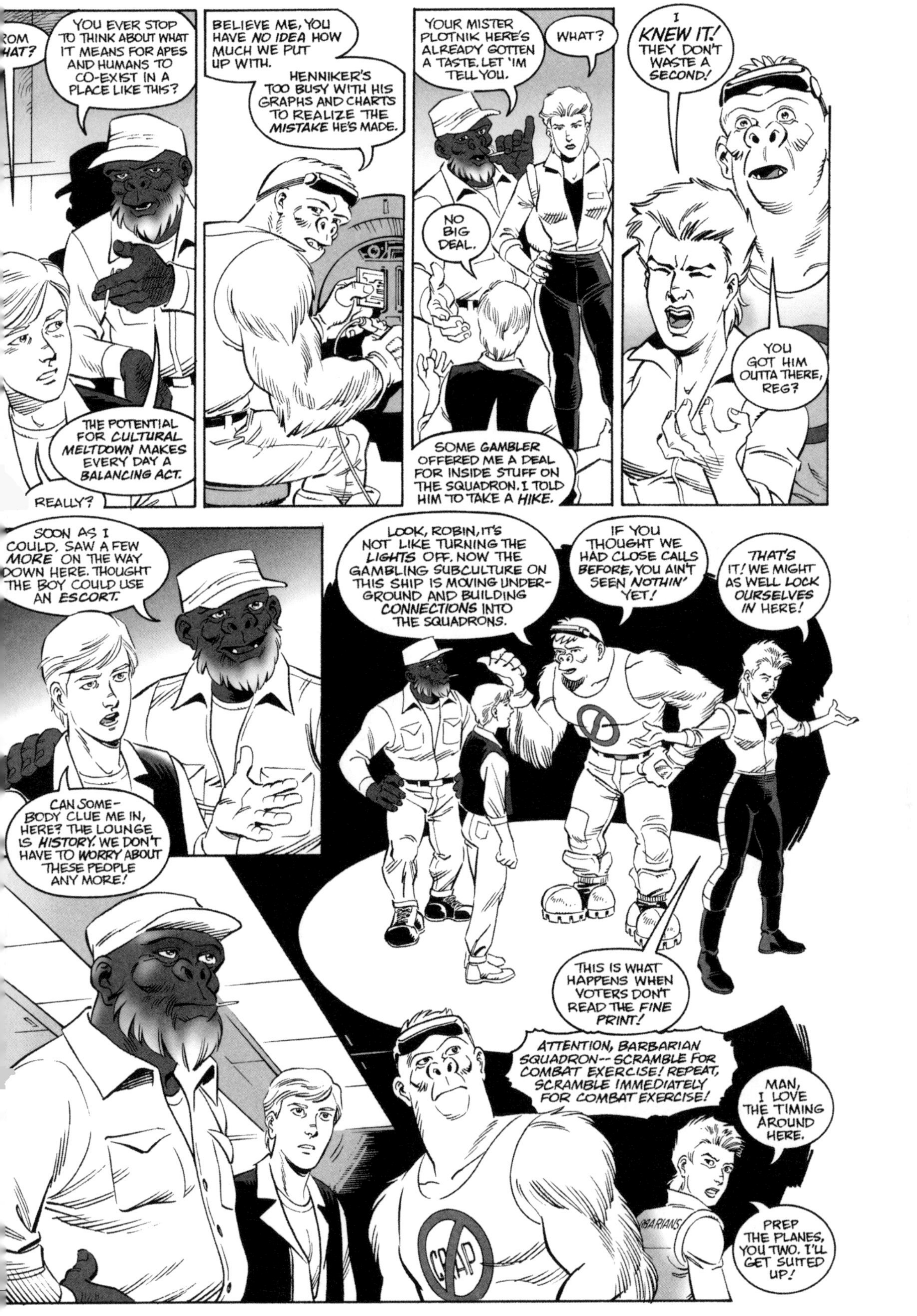
ROM
HAT?
YOU EVER STOP TO THINK ABOUT WHAT IT MEANS FOR APES AND HUMANS TO CO-EXIST IN A PLACE LIKE THIS?
THE POTENTIAL FOR CULTURAL MELTDOWN MAKES EVERY DAY A BALANCING ACT.
REALLY?
BELIEVE ME, YOU HAVE NO IDEA HOW MUCH WE PUT UP WITH.
HENNIKER'S TOO BUSY WITH HIS GRAPHS AND CHARTS TO REALIZE THE MISTAKE HE'S MADE.
YOUR MISTER PLOTNIK HERE'S ALREADY GOTTEN A TASTE. LET 'IM TELL YOU.
WHAT?
NO BIG DEAL.
SOME GAMBLER OFFERED ME A DEAL FOR INSIDE STUFF ON THE SQUADRON. I TOLD HIM TO TAKE A HIKE.
I KNEW IT! THEY DON'T WASTE A SECOND!
YOU GOT HIM OUTTA THERE, REG?
SOON AS I COULD. SAW A FEW MORE ON THE WAY DOWN HERE. THOUGHT THE BOY COULD USE AN ESCORT.
CAN SOMEBODY CLUE ME IN, HERE? THE LOUNGE IS HISTORY. WE DON'T HAVE TO WORRY ABOUT THESE PEOPLE ANY MORE!
LOOK, ROBIN, IT'S NOT LIKE TURNING THE LIGHTS OFF. NOW THE GAMBLING SUBCULTURE ON THIS SHIP IS MOVING UNDERGROUND AND BUILDING CONNECTIONS INTO THE SQUADRONS.
IF YOU THOUGHT WE HAD CLOSE CALLS BEFORE, YOU AIN'T SEEN NOTHIN' YET!
THAT'S IT! WE MIGHT AS WELL LOCK OURSELVES IN HERE!
THIS IS WHAT HAPPENS WHEN VOTERS DON'T READ THE FINE PRINT!
ATTENTION, BARBARIAN SQUADRON-- SCRAMBLE FOR COMBAT EXERCISE! REPEAT, SCRAMBLE IMMEDIATELY FOR COMBAT EXERCISE!
MAN, I LOVE THE TIMING AROUND HERE.
PREP THE PLANES, YOU TWO. I'LL GET SUITED UP!
CRAP
BARBARIANS

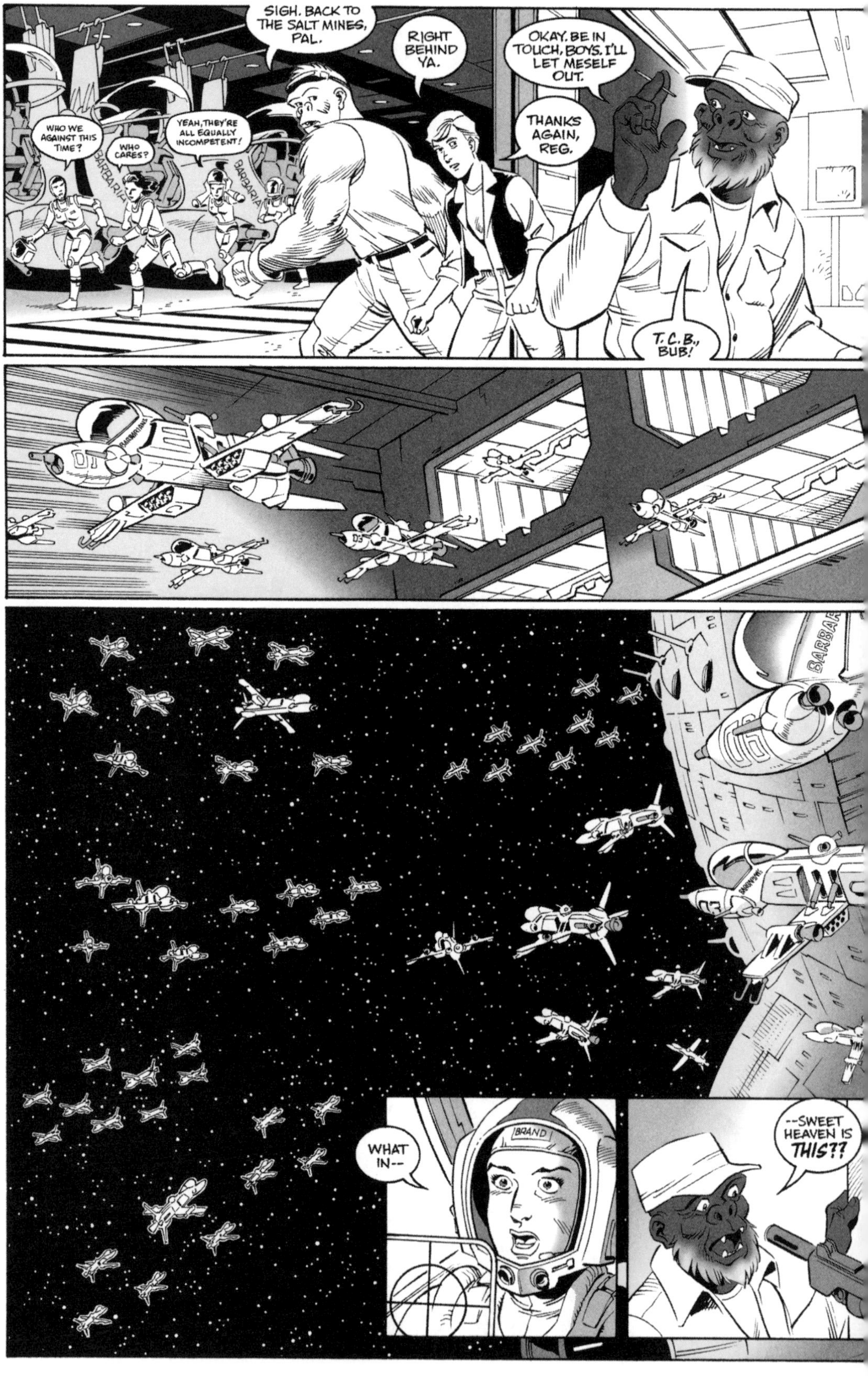
SIGH. BACK TO THE SALT MINES, PAL.
RIGHT BEHIND YA.
OKAY. BE IN TOUCH, BOYS. I'LL LET MESELF OUT.
THANKS AGAIN, REG.
T.C.B., BUB!
WHO WE AGAINST THIS TIME?
WHO CARES?
YEAH, THEY'RE ALL EQUALLY INCOMPETENT!
BARBARIA
BARBARIA
BARBARIA
BRAND
WHAT IN--
--SWEET HEAVEN IS THIS??

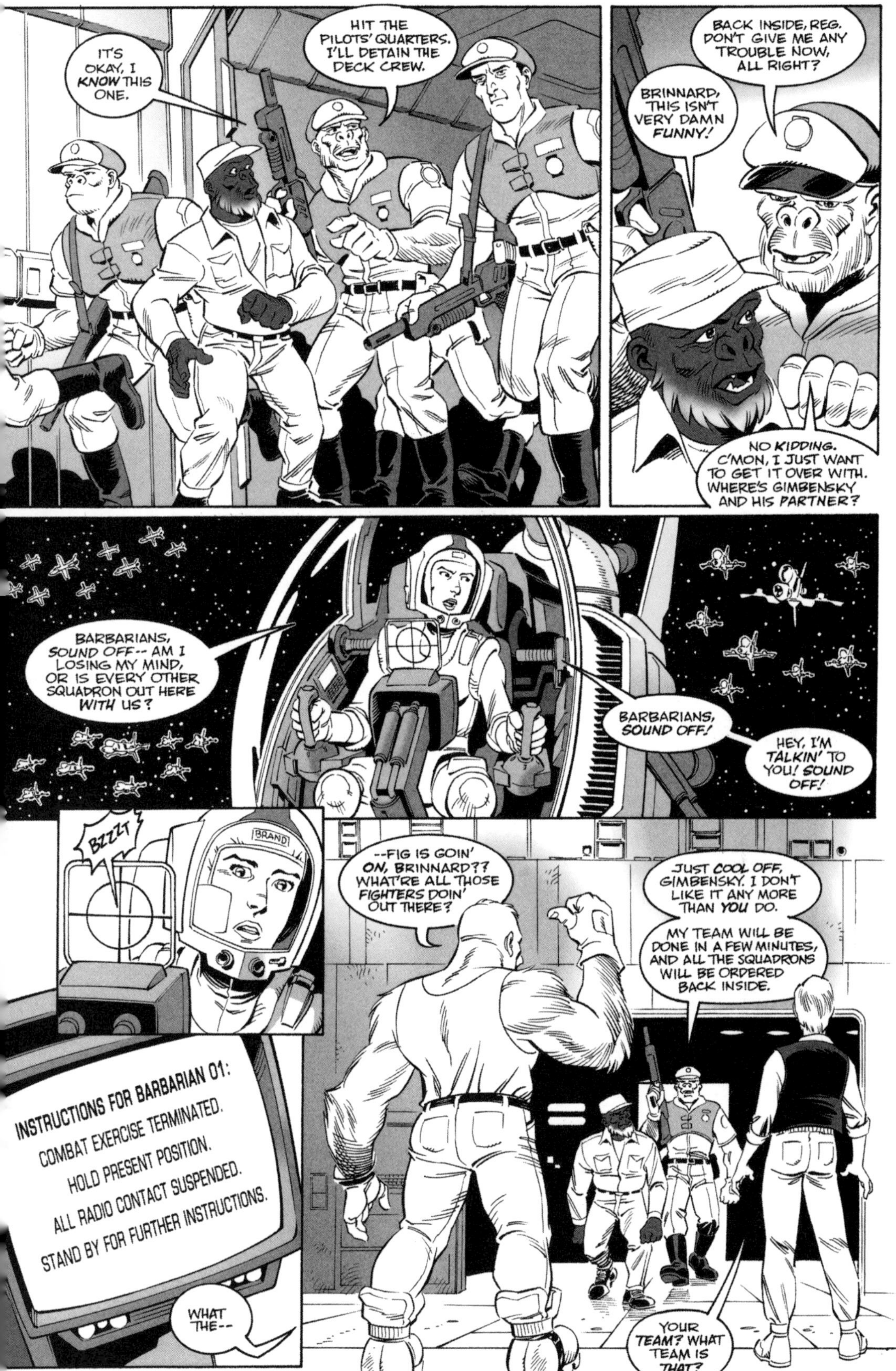
IT'S OKAY, I KNOW THIS ONE.
HIT THE PILOTS' QUARTERS. I'LL DETAIN THE DECK CREW.
BACK INSIDE, REG. DON'T GIVE ME ANY TROUBLE NOW, ALL RIGHT?
BRINNARD, THIS ISN'T VERY DAMN FUNNY!
NO KIDDING. C'MON, I JUST WANT TO GET IT OVER WITH. WHERE'S GIMBENSKY AND HIS PARTNER?
BARBARIANS, SOUND OFF-- AM I LOSING MY MIND, OR IS EVERY OTHER SQUADRON OUT HERE WITH US?
BARBARIANS, SOUND OFF!
HEY, I'M TALKIN' TO YOU! SOUND OFF!
BZZZT
BRAND
--FIG IS GOIN' ON, BRINNARD?? WHAT'RE ALL THOSE FIGHTERS DOIN' OUT THERE?
JUST COOL OFF, GIMBENSKY. I DON'T LIKE IT ANY MORE THAN YOU DO.
MY TEAM WILL BE DONE IN A FEW MINUTES, AND ALL THE SQUADRONS WILL BE ORDERED BACK INSIDE.
INSTRUCTIONS FOR BARBARIAN 01:
COMBAT EXERCISE TERMINATED.
HOLD PRESENT POSITION.
ALL RADIO CONTACT SUSPENDED.
STAND BY FOR FURTHER INSTRUCTIONS.
WHAT THE--
YOUR TEAM? WHAT TEAM IS THAT?

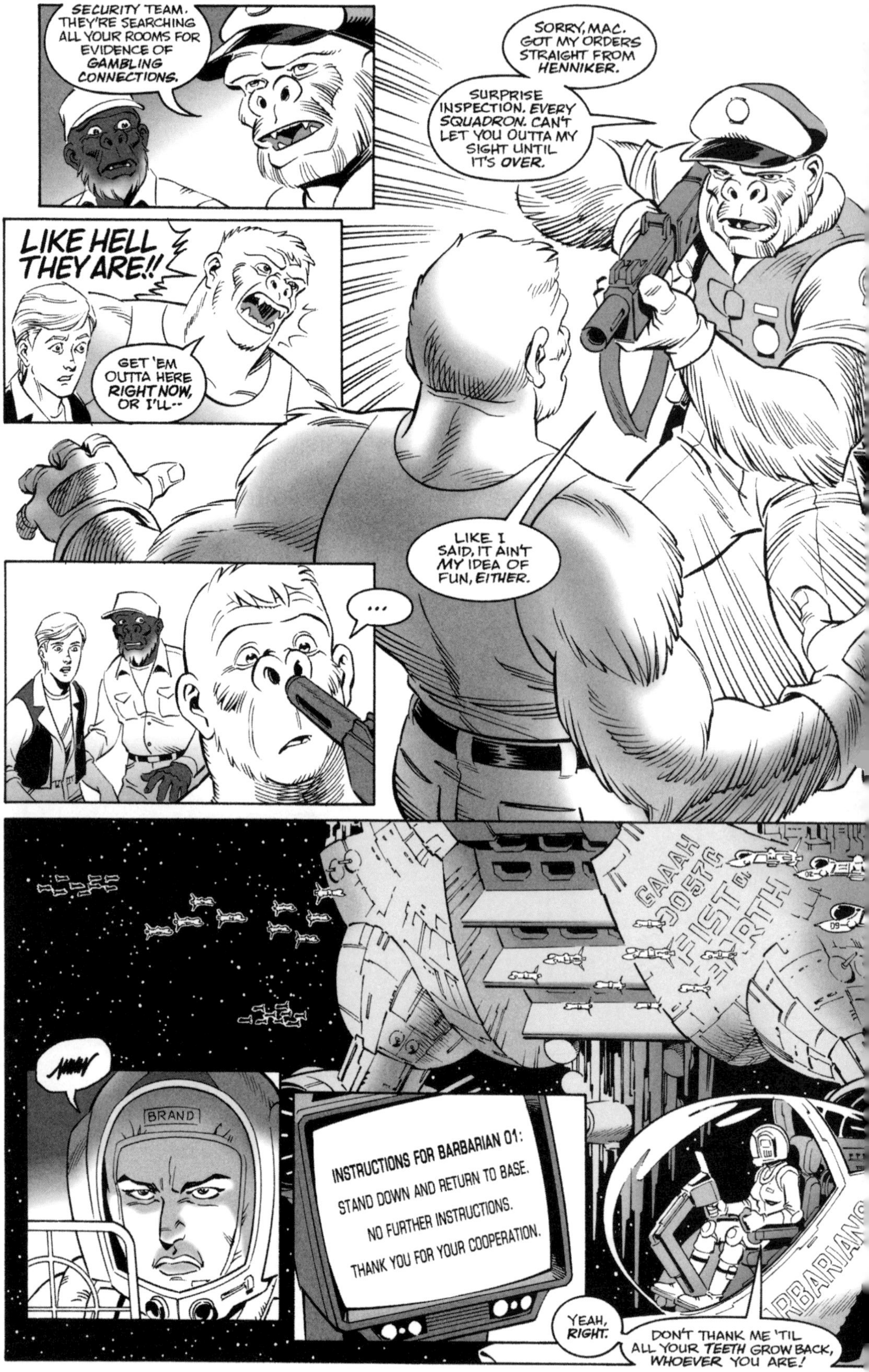
SECURITY TEAM. THEY'RE SEARCHING ALL YOUR ROOMS FOR EVIDENCE OF GAMBLING CONNECTIONS.
SORRY, MAC. GOT MY ORDERS STRAIGHT FROM HENNIKER.
SURPRISE INSPECTION. EVERY SQUADRON. CAN'T LET YOU OUTTA MY SIGHT UNTIL IT'S OVER.
LIKE HELL THEY ARE!!
GET 'EM OUTTA HERE RIGHT NOW, OR I'LL--
LIKE I SAID, IT AIN'T MY IDEA OF FUN, EITHER.
...
BRAND
INSTRUCTIONS FOR BARBARIAN 01:
STAND DOWN AND RETURN TO BASE.
NO FURTHER INSTRUCTIONS.
THANK YOU FOR YOUR COOPERATION.
YEAH, RIGHT.
DON'T THANK ME 'TIL ALL YOUR TEETH GROW BACK, WHOEVER YOU ARE!

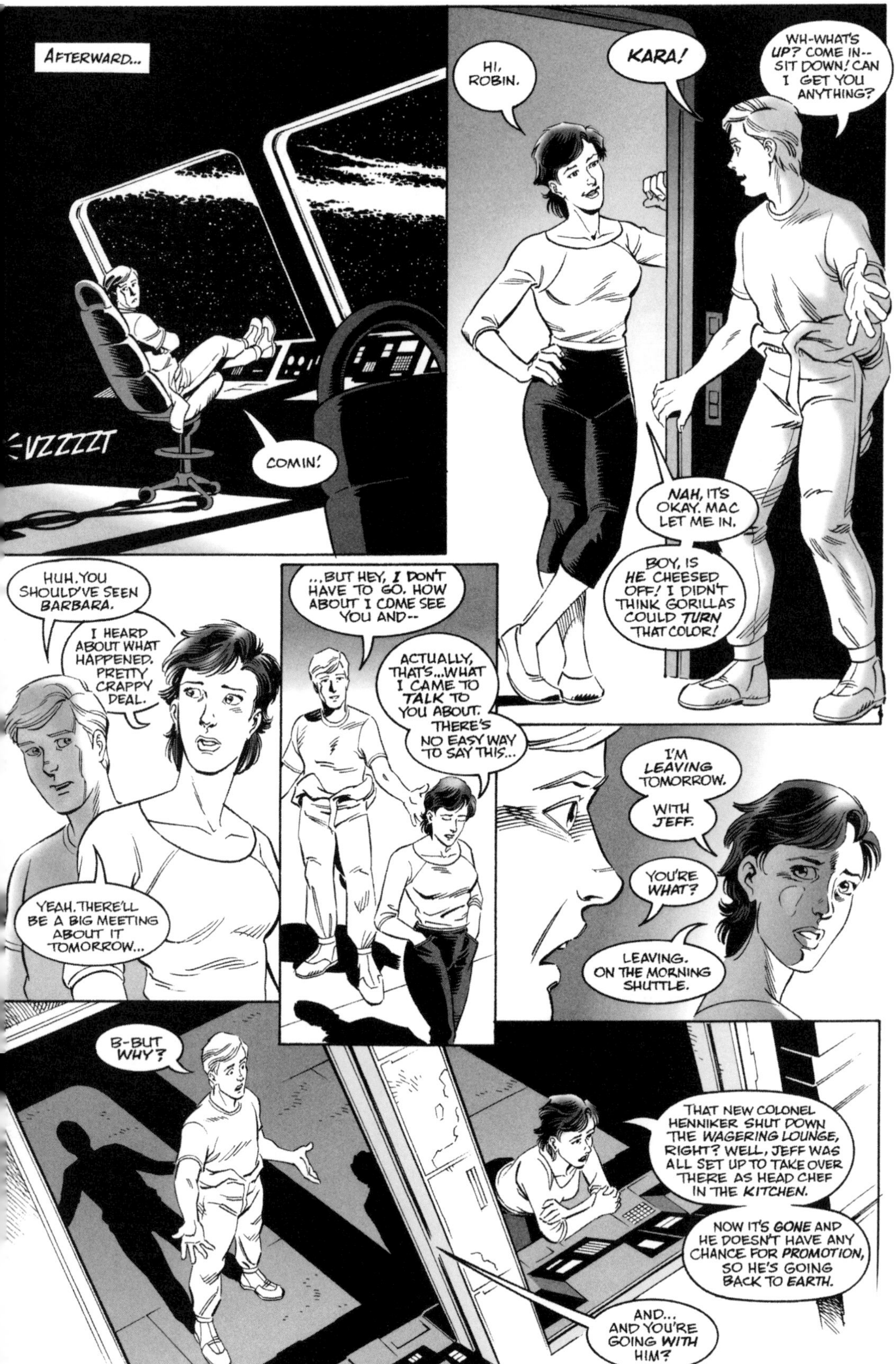
AFTERWARD...
VZZZZT
COMIN'!
KARA!
HI, ROBIN.
WH-WHAT'S UP? COME IN-- SIT DOWN! CAN I GET YOU ANYTHING?
NAH, IT'S OKAY. MAC LET ME IN.
BOY, IS HE CHEESED OFF! I DIDN'T THINK GORILLAS COULD TURN THAT COLOR!
HUH. YOU SHOULD'VE SEEN BARBARA.
I HEARD ABOUT WHAT HAPPENED. PRETTY CRAPPY DEAL.
YEAH. THERE'LL BE A BIG MEETING ABOUT IT TOMORROW...
...BUT HEY, I DON'T HAVE TO GO. HOW ABOUT I COME SEE YOU AND--
ACTUALLY, THAT'S...WHAT I CAME TO TALK TO YOU ABOUT. THERE'S NO EASY WAY TO SAY THIS...
I'M LEAVING TOMORROW.
WITH JEFF.
YOU'RE WHAT?
LEAVING. ON THE MORNING SHUTTLE.
B-BUT WHY?
THAT NEW COLONEL HENNIKER SHUT DOWN THE WAGERING LOUNGE, RIGHT? WELL, JEFF WAS ALL SET UP TO TAKE OVER THERE AS HEAD CHEF IN THE KITCHEN.
NOW IT'S GONE AND HE DOESN'T HAVE ANY CHANCE FOR PROMOTION, SO HE'S GOING BACK TO EARTH.
AND... AND YOU'RE GOING WITH HIM?

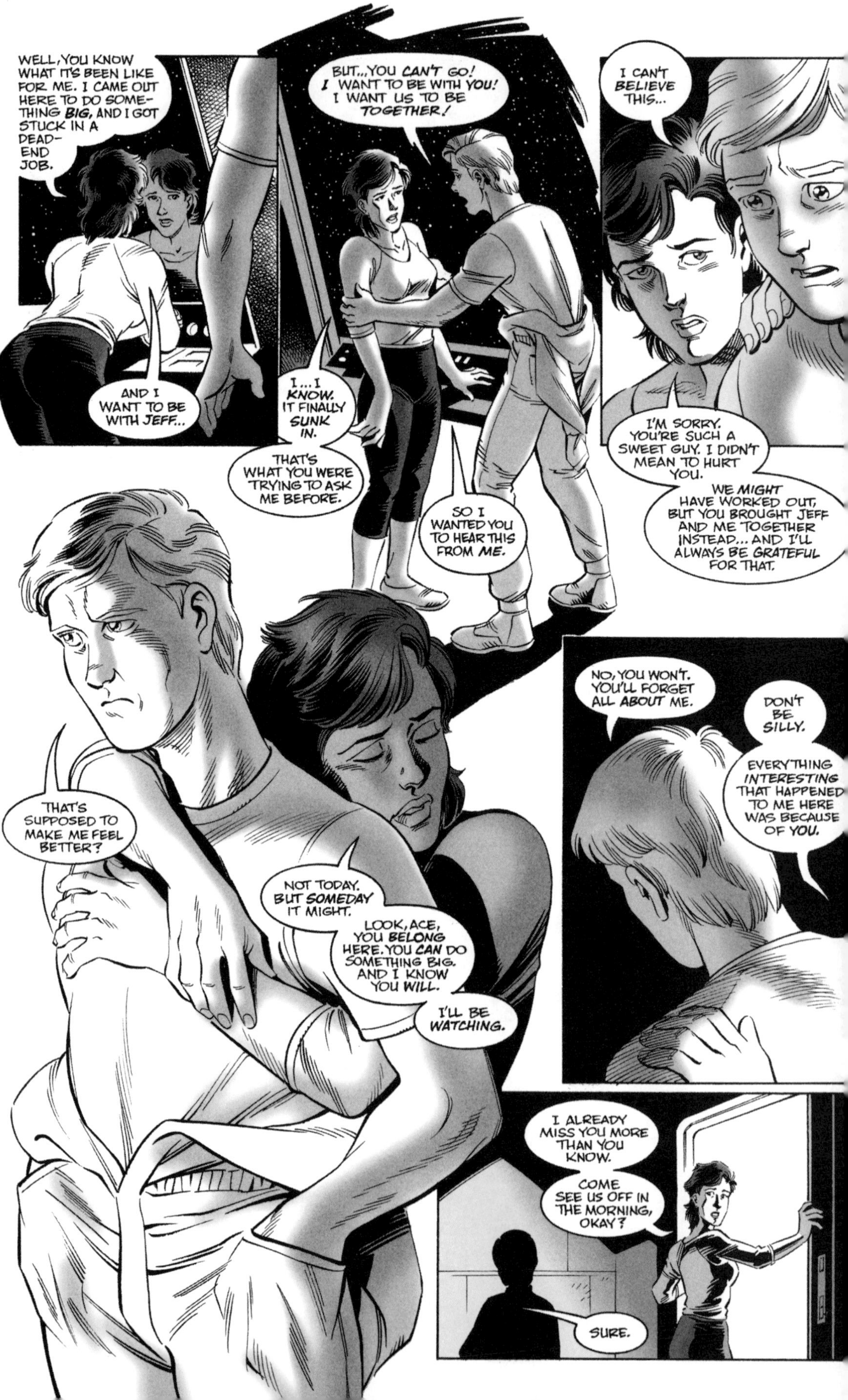

WELL, YOU KNOW WHAT IT'S BEEN LIKE FOR ME. I CAME OUT HERE TO DO SOMETHING BIG, AND I GOT STUCK IN A DEAD-END JOB.
AND I WANT TO BE WITH JEFF...
BUT... YOU CAN'T GO! I WANT TO BE WITH YOU! I WANT US TO BE TOGETHER!
I... I KNOW. IT FINALLY SUNK IN.
THAT'S WHAT YOU WERE TRYING TO ASK ME BEFORE.
SO I WANTED YOU TO HEAR THIS FROM ME.
I CAN'T BELIEVE THIS...
I'M SORRY. YOU'RE SUCH A SWEET GUY. I DIDN'T MEAN TO HURT YOU.
WE MIGHT HAVE WORKED OUT, BUT YOU BROUGHT JEFF AND ME TOGETHER INSTEAD... AND I'LL ALWAYS BE GRATEFUL FOR THAT.
THAT'S SUPPOSED TO MAKE ME FEEL BETTER?
NOT TODAY. BUT SOMEDAY IT MIGHT.
LOOK, ACE, YOU BELONG HERE. YOU CAN DO SOMETHING BIG. AND I KNOW YOU WILL.
I'LL BE WATCHING.
NO, YOU WON'T. YOU'LL FORGET ALL ABOUT ME.
DON'T BE SILLY.
EVERYTHING INTERESTING THAT HAPPENED TO ME HERE WAS BECAUSE OF YOU.
I ALREADY MISS YOU MORE THAN YOU KNOW.
COME SEE US OFF IN THE MORNING, OKAY?
SURE.

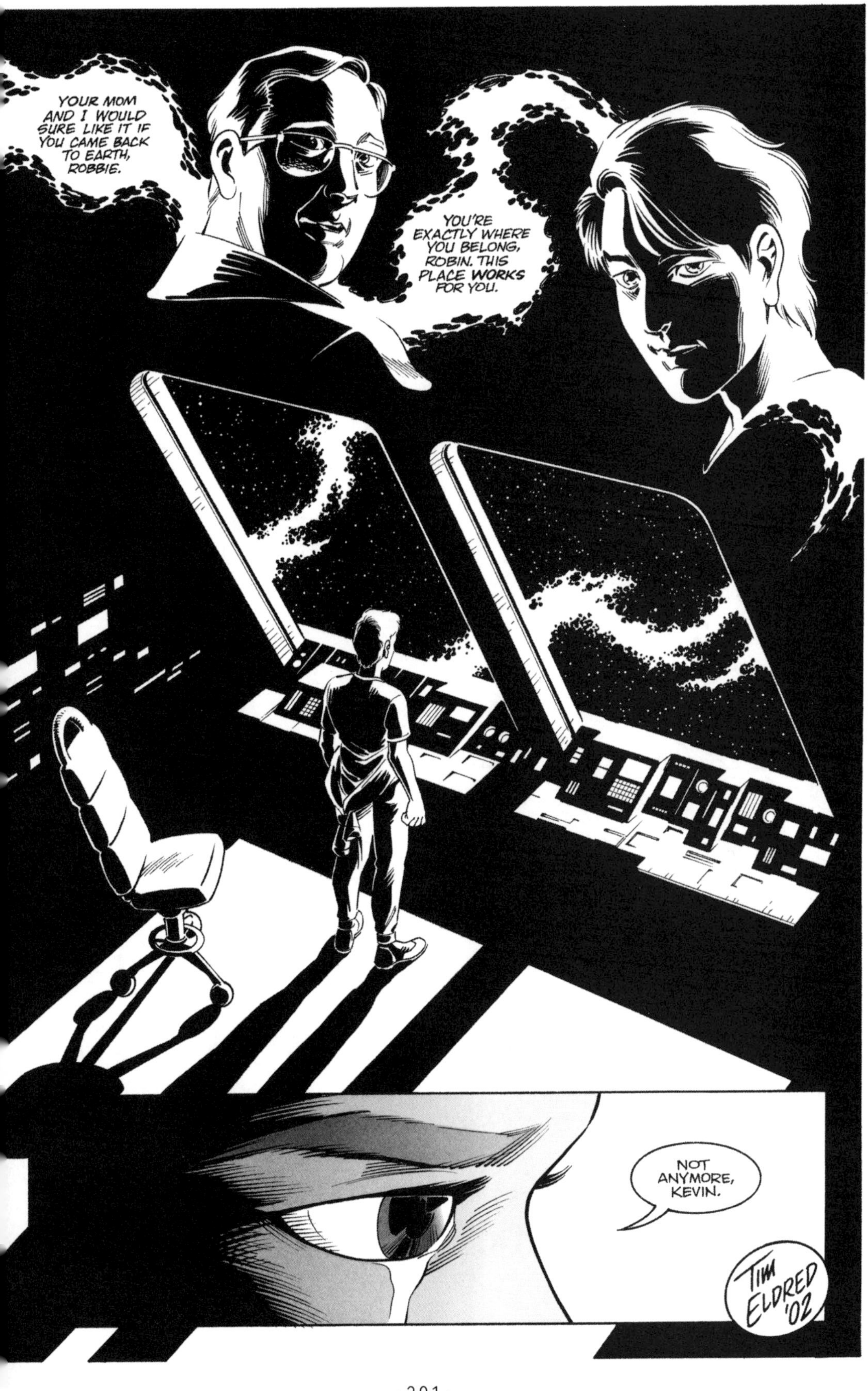
YOUR MOM AND I WOULD SURE LIKE IT IF YOU CAME BACK TO EARTH, ROBBIE.
YOU'RE EXACTLY WHERE YOU BELONG, ROBIN. THIS PLACE WORKS FOR YOU.
NOT ANYMORE, KEVIN.
TIM ELDRED '02

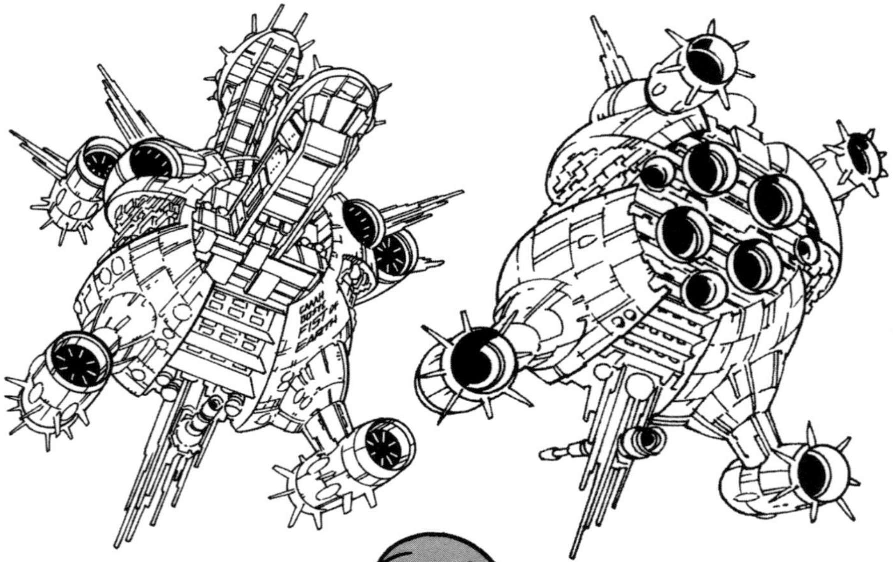

FLAGSHIP *FIST OF EARTH*

The *Fist*'s unique particle drive system (which scoops up heavy atoms and free-ranging photons) was a gift of the Benefactors along with a relativity-inversion field generator to allow faster-than-light travel without time dilation.

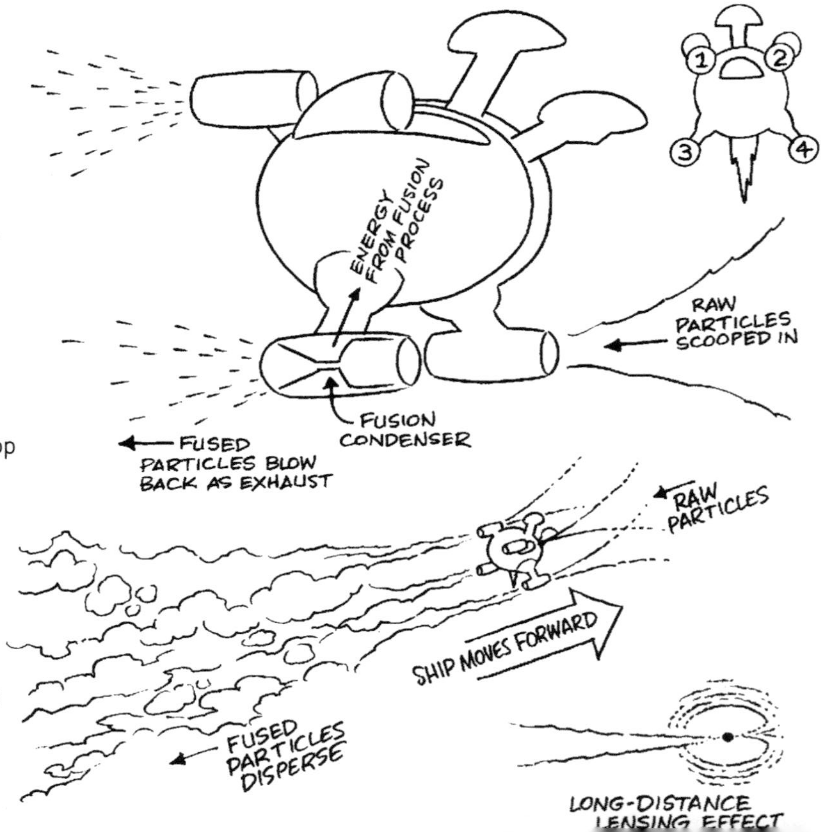

1
2
3
4
ENERGY FROM FUSION PROCESS
RAW PARTICLES SCOOPED IN
FUSION CONDENSER
FUSED PARTICLES BLOW BACK AS EXHAUST
RAW PARTICLES
SHIP MOVES FORWARD
FUSED PARTICLES DISPERSE
LONG-DISTANCE LENSING EFFECT

The *Fist*'s designation is 0057C:
00: priority code (topmost)
57: year of launch
C: for Carrier

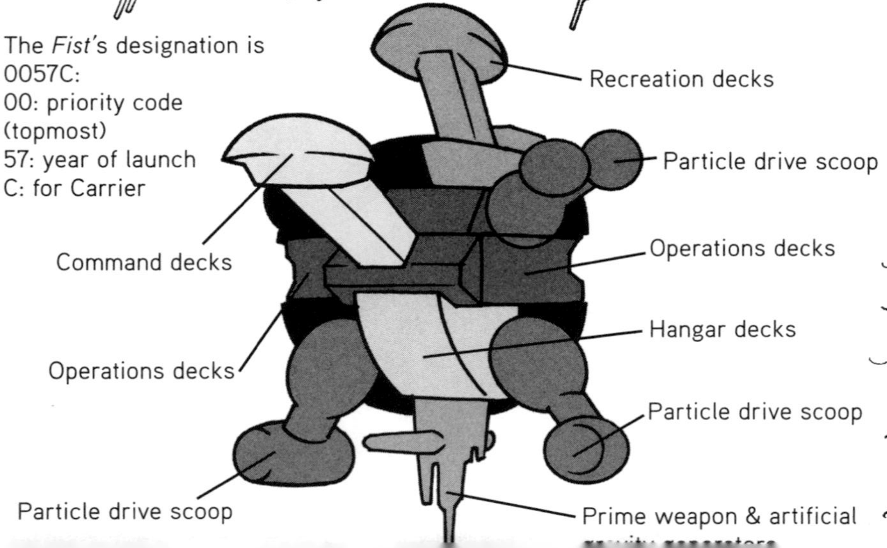

Recreation decks
Particle drive scoop
Command decks
Operations decks
Hangar decks
Operations decks
Particle drive scoop
Particle drive scoop
Prime weapon & artificial

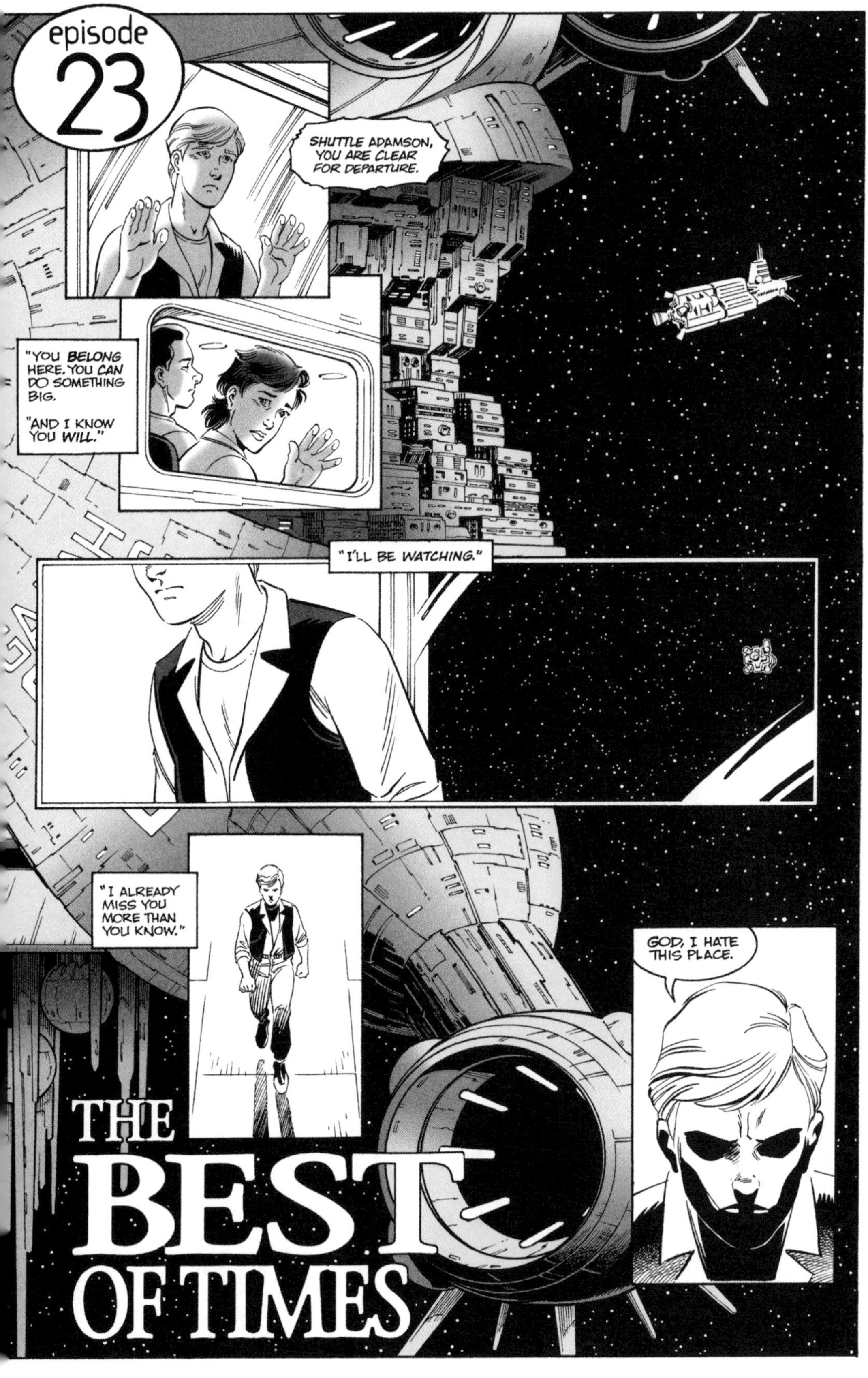
episode
23
SHUTTLE ADAMSON, YOU ARE CLEAR FOR DEPARTURE.
"YOU BELONG HERE. YOU CAN DO SOMETHING BIG.
"AND I KNOW YOU WILL."
"I'LL BE WATCHING."
"I ALREADY MISS YOU MORE THAN YOU KNOW."
GOD, I HATE THIS PLACE.
THE BEST OF TIMES

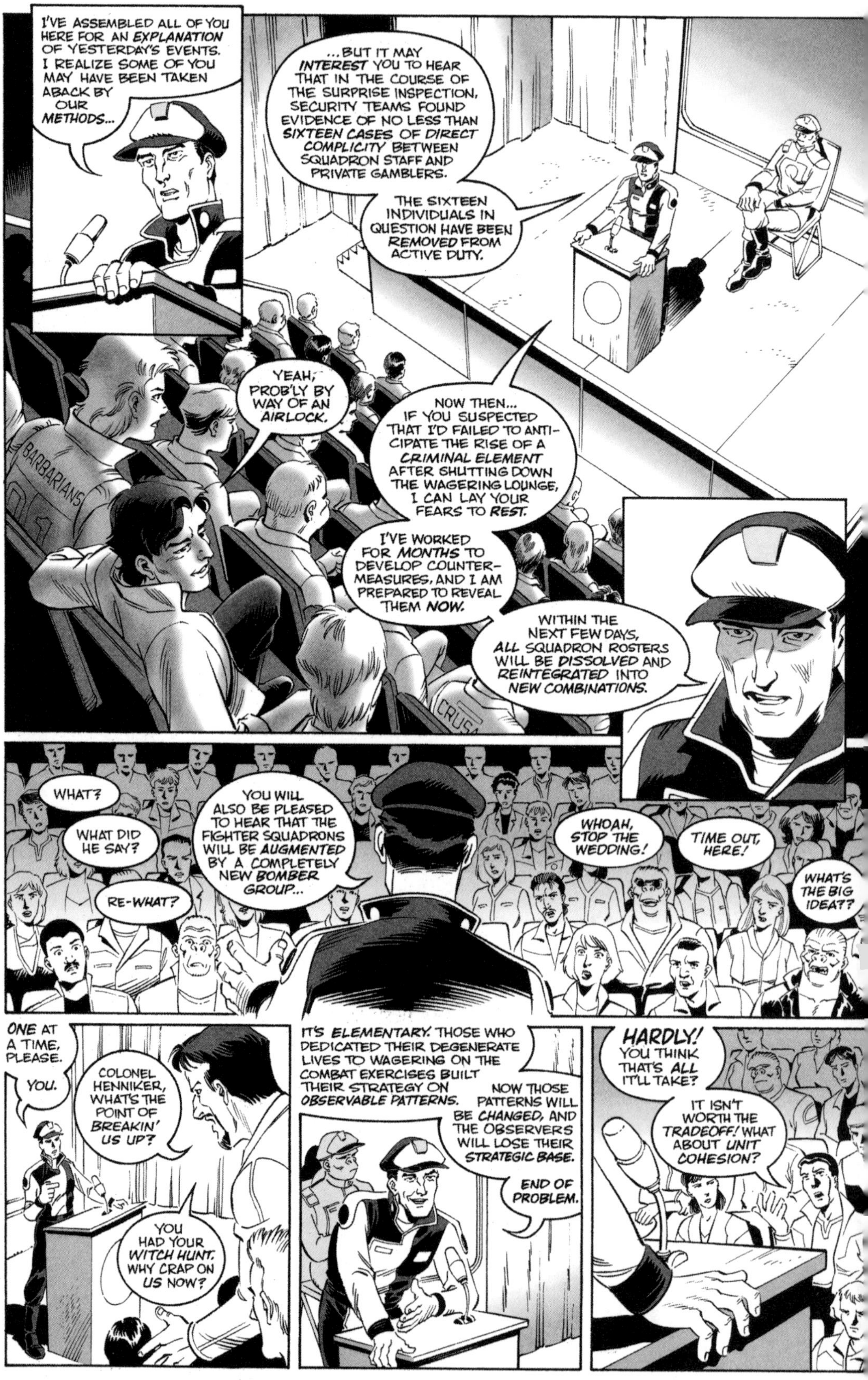
I'VE ASSEMBLED ALL OF YOU HERE FOR AN EXPLANATION OF YESTERDAY'S EVENTS. I REALIZE SOME OF YOU MAY HAVE BEEN TAKEN ABACK BY OUR METHODS...
...BUT IT MAY INTEREST YOU TO HEAR THAT IN THE COURSE OF THE SURPRISE INSPECTION, SECURITY TEAMS FOUND EVIDENCE OF NO LESS THAN SIXTEEN CASES OF DIRECT COMPLICITY BETWEEN SQUADRON STAFF AND PRIVATE GAMBLERS.
THE SIXTEEN INDIVIDUALS IN QUESTION HAVE BEEN REMOVED FROM ACTIVE DUTY.
YEAH, PROB'LY BY WAY OF AN AIRLOCK.
BARBARIANS
NOW THEN... IF YOU SUSPECTED THAT I'D FAILED TO ANTI-CIPATE THE RISE OF A CRIMINAL ELEMENT AFTER SHUTTING DOWN THE WAGERING LOUNGE, I CAN LAY YOUR FEARS TO REST.
I'VE WORKED FOR MONTHS TO DEVELOP COUNTER-MEASURES, AND I AM PREPARED TO REVEAL THEM NOW.
WITHIN THE NEXT FEW DAYS, ALL SQUADRON ROSTERS WILL BE DISSOLVED AND REINTEGRATED INTO NEW COMBINATIONS.
WHAT?
WHAT DID HE SAY?
RE-WHAT?
YOU WILL ALSO BE PLEASED TO HEAR THAT THE FIGHTER SQUADRONS WILL BE AUGMENTED BY A COMPLETELY NEW BOMBER GROUP...
WHOAH, STOP THE WEDDING!
TIME OUT, HERE!
WHAT'S THE BIG IDEA??
ONE AT A TIME, PLEASE.
YOU.
COLONEL HENNIKER, WHAT'S THE POINT OF BREAKIN' US UP?
YOU HAD YOUR WITCH HUNT. WHY CRAP ON US NOW?
IT'S ELEMENTARY. THOSE WHO DEDICATED THEIR DEGENERATE LIVES TO WAGERING ON THE COMBAT EXERCISES BUILT THEIR STRATEGY ON OBSERVABLE PATTERNS.
NOW THOSE PATTERNS WILL BE CHANGED, AND THE OBSERVERS WILL LOSE THEIR STRATEGIC BASE.
END OF PROBLEM.
HARDLY! YOU THINK THAT'S ALL IT'LL TAKE?
IT ISN'T WORTH THE TRADEOFF! WHAT ABOUT UNIT COHESION?

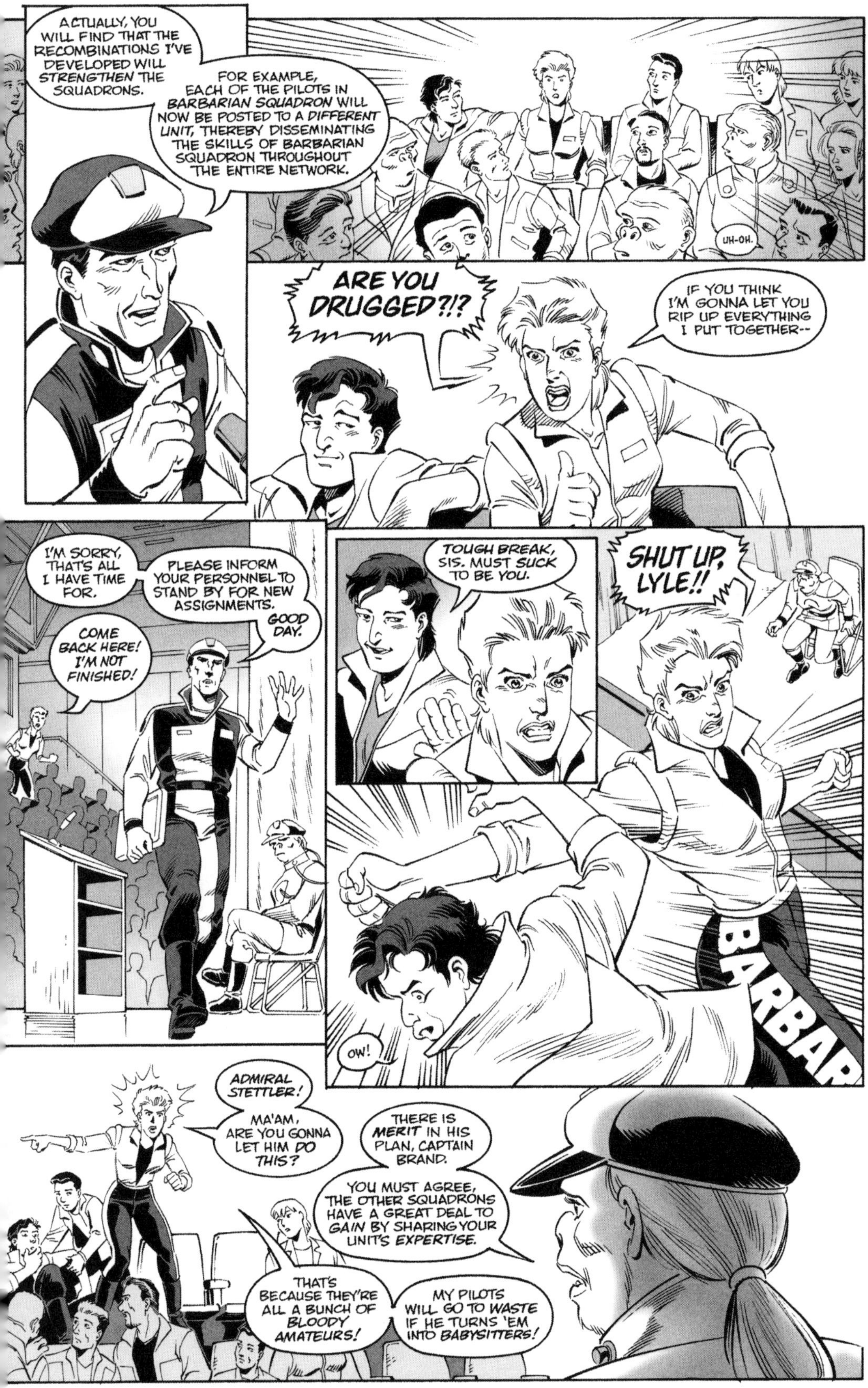
ACTUALLY, YOU WILL FIND THAT THE RECOMBINATIONS I'VE DEVELOPED WILL STRENGTHEN THE SQUADRONS.
FOR EXAMPLE, EACH OF THE PILOTS IN BARBARIAN SQUADRON WILL NOW BE POSTED TO A DIFFERENT UNIT, THEREBY DISSEMINATING THE SKILLS OF BARBARIAN SQUADRON THROUGHOUT THE ENTIRE NETWORK.
UH-OH.
ARE YOU DRUGGED?!?
IF YOU THINK I'M GONNA LET YOU RIP UP EVERYTHING I PUT TOGETHER--
I'M SORRY, THAT'S ALL I HAVE TIME FOR.
PLEASE INFORM YOUR PERSONNEL TO STAND BY FOR NEW ASSIGNMENTS.
GOOD DAY.
COME BACK HERE! I'M NOT FINISHED!
TOUGH BREAK, SIS. MUST SUCK TO BE YOU.
SHUT UP, LYLE!!
BARBAR
OW!
ADMIRAL STETTLER!
MA'AM, ARE YOU GONNA LET HIM DO THIS?
THERE IS MERIT IN HIS PLAN, CAPTAIN BRAND.
YOU MUST AGREE, THE OTHER SQUADRONS HAVE A GREAT DEAL TO GAIN BY SHARING YOUR UNIT'S EXPERTISE.
THAT'S BECAUSE THEY'RE ALL A BUNCH OF BLOODY AMATEURS!
MY PILOTS WILL GO TO WASTE IF HE TURNS 'EM INTO BABYSITTERS!

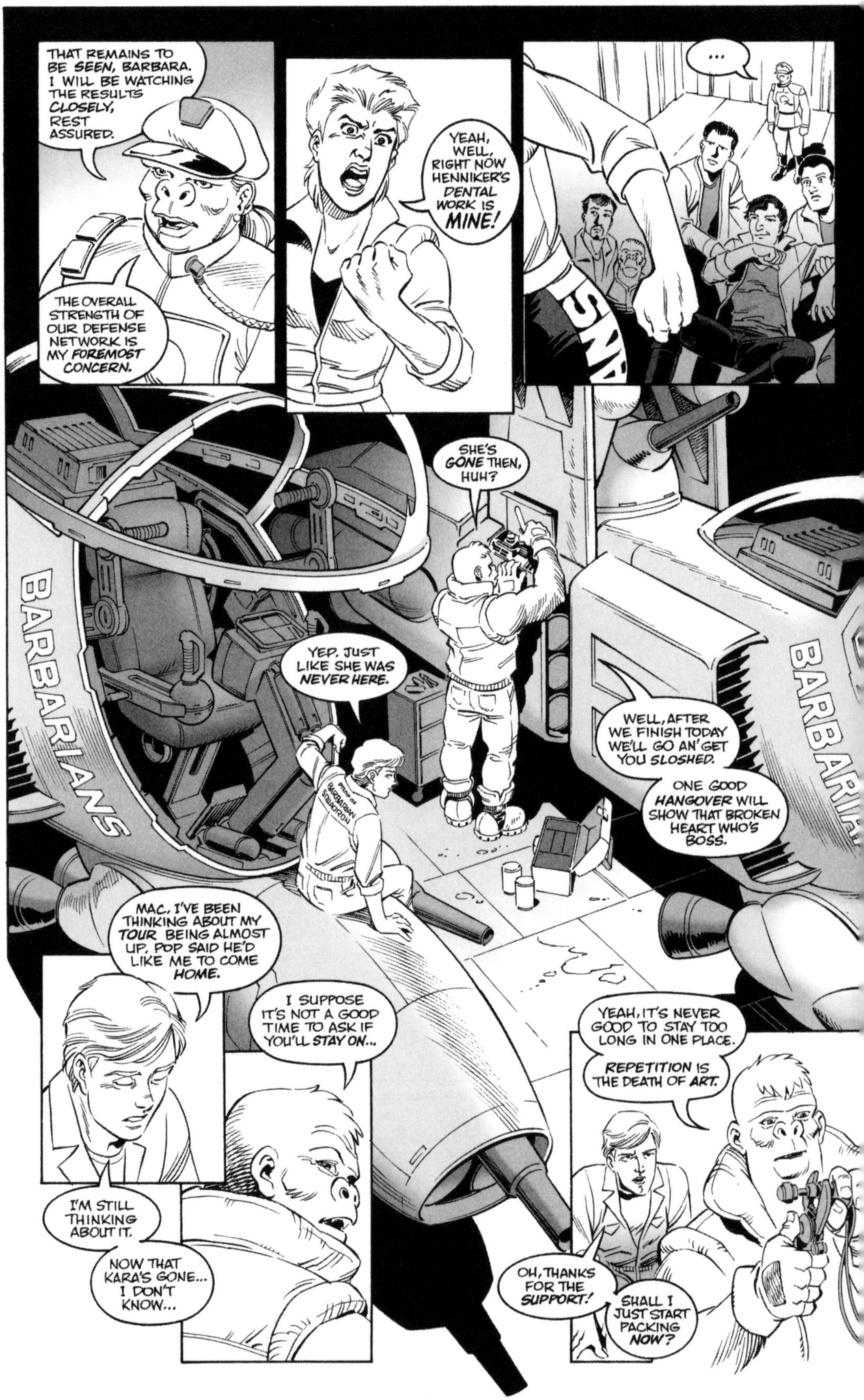
THAT REMAINS TO BE SEEN, BARBARA. I WILL BE WATCHING THE RESULTS CLOSELY, REST ASSURED.
THE OVERALL STRENGTH OF OUR DEFENSE NETWORK IS MY FOREMOST CONCERN.
YEAH, WELL, RIGHT NOW HENNIKER'S DENTAL WORK IS MINE!
...
SHE'S GONE THEN, HUH?
YEP. JUST LIKE SHE WAS NEVER HERE.
WELL, AFTER WE FINISH TODAY WE'LL GO AN' GET YOU SLOSHED.
ONE GOOD HANGOVER WILL SHOW THAT BROKEN HEART WHO'S BOSS.
BARBARIANS
MAC, I'VE BEEN THINKING ABOUT MY TOUR BEING ALMOST UP. POP SAID HE'D LIKE ME TO COME HOME.
I SUPPOSE IT'S NOT A GOOD TIME TO ASK IF YOU'LL STAY ON...
I'M STILL THINKING ABOUT IT.
NOW THAT KARA'S GONE... I DON'T KNOW...
YEAH, IT'S NEVER GOOD TO STAY TOO LONG IN ONE PLACE.
REPETITION IS THE DEATH OF ART.
OH, THANKS FOR THE SUPPORT!
SHALL I JUST START PACKING NOW?

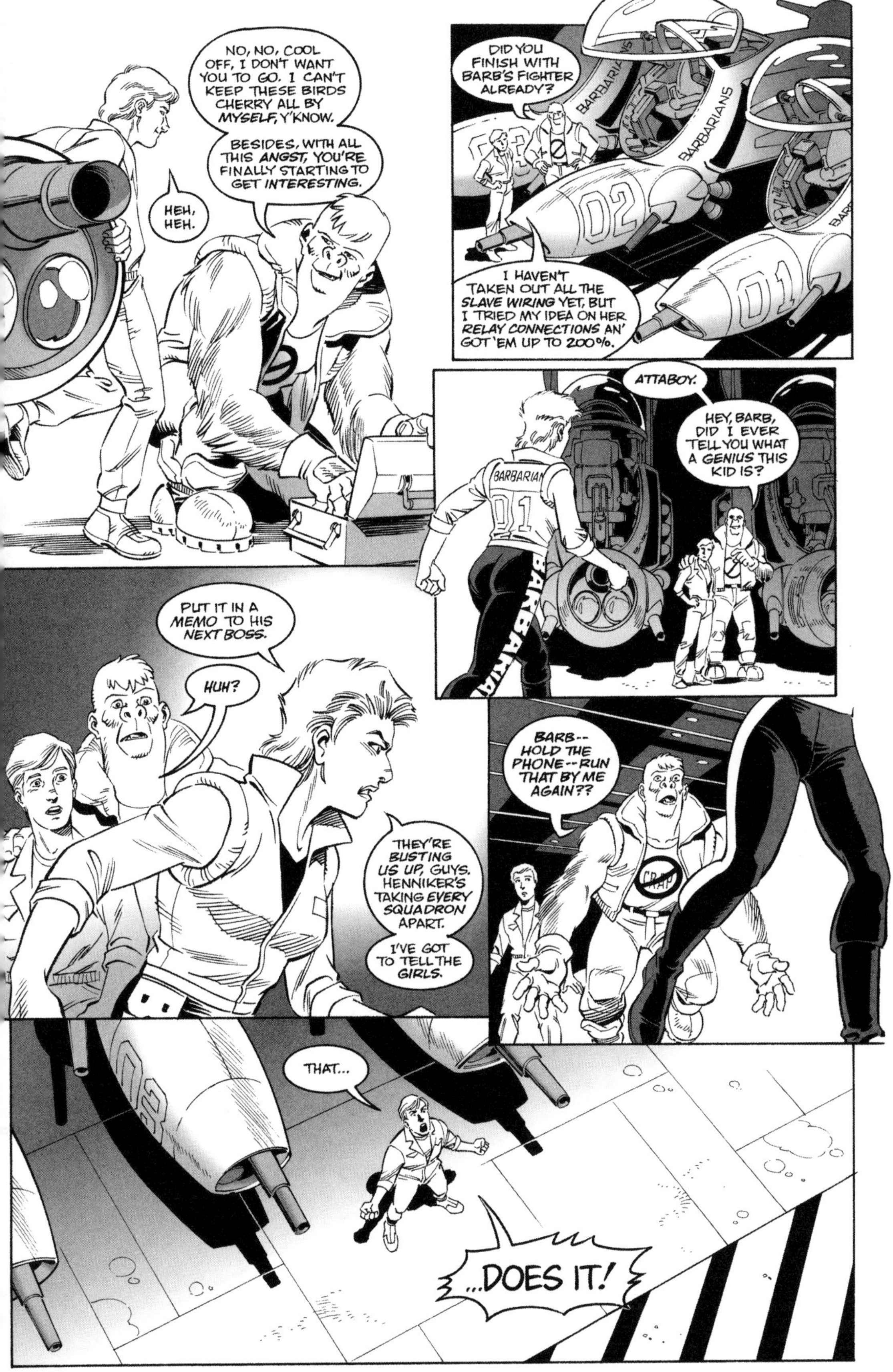
NO, NO, COOL OFF, I DON'T WANT YOU TO GO. I CAN'T KEEP THESE BIRDS CHERRY ALL BY MYSELF, Y'KNOW.
BESIDES, WITH ALL THIS ANGST, YOU'RE FINALLY STARTING TO GET INTERESTING.
HEH, HEH.
DID YOU FINISH WITH BARB'S FIGHTER ALREADY?
BARBARIANS
02
01
I HAVEN'T TAKEN OUT ALL THE SLAVE WIRING YET, BUT I TRIED MY IDEA ON HER RELAY CONNECTIONS AN' GOT 'EM UP TO 200%.
ATTABOY.
HEY, BARB, DID I EVER TELL YOU WHAT A GENIUS THIS KID IS?
BARBARIAN 01
PUT IT IN A MEMO TO HIS NEXT BOSS.
HUH?
THEY'RE BUSTING US UP, GUYS. HENNIKER'S TAKING EVERY SQUADRON APART.
I'VE GOT TO TELL THE GIRLS.
BARB-- HOLD THE PHONE--RUN THAT BY ME AGAIN??
THAT...
...DOES IT!

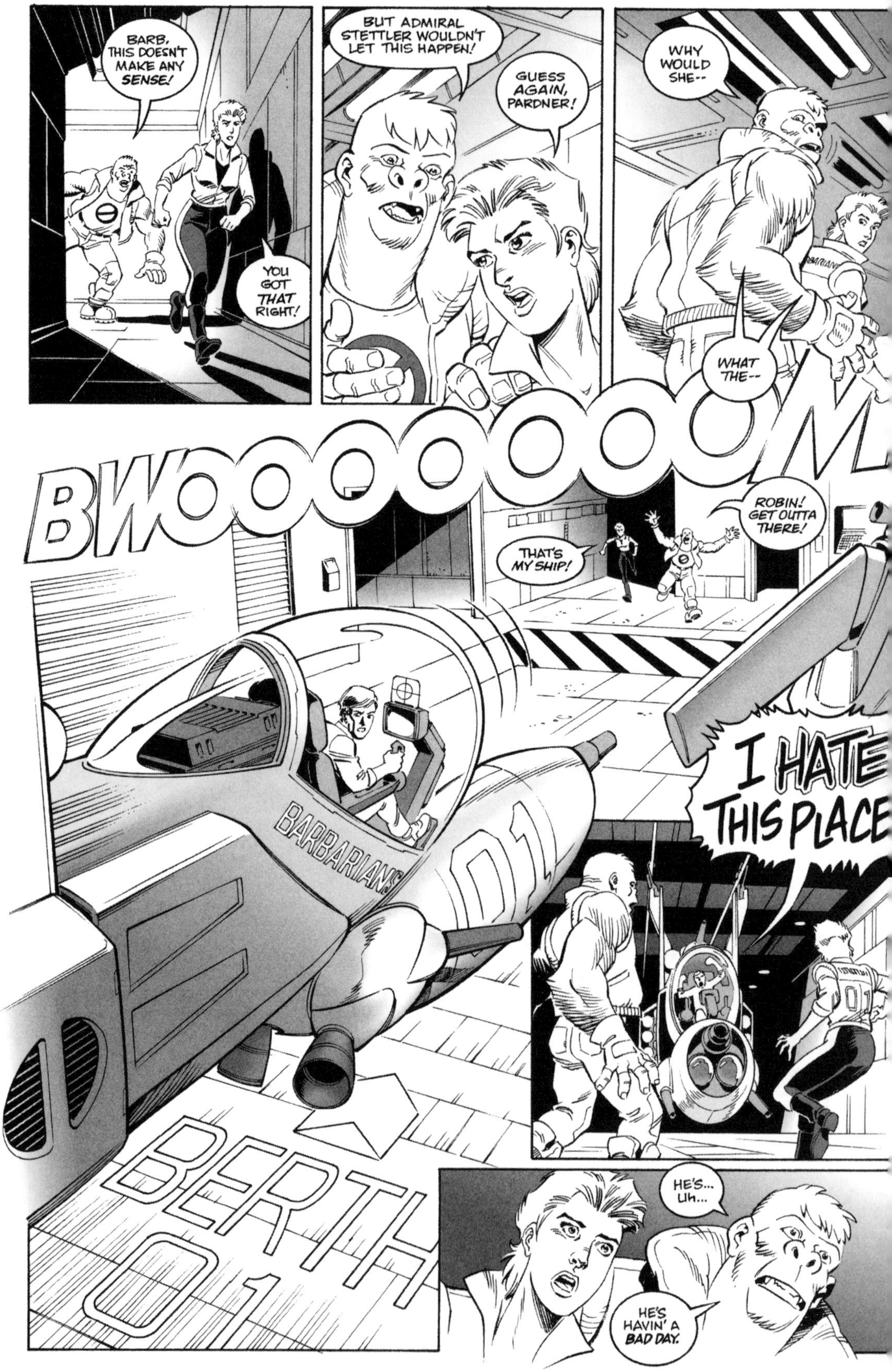
BARB, THIS DOESN'T MAKE ANY SENSE!
YOU GOT THAT RIGHT!
BUT ADMIRAL STETTLER WOULDN'T LET THIS HAPPEN!
GUESS AGAIN, PARDNER!
WHY WOULD SHE--
WHAT THE--
BWOOOOOOOM
ROBIN! GET OUTTA THERE!
THAT'S MY SHIP!
BARBARIANS
01
I HATE THIS PLACE
BERTH 01
HE'S... UH...
HE'S HAVIN' A BAD DAY.

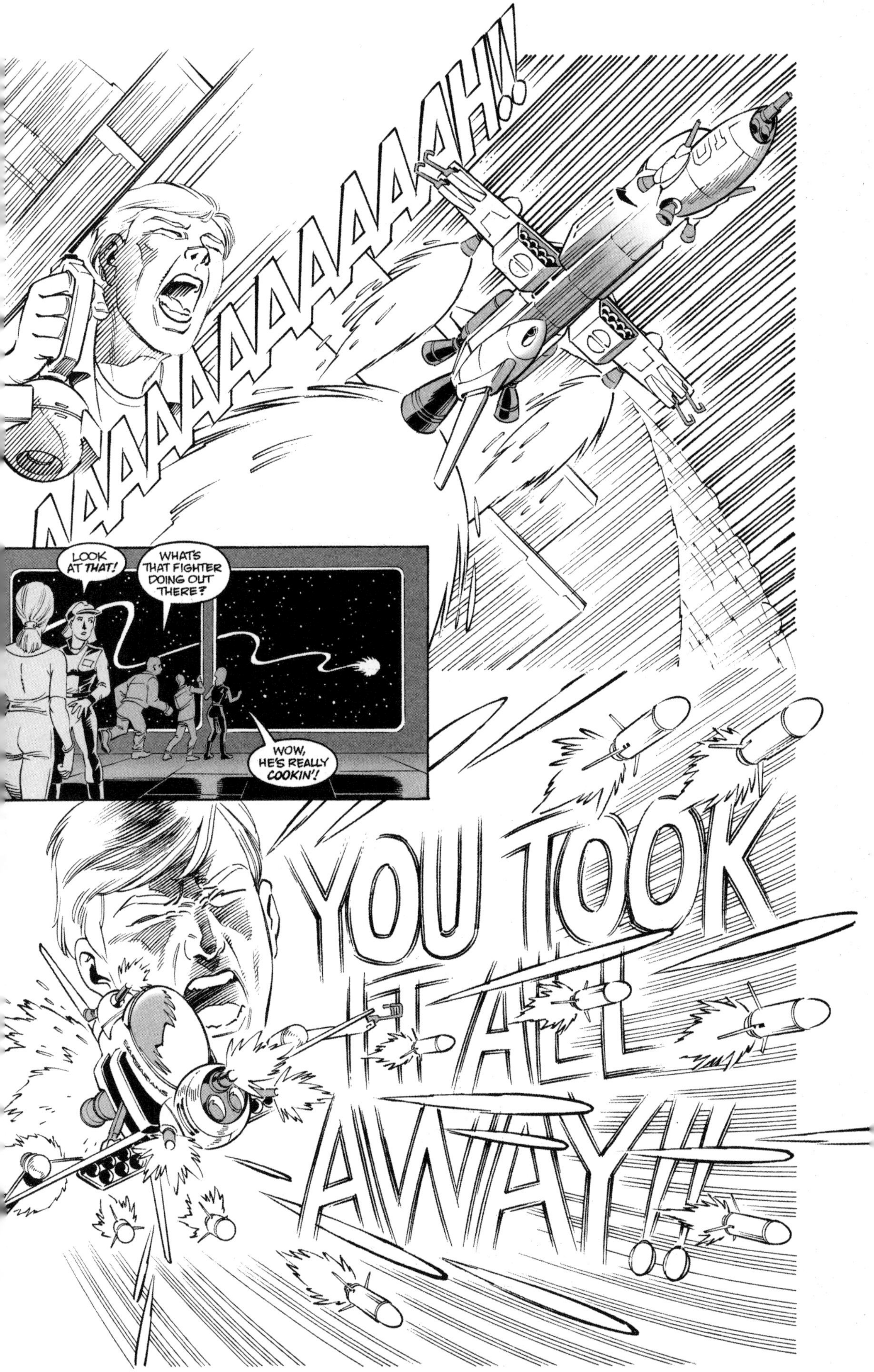
AAAAAAAAAAAH!!
LOOK AT THAT!
WHAT'S THAT FIGHTER DOING OUT THERE?
WOW, HE'S REALLY COOKIN'!
YOU TOOK IT ALL AWAY!!

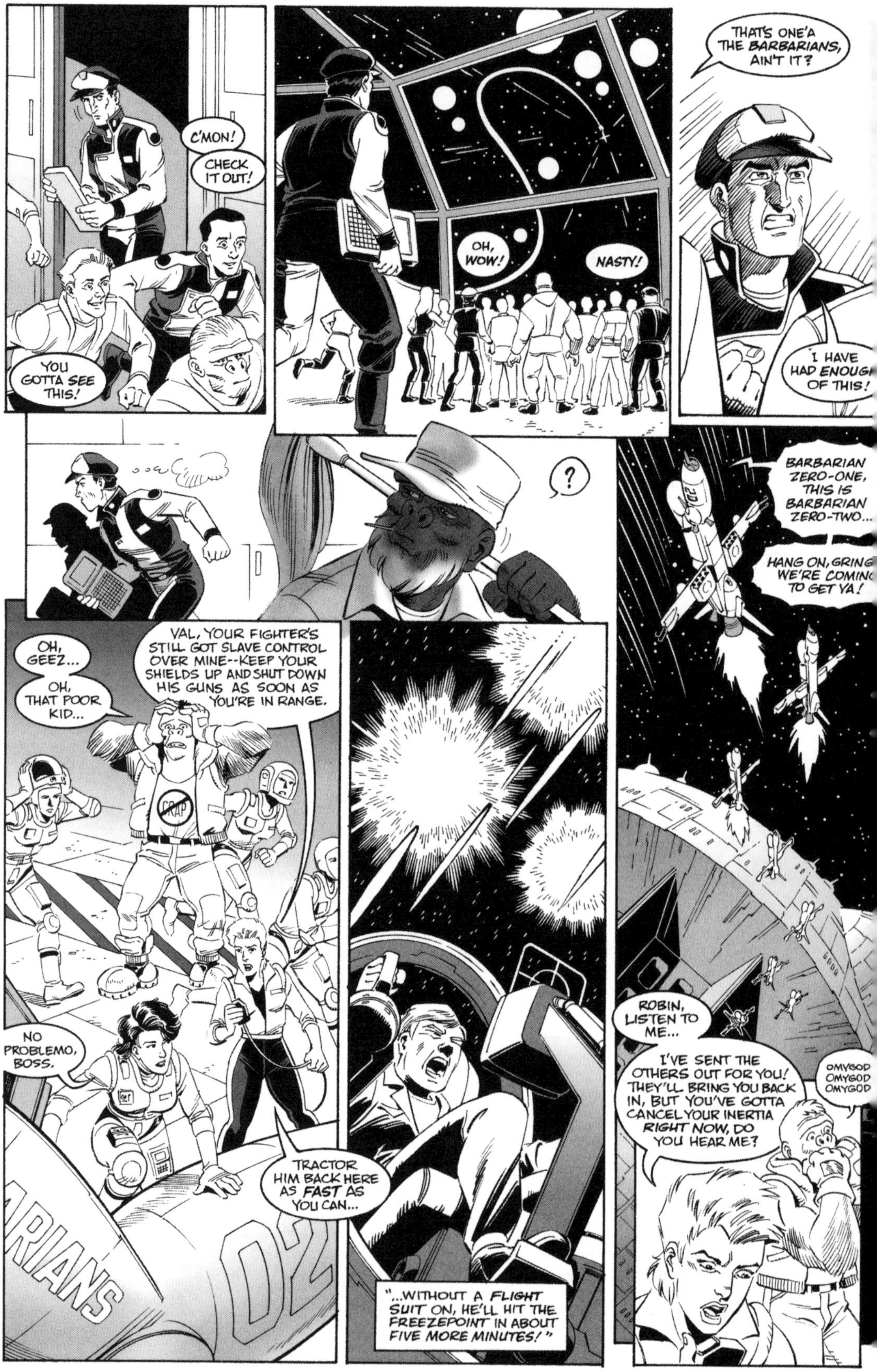
C'MON!
CHECK IT OUT!
YOU GOTTA SEE THIS!
OH, WOW!
NASTY!
THAT'S ONE'A THE BARBARIANS, AIN'T IT?
I HAVE HAD ENOUG OF THIS!
?
BARBARIAN ZERO-ONE, THIS IS BARBARIAN ZERO-TWO...
HANG ON, GRING WE'RE COMIN TO GET YA!
OH, GEEZ...
OH, THAT POOR KID...
VAL, YOUR FIGHTER'S STILL GOT SLAVE CONTROL OVER MINE--KEEP YOUR SHIELDS UP AND SHUT DOWN HIS GUNS AS SOON AS YOU'RE IN RANGE.
NO PROBLEMO, BOSS.
TRACTOR HIM BACK HERE AS FAST AS YOU CAN...
"...WITHOUT A FLIGHT SUIT ON, HE'LL HIT THE FREEZEPOINT IN ABOUT FIVE MORE MINUTES!"
ROBIN, LISTEN TO ME...
I'VE SENT THE OTHERS OUT FOR YOU! THEY'LL BRING YOU BACK IN, BUT YOU'VE GOTTA CANCEL YOUR INERTIA RIGHT NOW, DO YOU HEAR ME?
OMYGOD OMYGOD OMYGOD
CRAP
RIANS
02

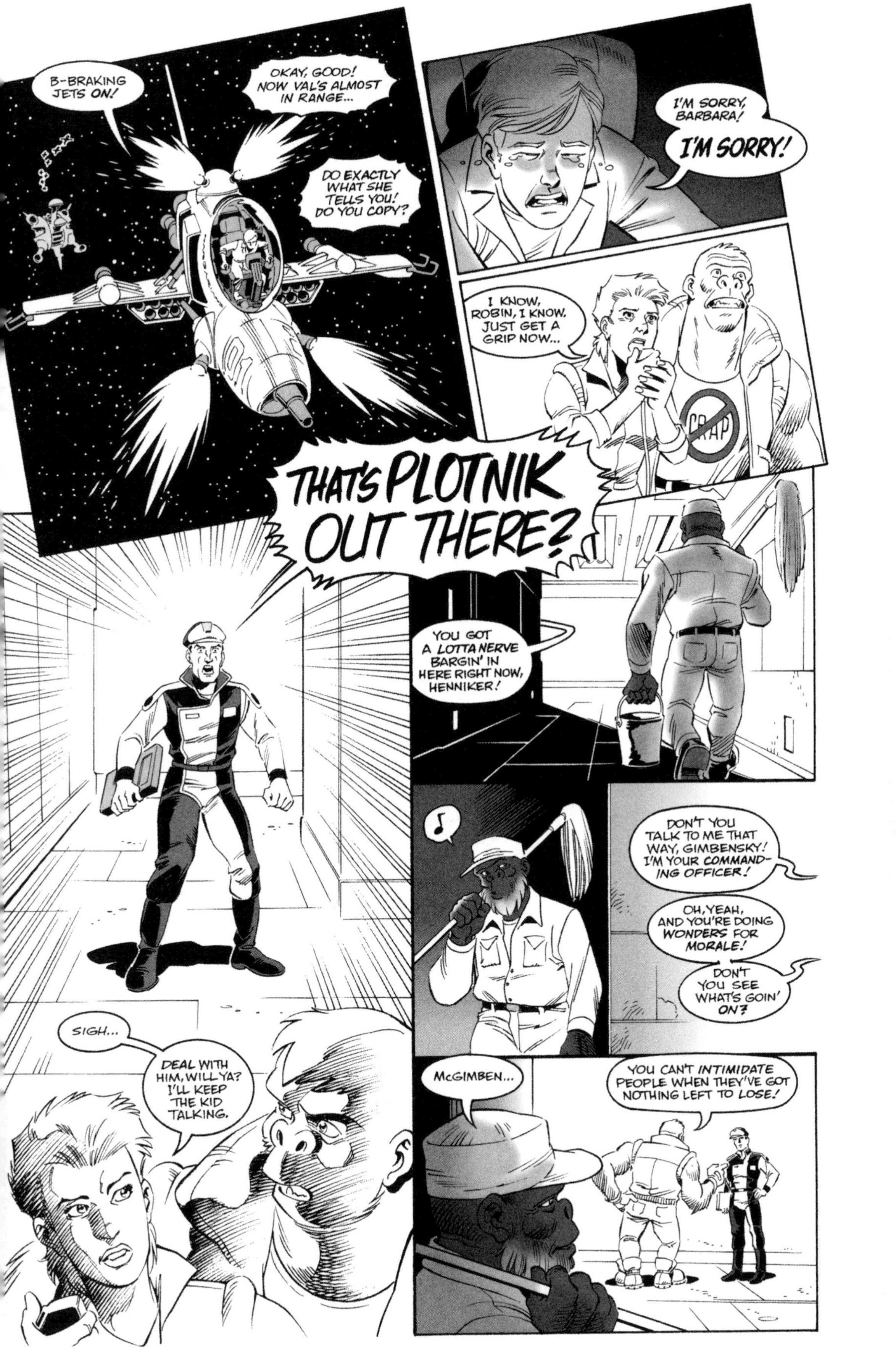
B-BRAKING JETS ON!
OKAY, GOOD! NOW VAL'S ALMOST IN RANGE...
DO EXACTLY WHAT SHE TELLS YOU! DO YOU COPY?
I'M SORRY, BARBARA!
I'M SORRY!
I KNOW, ROBIN, I KNOW. JUST GET A GRIP NOW...
CRAP
THAT'S PLOTNIK OUT THERE?
YOU GOT A LOTTA NERVE BARGIN' IN HERE RIGHT NOW, HENNIKER!
DON'T YOU TALK TO ME THAT WAY, GIMBENSKY! I'M YOUR COMMANDING OFFICER!
OH, YEAH, AND YOU'RE DOING WONDERS FOR MORALE!
DON'T YOU SEE WHAT'S GOIN' ON?
SIGH...
DEAL WITH HIM, WILL YA? I'LL KEEP THE KID TALKING.
McGIMBEN...
YOU CAN'T INTIMIDATE PEOPLE WHEN THEY'VE GOT NOTHING LEFT TO LOSE!

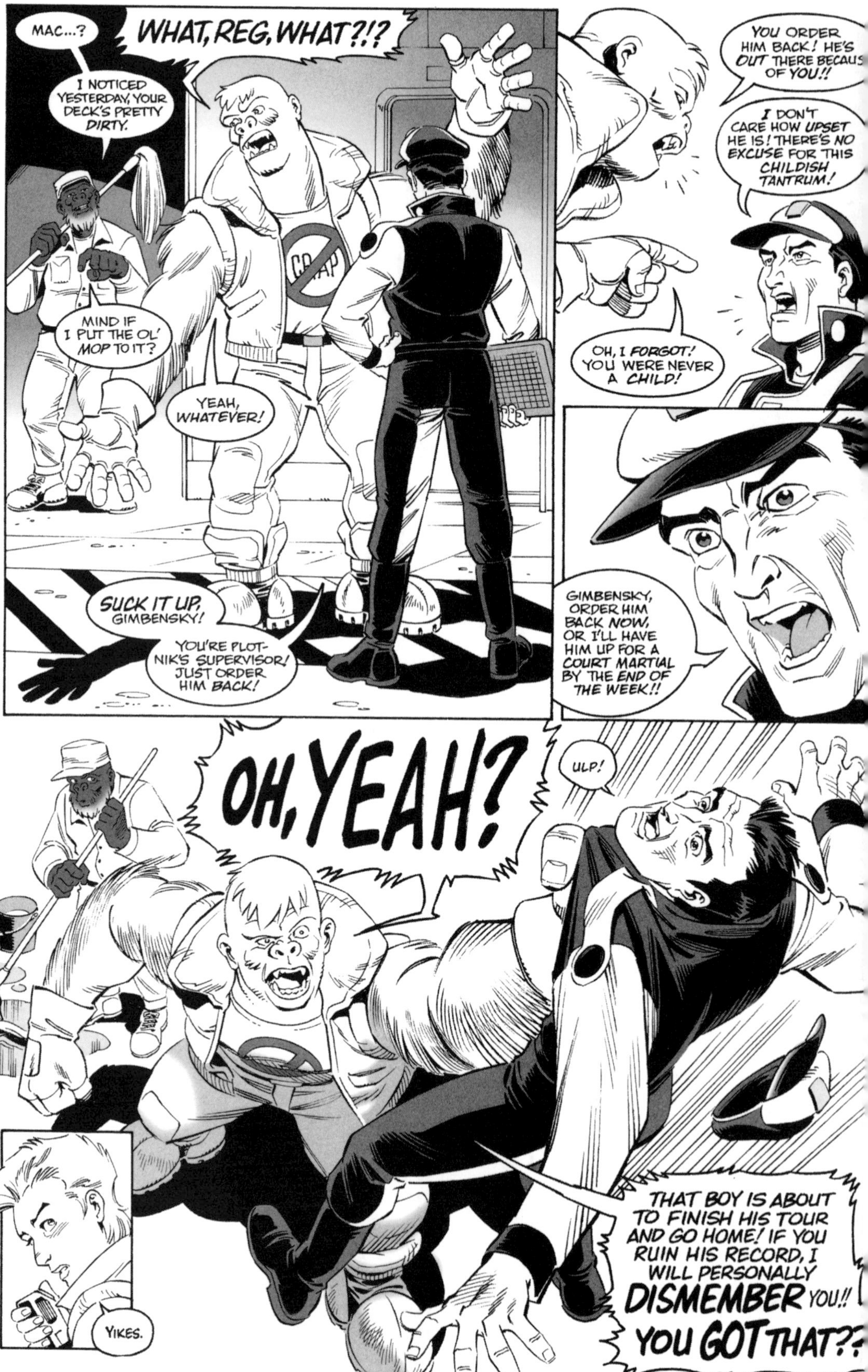

MAC...?
WHAT, REG, WHAT?!?
I NOTICED YESTERDAY, YOUR DECK'S PRETTY DIRTY.
MIND IF I PUT THE OL' MOP TO IT?
YEAH, WHATEVER!
SUCK IT UP, GIMBENSKY!
YOU'RE PLOTNIK'S SUPERVISOR! JUST ORDER HIM BACK!
YOU ORDER HIM BACK! HE'S OUT THERE BECAUS OF YOU!!
I DON'T CARE HOW UPSET HE IS! THERE'S NO EXCUSE FOR THIS CHILDISH TANTRUM!
OH, I FORGOT! YOU WERE NEVER A CHILD!
GIMBENSKY, ORDER HIM BACK NOW, OR I'LL HAVE HIM UP FOR A COURT MARTIAL BY THE END OF THE WEEK!!
OH, YEAH?
ULP!
THAT BOY IS ABOUT TO FINISH HIS TOUR AND GO HOME! IF YOU RUIN HIS RECORD, I WILL PERSONALLY DISMEMBER YOU!! YOU GOT THAT??
YIKES.

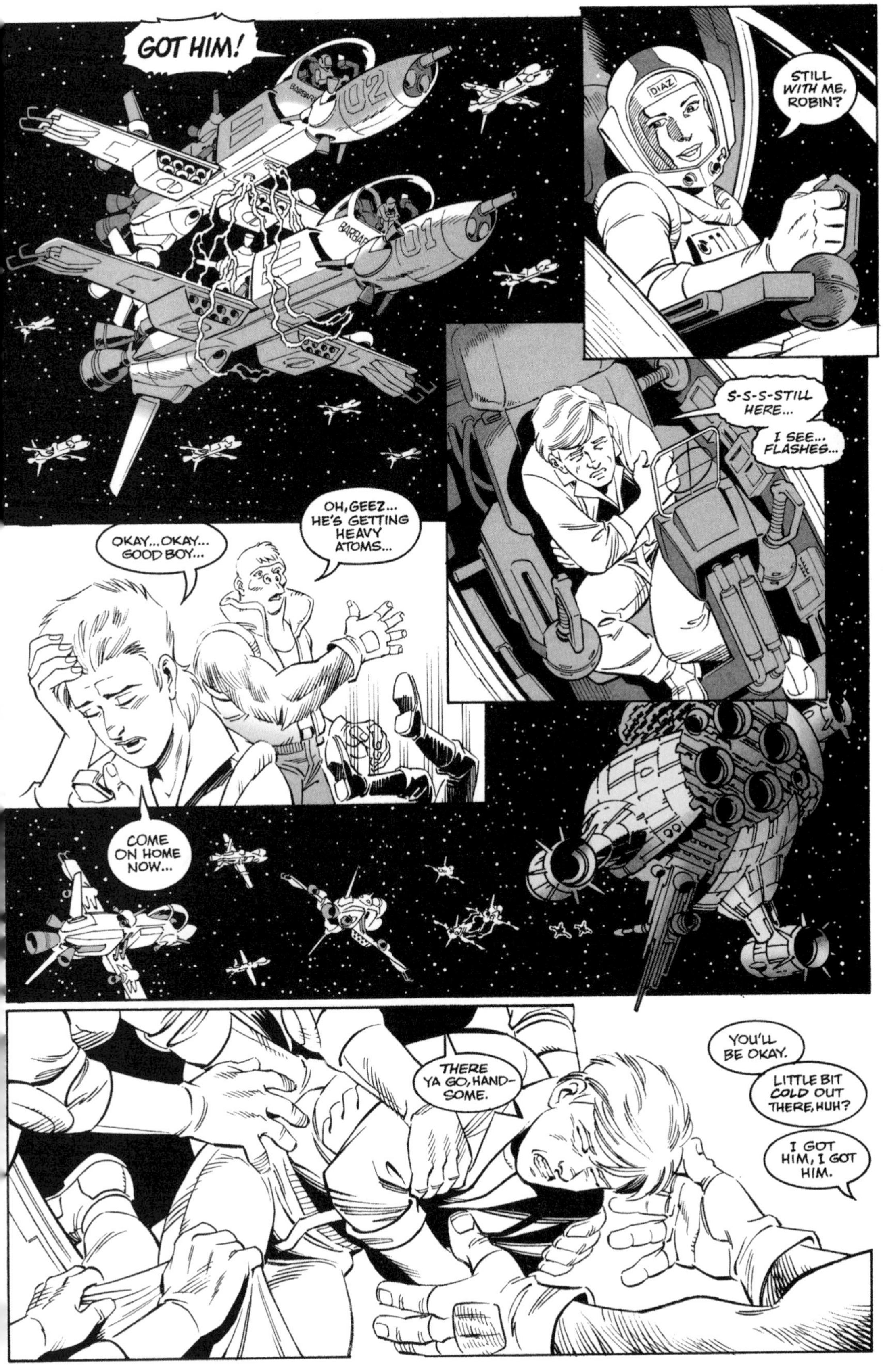
GOT HIM!
STILL WITH ME, ROBIN?
S-S-S-STILL HERE...
I SEE... FLASHES...
OKAY... OKAY... GOOD BOY...
OH, GEEZ... HE'S GETTING HEAVY ATOMS...
COME ON HOME NOW...
THERE YA GO, HAND-SOME.
YOU'LL BE OKAY.
LITTLE BIT COLD OUT THERE, HUH?
I GOT HIM, I GOT HIM.

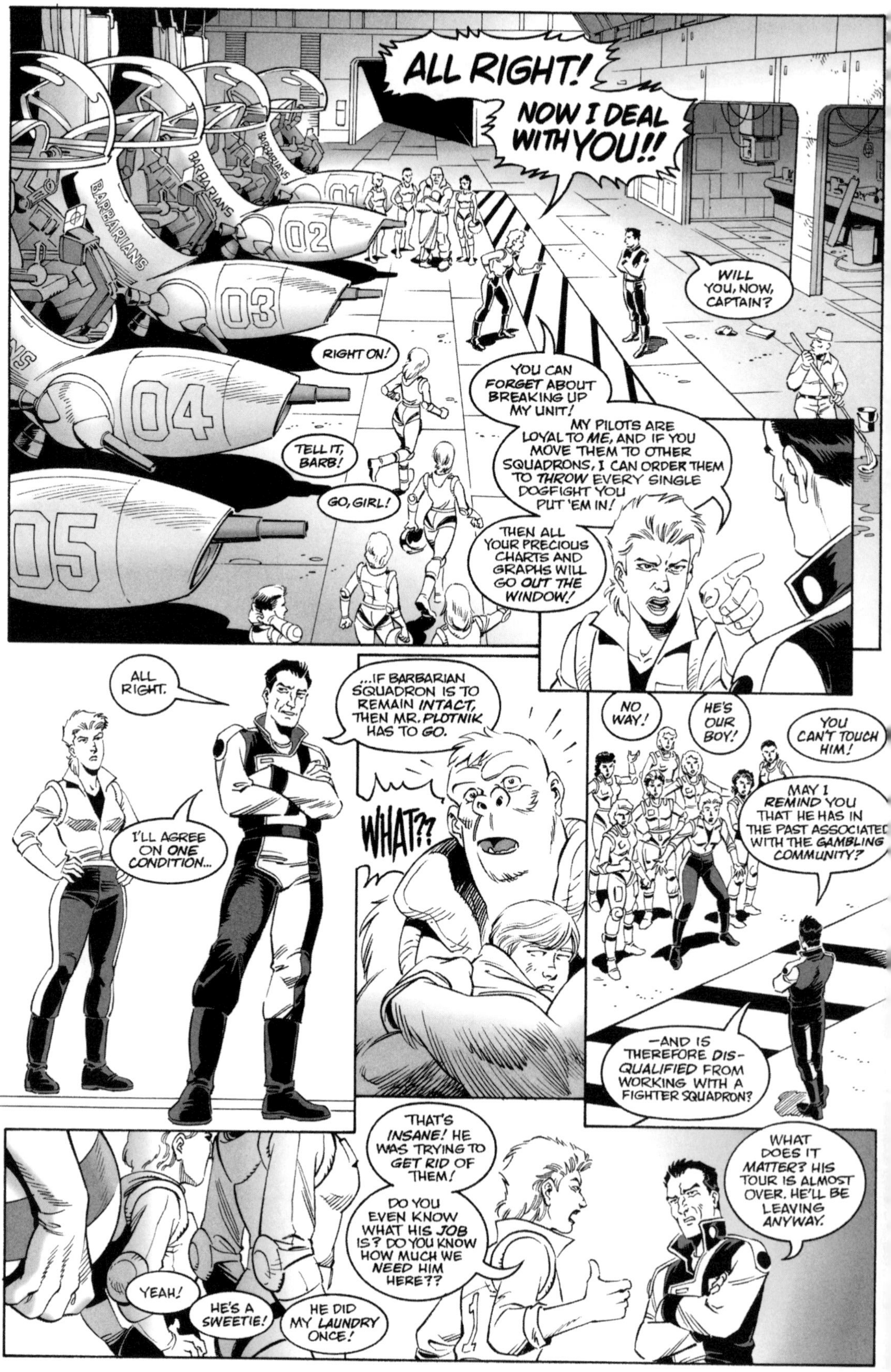
ALL RIGHT!
NOW I DEAL WITH YOU!!
WILL YOU, NOW, CAPTAIN?
RIGHT ON!
TELL IT, BARB!
GO, GIRL!
YOU CAN FORGET ABOUT BREAKING UP MY UNIT!
MY PILOTS ARE LOYAL TO ME, AND IF YOU MOVE THEM TO OTHER SQUADRONS, I CAN ORDER THEM TO THROW EVERY SINGLE DOGFIGHT YOU PUT 'EM IN!
THEN ALL YOUR PRECIOUS CHARTS AND GRAPHS WILL GO OUT THE WINDOW!
ALL RIGHT.
I'LL AGREE ON ONE CONDITION...
...IF BARBARIAN SQUADRON IS TO REMAIN INTACT, THEN MR. PLOTNIK HAS TO GO.
WHAT??
NO WAY!
HE'S OUR BOY!
YOU CAN'T TOUCH HIM!
MAY I REMIND YOU THAT HE HAS IN THE PAST ASSOCIATED WITH THE GAMBLING COMMUNITY?
—AND IS THEREFORE DIS-QUALIFIED FROM WORKING WITH A FIGHTER SQUADRON?
YEAH!
HE'S A SWEETIE!
HE DID MY LAUNDRY ONCE!
THAT'S INSANE! HE WAS TRYING TO GET RID OF THEM!
DO YOU EVEN KNOW WHAT HIS JOB IS? DO YOU KNOW HOW MUCH WE NEED HIM HERE??
WHAT DOES IT MATTER? HIS TOUR IS ALMOST OVER. HE'LL BE LEAVING ANYWAY.

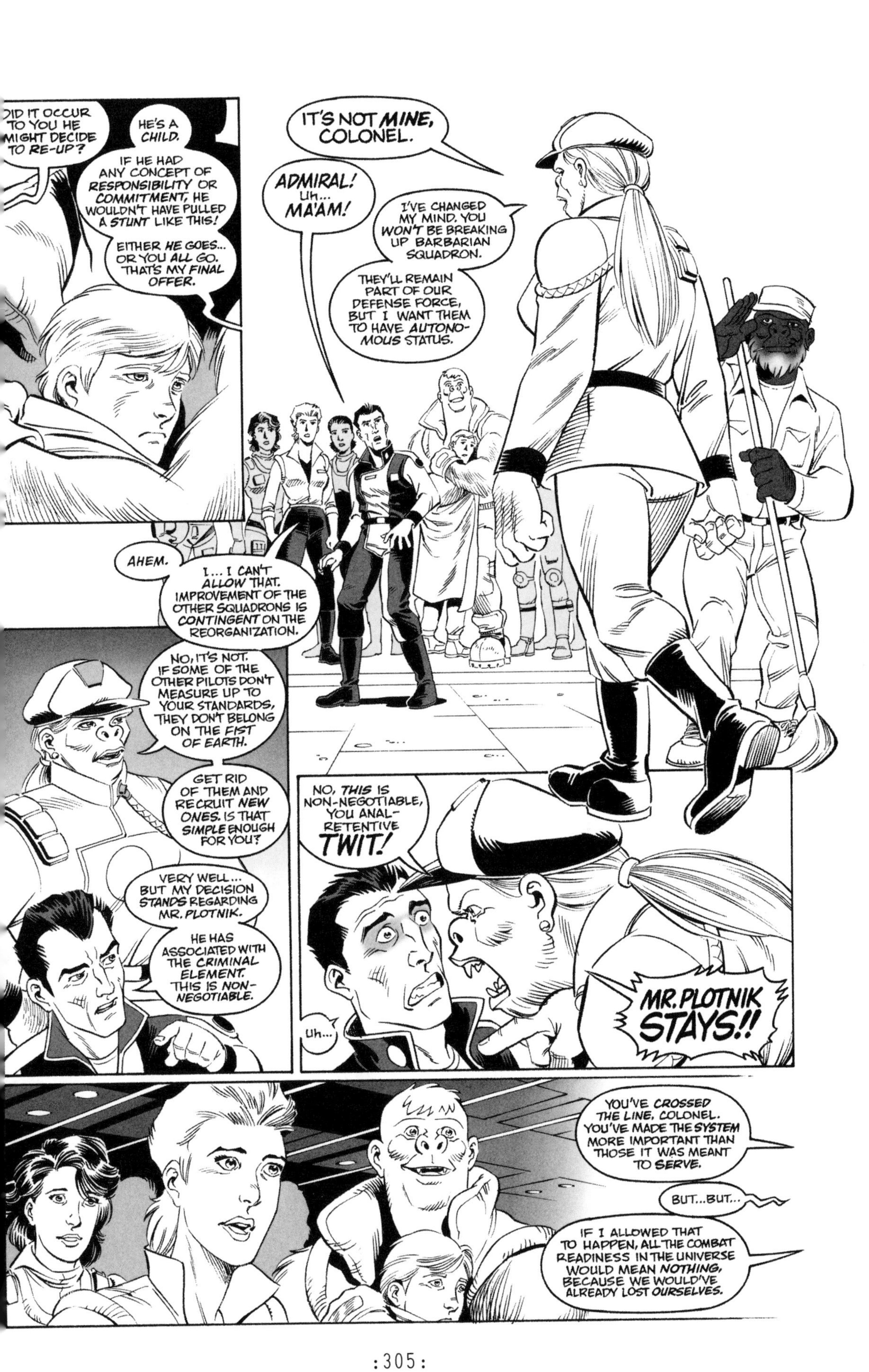
DID IT OCCUR TO YOU HE MIGHT DECIDE TO RE-UP?
HE'S A CHILD.
IF HE HAD ANY CONCEPT OF RESPONSIBILITY OR COMMITMENT, HE WOULDN'T HAVE PULLED A STUNT LIKE THIS!
EITHER HE GOES... OR YOU ALL GO. THAT'S MY FINAL OFFER.
IT'S NOT MINE, COLONEL.
ADMIRAL! Uh... MA'AM!
I'VE CHANGED MY MIND. YOU WON'T BE BREAKING UP BARBARIAN SQUADRON.
THEY'LL REMAIN PART OF OUR DEFENSE FORCE, BUT I WANT THEM TO HAVE AUTONOMOUS STATUS.
AHEM.
I... I CAN'T ALLOW THAT. IMPROVEMENT OF THE OTHER SQUADRONS IS CONTINGENT ON THE REORGANIZATION.
NO, IT'S NOT. IF SOME OF THE OTHER PILOTS DON'T MEASURE UP TO YOUR STANDARDS, THEY DON'T BELONG ON THE FIST OF EARTH.
GET RID OF THEM AND RECRUIT NEW ONES. IS THAT SIMPLE ENOUGH FOR YOU?
VERY WELL... BUT MY DECISION STANDS REGARDING MR. PLOTNIK.
HE HAS ASSOCIATED WITH THE CRIMINAL ELEMENT. THIS IS NON-NEGOTIABLE.
NO, THIS IS NON-NEGOTIABLE, YOU ANAL-RETENTIVE TWIT!
Uh...
MR. PLOTNIK STAYS!!
YOU'VE CROSSED THE LINE, COLONEL. YOU'VE MADE THE SYSTEM MORE IMPORTANT THAN THOSE IT WAS MEANT TO SERVE.
BUT...BUT...
IF I ALLOWED THAT TO HAPPEN, ALL THE COMBAT READINESS IN THE UNIVERSE WOULD MEAN NOTHING, BECAUSE WE WOULD'VE ALREADY LOST OURSELVES.

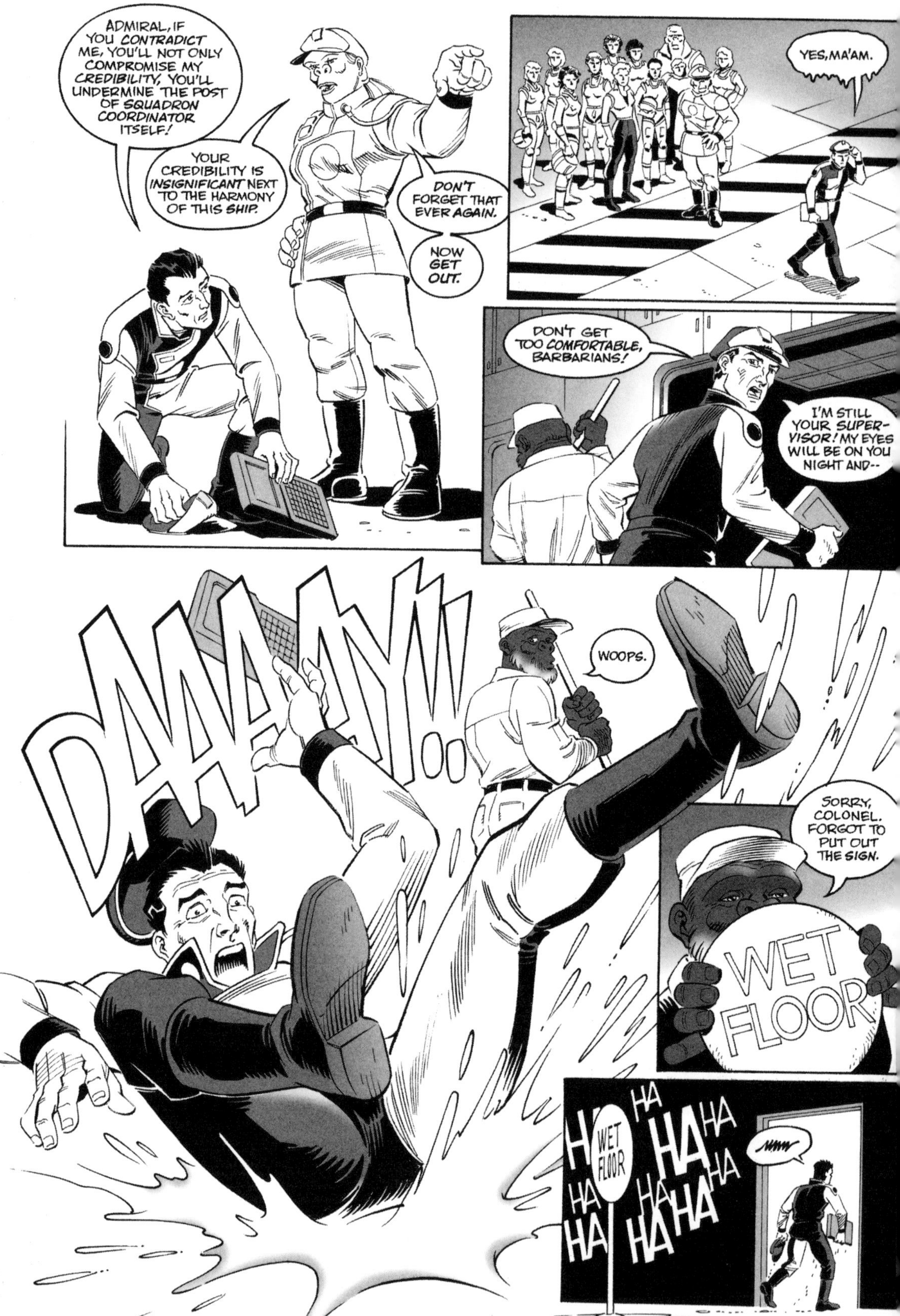
ADMIRAL, IF YOU CONTRADICT ME, YOU'LL NOT ONLY COMPROMISE MY CREDIBILITY, YOU'LL UNDERMINE THE POST OF SQUADRON COORDINATOR ITSELF!
YOUR CREDIBILITY IS INSIGNIFICANT NEXT TO THE HARMONY OF THIS SHIP.
DON'T FORGET THAT EVER AGAIN.
NOW GET OUT.
YES, MA'AM.
DON'T GET TOO COMFORTABLE, BARBARIANS!
I'M STILL YOUR SUPER-VISOR! MY EYES WILL BE ON YOU NIGHT AND--
DAAAAY!!
WOOPS.
SORRY, COLONEL. FORGOT TO PUT OUT THE SIGN.
WET FLOOR
HA HA HA HA HA HA HA HA HA HA HA HA
WET FLOOR

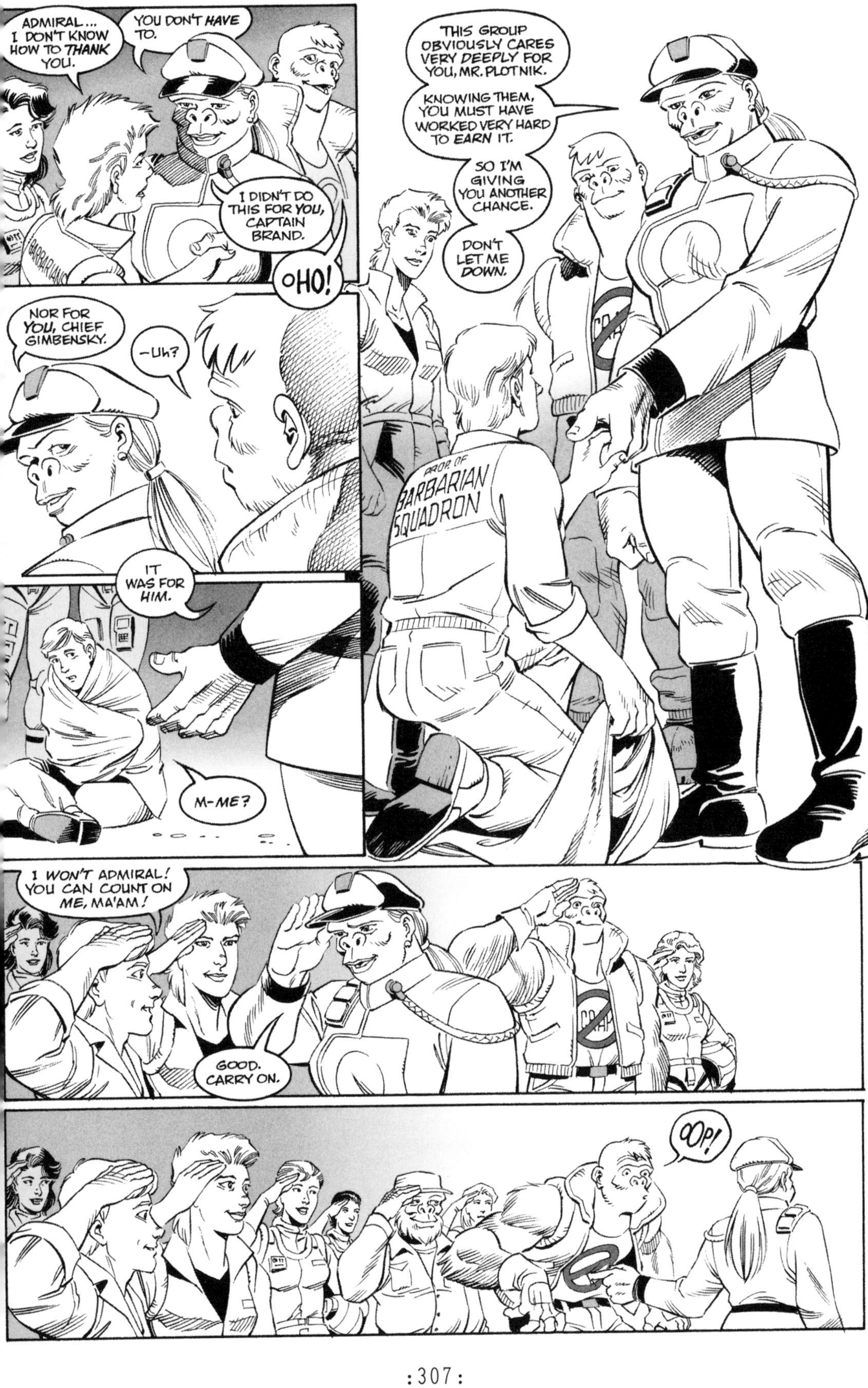
ADMIRAL... I DON'T KNOW HOW TO *THANK* YOU.
YOU DON'T *HAVE* TO.
I DIDN'T DO THIS FOR *YOU*, CAPTAIN BRAND.
OHO!
NOR FOR *YOU*, CHIEF GIMBENSKY.
-Uh?
IT WAS FOR *HIM*.
M-*ME*?
THIS GROUP OBVIOUSLY CARES VERY *DEEPLY* FOR YOU, MR. PLOTNIK.
KNOWING THEM, YOU MUST HAVE WORKED VERY HARD TO *EARN* IT.
SO I'M GIVING YOU ANOTHER CHANCE.
DON'T LET ME *DOWN*.
PROP. OF BARBARIAN SQUADRON
I *WON'T* ADMIRAL! YOU CAN COUNT ON *ME*, MA'AM!
GOOD. CARRY ON.
OOP!

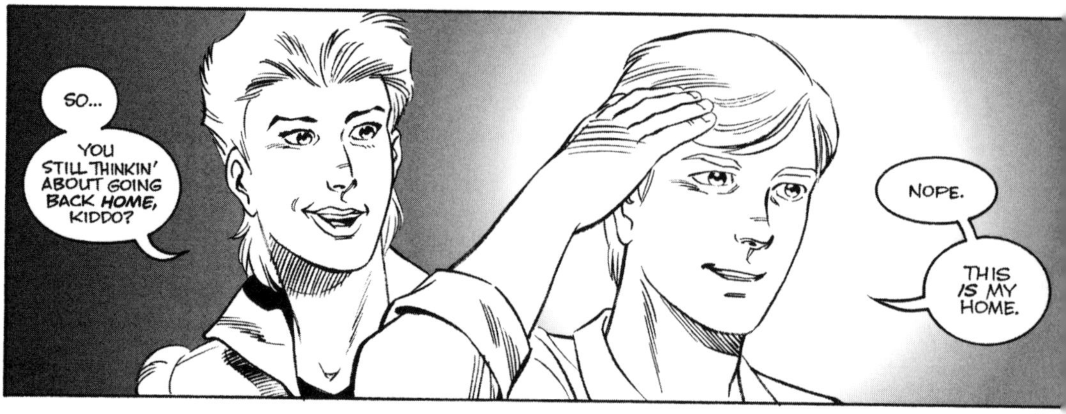
SO...
YOU STILL THINKIN' ABOUT GOING BACK HOME, KIDDO?
NOPE.
THIS IS MY HOME.

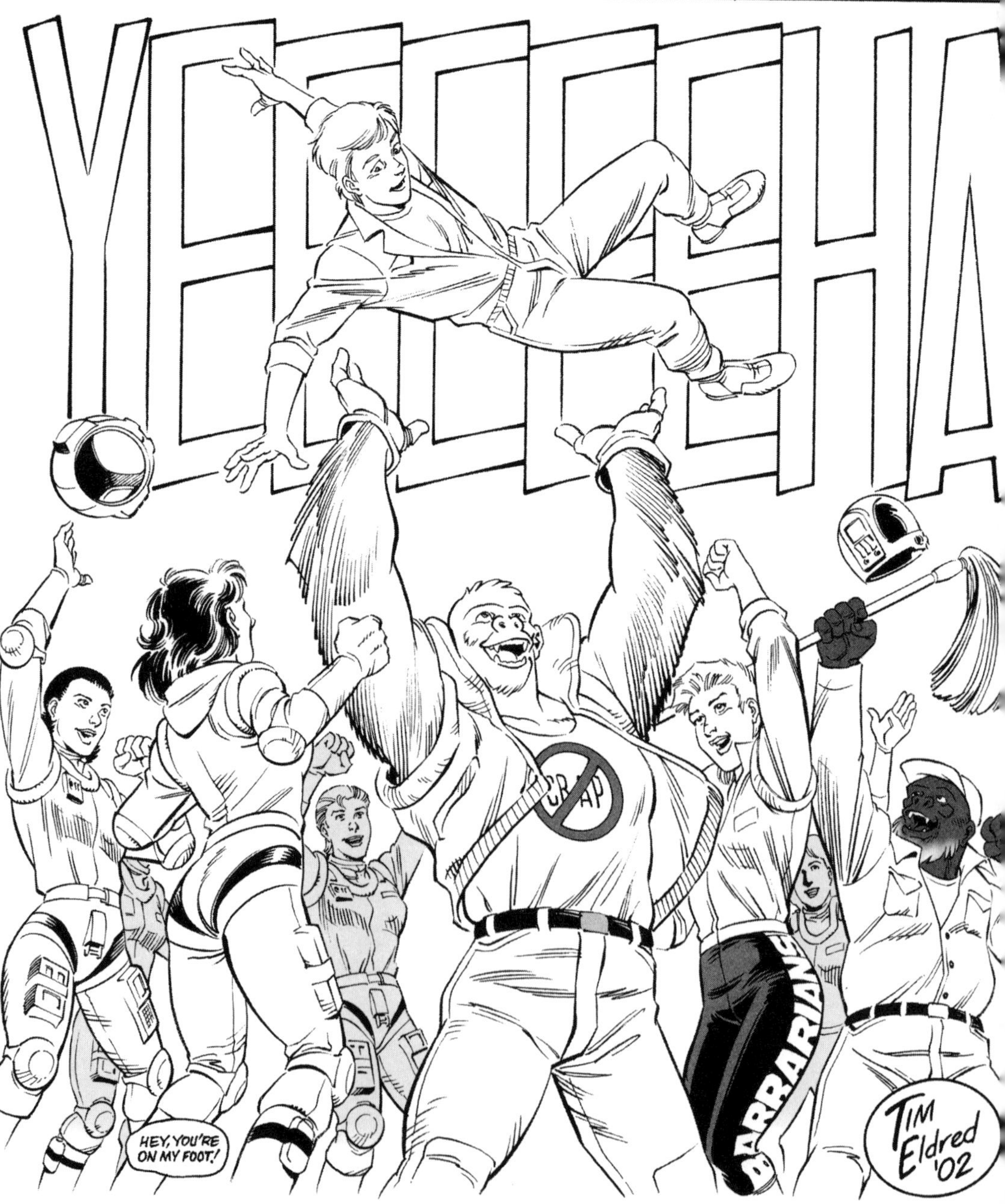
YEEEEEHA
CRAP
BARBARIANS
HEY, YOU'RE ON MY FOOT!
TIM Eldred '02

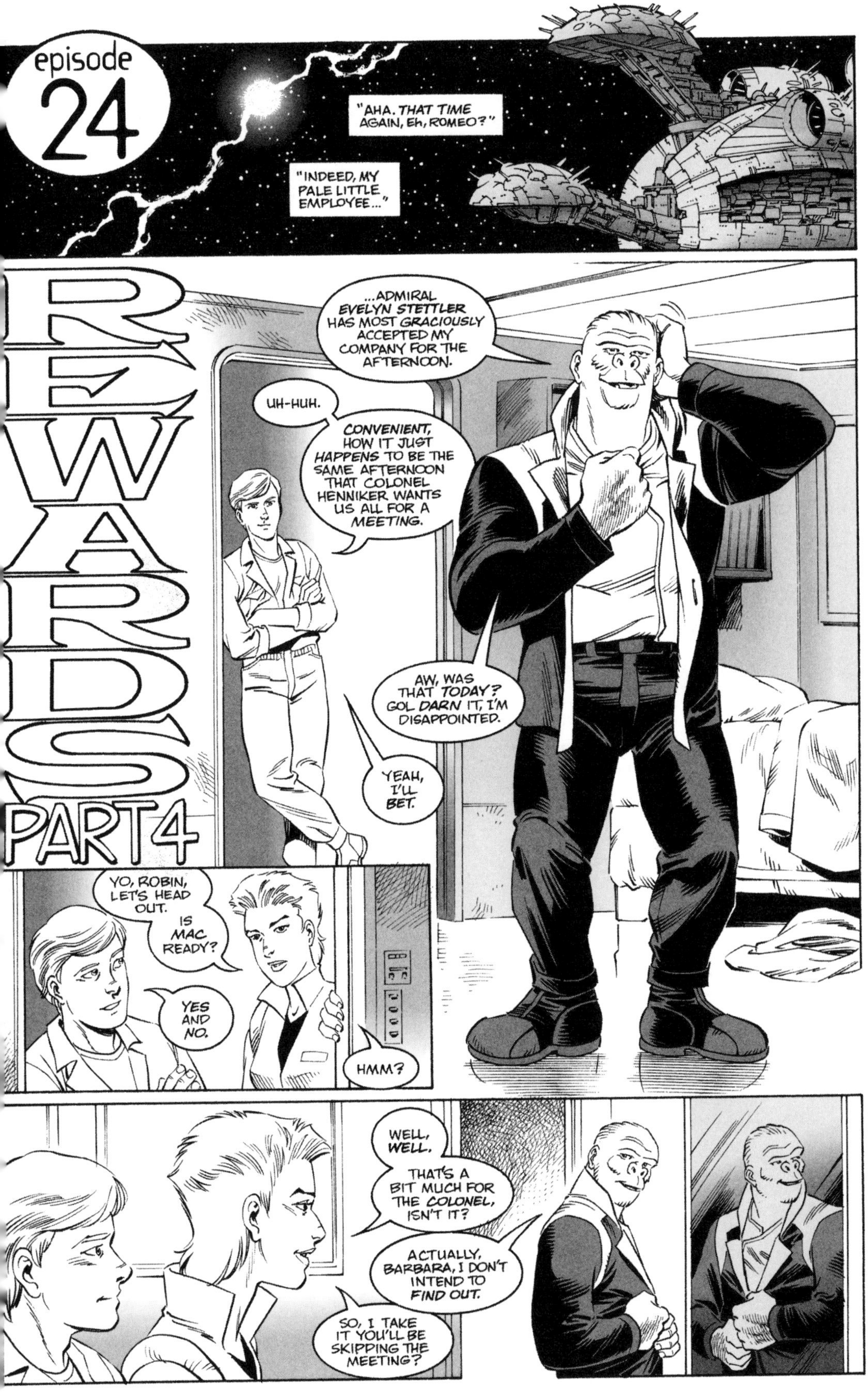
episode 24
"INDEED, MY PALE LITTLE EMPLOYEE..."
"AHA. THAT TIME AGAIN, Eh, ROMEO?"
REWARDS PART 4
...ADMIRAL EVELYN STETTLER HAS MOST GRACIOUSLY ACCEPTED MY COMPANY FOR THE AFTERNOON.
UH-HUH.
CONVENIENT, HOW IT JUST HAPPENS TO BE THE SAME AFTERNOON THAT COLONEL HENNIKER WANTS US ALL FOR A MEETING.
AW, WAS THAT TODAY? GOL DARN IT, I'M DISAPPOINTED.
YEAH, I'LL BET.
YO, ROBIN, LET'S HEAD OUT.
IS MAC READY?
YES AND NO.
HMM?
WELL, WELL.
THAT'S A BIT MUCH FOR THE COLONEL, ISN'T IT?
SO, I TAKE IT YOU'LL BE SKIPPING THE MEETING?
ACTUALLY, BARBARA, I DON'T INTEND TO FIND OUT.

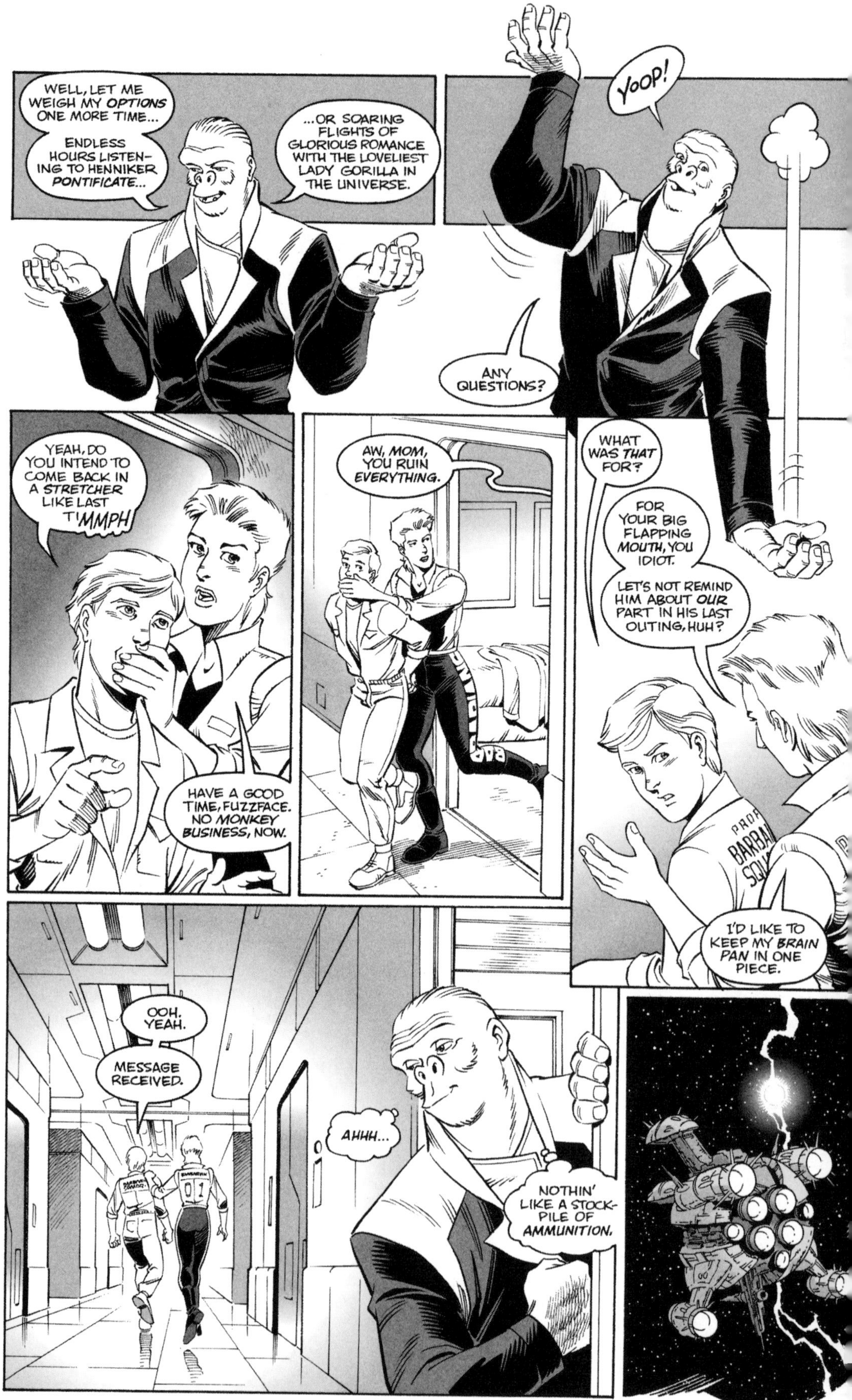

WELL, LET ME WEIGH MY OPTIONS ONE MORE TIME...
ENDLESS HOURS LISTENING TO HENNIKER PONTIFICATE...
...OR SOARING FLIGHTS OF GLORIOUS ROMANCE WITH THE LOVELIEST LADY GORILLA IN THE UNIVERSE.
YOOP!
ANY QUESTIONS?
YEAH, DO YOU INTEND TO COME BACK IN A STRETCHER LIKE LAST T'MMPH
HAVE A GOOD TIME, FUZZFACE. NO MONKEY BUSINESS, NOW.
AW, MOM, YOU RUIN EVERYTHING.
WHAT WAS THAT FOR?
FOR YOUR BIG FLAPPING MOUTH, YOU IDIOT.
LET'S NOT REMIND HIM ABOUT OUR PART IN HIS LAST OUTING, HUH?
I'D LIKE TO KEEP MY BRAIN PAN IN ONE PIECE.
OOH. YEAH.
MESSAGE RECEIVED.
AHHH...
NOTHIN' LIKE A STOCKPILE OF AMMUNITION.

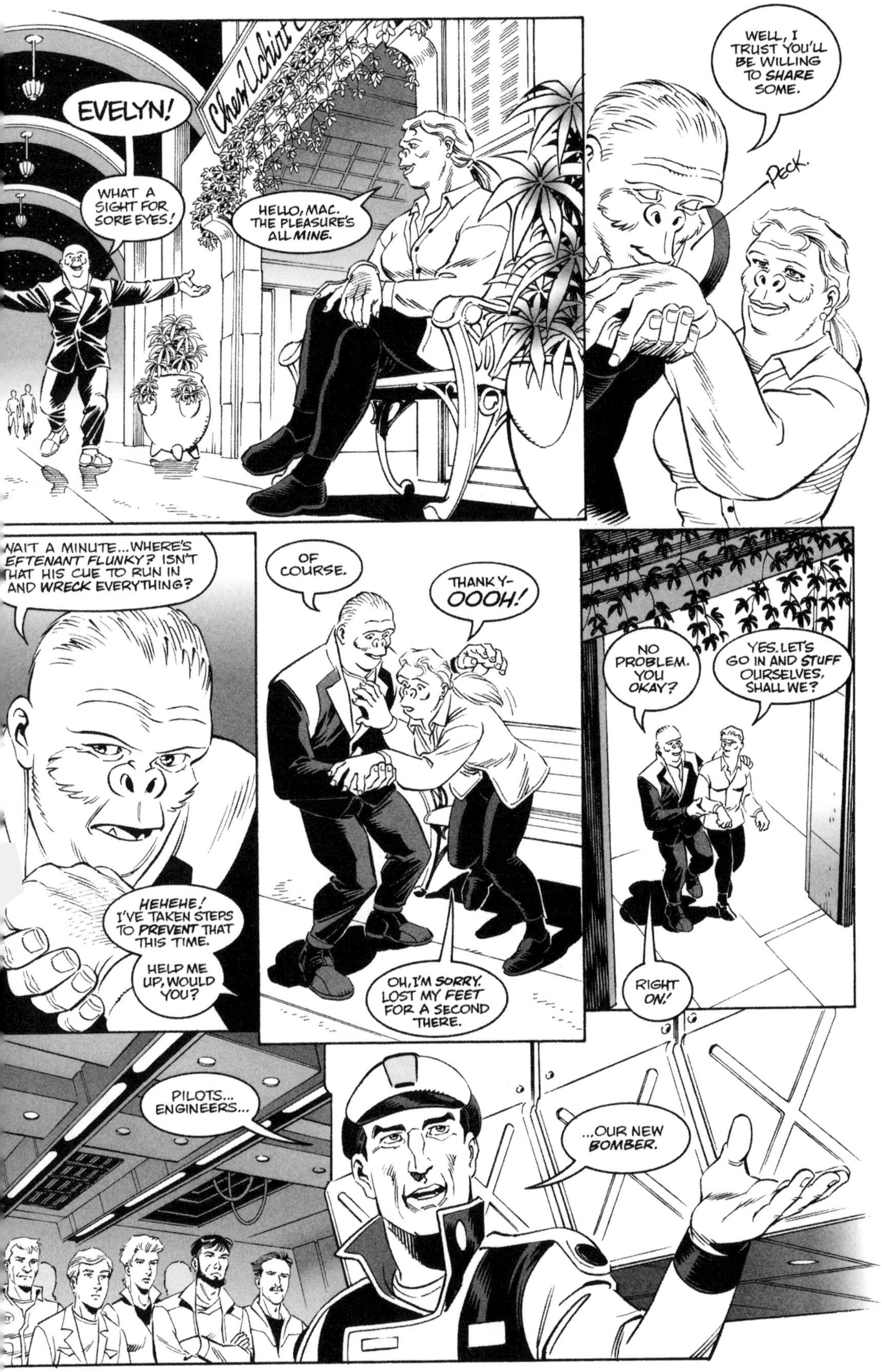
EVELYN!
WHAT A SIGHT FOR SORE EYES!
HELLO, MAC. THE PLEASURE'S ALL MINE.
WELL, I TRUST YOU'LL BE WILLING TO SHARE SOME.
PECK.
WAIT A MINUTE... WHERE'S LEFTENANT FLUNKY? ISN'T THAT HIS CUE TO RUN IN AND WRECK EVERYTHING?
HEHEHE! I'VE TAKEN STEPS TO PREVENT THAT THIS TIME.
HELP ME UP, WOULD YOU?
OF COURSE.
THANK Y-OOOH!
OH, I'M SORRY. LOST MY FEET FOR A SECOND THERE.
NO PROBLEM. YOU OKAY?
YES. LET'S GO IN AND STUFF OURSELVES, SHALL WE?
RIGHT ON!
PILOTS... ENGINEERS...
...OUR NEW BOMBER.

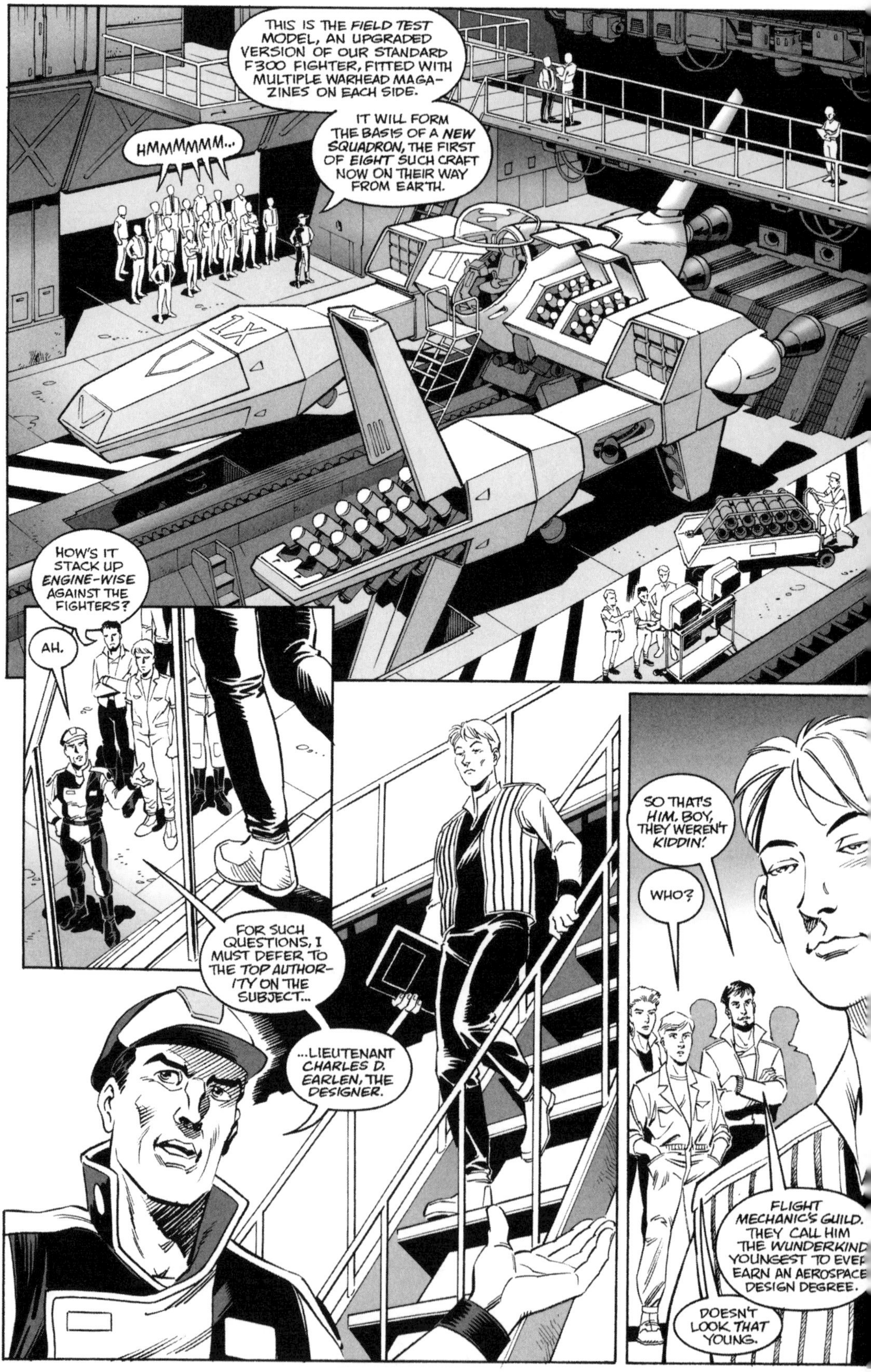
THIS IS THE FIELD TEST MODEL, AN UPGRADED VERSION OF OUR STANDARD F300 FIGHTER, FITTED WITH MULTIPLE WARHEAD MAGA-ZINES ON EACH SIDE.
IT WILL FORM THE BASIS OF A NEW SQUADRON, THE FIRST OF EIGHT SUCH CRAFT NOW ON THEIR WAY FROM EARTH.
HMMMMMM...
XI
HOW'S IT STACK UP ENGINE-WISE AGAINST THE FIGHTERS?
AH.
FOR SUCH QUESTIONS, I MUST DEFER TO THE TOP AUTHOR-ITY ON THE SUBJECT...
...LIEUTENANT CHARLES D. EARLEN, THE DESIGNER.
SO THAT'S HIM. BOY, THEY WEREN'T KIDDIN'!
WHO?
FLIGHT MECHANIC'S GUILD. THEY CALL HIM THE WUNDERKIND YOUNGEST TO EVER EARN AN AEROSPACE DESIGN DEGREE.
DOESN'T LOOK THAT YOUNG.

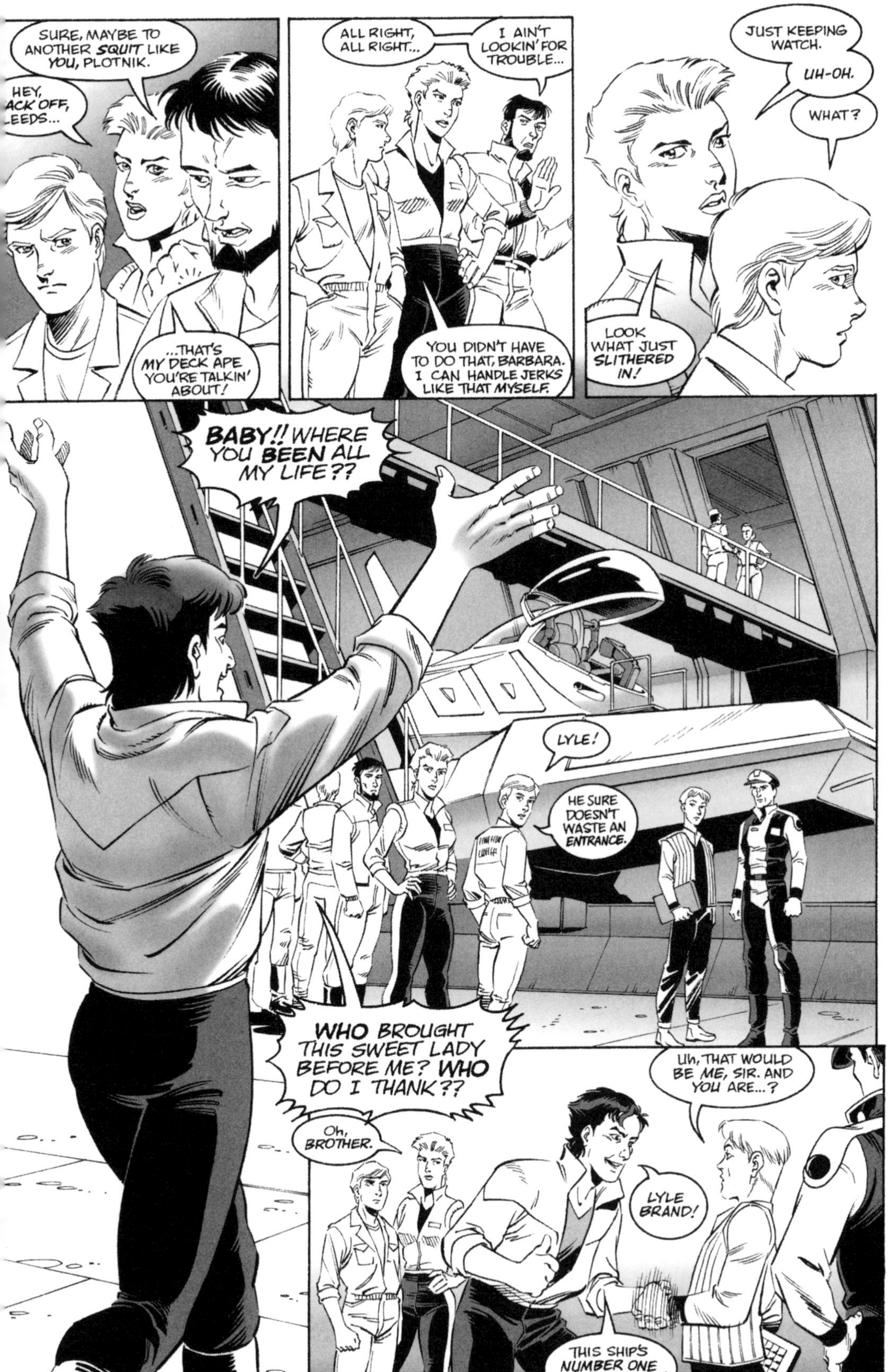
SURE, MAYBE TO ANOTHER SQUIT LIKE YOU, PLOTNIK.
HEY, ACK OFF, LEEDS...
...THAT'S MY DECK APE YOU'RE TALKIN' ABOUT!
ALL RIGHT, ALL RIGHT...
I AIN'T LOOKIN' FOR TROUBLE...
YOU DIDN'T HAVE TO DO THAT, BARBARA. I CAN HANDLE JERKS LIKE THAT MYSELF.
JUST KEEPING WATCH.
UH-OH.
WHAT?
LOOK WHAT JUST SLITHERED IN!
BABY!! WHERE YOU BEEN ALL MY LIFE??
LYLE!
HE SURE DOESN'T WASTE AN ENTRANCE.
WHO BROUGHT THIS SWEET LADY BEFORE ME? WHO DO I THANK??
Oh, BROTHER.
Uh, THAT WOULD BE ME, SIR. AND YOU ARE...?
LYLE BRAND!
THIS SHIP'S NUMBER ONE FIGHTER JOCK!

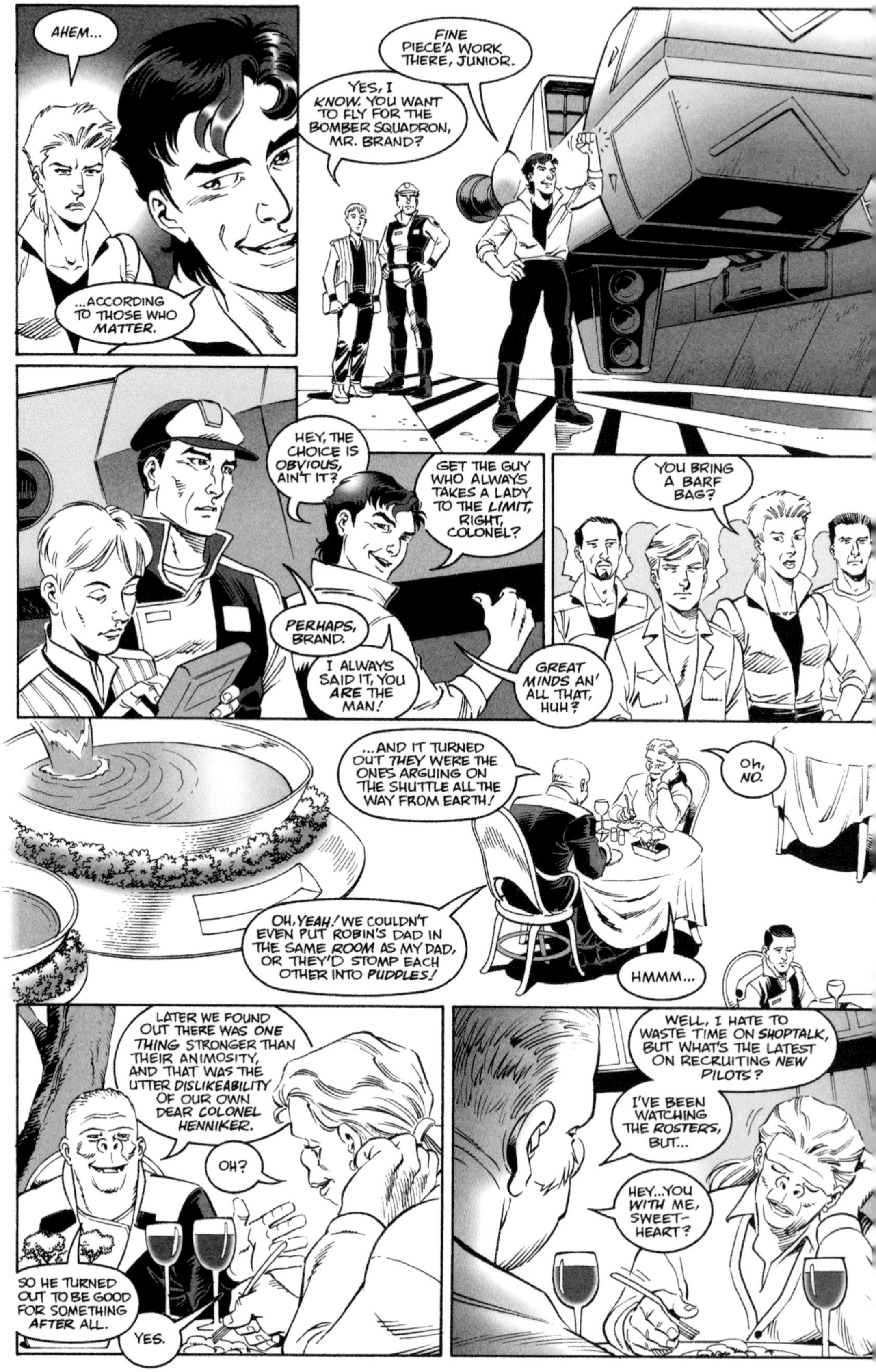
AHEM...
...ACCORDING TO THOSE WHO MATTER.
FINE PIECE'A WORK THERE, JUNIOR.
YES, I KNOW. YOU WANT TO FLY FOR THE BOMBER SQUADRON, MR. BRAND?
HEY, THE CHOICE IS OBVIOUS, AIN'T IT?
GET THE GUY WHO ALWAYS TAKES A LADY TO THE LIMIT, RIGHT, COLONEL?
PERHAPS, BRAND.
I ALWAYS SAID IT, YOU ARE THE MAN!
YOU BRING A BARF BAG?
GREAT MINDS AN' ALL THAT, HUH?
...AND IT TURNED OUT THEY WERE THE ONES ARGUING ON THE SHUTTLE ALL THE WAY FROM EARTH!
OH, NO.
OH, YEAH! WE COULDN'T EVEN PUT ROBIN'S DAD IN THE SAME ROOM AS MY DAD, OR THEY'D STOMP EACH OTHER INTO PUDDLES!
HMMM...
LATER WE FOUND OUT THERE WAS ONE THING STRONGER THAN THEIR ANIMOSITY, AND THAT WAS THE UTTER DISLIKEABILITY OF OUR OWN DEAR COLONEL HENNIKER.
OH?
SO HE TURNED OUT TO BE GOOD FOR SOMETHING AFTER ALL.
YES.
WELL, I HATE TO WASTE TIME ON SHOPTALK, BUT WHAT'S THE LATEST ON RECRUITING NEW PILOTS?
I'VE BEEN WATCHING THE ROSTERS, BUT...
HEY...YOU WITH ME, SWEETHEART?

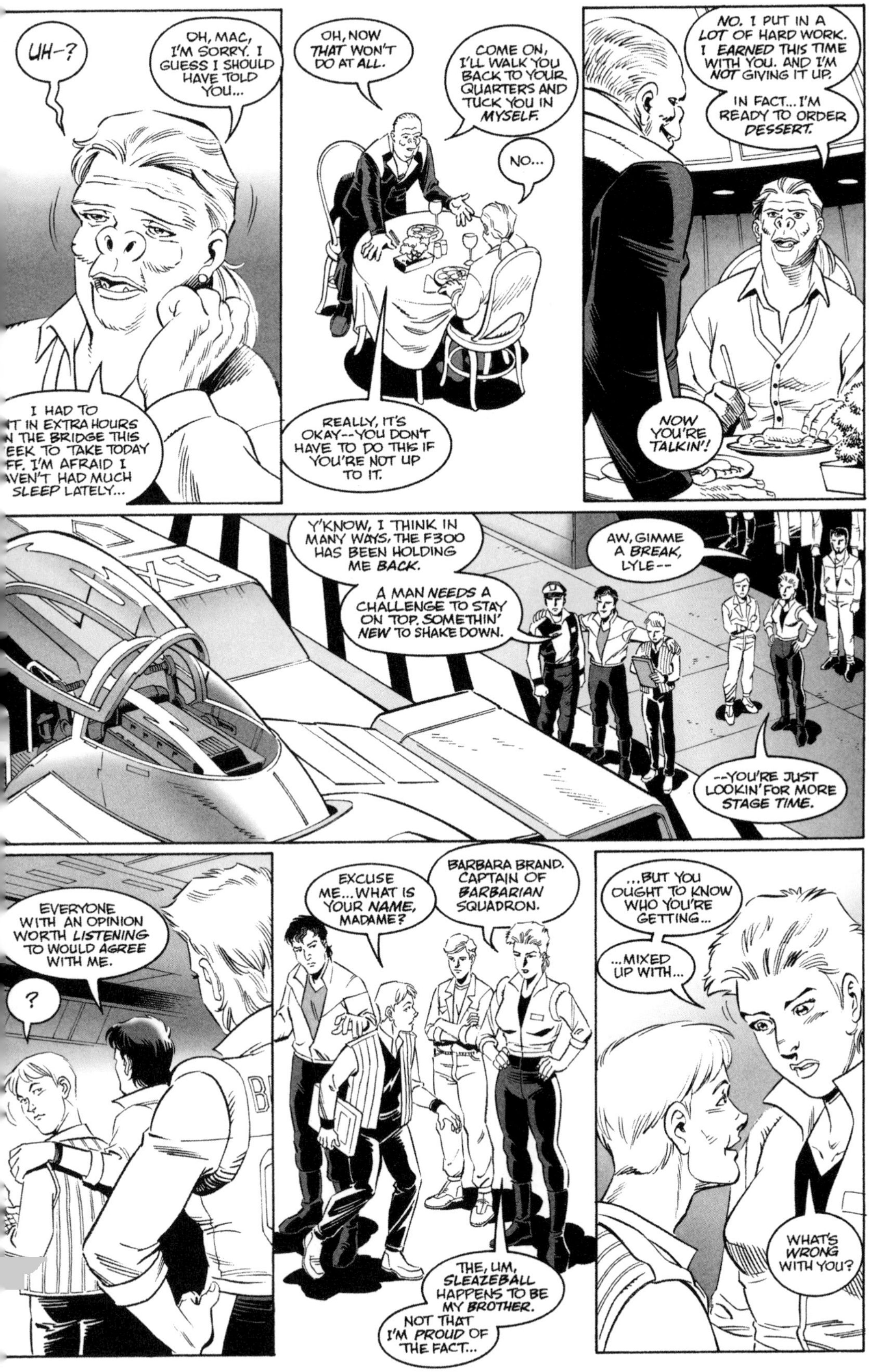
UH-?
OH, MAC, I'M SORRY. I GUESS I SHOULD HAVE TOLD YOU...
I HAD TO PUT IN EXTRA HOURS ON THE BRIDGE THIS WEEK TO TAKE TODAY OFF. I'M AFRAID I HAVEN'T HAD MUCH SLEEP LATELY...
OH, NOW THAT WON'T DO AT ALL.
COME ON, I'LL WALK YOU BACK TO YOUR QUARTERS AND TUCK YOU IN MYSELF.
NO...
REALLY, IT'S OKAY--YOU DON'T HAVE TO DO THIS IF YOU'RE NOT UP TO IT.
NO. I PUT IN A LOT OF HARD WORK. I EARNED THIS TIME WITH YOU. AND I'M NOT GIVING IT UP.
IN FACT... I'M READY TO ORDER DESSERT.
NOW YOU'RE TALKIN'!
Y'KNOW, I THINK IN MANY WAYS, THE F300 HAS BEEN HOLDING ME BACK.
A MAN NEEDS A CHALLENGE TO STAY ON TOP. SOMETHIN' NEW TO SHAKE DOWN.
AW, GIMME A BREAK, LYLE--
--YOU'RE JUST LOOKIN' FOR MORE STAGE TIME.
EVERYONE WITH AN OPINION WORTH LISTENING TO WOULD AGREE WITH ME.
?
EXCUSE ME... WHAT IS YOUR NAME, MADAME?
BARBARA BRAND. CAPTAIN OF BARBARIAN SQUADRON.
THE, UM, SLEAZEBALL HAPPENS TO BE MY BROTHER.
NOT THAT I'M PROUD OF THE FACT...
...BUT YOU OUGHT TO KNOW WHO YOU'RE GETTING...
...MIXED UP WITH...
WHAT'S WRONG WITH YOU?

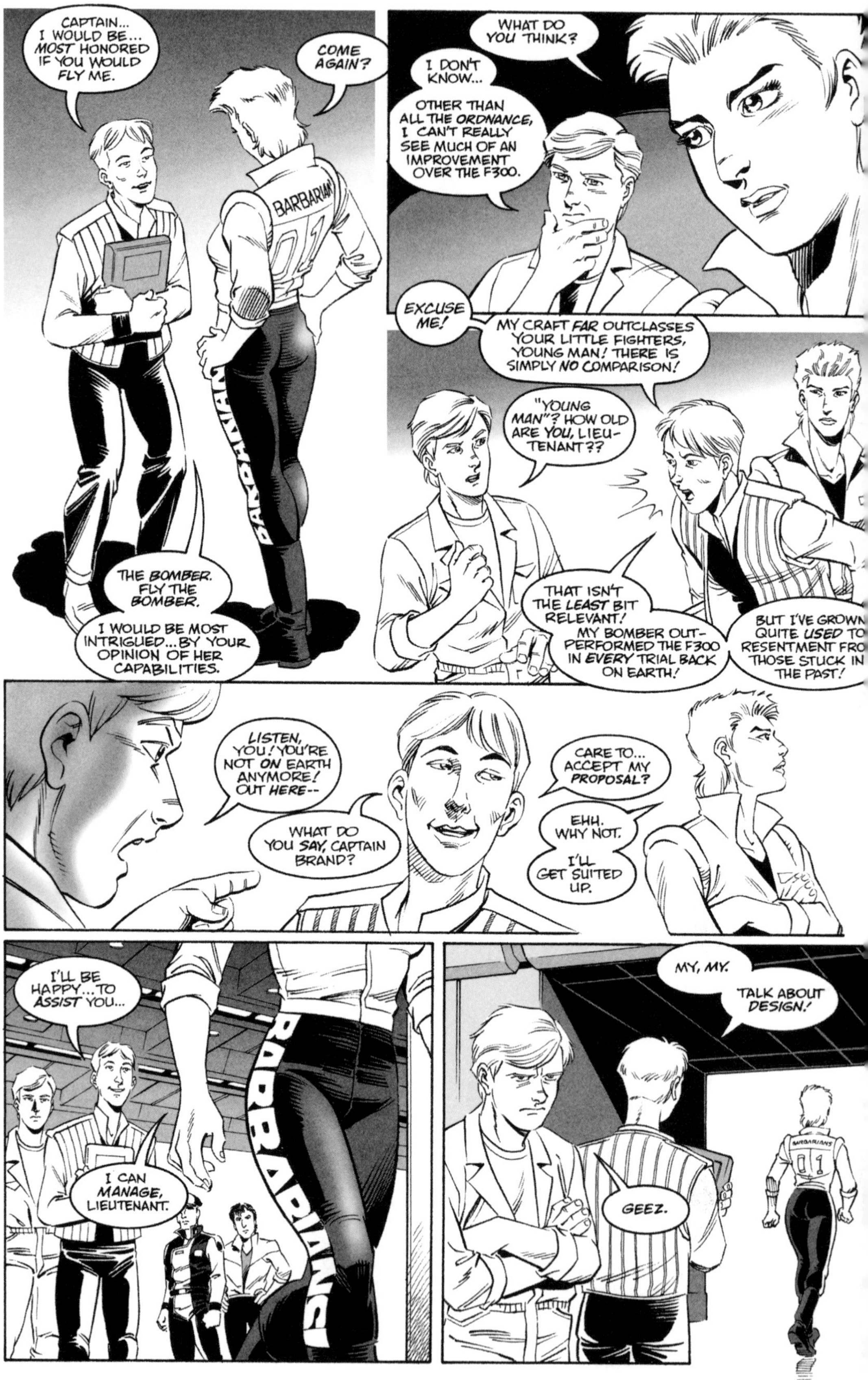
CAPTAIN... I WOULD BE... MOST HONORED IF YOU WOULD FLY ME.
COME AGAIN?
THE BOMBER. FLY THE BOMBER.
I WOULD BE MOST INTRIGUED... BY YOUR OPINION OF HER CAPABILITIES.
BARBARIAN
BARBARIAN
WHAT DO YOU THINK?
I DON'T KNOW...
OTHER THAN ALL THE ORDNANCE, I CAN'T REALLY SEE MUCH OF AN IMPROVEMENT OVER THE F300.
EXCUSE ME!
MY CRAFT FAR OUTCLASSES YOUR LITTLE FIGHTERS, YOUNG MAN! THERE IS SIMPLY NO COMPARISON!
"YOUNG MAN"? HOW OLD ARE YOU, LIEUTENANT??
THAT ISN'T THE LEAST BIT RELEVANT!
MY BOMBER OUT-PERFORMED THE F300 IN EVERY TRIAL BACK ON EARTH!
BUT I'VE GROWN QUITE USED TO RESENTMENT FROM THOSE STUCK IN THE PAST!
LISTEN, YOU! YOU'RE NOT ON EARTH ANYMORE! OUT HERE--
WHAT DO YOU SAY, CAPTAIN BRAND?
CARE TO... ACCEPT MY PROPOSAL?
EHH. WHY NOT.
I'LL GET SUITED UP.
I'LL BE HAPPY... TO ASSIST YOU...
I CAN MANAGE, LIEUTENANT.
BARBARIANS
MY, MY.
TALK ABOUT DESIGN!
GEEZ.

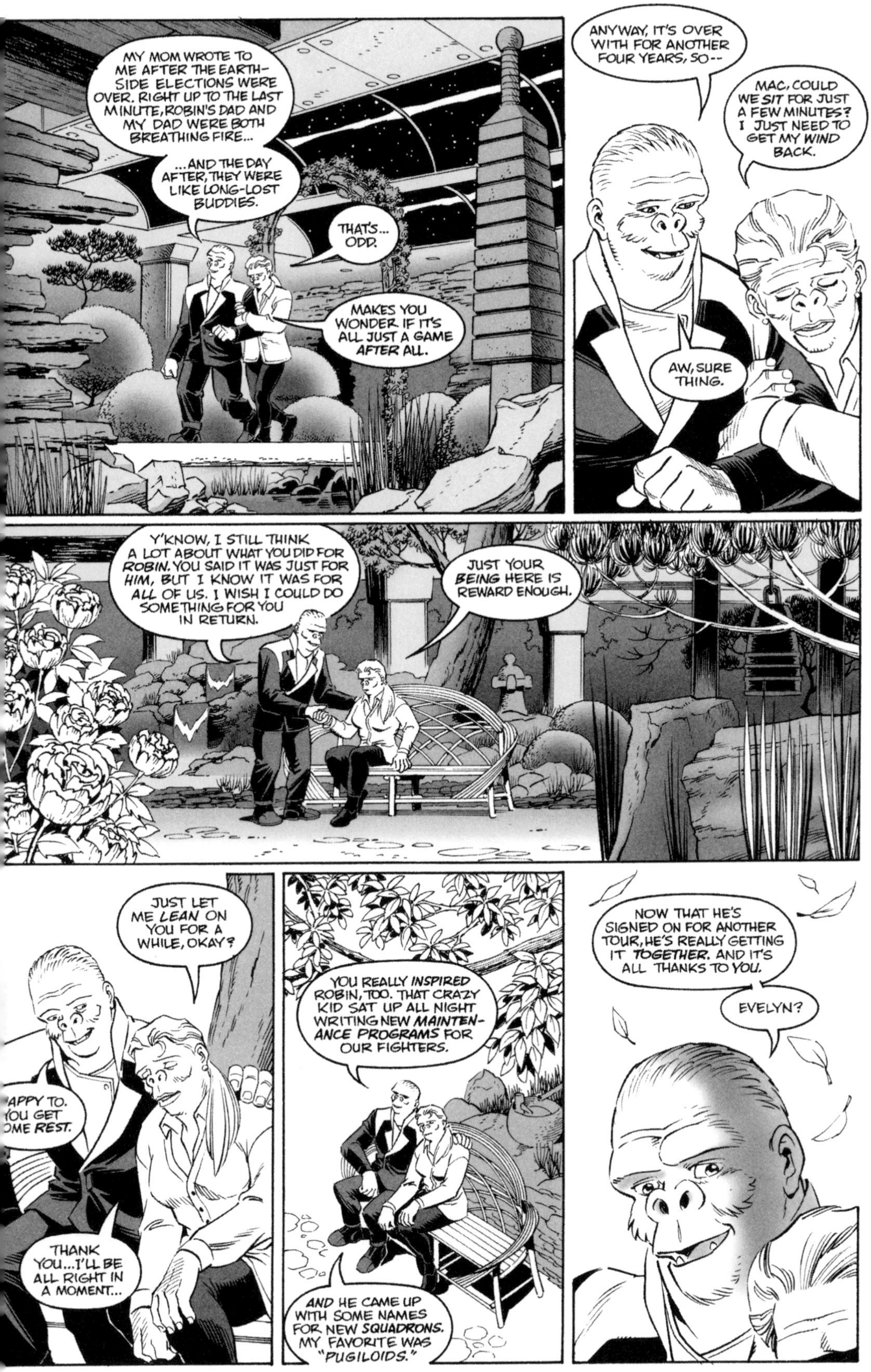
MY MOM WROTE TO ME AFTER THE EARTH-SIDE ELECTIONS WERE OVER. RIGHT UP TO THE LAST MINUTE, ROBIN'S DAD AND MY DAD WERE BOTH BREATHING FIRE...
...AND THE DAY AFTER, THEY WERE LIKE LONG-LOST BUDDIES.
THAT'S... ODD.
MAKES YOU WONDER IF IT'S ALL JUST A GAME AFTER ALL.
ANYWAY, IT'S OVER WITH FOR ANOTHER FOUR YEARS, SO--
MAC, COULD WE SIT FOR JUST A FEW MINUTES? I JUST NEED TO GET MY WIND BACK.
AW, SURE THING.
Y'KNOW, I STILL THINK A LOT ABOUT WHAT YOU DID FOR ROBIN. YOU SAID IT WAS JUST FOR HIM, BUT I KNOW IT WAS FOR ALL OF US. I WISH I COULD DO SOMETHING FOR YOU IN RETURN.
JUST YOUR BEING HERE IS REWARD ENOUGH.
JUST LET ME LEAN ON YOU FOR A WHILE, OKAY?
APPY TO. YOU GET OME REST.
THANK YOU... I'LL BE ALL RIGHT IN A MOMENT...
YOU REALLY INSPIRED ROBIN, TOO. THAT CRAZY KID SAT UP ALL NIGHT WRITING NEW MAINTENANCE PROGRAMS FOR OUR FIGHTERS.
AND HE CAME UP WITH SOME NAMES FOR NEW SQUADRONS. MY FAVORITE WAS "PUGILOIDS."
NOW THAT HE'S SIGNED ON FOR ANOTHER TOUR, HE'S REALLY GETTING IT TOGETHER. AND IT'S ALL THANKS TO YOU.
EVELYN?

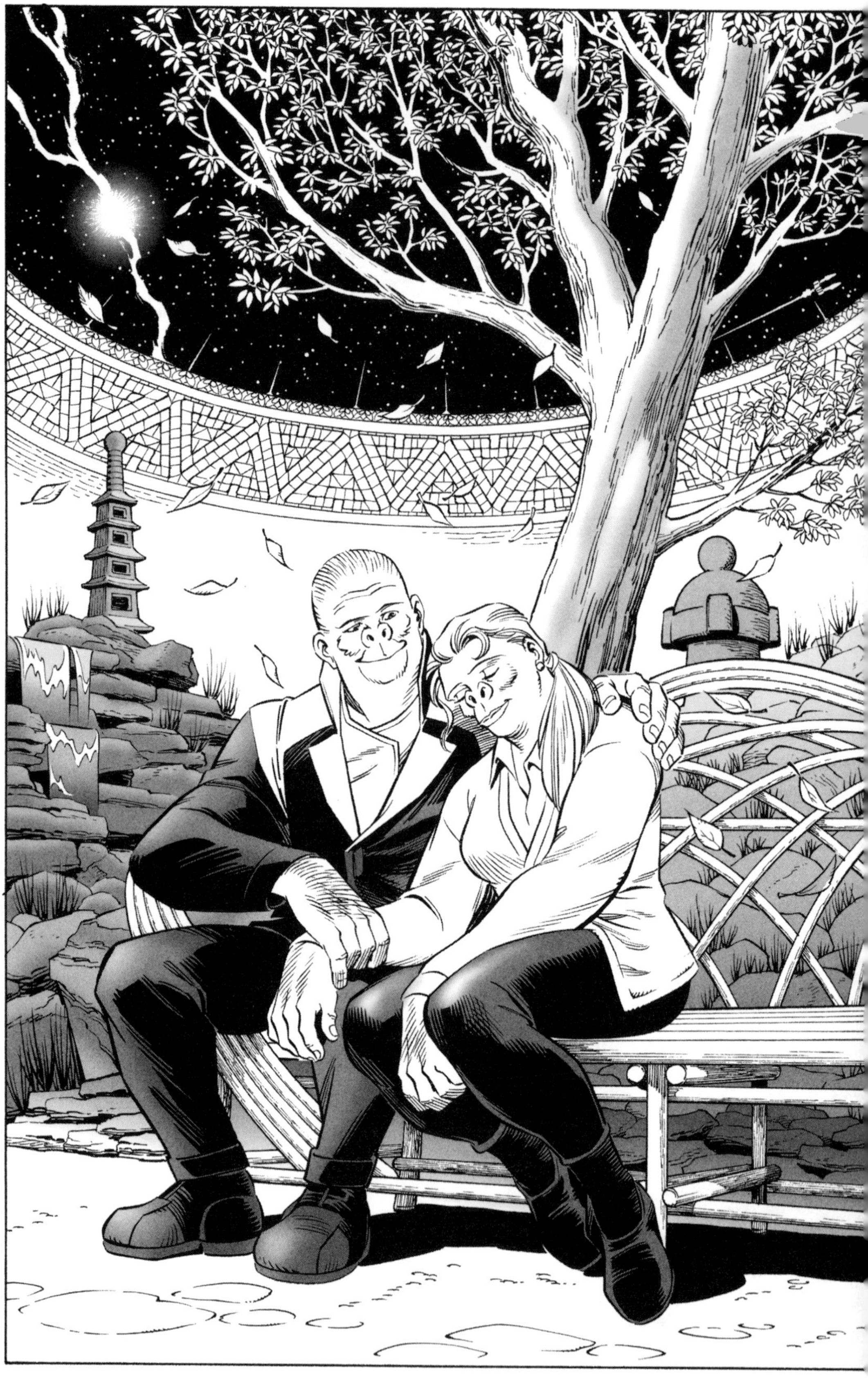

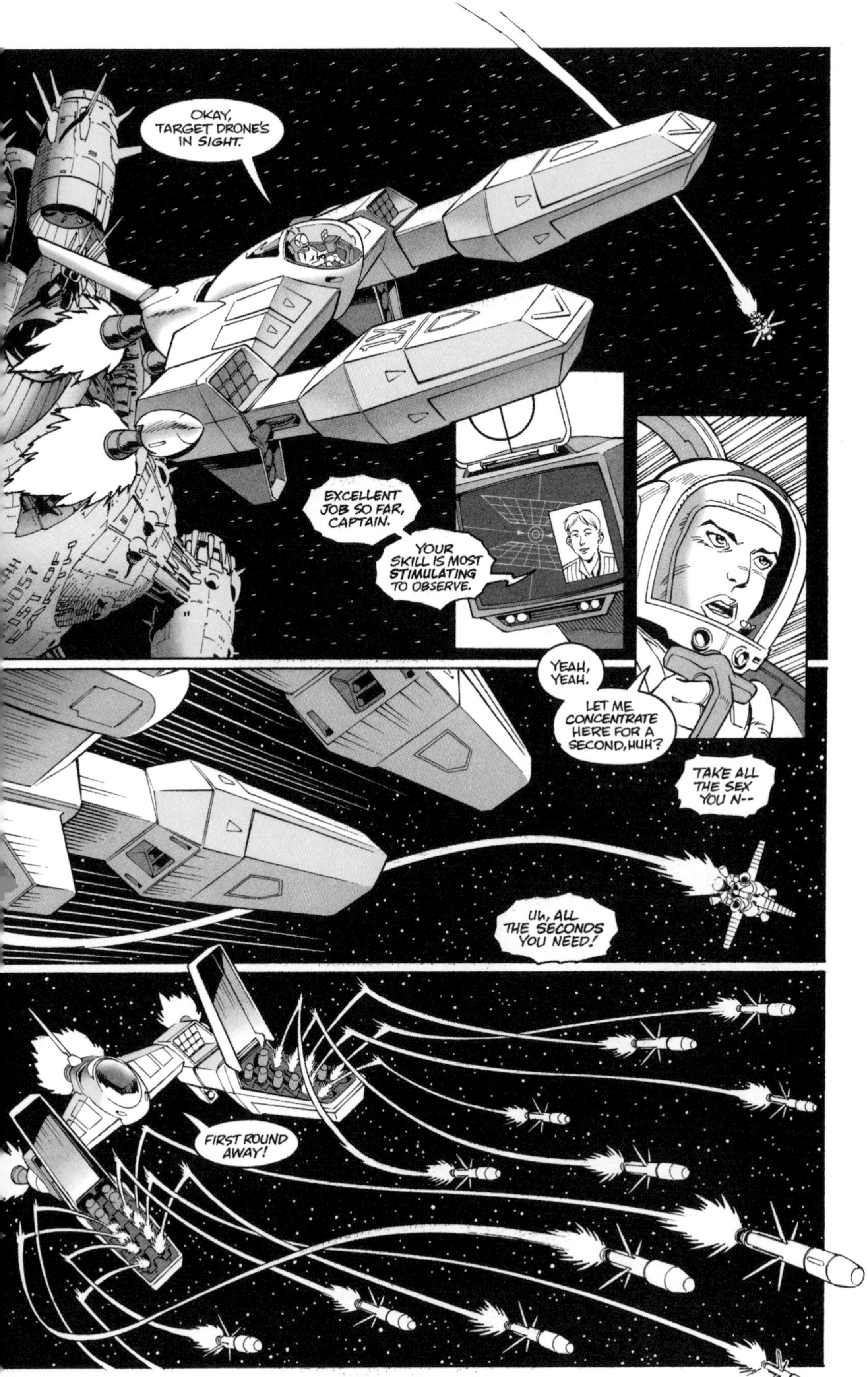
OKAY, TARGET DRONE'S IN SIGHT.
EXCELLENT JOB SO FAR, CAPTAIN.
YOUR SKILL IS MOST STIMULATING TO OBSERVE.
YEAH, YEAH.
LET ME CONCENTRATE HERE FOR A SECOND, HUH?
TAKE ALL THE SEX YOU N--
UH, ALL THE SECONDS YOU NEED!
FIRST ROUND AWAY!

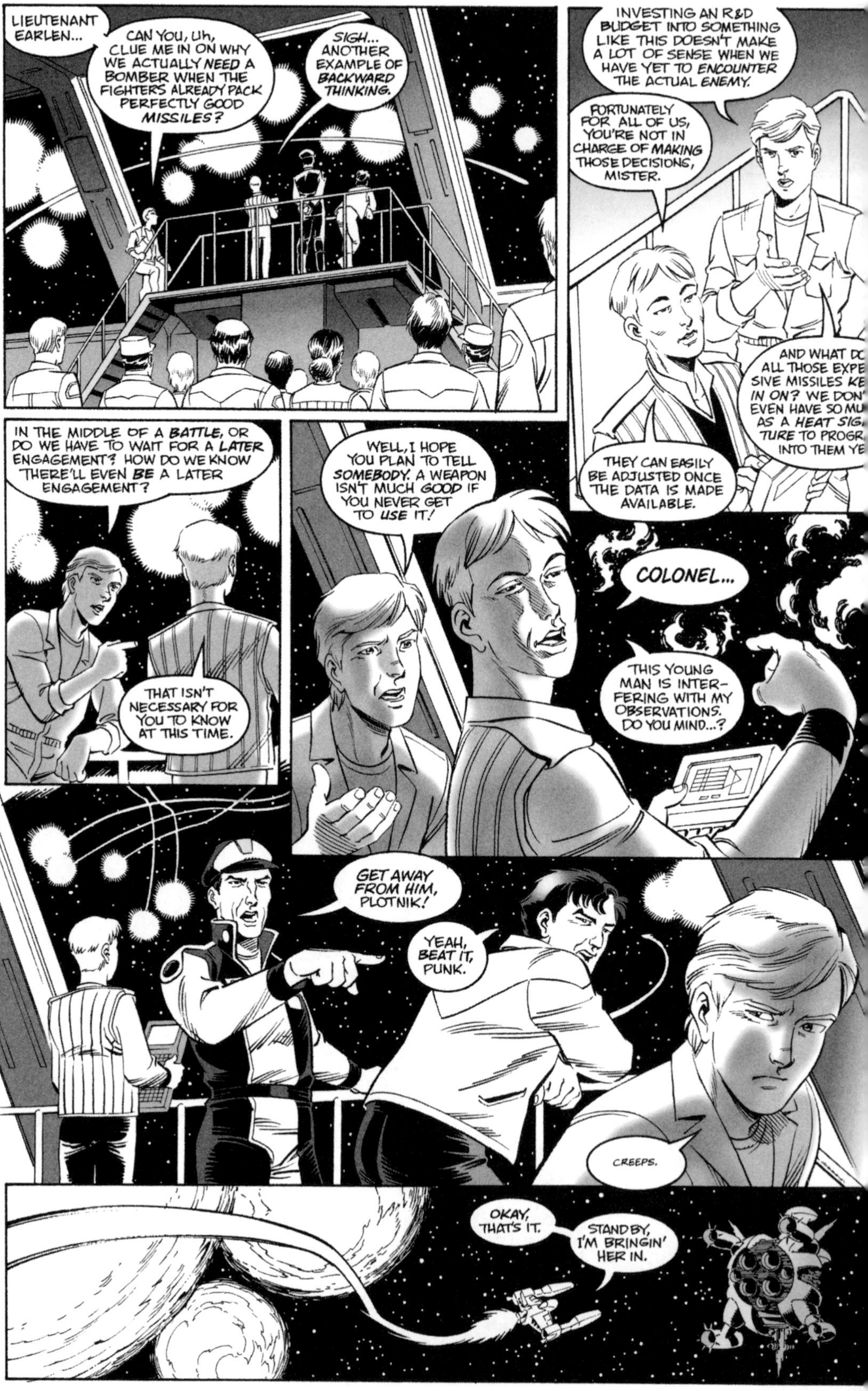

LIEUTENANT EARLEN...
CAN YOU, UH, CLUE ME IN ON WHY WE ACTUALLY NEED A BOMBER WHEN THE FIGHTERS ALREADY PACK PERFECTLY GOOD MISSILES?
SIGH... ANOTHER EXAMPLE OF BACKWARD THINKING.
INVESTING AN R&D BUDGET INTO SOMETHING LIKE THIS DOESN'T MAKE A LOT OF SENSE WHEN WE HAVE YET TO ENCOUNTER THE ACTUAL ENEMY.
FORTUNATELY FOR ALL OF US, YOU'RE NOT IN CHARGE OF MAKING THOSE DECISIONS, MISTER.
AND WHAT DO ALL THOSE EXPE SIVE MISSILES KE IN ON? WE DON' EVEN HAVE SO MU AS A HEAT SIG TURE TO PROGR INTO THEM YE
THEY CAN EASILY BE ADJUSTED ONCE THE DATA IS MADE AVAILABLE.
IN THE MIDDLE OF A BATTLE, OR DO WE HAVE TO WAIT FOR A LATER ENGAGEMENT? HOW DO WE KNOW THERE'LL EVEN BE A LATER ENGAGEMENT?
THAT ISN'T NECESSARY FOR YOU TO KNOW AT THIS TIME.
WELL, I HOPE YOU PLAN TO TELL SOMEBODY. A WEAPON ISN'T MUCH GOOD IF YOU NEVER GET TO USE IT!
COLONEL...
THIS YOUNG MAN IS INTERFERING WITH MY OBSERVATIONS. DO YOU MIND...?
GET AWAY FROM HIM, PLOTNIK!
YEAH, BEAT IT, PUNK.
CREEPS.
OKAY, THAT'S IT.
STAND BY, I'M BRINGIN' HER IN.

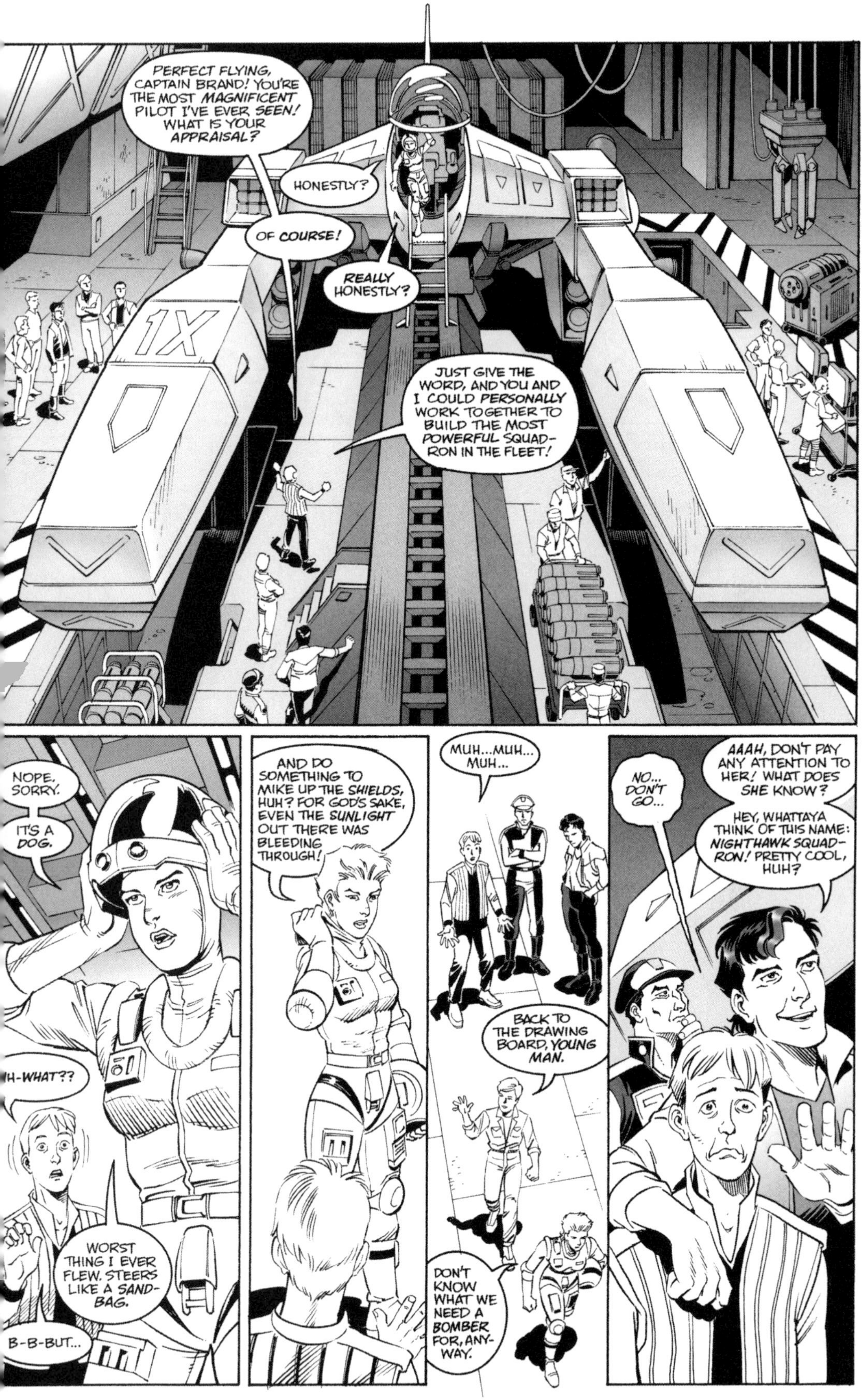
PERFECT FLYING, CAPTAIN BRAND! YOU'RE THE MOST MAGNIFICENT PILOT I'VE EVER SEEN! WHAT IS YOUR APPRAISAL?
HONESTLY?
OF COURSE!
REALLY HONESTLY?
JUST GIVE THE WORD, AND YOU AND I COULD PERSONALLY WORK TOGETHER TO BUILD THE MOST POWERFUL SQUADRON IN THE FLEET!
1X
NOPE. SORRY.
IT'S A DOG.
H-WHAT??
WORST THING I EVER FLEW. STEERS LIKE A SANDBAG.
B-B-BUT...
AND DO SOMETHING TO MIKE UP THE SHIELDS, HUH? FOR GOD'S SAKE, EVEN THE SUNLIGHT OUT THERE WAS BLEEDING THROUGH!
MUH...MUH... MUH...
BACK TO THE DRAWING BOARD, YOUNG MAN.
DON'T KNOW WHAT WE NEED A BOMBER FOR, ANYWAY.
NO... DON'T GO...
AAAH, DON'T PAY ANY ATTENTION TO HER! WHAT DOES SHE KNOW?
HEY, WHATTAYA THINK OF THIS NAME: NIGHTHAWK SQUADRON! PRETTY COOL, HUH?

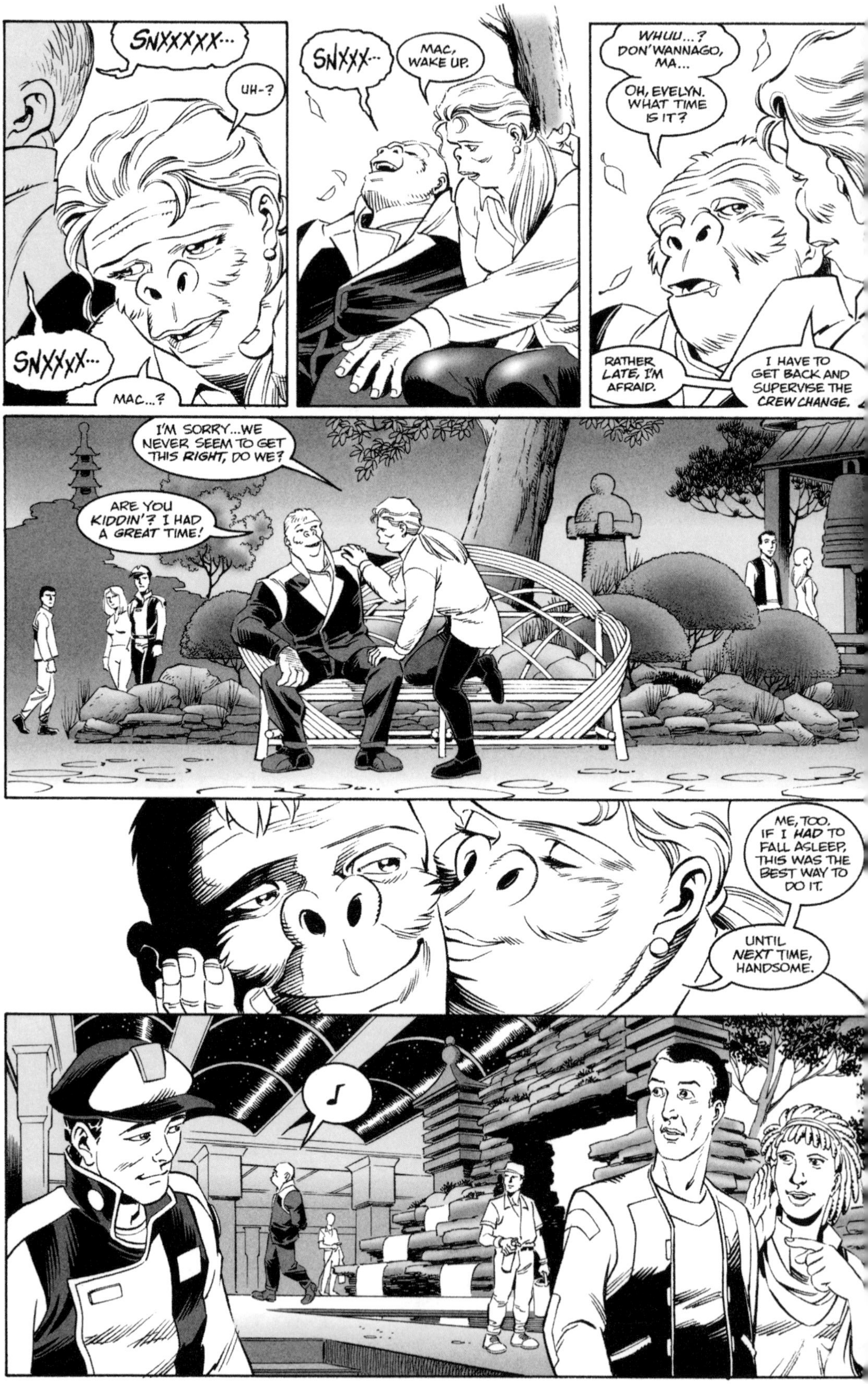
SNXXXXX...
UH-?
SNXXXX...
MAC...?
SNXXX...
MAC, WAKE UP.
WHUU...? DON'WANNAGO, MA...
OH, EVELYN. WHAT TIME IS IT?
RATHER LATE, I'M AFRAID.
I HAVE TO GET BACK AND SUPERVISE THE CREW CHANGE.
I'M SORRY...WE NEVER SEEM TO GET THIS RIGHT, DO WE?
ARE YOU KIDDIN'? I HAD A GREAT TIME!
ME, TOO. IF I HAD TO FALL ASLEEP, THIS WAS THE BEST WAY TO DO IT.
UNTIL NEXT TIME, HANDSOME.

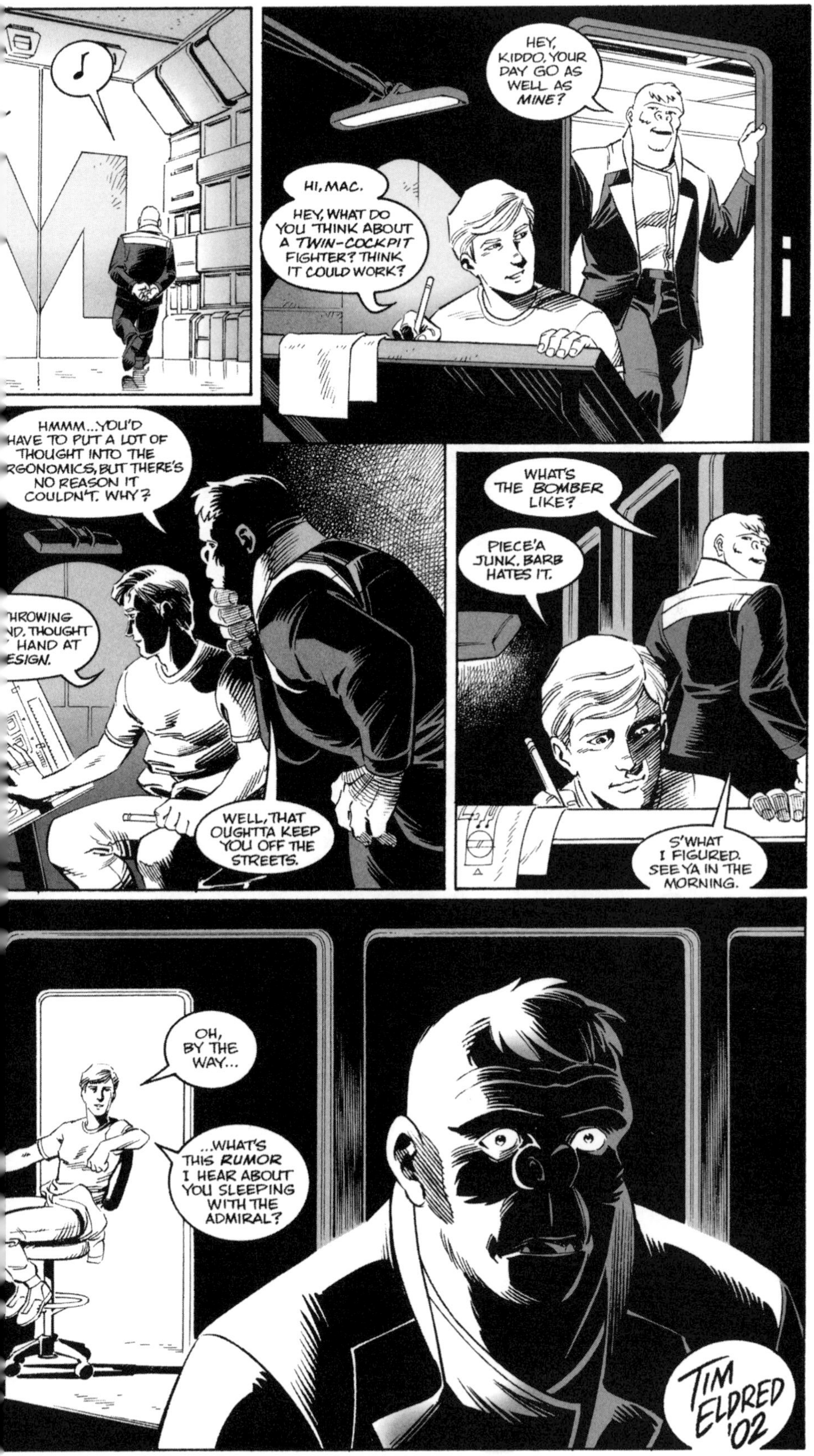
HEY, KIDDO, YOUR DAY GO AS WELL AS MINE?
HI, MAC.
HEY, WHAT DO YOU THINK ABOUT A TWIN-COCKPIT FIGHTER? THINK IT COULD WORK?
HMMM... YOU'D HAVE TO PUT A LOT OF THOUGHT INTO THE RGONOMICS, BUT THERE'S NO REASON IT COULDN'T. WHY?
THROWING ND, THOUGHT HAND AT ESIGN.
WELL, THAT OUGHTTA KEEP YOU OFF THE STREETS.
WHAT'S THE BOMBER LIKE?
PIECE'A JUNK. BARB HATES IT.
S'WHAT I FIGURED. SEE YA IN THE MORNING.
OH, BY THE WAY...
...WHAT'S THIS RUMOR I HEAR ABOUT YOU SLEEPING WITH THE ADMIRAL?
TIM ELDRED '02

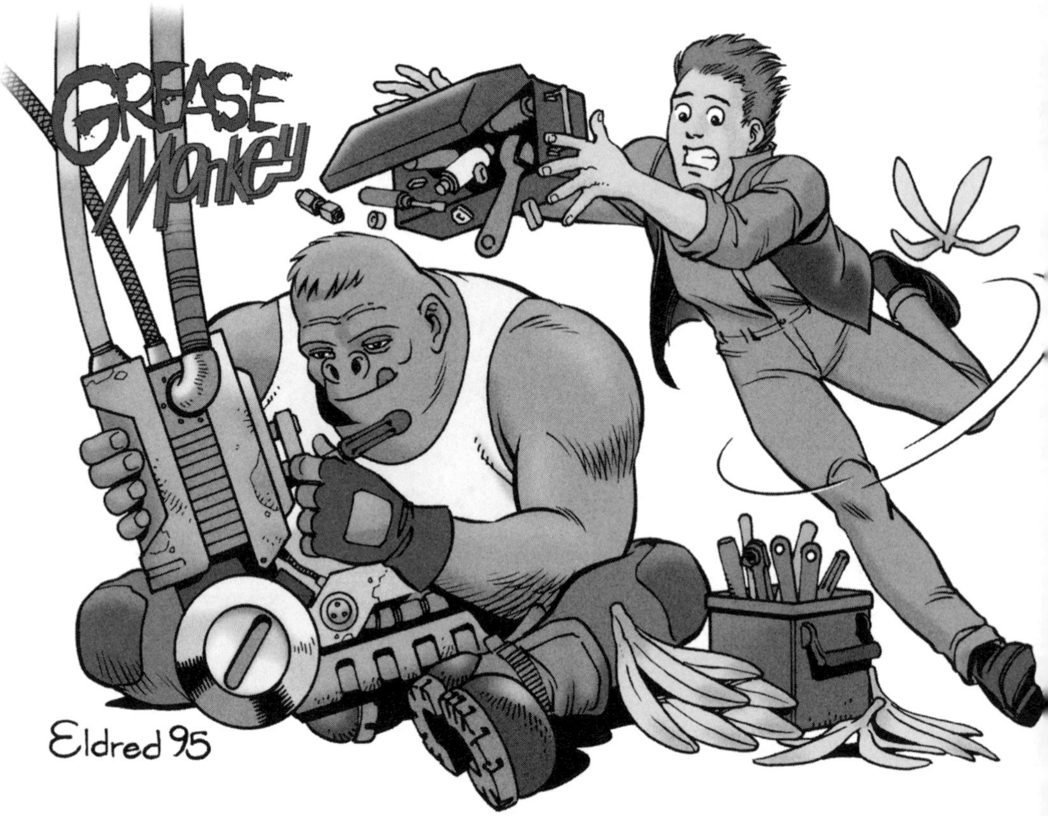
GREASE Monkey
Eldred 95

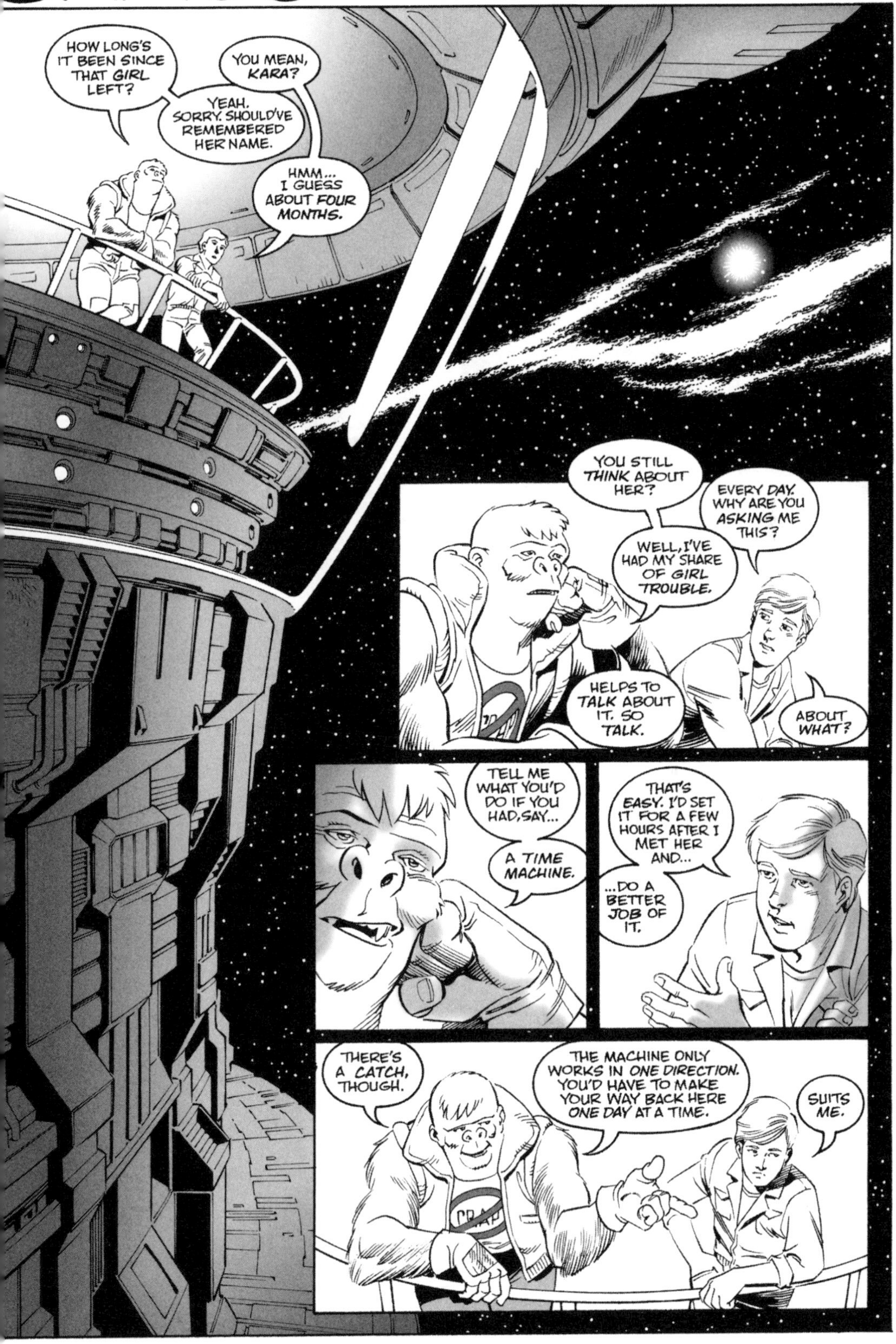
HOW LONG'S IT BEEN SINCE THAT GIRL LEFT?
YOU MEAN, KARA?
YEAH. SORRY. SHOULD'VE REMEMBERED HER NAME.
HMM... I GUESS ABOUT FOUR MONTHS.
YOU STILL THINK ABOUT HER?
EVERY DAY. WHY ARE YOU ASKING ME THIS?
WELL, I'VE HAD MY SHARE OF GIRL TROUBLE.
HELPS TO TALK ABOUT IT. SO TALK.
ABOUT WHAT?
TELL ME WHAT YOU'D DO IF YOU HAD, SAY...
A TIME MACHINE.
THAT'S EASY. I'D SET IT FOR A FEW HOURS AFTER I MET HER AND...
...DO A BETTER JOB OF IT.
THERE'S A CATCH, THOUGH.
THE MACHINE ONLY WORKS IN ONE DIRECTION. YOU'D HAVE TO MAKE YOUR WAY BACK HERE ONE DAY AT A TIME.
SUITS ME.

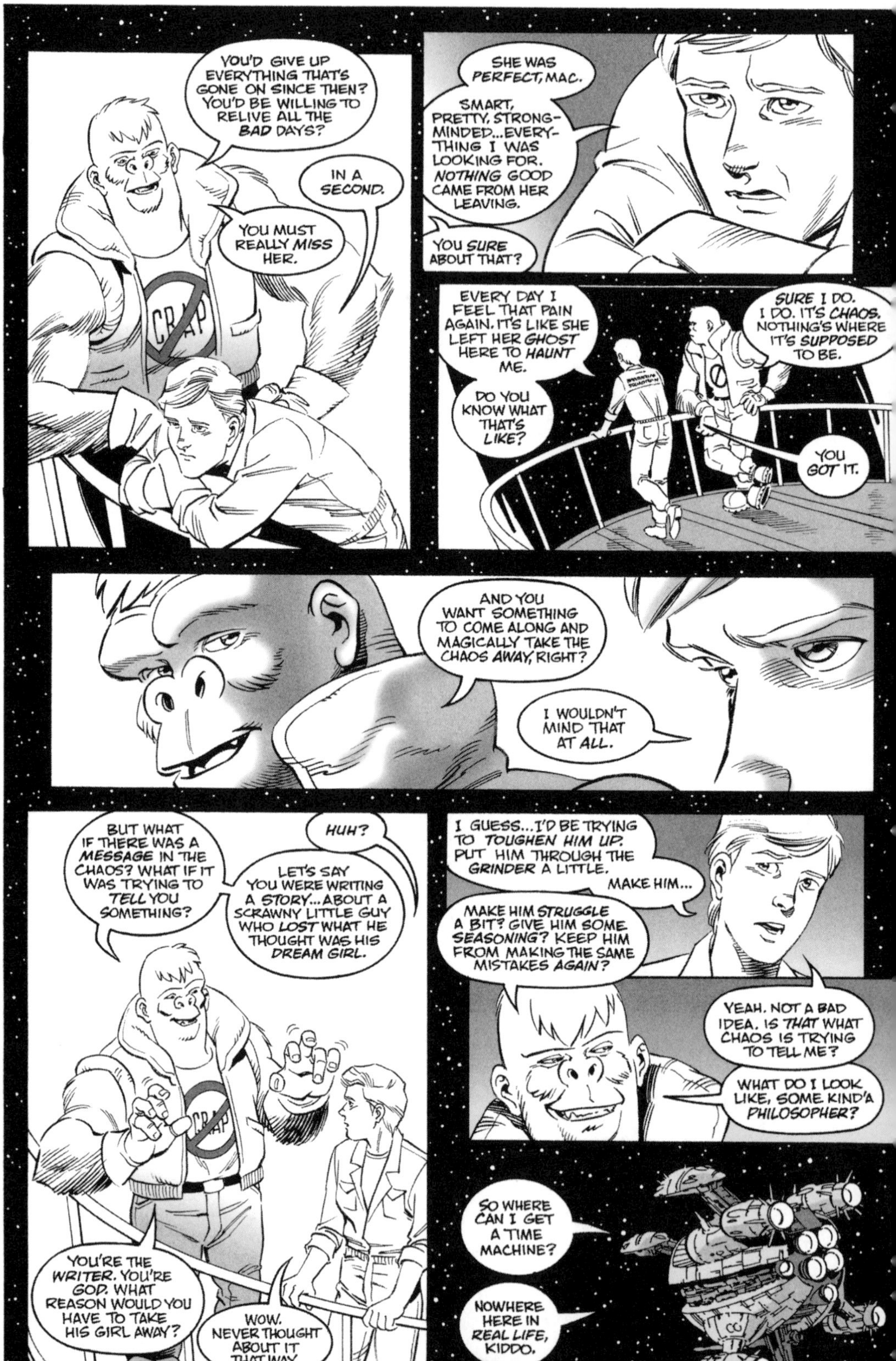

YOU'D GIVE UP EVERYTHING THAT'S GONE ON SINCE THEN? YOU'D BE WILLING TO RELIVE ALL THE BAD DAYS?
IN A SECOND.
YOU MUST REALLY MISS HER.
SHE WAS PERFECT, MAC.
SMART, PRETTY, STRONG-MINDED...EVERY-THING I WAS LOOKING FOR. NOTHING GOOD CAME FROM HER LEAVING.
YOU SURE ABOUT THAT?
EVERY DAY I FEEL THAT PAIN AGAIN. IT'S LIKE SHE LEFT HER GHOST HERE TO HAUNT ME.
DO YOU KNOW WHAT THAT'S LIKE?
SURE I DO. I DO. IT'S CHAOS. NOTHING'S WHERE IT'S SUPPOSED TO BE.
YOU GOT IT.
AND YOU WANT SOMETHING TO COME ALONG AND MAGICALLY TAKE THE CHAOS AWAY, RIGHT?
I WOULDN'T MIND THAT AT ALL.
BUT WHAT IF THERE WAS A MESSAGE IN THE CHAOS? WHAT IF IT WAS TRYING TO TELL YOU SOMETHING?
HUH?
LET'S SAY YOU WERE WRITING A STORY...ABOUT A SCRAWNY LITTLE GUY WHO LOST WHAT HE THOUGHT WAS HIS DREAM GIRL.
YOU'RE THE WRITER. YOU'RE GOD. WHAT REASON WOULD YOU HAVE TO TAKE HIS GIRL AWAY?
WOW. NEVER THOUGHT ABOUT IT THAT WAY.
I GUESS...I'D BE TRYING TO TOUGHEN HIM UP. PUT HIM THROUGH THE GRINDER A LITTLE.
MAKE HIM...
MAKE HIM STRUGGLE A BIT? GIVE HIM SOME SEASONING? KEEP HIM FROM MAKING THE SAME MISTAKES AGAIN?
YEAH. NOT A BAD IDEA. IS THAT WHAT CHAOS IS TRYING TO TELL ME?
WHAT DO I LOOK LIKE, SOME KIND'A PHILOSOPHER?
SO WHERE CAN I GET A TIME MACHINE?
NOWHERE HERE IN REAL LIFE, KIDDO.

DEDICATED to ALL BROKEN HEARTS. Tim Eldred '02

END OF THE TUNNEL

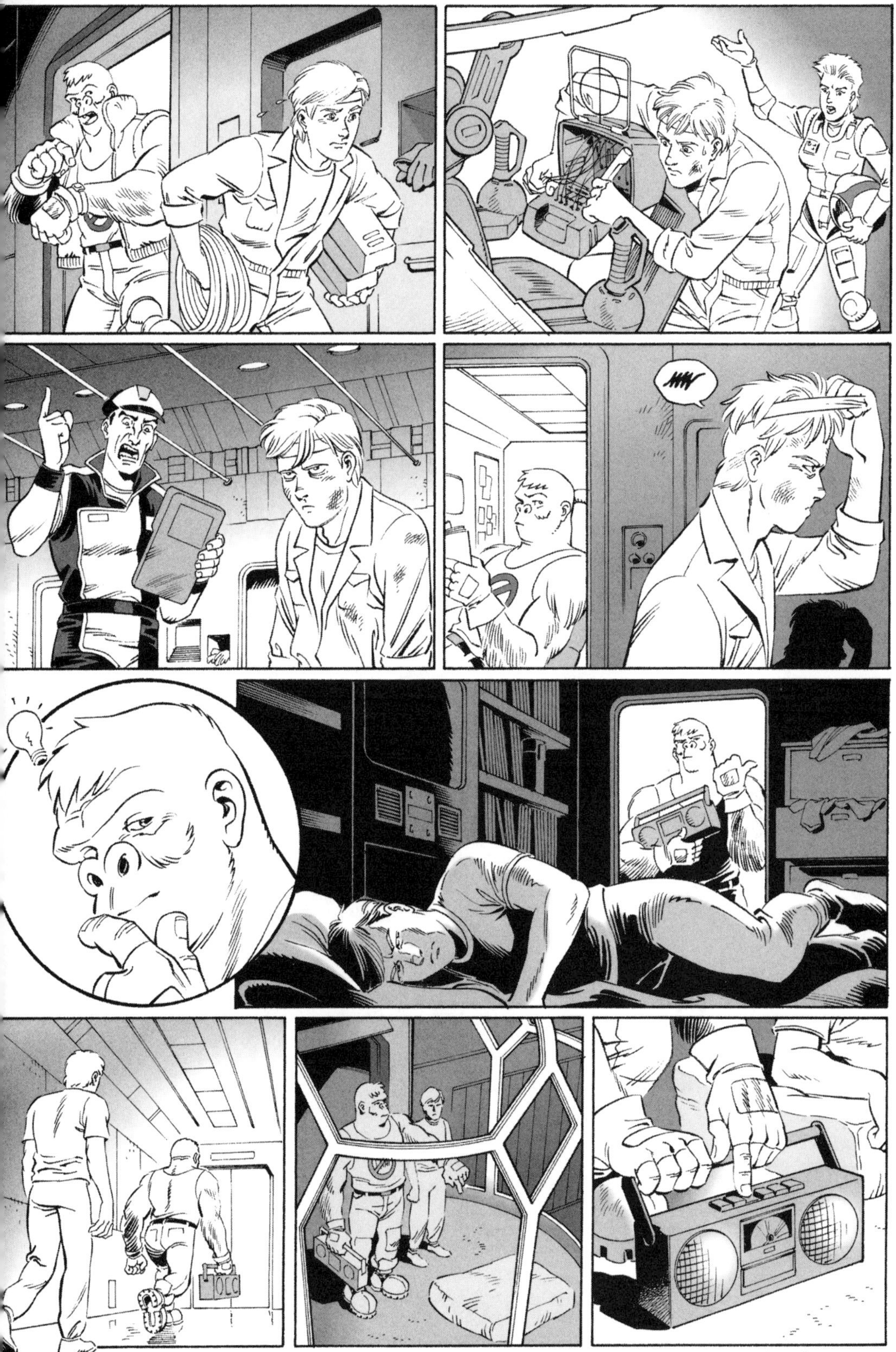

Start music now.

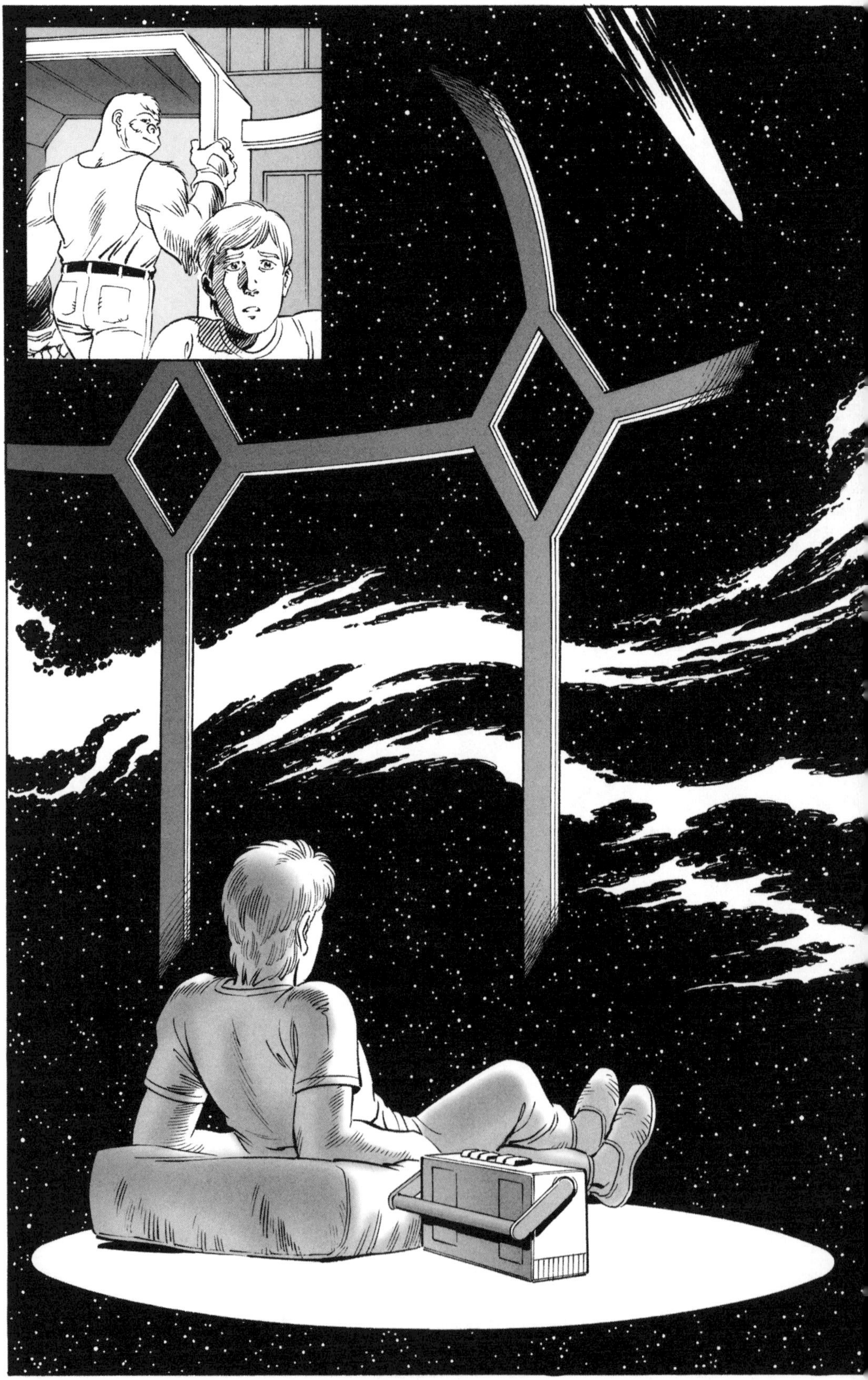

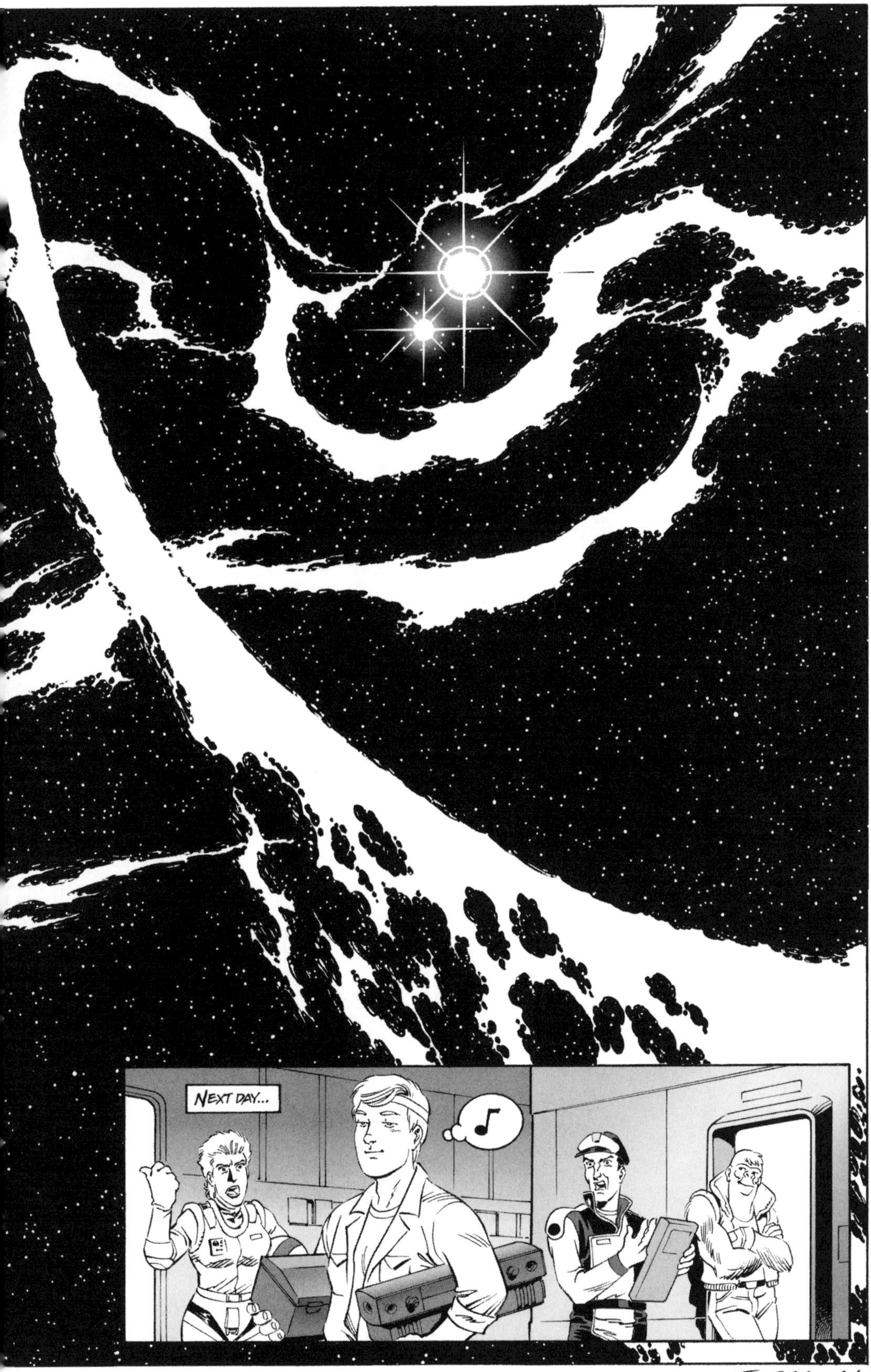
NEXT DAY...

Tim Eldred '02

BARFLY

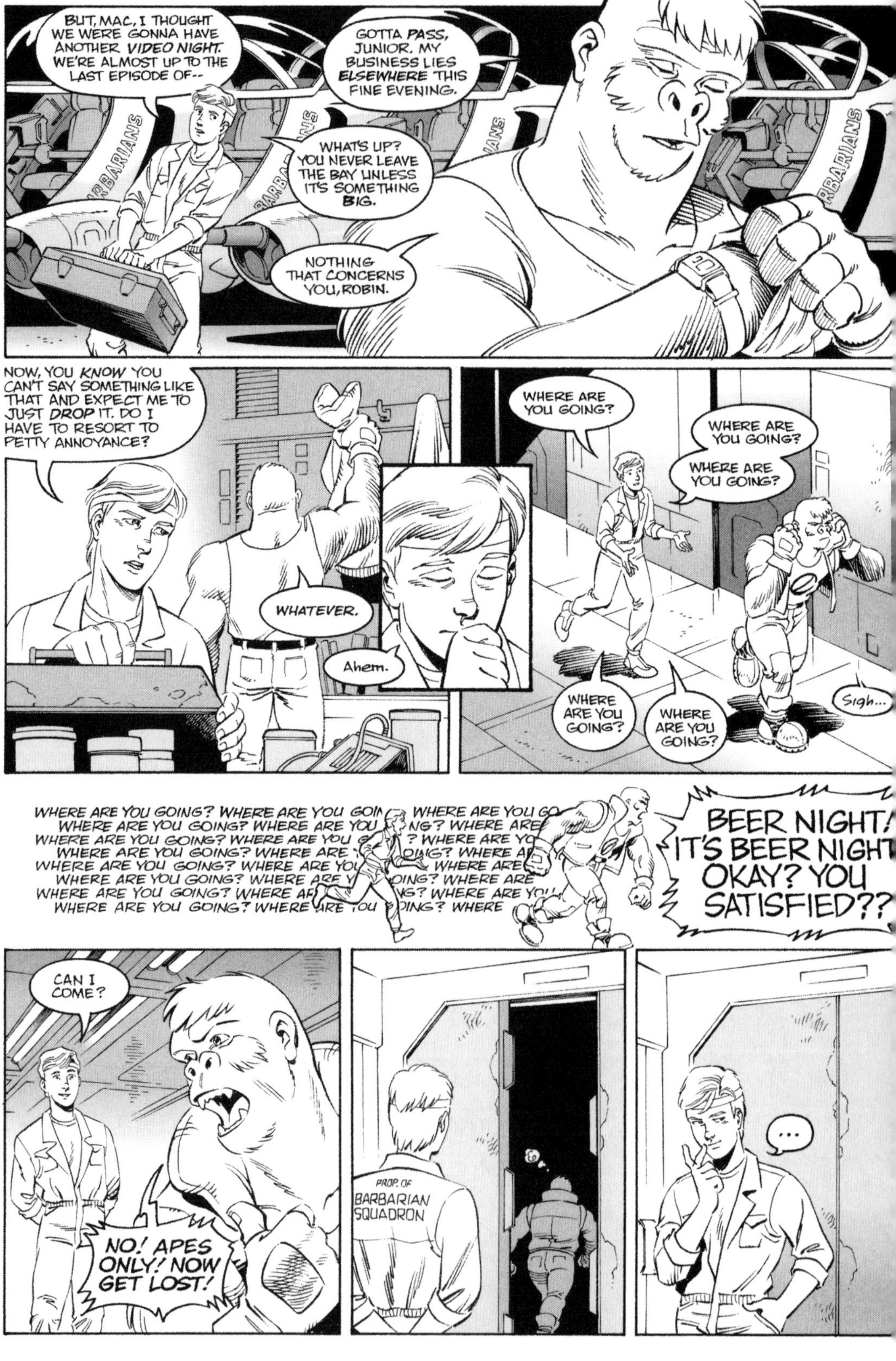

BUT, MAC, I THOUGHT WE WERE GONNA HAVE ANOTHER VIDEO NIGHT. WE'RE ALMOST UP TO THE LAST EPISODE OF--
GOTTA PASS, JUNIOR. MY BUSINESS LIES ELSEWHERE THIS FINE EVENING.
WHAT'S UP? YOU NEVER LEAVE THE BAY UNLESS IT'S SOMETHING BIG.
NOTHING THAT CONCERNS YOU, ROBIN.
BARBARIANS
NOW, YOU KNOW YOU CAN'T SAY SOMETHING LIKE THAT AND EXPECT ME TO JUST DROP IT. DO I HAVE TO RESORT TO PETTY ANNOYANCE?
WHATEVER.
Ahem.
WHERE ARE YOU GOING?
WHERE ARE YOU GOING?
WHERE ARE YOU GOING?
WHERE ARE YOU GOING?
WHERE ARE YOU GOING?
Sigh...
WHERE ARE YOU GOING? WHERE ARE YOU GOING? WHERE ARE YOU GOING? WHERE ARE YOU GOING? WHERE ARE YOU GOING? WHERE ARE YOU GOING? WHERE ARE YOU GOING? WHERE ARE YOU GOING? WHERE ARE YOU GOING? WHERE ARE YOU GOING? WHERE ARE YOU GOING? WHERE ARE YOU GOING? WHERE ARE YOU GOING? WHERE ARE YOU GOING? WHERE
BEER NIGHT! IT'S BEER NIGHT OKAY? YOU SATISFIED??
CAN I COME?
NO! APES ONLY! NOW GET LOST!
PROP. OF BARBARIAN SQUADRON
...

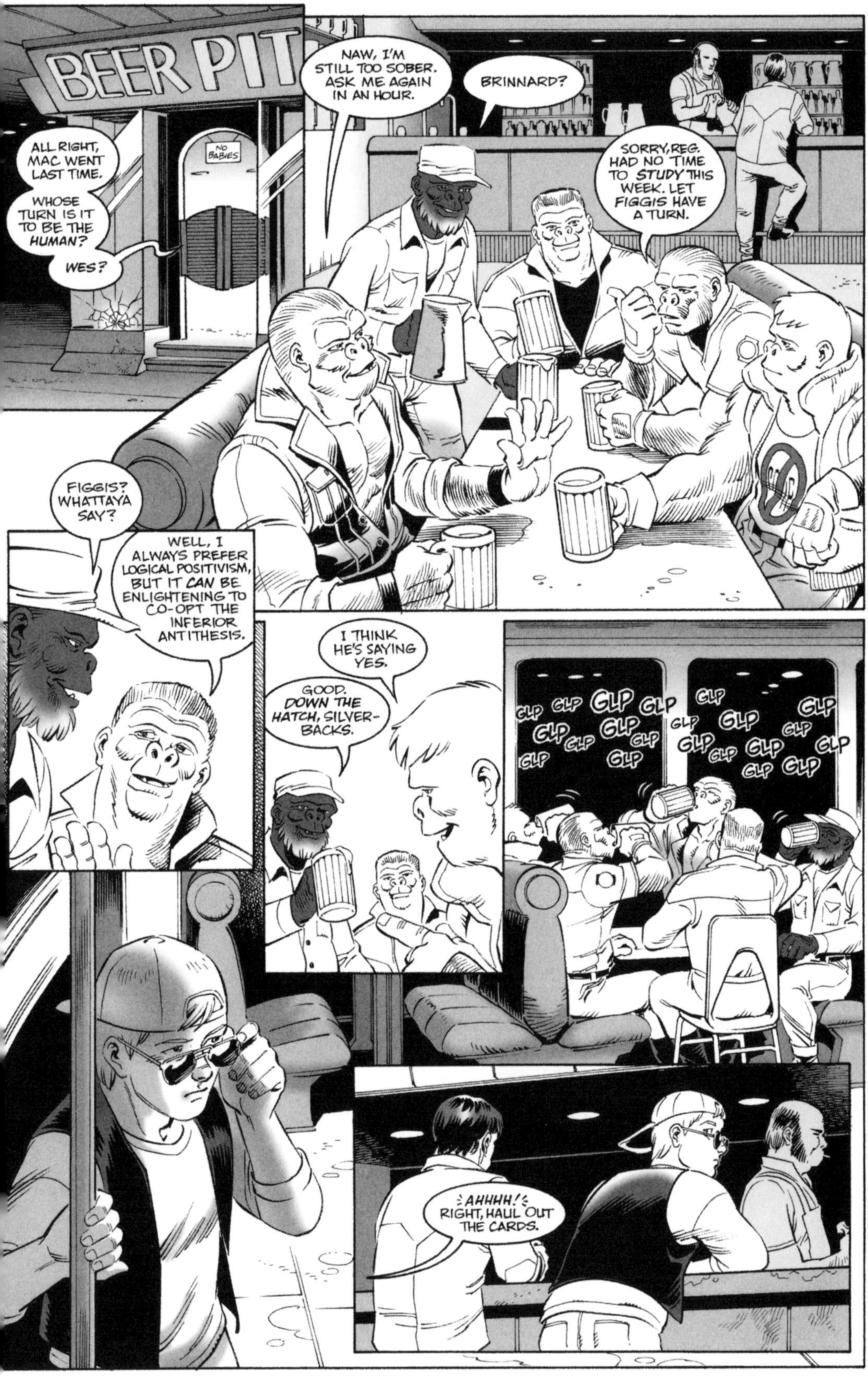
BEER PIT
NO BABIES
ALL RIGHT, MAC WENT LAST TIME.
WHOSE TURN IS IT TO BE THE HUMAN?
WES?
NAW, I'M STILL TOO SOBER. ASK ME AGAIN IN AN HOUR.
BRINNARD?
SORRY, REG. HAD NO TIME TO STUDY THIS WEEK. LET FIGGIS HAVE A TURN.
FIGGIS? WHATTAYA SAY?
WELL, I ALWAYS PREFER LOGICAL POSITIVISM, BUT IT CAN BE ENLIGHTENING TO CO-OPT THE INFERIOR ANTITHESIS.
I THINK HE'S SAYING YES.
GOOD. DOWN THE HATCH, SILVER-BACKS.
GLP GLP GLP GLP GLP GLP GLP GLP GLP GLP GLP GLP GLP GLP GLP GLP GLP GLP GLP GLP GLP
AHHHH! RIGHT, HAUL OUT THE CARDS.

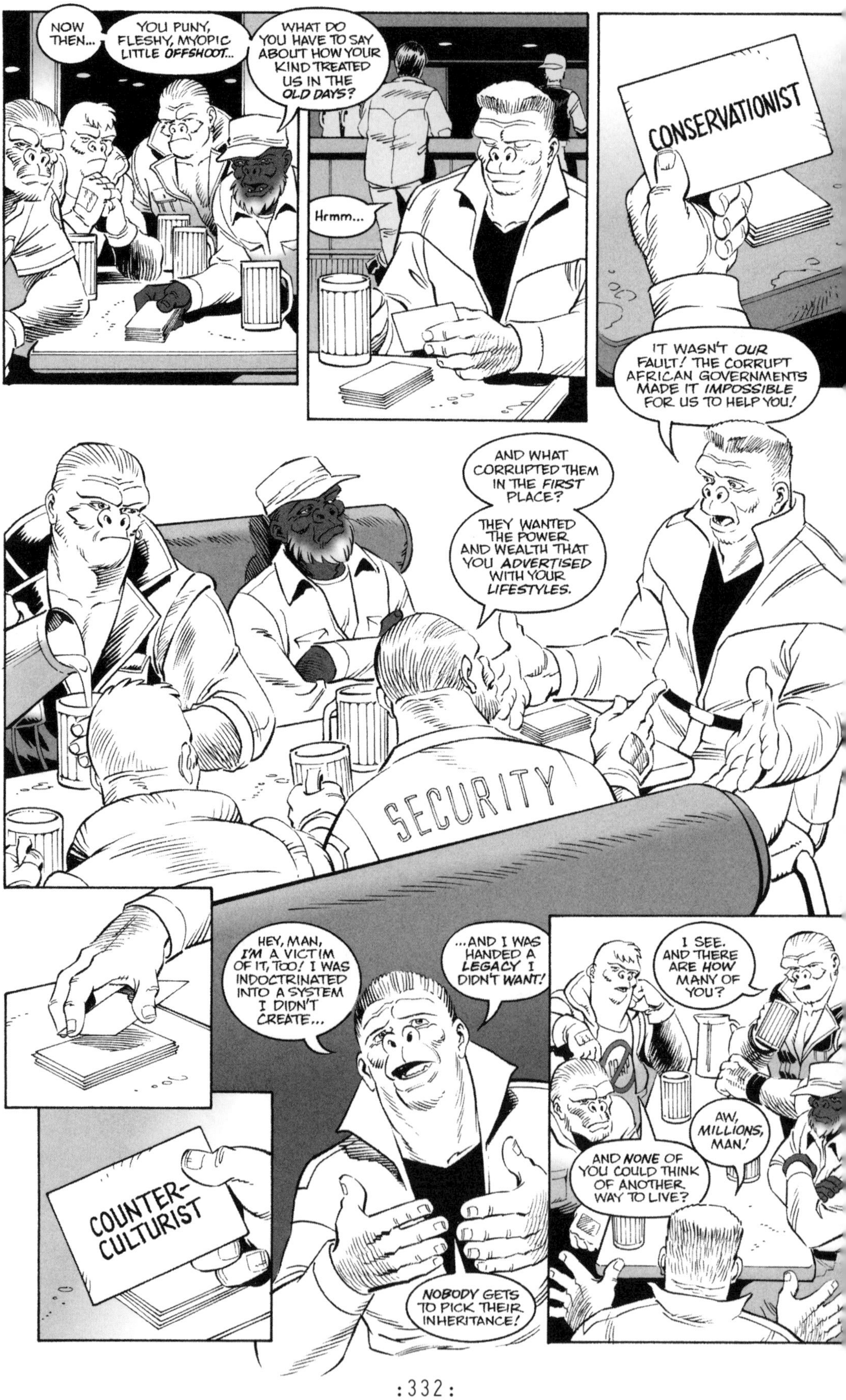
NOW THEN...
YOU PUNY, FLESHY, MYOPIC LITTLE OFFSHOOT...
WHAT DO YOU HAVE TO SAY ABOUT HOW YOUR KIND TREATED US IN THE OLD DAYS?
Hrmm...
CONSERVATIONIST
IT WASN'T OUR FAULT! THE CORRUPT AFRICAN GOVERNMENTS MADE IT IMPOSSIBLE FOR US TO HELP YOU!
AND WHAT CORRUPTED THEM IN THE FIRST PLACE?
THEY WANTED THE POWER AND WEALTH THAT YOU ADVERTISED WITH YOUR LIFESTYLES.
SECURITY
HEY, MAN, I'M A VICTIM OF IT, TOO! I WAS INDOCTRINATED INTO A SYSTEM I DIDN'T CREATE...
...AND I WAS HANDED A LEGACY I DIDN'T WANT!
COUNTER-CULTURIST
NOBODY GETS TO PICK THEIR INHERITANCE!
I SEE. AND THERE ARE HOW MANY OF YOU?
AW, MILLIONS, MAN!
AND NONE OF YOU COULD THINK OF ANOTHER WAY TO LIVE?

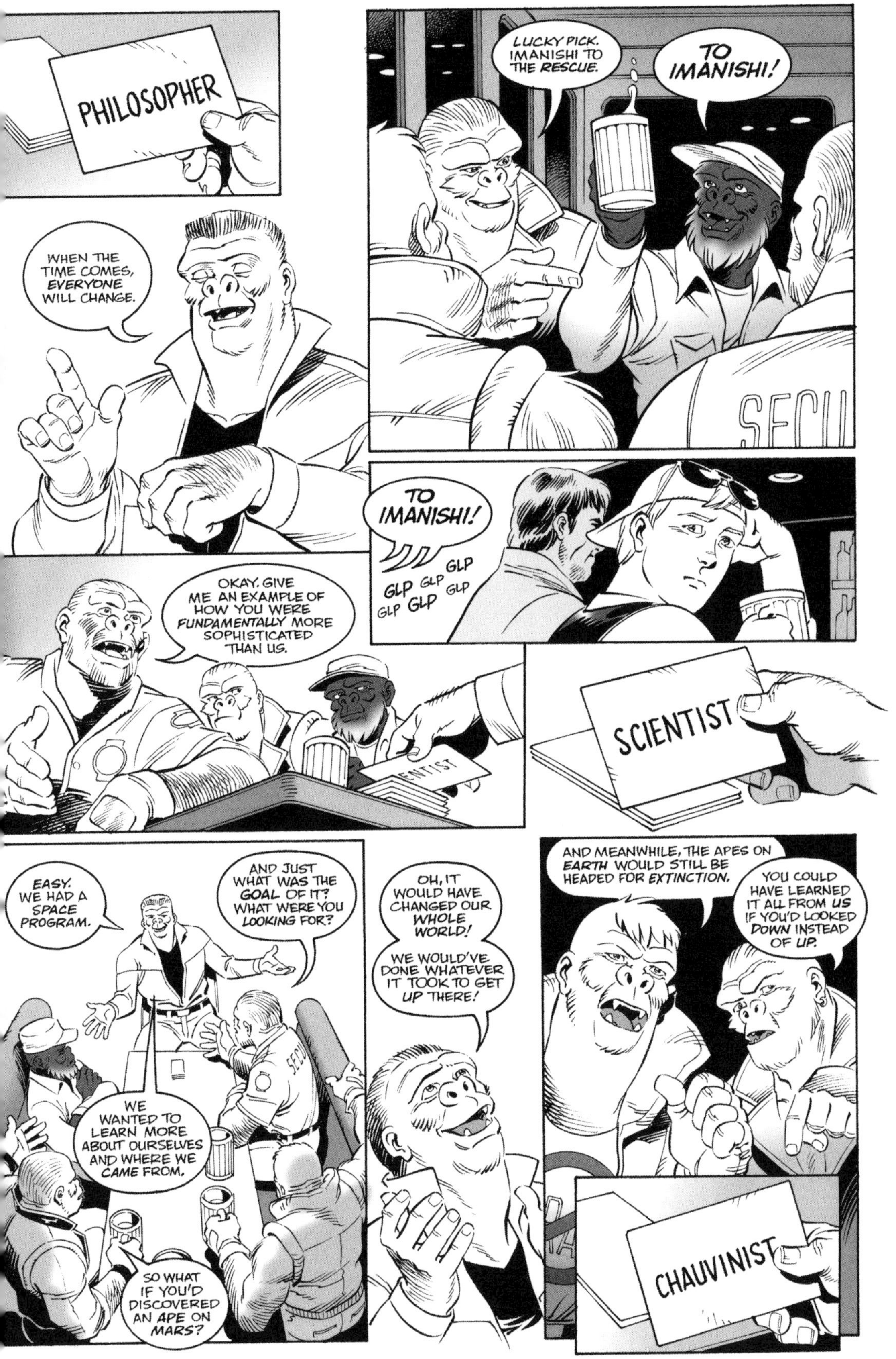
PHILOSOPHER
LUCKY PICK. IMANISHI TO THE RESCUE.
TO IMANISHI!
WHEN THE TIME COMES, EVERYONE WILL CHANGE.
TO IMANISHI!
GLP GLP GLP GLP GLP GLP GLP
OKAY. GIVE ME AN EXAMPLE OF HOW YOU WERE FUNDAMENTALLY MORE SOPHISTICATED THAN US.
SCIENTIST
EASY. WE HAD A SPACE PROGRAM.
AND JUST WHAT WAS THE GOAL OF IT? WHAT WERE YOU LOOKING FOR?
WE WANTED TO LEARN MORE ABOUT OURSELVES AND WHERE WE CAME FROM.
SO WHAT IF YOU'D DISCOVERED AN APE ON MARS?
OH, IT WOULD HAVE CHANGED OUR WHOLE WORLD!
WE WOULD'VE DONE WHATEVER IT TOOK TO GET UP THERE!
AND MEANWHILE, THE APES ON EARTH WOULD STILL BE HEADED FOR EXTINCTION.
YOU COULD HAVE LEARNED IT ALL FROM US IF YOU'D LOOKED DOWN INSTEAD OF UP.
CHAUVINIST

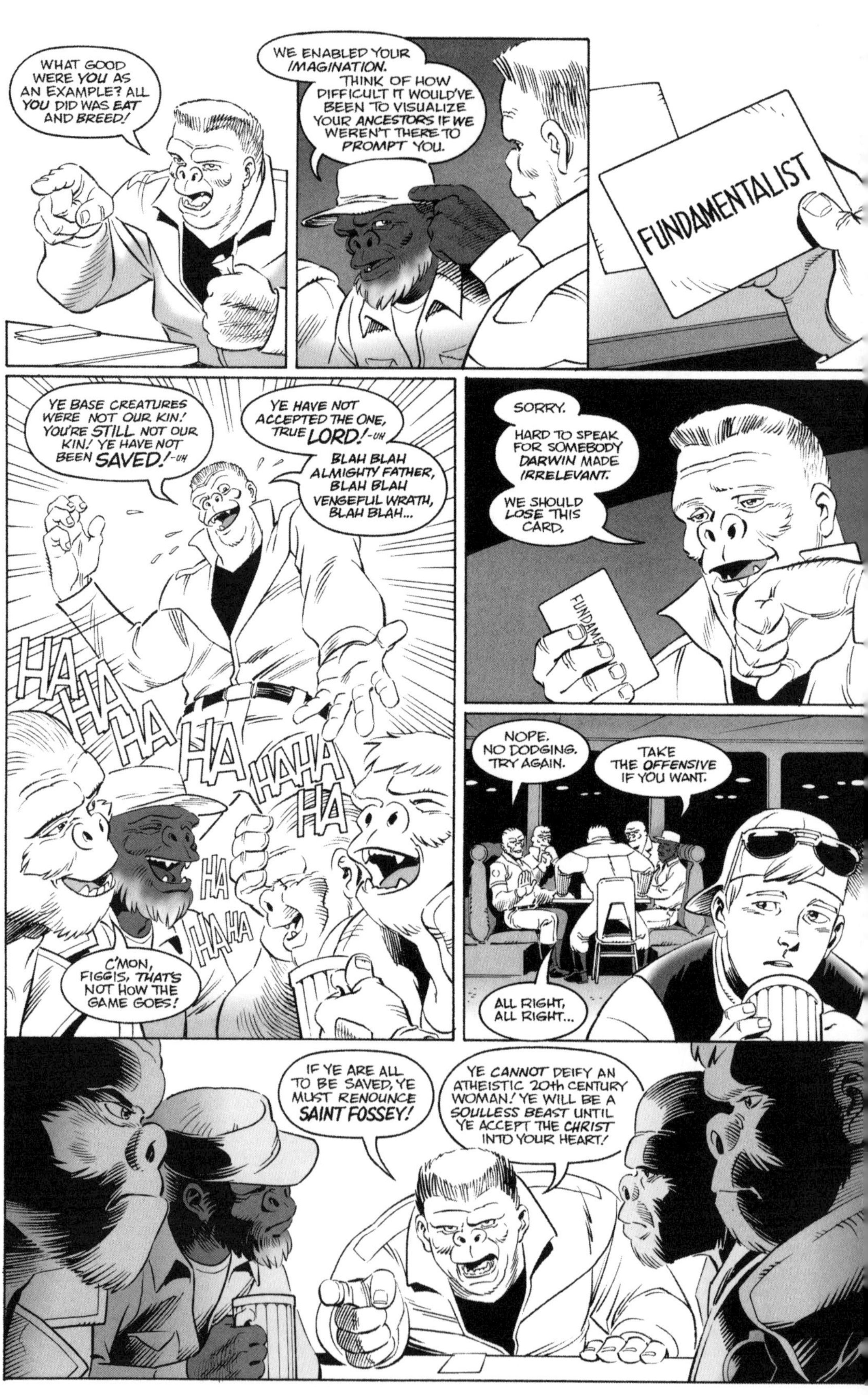

WHAT GOOD WERE YOU AS AN EXAMPLE? ALL YOU DID WAS EAT AND BREED!
WE ENABLED YOUR IMAGINATION.
THINK OF HOW DIFFICULT IT WOULD'VE BEEN TO VISUALIZE YOUR ANCESTORS IF WE WEREN'T THERE TO PROMPT YOU.
FUNDAMENTALIST
YE BASE CREATURES WERE NOT OUR KIN! YOU'RE STILL NOT OUR KIN! YE HAVE NOT BEEN SAVED!-UH
YE HAVE NOT ACCEPTED THE ONE, TRUE LORD!-UH
BLAH BLAH ALMIGHTY FATHER, BLAH BLAH VENGEFUL WRATH, BLAH BLAH...
HAHAHAHA HA HAHAHA HA HA HAHA
C'MON, FIGGIS, THAT'S NOT HOW THE GAME GOES!
SORRY.
HARD TO SPEAK FOR SOMEBODY DARWIN MADE IRRELEVANT.
WE SHOULD LOSE THIS CARD.
FUNDAME
NOPE. NO DODGING. TRY AGAIN.
TAKE THE OFFENSIVE IF YOU WANT.
ALL RIGHT, ALL RIGHT...
IF YE ARE ALL TO BE SAVED, YE MUST RENOUNCE SAINT FOSSEY!
YE CANNOT DEIFY AN ATHEISTIC 20th CENTURY WOMAN! YE WILL BE A SOULLESS BEAST UNTIL YE ACCEPT THE CHRIST INTO YOUR HEART!

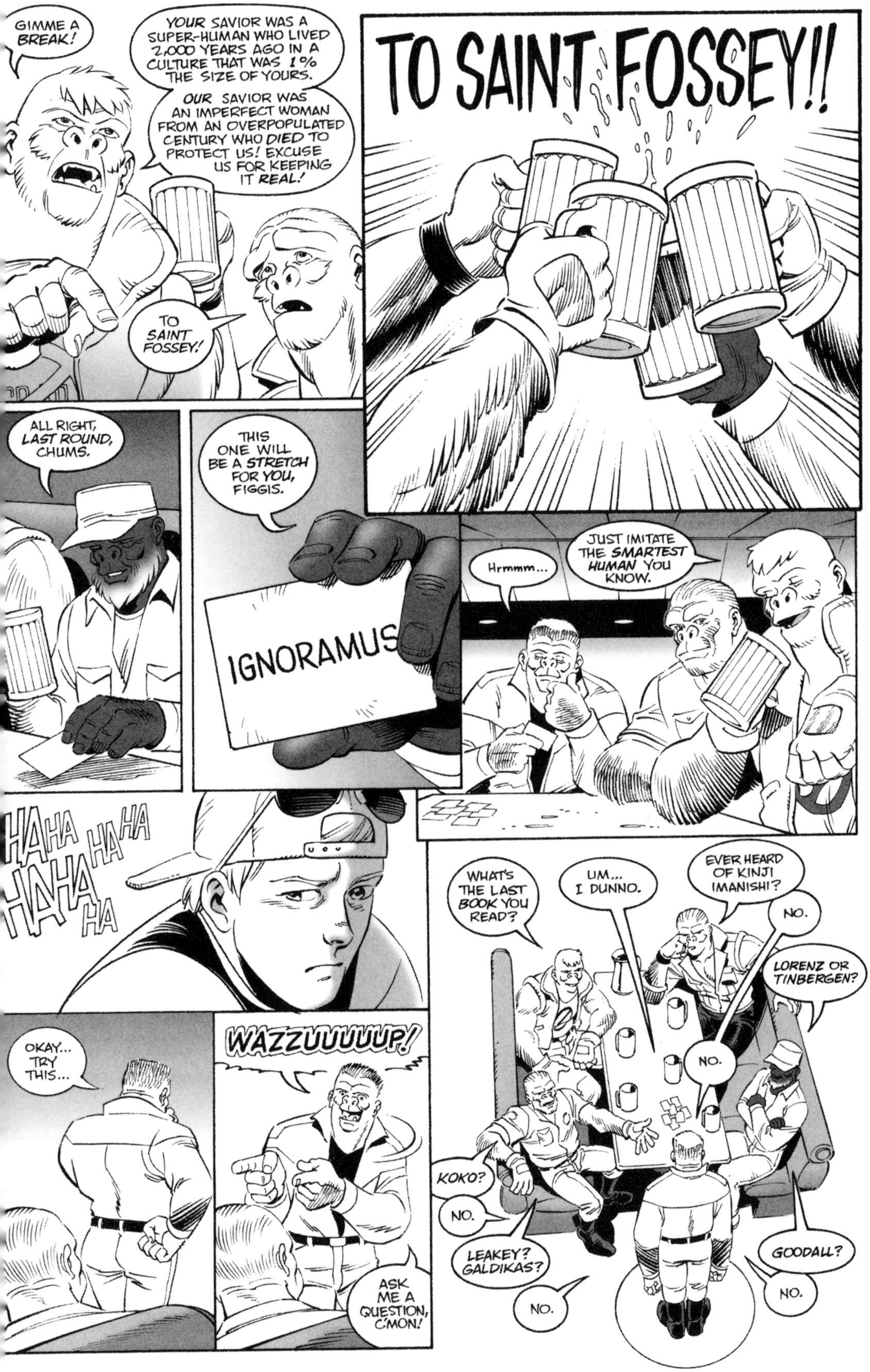
GIMME A BREAK!
YOUR SAVIOR WAS A SUPER-HUMAN WHO LIVED 2,000 YEARS AGO IN A CULTURE THAT WAS 1% THE SIZE OF YOURS.
OUR SAVIOR WAS AN IMPERFECT WOMAN FROM AN OVERPOPULATED CENTURY WHO DIED TO PROTECT US! EXCUSE US FOR KEEPING IT REAL!
TO SAINT FOSSEY!
TO SAINT FOSSEY!!
ALL RIGHT, LAST ROUND, CHUMS.
THIS ONE WILL BE A STRETCH FOR YOU, FIGGIS.
IGNORAMUS
Hrmmm...
JUST IMITATE THE SMARTEST HUMAN YOU KNOW.
HAHA HAHA HAHA HAHA HA
OKAY... TRY THIS...
WAZZUUUUUP!
ASK ME A QUESTION, C'MON!
WHAT'S THE LAST BOOK YOU READ?
UM... I DUNNO.
EVER HEARD OF KINJI IMANISHI?
NO.
LORENZ OR TINBERGEN?
NO.
KOKO?
NO.
LEAKEY? GALDIKAS?
NO.
GOODALL?
NO.

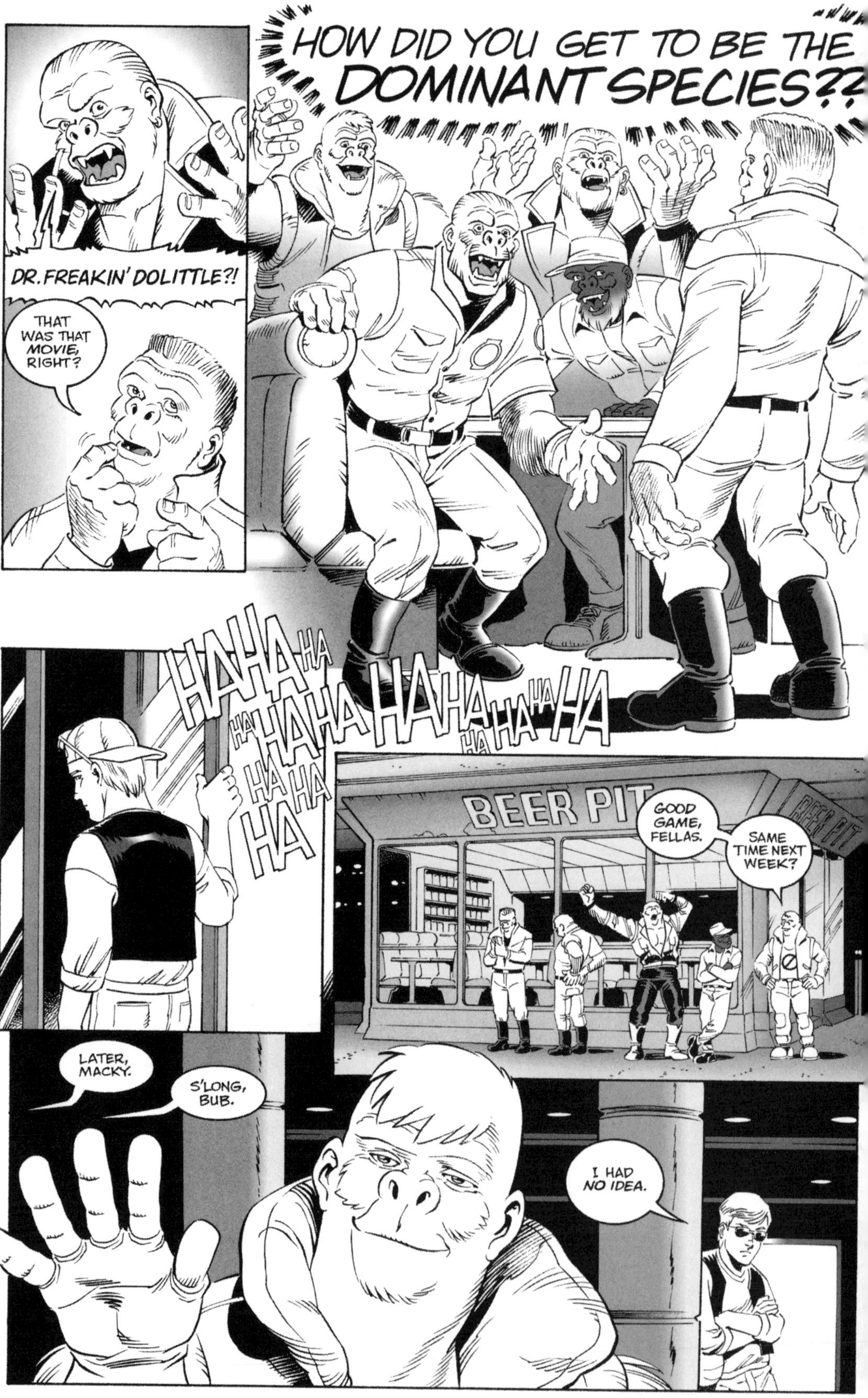
HOW DID YOU GET TO BE THE DOMINANT SPECIES??
DR. FREAKIN' DOLITTLE?!
THAT WAS THAT MOVIE, RIGHT?
HAHAHA HAHAHA HAHAHA HAHAHA HAHAHA HA
BEER PIT
GOOD GAME, FELLAS.
SAME TIME NEXT WEEK?
LATER, MACKY.
S'LONG, BUB.
I HAD NO IDEA.

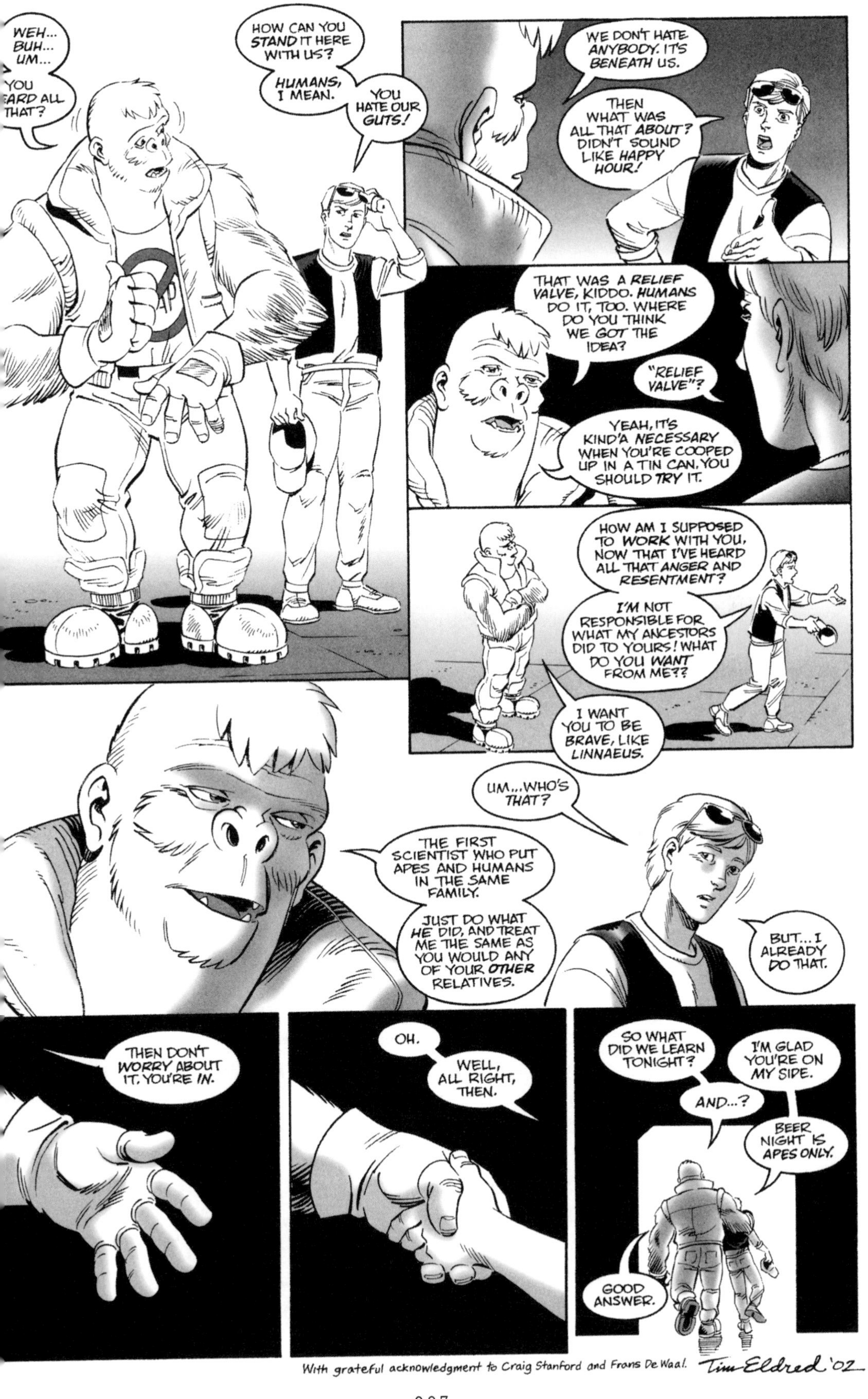
WEH... BUH... UM...
YOU EARD ALL THAT?
HOW CAN YOU STAND IT HERE WITH US?
HUMANS, I MEAN.
YOU HATE OUR GUTS!
WE DON'T HATE ANYBODY. IT'S BENEATH US.
THEN WHAT WAS ALL THAT ABOUT? DIDN'T SOUND LIKE HAPPY HOUR!
THAT WAS A RELIEF VALVE, KIDDO. HUMANS DO IT, TOO. WHERE DO YOU THINK WE GOT THE IDEA?
"RELIEF VALVE"?
YEAH, IT'S KIND'A NECESSARY WHEN YOU'RE COOPED UP IN A TIN CAN. YOU SHOULD TRY IT.
HOW AM I SUPPOSED TO WORK WITH YOU, NOW THAT I'VE HEARD ALL THAT ANGER AND RESENTMENT?
I'M NOT RESPONSIBLE FOR WHAT MY ANCESTORS DID TO YOURS! WHAT DO YOU WANT FROM ME??
I WANT YOU TO BE BRAVE, LIKE LINNAEUS.
UM...WHO'S THAT?
THE FIRST SCIENTIST WHO PUT APES AND HUMANS IN THE SAME FAMILY.
JUST DO WHAT HE DID, AND TREAT ME THE SAME AS YOU WOULD ANY OF YOUR OTHER RELATIVES.
BUT... I ALREADY DO THAT.
THEN DON'T WORRY ABOUT IT. YOU'RE IN.
OH.
WELL, ALL RIGHT, THEN.
SO WHAT DID WE LEARN TONIGHT?
I'M GLAD YOU'RE ON MY SIDE.
AND...?
BEER NIGHT IS APES ONLY.
GOOD ANSWER.

With grateful acknowledgment to Craig Stanford and Frans De Waal. Tim Eldred '02

THE WHOLE HISTORY OF
GREASE MONKEY

As I write these words, ten years have passed since the idea first crossed my mind to write and draw comics about a gorilla in space. In all that time, the thing has never left my side, even when I neglected it. This isn't the first time I've written about the creation of this comic, so those of you who have been here before can feel free to skip ahead to the later paragraphs. But for anyone who likes a tale about the flow of ideas or the rewards of unswerving dedication, here is the story in full. None of the names have been changed, and no one is innocent.

PHASE 1 (EARLY 1990s)

It all started on a tiny little creative whim and a great big throbbing pustule of righteous anger.

The whim was this: to create a fun little comic strip about a diverse cast of non-super-powered characters finding their way through life. The anger came from the comic book industry's lack of concern over the need for such comics—and its occasional hostility toward the very idea of them.

It was 1992, and the future didn't look promising. More and more of the same old stuff was coming down the pike. More superheroes, more bad girls, and more of the same junk that didn't appeal to the mainstream public. It

was always my feeling that this industry would stagnate if it didn't work harder to broaden its readership, and it often seemed like I was alone in my concern. What was to be done? Well, everything starts with an act of creation, and as a comic book creator I felt it was my responsibility to come up with something to address this need.

So where did *Grease Monkey* come from? The answer lies in several directions. First, I'd always loved outer space SF action, so that was my backdrop of choice. Second, I've always had a respect for well-crafted war stories. War, like love, forces people to dig deep into themselves and learn the true source of their humanity. Against this tapestry, you can learn a lot about what makes us tick.

Above and below: The very first drawings of Mac and Robin, before I got to know them.

The thing about war, though, is that increasingly few of us have actually experienced one, so its value as a literary tool is slowly eroding. For writing to endure and find a wide audience, it needs something universal and relevant to our daily lives. Therefore, I started thinking about the role of non-combatants—people living in a wartime environment, but not constantly placed in life-and-death situations. The non-combatant's life is beset on all sides by bureaucracy, personal politics, stifling regulations, and emotional conflict—not unlike the lives of us "normal" people.

I'd been kicking around this notion for a few years, looking for a way to focus it, when inspiration came from a Stan Ridgway song called "The Overlords." The narrator of this song was a man laboring under alien domination, dreaming about going underground and "monkeywrenching" for the resistance. This is a term for acts of sabotage, but it also planted the image in my head of a battlefield mechanic whose job it is to keep the maines running. This was a character I could work with. Still keying off e word "monkeywrenching," I wondered what it might be like if the char- ter were a gorilla. (Because, of course, as everyone knows, gorillas are e coolest animals on Earth.) That lit the fuse for everything that has hap- ened since.

The next step was to decide where the gorilla came from and how he und himself among humans. I wrote an extensive backstory to explain this, hich I've tinkered with over the years and plan to reveal as the bits and eces become germane.

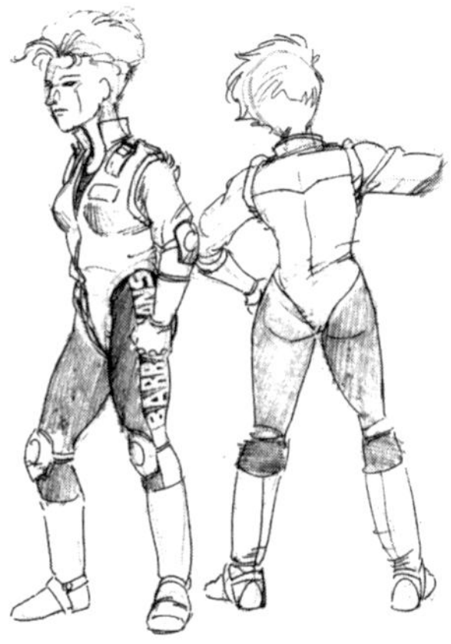

Early design for Barbara Brand

In establishing the setting for the story, I decided to place it inside a paceship, a giant pressure cooker. And there would be many gorillas work- g alongside humans, not just one. A whole culture was beginning to form, which the idea of a diverse cast expanded from gender and race to include whole separate species. The possibilities for tension and conflict expanded ght along with it.

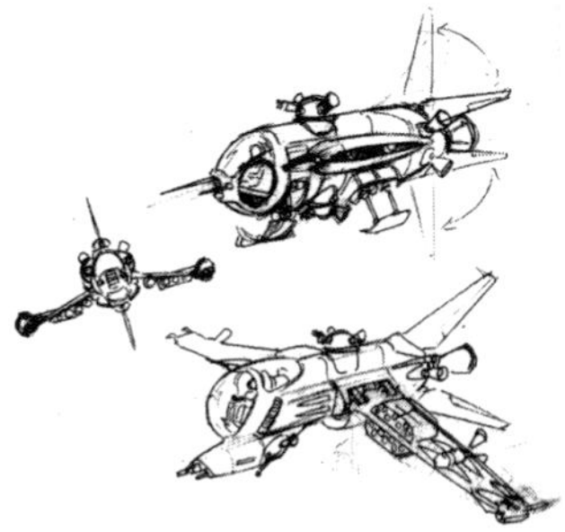

Working out the F300 Fightercraft

The concept was getting complex enough now to convince me that the tory needed a human focal character, who would be immersed in this cul- ure on behalf of the reader. To my surprise, that character turned out to e me. Robin Plotnik is exactly who I saw myself as most of the time, at east back in 1992; a hopeful, optimistic, well-meaning young buck who hinks he's got it all figured out but is in for a lot of surprises. Robin's per- onality and his reactions to things are much more like mine than I first ntended, and I was utterly blind to this until other people began pointing t out. Once it became clear, the purpose of the project took on a whole ew meaning.

I put a few more pieces into place and created the first episode, "Art overs," in the summer of '92. (See the liner notes for more detail.)

Below: Mac and Robin in their first fully rendered form (but not quite finished yet).

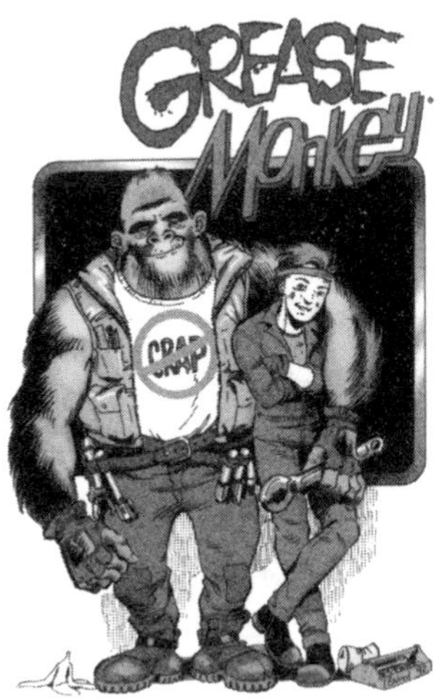
GREASE
Monkey
CRAP

What continues to amaze me the most about *Grease Monkey* is the wealth f unexpected rewards it has brought my way. I should explain that I've al- vays been a staunch advocate for the creative impulse. Whenever talking vith young artists who want to draw comics for a living, I always make it a oint to value originality and self-determination. Traditionally, the measure f true long-term success comes from how unique your vision is, not how vell you follow someone else's lead. To that end, I advocate that instead of vaiting around for a big break, young artists should look for ways to satisfy heir own creative goals on their own time and use their freedom to their ad- vantage.

Anyone who wants to see the value of this approach need look no fur- ther than these very pages. When I started it, *Grease Monkey* only existed for an audience of one: me. I took time off from paying projects just to en- tertain myself with it. I knew one day I'd offer it to a publisher, but my primary purpose was to have the simple joy of creating it. I didn't know then that when you risk a break from the daily routine to pursue your dream, you place yourself in the hands of fate, and there's no telling what will happen.

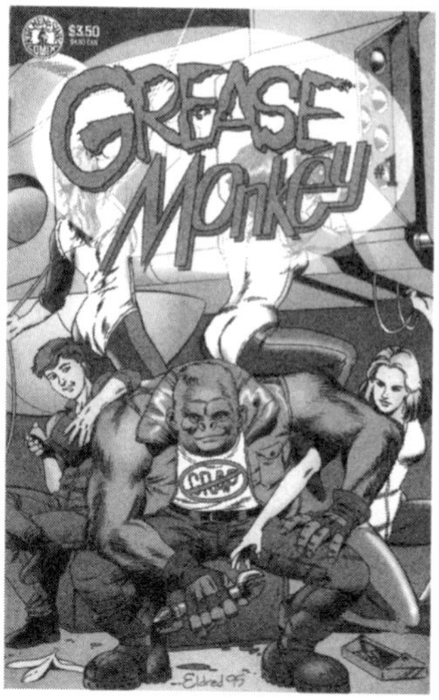
$3.50
GREASE
Monkey
#1
CRAP

Covers, Kitchen Sink Press, 1996

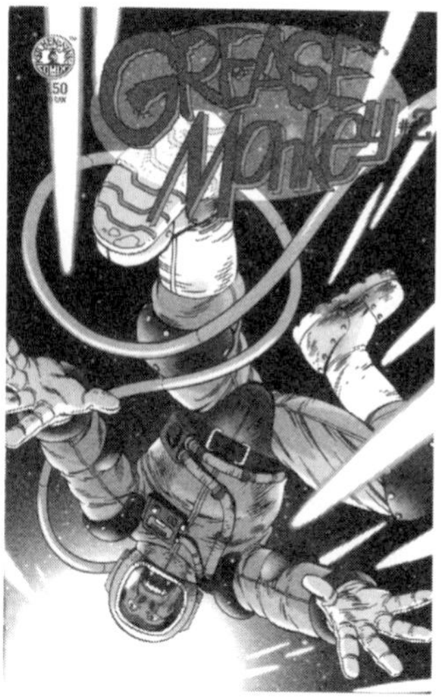
GREASE
Monkey

Below: A promotional button for the Kitchen Sink Press release. Sure to be a collector's item in a few hundred years. . .

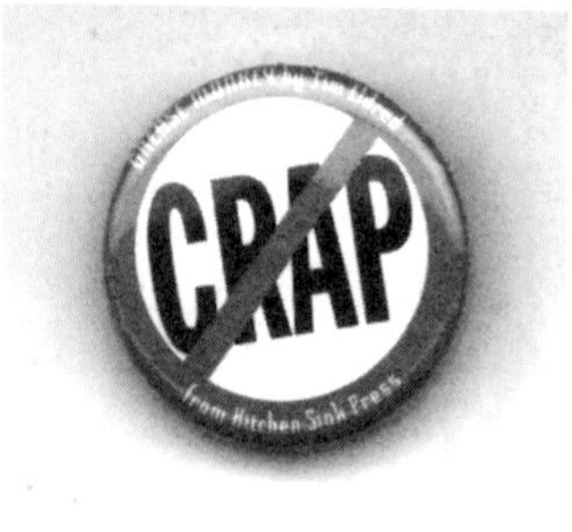
CRAP

So imagine my surprise when this happened: a few days after I finished drawing the first episode, I contacted a Canadian comics distributor, Styx International, on an unrelated matter and they asked if I had anything new they could publish in their magazine, *Up'N'Coming*. As a matter of fact, I did. A few more days later, the deal was done.

Joe Krolik and Brent Richard loved the first strip and immediately hired me to come up with five more. Fate had rewarded me for taking a chance. And this was only the beginning.

Writing and drawing these six episodes carried me into 1993, by which time I'd moved across the country from snow-locked Michigan to sunny Southern California. This put me a lot closer to Hollywood, the magical kingdom where anything goes. . . .

PHASE 2 (MID 1990s)

A year passed, and in the spring of 1994 I found myself at an industry convention in the presence of Denis Kitchen. I'd always respected Denis' company, Kitchen Sink Press, and was intrigued by the transformation of Mark Schulz' magnificent *Xenozoic Tales* into the highly underrated *Cadillacs and Dinosaurs* cartoon for CBS. This seemed like an ideal blueprint for *Grease Monkey*, so I approached Denis about publishing it as a regular series. To my delight, he asked me to colorize the six existing strips, and KSP would collect them into two standard-format comic books. Getting a second lease on life was amazing enough, but having the chance to go back and upgrade the strip was quite a bonus.

Grease Monkey #1 and #2 came out from Kitchen Sink Press in early 1996, and though they didn't quite set the world on fire, they did open the gate into the world of animation via Kitchen's Hollywood rep, Brad Neufeld. Developing the strip for animation turned out to be a thoroughly eye-opening, occasionally frustrating, and infinitely educational experience. I gained a front-row view of what TV execs insist is appropriate for children and acceptable to sponsors. I won't disgust you with the details just now. Suffice to say, the cart often comes before the horse and the tail nearly always wags the dog.

Nevertheless, this experience too handed me an unexpected reward. The Neufeld connection put me together with an animation writer (Jymn Magon), an agent (Ellen Vein), and ultimately a career in the cartoon biz. In the fall of 1995, *Grease Monkey* was pitched as an animated TV series to several networks and studios, including MCA/Universal. Producer Ralph Sanchez took a shine to it, particularly the artwork on my presentation boards, and he offered me a job on an upcoming series called *Wing Commander Academy* (based on the popular computer game starring Mark Hamill).

The timing couldn't have been better. Things were slowing down in the comics industry, because not enough had been done to broaden the audience (ah, you could cut the irony with a knife), and animation was the next logical stomping ground. I hadn't any practical experience in animation storyarding, but Ralph and Universal took a chance on me anyway, and I didn't t them down. I ended up storyboarding several episodes of *WCA* and serv- g as a character designer for the series during the summer of 1996. The ow debuted on USA Network that fall, and it gave me my first official reen credits.

This led directly to a gig at Columbia/Tristar TV animation. I began as a oryboard artist there at the end of 1996, but one look at *Grease Monkey* nvinced producer extraordinaire Audu Paden that I had the chops to be a irector. In very little time, I found myself helming several episodes of *Ex- eme Ghostbusters*, which premiered in September 1997.

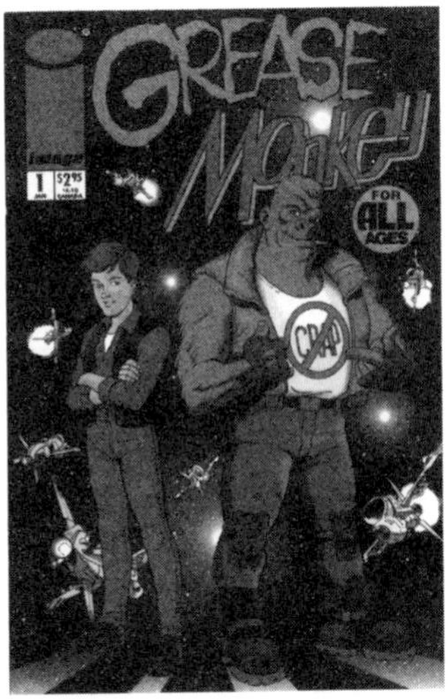
image
GREASE Monkey
FOR ALL AGES

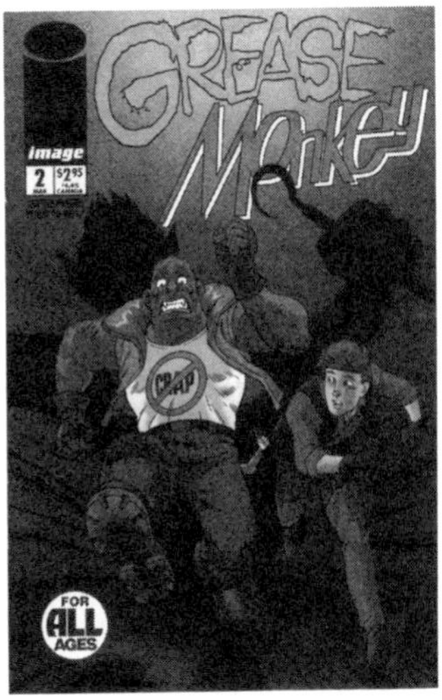
image
GREASE Monkey
FOR ALL AGES

Covers, Image Comics, 1998

HASE 3 (LATE 1990s)

In the summer of '96, Ralph Sanchez had moved from Universal to Film oman (home of *The Simpsons*) and engineered a development deal there for *rease Monkey*. This meant developing new concepts for a TV series, and it spired me to write some new comics. In the space of a few months, I anked out 18 new stories, bringing the total up to 24. I'd intended to start awing them right away, but with a full-time job in animation my plate was retty full. Regardless, more rewards appeared anyway. And this time, they ere far more valuable than jobs or money.

Something happens when you place yourself into your own works of fic- ion, as I unwittingly did with young Robin Plotnik. When your characters re extensions of you, and react to things as you would, it puts you in a ather Godlike position. Writing the new stories gave me that experience. Then I put Mac and Robin through one crisis after another, it was up to me o work out the solutions to their problems. Unwittingly, I was writing my- elf a manual for crisis management.

This manual, such as it was, gave me a vital reference point throughout 997, as I faced trials in my personal life that I wasn't equipped to deal with t an earlier time. This brought me a nice revelation: that not only does life mitate art, my life was imitating my own art. For practically everything that appened to me, I could find some parallel in a *Grease Monkey* story. I'd already faced these crises on paper, and I new how to handle them. The chance to live one's own art must be one of life's greatest rewards, and all it took vas the resolve to break with routine back in 1992. But it wasn't over yet—not by a long shot.

Something else that happened in '97 was a surprise connection with Image Comics. Like everyone else in omicdom, I had watched the rise of this aggressive publisher with interest. I had not, however, found much to nterest me in their actual comics, which seemed intent on treading where others had already gone. So when my riend Kurt Busiek (writer of such magnificent comics as *Marvels* and *Astro City*) recommended that I approach mage's editor-in-chief Larry Marder with *Grease Monkey*, it seemed slightly insane. When Kurt told me that here was more to Image than I originally thought, I took his word for it—and damned if he didn't turn out to be ight.

Marder put me in touch with one of the Image principals, Jim Valentino, who turned out to be just as passion- ate as I was about broadening the readership. He had turned this passion into his own sub-group of black & white comics that followed the tenets of do-it-yourself creator ownership . . . but with the Image Comics logo on the cover. This was an idea I could warm to.

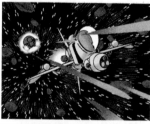

Above: Stills from the first animated *Grease Monkey* pilot film.

Jim was impressed with *Grease Monkey,* and in a few short months the original stories saw their third time in print (spring 1998). Despite critical acclaim, the sales figures were barely high enough to cover the printing costs, so the series fizzled out before I could begin drawing the 18 stories that were lying in wait.

Disappointing, yes, but not discouraging. There was much still to do. The rest of 1998 and most of 1999 was filled up with work on a graphic novel, which was yet another of the many rewards. Let me back up again to 1992 for an explanation. At about the same time I was working on the first six episodes of *Grease Monkey*, author Daniel Quinn was publishing a novel called *Ishmael*. Daniel and I had something remarkable in common: the main characters in both our stories were talking gorillas. When I heard about *Ishmael*, I devoured it instantly and found it to be one of the most amazing books I'd ever read. I contacted Daniel to say hello, and sent him some *Grease Monkey* comics just for laughs. What I got back was an offer to work together.

Daniel has written a lot of books along the lines of *Ishmael*, all dealing with the heady subject of where our species is headed. He'd also written a screenplay in this vein called *The Man Who Grew Young*. It didn't look as if it would get made into a film, so Daniel asked if I'd be interested in turning it into a graphic novel instead. I thought about it for approximately three seconds and that was that. I'll cut to the chase and say that *The Man Who Grew Young* was published by Context Books in the summer of 2001, and I'm immensely proud of it. All the while I was working on it, I vowed that afterward I would return my attention to *Grease Monkey* and finally start drawing those later episodes. I managed to fulfill half of that vow. I would indeed return to *Grease Monkey*, but not in the way I'd planned.

PHASE 4 (2000 PLUS)

1999 was drawing to a close, and a brainstorm had struck. By day, I was still working in TV animation, and I had gained a lot of skills since '96. One part of the process of making cartoons is to assemble the storyboards and voice tracks into an animatic—a sort of slideshow version of the finished program that is used to blueprint the timing and editing. Technology had reached a point where animatics could be assembled on a home computer. Hence, the brainstorm: why not make a *Grease Monkey* animatic and use it to pitch the series again for TV? I had everything I needed, including friends who could supply the voices. The only thing I lacked was a sense of what a monumental undertaking it would be.

In the fall of 1999 I wrote a script for a *Grease Monkey* pilot film entitled "All You Need Is Love." I thought it would run about 5 minutes and I could do the whole animatic—start to finish—in a month or two. The script actually timed out to about 7 minutes, so I figured maybe three months. Then I started drawing and the thing just kept growing. The more I worked on it, the more I added. I also decided the finished animatic would be in full color, hich meant even more production time. In the end, it required over 2,000 awings, took 6 months to make, and it totaled 17 minutes of screen ne . . . just 5 minutes shy of a standard made-for-TV episode. But it was much fun, I had to make another one!

The first cartoon wrapped in July 2000 and a month later I got going on a cond short entitled "Black Holes Suck." It was more fully animated than e first film, and although it totaled only 6 minutes, it took another 6 onths to finish. It became obvious that I couldn't do this for a living, but I t the job done—both of these animated visions really exist! Now I could arch into a Hollywood studio, shove a tape into a VCR, and say "Look— ere's my show!" Did it work? Of course not. Why? Lousy timing.

The first time I pitched *Grease Monkey*, the animation industry was retty unstable. A lot of studios were being bought by other studios, or management was changing, or execs were just too scared to start anything new. he year 2000 was also pretty unstable. The TV animation biz was shrinking gain (it does this every 10 years or so) and everyone wanted goofy slapstick hows like the ones that were successful the year before. I tried Internet ompanies, but they only wanted adult (i.e., shock-humor or soft-porn) cartoons. Once again, *Grease Monkey* was a misfit. The odd thing was, everyone utside Hollywood loved the cartoons and demanded more. The guy who said nobody in Hollywood knows anything" must have gone through something ke this.

One more thing occurred during the whole cartoon-making experience. hinking that *Grease Monkey* could also be pitched as a feature film, I decided to write a screenplay for one. This was easier than it sounds, since I lready had the mini-bible from 1996 to fall back on. The 17-minute pilot ilm worked perfectly as an opening act, so I just took off from there and tarted writing. This took about a month, and in late July of 2000 I finished a 95-page first draft. Thoughts entered my head about turning the whole thing into either a long-running animatic or a graphic novel, but here were other things to do first. To be precise, there were 18 other hings to do first.

In January 2001, I finally started drawing *Grease Monkey* comics again. Having all those scripts sitting in reserve was often a great comfort in previous times, sort of like having a dresser drawer full of warm socks. I'd often heard that "real" writers had an archive of unpublished work sitting in their iles to be discovered after they die, so for that brief time I felt like a "real" writer. (In fact, after I started drawing again I occasionally thought I might not live long enough to finish. Fortunately, this turned out to be simple dementia.)

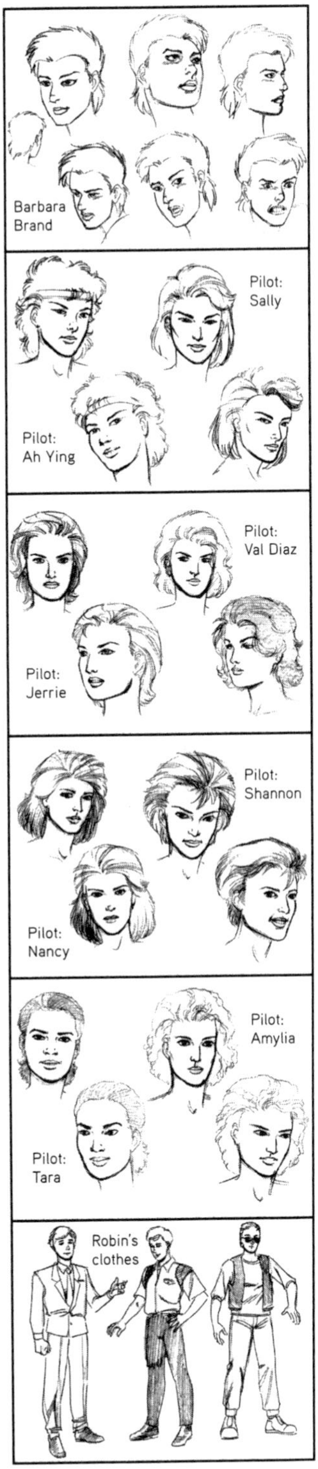
Barbara
Brand
Pilot:
Sally
Pilot:
Ah Ying
Pilot:
Val Diaz
Pilot:
Jerrie
Pilot:
Shannon
Pilot:
Nancy
Pilot:
Amylia
Pilot:
Tara
Robin's
clothes

Character model sheets

For reasons that were entirely aesthetic, I decided to continue with the 12-page episodic format that I'd established in the very beginning. Because of this, there was always a charge of anxiety during the first step, where I broke each script down into thumbnail sketches. I placed a rigorous 12-page rule on myself, and like all rules it was bound to be broken. Some stories contained themselves effortlessly. Others fought like demons. The first time

Kevin Nedelmat

Jeff Simons

Kara Solu

Kara's clothes

Kara's room-mates

Ms. Ann Thrope

I allowed myself to break the rule (on episode 11), all bets were off. So muc[h] for discipline.

An interesting aspect of the whole creative process is the transfer of im[-]portance from one stage to another. Every story makes the passage throug[h] script, thumbnail, rough layout, pencil, ink, and printing. Whatever stage I[']m on at any given time is the most important. For a while, the script is indis-pensable. When I finish the rough, the script is yesterday's newspaper. By the time I get to the inking, the rough is waste paper. When these things were merely hypothetical, they were priceless. Now that there's a finished product, they're just taking up space. Following this premise to its natural conclusion, the paper is just the transient vehicle of the idea. In the end, th[e] book you're reading will be less important than the ideas it communicates. I[f] I got it right, the ideas will resonate for a good long time and the book itself can vanish. (Not that I want it to, of course.)

PHASE 5 (THIS BOOK)

By now it should be obvious that getting this work into your hands was quite an undertaking, with a full fourteen years between initial conception and finished product. The last phase began when the art was finished in 2002, and I decided to approach a large book publisher, rather than one lim-ited only to the comic book market. This required the support of a canny lit-erary agent named Ashley Grayson, who received my introductory letter at precisely the same moment he decided he'd like to add a graphic novel to hi[s] already impressive credentials. Ashley suspected that Tor Books might feel the same way, and about a year later his hunch paid off.

From there, my editor Teresa Nielsen Hayden took me under her wing and pulled me into this entirely new realm. She knew it would be a chal-lenge, since the production leap from prose fiction to graphic novels brings a huge number of variables into play, but to my relief and her credit, there was never any question that it could be done. She was one o[f] those people who "got it" upon her first reading of the book, and her de-sire for others to have that experience kept the entire project buoyant. I owe a huge debt of gratitude to both Teresa and her mighty crew, and I have no doubt that they committed many untold acts of heroism to ensur[e] that *Grease Monkey* stayed on course. If we're all lucky, we'll get to do it again with the sequel.

Yes, there is already a sequel in the works. In late 2003 I began to turn my movie script into a graphic novel, and as of this writing (March 2006), all 229 pages of *Grease Monkey Book 2: A Tale of Two Species* exist in roug[h] form. As you can imagine, finishing it is going to require a lot of time and energy. I can supply the lion's share, but I need your help. If you like this book enough to want another, share that enthusiasm with your friends and, just as important, your favorite bookseller.

Something else you can do is check in from time to time at www.greasemonkeybook.com. There you can find all sorts of goodies that didn't make it into this volume, plus the first few chapters in their original full color glory[.]

LINER NOTES

PISODE 1: ART LOVERS

Debut episodes can be intimidating to write unless you first figure out here you want them to end, with everyone on stage and set up for things come. Writing this story became a matter of stringing the right scenes gether until they reached that point. This simplicity was offset, however, a truly bizarre series of events surrounding page one. I wrote the script r this page on my first computer, then promptly lost it to the digital therworld and had to re-create it from memory (not always as easy as it unds). After finishing the art for page one, I discovered that my then- ree-year-old daughter apparently didn't like one of my panels and lav- hed it with White-Out a mere half hour before I had to ship it to my blisher. Then, three years later, I colored page one on my second com- ter and lost it AGAIN. I have to say, three times makes it a genuine rse. Now I save computer files frequently and keep the White-Out at a fe distance. (By the way, the original art for page one—and every other ge of this story—has seemingly vanished from the face of the Earth. Make this what you will.)

PISODE 2: THE PRICE

The task for this story was to depict Robin's rite of passage, his initiation ith all its requisite pain) into the new life that stretches out before him. hat surprises me the most about this episode is how closely it follows the ructure of the classic hero's journey myth. I wasn't introduced to the orks of Joseph Campbell until a few years after I wrote this, but all the tra- tional motifs are here. Robin is still held back by the constraints and pre- nceptions of his old sphere of existence, represented by his increasingly solete attachment to Kevin. Mac is the shaman who has to guide Robin—by hatever means necessary—through a death and rebirth. Robin has to break e chains he was born with. As a writer, I instinctively knew these things d to happen, but I was completely unaware of how universal the concepts ere. Few things astonish me more than mythology's power to influence us ross the span of history.

PISODE 3: GORILLA TACTICS

Now that Robin and Mac had overcome their initial teething pains, it was me for them to take a step into their surrounding environment. The *Fist of rth*, after all, is a colorful microcosm of all manner of deviants, rogues, d monsters. I should probably explain that although it's a ship of war, it n't at war yet, and everybody has a job to do but they can also relax and let

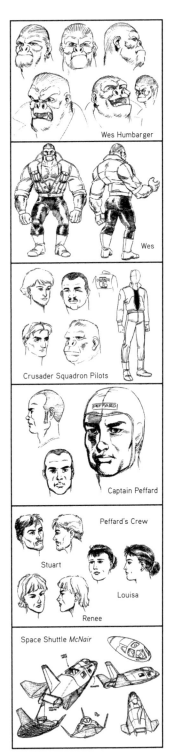

Wes Humbarger

Wes

Crusader Squadron Pilots

Captain Peffard

Peffard's Crew

Stuart

Louisa

Renee

Space Shuttle *McNair*

Henniker

Rosco

Rosco

Lyle Brand

Lieutenant Flunky

Mac on a date

in some comedy. After years of writing hard-edged SF dramas, it was quite liberating to discover this.

EPISODE 4: THE GIFT

Robin does in this story exactly what I would do if I suddenly found myself surrounded by women like the Barbarians: lose my cool, my confidence and any semblance of self-esteem. Unlike me, however, Robin has a highly sensible and infinitely devious benefactor on his side. And next to some of the other human males on the *Fist of Earth*, Robin is a prize whether he believes it or not.

EPISODE 5: THE CALLING

By this time, I figured any readers who were hooked by the first four stories deserved something of an explanation for exactly what happened to the Earth and why intelligent gorillas are bunking with human beings. I also knew I wouldn't be satisfied with *Grease Monkey* until I found some way to render a profile of Mac looking heavenward. Something about that image stuck in my mind as a symbol for the particular sense of wonder I wanted the series to convey.

EPISODE 6: REWARDS

No doubt about it, of the first six episodes this one is my personal fave. When this story came out of my pen, I wished all these characters were actors so I could send them flowers after their masterful performance. After this one, the story had taken over and I no longer considered these to be fictional characters. I was just the guy holding the pen, reporting on their lives. How disturbed is that?

EPISODE 7: KISMET

I dearly hope that two things from our time will still be around in a future of space travel. First, I hope there are still books that you have to pick up and open to read. Even though it makes more sense in a closed environment to store all your text electronically, I doubt that any piece of literature would have the kind of weight—and meaning—that it gains by virtue of taking up physical space. Second, I hope that being surrounded by ultra-high-tech hardware and exotic circumstances will not supplant a hearty taste for science fiction adventure. Even now, most of us don't get excited about stories centered on what surrounds us in our daily lives. These two thoughts tugged at me as I created this story, and I cheerfully addressed them both. *Fist of Earth*'s library contains digital books, but they each demand their own package, unwilling to be denigrated. And when Robin declares that the ship is full of stiffs, he is observing precisely what happens when people lose their appetite for imagination. Kara is a casualty of this, someone whose creative mind serves little purpose to the society and goes to waste by running itself in circles. Let's all promise each other we won't let it come to this, okay?

?ISODE 8: GORILLA WARFARE

Few obstacles in life are as insurmountable as our reactions to them. hoever learns how to manipulate our reactions will be the true master of e world. The scary part is that maybe they're already in charge.

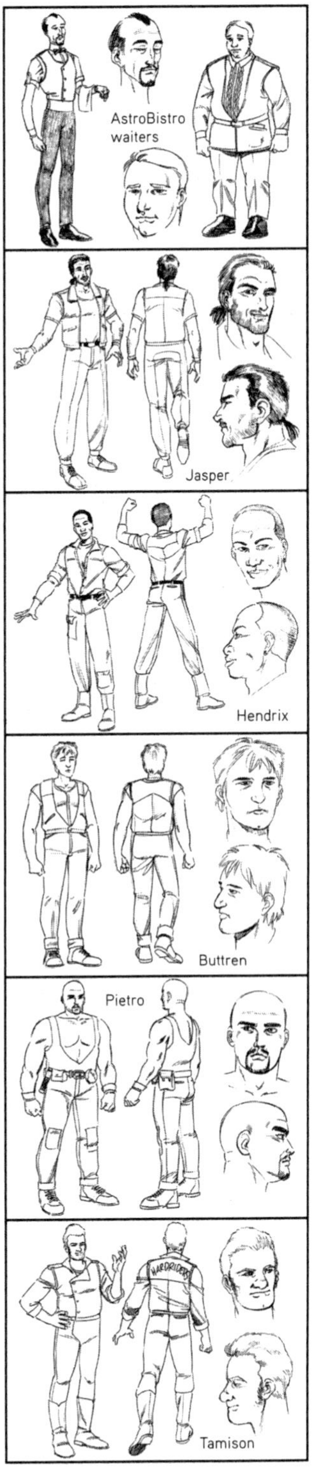

AstroBistro waiters
Jasper
Hendrix
Buttren
Pietro
Tamison

?ISODE 9: END OF THE WORLD

This story has a bit of a checkered past. As a fervent NASA supporter, I anted to be completely accurate in my depiction of a next-generation space uttle, which for the longest time looked like it would be the X-33 Ven- restar. Ever since I wrote this script in 1996, I was on the lookout for X-33 ferences, but I was never happy with what I found, not to mention an- yed by the ship's lack of a human crew. This had me stymied for three ars until NASA (bless their hearts) rolled out the X-38, a smaller shuttle signed as an escape vehicle for the International Space Station. The shut- e that appears in this episode isn't exactly the X-38 (its aerospike engine ould be a dead giveaway to those in the know), but it's founded on the same ncept, which serves this story far better than the X-33 ever would. Be- des, it was announced as I was drawing this story that the X-33 project as finally being scrapped after five years of study. Nonetheless, I hope mething like it does eventually fly—with humans at the helm—and that ople like Captain H.E. Peffard are among them.

Special thanks to my pal Glenn Swanson at the Johnson Space Center for ference on the vitally important SAFER unit!

PISODE 10: ENEMIES

Political correctness gets a bad rap these days. I see it as a much-abused ea with noble roots. If you accept that words and thoughts can be the same ing, then changing the words we use can have a strong impact on how we ink. We struggle mightily against modes of thought that are forced upon s—as well we should—but since we humans have gained a virtual strangle- old on the planet, I think it behooves us to recognize that little will improve ntil the quality of our thoughts improves. If that means paying closer atten- on to the words we use, then so be it.

PISODE 11: THE RIVAL

So far it seems to be an inescapable truth that within any group you will nd at least one obnoxious jerk who seems unaware of, or uninterested in, e effect they have on the people around them. You know the type. A human emorrhoid. One whose primary function is to make life harder for everyone se. If this is indeed a given pattern in human affairs, we can do one of two ings in response: either compromise ourselves into ambivalence, or try to nd a purpose in it. My thinking is that human obstacles are here to teach us more about ourselves, to heighten ur awareness of the impact we have on each other's lives. And if that doesn't quite work, they can at least give s an excuse to sharpen our wit and sarcasm (two of humanity's most vital resources, if you ask me).

Colonel
Lawrence
Craine

Accelerated
Dolphin

Dolphin Detail

U.N. Speaker

U.N. Bureaucrats

Fist of Earth
Broadcasters

EPISODE 12: REWARDS, PART 2

When I wrote the first six episodes in 1992, they sort of naturally fell into a story arc culminating with Mac almost getting a date with Admiral Stettler. When I made up my mind to write more episodes in 1996, it felt right to construct the entire series this way, in arcs of six stories that would each end with a follow-up to "Rewards." And I have to say that although each story is special to me in its own unique way, these episodes stand out because they pretty much wrote themselves. It's an undefinable kind of magic when your characters tell you what's supposed to happen to them, like the thing you created is alive and independent of you. It's just like all the best moments of being a parent, and I wouldn't trade the experience for anything.

EPISODE 13: EXCHANGE DAY

My daughter, like just about any kid in the world, goes through occasional bad-patch moments where nothing is fair and she never gets her way and everybody around her is mean for no reason. A while ago, my daughter and I took a weekend off in a major American city (I won't say which one) and wound up staying in a shabby hotel on the anarchic side of town. Lots of homeless people, an atmosphere of violence, and oppressive cityscapes were just some of the highlights. In the midst of this, she turned to me and said, "You know what, Dad? I really like my life." Until that moment, I hadn't quite realized how valuable it is to have context.

EPISODE 14: GRAIL TIME

Since day one of this project, I've always puzzled over how much I want to make Mac and the others like real gorillas from our time. I've often worried that they just come off as humans in ape costumes. Beyond the cheap banana jokes and monkey puns, there ought to be many subtle and complex levels of gorilla behavior. As it turns out, they were subtle enough to sneak into the fabric of the story on their own. First, gorilla troops consist mainly of females grouped around an alpha male and one or two juvenile males, precisely the makeup of Barbarian Squadron. Also, since the female gorillas choose which male to join up with, he has to audition for the role—he has to show leadership and responsibility in order to win her over. Which is precisely what Mac does in his long-term attempt to impress and charm Admiral Stettler. So the gorilla culture as we have come to know it is in there, it just took its own subtle and complex route. Believe me, I'm as surprised as anyone by this.

By the way, the philosophy in this story has helped me to cope with some interesting times. Who knows, maybe it will help someone else.

EPISODE 15: SEPARATION

Here was a genuine case of history overtaking me. When I originally wrote this story, it included this line as part of the VR movie: "Only twice before had humanity been touched by such power." The two events were the st atomic bomb explosion and the first moon landing. To me, it seemed at nothing could compare with those two utterly different but equally significant moments in history. But that was before September 11, 2001. It occurred to me on that horrible day that my concept of a worldwide alien attack ould look something like what happened in New York. But, of course, it had e built-in buffer of being fictional. I drew this story a month after 9/11, d it already seemed historically inept to stick with the original script. ars from now, I'm certain that 9/11 will be remembered in just this fashn. If something worse is yet to come, I'd rather keep it fictional.

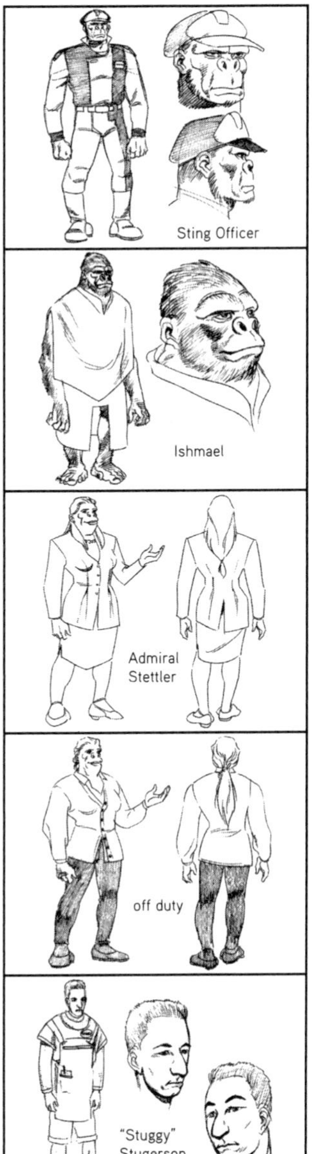
Sting Officer
Ishmael
Admiral
Stettler
off duty
"Stuggy"
Stugerson
(waiter)
Jace (Captain of
Vulture Squadron)

ISODE 16: THE LONG ROAD

During the first half of the 1990s when I began this project, a few of my ntemporary comic book creators suddenly received explosive popularity in turn for what looked to me like not very much effort. Those of us in the ger sector of the artform (the lesser known but harder working) kept our ads down and toiled onward, quietly resenting the hell out of this paradox. now I'm not the only one in the world who believes that reward should be mmensurate—not reciprocal—to the time and effort you give to your work. hen evidence piles up in support of the opposing theory, when it looks like e manipulation of easy formulas is the fast track to both financial and creive success, you begin to question some of your fundamental beliefs. Some us were irresistibly tempted, and jumped onto the bandwagon. And nearly eryone who did has dropped out of sight in the years since. We should all ve realized how hollow it actually was. Observing this led me to my short ad vs. long road ethic, which I hope I've mapped out clearly in this isode. Perhaps an amusing coda is that this particular story was the most fficult of them all to lay out, and it refused to be contained in my preferred pages. In other words, I had to work harder to tell a story that applauds rd work.

ISODE 17: THE WAY OF ART

I won't go on and on about the real-life influences in this story, beuse I find it's much better when you can be pointed toward great books d ideas with minimal hype. Instead, I will sing some praises. When I rote this story, I deluded myself into thinking I could draw the whole ing myself and adjust my style slightly for "the comic within the comic." th time came wisdom, and when I finally dissuaded myself from the non I had to figure out who else could do it. This led me to my pal David artman, a wicked genius if there ever was one. He pays his bills as an imation director, and spends his funtime on his misanthropalyptic (my ord) comic series *Rite,* endless homemade monster movies, and more armingly disgusting cartoons than any other human I've met. His work contains the same wit, irreverence, d silliness with which he lives his life, and he was my first and only choice to stand in for the fictional E.C. urels. The writing and layouts are mine, but every grain of character and texture are pure Hartman. I hope u enjoy it as much as I do.

Richard Plotnik

Garvin Gimbensky

Mr. Shady

Brinnard

Brinnard

Charles D. Earlen

EPISODE 18: REWARDS, PART 3

This one is my favorite.

EPISODE 19: POLITICS

I'm gonna go out on a limb here and predict that unless somebody inven[t] telepathy, boys will always find the workings of the female mind a complete mystery whether it actually is or not. Moreover, I'm gonna predict that even when the answers to their most fundamental questions are sitting right in front of them, people will still insist on looking for something else. Try as w[e] might, we still prefer the chase over the prize. But that's okay, because ver[y] few of us know what to do with the prize once we've got it. I wish there were more tales about that.

EPISODE 20: STALEMATES

This was the single toughest story for me to write. Most of the previous scripts were written at a breakneck pace, which came to a screeching halt on this one. It was because I had only a meager grip on the character of the fathers, and looking back, I realized that I had no template to follow. Most o[f] the men in my family did not flow with reckless passion when I grew up, an[d] I simply didn't know what it would be like to live with that. After about a month of creative constipation, I gave up the research angle and just put th[e] two fathers together in their first scene. Imagine my surprise when the fin[-]ished script clocked in at twice normal length! Those guys just took the sta[ge] and ran with it, exhausting everyone in the process. In the end, this proba[-]bly gave me the experience I lacked before.

EPISODE 21: ELECTION DAY

Although this story was written shortly after the '96 presidential elec[-]tion, the political views I built into it turned out to have a lot more rele-vance to the fiasco of four years later. If these views are still relevant in [a] hundred years or so, we will have a lot to answer for as the caretakers of democracy.

EPISODE 22: UPHEAVAL

There comes a time for all of us when larger forces—vast, cool, and un[-]sympathetic, in the words of H.G. Wells—emerge from silence and cast strange, discomforting shadows over our lives. I imagine that each of us has known a time when our fates were suddenly, frighteningly, placed in the control of someone who had little notion or concern about the power they could wield. Bank manager, landlord, employer, lover, whatever. It doesn't take much to crack our armor sometimes, and make us feel insigni[f]icant. This is often the result when a system becomes more important than the people it was meant to serve. Y[ou] won't find many laughs in this story, because it's a topic I don't find terribly amusing.

ISODE 23: THE BEST OF TIMES

At last, the payoff. What I like best about payoff stories is that they are usually so unique to their context that other combination of elements could have created them. One of the best things about a payoff story is that it n give a writer genuine opportunities for wish fulfillment. In this case, I had two wishes: that your friends will me to your rescue when you need them the most, and that once in a while your leaders actually do know what ey're doing. I think those are wishes we can all get behind.

ISODE 24: REWARDS, PART 4

Okay, I'll come clean. The whole reason I did this book was so I could draw that one big page of Mac & Stettler ether. There. I said it.

GNETTE 1: CHAOS

After I wrote the entire Robin meets-and-loses Kara storyline, it all happened to me in real life. The details re different, but the impact on me was the same as on my paper persona, and my reaction was (naturally) just e his. I wrote this in response, bringing together a little formula for dealing with life that still usually works ıen I remember to apply it. By the way, my Kara came back to me a couple of years later. Maybe someday the me will happen to Robin.

GNETTE 2: END OF THE TUNNEL

I almost always listen to music or have some riff going through my head while I draw. Music is such an ener-ing, inspirational, creative force, I can't imagine getting through a workday without it. This made me want to d some way of including music in a comic strip without just providing a dopey playlist. So here it is: YOU pick music. When you read this story, you can play your own favorite piece behind it (preferably something classi-) and maybe you'll get to have the same experience as Robin.

GNETTE 3: BARFLY

The last time I visited the San Diego Wild Animal Park, I was stunned when the tour guide claimed that wild rican gorillas were now extinct. It felt like someone had kicked me in the stomach, as if a family member had ddenly died. Gorillas were endangered when I started writing these stories, but it never occurred to me that se most magnificent creatures wouldn't be around by the time I finished. Fortunately, I was able to learn from fine people at the Dian Fossey Gorilla Fund that this tour guide was, in fact, exaggerating. The mountain goril- of Rwanda are most definitely in trouble, but lowland gorillas can still be found in the thousands. So there's a of a relief. Anyway, I cooked up this story while I wandered around the park that day, sick with the shock I felt on hearing the "e" word and feeling very raw toward my fellow human beings. My mood has improved since n.

Thanks for reading!

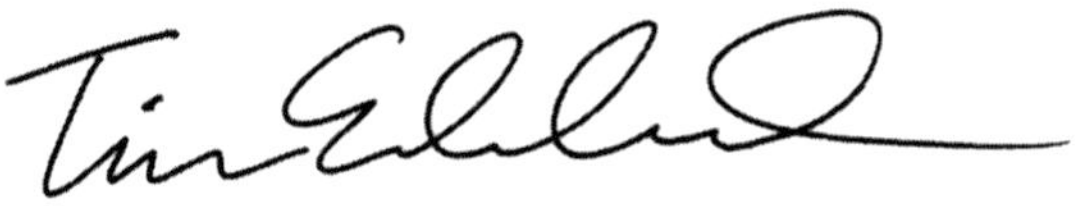

ACKNOWLEDGMENTS

I wouldn't be able to look at myself in a mirror if I didn't use this page to thank every one of the outstanding individuals who believed in this project and helped it along at various key points.
They know who they are, but they don't all know each other.

Eileen Kane
Brent Richard
Joe Krolik
Albert Deschesne
Denis Kitchen
Chris Couch
Maggie Thompson
Brad Neufeld
Ralph Sanchez
Jymn Magon
Kurt Busiek
Jim Valentino
Ellen Vein
Julie Kane-Ritsch
Eric Vesbit
Cassy Harlo
Tresa Harrington
Chip Kocel
Michelle Durnell
Travis Clark
Aaron Williams
Amy Raasch
Ashley Grayson
Teresa Nielsen Hayden
Genevieve Eldred
my long-suffering daughter
and
Monique Beatty
my one true Admiral